BUSINESS AND GOVERNMENT IN AMERICA SINCE 1870

A Twelve-Volume Anthology of Scholarly Articles

Series Editor

ROBERT F. HIMMELBERG
Fordham University

A GARLAND SERIES

131322

SERIES CONTENTS

VOLUME

12

NEW ISSUES IN GOVERNMENT-BUSINESS RELATIONS SINCE 1964

CONSUMERIST AND
SAFETY REGULATION,
AND THE DEBATE OVER
INDUSTRIAL POLICY

Edited with introductions by

ROBERT F. HIMMELBERG

GARLAND PUBLISHING, INC.
New York & London
1994

Library of Congress Cataloging-in-Publication Data

New issues in government-business relations since 1964 : consumerist and safety regulation, and the debate over industrial policy /
edited with introductions by Robert F. Himmelberg.
        p.   cm. — (Business and government in America since
1870 ; v. 12)
        Includes bibliographical references.
        ISBN 0–8153–1414–0 (alk. paper)
        1. Industry and state—United States.   2. Trade regulation—
United States.   I. Himmelberg, Robert F.   II. Series.
HD3616.U47N48   1994
338.973—dc20   93–45892
                                                              CIP

Printed on acid-free, 250-year-life paper
Manufactured in the United States of America

CONTENTS

SERIES INTRODUCTION

This compilation of articles provides a very broad and representative selection of the scholarly literature found in learned journals on the subject of government-business relations in the age of industry, the period since 1870. The scope of this collection is wide, covering all the arenas of business-government interaction. Sectorially, the focus is on manufacturing and transportation, upon whose rapid expansion after the Civil War the modern industrial economy was founded.

For the volumes covering the years from 1870 to 1965 (Volumes I through IX) it has been possible, while exercising selectivity, to include a very high proportion of everything published within the past thirty years. This literature is found largely in historical journals. More selectivity had to be employed for Volumes X through XII, which cover the period since 1965. Historians have not yet trodden much on the ground of the very recent past but social scientists and legal scholars have offered abundant materials, so abundant as to require a relatively severe selectivity. By choosing articles that appear to have a long-term analytical value and by excluding those too narrow in scope, too preoccupied with methodological questions or otherwise unsuitable for a non-specialized audience, an extensive and accessible body of writing has, however, been assembled for the post-1965 period, mainly from economics and legal periodicals.

The volumes are designed to contain articles relating to a particular period and to one or more topics within a period. The literature of business-government relations has four logically distinct major topics: antitrust, regulation, promotion, and cooperation. These topics define distinctive aspects of the relationship. Yet, the distinctions sometimes in practice blur, the ostensible, publicly proclaimed purposes of policy sometimes differing from the actually intended purposes or the actual outcomes.

Antitrust policy emerges in Volume I, which covers the era 1870–1900 when big business appeared, and figures prominently throughout the series. Several volumes are devoted entirely to it. Uniquely American, at least until relatively recently, antitrust policy has a complex history and much of what scholars have discovered about its origin and evolution is recorded only in the articles gathered in this collection. The literature reproduced here makes clear that the intent and impact of antitrust policy has varied enormously during its one-hundred-year history, which dates from the Sherman Act of 1890. Tension between competing objectives has existed from the outset. Should the "trusts" be broken up on the grounds that super-corporations inevitably conflict with democratic government and entrepreneurial opportunity? Or should only "bad trusts", those guilty of crushing competitors through unfair methods, suffer dissolution? Is cartelistic behavior always an illegal restraint of trade, or should it sometimes be tolerated if it helps small business to survive? Put most broadly, should the aim of antitrust policy be simply promoting competition, or should other conflicting social and economic values be recognized?

Business regulation also arose during the early stages of industrialization, appearing at the federal level with the enactment of the Interstate Commerce Act in 1887. The term "regulation" is used here to denote government policies intended, not to promote or restore competition, but to require specific behavior from business. The classic justification for regulation was the argument that in some situations the public interest could be served only through governmental prescription, that in some instances a remedy simply could not be obtained through the workings of the marketplace. Theoretically there are two such instances. The first occurs in the case of "natural monopoly," market situations in which competition would be wasteful and competing firms do not and should not exist. Railroads and public utilities were early identified as industries of this sort and were the first targets of government regulation. Would-be regulators early discovered a second justification for applying the regulatory approach, the situation in which competition fails to provide rival firms with incentives to avoid methods that may injure public health or well being. The argument found early expression in regulation of the meat-packing industry and has over the course of the twentieth century created a remarkable body of federal regulatory practices. The history of regulation, however, has not unfolded, any more than the history of antitrust, according to the logic of theory. It has been determined by the interplay between many factors, including the ideas of reformers, the complaints of those who have felt injured, policy rivalries among businessmen themselves, and the capacity or incapacity of government to execute planned reform. A major focus of recent literature on regulation, and to an extent on antitrust also, is the thesis of capture, the notion that regulatory efforts have often fallen captive to the interests they were intended to oppose.

The third theme of relations between government and business, promotion and encouragement, also emerged during the initial stages of the industrial era. Railroad subsidies abounded during the age of building the transcontinentals, of course, and protective tariffs were almost as old as the Republic itself. In the early twentieth century government support of trade expansion abroad enlarged and gradually became a major thread of government policy. Resembling promotion but logically distinct in many respects is the fourth category of business-government interaction, the area of cooperative relationships. Few scholars, even those who believe ongoing conflict has chiefly characterized business-government relations, would deny that cooperation has occurred at certain points, as during American participation in the major wars of the twentieth century. But in recent years many writers who conceive of business-government relations as taking place within a "corporatist" framework have perceived the scope and continuity of cooperative tendencies as very broad.

These four categories describe the subjects or topics around which scholarly investigation of business-government relations has revolved. There is, however, another approach to analyzing the literature of this relationship, one in which we ask about a writer's interpretive perspective, the conceptualizations the writer brings to the subject. All historians and social scientists, including those who created the literature collected here, adopt an interpretive standpoint from which to view society and its workings. An interpretive standpoint is a way of understanding the structure of society and the way those structural elements relate and interact; in other words, it is a "model" of society. Several rival models have competed for acceptance among scholars in recent times. Readers will be better equipped for informed reading of the literature assembled in these volumes if they are knowledgeable about these interpretive standpoints and the aim here therefore is to define the most important of these and give them appropriate labels.

Until the 1950s the prevailing interpretation of business-government relations—indeed, of American history generally—was the progressive viewpoint. The term progressive refers in the first place to the reform ideology and activity of the early twentieth century, the period before World War I. The perspective of the progressive generation continued for many years to dominate historical writing, not only on the period itself but on the whole of American history. According to the progressive perspective, the rise of big business during the late nineteenth and early twentieth centuries created a radical shift in the balance of economic and political power in America in favor of concentrated wealth. The rise of the "trusts", the powerful firms that came to predominate in many industries in the years after 1880, and the creation of cartels and other arrangements for suppressing competition, threatened independent capitalists and consumers with raw economic exploitation. This concentration of economic power threatened to utterly suborn representative political institutions as well and reduce American democracy to a plutocracy. In the progressive view the predominating tone of business-government relations was therefore necessarily antagonistic and conflictual.

The progressive paradigm became deeply embedded in the American consciousness. Reformist politicians have often reverted to it in shaping their ideological and rhetorical appeals. Franklin D. Roosevelt's attack in the campaign of 1936 upon "economic royalists" and John Kennedy's denunciation in 1962 of Big Steel during the controversy over price guidelines as "utterly contemptuous of the public interest" are vivid examples. The progressive outlook is evidently a persistent element in the popular historical consciousness. The power of the progressive conception of American history is in fact readily confirmed by reference to the way twentieth-century history is periodized, in textbooks and popular histories, into epochs of reform (the Progressive, New Deal, Fair Deal and Great Society periods) and of reaction (the Twenties, the Eisenhower and Reagan eras).

But if the progressive interpretation of business government relations retains some force among some historians and in the consciousness of liberal opinion makers and the public, its hold on much of the academic mind has long since weakened. A reaction among historians and other academics against the progressive paradigm emerged soon after the end of the Second World War and gathered force during the 1950s. The reaction was especially sharp among historians writing business history. Writing at a time when a reinvigorated American economy appeared to have overcome the doldrums of the 1930s and to be demonstrating the superiority of capitalism over other systems, energetic business and economic historians completely revised the progressive interpretation of the founders of American big business. The revisionists interpreted the founders not as greedy robber barons but as heroes of the entrepreneurial spirit, the spirit of enterprise and productivity. This revisionist interpretation proved too one-dimensional and celebratory to be maintained without modification. Revisionism, however, did succeed in thoroughly discrediting the progressive point of view. This circumstance, together with the impact of interpretive concepts emanating from post-war social science, moved historians to replace the progressive paradigm with a new and more sophisticated framework for understanding American political economy, the pluralist framework.

Pluralism as the dominant interpretive mode replaced progressivism in the 1950s and 60s. Speaking broadly, the pluralist model understands public policy as the result of struggle between economic and social groups. A major by-product of industrialization is the sharpening of differences between groups playing distinctive economic roles and a heightened articulation of self-interested goals and purposes on the part of such groups. Thus, government-business relations, that is, the shape of government policies towards business, are the result of rivalries among the major interest groups, business, labor, consumers, and so on. But the nature of the struggle is complex because the major groups are themselves divided into more or less rivalrous sub-groups. Business itself is divided; both intra- and inter-industry rivalries exist, sometimes in acute forms. Government policy is not merely the result of nonbusiness groups seeking to shape that policy but also of some business interests seeking to impose their own wishes on others.

During the 1960s pluralist interpretation became more complex. One important source of this heightened complexity was what some commentators have called the "organizational" outlook. Again influenced by currents in American social science, this time sociology, practitioners employing the organizational perspective are struck by the ever-increasing importance of large bureaucratic organizations in American life since the onset of industrialization. Business has continuously evolved in terms of an ever larger role for the large corporation, but other spheres, including government and the professions, also are organized in terms of large hierarchical bureaucracies. Borrowing from Weberian sociological traditions, writers impressed by the organizational perspective have explored the thesis that large bureaucracies wherever situated have similar requirements and tend to develop in those who manage them similar values and expectations. Thus, this brand of pluralism stresses the extent to which group leaders, including the managers and technicians who run the large corporations, developed accommodative as well as merely self-seeking motives. Business leaders, many of them at least, came to share certain values, such as respect for stability in the overall economy, which leads them to seek harmonious and cooperative relationships between interest groups and between them and the government. Government is assigned the role, in this construct, of facilitating and stimulating cooperative modes of behavior and umpiring conflicts. In the literature on business and government, figures who have advocated this kind of polity are often dubbed "corporatists" or "corporate liberals." Broadly defined, corporatism is the practice of cooperation between government and the corporate world to resolve economic issues. The existence and the importance of corporatist relationships has been one of the major emphases of recent scholarship but there is much disagreement as to the intentions of its practitioners and its impact. Some scholars have interpreted corporatism in a more or less positive light, as an ideology and a practice entailing cooperation rather than conflict between government and business, as an alternative to an adversarial relationship, a way of obtaining desirable economic performance from business without resorting to governmental coercion.

But others, especially but not only those writing in the vein of the "New Left", have argued that members of the corporate elite have frequently pursued their own narrow interests under the cover of ostensibly cooperative endeavors. The New Leftists emerged in the 1960s, expounding a more radical criticism of business than the progressive-liberal historians had advanced. The New Leftists doubted or denied outright that the American system was pluralist at all in any meaningful sense. Control of public policy might appear as a contest between social groups, but in fact one group, or rather class, those who controlled big business, enjoyed such lopsided power that the contest was apparently not real. Behind the facade of political infighting over government policy toward business, the masters of the corporate world quietly steered events toward outcomes which cemented in place control of the economy by monopoly capital.

These four conceptualizations, the progressive, the pluralist, the corporatist, and the New Leftist, are essentially theories of the structure and process of American political economy. However, rarely are researchers slavishly devoted to a theoretical perspective. Thus, those who see, in the progressive vein, an ongoing conflictual relationship between the people and business sometimes argue against the reformers and in favor of the businessmen. Even more significant and widespread is the conclusion of many writers using the pluralist or corporatist modes of interpretation, that regulation has not fostered equity and economic progress but rather has hardened the economy's vital arteries. Pluralists initially assumed that policies arising from a political arena to which all organized interests have access will inevitably achieve benign results, that the policy outputs will construct a system of "countervailing power" among organized interest groups. The assumption of acceptable outcomes is still prevalent, but a skeptical version of the results of interest group rivalries became manifest in the late

1960s, holding that both in origin and ongoing impact, business regulation was too often subject to "capture." In this view, regulatory measures and agencies and other policies seeking to guide business behavior toward balanced and generally acceptable outcomes readily fall under the control of the very interests they were intended to regulate.

There has emerged in recent years still another approach to the origin and process of social-economic policy that has been applied to the business-government connection. In this interpretation of the connection, a few examples of which will be found in articles collected here, emphasis is placed on the relative autonomy of government administrators and regulators. Seen by the pluralists as merely the creatures of the organizational struggles that result in public policies, in this new view regulators are seen as possessing substantial room for independent action. Thus the state is not merely to be seen as a passive receptor and executor of outcomes that social forces determine but as having a partially autonomous role which the officers of the state presumably will use to extend their own interests rather than the interests articulated by social groups.

These categories, progressivism, pluralism, corporatism, Leftism and the "autonomous officialdom" viewpoint, represent the major schools of thought and interpretation that readers will discover in the literature reproduced in these volumes. Writers investigating specific historical incidents, trends or problems have, in most cases, written through the framework provided by one or another of these interpretive models. As an alert reader will discover, most writers do have certain assumptions about the structure and dynamics of social relationships, and these assumptions stem from one of the models that have been described.

Interpretation of the relationship between business and government in the age of industry has given rise to a literature that is large and complex. It presents a stimulating intellectual challenge and is certainly relevant for anyone seeking understanding of contemporary business-government relations and endeavoring to predict, or to shape, their future course.

INTRODUCTION

As the reformist spirit that enlivened much of the political discourse of the 1960s turned to environmental and quality-of-life issues, the business system came under increasingly hostile fire. The deregulation movement, seen in the preceding volume, was one result. But reformism also produced remarkably enthusiastic movements for consumer and environmental protection and regulation of workplace safety. These movements blossomed during the 1970s, producing a new kind of regulation on an immense scale. At the same time, the increasing difficulty business experienced in meeting foreign competition at home and in successfully competing in world markets led to a debate over whether a new "industrial policy" to protect, promote and guide American business should be adopted. This volume contains much of the best journal literature on these topics.

The remarkable extent of enthusiasm for the new regulation is displayed by the number of people involved in federal regulation; it rose between 1970 and 1979 from under 10,000 to over 60,000. This wave of regulation emphasized issues different from those stressed in earlier eras of regulatory innovation. The new wave was fueled by the political struggle that arose in the later 60s and early 70s over quality-of-life issues. It was the era of the Vietnam war, a time of bitter division in American society. The political atmosphere became supercharged with passion. New issues came into vogue, equality for all, protection of the environment, and occupational safety and consumer protection. Demands concerning these issues reached levels that in the previous political setting would have in some cases been dismissed as extreme. In response, Congress hastily legislated a new array of regulatory policies compelling business to incur large costs to improve environmental protection and occupational health and safety and fulfill society's expectation of a society more just to minorities and women.

The new regulation was unmistakably motivated, in part at least, by anti-business hostility. In any case, the business community felt the consumerist, environmental and social burdens laid upon the corporations were unduly heavy and costly, and they soon mounted a strong counterattack, hoping to avoid additional burdens. The impact of the new regulation coincided, in the 1970's, with a drastic slump in productivity gains for American industry, double-digit inflation and recurrent, serious recessions. But hard times somewhat diminished public enthusiasm for the new regulationism and they created an atmosphere more disposed to heed businessmen's protests and to listen to voices advancing new remedies for the great economic problems of the later 70s, falling productivity, soaring prices and foreign competition. This fierce competition from abroad, most importantly from Japan, threatened to devour the markets of American manufacturers and to turn the heavy industry cities of the upper Middlewest into a "rust belt."

By the late 1970s, spokesmen for the corporatist outlook began to find an attentive audience for their argument that American industry was beset by too much government meddling. They took up the campaign the economists of the Chicago School had launched for relaxation of antitrust restrictions on mergers and proposed adoption of a new "industrial policy." The specific proposals covered by this elastic concept varied widely, but proponents of an industrial policy began with the premise that American businessmen, distracted by competitive pressures at home and over-regulated by multiple government agencies, were being robbed of the capacity to respond effectively to competition from abroad.

The solutions advocated by these new voices were of course not really novel; their message was merely a revival of the corporatist point of view. Muted by the sounds of popular anti-business rhetoric during the late 60s and 70s, the corporatist ideology, adapted to new conditions, is clearly discernible in two major themes emerging in the mid-seventies. One of these is the demand for liberalizing the antitrust laws, the other the demand for an "industrial policy."

The solutions proposed ranged from relaxation of antitrust and regulatory interference to government incentives for research, but they generally were founded upon the principle that improved cooperation among an industry's firms and between industry and government was the essential formula for recovery of America's capacity to innovate and produce efficiently. This, of course, is the traditional corporatist thesis. Industrial policy thus is best understood as the latest phase in the evolution of a concept that has guided the most influential leaders of the business establishment during the twentieth century. In this volume, both the movement to soften antitrust enforcement and to adopt an industrial policy are thoroughly covered.

Jei *JOURNAL OF ECONOMIC ISSUES*
Vol. XIX   Number 2   June 1985

Industrial Policy and Corporate Power

William S. Brown

The industrial policy debate has become almost "pop" in recent years. As is frequently the case in policy debates, the sides were drawn almost before the debate began. Conservatives continue to oppose all forms of government intervention, including industrial policy, and liberals seem unable to make up their minds, but most post Keynesians and institutionalists favor industrial policy—and have for sometime now.[1] The fact that conventional economists are at least discussing an institutionalist policy gives institutional economics a kind of credibility that has been too infrequent in recent years.

The purpose of this article is to suggest that, because of the particular nature of U.S. corporate power, the United States is especially in need of industrial policy. The first part serves as an introduction and briefly reviews the industrial policy debate. In the second part, it is suggested that coalescing labor and management power has established distributional coalitions, to society's detriment. The result is an unplanned, disorganized, inefficient industrial policy—the state that exists in the United States today. The third part outlines the basics of an industrial policy designed to overcome the abuses of economic power. A summary and conclusions follow.

Pros and Cons of Industrial Policy

Industrial policy means different things to different people. In the context used here, it is meant to accomplish two things: increase aggregate

---

The author is Associate Professor of Economics, Rollins College, Winter Park, Florida. This article was presented at the Annual Meeting of Association for Evolutionary Economics, Dallas, Texas, 28-30 December 1984.

productivity and income growth, and ease the transfer of resources between industries. Interest in industrial policy began in response to the stagflation and productivity crisis of the 1970s. Between 1963 and 1973, productivity growth averaged only 1.9 percent in the United States, less than half of the average rate for the seven largest OECD countries, but it fell to zero between 1974 and 1981. By comparison, productivity grew at 8.7 percent annually between 1963 and 1973 in Japan; in the period 1974-1981, it fell to 3.3 percent, a rate that exceeded the *good* years in the United States by more than 50 percent [Cornwall 1983, p. 23].

What was Japan doing differently? Among other things, Japan had MITI, the Ministry of International Trade and Industry, which promoted and coordinated policies for economic development. MITI's functions are diverse. It targets industries and products for development, eases adjustments resulting from industrial dislocation, assists in regional development, and is involved in many other areas. Perhaps the most important function of MITI is to provide visions of future Japanese industrial development. In the past, these visions have frequently been at odds with the law of comparative advantage. In the 1950s, instead of encouraging the growth of labor-intensive production, MITI acted to encourage steel, autos, and other areas of high value added production. Dynamic considerations—expected world income growth and income elasticity—were used as criteria for selection [Ozaki 1984]. MITI is not an autonomous planning agency—its actions are subject to review by the Diet, the Prime Minister, the Ministry of Finance, and other groups [Reich 1984]. Neither is it infallible—it tried to discourage Honda from entering the auto business and Sony from consumer electronics [Lararus and Litan 1984]. But it must have been doing something right, unless we want to believe that the Japanese people are smarter or better workers.

Whether the United States could or should establish an industrial policy and a MITI-type agency has become the subject of intense controversy. Those opposed to industrial policy generally make one of three arguments. First, they frequently argue that the market is the most efficient allocator of resources. Deregulation, antitrust, or perhaps union-busting is all that is necessary to achieve economic efficiency. Second, though the market *occasionally* makes mistakes, the government *frequently* makes mistakes. To allow the government to "pick winners and losers" would be an unmitigated disaster. A much better strategy would be to pursue traditional policies to promote economic growth. Finally, many argue that the U.S. economy is simply not in trouble: bad figures on productivity are dismissed as a result of the move to a service economy, unemployment increases result from an increase in the natural rate, and so on.

Those in favor of industrial policy make several arguments. First, they emphasize not the efficacy of the market, but the decline of the market. As comfortable as it is to have faith in the market, supply and demand no longer rule the corporate international economy. Nations use subsidies, tariffs, and other measures to help particular industries and interest groups. The notion of equilibrium and the optimal allocation of resources is misleading, at best. Second, in a world of modern technology, work skills can be quickly outmoded. Blue collar and white collar workers are losing jobs to other industrialized nations and the LDCs. Capitalism never has been very good at disinvestment—the process of replacing old capital with new [Thurow 1980]. This is true for both human and physical capital (though not necessarily for financial capital). Since technology changes and moves across borders so fast, some help is needed to reduce the costs of change.

Finally, and most significant for this article, many have argued that an industrial policy is necessary because the United States already has one, albeit an inefficient, disorganized one, that caters to special interest groups with no social goal in mind.[2] One way to dismantle a bad program, perhaps the only way, is to establish a new program.

Distributional Coalitions and Coalescing Power

One would hope that the miserable economic performance of the 1970s would lead to enlightened collective action to better society, but as Mancur Olson [1982] has pointed out, it is extremely difficult for large social groups to organize for action. It is much easier for small groups to establish political and economic power to effect change. These groups, *distributional coalitions*, can increase their share of income much more easily than they can increase aggregate income. In fact, in stable, modern societies, "the incentive to produce is diminished; the incentive to seek a larger share of what is produced increases" [Olson 1982, p. 72]. To briefly summarize Olson's argument: Not only is it inevitably difficult for "large" groups to agree on strategies, but a group encompassing, say, 25 percent of society would incur all of the costs involved with increasing social efficiency but enjoy only 25 percent of the benefits. A "small" group would enjoy proportionately less of the benefits of an improvement in economic efficiency. A better strategy is to lobby for specific help; that is, import restrictions. Such restrictions may reduce economic effi-

ciency and aggregate income, but the share of national income going to
the small group will increase. As long as the group share increases by
more than aggregate income falls, the distributional coalition is better
off. Olson concludes that since distributional coalitions often act to suppress market pressures, they impair the ability of society to "adopt new
technologies and reallocate resources in response to changing conditions"
[Olson 1982, p. 65].

The ability of distributional coalitions to influence policy makers depends on their power. An extremely small group should not be able to
win policy concessions, despite its ability to reach internal agreement.[3]
And groups that have visible opposition may tend to cancel out in the
political arena; that it, if passing a program that favors labor caused management to support the opposition, politicians would hesitate to promote
such legislation.

A particular kind of distributional coalition has recently evolved in the
United States. According to Walter Adams and James Brock [1983-84 ,
labor and management power have *coalesced* in many industries. This is
especially apparent in the auto and steel industries, where labor and management have coordinated their efforts to keep out foreign competition.
This has important implications. With labor and management agreeing
on goals, they can more effectively lobby for protectionist policies. Also,
their strength in the political arena is greatly enhanced, because pro-labor
policies are not always interpreted as being anti-management. The result
of coalescing power in establishing industries is just what Olson would
predict: social inefficiency but an increasing share and higher income for
the coalitions. Adams and Brock note that despite lower than average
productivity growth, wages in the auto and steel industries have risen
faster than average [Adams and Brock 1983-84, pp. 186-91].

While economic power usually develops in response to technological
uncertainty [Gruchy 1984], distributional coalitions grow best in stable
societies. This is because it is difficult and takes time to establish collective organizations and new patterns of cooperation. But once established,
such organizations tend to develop strength over time and frequently last
beyond their usefulness—until some form of social upheaval occurs
[Olson 1982, pp. 38-41]. This explains why stable societies—Britain and
the United States—seem to be dominated more by special interest organizations than Germany and Japan, countries whose internal power
structures were eliminated in World War II [Olson 1982, chap. 4].

The examples of autos and steel are but two cases where corporate
power works to sway government decisions and economic policies. Sim-

ilar arguments can be made concerning the defense industry [DeGrasse 1983], textiles, and others [Markre and Tarr 1980]. These programs amount to nothing less than an industrial policy, but one with the goals of only a small segment of society in mind. A more productive economy would prevail in the absence of these power blocs, but that is to deny a truth: power blocs exist as an evolutionary response to the uncertainty of economic change. And contrary to the conventional wisdom, the market is not always able to eliminate economic power. As John Kenneth Galbraith says: "The only thing that now disguises this concentration of economic power (and then not very well) is the increasingly obsolescent conditioning that asserts the continued power-dissolving subordination of the firm to the classical market" [Galbraith 1983, p. 182].[4]

Components of an Industrial Policy

The recent "success" of the auto and steel industries—voluntary import quotas and trigger prices—may serve as a model for other industries. Without deliberate action, we can expect only to see more of these kinds of policies. What is needed is a national industrial policy that coordinates incentives and subsidies in a socially responsible manner.

There have been many different industrial policies proposed recently, but even a casual first reading makes one thing clear: The industrial policies espoused by big labor [AFL-CIO 1983] lean heavily toward protection of established industries where unionized labor is strongest; the industrial policy proposed by the "Atari Democrats" favors aid to high tech industries [Lundine 1983], that just happen to be located in the home states of many of the sponsors;[5] and the few conservatives who espouse industrial policy call for an explicitly "pro-business" program [Phillips 1984]. In short, the policymakers want to make policies in their own interest. This cannot be allowed to happen. For an industrial policy to succeed, it must not be perceived as an institutionalization of existing power. At the same time, the expertise of business and labor must be called upon if the policy is to succeed. Industrial policy will evolve as a learning process; its form will change over time just as technology and the nature of work change. But as a starting place, an effective industrial policy needs the following:

Incomes Policy. The standard medicine for inflation in the United States has been recession. Recessions do halt inflation, at least temporarily, but they also reduce the productivity advances that accompany economic growth.[6] Fear of inflation results in contractionary policies be-

5

ing applied before anything approaching full employment is reached. An effective incomes policy would allow policymakers to pursue full empolyment policies without this fear.

Economic Cooperation Council. Patterned after MITI and with membership from labor, management, and the public, the ECC would study requests from different groups for economic aid and recommend policies to Congress. A spirit of economic cooperation may seem foreign to the U.S. economic experience, but the trend toward coalescing labor-management power may be a first step in this direction.

National Investment Bank. The investment bank would serve several functions. First, when the recessions of the 1970s and 1980s turned the Midwest into the "Rust Belt," financial capital left the region—a response to market signals. Investment in that area may yield large social returns, but not as quickly as money spent elsewhere on mergers or fast food restaurants. As a partner to private industry, the government would be able to target investment to regions so as to minimize the human costs of displacement. More importantly, had an investment bank been operative during the structural shocks of the 1970s, the term "Rust Belt" never would have been coined. Japan is already planning for the demise of its steel industry [*Business Week* 1984].

The investment bank would also make loans to companies for research and development. Studies by Edwin Mansfeld [1983] and Eileen Collins [1982] show that the average and marginal rates of return on industrial R&D can be as high as 30 percent, yet there is too little R&D expenditure. Further, tax incentives for R&D simply do not work. The 1981 ERTA provided a 25 percent tax credit for R&D expenditures in excess of average R&D expenditures in the base period with hardly any effect: company-financed R&D would have been only .3 percent lower in 1981 and 1 percent lower in 1982 without the incentive.

Cooperative Corporate R&D. Shlomo Maital and Sharone Maital [1984] have used game theory to show that competition among firms is likely to lead to one of two R&D results: either all firms engage in the same research, or all firms wait for the other to take the innovative risk. In the first case, research dollars are wasted in redundancy. In the second case, the R&D never takes place. The optimal solution results from cooperation. Such cooperation is now illegal in the United Sates, but not in Japan—and may explain why Japan is a world leader in industrial R&D. Cooperative corporate research need not be anti-competitive. Process, not product, development would be the aim of the centers. Once a process was developed, firms would be free to adopt it to their specific uses.

Social Accounting Methods. To keep the ECC from becoming the tool of vested interests, social accounting criteria would be used in making decisions. Social accounting can result in policies contrary to the naive free market solution. For example, few orthodox economists favor import restrictions to protect jobs in declining industries since the cost per job saved appears too high. But from·a social accounting perspective, allowing those workers to be displaced represents tremendous waste. A more efficient strategy might be to slow the demise of the sunset industry while retraining takes place. For example, Peter Gray [1984] has shown that temporary protection should be allowed if the present value of displaced, nontransferable workers minus the cost of protection exceeds the capitalized value of transferable displaced workers. He suggests a similar rule for determining the optimality of worker retraining programs. Gray's work draws upon the vita labor market theory that emphasizes that the labor "market" is composed of specific skills and skill levels rather than a homogeneous lump of workers. To argue that import protection is always bad implies that workers are readily transferable between jobs; a "simplifying" assumption of the neoclassical model and one that is implicitly accepted by free trade policies. But no worse than this is to suggest that *no* displaced workers will find jobs, which is apparently what many groups calling for protection suppose. A reasoned policy, administered with social goals and equity, would *have* to be better than either of these polar cases.

Summary and Conclusions

In the modern corporate economy, there are several forces working against the proper kinds and level of investment: the Maital and Maital game theoretic argument, the separation of ownership from control, policy uncertainty, and so on. But the factor that may be most responsible is *time*. As social scientists, we know the benefits of investment, but we also know that the payoff is frequently years in the future—easily discounted with a $1/(1 + r)^n$ formula. Economic actors do not want to wait that long, but they do not have to—provided they can influence policy to their benefit. In this society of instant gratification, long-term, productivity-enhancing investment is not the maximand of any economic actor, save perhaps the weakest of all interest groups, those yet to be born. Unchecked, modern capitalism provides incentives for groups to rob from the whole of this, and the next generation. If these arguments are correct, an industrial policy is mandatory before the United States can hope to catch up in the "productivity race."

Clearly the crucial aspect determining the success of an industrial policy is the adoption of social accounting methods. This is necessary not only to prevent established power blocs from controlling policy, but also to allow consideration of the true costs and benefits of special interest policies. An example may press home this point: Current trade barriers restrict imports from LDCs, much to the detriment of their economies. This makes it more difficult for LDCs to pay off debts and affects the stability of U.S. banks. Lost export earnings result in economic instability in the LDCs and can lead to political instability. The response from the United States has been economic and military aid as well as measures to bail out U.S. banks. These are the real costs of measures designed to protect U.S. distributional coalitions, but a kind that the market does not and *cannot* recognize.

Notes

1. The literature on industrial policy is voluminous. Two valuable collections which present different points of view are Johnson [1984] and Wachter and Wachter [1983]. Richard McKenzie [1984] makes the conservative anti-industrial policy case. Charles Schultz [1983] presents the liberal case against industrial policy. Robert Reich, a liberal, is perhaps the writer most responsible for renewed interest in industrial policy. His *Next American Frontier* [1983] and, with Ira Magaziner, *Minding America's Business* [1982], are essential reading in the area. The institutionalist view is well represented by Gar Alperovitz and Jeff Faux [1984] and William Dugger [1984].
2. At least one additional pro-industrial policy argument must be mentioned: the Democrats needed it as an alternative to Ronald Reagan's supply-side economics. The two ideas address similar issues, but from an entirely different perspective. Donald Regan [1983] even calls Reaganomics an "industrial policy."
3. Of course there are always exceptions. Reagan's decision to protect the domestic motorcycle industry (which consists of one company) doesn't make political or economic sense. And this talk of protecting California kiwi farmers fits in the same category [Bandow 1984].
4. William Baumol's [1982] contestable markets theory may be a new example of this increasing obsolescent conditioning. See William Shepard [1984] for critique of the theory.
5. To be fair, the labor and the "Atari Democrat" arguments can be supported on their own merits. Under some circumstances, it may make sense to help established industries since the high-tech industries are growing fast enough without special help; or it could be contended that since heavy industry is collapsing so fast, it is necessary to provide incentives for high-tech to absorb new workers. But which strategy should be pursued must be decided by an unbiased group.

6. That productivity growth is the result of economic growth is the essential result of Verdoorn's or Kaldor's Law. See A. Thirwall [1983]. The same issue of *JPKE* contains a symposium on Kaldor's growth laws.

References

Adams, Walter, and James Brock. 1983-84. "Countervailing or Coalescing Power? The Problem of Labor/Management Coalitions." *Journal of Post Keynesian Economics* 6 (Winter) : 180-97.

Alperovitz, Gar, and Jeff Faux. 1984. *Rebuilding America*. New York: Random House.

Bandow, Doug. 1984. "Kiwi May Peel Off Reagan's Pro-Free Market Mask." *Rocky Mountain News*. 11 July, p. 55.

Baumol, William. 1982. "Contestable Markets: An Uprising in the Theory of Industry Structure." *American Economic Review* 72 (March) : 1-15.

Business Week. 1984. "The Worldwide Steel Industry: Reshaping to Survive." 20 August, pp. 150-54.

Collins, Eileen. 1982. "Tax Incentives for Innovation—Productivity Miracle or Media Hype?" *Journal of Post Keynesian Economics* 5 (Fall) : 68-74.

Cornwall, John. 1983. *The Conditions for Economic Recovery*. New York: M. E. Sharpe.

DeGrasse, Robert. 1983. *Military Expansion, Economic Decline*. New York: M. E. Sharpe.

Dugger, William. 1984. *An Alternative to Economic Retrenchment*. New York: Petrocelli Books.

Galbraith, John Kenneth. 1983. *The Anatomy of Power*. Boston: Houghton Mifflin.

Gray, Peter. 1984. "Employment Arguments for Protection and the Vita Theory." *Eastern Economic Journal* 10 (January-March) : 1-14.

Gruchy, Allan. 1984. "Uncertainty, Indicative Planning, and Industrial Policy." *Journal of Economic Issues* 18 (March) : 159-80.

Johnson, Chalmers, ed. 1984. *The Industrial Policy Debate*. San Francisco: ICS Press.

Lararus, Simon, and Robert Litan. 1984. "The Democrats' Coming Civil War Over Industrial Policy." *The Atlantic* 254 (September) : 92-98.

Lundine, Stan. 1983. "Now Is the Time for a National Industrial Strategy." *Challenge* 26 (July/August) : 16-21.

Magaziner, Ira, and Robert Reich. 1982. *Minding America's Business*. New York: Vintage Books.

Maital, Shlomo, and Sharone Maital. 1984. *Economic Games People Play*. New York: Basic Books.

Mansfield, Edwin. 1983. "Commentary," in *Industrial Change and Public Policy*. Symposium sponsored by the Federal Reserve Bank of Kansas City.

Markre, M., and D. Tarr. 1980. *Effects of Restrictions on United States Imports: Five Case Studies and Theory*. Washington, D.C.: U.S. Federal Trade Commission.

McKenzie, Richard. 1984. *Fugitive Industry*. San Francisco: Pacific Institute for Policy Research.

Olson, Mancur. 1982. *The Rise and Decline of Nations*. New Haven: Yale University Press.

Olson, Mancur. 1984. "Why Nations Rise and Fall" (interview). *Challenge* 27 (March/April): 15-23.

Ozaki, Robert. 1984. "How Japanese Industrial Policy Works." In *The Industrial Policy Debate*. Edited by Chalmers Johnson. San Francisco: ICS Press.

Phillips, Kevin. 1984. *Staying on Top: The Business Case for a National Industrial Strategy*. New York: Random House.

"Rebuilding America: A National Industrial Policy," *The AFL-CIO American Federationist*, 22 October 1983. Reprinted in *Economics 84/85*, edited by Reuben Slesinger and Glen Beeson. Guilford, Conn.: Dushkin Publishing.

Regan, Donald. 1983. "Peas, People, and the Economy." In *Toward a New U.S. Industrial Policy?* Edited by Michael Wachter and Susan Wachter. Philadelphia: University of Pennsylvania Press.

Reich, Robert. 1983. *The Next American Frontier*. New York: Penguin Books.

Rohatyn, Felix. 1983. *The Twenty-Year Century*. New York: Random House.

Schultze, Charles. 1983. "Industrial Policy: A Dissent." *The Brookings Review* 2 (Fall): 3-13.

Shepard, William. 1984. " 'Contestability' vs. Competition." *The American Economic Review* 74 (September): 572-87.

Thirwall, A. 1983. "A Plain Man's Guide to Kaldor's Growth Laws." *Journal of Post Keynesian Economics* 5 (Spring): 345-58.

Thurow, Lester. 1980. *The Zero-Sum Society*. New York: Penguin.

Wachter, Michael, and Susan Wachter, eds. 1983. *Toward a New U.S. Industrial Policy?* Philadelphia: University of Pennsylvania Press.

U.S. TRADE POLICY: HISTORY AND EVIDENCE

Victor A. Canto

Introduction

For the past 13 years, U.S. trade policy has been on a steady course toward increased protectionism. A policy to reduce tariffs across the board among all trading nations has been paralleled by efforts to protect selected industries from foreign competition. In the vernacular, the call for "free" trade has been joined by the admonition to seek "fair" trade. An increasing number of people have advocated protectionist policies in an effort to create a favorable balance of trade. Foreign competition increasingly is blamed for the decline in the health of the U.S. economy while problems of several of the economy's weakest sectors, including steel and autos, are attributed to an uncontrolled surge of imports.

The debate now is much the same as it was 200 years ago. Arguments today that favor increased protectionism incorporate several of the mercantilist concepts, including the importance of a positive trade balance to a nation's prosperity. By contrast, the economic principles invoked by those advocating free trade can be found in the writing of Adam Smith and his predecessors. The trade account is viewed as a means to provide consumers and producers with the widest possible access to foreign goods and markets. Though restrictions placed on trade by foreign nations can be harmful to the domestic economy, imposing additional restrictions on trade at the domestic level serves only to compound the loss of economic efficiency, limiting further the opportunities to realize the benefits of trade.

The historical account of the U.S. trade policy presented in this paper suggests that the rise of protectionist policies can be linked to

Cato Journal, Vol. 3, No. 3 (Winter 1983/84). Copyright © Cato Institute. All rights reserved.

The author is Associate Professor of Finance and Business Economics at the University of Southern California, Los Angeles, Calif. 90089. He wishes to thank A. B. Laffer, R. V. Eastin, and C. W. Kadlec for their comments and suggestions.

the concern for the international competitiveness of U.S. products. The enthusiasm for restricting trade as a means to improve the domestic economy and protect selected industries, however, is tempered by the realization that trade restrictions can become counterproductive, impoverishing domestic and foreign producers and consumers alike.

Historical Survey of U.S. Trade Policies

The Trade Agreements Act of 1934

The roots of current U.S. trade policies can be traced back to the Trade Agreements Act of 1934. The purpose of this act, passed by the U.S. Congress, was to increase United States exports to foreign countries. There was a need for such an act for two reasons. First, the Smoot-Hawley Tariff Act of 1930 raised duties on imports to 53 percent in 1931 and 59 percent in 1932. This action provoked other countries to retaliate against the U.S., shrinking world trade. Second, the ensuing worldwide contraction in economic activity in the early 1930s caused world trade to decline even further. Between 1929 and 1933, world trade shrank 25 percent.

The Trade Agreements Act of 1934 delegated to the president the authority to negotiate U.S. trade agreements. It also allowed the president to participate in negotiations for the purpose of lowering tariffs to a level as low as 50 percent of the rates established by the Smoot-Hawley Act.

Extensions of the Trade Agreements Act, particularly after World War II, permitted the imposition of restrictions when harmful domestic effects could be shown to result from tariff cuts. Nevertheless, under the act, the United States signed bilateral trade agreements with 20 foreign nations. And, by 1947, tariff rates had been reduced to one-half their 1934 levels.

The General Agreement on Tariffs and Trade

In spite of this progress, it was apparent that, in the years preceding World War II, an alarming number of nations had adopted a neo-mercantilist, "beggar-thy-neighbor" approach to trade policy. Many politicians and commentators specifically attributed the outbreak of war to that trade environment.

This feeling served as the underpinning for the major international efforts following the war in which open communication, free trade and international economic interdependence were basic goals. Thus, the United Nations, the Bretton Woods agreement, and the General Agreement on Tariffs and Trade (GATT) were formed—all through the leadership of the United States.

GATT is particularly noteworthy for purposes of this study. It institutionalized the following basic goals:

1. Trade without discrimination (general, most-favored-nation treatment);
2. Protection of domestic industries only through tariffs;
3. Establishment of a predictable and stable basis for trade;
4. Consultation when trade problems arise;
5. Waivers and emergency actions that serve as exceptions to the general rules (e.g., escape clauses); and
6. Acceptance of regional trading arrangements.

Under the provisions of GATT, seven rounds of trade negotiations occurred: in 1947 (Geneva), 1949 (Annecy, France), 1951 (Torquay, England), 1956 (Geneva), 1961 (Dillon Round, Geneva), 1964 (Kennedy Round, Geneva), and 1975 (Tokyo Round, Geneva).

The Trade Expansion Act of 1962

During the span between 1947 and the mid-1950s, trade barriers were reduced on a commodity-by-commodity basis. After the mid-1950s, however, this method was considered ineffective for large-scale reductions. Participants in GATT therefore requested a "linear," or across-the-board, approach to tariff cuts. Such an approach was authorized when Congress passed the Trade Expansion Act of 1962.

The Trade Expansion Act was the most significant piece of trade legislation since the adoption of the Reciprocal Trade Agreements Act in 1934. This legislation was the statutory mandate for the president to negotiate tariff cuts at the next GATT-sponsored multilateral trade negotiations, later to be called the Kennedy Round. This act was significant for another reason: It established the office of the special trade representative (now the U.S. trade representative) to conduct the negotiations, replacing the State Department in this role. The purpose behind this shift was to meet congressional concerns that the State Department was too prone to negotiate trade agreements based on nebulous foreign policy grounds. Thus, trade policy was made less a stepchild of foreign policy and more subject to commercial realities and special-interest pressures.

The Kennedy Round. The Kennedy Round had three major objectives: (1) Overall reduction in tariffs, (2) reduction of nontariff barriers, and (3) participation of less-developed countries. Of these three objectives, reduction of tariffs was the most successful. The reduction of nontariff barriers was not as successful as had been hoped.

681

13

Import duties were cut an average of 35 percent on manufactured goods and 20 percent on agricultural products (excluding cereals, meat and dairy products). In all, about 70 percent of imported items were included in the cuts. By the end of the Kennedy Round, tariffs in the United States, the European Community, and Japan averaged only about 10 percent.

The Kennedy Round was also the first set of negotiations that addressed the problem of nontariff barriers, including:

1. Technical Barriers—mainly product standards, labeling and packaging restrictions, statements of origin, etc.;

2. Anti-dumping Policies—selling a product in a foreign market below the price charged by manufacturers in its home market or below cost;

3. The Government Procurement Code—regularizing and opening up procedures for government so that international sellers have better access to government contracts; and

4. The Customs Valuation Code—the evaluation of products for tariff purposes, nomenclature, and related customs procedures.

The inability of the participants to reach agreement in the reduction of nontariff barriers, however, anticipated many of the trade-related problems of the 1970s.

The Kennedy Round was concluded on June 30, 1967, when 53 nations signed agreements to put four years of negotiations into effect. The agreements were implemented over a five-year period ending in 1972. During the late 1960s, however, the steel and textile industries became primary advocates of restricting import competition. The Nixon administration responded to this pressure by endorsing textile and steel quotas. Also, the lack of international negotiations and the failure of GATT as an institution to resolve trade problems caused protectionist legislation to be introduced in Congress. While such legislation, epitomized by the Mills bill and the Burke-Hartke bill, never became law, it emphasized the growing pressure by special domestic interests to cope with the increasing pains of free trade and open-market policies.

New Forms of Trade Restraints

"Voluntary" Restraints. On January 1, 1969, the United States entered into voluntary restraint agreements with countries exporting all types of steel into the United States. Domestic manufacturers of steel called for these restraints because they feared injury from

the tremendous increase of imported steel.[1] These restrictions were in effect until December 31, 1971. A second set of "voluntary" restraints was imposed January 1, 1972, which extended the restrictions until December 31, 1974.

President Nixon, in an effort to adhere to a 1968 campaign pledge, asked Japan and other countries to apply "voluntary" quotas on their exports of woolens and synthetic textiles to the United States. Because Japan was reluctant to abide by the "voluntary" quotas, the chairman of the House Ways and Means Committee, Wilbur Mills, with encouragement from the administration, introduced a bill in May 1969 to limit textile imports to their average annual level recorded in 1967 and 1968.

The Trade Bill of 1970. This action was a sharp departure from more than 30 years of U.S. leadership toward liberalizing trade. In the closed sessions that followed, the committee converted the president's bill into the most protectionist legislation since the Smoot-Hawley Act of 1930. It permitted any industry, when threatened by imports, to seek and obtain protection.

The bill was opposed by the European Economic Community. European governments threatened to retaliate if the bill became law. In spite of heavy opposition to the bill within the United States, especially among major exporters and multinationals, the House of Representatives passed it in November 1970. The Senate also appeared ready to pass the bill. But it adjourned before the vote could be taken, leaving the trade issue to be taken up anew by the next Congress as it convened in January 1971.[2]

The Burke-Hartke Bill. The near passage of the Trade Act of 1970 encouraged protectionist groups to seek even greater limits to free trade. Representative Burke and Senator Hartke placed a bill before Congress called the Foreign Trade and Investment Act of 1972, the Burke-Hartke bill. The objective of this bill was to provide for significant increases in government intrusion and regulation of the international flow of goods and capital. This bill was never passed, but it set the terms of the trade debate for the first half of the decade.

The Burke-Hartke bill combined traditional protectionism (import restrictions) with new forms of protectionism, including restrictions

[1]See "The Attractions of Quotas," *Wall Street Journal,* 15 January 1969, p. 18.
[2]For a discussion of the debate on the 1970 trade bill, see "Economists Warn Peril of SST if Trade Bill Passes," and "Trade Bill Foes Lose Hard Fight on Amendment," *Wall Street Journal,* 19 November 1970, p. 3; "House Approves Controversial Trade Measure," *Wall Street Journal,* 20 November 1970, p. 4.

683

15

on direct foreign investment. In addition, a foreign trade and investment commission, composed of three persons appointed by the president and confirmed by the Senate, would have been established. The commission would have been required to restrict imports to the average quantity for the period 1965–69. The commission's other responsibilities would have included estimating production schedules for various categories of goods from the previous year and fixing import quotas for each category and its supplying country. In order to grant an exception to these limits, the commission was supposed to act, in effect, as a central planning agency for the major sectors of the U.S. economy. The protectionist movement of Burke-Hartke would have frozen the 1967–69 ratio of imported goods to the production of "similar" domestic goods for an undetermined amount of time. It also attempted to freeze the geographic patterns of goods in each category.

The Demise of Bretton Woods. During this same period, the Bretton Woods agreement on international monetary policy collapsed. In August 1971, President Nixon, in violation of the Bretton Woods agreement, refused to convert dollars into gold for foreign central banks. The dollar was devalued 8.6 percent relative to gold, making the official price of an ounce of gold $38. Tariffs were increased across the board by 10 percent, and wage and price controls were imposed on the domestic economy. In December of that year, the tariff increase was rescinded and, under the Smithsonian agreement, the devaluation of the dollar against gold was "approved." A general realignment of currency values relative to the dollar also was established. The value of the dollar, however, remained under pressure. Gold convertibility was not restored. And, in February 1973, the United States devalued the dollar by another 10 percent relative to gold and, implicitly, relative to most foreign currencies as well.[3] In the months that followed, one country after another halted efforts to maintain a fixed exchange rate with the dollar, ushering in the present system of floating exchange rates. Efforts to restore dollar/gold convertibility ceased.

The fracturing of the international monetary system and the shift in the trade debate toward extreme protectionism represented by the Burke-Hartke bill paved the way for advocates of selective limits on foreign competition to appear moderate and constructive.

[3]For a discussion of the major trade issues at the time, see "U.S. Devalues Dollar 10% by Raising Price of Gold; Japan Agrees to Let Yen Float," *Wall Street Journal*, 13 February 1973, p. 3.

684

16

The Trade Act of 1974

The Trade Act of 1974 provided the broadest congressional mandate in history for the conduct of trade negotiations regarding the reduction of both tariff and nontariff barriers. The president was authorized to reduce tariffs as much as 60 percent below the levels that prevailed at the close of the Kennedy Round. It also called upon the president to begin negotiations for the purpose of strengthening the GATT system so that it could serve the purpose that the multilateral negotiations had served: diffusing and resolving trade conflicts.

However, in response to industry and congressional pressure, the cost of this broad mandate was the adoption of several provisions that eased the criteria necessary for imposing trade restraints. These included more flexible criteria for relief from increasing (but "fair") import competition, as well as substantive and procedural revisions of unfair trade practice laws (such as the antidumping and countervailing duty statutes). Thus, in addressing problems created by import competition that is considered to be "fair," the Trade Act of 1974 provided that an industry no longer need demonstrate that its injury was caused by imports resulting from an earlier tariff concession or that imports are the "major" cause—i.e., a cause no less important than any other cause—of its injury. Under the 1974 Trade Act, an industry need only show that imports are a "substantial" cause. If the International Trade Commission (ITC) finds injury, the president then must consider what impact trade restrictions would have on the domestic economy, consumers, and the overall national interests. The final determination of what action, if any, should be taken is, essentially, at his discretion. The ITC may, however, recommend adjustment assistance instead of trade restrictions. If the president does not proclaim the relief recommended by the ITC, Congress may override the president and institute the relief recommended by the commission.

The authority of the president to impose quantity restrictions was increased: For the first time, the president was authorized to negotiate orderly marketing agreements as a form of relief under the escape clause. The act also required the fulfillment of reciprocity in trade concessions before a trade agreement could be binding between the United States and another major industrial country. The Trade Act of 1974 triggered a rash of demands by U.S. industries for relief from import competition. These included requests for antidumping and countervailing duties, as well as escape clause restrictions on such items as chemical products, steel products, consumer electronics, industrial fasteners, canned hams, and vinyl shoes.

685

Changes in tariff policies were specifically circumscribed by GATT.[4] The GATT agreements also sought to prohibit the use of quantitative restrictions, which were viewed as more harmful than tariffs. However, these prohibitions were not specific enough to prevent circumvention through quantitative restrictions that were quotas in all but name. Moreover, various kinds of nontariff barriers were introduced on a plethora of products. Among the most complex of these arrangements were the multifiber arrangements, establishing the parameters for restricting textile imports by the industrialized countries (effective January 1, 1974).

The use of "voluntary export restraints" also expanded during the 1970s. Under this arrangement, the importing country negotiates an agreement with the exporting country for that country to limit "voluntarily" the amounts of certain exports. In the United States, such negotiated trade restrictions, in the form of orderly marketing agreements, have been imposed on specialty steels, color TV receivers, nonrubber footwear, certain meats, mushrooms, textiles and automobiles. In 1976 the president obtained an orderly marketing agreement to limit specialty steel exports with Japan, and unilateral quotas were imposed on imports from the EEC and various countries.

The Tokyo Round. Under the Trade Act of 1974, the president entered into the Tokyo Round of Multilateral Trade Negotiations. Once again, tariff reductions were high on the agenda. But reduction of nontariff barriers also were considered an integral part of the negotiations. The agreements reached were signed in December 1978, and represented potential progress in both tariff and nontariff reductions.

Tariff reductions averaged about 30 percent for the United States, 22 percent for Japan, and 27 percent for the European Economic Community. Nontariff reductions centered on the codes discussed earlier but generally were attempts to make trade-barrier activities transparent and explicit rather than hidden. The tariff reductions centered on "harmonization," wherein higher tariffs are reduced by a higher percentage than lower tariffs. Agreement was achieved on the "Swiss formula" with exceptions made for particularly sensitive commodities.[5] Had the Swiss formula been applied in its strictest

---

[4]The views of GATT's director general on bilateral trade are detailed in B. Bahree, "Bilateral Trade Accords are Blasted by Head of GATT in Appeal for Unity," *Wall Street Journal*, 20 August 1981, p. 34.

[5]Specifically, the Swiss formula called for a tariff rate x to be reduced to a lower rate z, according to the formula, $z = 4x/(x + 14)$. This formula would result in larger percentage cuts for higher rates. There was no historical or intellectual reason for the choice of this particular formula. It was chosen principally because it was simple and implied an acceptable cut in the average tariff levels.

sense, tariff reductions on average would have been 41 percent for the United States, 43 percent for the EEC, 68 percent (in applied rates) for Japan, and 39 percent (in applied rates) for Canada.

Failure of the United States and other countries to meet the tariff reductions dictated by the Swiss formula created a general environment of tariff reduction avoidance. When concessions were made for one country, other countries felt it in their best interest to protect themselves by maintaining higher tariffs on items of particular sensitivity in their countries. Agreements affecting nontariff barriers were reached in three major areas: codes for conduct of international trade, reform of the GATT framework, and the reductions of nontariff barriers in specific products.

Six codes were agreed upon in Geneva. They addressed such trade problems as government procurement, the use of export subsidies, the imposition of countervailing duties, "dumping" of goods in foreign markets, customs valuation, the setting of standards for imports, and the issuance of import licenses. In addition, two other codes were discussed but no agreement was reached. GATT allowed countries to protect themselves against import surges in order to safeguard domestic industries. But increasingly, major industrial nations ignored the GATT mechanisms and used bilateral negotiations that allowed countries to "voluntarily" limit their exports of industry-threatening products.

Recent Developments

In March 1979, the U.S. International Trade Commission determined that Korean bicycle tires and tube imports were injuring domestic producers.[6] In October, the ITC recommended that President Carter impose three years of quotas on Russian anhydrous ammonia. In November, the commission proposed a sharp increase in U.S. import duties on low-priced porcelain and on steel cookware. By late spring of 1980, pressure was building to impose significantly higher import duties on small trucks imported from Japan. In August 1980, that pressure resulted in a 25 percent duty on lightweight truck chassis originating in Japan.[7]

A significant increase in the use of trade restrictions as a foreign policy weapon was witnessed in 1980.[8] In response to the Soviet

[6]See "U.S. Ruling Faults Imports of Korean Bicycle Tires," Wall Street Journal, 23 March 1979, p. 36.

[7]See A. Pasztos, "Sharp Boost in Duties on Foreign Trucks is not Expected to Aid Sales of U.S. Models," Wall Street Journal, 20 August 1982, p. 9.

[8]Support for these actions can be found in F. Allen, "Executives Say Imports Pose Serious Threat," Wall Street Journal, 27 August 1980, p. 11.

687

invasion of Afghanistan, the United States forbade domestic exporters to sell corn, wheat, and certain fertilizer products to the Soviet Union. Severe restrictions also were placed on the export of high technology products.

In the summer of 1980, Ford Motor Company joined with the United Auto Workers to petition the ITC to grant protection from import competition from Japan. The U.S. International Trade Commission determined that imports were not a substantial cause of the domestic auto industry's sales problem. But Congress and the executive branch responded to political pressure and "voluntary" export restraints were discussed with the Japanese government. In effect, the Japanese automakers agreed—under pressure from the Japanese government—to restrict exports to the United States to 1.68 million units in the year following April 1981, and not to increase their exports unless the U.S. sales of all autos expand. Currently, Japanese auto company spokesmen are indicating reluctance to abide by the voluntary restraints. Thus the stage is set for yet another round of calls for tighter protection from U.S. automakers and labor organizations.

Although the Reagan administration endorses free trade, it is considering a new trade policy based on "reciprocity." The goal is to force other industrial nations to reduce their trade barriers to American-made goods and to reduce subsidies to their export industries. If a nation fails to meet these conditions, special restrictions and/or tariffs conceivably would be imposed on its exports to the United States.

The approach represents a radical change in U.S. trade policy. In essence, it is a bilateral framework that requires negotiations with all countries that trade with the United States before extension of the U.S. most-favored-nation (minimum) tariff structure. This policy would represent an abandonment of the unconditional most-favored-nation principle that has been the foundation of trade policy among the industrial nations since 1923. As such, it invites increased protectionism among the industrial countries, and threatens a return to the "beggar-thy-neighbor" policies of the early 1930s.

The move toward protectionism got another push when the domestic steel industry on January 11, 1982, filed forms with the Commerce Department and the International Trade Commission charging nine European countries, Brazil, and South Africa with unfair trade practices. In its preliminary rulings, the Commerce Department found that nine foreign governments had been unfairly subsidizing steel exports. The International Trade Commission agreed that 90 percent of the unfair trade complaints represented reasonable injury to

688

domestic steel products. The Commerce Department's final ruling reduced most of the subsidy margins cited in its preliminary determination and narrowed the list of offenders to six Western European countries.

On October 21, just hours before the Commerce Department would have been required to impose countervailing and penalty duties—selective increases in U.S. tariffs and duties—quota negotiations were finalized limiting European steel imports to about 85 percent of 1981 levels. In addition, the quotas were extended to pipe and tube products. The accord has two parts:

1. Carbon and alloy steel shipments will be limited to an average 5.44 percent of the projected U.S. market. The pact also sets individual ceilings for specific categories. The Europeans will set up a new export licensing system to enforce this part of the accord.

2. Pipe and tube exports will be restricted to 5.9 percent of expected U.S. demand. If it seems likely that the limit will be breached, the two sides will have 60 days to find a settlement. Otherwise, either may impose new restrictions.

The United States will help enforce the agreement by invoking a newly enacted law that allows the customs service to block specified steel imports that have not received foreign export licenses. Such actions could undercut U.S. efforts to persuade the Western Europeans and Japanese to move toward freer trade by dropping some nontariff barriers.

Restrictions on U.S. exports to the Soviet Union and U.S. efforts to curtail East-West trade in the aftermath of martial law in Poland also threaten to disrupt trading patterns that have been established during the past 10 years. That, too, will detract from economic growth both in Western Europe and Japan, increasing economic tensions among the industrial countries.

With record trade deficits persisting, implementation of the new GATT codes of conduct only beginning, and unemployment rates in the United States near their postwar high, pressure will be intense to protect American industries, from autos and steel to textiles and footwear. The influence of the protectionist groups is fairly apparent in the various trade legislation currently on Congress' agenda. The influence of protectionist groups is felt both in the formulation of protectionist legislation and free trade policies. An example of the push for protectionism on Capitol Hill is the local content legislation that is aimed at largely eliminating Japanese auto imports. Protectionist influence is also evident in the supposedly "free trade" type

689

21

of legislation such as the Carribean Basin Initiative. This legislation would reduce trade barriers for numerous commodities but retain protection for textiles and sugarcane—commodities in which the Carribean region has a clear comparative advantage.[9]

The November 1982 GATT Meeting. In November 1982, for the first time since 1973, a GATT ministerial meeting was held. The following major issues appeared on the GATT agenda:[10]

1. A moratorium on protectionism, designed to stem the proliferation of new trade barriers;
2. A new safeguards system that would limit the import restraints a country may impose to protect industries threatened by foreign competition;
3. Extension of the GATT rules to cover trade in services, investments, and high-technology products;
4. Common Market subsidies on agricultural exports;
5. A proposed round of negotiations between rich and poor countries aimed at opening the developing countries; and
6. The development of a dispute-settling mechanism.

One of the objectives of the meetings was to reassure the world that the major trading countries would resist the kind of protectionism that could result in a worsened worldwide recession. However, due to the disagreement among member countries, the meetings were doomed to failure.[11] Even the GATT director doubted that much agreement could be reached on the major issues, such as import safeguards.[12]

At best, the results of the ministerial meeting can be considered a symbolic victory for free trade. The member countries committed themselves in principle to avoid further violations of GATT rules and to correct existing ones. The document, however, lacks any new measures to reinforce that pledge.[13]

---

[9]See G. Sieb, "Reagan Sends Caribbean Plan to Congress," *Wall Street Journal*, 18 March 1982.

[10]For a more detailed account of the basic issues, see A. Pine, "Ministers Mull World Trade," *Wall Street Journal*, 11 November 1982, p. 6.

[11]See A. Pine, "U.S. Worries that . . . GATT Parley Will Increase Protectionism not Trade," *Wall Street Journal*, 5 November 1982, p. 36; and idem, "GATT Talks Face Problems as Negotiators Fail to Agree on any Big Issue on Agenda," *Wall Street Journal*, 10 November 1982, p. 25.

[12]See World Briefs column in the *Wall Street Journal*, 8 October 1982.

[13]See A. Pine, "GATT Meeting Communique Isn't Likely to Have Much Influence on World Trade," *Wall Street Journal*, 30 November 1982, p. 2.

The lack of agreement on the major policy issues discussed at the GATT ministerial session should not be surprising to an economist. The dismantling, as well as the imposition, of trade restrictions alters the incentive structure of different interest groups in the member countries. The restrictions clearly increase the well-being of some the poor member countries. However, to the extent that the restrictions do not benefit the world as a whole, countries negatively affected will either try to circumvent the regulations[14] or lobby for more favorable restrictions.[15]

Trade restrictions give rise to economic rents. This is turn gives rise to rent-seeking behavior. To the extent that those countries that benefit from the actions can organize effectively, the political process may result in protectionist policies.[16] Thus one of the problems for advocates of free trade is to keep protectionist pressures within bounds and to avoid repeating the experience of the Smoot-Hawley Act of 1930.[17]

The Williamsburg Summit. Recent developments are not encouraging to those who advocate free trade. At first glance, the trade restrictions of high tariffs and new quotas on specialty steel and an effective increase in tariffs on frozen concentrated orange juice from Brazil seem too superficial to be concerned about. But a close look reveals that the threat posed by these restrictions is potentially far more than a mere blemish on the economic recovery of the world economy. The actions suggest a retaliatory behavior on the part of the United States. The view becomes more credible as one takes into consideration the fact that the countries affected were the

---

[14]For an analysis of individual behavior and smuggling activity in the presence of trade restrictions, see J. N. Bhagwati and B. Hansen, "A Theoretical Analysis of Smuggling," *Quarterly Journal of Economics* 87 (May 1973): 172–87; J. N. Bhagwati and T. N. Srinivasan, "Smuggling and Trade Policy," *Journal of Public Economics* 2 (November 1973): 377–89; and R.E. Falvey, "A Note on Preferential and Illegal Trade under Quantitative Restrictions," *Quarterly Journal of Economics* 92 (February 1978): 175–78.

[15]For a discussion of the politics of special interest groups, see W. A. Brock and S. P. Magee, "The Economics of Special Interest Politics: The Case of the Tariff," *American Economic Review* 68 (May 1978): 246–50.

[16]Analysis of rent-seeking behavior can be traced to A.O. Krueger's seminal paper. "The Political Economy of the Rent-Seeking Society," *American Economic Review* 64 (June 1974): 291–303. Krueger's analysis has been further refined and generalized by J. N. Bhagwati and T. N. Srinivasan, "Revenue Seeking: A Generalization of the Theory of Tariffs," *Journal of Political Economy* 88 (December 1980): 1069–87.

[17]On this issue, see R. Straus, "The Mercantilist Threat to World Trade," *Wall Street Journal*, 24 November 1982.

691

23

ones opposed to the major issues discussed at the November 1982 GATT meeting.

The decision by the president to provide protection to the specialty steel industry, little more than a month after the May 1983 Williamsburg economic summit, undercuts the U.S. efforts to ease trade barriers among the industrialized countries. To add insult to injury, the new restrictions on steel—ranging from higher tariffs on stainless steel sheet strips and plates to quotas on stainless steel bar and plates, and alloy tool steel products, which reduce imports by as much as 44 percent below their 1982 levels—fall largely on six industrial nations: Canada, France, West Germany, Italy, Japan, and the United Kingdom.

Administration arguments that the new trade restrictions are designed to foster the goals of the Williamsburg summit by pressuring other nations to get rid of practices injuring U.S. producers are fatuous. The European response was to threaten to retaliate with higher tariffs on U.S. exports to the Common Market. Furthermore, the U.S. actions ignore recent European moves reducing "unfair" trade practices. Prior to the economic summit, the Common Market countries had agreed to phase out, over the next 18 months, the steel subsidies that are so offensive to U.S. producers and the administration. Yet, the higher tariffs and quotas will prevail for four years.

Effect of Trade Policies on the U.S. Economy

Sectoral Impact of Trade Policies

This section presents two case studies analyzing the effectiveness of trade policies used to aid a domestic industry. First, the apparently successful case of temporary import restraints on color televisions is explored. Next, the more complex, and apparently unsuccessful, attempt to assist the domestic steel industry adjust to foreign competition is presented.

Color Televisions. In the spring of 1977, the United States negotiated an orderly marketing agreement with Japan that reduced the number of Japanese color television imports into the United States to 1.56 million units from their high of 2.5 million units reached in 1976.[18] The Japanese producers more than complied with these restrictions, reducing exports to the United States to 1.4 million units in 1978.

---

[18]A more detailed analysis of the effects of the orderly marketing agreement can be found in V. A. Canto and A. B. Laffer, "The Effectiveness of Orderly Marketing Agreements: The Color TV Case," *Business Economics* 18 (January 1983): 38–45.

U.S. producers, however, did not benefit from this restriction. Instead, foreign producers (especially in South Korea, Taiwan and Canada) increased dramatically their exports to the United States. As a result, color television imports in 1978 were above their 1977 level and nearly as high as their record 1976 level. The sudden success of these foreign producers led to new or extended import quotas for Taiwan and South Korea. As a result, total color television imports in 1980 were 1.3 million units, less than half of their 1976 peak.

The apparent success of the effort to protect the domestic color television manufacturers is misleading. Domestic producers (both U.S. and foreign-owned) circumvented these restrictions by beginning the production of their televisions in the United States, exporting the incomplete sets for the bulk of the manufacturing and assembly, and then "reimporting" the televisions for final assembly in the United States. The tariff imposed on the "reimported" TVs is only 5 percent of the foreign value added.

During the 1977–80 period, incomplete color TV imports rose to nearly three million units from virtually zero in 1976. Subtracting these from total "U.S.-produced" TVs indicates that the domestic production of color TVs has increased only slightly since the imposition of the trade restrictions. Moreover, since 1977, the number of persons employed and the average number of man-hours worked in the domestic industry have declined.

Steel.[19] In response to the steadily growing market share of Japanese steel imports, the United States in 1968 negotiated a three-year voluntary restraint agreement with Japanese and European exporters. Exports of steel to the United States were limited to a target of 14 million tons in 1969—22 percent below their 1968 level. The target was allowed to increase gradually during the subsequent years. And the agreement was extended in 1971 for three additional years.

In the face of the quantity restriction, the Japanese and European exporters shifted their product mix from lower-valued steels—where they had made the largest inroads—to higher-valued products. During the six years of the import restrictions, domestic prices of higher-valued steel products, such as cold- and hot-rolled steel, remained fairly close to those of the Japanese. The price of lower-valued steel products, such as structurals, however, increased well above the

[19]The analysis in this section is based on V. A. Canto, R. V. Eastin, and A. B. Laffer, "Failure of Protectionism: A Study of the Steel Industry," *Columbia Journal of World Business* 17 (Winter 1982): 43–57.

693

world price. As a result of this shift, even though the tonnage of steel imports was reduced, the overall value of imports remained approximately the same.

The net effect of increased competition in higher-valued steels and less competition in lower-valued steels was, if anything, to hurt the U.S. steel industry. The rate of return of the industry during the period of import restrictions (1969–74) was lower than during the three years prior to the period of import protection and the two years subsequent to import protection. During the protected period, capital expenditures in constant dollars declined relative to 1967 as well as to the years subsequent to the expiration of the voluntary restraint agreements. Moreover, the voluntary import restraints did not stop the decline in the steel industry's employment levels.

Trigger prices, too, have been unsuccessful in fostering a healthy, domestic steel industry. The trigger prices have been successful in reducing the market share of steel imports from Japan and the European Economic Community. But the bulk of this gap has been filled by imports from other foreign producers. Moreover, the trigger price mechanism acts to increase the profit margin of foreign producers as soon as it becomes effective. As such, it provides them with an incentive to increase their production, even if sold at prices below the trigger and prevailing market prices. This distortion of incentives can be expected to lead directly to an increase in the incidence of dumping charges by U.S. producers.

The 1950-to-1983 experience of the U.S. steel industry can be explained largely in terms of the standard trade theory without any reference to government interference in world steel markets. Following World War II, as Japan rebuilt its steel industry, resulting in larger and more efficient plants, the cost advantage of producing steel shifted from U.S. producers to Japanese producers. The steady loss of market share by U.S producers is, to a large extent, due this shift in cost effectiveness.

In January 1982, major U.S. steel companies sought relief from government-subsidized competitors. As a result of these legal actions, the U.S. government dropped enforcement of the trigger price mechanism. Preliminarily in June and finally in late August, the Commerce Department upheld charges of government-subsidized steel prices against six Western European nations. Under the law, high tariffs in the form of countervailing and penalty duties would have been levied to offset the advantages of foreign subsidies and dumping. In their stead, the Commerce Department negotiated quotas on European steelmakers. Individual ceilings for specific categories also were set.

694

The Impact of Trade Policies on the National Economy

Import tariffs and export subsidies represent another set of policies attempting to improve the balance of trade. Advocates of these policies observe that tariffs raise the domestic prices of imported goods and subsidies reduce the prices of exported products to foreigners. This reduction in imports and the stimulus to exports are believed to improve the balance of trade and, consequently, domestic economic conditions.

An analysis of the effects of changes in average tariff rates on the trade balance, however, indicates that the real-world effects of tariffs on the balance of trade are more complex. Not only do tariffs reduce imports but they are associated with a decline in exports as well. Thus, the impact of tariffs on the trade balance is ambiguous (with the exception of the extreme case in which a country is running a trade balance deficit and then bans all imports). The decline in exports and imports indicates that the overall volume of trade is reduced by tariffs. Moreover, since both exports and imports are reduced by import tariffs, the trade balance (exports less imports) would be little changed. This result can be understood by realizing that exports and imports are two sides of the same transaction: The object of producing goods for export is to be able to import and consume goods produced by foreigners.

Suppose that a tariff successfully reduces the volume of imports by one-half. There are now only half as many foreign goods available to exchange for domestically produced goods, given the world terms of trade. So, the volume of exports must be reduced symmetrically by one-half. The net effect on the trade balance is zero. In other words, a tax on imports is equivalent in effect to a tax on exports. This principle is referred to as Lerner's symmetry theorem, a well-known principle of trade theory.[20]

Quantitative restrictions in the form of import quotas and self-imposed foreign export quotas also are on the menu of protectionist policies. In principle, there is a precise correspondence between quotas and tariffs: For any quota (or quantitative restriction) imposed, there exists a tariff that will produce exactly the same price and quantity effects on the volume of imports and exports. The Lerner symmetry theorem is equally applicable to quotas. A restriction on imports is equivalent to a restriction on exports and can be expected to have little or no effect on the balance of trade. Thus, the efficacy

---

[20]A.P. Lerner, "The Symmetry between Import and Export Taxes," *Economica* 3 (August 1936): 306–13.

of protectionist measures to improve the trade balance is dubious on both theoretical and empirical grounds.

Trade restrictions reduce the efficiency of the world economy and reduce the standard of living of all trading partners.[21] To the extent that trade restrictions are effective, the gains from trade in both production and consumption are lost. Production incentives shift away from those goods that are produced more efficiently domestically. And consumers are no longer able to choose goods produced more efficiently abroad. Trade restrictions devised to protect a particular industry may well accomplish that task for a period of time. But the cost of protecting that industry is borne by the rest of the economy.

Further, tariffs and quotas on imports constitute tax wedges for the world economy. With fewer goods available in each domestic economy, at higher prices, the rewards for work effort are reduced. The Smoot-Hawley Act tariffs offer grim evidence of the tax wedge imposed by tariffs.

Conclusion

The increase in protectionist legislation and the Reagan administration's new trade policy based on "reciprocity" represent a departure from the postwar trade liberalization movement. The administration hopes to convince other nations to lower their trade barriers and to reduce subsidies to their export industries. In order to achieve these objectives, the United States stands ready to increase its trade barriers on a bilateral basis and increase subsidies to its import-competing industries. This policy is supposed to be sufficient to further the goal of freer world trade.

The policy issue therefore centers on whether judiciously applied protectionist measures can contribute to domestic economic stability and growth. In particular, can instruments of trade policy be used to improve a country's balance of trade and its overall economic performance? Furthermore, can specific industries suffering from import competition be assisted through protectionist measures, thereby reducing unemployment and increasing total output and income?

The grim experience of the early 1930s amply demonstrates that the movement toward protectionism carries with it major implications for the U.S. economy. Virtually all economists and policy makers agree that, in the extreme, trade restrictions are self-defeating, impoverishing foreign countries and U.S. citizens alike.

[21]See V. A. Canto, A. B. Laffer, and J. C. Turney, "Trade Policy and the U.S. Economy," *Financial Analyst Journal* (September/October 1982): 237–46.

Quarterly Review of Economics and Business
Vol. 24, No. 2 (Summer 1984)

Review Article

Reindustrialization of the United States: Three Perspectives on Organizational Adaptation

Alok K. Chakrabarti

Reindustrialization and industrial policy have become almost household words through the discussions and debates occurring in the mass media, business magazines and periodicals, and political speeches. The lure of "high tech" is strongly eluding many public officials, business leaders, and political pundits as the ultimate panacea for all the economic ills of the country. The objective of this review is to take a close look at the various views on industrial policy and go beyond the usual political rhetoric to understand the differences and similarities among them.

Robert B. Reich, a professor of industrial policy at the Kennedy School of Government at Harvard, has articulated the issues concerning industrial policy in his book, *The New American Frontier* [3]. Reich has an impressive following, including the presidential aspirants in the Democratic party. Professor Reich, a lawyer by training, assents that political, social, and organizational "adaptation is America's challenge" and her "next frontier."

"Organizational adaptation" has been advocated as the key in *Renewing American Industry* by Paul R. Lawrence and Davis Dyer of the Harvard Business School [2]. Lawrence, an organizational behavior expert, teamed with business historian Dyer to analyze key industries such as autos, steel, hospitals, agriculture, residential construction, coal, and telecommunications. The outcome of this massive historical analysis is the development of an organizational theory for adaptation and readaptation.

William J. Abernathy along with his colleagues Kim B. Clark and Alan M. Kantrow from the Operations Management Group at the Harvard Business School in their *Industrial Renaissance* [1] make suggestions for "producing a competitive future for America." Abernathy and his associates have studied the US auto industry in great depth and have developed a theory of industrial competition over time, along with relevant policy suggestions and guidelines.

Although the background and training of the authors of these three books differ significantly, they all have used historical analysis to substantiate their theories. The relative emphasis on micro (firm-specific) and macro (general government-policy-oriented) issues is related closely to the authors' background. Reich is mostly macro-policy-oriented; he dealt with macro trends in industries, making broad generalizations, while Lawrence and Dyer are oriented to firm-specific issues. They are concerned with relating their hypotheses and conclusions in empirically testable terms. Abernathy, Clark, and Kantrow are also deeply empirically oriented and maintained a micro focus on the auto industry.

The authors of these three books agree about the impact of international competition and resource scarcity on the problems of American industry. Abernathy, Clark, and Kantrow observe,

High quality, reliable performance, relatively low cost based on real manufacturing efficiencies — these have been, time and again, at the heart of the competitive strategy that has enabled foreign producers to outflank, outfox, and outperform their American counterparts.

Lawrence and Dyer's book opens,

In industry after industry, U.S. firms are loosing their competitive advantage to foreign firms. This loss is the underlying cause for the country's present, serious, economic distress and the many financial problems closely related to it. Unemployment, adverse balance of payments, decline in the growth of the gross national product, low rate of productivity gain, and the high level of interest rates and inflation are but symptoms of a seriously weakened position industry by industry, firm by firm.

Reich also identifies the changes in the world market as the root cause for the economic decline of the United States. Through a historical analysis of the US management system, Reich has tried to make a convincing argument that our inability to adapt to the demands of the changing world market has led to significant economic decline.

Although the diagnosis of the symptoms seems to be the same, the authors differ on their prognosis of the situation. Reich advocates that the federal government adopt industrial policy that would provide a proactive, rather than the reactive role that the Congress and the executive branch usually take, and guide investment, employment, and development of market opportunity. As a very competent legal scholar, he convincingly steers the reader towards the conclusion. Reich's argument is based on several hypotheses and conclusions about the US system.

Reich points out the dichotomy of two cultures: civic and business. The civic culture is rooted in the concept of social justice and welfare while the business culture is rooted in the concept of individual freedom, entrepreneurship, and innovation. Reich traces the adversary relationship between these two cultures and calls for a basic adaptation to end the polarity. The industrial development of the United States has been explained through the tension between these two opposing cultures. The growth of the management system has been accounted for primarily by the dominance of business culture. In Reich's analysis, we get an implied picture of conspiracy, manipulation, and political control by the opposing camps of culture. Reich painstakingly demonstrates the government's involvement in these feuds, conspiracies, interventions, and market control by industries and firms.

This system of opposing cultures, the adversary relationship between management and labor, and the sporadic involvement of government agencies and regulatory boards worked fine until the mid-1960s when we encountered major global change in market and production systems. The US system of production and distribution is just not competitive in the international marketplace. Reich prescribes a few remedies.

First of all, he wants a major change in the sociopolitical culture and outlook emphasizing collectivism over individualism. In the international marketplace, we will see more competition between complex organizations than between individuals.

Second, he advocates a political institution "less concerned with *correct* decisions than with making correctable ones; less obsessed with avoiding error than with detecting and correcting error." He carefully points out that such a political institution is not a "national planning" agency.

Third, Reich contends that certain types of industries and businesses are beyond redemption and that we would be better off without them. The United States should, according to Reich, be involved in "flexible system production" of precision products, custom products, and technology-driven products, dependent on skilled labor.

Fourth, Reich wants more active, strategic intervention through fiscal and financial measures by the government to steer industries towards some desired courses of action.

Technology, skill, and knowledge are key ingredients in Reich's "flexible system." He considers capital and technology highly mobile; however, skilled labor that is consistently developing its skill and technical level is not mobile across geographical boundaries and, therefore, would provide stability to the United States.

Abernathy, Clark, and Kantrow believe in technology and operational efficiency as key to the "industrial renaissance" of the United States. Their method of analysis differs substantially from Reich's. By using the product-life-cycle model and relating the differences in relative emphasis on product performance and cost of production, Abernathy and his colleagues presented the three stages of industrial growth. The appropriate management policy and strategies have been outlined for these different stages. Abernathy's finding about the evolution of the American manufacturing system is less dialectical than Reich's. According to Abernathy, Clark, and Kantrow, the United States manufacturing system has gone through the following developmental stages:

(1) "development of factories well suited to the sequential production of simple, imitative, and not-very-capital-intensive products which were assembled from machine-made and largely interchangeable parts";

31

(2) the example of Singer Machine Company led to "building a manufacturing organization flexible enough to assimilate technological advances while offering substantial variety at low cost and at uniformly high levels of quality";

(3) the initiation by Samuel Colt of "institutionalizing constant improvements in process and product technology as a deliberately chosen means for achieving competitive advantage";

(4) the stage of dependence on suppliers that facilitated access to new technology at low costs.

The problem, according to Abernathy, Clark, and Kantrow, is deemphasis of production and technology in the mid-1960s, just when the United States faced increasingly intensive international competition. The productivity of labor and capital became badly affected compared with other countries, such as Japan. The result is a net cost disadvantage of $1,500 per car for US manufacturers compared with Japanese producers. Abernathy, Clark, and Kantrow concluded,

The fact remains that consumer perceptions about quality do influence sales, and the landed-cost advantage enjoyed by Japanese producers translates those sales into a highly profitable stream of revenues. This is the basis on which Japanese manufacturers of automobiles — and for that matter, a host of other products — have been able to compete so very successfully with domestic American producers.

The solution to America's problems lies in technological innovations with a high degree of "transilience," that is, "capacity to influence production systems and their linkage to market." Based on the transilience factor, Abernathy, Clark, and Kantrow defined four classes of innovations:

(1) *Innovations leading to architectural phase.* They have a high impact on productive as well as market linkages. The innovations establish "design hierarchies that set the agenda for later development and new application possibilities."

(2) *Innovations leading to niche-creation phase.* Innovations with minor impact on the productive system try to achieve high profitable impact on the market through repackaging of existing technology. Here the technical and manufacturing challenges are of little importance. "Fine tuning of production systems to offer entrenched design concepts to new users" is of strategic importance.

(3) *Innovations leading to regular phase.* Innovations leading to the regular phase take place after the "basic architecture of the product has been established and its market linkages have begun to crystallize." Innovations at this stage are incremental in nature and reinforce the existing productive system and market linkages.

(4) *Innovations leading to revolutionary phase.* The revolutionary phase is precipitated when the "regular and niche-creation innovations" are inadequate to restore the "competitive vitality" of the industry. Radical

32

changes in design and technology challenge the core technical concepts. The existing market linkages are utilized to apply these revolutionary technological developments.

Abernathy, Clark, and Kantrow suggest that industrial renaissance would be possible through a better understanding of the different types of innovations at maturity level. The US firms are too preoccupied with innovations related to the niche-creation and regular phases. The industrial structure now demands more revolutionary and architectural types of innovation. New organizational adaptation and reward systems are needed to stimulate and foster innovation.

Lawrence and Dyer provide a complex model of the different industries, relating their characteristics in terms of "information complexity" domain and the "resource scarcity" domain. The beauty of this complex model is that it takes into account the interaction of the various factors, rather than providing a simplistic political panacea. Lawrence and Dyer deal with the human-resource management in various industrial sectors at much more depth than the other authors. The need for different types of technologies is explained with reference to the "information complexity" and "resource scarcity" domains. Finally, Lawrence and Dyer have found a place for all types of organizations — owner entrepreneurs, and professional-dominated, consumer-dominated, and salaried-manager-dominated ones.

In fairness to all the authors, one would detect a common theme in these three books — change and adaptation. Reich advocates change at the macro level more intensely than at the micro level. Government participation is the central theme in his prescription. Predictably, one would encounter opposition to industrial policy. *Business Week* (4 July 1983) quoted several economists opposing the concept of government industrial policymaking. Their criticism can be summarized as follows:

- Policy would be vague to the point of being meaningless;
- Government is a poor performer as an entrepreneur;
- Policy would parcel out tax dollars to politically powerful groups;
- Government subsidy to industries are ineffective measures to raise competitive strength;
- Adequacy of knowledge of government bureaucrats to make proper decisions is doubtful;
- The market place should be ultimate arbiter of capital allocation.

Although one agrees with Reich about the need to dismantle the complex array of sometimes conflicting, sometimes self-defeating rules, regulations, and incentives, it is difficult to transfer great power and authority to central bureaucracies for the final decisions. The decentralized — somewhat inefficient and cumbersome — decision-making process of the United States is our best strength. History has taught us the danger of centralized, absolute power for a country. The utopian picture of political and social change depicted by Reich may well suit a presidential campaign, but it is not what should be implemented.

33

Abernathy and his associates as well as Lawrence and Dyer provide a more sober, realistic path for dealing with industrial-revival issues. A change in sociopolitical philosophy cannot be legislated, but must be implemented slowly through debate, discussions, and education. To that extent, Reich, the professor, has done us an enormous service through his book. His colleagues across the river in the business school presented the complexity of the issues in a more realistic and empirically validated manner.

Whomever one agrees with, the choice is clear — we need some radical change and adaptation in our sociopolitical and technological areas. No country may serve as a model to imitate. The real new frontier ahead of us is unknown, and Americans have to pioneer in that frontier through adaptation and readaptation of its organizational systems.

REFERENCES

1. William J. Abernathy, Kim B. Clark, and Alan M. Kantrow, *Industrial Renaissance: Producing a Competitive Future for America* (New York: Basic Books, 1983).

2. Paul R. Lawrence and Davis Dyer, *Renewing American Industry* (New York: The Free Press, 1983).

3. Robert B. Reich, *The Next American Frontier* (New York: Times Books, 1983).

THE POLITICAL ECONOMY OF NATIONAL INDUSTRIAL POLICY

Thomas J. DiLorenzo

Introduction

The phrase "national industrial policy" (NIP) can be viewed as a euphemism for national economic planning and an expanded welfare state.[1] This can be seen by examining some of the NIP proposals, which include greater governmental control over credit allocation, government domination of plant-closing decisions, governmental promotion or penalization of "winning" and "losing" industries through selective tax and subsidy schemes, and legislatively enacted co-determination.[2] Although the volume and variety of NIP proposals is mind boggling, the current debate over national industrial policy centers on one basic issue: Does economic growth best proceed through the spontaneous forces of the market or the coercive powers of the state? In short, the debate over industrial policy concerns the basic role of government in a free society: Should the powers of the state be used to cultivate the market order or to supersede the market and replace planning by individuals with planning by government bureaucracies? According to Hayek (1978, p. 234), this and other disputes over economic planning really hinge upon whether

> it is better that the holder of coercive power should confine himself
> in general to creating conditions under which the knowledge and
> initiative of individuals are given the best scope so that *they* can

---

Cato Journal, Vol. 4, No. 2 (Fall 1984). Copyright © Cato Institute. All rights reserved.

The author is Assistant Professor of Economics at George Mason University. He was awarded second prize in the 1984 Olive W. Garvey essay contest sponsored by the Mont Pelerin Society for an earlier version of this paper.

[1]Few NIP advocates voice a preference for comprehensive national economic planning in view of the debacles created by all previous attempts. Instead, they urge more of a "halfway house" between comprehensive economic planning and a free market economy. As shown below, such partial attempts are doomed to fail for the same reasons comprehensive planning has failed.

[2]For an overview of these proposals see McKenzie (1983).

plan most successfully; or whether a rational utilization of our resources requires *central* direction and organization of all our activities according to some consciously constructed 'blueprint.'

This paper evaluates the current NIP proposals by first explaining the general economic consequences of the "protective state" that facilitates market exchange and economic efficiency, and the "redistributive state" that arbitrarily directs the organization of individual activity according to political criteria. It is shown how government promotes economic cooperation and prosperity when it is restricted to protecting private property rights and the freedom of exchange, and how the redistributive or "planning" role of government leads to economic conflict, stagnation, and a loss of individual liberty.

The adverse effects of government planning are illustrated by examining the consequences of the NIP proposal to extend greater governmental control over the allocation of credit. It is explained how NIP proponents are deluded by the fallacious assumption that politics is inherently "cooperative" whereas market behavior is conflictual, and is therefore the source of economic instability. This is followed by a discussion of how the current debate over industrial policy is part of an ongoing struggle by political forces to supersede the market economy.

Markets, Politics, and Economic Growth

The market is a process in which individuals voluntarily interact with one another in pursuit of their own interests. With appropriately designed institutions—such as well-defined, enforced, and respected property rights and freedom of contract, freedom of exchange, and the enforcement of contracts—self-interested behavior generates a spontaneous order. This order is chosen by no one, yet it tends to maximize the subjective values of all the market participants. Only in this sense can the market process be termed "efficient." The maximization of subjective values, as individuals perceive them, is the end result of the market process and cannot be defined or "maximized" by any outside observer. A market situation can be judged "efficient" to the extent that it allows individuals to exercise their preferences subject only to the principles of mutual agreement and noninterference with the equal rights of others. The determination of what is efficient by some third party, such as government, would require interpersonal utility comparisons that are arbitrary and meaningless. In the absence of an omniscient and benevolent despot, market efficiency can be defined only in terms of the extent to which

588

existing institutions facilitate mutually advantageous trade, subjectively valued.

Voluntary trade is a positive-sum game that increases the wealth of nations *as long as rights are exclusive*. That is, as long as property rights are defined, enforced, and transferable, productive activity will take place. If, by contrast, rights are attenuated, less trade and productive activity will take place. This amplifies the importance of one role that government has played in the economic system: the definition and enforcement of property rights. By establishing and enforcing the "rules of the game," government can encourage market efficiency and productive activity.

Of crucial importance is the protection of a well-functioning price system, for it provides the information individuals need to coordinate their plans and to engage in trade. Through the process of competition the price system reveals information on changing consumer preferences, changing relative scarcities, alternative levels of risk, and other information that is invaluable to decision makers, whether they are consumers or businessmen.

The fatal mistake of NIP proponents is that they ignore the fact that only through the competitive market process can we learn, via the price system, the relevant information for making economic decisions. To the extent that NIP proposals interfere with the price system (and they would), economic decision making and economic efficiency would be impaired. As Hayek stated (1978, p. 236):

> The chief reason why we cannot hope by central direction to achieve anything like the efficiency in the use of resources which the market makes possible is that the economic order of any large society rests on a utilization of the knowledge of particular circumstances widely dispersed among thousands or millions of individuals. . . . But among the alternative possibilities for coping with these difficulties—either conveying to a central directing authority all the relevant information possessed by the different individuals, or communicating to the separate individuals as much as possible of the information relevant for their decisions—we have discovered a solution for the second task only: the market and the competitive determination of prices have provided a procedure by which it is possible to convey to the individual managers of productive units as much information in condensed form as they need in order to fit their plans into the order of the rest of the system.

Furthermore, as an economy gains in size and complexity, it becomes even more necessary to rely on the market; for it is the only known mechanism that can effectively deal with such complexity. Subjecting private decision makers to further governmental interference through credit "controls," plant-closing boards, and other means can only increase uncertainty in the minds of entrepreneurs who must then refocus their efforts from serving consumers to dealing with red tape, directives, and regulations.

Thus, if economic growth is the objective, the most effective "industrial policy" would be for government to protect private property rights, safeguard freedom of trade and contract, and preserve the price system. In short, the proper role for government is to be the referee who watches over and enforces these rules of the game.

Politicial Resource Allocation

In recent decades the government's role has shifted away from being a referee to actively rearranging and redistributing property rights. In modern politics, ownership rights are not well respected. The state seems to operate with the notion that those within government can lay claim to all property rights and have the power to rearrange these rights arbitrarily through legislation. As individuals, politicians and bureaucrats are no different than the rest of us: They too prefer more rights to the use of resources to less and seek to maximize their utility. The utility of the politician or bureaucrat, however, is not enhanced primarily by acquiring ownership rights in goods and services through market activity. Politicians and bureaucrats gain access to goods and services by using their positions in government to bestow special privileges—to rearrange property rights—in favor of politically active individuals or groups. They do this in exchange for votes, campaign contributions, and other forms of political support. And they can do so at little cost; for those whose rights are consequently abridged are usually not politically well organized. In essence, the attenuation of property rights is the business of modern politics, and always has been. Politicians are continually seeking to expand the market for their services. Stability in private property rights is anathema to them because it imposes constraints on their abilities to accumulate power and wealth. Bernard Siegan (1980) has shown that since the early 1940s, there has been a progressive attenuation of property rights in the United States. The Supreme Court has failed, in effect, to protect our economic liberties by letting the legislative branch redistribute property almost at will.

The net effect of political resource allocation is to inhibit trade and production by reducing the expected benefits (for example, by restricting land use) and by increasing the costs. As more rights and resources come under political control, the returns to lobbying and other forms of political activity increase. This reduces the nation's productive capacity even further, because many of the resources spent by individuals and groups who seek special interest legislation are necessarily withdrawn from the process of production. Thus, by defining and enforcing property rights the state encourages productive activity, whereas by redefining and reallocating rights and interfering with the price system the state discourages production and encourages rent-seeking behavior.[3]

The importance of the government's role in protecting rather than rearranging property rights has long been recognized. Over 100 years ago Frédéric Bastiat wrote that governmental attempts to redistribute income will create "a frightful uncertainty . . . over the whole domain of private activity" (1964, p. 127). The value of individual responsibility, said Bastiat (1860, p. 10), will then be rendered

> more and more inert and inefficacious. By an improper application of the public force [to redistribute income], we alter the relation of labour to its remuneration, we disturb the laws of industry and of exchange . . . we give wrong direction to capital and labour. . . .

Bastiat (1964, p. 128) feared that once it is accepted among citizens that it is "legitimate" for government to arbitrarily redistribute income,

> we shall see the entire people transformed into petitioners. Landed property, agriculture, industry, commerce, shipping, industrial companies, all will bestir themselves to claim favors from the state. The public treasury will be literally pillaged.[4]

In sum, the NIP proposals, by expanding the domain of rent-seeking behavior, are inherently biased toward stifling, not stimulating, economic growth. As economic growth takes place over time, circumstances constantly change; and the market system best facilitates adaptation to change. Since it is precisely this adaptation that NIP proposals will delay or eliminate, they will stifle the source of long-term economic growth only for the short-term benefit of a few powerful special interests, including various businesses, unions, and other groups. As Hayek (1979, p. 94) recently noted, the social benefits of competitive markets and economic growth "are the results of such changes, and will be maintained only if the changes are allowed to continue." But every change hurts some organized interests; thus the preservation of the market order hinges upon our ability to stop these interests from preventing, through government, changes they do not like. Perhaps the major NIP proposal is for an expanded role of government in the allocation of capital. This practice provides a clear example of how allocating resources through politics rather

---

[3]Tollison (1982) provides a survey of the rent-seeking literature. Olson's (1982) work includes empirical estimates of the effects of rent-seeking behavior on economic growth.
[4]See Dorn (1981) for a fuller discussion of Bastiat's ideas on the role of government.

591

than markets benefits only a few at great expense to the rest of the nation.

The Political Economy of Government Credit Allocation

One of the most common themes of NIP enthusiasts is that there is an alleged need to "reindustrialize America . . . through a new partnership between government, management and labor" (Kirkland 1982, p. 20). That is, the market should be replaced by a "panel of experts," including businessmen, politicians, and union leaders. Lane Kirkland (1982, p. 20), president of the AFL-CIO, holds a view that all NIP proponents seem to share. He proposes

> the creation of a tripartite National Reindustrialization Board— including representatives of labor, business, and government—which would . . . insure the revitalization of the nation's sick industries and decaying communities, while at the same time encouraging the development of new industries with promise for the future. . . . This board would also direct the activities of a financing agency, patterned after the Reconstruction Finance Corporation of the 1930s and 1940s, which would be authorized to make and guarantee loans to finance approved reindustrialization ventures.

Proponents of a new Reconstruction Finance Corporation (RFC) claim benefits that such a program could not possibly produce. Supposedly an RFC is needed to better pursue "the longer-term perspective of the needs and aspirations of the American people" and to "target industrial sectors and regions that particularly need help" (Kirkland 1982, p. 21). It is impossible, however, for a government "planner" to obtain results that are superior (or even similar) to what an unregulated market economy can produce. Resource allocation by a resurrected RFC would subvert the role of the price system in allocating resources to their highest-valued uses, a role which, ironically, RFC proponents claim to be one of their chief objectives.

The idea that an RFC can improve the allocation of resources by "targeting" certain industries is absurd, regardless of the good intentions of its proponents. For this to be feasible, one must assume that government bureaucrats would be consistently better at forecasting consumer demands than are private firms and therefore will make better use of information (on behalf of consumers) than will private entrepreneurs. This argument is inherently flawed. In the private sector those firms that fail to accurately anticipate or forecast changes in consumer demands will not prosper and may not survive. Only firms that can best anticipate consumer demands and channel resources

592

40

accordingly will survive in the marketplace. Those individuals and firms that have all the detailed knowledge of particular industries— knowledge of consumer tastes, the likely success of various technological advances, changes in relative scarcities of raw materials, and so on—are best able to "plan" for the future. By contrast, government bureaucrats are subject to no such forces. Failure to correctly and consistently forecast consumer demands is not met with "losses," for there are no profits or losses, in an accounting sense, in the public sector. Moreover, the bureaucrat often judges failure as success, because this provides him with opportunity to make a plea for even more funding for his bureau.

Government bureaucrats, by definition, are detached from the everyday workings of an industry and simply cannot plan as effectively as can private individuals or firms. They are not in a position to obtain all the "information of time and place" that is necessary to operate successful business enterprises (namely, ones that satisfy consumers), even if they had an incentive to do so. It is odd that in light of the well-documented failure of government bureaucracies to plan their own affairs efficiently, NIP proponents are attempting to convince the public that additional governmental control over *private* enterprise is desirable. Moreover, only the competitive market process can reveal the appropriate information in the first place.

An RFC would also subvert the very important role credit markets play in allocating risk. Credit markets evaluate the riskiness of alternative projects, and those with higher probabilities of failure (to meet consumer demands) are charged higher borrowing costs. In this way the credit markets give consumers and producers invaluable information about the most productive uses of resources. By socializing risk an RFC would make it impossible for consumers and producers to make truly accurate benefit-cost calculations; and resources are put to lower-valued, not higher-valued, uses once politics is used to allocate credit. For example, at times when high interest rates force private firms to invest in only the most productive projects promising very high yields, politically favored firms and industries would invest in projects yielding only a fraction of the return of the "unfavored" investments. Thus, by subsidizing economically inefficient but politically popular investments, an RFC would surely reduce the productivity of the nation's capital stock, thereby *lowering* the rate of economic growth.

In sum, by interfering with the market allocation of credit, governmentally controlled credit allocation would be very harmful to the nation's economy, even though it may confer short-lived benefits on politically favored industries, unions, and regions.

593

41

Political Versus Market Allocation of Capital

The establishment of an RFC is directly at odds with the growth-facilitating forces of the price system and, therefore, with consumer sovereignty. The whole purpose of an RFC is to prevent the price system from allocating resources and, instead, to assign that task to selected politicians, bureaucrats, businessmen, and union leaders. The creation of an RFC would convey the message that consumers are no longer to be trusted to register their true preferences via the price system. Rather, government bureaucrats would inform us what our preferences are and then "target" governmentally controlled credit into those areas. But even if government authorities were omniscient and could read the consumers' minds, there is no reason to believe that resources would be used efficiently. Equity, however defined, is equally unlikely, and political resource allocation often generates greater inequities than does the market. How politicians allocate resources under their control will depend on their perceptions of the personal benefits, such as votes and campaign contributions, that accrue from alternative allocations. As James Buchanan observed (1977, p. 13):

> Politicians are politicians because they want to be. They are no more robots than other men. Yet the politician who would do nothing other than reflect the preferences of his constituents would, in fact, be robotlike in his behavior. Few, if any, politicians are so restricted. They seek office because they seek 'profit' in the form of 'political income' which will normally be obtained only if their behavior is not fully in accord with the desires of electoral majorities. Those men who are attracted to politics as a profession are likely to be precisely those who have considerable interest in promoting their own version of good government, along with those who see the opportunities for direct and indirect bribes, and those who evaluate political office as a means toward other ends.

And as Senator William Proxmire stated during the July 25, 1983, Senate debates on industrial policy:

> Money will go where the political power is. . . . It will go where the union power is mobilized. It will go where the campaign contributors want it to go. It will go where the mayors and governors as well as congressmen and senators have the power to push it. Anyone who thinks government funds will be allocated to firms according to merit has not lived or served in Washington very long.[5]

Thus, an RFC can be expected to allocate credit in a way that is the most profitable politically: It will reward the most politically

---

[5]Cited in Poole (1983, p. 6).

active unions, industries, and regions. Such a strategy will promote "reindustrialization" only by accident. It can be expected to stifle economic growth by subsidizing economically inefficient but politically popular firms and industries.

The role of the federal government in allocating credit did not end with the original RFC in the mid–1950s. The RFC was just one among many tools used by federal politicians to control the allocation of credit during the Great Depression, and many of its remnants are alive and well. A survey of some of these practices will help in understanding the consequences of political credit allocation.

Loan Guarantees and the Allocation of Credit

Proponents of a new RFC rarely mention that in addition to about $30 billion in direct loans, there are already more than 150 federal loan guarantee programs administered by federal agencies that guide the allocation of more than $100 billion in loans annually.[6] Loan guarantees are part of the legacy of the original RFC, and expanded guarantees are an integral part of the more recent proposals.

The costs of federal loan guarantee programs, like the benefits, are indirect. A major difference, however, is that the benefits accrue to well-organized interest groups but the costs are widely dispersed among the general public. The predominant indirect cost of federal loan guarantees is borne by less-favored borrowers who are crowded out of the credit market or who must pay higher interest rates on the loans that are obtained. Loan guarantees tend to increase the overall demand for credit while at the same time reducing the supply of credit available to nonguaranteed borrowers. The effect is to increase the rates charged to nonguaranteed borrowers to levels higher than they would otherwise be, which crowds out much private borrowing. This seriously distorts the market process whereby unregulated markets allocate credit to its most highly valued uses, enhancing economic growth.

As an example of how private-sector investments are crowded out in favor of government-sponsored investments, consider the following: In 1980, when a 20 percent prime rate and a 16 percent consumer loan rate contributed to the bankruptcy of thousands of small businesses, such as auto dealerships and grocery stores, the Rural Electrification Administration began a new program to provide 35–year loans at 5 percent interest to finance rural cable television systems; rural home mortgages were available at 3.3 percent; and insured student loans went for 7 percent. Also during that year, while many

---

[6]The following discussion is based on Bennett and DiLorenzo (1983).

private utilities were paying 16 percent on their long-term bonds, the Tennessee Valley Authority (TVA) was borrowing at a rate that was several percentage points lower. As a result of this and other subsidies, the cost of electricity supplied by TVA is lower than it is in many areas served by less-favored private companies. In 1979, for example, TVA rates were about 50 percent lower than rates in such "frostbelt" states as New York and Massachusetts and about 38 percent below the national average.

It is very difficult, if not impossible, to gauge the extent of crowding out caused by federal loan guarantees, but some preliminary estimates have been made. Economist Herbert M. Kaufman of the University of Arizona conducted an empirical study of federal loan guarantees, in which he estimated that for every $1 billion in loan guarantees, between $736 million and $1.2 billion in private investment is crowded out. These are rough estimates, but they indicate that loan guarantees, which are being extended at a rate of over $100 billion per year, are certain to have a profound, negative impact on economic growth, employment, and price stability.

The federal government uses loan guarantees in a more subtle way to control the allocation of resources by influencing the recipients. For example the Federal Housing Administration (FHA), which administers the largest loan guarantee program, attempts to implement various social policies by vetoing a loan application if a builder does not comply with FHA's regulations regarding marketing to minority groups, environmental impact statements, architectural review, underwriting minimum wages, and so on. Because of the division of responsibility for these objectives, there is considerable confusion and delay, which increases the cost of housing construction. Further, once a firm or an industry is dependent upon financial assistance from the government, the dependence is often used as a lever to impose additional regulatory controls that may be totally unrelated to the government's contingent liability.

Equity Aspects of Federal Loan Guarantees

In addition to fostering a less efficient allocation of resources and hindering economic growth, many of the loan guarantee programs would be considered by many to be inequitable. An extreme case is the student loan program that, with few eligibility requirements, creates generous subsidies for higher-income households. With such loans available to students and their parents at a 7 percent interest rate regardless of income, the high market interest rates of the late 1970s and early 1980s provided many lucrative investment opportunities for wealthy families. As the spread widened between interest

596

rates on student loans and market rates, new student loans rose from $2.7 billion in 1979 to $7.2 billion in 1981, reflecting the growing recognition of the opportunities to borrow thousands of dollars at 7 percent interest and invest the proceeds in long-term bonds or money market funds paying 14 to 16 percent. Futhermore, hundreds of millions of dollars in student loans are now in default, rendering these loans outright gifts to the students and their parents.

Regardless of the rhetoric associated with such programs, the vast majority of federal loan guarantee programs provide subsidies to individuals who are not generally considered to be financially disadvantaged. There is a very strong incentive for the administrators of loan guarantee programs to subsidize politically powerful groups, regardless of income, who will, in return, provide support for the agency at appropriations time. Even though the chief goals of the Department of Housing and Urban Development (HUD) are supposedly "the elimination of substandard and inadequate housing through the clearance of slums and blighted areas," it has established hundreds of programs that have nothing to do with slum clearance. For example, HUD's housing rehabilitation loan program has extended 3 percent guaranteed loans to individuals earning over $50,000 per year to finance skylights and greenhouses.[7]

If there is a pattern of behavior that guides the granting of federal loan guarantees, it is based on the ability of the subsidized group to provide political support for the agency and its legislative sponsors, and not on efficiency or equity grounds. There is no reason to believe that a new RFC would behave any differently. Additional loan guarantees are an integral part of the current proposals for a resurrected RFC and would undoubtedly inflict further harm on the economy.

NIP enthusiasts apparently believe that the original RFC was a success, for its resurrection is the main plank in their industrial policy platform. A closer look at Hoover's original invention, however, indicates otherwise.

Hoover's Reconstruction Finance Corporation

Contrary to popular belief, the original RFC was not a product of Franklin Roosevelt's "New Deal" but was an offspring of Herbert Hoover's administration. After over a year of intensive lobbying, Hoover signed the RFC into law on January 11, 1932. Also contrary to popular belief, the RFC was a dismal failure that most assuredly made the Depression worse. Even though tens of billions of dollars were spent, unemployment stood at 9 million in 1939 and increased

---

[7]See Lambro (1980) for dozens of similar examples.

597

to the level reached in 1932 as the United States entered World War II.[8] This is hardly evidence of the alleged success of the RFC, and should come as no surprise, for the sole purpose of the RFC was to make unsound investments; that is, those that had been shunned by private capital markets. For this reason the RFC also severely reduced consumer welfare during the Depression years. That a private business venture is unable to obtain credit is evidence that the venture is not likely to satisfy consumer demands as well as alternative uses of that credit. Therefore, the private capital markets channel those funds into uses that would better serve consumers. Thus, the effect of the RFC was to *reduce* economic growth *and* to replace consumer demand with the preferences of politicians and bureaucrats.

The RFC could not possibly have aided economic recovery during the Depression, nor could it do so today. It only served to delay the market adjustments that are necessary to attain economic recovery. During an economic downturn, market forces work to channel resources into their most productive uses, enhancing economic growth and spurring a recovery. Subsidizing less productive resources through the aegis of the RFC only delayed or aborted the recovery.

The true character of the RFC was revealed during congressional floor debates on the RFC bill in 1931. There was little pretense that the bill was anything but a means of subsidizing economically inefficient but politically popular businesses. As historian James Olson stated (1977, p. 112):

> The response of businessmen to the bill was so overwhelmingly positive that Congressmen were immediately suspicious. Representatives of commercial banks, railroads, savings banks, building and loan associations, and life insurance companies all praised the bill in glowing terms. [T]heir commitment to the bill was absolute.

Several congressmen harshly criticized the bill. Representative Fiorello LaGuardia of New York, for example, called the bill

> a millionare's dole and you cannot get away from it. It is a subsidy for broken bankers—a subsidy for bankrupt railroads—a reward for speculation and unscrupulous bond pluggers.[9]

Representative Louis McFadden of Pennsylvania was even more critical, calling the bill a scheme by "financial criminals" for

> gouging $500,000,000 out of the Treasury of the United States. It is a scheme for taking $500,000,000 of the people's money produced by labor at a cost of toil and suffering and giving it to a supercorporation

---

[8]Cited in Rothbard (1972).
[9]*Congressional Record*, 11 January 1932, p. 1742.

for the sinister purpose of helping a gang of financial looters to cover up their tracks.[10]

As long as it was in their self-interest to do so, these and other congressmen "spoke their minds" about the RFC and what it was designed to accomplish. But attitudes changed as soon as President Hoover showed them how it could work to their own political advantage. For example, Arkansas Senator Joseph Robinson's objections were eliminated by the promise to grant loans to livestock and agricultural credit corporations, to federal land banks, and to joint stock land banks (Olson 1977, p. 38). Senator Ellision ("Cotton Ed") Smith of South Carolina became a true believer because of a promise to grant $50 million to the Secretary of Agriculture for small crop loans. Other congressmen were similarly convinced of the so-called merits of the RFC when Hoover asked *them* to select the members of the RFC's board of directors. Thus it was that a process of arm twisting and logrolling produced the RFC in January 1932, despite earlier protests. Hoover then praised the "patriotism of the men of both houses of Congress who have given proof of their devotion to the welfare of their country, irrespective of political affiliation."[11]

The RFC act provided for massive government intervention in the economy by extending loans and loan guarantees to such enterprises as banks, insurance companies, trust companies, building and loan associations, mortgage companies, credit unions, federal land banks, agricultural credit corporations, livestock credit companies, railroads, and, eventually, even topless bars and massage parlors.[12]

As with the proposals for a new RFC, the original RFC's board of directors included businessmen, bankers, and bureaucrats. It is no surprise, therefore, that big business, big banks, and government bureaucracies were the major beneficiaries of the RFC, all at the expense of the American taxpayer, who was subjected to one of the largest tax increases in history (up to that time) in 1932. The large tax increases of 1932 surely stifled private economic activity even further, thereby deepening the Depression.

Once the RFC began its operations in early 1932 it attempted to make every individual, group, and industry a "preferred borrower," as each congressman scrambled to ensure that his constituents would receive their share of the largesse. Jesse H. Jones, director of the RFC from 1932 to 1945, wrote a book boasting about how he spent

[10]*Congressional Record,* 11 January 1932, p. 1924.

[11]*Congressional Record,* 11 January 1932, p. 1705.

[12]For a history and analysis of the loans made by the original RFC, see Denzau and Hardin (1984).

599

$50 billion of taxpayers' funds during that time "with almost unlimited authority" (Jones 1951, p. 3). The enormous scope of government intervention in the credit markets is revealed in the volume by Jones, and is exemplified by such statements as, "we even loaned money on a drove of reindeer in Alaska," and "when the grape growers of California felt the pinch of hard times, they, like almost everyone else, hollered for help in Washington" (1951, p. 183).

The RFC bailed out thousands of failing businesses and, by law, it was designed to do exactly that. As Jones stated, "The law specified that we should lend only where the borrower could not get the money from others on reasonable terms" (1951, p. 183). Thus, the RFC was to make only inefficient investments, those that would reduce both economic growth and consumer welfare. It was merely a tool Jones and his political allies used to forcefully impose their preferences on the general public at the great expense of intensifying the Depression. That RFC bureaucrats were among the chief beneficiaries of the RFC's operations is indicated in Appendix IV of Jones's book, "Some RFC Alumni Who Have Done Well," which reads like a "who's who" of the Fortune 500. For example, the first page of the appendix lists former RFC loan executives, auditors, and attorneys who, after they left the RFC, attained such positions as vice president of Greenwich Savings Bank, general solicitor of the Baltimore and Ohio Railroad, and various bank presidencies. For these individuals, working at the RFC was an investment in human capital, a time spent feathering the nests of banks and businesses (at taxpayers' expense) in return for future employment opportunities with those businesses. Other researchers (Eckert 1981) have found this to be a general consequence of government regulation of industry. Regardless of the "public interest" rhetoric, much regulation merely serves to benefit regulators and various regulated industries, not the general public, and the RFC was no exception. It is easy to understand why so many bankers, businessmen, union leaders, and politicians have chosen to ignore history and reality by making appeals for a new RFC.

In summary, government control of credit allocation is inherently incompatible with economic growth. The argument that if only done "right," government bureaucracies can outperform private markets is nonsense that simply should not be countenanced. Moreover, arguments that greater government involvement is essential for reasons of "fairness" or "social justice" are equally unfathomable. In a free market economy, those who make the best use of resources are those who can best serve others in the society. Those who offer consumers the best products at the lowest prices will be "targeted" by the capital markets. Politics can only obstruct this process by arbitrarily redirecting resources to politically popular but economically inefficient uses, and at great expense to consumers. The loss of individual freedom is heightened by this process, for individuals are encouraged to put less effort into pleasing others in the society (that is, consumers) and more toward catering to the whims of the political authorities.

Cooperation and Conflict:
The Industrial Policy Delusion

A basic premise of most, if not all, of the NIP proposals is that the problem of slow economic growth is best addressed through "cooperation," most notably between "government, labor, and business," an arbitrarily chosen collection of special interests. The political process is said to embody a spirit of cooperation among businessmen, union leaders, and politicians that will help solve the nation's problems (as though nations, not individuals, have problems). However, there are two basic misconceptions here. First is the age-old myth that collective, as opposed to individual, decisions are made for the "public interest," in a spirit of selflessness or concern for others. "Good" motivation is thought to lead to "good" results. By contrast, "bad" motivation (for example, self interest and the profit motive) leads to "bad" results. In other words economic problems are often caused by perverse individual behavior, but they can be corrected by a sufficiently benevolent group of enlightened statesmen. Clearly, we do not observe this type of schizophrenic behavior: There is no logical basis for believing that individuals are any more or less self-interested when they make collective decisions than they are when making individual decisions. No divine transformation takes place when individuals leave the private sector for the public sector; nor do halos turn to horns when the opposite occurs.

This has given rise to the second major misconception, a confusion over the meaning of "cooperation" in market as opposed to nonmarket (that is, political) settings. As stated earlier, the market is essentially a process through which individuals, acting in their own interests, cooperate to get what they want, subject only to the principle of mutual agreement. Adam Smith's well-worn dictum is as trite as it is true: It is not the benevolence of the butcher or baker that provides us with our meat and our bread, but concern for their self-interest.

By contrast, *political* cooperation is inherently conflictual, for political "exchange" is necessarily zero-sum, at best. In politics, one party or coalition can gain *only at the expense of others* through a

601

49

rearrangement of property rights. This will always be true in the absence of a voting rule of unanimity. The coercive powers of the state are used to enforce such changes, which are the source of much social conflict. Market exchange, since it is voluntary, is necessarily positive-sum or "unanimous," benefiting *all* parties involved.

Recent events in the transportation industry illustrate what can be expected from "cooperation" in politics. It is well known that in the trucking industry, for example, business, labor, and government have cooperated and the Interstate Commerce Commission was part of an earlier industrial policy aimed at fostering such cooperation. With the aid of the coercive powers of government, trucking firms and the Teamsters union were able to cartelize the trucking industry, thereby redistributing wealth from the general population to themselves. Politicians gladly cooperated, for they shared in the government-sanctioned monopoly profits in the form of votes, campaign contributions, and other means of political support. Strong taxpayer support for deregulation of the trucking industry is evidence that taxpayers do not find this particular industrial policy to be in their best interest. This, however, is precisely the type of cooperation NIP enthusiasts urge upon us.

Business, government, and unions can also be expected to cooperate on the issue of protectionism. The notion that businesses and unions are generally adversaries who deal with each other on an "arms length" basis is becoming increasingly untenable. This is so because in many areas businesses and unions cooperate or conspire to secure common objectives, such as protection from international competition. In recent years U.S. automobile producers have joined forces with the United Auto Workers to lobby for import quotas, "domestic content" legislation to require foreign cars to be constructed in the United States, and other forms of protectionism. And they have been quite successful; the Reagan administration has succumbed to protectionist pressures in the automobile, steel, textiles, motorcycle, and even clothespin industries, to name a few.

In sum, because government is the chief agent of coercion in society, it is misleading, at best, to suggest that political cooperation will lead to such lofty goals as "economic progress" or "social justice." A coalition of business, labor, and government is more likely to conspire against the general public than cooperate to serve it. In contrast, since free trade is voluntary, no individual or group can coerce or exploit another in market exchange. It is in every individual's self-interest to cooperate with others (most of whom he does not know) by trying to produce what they want. By doing so the welfare of society as a whole is enhanced. If one wishes to stress the importance of cooperation in economic affairs, the appropriate emphasis should be on *market* exchange or cooperation, not political cooperation. The former tends to increase the wealth of nations, whereas the latter is a major source of economic stagnation.

The Industrial Policy Cycle

In essence the NIP proposals are nothing other than a thinly disguised plea for an expanded welfare state and some version of national economic planning. It is sufficiently clear, however, that these policies are the root causes of economic stagnation. In recent decades government intervention has severely stifled productivity in the United States and elsewhere largely because of accelerated inflation, high taxes (and tax rates), price controls, and other regulations (Kendrick 1981). All of these government policies stifle individual incentives to work, save, and invest, which are the ingredients of economic growth. These policies also increase the power and prestige of politicians, bureaucrats, and other supporters of the welfare state and governmental planning. This is why, despite overwhelming evidence accumulated ever since Adam Smith exposed the fallacies of mercantilism, there are renewed pleas for even greater government intervention. When NIP proponents simply ignore all the lessons of history and economic theory, they participate in a con game that must be exposed.

It has often been said that in government, "failure is success." That is, when government policies cause economic instability there is inevitably a public demand for the government to "do something" about it. It is the natural proclivity of politicians to avoid admitting that their own actions caused the problems in the first place and to undo their mistakes. Instead, they typically offer new programs and policies to "solve" the problems. The end result is even more economic instability, and even greater power placed in the hands of the political authorities. The current industrial policy hype is part of this cycle and is largely a political response to the failed governmental policies of the 1960s and 1970s.

NIP proponents have distorted the facts about the U.S. economy. Government intervention is clearly the cause of, not the cure for, our economic problems. NIP enthusiasts have also reversed reality when they cite the Japanese economy as a successful prototype of their brand of industrial policy. If one considers the *facts,* the Japanese experience provides an invaluable lesson for the United States and the rest of the world, but the lesion is not that an interventionist industrial policy works. Dr. Katsuro Sakoh (1983) conducted an

603

51

extensive empirical study of the relatively prosperous Japanese economy of the early 1970s and concluded that Japan's success was the result of

> [a] basically free market economy, functioning effectively with minimal government intervention. The collapse of Japan's traditional feudal society in the 1940s and the emergence of a more open society triggered an explosion of creative energy. Free speech, human rights, and freedom of investment and pricing changed the country's political and economic dynamics. Any Japanese—regardless of age, class, or family background—could venture into business and succeed through hard work, imagination, willingness to take risks, and luck. Many dynamic and exciting new enterprises, such as Honda, Yamaha, Sony, and Suzuki, to name but a few, sprouted in this climate. In short, individual entrepreneurs did not invest in capital goods and equipment because MITI officials suggested it, but because these entrepreneurs glimpsed the potential for future profits by beating the competition in both domestic and foreign markets. The market mechanism allowed Japan's industrial structure to be transformed by the 1970s, as older industries were replaced by these new manufacturing industries.

The "Japanese miracle" has now apparently ended, as the Japanese economy became very sluggish beginning in the mid–1970s. It is no surprise that as this occurred, there was a marked increase in government intervention. In 1982 Japan experienced its first large quarterly drop in real GNP in 30 years, and economic growth during that year was only about a third of what it had been during the previous 25 years (Drucker 1982, p. 28). Furthermore, productivity growth has fallen even more steeply in Japan in recent years than in either the United States or Western Europe, and savings are only two-thirds of the average levels of the 1970s. The reasons for this little-publicized economic decline are not that Japan has abandoned what little efforts it had made at "industrial policy," but rather the familiar problems of uncontrolled government spending and rising federal deficits and regulation. As Drucker recently stated (1982, p. 28):

> Throughout its years of rapid economic growth, from the early 1950s to the mid 1970s, Japan's budget was balanced or in slight surplus. Japan shifted to deficit spending in 1975–76 and the economy promptly began to slow down. The deficit is now more than three times larger than seven years ago. It is larger, both per capita and as a proportion of GNP, than the deficit of any other highly industrialized country except Canada. And, just as in the highly developed countries of the West, government in Japan is now beginning

to crowd private borrowers out of the capital markets. This is occurring just when Japan needs to make heavy investments in automation, in new technologies and in manufacturing subsidiaries abroad. . . .

The question that must be posed to those who advocate an interventionist industrial policy for the United States is: If such a policy is responsible for Japan's success, why has the Japanese economy stagnated during the past eight years (in many ways far more severely than the economies of either the United States and Western Europe)?

Conclusion

One positive aspect of the industrial policy debate is that it has refocused attention on the important issue of the role of government in a free society. One role of government is to protect private property, freedom of exchange, and freedom of contract. In short, the government's responsibility is to cultivate an institutional environment in which the spontaneous forces of the market can best coordinate individual plans so as to enhance individual welfare. Government, however, has strayed far from this role, and it now actively supersedes the forces of the market and is, therefore, the cause of many of our economic problems. Furthermore, the redistributive role of government is a major source of interpersonal conflict, despite the much-touted pleas for greater "cooperation" among politicians, businessmen, and union leaders. The industrial policy proposals would empower the government to expand its activities of favoring some groups at the expense of others in society, which violates the principles of justice and equality of treatment—principles that NIP proponents ironically claim to be their concern. Neomercantilism is perhaps a better name for an interventionist industrial policy. Adam Smith described what he thought was the immorality of such policies more than 200 years ago (1960, p. 152):

> To hurt in any degree the interest of any one order of citizens, for no other purpose but to promote that of some other, it is evidently contrary to that justice and equality of treatment which the sovereign owes to all the different orders of his subjects.

To invigorate industry and to pursue the principles of justice and equality of treatment requires reducing the size and scope of government, not expanding it. Accordingly, an appropriate industrial policy is one that reduces the burden of taxation, encourages privatization of government-run enterprises, eliminates regulatory restrictions on the freedom of exchange, and places strict limitations, perhaps

605

constitutionally imposed, on the size and growth of government and on the destruction of wealth and welfare it inevitably entails.

References

Bastiat, Frédéric. *Harmonies of Political Economy.* Translated by Patrick James Stirling. London: John Murray, 1860.

Bastiat, Frédéric. "Justice and Fraternity." In *Selected Essays on Political Economy,* pp. 116–39. Translated by Seymour Cain and edited by George B. de Huszar. Irvington-on-Hudson, N.Y.: Foundation for Economic Education, 1964.

Bennett, James T., and DiLorenzo, Thomas J. *Underground Government: The Off-Budget Public Sector.* Washington, D.C.: Cato Institute, 1983.

Buchanan, James M. "Why Does Government Grow?" In *Budgets and Bureaucrats: The Sources of Government Growth.* Edited by Thomas Borcherding. Durham, N.C.: Duke University Press, 1977.

Denzau, Arthur T., and Hardin, Clifford M. *A National Development Bank: Ghost of the RFC Past.* St. Louis: Center for the Study of American Business, Washington University, 1984.

Dorn, James A. "Law and Liberty: A Comparison of Hayek and Bastiat." *Journal of Libertarian Studies* 5 (Fall 1981): 375–97.

Drucker, Peter F. "Clouds Forming Across the Japanese Sun." *Wall Street Journal,* 13 July 1982, p. 28.

Eckert, Ross. "The Life Cycle of Regulatory Commissioners." *Journal of Law and Economics* 24 (April 1981): 113–20.

Hayek, F[riedrich] A. *New Studies in Philosophy, Economics, and The History of Ideas.* Chicago: University of Chicago Press, 1978.

Hayek, Friedrich A. *Law, Legislation, and Liberty,* Vol. 3, *The Political Order of a Free People.* Chicago: University of Chicago Press, 1979.

Jones, Jesse. *Fifty Billion Dollars: My Thirteen Years With the Reconstruction Finance Corporation.* New York: Macmillan, 1951.

Kendrick, John W. "International Comparisons of Recent Productivity Trends." In *Issues in Contemporary Economic Problems,* pp. 125–70. Edited by William Fellner. Washington, D.C.: American Enterprise Institute, 1981.

Kirkland, Lane. "An Alternative to Reaganomics." *USA Today,* May 1982.

Lambro, Don. *Fat City: How Washington Wastes Your Taxes.* Southbend, Ind.: Regnery Gateway, Inc., 1980.

McKenzie, Richard B. "National Industrial Policy: An Overview of the Debate." Heritage Foundation *Backgrounder* No. 275, Washington, D.C., 12 July 1983.

Olson, James. *Herbert Hoover and the Reconstruction Finance Corporation.* Ames, Iowa: Iowa State University Press, 1977.

Olson, Mancur. *The Rise and Decline of Nations.* New Haven: Yale University Press, 1982.

Poole, Robert, Jr. "Healing American Industry" (editorial). *Reason* 15 (August 1983): 6.

Rothbard, Murray. *America's Great Depression.* Kansas City, Kans.: Sheed and Ward, 1972.

Sakoh, Katsuro. "Industrial Policy: The Super Myth of Japan's Super Success." Heritage Foundation, Asian Studies Center *Backgrounder* No. 3, Washington, D.C., 13 July 1983.

Siegan, Bernard H. *Economic Liberties and the Constitution*. Chicago: University of Chicago Press, 1980.

Smith, Adam. *The Wealth of Nations*. London: Cannon, 1960.

Tollison, Robert D. "Rent Seeking: A Survey." *Kylos* 35 (Winter 1982): 575–602.

SOCIAL PROBLEMS, Vol. 30, No. 1, October 1982

THE ORIGINS OF THE OCCUPATIONAL SAFETY AND HEALTH ACT OF 1970*

PATRICK G. DONNELLY
University of Dayton

This paper analyzes the emergence of the Occupational Safety and Health Act of 1970 and finds previous explanations of its origin inadequate. I trace the roots of this law to the protests of rank-and-file workers across the United States at a time when the support of these workers was particularly important to the two main political parties. The protest was directed not only at those employers who operated unsafe and unhealthy workplaces, but also at union officials who paid little or no attention to safety and health issues in negotiating new contracts.

In 1980, 13,000 workers were killed and 2.2 million workers suffered disabling injuries in workplace accidents in the United States (National Safety Council, 1981:25). Government estimates indicate that occupational diseases and illnesses kill another 100,000 workers and afflict 390,000 workers each year (U.S. Department of Health, Education, and Welfare, 1972). Both sets of figures are conservative estimates since they rely only on cases reported by employers, who have an economic incentive not to report accidents and illnesses. Furthermore, the medical and scientific community does not know whether many commonly-used chemicals and other substances are dangerous, since the onset of the disease or illness may occur up to 30 years after a worker was exposed to the substance. The Occupational Safety and Health Act of 1970 (OSHAct) was designed to protect over 55 million workers in 4.1 million workplaces. It is the first comprehensive federal legislation in the United States to recognize the right of the government to inspect, cite, and penalize employers for infringements of the right of workers to labor under safe and healthy conditions.

The OSHAct can be traced back to 1968 when legislation on worker safety and health was introduced in Congress. The legislative debate shows that the business community was vehemently opposed to the strong bill proposed by the Democrats (Bureau of National Affairs, 1971; Page and O'Brien, 1973). When the Republican administration of President Nixon introduced its bill in 1969, it differed significantly from the Democrat's bill: it gave less power to the Labor Department, relied more on state governments, and put the final enforcement responsibilities in the hands of a presidentially-appointed commission. Business representatives had suggested all of these changes earlier, arguing that a worker safety and health bill should not centralize power in any one department or level of government. While this analysis of Congressional debate is important for an understanding of the law-creation process, it does not consider the social, political, and economic factors that led to the bill's introduction in Congress. In this paper, I first assess previous explanations of the origins of the OSHAct and then examine two factors which have been consistently overlooked; rank-and-file activism and the political climate of the 1960s.

FOUR PREVIOUS EXPLANATIONS

The Objective Condition

Some authors suggest that the key factor in the birth of the OSHAct was the number of

---

* An earlier version of this paper was presented at the annual meeting of the Society for the Study of Social Problems, New York, 1980. The author thanks Bill Chambliss, Gerry Turkel, Dave Ermann, Brenda Wixson Donnelly, Steve McNamee, Dan Miller, Ron Kramer and the *Social Problems* reviewers for their comments. Correspondence to: Department of Sociology, University of Dayton, Dayton, Ohio 45469.

workers killed and injured in the United States or the increase in these figures during the 1960s (Altman, 1976; Bureau of National Affairs, 1971; Gersuny, 1981). The number of workers injured rose from 1,950,000 in 1960 to 2,200,000 in 1967. Deaths from workplace accidents increased from 13,800 to 14,200 during the same period (National Safety Council, 1981:25). Much research was published during this period revealing previously unknown health hazards or demonstrating a greater seriousness of already recognized hazards. Ashford (1976) argues that legislation was the federal government's natural response to a growing social problem. However, such explanations fail to explain why the government remained inactive for decades when the number of workers killed and injured by accidents was as high or higher than it was in 1967. During the 1920s, for example, an estimated 20,000 workers were killed each year and another 2.6 million were disabled (Woodbury, 1927). In 1945, 16,500 workers were killed and 2 million were injured (National Safety Council, 1981:25). Furthermore, while the number of workers killed and injured increased between 1960 and 1967, the ratio of injury and death to the total work force decreased. In 1960, there were 3,028 injured per 100,000 workers; by 1967 the ratio had fallen to 2,945. Deaths from workplace accidents decreased from 21 per 100,000 workers in 1960 to 19 in 1967 (National Safety Council, 1981:25). While these statistics cannot minimize the seriousness of the problem in 1967, they do show that workplace safety was not deteriorating as others have implied.

Public Opinion and Mass Media

However serious a condition may be, little will be done to solve it unless a segment of the public considers it worthy of concern (Blumer, 1971; Piven and Cloward, 1971; Ross and Staines, 1972). Ashford (1976) suggests that the public attention given to workplace disasters in the 1960s was a major factor leading to legislation. This implies that the OSHAct was a response to an increasingly aware public. However, neither public opinion polls nor media coverage suggests that unsafe and unhealthy working conditions were perceived as a major social problem by the public during the 1960s. The Gallup polls found people most concerned about the Vietnam War, crime, race-related issues including the urban riots, the high cost of living, and poverty. In fact, at no time during the 1960s were workplace conditions mentioned frequently enough to warrant reporting by the Gallup poll (Gallup, 1972).

Media coverage of worker safety and health issues was sparse prior to the introduction of legislation. I examined the *New York Times Index* and the *Readers' Guide to Periodical Literature* to evaluate media coverage.[1] The key year in assessing whether the media directed government attention to worker safety and health is 1967. Although the first worker safety and health bill was not introduced in Congress until 1968, Labor Department lawyers drafted the legislation in 1967. Only seven articles dealing with the issue appeared in the *New York Times* during 1967, and only six articles appeared in any of the 128 U.S. magazines indexed in the

---

1. The use of such indexes to indicate the importance of social issues is widespread (Becker, 1963; Dickson, 1968; Funkhouser, 1973; Galliher and Walker, 1977; Schoenfeld *et al.*, 1979). I counted the number of articles in the *New York Times Index* and the *Readers' Guide to Periodical Literature* under the subject headings related to worker safety and health. In the *New York Times Index*, the categories were: Accidents, Industrial; Accidents, Mining; Occupational Health; and Labor—U.S.—Occupational Hazards and Safety. The main subject headings in the *Readers' Guide* were: Industrial Safety; Diseases, Industrial; Industrial Hygiene; Coal Mine and Mining—Accidents and Explosions; and Accidents, Industrial. In both indexes, when cross-references referred to another category, I counted only those articles which clearly related to worker safety and health hazards. The *Monthly Labor Review*, published by the U.S. Department of Labor, is indexed in the *Readers' Guide* but I did not count articles appearing in it because of the purpose of my analysis—to determine whether the social issue created government interest or vice versa.

Readers' Guide. In 1966, there were 12 articles in the *New York Times* and only one in the indexed magazines. Furthermore, the magazines that published articles on worker safety and health in 1966 and 1967 were *Science News, Business Week,* the *U.N. Monthly Chronicle,* and *Science* — all special-interest publications.

The few newspaper and magazine articles appearing in 1966 and 1967 might have had an impact if they had represented a drastic increase in media coverage of the problem. Yet, as Table 1 shows, there is little discernible pattern to media coverage of the problem in either the *New York Times* or the indexed magazines. The seven articles in the *New York Times* in 1967 represent the second lowest number of articles from 1950 to 1967. The six 1967 magazine articles represent a significant increase over the one article in 1966, but are still fewer than the number of articles in 11 of the preceding 17 years.

It is unlikely, then, that media coverage played a major role in the creation of a law to deal with the problem of worker safety and health. Table 1 shows a sharp increase in the number of articles dealing with the problem only after government officials drafted legislation. Thus, government action played a major role in the creation of a social issue.

An examination of the data on the attention paid to several major industrial disasters during the 1960s reveals a similar pattern. In 1963, two accidents in mines, one in Utah that killed 18 and another in Pennsylvania in which two trapped miners were dramatically rescued, triggered seven

TABLE 1

Media Coverage of Issues Related to Worker Safety and Health, 1950–1975

	Number of Articles in	
Year	New York Times Index	Readers' Guide to Periodical Literature
1950	53	11
1951	44	11
1952	73	17
1953	38	7
1954	18	4
1955	16	4
1956	29	21
1957	24	8
1958	35	7
1959	7	6
1960	21	8
1961	9	15
1962	14	3
1963	39	8
1964	6	7
1965	10	2
1966	12	1
1967	7	6
1968	53	17
1969	111	26
1970	104	18
1971	99	25
1972	81	16
1973	56	18
1974	65	26
1975	74	21

magazine articles within six weeks of the events. In the two years that followed these accidents, there were 12 magazine articles indexed under the category "Coal Mines and Mining: Accidents and Disasters." However, many industrial disasters in the past received considerable attention without leading to any large-scale attempt to eliminate the problem. On December 6, 1907, a mine explosion in West Virginia killed 361 workers. Only 13 days later, 239 workers were killed in a mine explosion in Pennsylvania. Within two years of these disasters there were 35 magazine articles indexed under the heading "Coal Mines and Mining: Accidents and Explosions." Yet no major legislative action was taken.

Environmental Interests

Some authors suggest that the environmental movement of the 1960s played a major role in the recognition of the need for worker safety and health legislation (Ashford, 1976; Berman, 1978; Bureau of National Affairs, 1971; Gersuny, 1981). It is plausible that the recognition of generally deteriorating environmental conditions would lead to concern over the well-being of workers, the persons closest to industrial air pollution. Yet there is little evidence to support this argument. Rarely have the environmental movement and the worker safety and health interests overlapped. One federal government study of occupational health, conducted in 1965, was done for the Public Health Service by the National Advisory Environmental Health Committee (NAEHC). The study was undertaken after committee members realized that most research examined pollution in the general environment rather than the work environment (Ashford, 1976). Another link between the environmental and worker safety and health issues is the launching by the American Medical Association (AMA), in 1960, of a journal entitled *The Archives of Environmental Health: Preventive, Occupational, and Aerospace Medicine.* However, the journal was a continuation of a previous AMA journal, *The Archives of Industrial Health.* The AMA's interest in industrial health preceded its interest in environmental health.

There is some evidence that the environmental movement did not generate interest in the worker safety and health issue. Media interest in worker safety and health and in environmental concerns both accelerated in 1969, while the OSHAct was already being debated in Congress (Schoenfeld *et al.*, 1979:48). Many of the links between the issues came after 1970. Ralph Nader's Health Research Group and Dr. Irving Selikoff's Society for Occupational and Environmental Health were both formed afterwards. Local groups such as PhilaPOSH, the Philadelphia Project on Occupational Safety and Health, began working with environmental groups on projects of mutual interest in the late 1970s.

The environmentalists were often at odds with workers prior to the OSHAct because of the different concerns of the two groups (Gunningham, 1974; Stellman and Daum, 1973). The environmentalists often pressed for the elimination of pollution even when it would mean a loss of jobs. There is little evidence that environmental interests played an active role in generating concern about the safety of the workplace.

Labor Union Interest

During the 1960s, a period of relative prosperity, unions did not have to struggle for higher wages, fringe benefits, and pensions, since industry was willing to share the fruits. But there is no evidence to support the claim that this freed unions to struggle for safer working conditions, as the Bureau of National Affairs (1971) argues. Unions traditionally have given little attention to safety and health (Cummins, 1932), and the 1960s were no exception. One indicator of organized labor's willingness to press for improved safety and health conditions is the extent of work stoppages over the issue. Yet, relatively few work stoppages occur over safety and health issues. Since 1961, the classification system used by the Bureau of Labor Statistics on the cause of strikes includes a category labeled "Safety Measures, Dangerous Equipment, Etc." At no time during the 1960s were more than 1.6 percent of all strikes in the United States over safety hazards (U.S. Department of Labor, 1961–70).

In May, 1966, President Johnson challenged unions to transcend the "bread and butter issues in order to join with us in the effort to improve the total environment" (Public Papers of the Presidents, 1966:237). He referred to new health hazards created by industry since the Second World War.

Neither George Meany, president of the AFL-CIO, nor Walter Reuther, head of the UAW, displayed any real interest in the issue, and their lack of enthusiasm undercut any desire on the part of the White House to press forward with a new program (Page and O'Brien, 1973:138).

It might be argued that organized labor settles safety and health problems through collective bargaining. Yet, a number of government surveys of collective bargaining agreements during the 1950s and 1960s demonstrate that this is not the case. A national survey of 1,594 agreements in effect in 1954–55 shows that only 356 (22 percent) contained clauses providing for committees concerned with plant safety, sanitation, and employee health. Among these agreements were 75 which did not specify that employers and unions were to participate jointly on the committees (U.S. Department of Labor, 1956). Bureau of Labor Statistics data on collective bargaining agreements a decade later, in 1963–64, again demonstrate the lack of concern on the part of organized labor. Only 21 of 450 major agreements (5 percent) sampled contained any provision for union-management cooperation in safety and health issues. Two clauses that the U.S. Department of Labor (1966:44) described as typical were: (a) The union agrees with the objective of achieving the highest level of employee performance and efficiency with safety, good health, and sustained effort; and (b) Consistent with the principle of a fair day's work for a fair day's pay and consistent with the employees' welfare in regard to safety, health, and sustained effort, the union agrees to cooperate with management in its efforts to increase employee effectiveness and productivity. Such clauses do not demonstrate organized labor's deep concern for safety and health since they balance workers' health and safety against productivity and profit.

The platforms of the American Federation of Labor-Congress of Industrial Organizations (AFL-CIO) that were presented to the Democratic and Republican national conventions in 1964 and 1968 also show the low priority given to safety and health conditions. In 1964, the AFL-CIO platform was 24 pages long and covered the following topics in order of discussion: economic issues and jobs, the Civil Rights Act of 1964, foreign policy and defense, social and public needs, labor and management (relations), social security and health, and government administration. The only mention of worker safety and health came on page 22, when 11 sentences were devoted to asking the federal government to help make state safety codes uniform (American Federation of Labor-Congress of Industrial Organizations, 1964). In 1968, the AFL-CIO platform expanded to 34 pages and added another issue, the urban crisis, to its program. This time, 13 sentences were devoted to worker safety and health on page 30. The AFL-CIO called for "federal leadership and support" to get prompt action from politicians "toward achieving a safe, healthy work environment for every American worker" (American Federation of Labor-Congress of Industrial Organizations, 1968), yet this proposal was submitted *after* the first version of the OSHAct had been introduced in Congress.

Suggestions that the extent of the condition, public opinion or media interest, the environmental movement's convergence with labor interests, or the push of organized labor motivated introduction of legislation clearly run contrary to fact. There is, however, much evidence to suggest that rank-and-file activism was an important factor leading to the OSHAct. Moreover, a particular set of political circumstances made it possible for the rank-and-file workers to exert more power than was usually available to them.

RANK-AND-FILE ACTIVISM

Throughout the 1960s, rank-and-file workers in many of the major labor unions expressed their dissatisfaction with working conditions in general and with safety and health conditions in particular. They also protested against the way their union officials were dealing with the problem. This dissatisfaction was seldom reported in the headlines of newspapers and magazines but was a recurrent sub-theme in many articles appearing in publications such as the *New York Times*, the *Wall Street Journal*, and *Business Week*. I surveyed articles indexed in the *New York Times Index* and the *Readers' Guide* dealing with labor unrest and worker dissatisfaction from 1960 to 1967.[2] These sources are used to describe the actions of rank-and-file workers in several major unions. Beginning in the mid-1960s, wage issues became less important as a source of worker unrest. Grievance procedure, union local autonomy, working conditions, speed-ups, and safety and health conditions were cited with increasing regularity as sources of conflict between the rank and file and their union officials and management.

The members of the United Auto Workers (UAW) were among the first groups to express their dissatisfaction with working conditions. Between 1953 and 1955, thousands of UAW members across the United States and in all major auto companies participated in wildcat strikes to protest industry-imposed and union-sanctioned production speed-ups (Aronowitz, 1973). This rank-and-file concern continued throughout the 1950s and 1960s. In July, 1966, 9,000 workers walked off their jobs at three Ford plants in Cleveland where 200 unsettled grievances — most of them involving inadequate safety and health standards — had accumulated (*Business Week*, 1966a). In October, 1966, 4,200 UAW workers at the Twinsburg, Ohio, Chrysler plant went on strike over unsettled grievances involving working conditions, including the dangers involved with fork-lift trucks at the plant (*Business Week*, 1966b). The elimination of fumes at a Ford foundry plant in Cleveland was a major demand by local leaders when the 1967 UAW contract was negotiated (Shafer, 1967). Health and safety conditions caused frequent conflicts between management and workers in the Ford plant in Livonia, Michigan. In 1967, the president of Local 182 in Livonia complained that expenditures for health and safety conditions were usually the first to be cut since they were not directly related to manufacturing the product (*Business Week*, 1967).

In February, 1967, a UAW local at a General Motors plant in Mansfield, Ohio, called a wildcat strike when two workers were fired for refusing to prepare materials and equipment for shipment to another plant. Certain work operations were being shifted to the Pontiac, Michigan, plant as a result of the Mansfield workers' complaints that safety conditions on that operation were poor. In all, 133,000 workers from 20 different shops walked off the job. Walter Reuther, the president of the UAW, called the strike illegal and sent representatives to Mansfield to convince local leaders to call it off. Reuther's officials told the local leaders that their strike was ill-timed because the national UAW organization was planning to give priority to higher salaries and profit-sharing in upcoming contract negotiations (Weir, 1967). This fact strongly undermines claims that the unions gave more attention to safety and health during the relatively prosperous sixties.

The United Mine Workers (UMW), usually one of the more militant unions, was also involved in a major dispute over safety conditions. In the summer of 1965, five UMW members in Moundsville, West Virginia, were fired for refusing to work under conditions that they considered unsafe. Employers had ordered the crew to work when the full mine operations were shut down. Within days, more than 17,000 miners in West Virginia, Ohio, and Pennsylvania went on a wildcat strike (U.S. Department of Labor, 1966). The members realized that their concern for worker safety and health issues could only be implemented if they had greater participation in contract negotia-

---

2. Once a date for a particular incident or issue dealing with safety and health conditions was found, I used other sources to supplement the sources found in these two indexes.

tions. They agreed to return to work only after the UMW International promised them a greater voice in the next contract negotiations (Weir, 1967).

In June, 1965, 12,000 Teamsters in the Philadelphia area walked off their jobs when four employees of one company were fired for refusing to work under conditions they considered dangerous. The workers claimed that obstructions in their path made unloading their truck a dangerous assignment. Jimmy Hoffa, then president of the Teamsters, called the strike illegal and told the workers to go back to their jobs. They refused. The employers obtained a court injunction ordering the truckers back to work, but the strikers ignored it. The lead paragraph in a *New York Times* story about the strike is reminiscent of scenes much more common in earlier periods of union-management relations:

> Armed with bats and iron pipes, gangs of striking truck drivers roamed the streets of Philadelphia today attempting to halt the movement of food and freight (Bigart, 1965a:16).

Mayor James Tate ordered the Philadelphia police to "break the siege by Teamsters who have paralyzed the distribution of fruit and vegetables in the city" (Bigart, 1965b:49). A judge in the Common Pleas Court suggested that the National Guard be called in if the police could not maintain law and order in a situation which he characterized as "a bit of anarchy" (Bigart, 1965c:36). Fines of $35,000 a day against the local and $1,500 a day against each union official finally convinced the workers to go back to their jobs after a week (*New York Times*, 1965b). Before the strike ended, officials of the city's four largest food chains announced that they were within a day of being forced to close all their stores because of food shortages. Many gas stations closed because deliveries were not made. One company laid off 1,200 of its 1,400 employees while another furloughed all of its 1,250 workers (*New York Times*, 1965a).

While the issue of safety and health did not cause as severe disruptions in the United Steelworkers of America union, it was a constant underlying factor in the complaints of many rank-and-file workers and local officials throughout the 1960s. The key issue in the Steelworkers' 1964 contract negotiations was not wages but working conditions. Weeks before the negotiating sessions began, Local 1011 in Youngstown, Ohio, placed a resolution before the union's district council demanding a stronger emphasis on plant safety. It also urged that locals be given the right to strike over local issues such as safety and health (*Business Week*, 1964). Members of a local near Pittsburgh complained that safety and health precautions were frequently neglected by management and appealed to the national leadership to give greater attention to the issue (Stetson, 1964).

Other unions also experienced rank-and-file discontent with officials' lack of concern over working conditions. During the 1960s, members of the International Longshoremen's Association, the International Longshoremen's and Warehousemen's Union, the International Association of Machinists Union, and the International Union of Electrical Workers sought to bring about better working conditions by striking and rejecting contracts negotiated by their officials. Some, but not all, of these actions centered on safety and health conditions.

Clearly, safety and health concerns were on the minds of workers. More clearly, many rank-and-file workers were protesting against unsafe and unhealthy workplace conditions. At the same time, the political climate of the 1960s increased the likelihood that such protests would not fall on deaf ears.

POLITICAL CLIMATE

In the summer of 1967, Labor Department lawyers began drafting an occupational safety and health bill. The bill was completed by late fall and included in a package of legislation sent to the White House by the Labor Department at the end of 1967. White House officials then met with Labor Department officials and representatives of several other agencies and departments to prepare the final version (Page and O'Brien, 1973). The bill was introduced in Congress in early 1968, an election year, at a time when the Johnson administration was coming under widespread criticism for its handling of the Vietnam War. From late 1966 on, both the Harris and Gallup polls indicated that the leading Republican slate, whether led by George Romney, Nelson Rockefeller, Ronald Reagan, or Richard Nixon, would defeat a Johnson-led ticket.

Organized labor's response to Johnson's candidacy was predictable. In January, 1967, George Meany, president of the AFL–CIO, personally endorsed Johnson for president. The UAW's Reuther, while voicing some concern over Johnson's handling of the war, followed suit eight months later. An AFL–CIO poll of union members taken in January, 1967, showed Johnson with a strong lead over any Republican challenger. Yet, as 1967 wore on, the support of the rank and file became both more crucial and more problematic. Governor George Wallace's potential candidacy further complicated the picture. Shannon (1967), a *New York Times* political analyst, wrote in the summer of 1967 that Wallace's entry would severely undermine Johnson's prospects for re-election. He pointed out that Johnson would need the strong united support of the traditional democratic allies, the trade unions, and liberal independents, but predicted that such support would not be forthcoming. It was clear that the Democratic party would not be unified and that most liberals and much of the academic community would find it difficult to support Johnson. This meant that labor's support was even more crucial for Johnson.

Concern over the loss of rank-and-file support was expressed most clearly in August, 1967, by John Bailey, then head of the Democratic National Committee. He noted that the party was in danger of losing its traditional support from the rank and file and suggested that prosperity "has virtually eliminated for the present and perhaps forever, many of the ties of traditional political leadership." Workers were no longer going along with the candidates endorsed by union officials (*New York Times*, 1967:30).

On January 23, 1968, Johnson announced to Congress that the protection of 75 million U.S. workers must become a national goal. The following day, the Occupational Safety and Health Act of 1968 was introduced in Congress. The swiftness with which the bill was drafted and introduced surprised Secretary Willard Wirtz, who testified that the bill "developed quickly," too quickly to allow adequate consultation with those responsible for safety and health programs at the state level (U.S. Congress: House, 1968:34). Wirtz later admitted that he did not even know Johnson "had decided to make occupational safety and health a principal element in his program this year" until several days before the president's address to Congress (Page and O'Brien, 1973:140). The legislation was drafted and introduced at a time when the political support of rank-and-file workers was desperately needed by the incumbent president. During Congressional hearings on the bill in 1968, the Southern States Industrial Council issued a statement calling it "an attempt to create in the public mind a crisis where none exists, in order to capitalize politically on the natural concern of all citizens" for worker safety and health. It referred to the administration's "obvious election year effort by [sic] develop an image as guardian and saviour of the production worker" (U.S. Congress: House, 1968:960). In the Senate, the bill was never reported out of the Committee on Labor and Public Welfare in 1968, while the House Committee on Education and Labor did adopt an amended version. However, the bill never reached the House floor. The priority usually given to administration bills disappeared when Johnson decided not to seek his party's nomination (Page and O'Brien, 1973).

The key issue of the 1968 presidential election campaign was the Vietnam War. Campaigning for "peace with honor," Nixon won despite Hubert Humphrey's 14 percent edge among union workers (Harris, 1973). Nixon had sought the support of the "silent majority," the "forgotten Americans, the non-shouters, the non-demonstrators," and continued to turn to them for support after the election. The "New American Majority" that Nixon sought to create had for its backbone the working and middle class. The majority was "middle America" with its emphasis on traditional values. Geographically, it was the South and the ethnic and working-class precincts of the North and Midwest that Nixon sought to use as a support base (Buchanan, 1973). The Nixon administration soon discovered that one segment of the rank and file actually supported his efforts to win the war. This point was driven home during May, 1970, following the U.S. invasion of Cambodia. As anti-war demonstrations grew in size and frequency, construction workers in New York City took to the streets in support of the president. One particular march, organized by the building trades union, erupted in violence when it was rumored that anti-war protestors had burned a U.S. flag. The workers attacked the demonstrators, mostly students, with fists, pipes, and wrenches. Within weeks, the leaders of the construction workers' march were received by Nixon in the White House and thanked for their support (Harris, 1973).

At the same time, Nixon continued to court the Teamsters. In the 1968 election, Nixon received almost $1 million in campaign contributions from Las Vegas supporters who had secured large loans from the Teamsters through their imprisoned leader, Jimmy Hoffa. Soon afterward, "the wheels began to grind in the Justice Department and White House for a Hoffa pardon" (Velie, 1977:41). Two hundred and fifty thousand Teamsters signed a petition urging Nixon to free Hoffa and suggesting that their political support was conditional upon Hoffa's release. Hoffa was pardoned in December, 1971 (Velie, 1977). While befriending both the new leadership and the rank-and-file Teamsters, Nixon also responded to an issue troubling many Teamsters. The Teamsters' strike in Philadelphia was one indication of this concern. To ignore the safety and health issue would not be politically expedient, particularly after the Democrats reintroduced their bill in 1969. So the Republicans countered several months later with their own, substantially weaker, bill. As long as the Republican administration played an active role and succeeded in passing a worker safety and health bill, it could and did argue that it was protecting the safety and health of the rank and file. The symbolic impact of the legislation would assure the Republicans a claim to the rank-and-file vote in the 1972 election.[3]

The OSHAct of 1970 was a compromise. While labor did not get all it wanted, the law does give the rank and file a mechanism to improve the safety and health conditions in workplaces.[4] Nor did business get what it originally wanted—no law at all. However, it did succeed in drastically diluting the original proposed legislation.

Struggles over the legal process do not end with the passage of legislation. Since 1970, the Occupational Safety and Health Administration has been attacked from many fronts: by management for being overly concerned with trivial standards; by labor for being too weak, lenient, and ineffective; and by other branches of government for proposing standards that would fuel inflation. The OSHAct awakened union interest in the issue. More management-union safety committees have been formed and more collective bargaining agreements include safety and health provisions than ever before. In 1963–64, only five percent of 450 major agreements contained provisions for management-union cooperation. In 1974–75, 44 percent of 1,724 agreements contained such provisions (U.S. Department of Labor, 1976). In 1954–55, 22 percent of the agreements

---

3. In the 1972 election, the AFL–CIO's Meany fought George McGovern's nomination and threatened to put on probation any local affiliate that endorsed him. Meany showed his personal preference for Nixon (Harris, 1973). In the course of the 1972 campaign, Nixon was known to have received $165,000 from labor, mostly from the Seafarers and the Teamsters. Hoffa suspected that the Teamsters contributed much more than they reported (Alexander, 1976). Fifty-six percent of union members voted for Nixon (Harris, 1973).
4. The OSHAct created the Occupational Safety and Health Administration in the Department of Labor. The Labor Department is responsible for setting standards for industry and for enforcing those standards through inspections and penalties, where appropriate. The Occupational Safety and Health Review Commission was established as an independent, quasi-judicial review board appointed by the president. It rules on all enforcement actions of the Occupational Safety and Health Administration. Workers have the right to call in inspectors when they feel hazardous conditions exist. Individual states may regain authority to operate their own programs if they can demonstrate that they will be at least as effective as the federal program.

contained clauses providing for joint committees, compared with 27 percent in 1974–75 (U.S. Department of Labor, 1976). Union members who feel their officials have not done enough in this area have filed suits against their unions (Drapkin, 1981), and numerous regional committees on worker safety and health have been organized (Berman, 1981). In addition, the Supreme Court of the United States provided a basis for workers to refuse unsafe and unhealthy work in the *Whirlpool v. Marshall* (1980) decision.

Businessmen have attempted to weaken the Occupational Safety and Health Administration by challenging its standards, causing delays in their enactment, and using the courts and Congress to limit its powers (Deutsch, 1981). Business has won its share of these battles, including the right of plant managers to refuse entrance to inspectors who do not have court-issued warrants (*Marshall v. Barlow*, 1978), and the requirement that the Occupational Safety and Health Administration must demonstrate scientifically that reductions in exposure limits be "reasonably necessary" to provide safe and healthy employment conditions (*Industrial Union Department, AFL–CIO v. American Petroleum Institute*, 1980).

SUMMARY

Previous explanations of the OSHAct are based on public statements made during Congressional hearings in which union officials and environmental groups painted a dismal picture of rapidly deteriorating safety and health conditions. However, the OSHAct was not spawned by a growing safety problem, by heightened public awareness of the problem, by a convergence of the environmental movement with worker health and safety interests, or by the concerted efforts of organized labor. Rather, the roots of the law can be traced to the rebellion of rank-and-file workers across the United States at a time when the political support of these workers was particularly important. Wildcat strikes, walkouts, rejected contracts, and violent confrontations expressed rank-and-file dissatisfaction with existing safety and health conditions. The low ratings of an incumbent president in a pre-election year made united rank-and-file support an essential ingredient for political success. These two factors together made possible the emergence of a worker safety and health law.

DISCUSSION

Since the origins of this law lie in the overt class struggle initiated by the rank and file, we must look more closely at the nature of that conflict. The conflict was directed at those employers who operated unsafe and unhealthy workplaces. The rank and file sought to change workplace conditions which, in the United States, are usually considered the sole domain of employers. In refusing to do hazardous work, in walking off unsafe work sites, and in stopping the flow of business traffic, the workers disrupted employers' operations. In some cases, entire businesses were forced to shut down. The rank and file employed its most potent weapon, its labor, in an attempt to force concessions relating to safety and health conditions.

However, the protests were not directed solely at those businesses who maintained unsafe and unhealthy workplaces. They were also directed at the union hierarchy, who consistently expressed little or no concern over hazardous working conditions. These protests indicated that the rank and file wanted their union officials to take a more active role in determining safety and health conditions. Rejected contracts and refusals to obey union officials' back-to-work orders cast doubt on the legitimacy of the union hierarchy. In unions with more democratic electoral systems, these protests threatened re-election for officials, whose problems were compounded when management realized that the officials could no longer guarantee acceptance of negotiated contracts. More generally, these protests showed that the union officials had lost touch with their constituency and that they no longer represented the workers' interests.

The rank-and-file struggles of the 1950s and 1960s that culminated in the OSHAct were an attempt by workers to protect their own health and safety. Deutsch (1981) suggests that such struggles cannot be separated from the broader issues of worker control and democracy in the workplace. In this case, the workers sought to force both employers to improve conditions and their union officials to assert more power in shaping these conditions. When the officials did not, the rank and file rejected negotiated contracts. Simultaneously, the rank and file sought to exert more influence in union decision-making by demanding more input into contract negotiations. In general, workers were demanding a greater voice in the operations of the workplace.

On a broader level, the law channels future conflict into bureaucratic procedures. By awakening union interest in safety and health, the OSHAct gives more union workers institutionalized conflict-resolution mechanisms in their collective bargaining agreements. They can work to eliminate hazards through their plant safety and health committees or through the established grievance procedures in their contracts. These mechanisms defuse overt conflict. In addition, the Occupational Safety and Health Administration and the Occupational Safety and Health Review Commission also act as institutionalized mechanisms to deal with issues relating to safety and health on the job. The rank and file may work through these agencies to resolve disputes over hazards. Instead of walking off the job when other attempts to eliminate workplace hazards fail, workers now have the right, which they are expected to exercise, to call in Occupational Safety and Health inspectors. Instead of open confrontations, legal mechanisms are available to improve working conditions. The nature of the conflict is changed. Problems of unsafe and unhealthy workplaces have become bureaucratic, legal issues rather than political ones. The conflict takes place in judicial or quasi-judicial settings rather than in the workplaces and the streets.

REFERENCES

Alexander, Herbert E.
    1976   Financing the 1972 Election. Lexington, Mass.: Lexington Books.
Altman, Stephen
    1976   "Growing pains: A portrait of developing occupational safety and health in America." Job Safety and Health 4 (August):24–32.
American Federation of Labor-Congress of Industrial Organizations
    1964   AFL–CIO Platform Proposals, 1964. Washington, D.C.: AFL–CIO.
    1968   AFL–CIO Platform Proposals, 1968. Washington, D.C.: AFL–CIO.
Aronowitz, Stanley
    1973   False Promises. New York: McGraw–Hill.
Ashford, Nicholas
    1976   Crisis in the Workplace: Occupational Disease and Injury. Cambridge, Mass.: MIT.
Becker, Howard
    1963   Outsiders. New York: The Free Press of Glencoe.
Berman, Daniel
    1978   Death on the Job. New York: Monthly Review Press.
    1981   "Grassroots coalitions in health and safety: The COSH groups." Labor Studies Journal 6 (Spring):104–113.
Bigart, Homer
    1965a   "Teamsters strike in Philadelphia." New York Times, June 22:16.
    1965b   "Strikers curbed in Philadelphia." New York Times, June 23:49.
    1965c   "Hoffa aid asked by Philadelphia." New York Times, June 24:36.
Blumer, Herbert
    1971   "Social problems as collective behavior." Social Problems 18:298–306.
Buchanan, Patrick
    1973   The New Majority. The Girard Company.
Bureau of National Affairs
    1971   The Job Safety and Health Act of 1970. Washington, D.C.: Bureau of National Affairs.
Business Week
    1964   "Steel locals turn restive." November 7:90.
    1966a   "Walkout at three Ford plants involves grievances over health and safety standards." July 16:58.
    1966b   "Chrysler gets back into production after strike closes most assembly lines." October 8:148.
    1967   "Where the auto talks are going smoothly." September 23:146.

Cummins, E. E.
    1932   The Labor Problem in the United States. New York: Van Nostrand.
Deutsch, Steven
    1981   "Extending workplace democracy: Struggles to come in job safety and health." Labor Studies
              Journal 6 (Spring):124-132.
Dickson, Donald
    1968   "Bureaucracy and morality: An organizational perspective on a moral crusade." Social Prob-
              lems 16:143-156.
Drapkin, Larry
    1981   "Bargaining for health and safety: Opening a Pandora's box of liability." Labor Studies Journal
              6 (Spring):82-94.
Funkhouser, G. Ray
    1973   "Trends in media coverage of the issues of the '60s." Journalism Quarterly 50
              (Autumn):533-538.
Galliher, John F., and Allyn Walker
    1977   "The puzzle of the social origins of the marijuana tax act of 1937." Social Problems 24:367-376.
Gallup, George
    1972   The Gallup Poll: Public Opinion 1935-1971. New York: Random House.
Gersuny, Carl
    1981   Work Hazards and Industrial Conflict. Hanover, New Hampshire: University Press of New En-
              gland, for University of Rhode Island.
Gunningham, Neil
    1974   Pollution, Social Interest, and the Law. Bath, England: The Pitman Press.
Harris, Louis
    1973   The Anguish of Change. New York: W.W. Norton and Company, Inc.
National Safety Council
    1981   Accident Facts. Washington, D.C.: National Safety Council.
New York Times
    1965a   "Strike pinch felt in Philadelphia." June 25:34.
    1965b   "Teamsters end wildcat strike." June 27:54.
    1967   "Prosperity role feared by Bailey." August 27:30.
Page, Joseph A., and Mary-Win O'Brien
    1973   Bitter Wages. New York: Grossman Brothers.
Piven, Frances Fox, and Richard Cloward
    1971   Regulating the Poor: The Functions of Public Welfare. New York: Pantheon Books.
Public Papers of the Presidents
    1966-71   Milwood, New York: Kraus-Thompson Organization Press.
Ross, Robert, and Graham Staines
    1972   "The politics of analyzing social problems." Social Problems 20:18-39.
Schoenfeld, A. Clay; Robert Meier; and Robert Griffin
    1979   "Constructing a social problem: The press and the environment." Social Problems 27:38-61.
Shafer, Ronald
    1967   "UAW's local issues." Wall Street Journal, August 25:1.
Shannon, William V.
    1967   "President Johnson and the peace democrats." New York Times, July 25:34.
Stellman, Jeanne, and Susan Daum
    1973   Work is Dangerous to Your Health. New York: Vintage Books.
Stetson, Damon
    1964   "Raise is a secondary issue in steel." New York Times, December 6:73.
U.S. Congress: House of Representatives
    1968   Occupational Safety and Health Act of 1968. Committee on Education and Labor, Select Sub-
              committee on Labor. 90th Congress, 2nd Session. Washington, D.C.: U.S. Government Print-
              ing Office.
U.S. Department of Health, Education, and Welfare
    1972   President's Report on Occupational Safety and Health. Washington, D.C. U.S. Government
              Printing Office.
U.S. Department of Labor
    1956   Collective Bargaining Clauses: Labor-Management, Safety, Production, and Industry Stabiliza-
              tion Committees. Bureau of Labor Statistics Bulletin 1201. Washington, D.C.: U.S. Govern-
              ment Printing Office.
    1961-70   Analysis of Work Stoppages. Bureau of Labor Statistics. Washington, D.C.: U.S. Government
              Printing Office.
    1966   Major Collective Bargaining Agreements: Management Rights and Union-Management Coop-
              eration. Bureau of Labor Statistics Bulletin 1425-5. Washington, D.C.: U.S. Government
              Printing Office.

1976   Major Collective Bargaining Agreements: Safety and Health Provisions. Bureau of Labor Sta-
            tistics Bulletin 1425-16. Washington, D.C.: U.S. Government Printing Office.
Velie, Lester
1977   Desperate Bargain. New York: Reader's Digest Press.
Weir, Stan
1967   U.S.A.: The Labor Revolt of the 1960s. Somerville, Mass.: New England Free Press.
Woodbury, Robert
1927   Workers' Health and Safety: A Statistical Program. New York: Macmillan.

Cases cited

Industrial Union Department, AFL-CIO v. American Petroleum Institute, 48 U.S.L.W. 5022, 1980.
Marshall v. Barlow, 46 U.S.L.W. 4483, 1978.
Whirlpool Corporation v. Marshall, 48 U.S.L.W. 4189, 1980.

Reply

Reindustrialization through Coordination or Chaos?

Stuart E. Eizenstat†

Jose Ortega y Gasset once said that "to define is to exclude and deny."[1] The authors of the preceding article[2] (hereinafter referred to collectively as Miller) attempt to discredit American-style industrial policy by mischaracterizing it. Miller does this through a series of historical and contemporary examples which in reality are easily criticized attempts at centralized planning[3] and which bear little relation to the industrial policy strategies proposed for the 1980's. These inapt examples lead Miller to dismiss industrial policy on the ground that it would lead to politicized, collectivist action against the public good.[4] They also compel him to favor reliance on the market, which Miller asserts "is the best coordinator of business, labor, and consumer decisions—especially in a complex industrial economy."[5] Perhaps the most serious defect in Miller's discussion, however, is its failure to address three important realities that must be considered when evaluating the desirability of implementing an industrial policy: (1) government's inevitable involvement in microeconomic policymaking, (2) the nature of international economic competition, and (3) the difficulties that attend the present transition of the American economy from a manufacturing to a service and information economy.

Section I of this Reply presents a more accurate picture of what American proponents of industrial policy envision, and shows that the historical examples relied on by Miller fail to establish the undesirability of such a policy. Section II describes the need for a coherent industrial policy. It

† Partner, Powell, Goldstein, Frazer & Murphy, Washington, D.C.; chief domestic policy adviser to President Carter from 1977 to 1981. The author wishes to acknowledge the valuable research assistance provided by Stephanie Epstein of Powell, Goldstein, Frazer & Murphy.

1. J. ORTEGA Y GASSET, THE MODERN THEME 99 (J. Cleugh trans. 1933).
2. Miller, Walton, Kovacic & Rabkin, *Industrial Policy: Reindustrialization through Competition or Coordinated Action?*, 2 YALE J. ON REG. 1 (1984) [hereinafter cited as Miller].
3. *See* Miller, *supra* note 2, at 10-11 (discussion of the War Industries Board) and 14-20 (discussion of the National Recovery Administration).
4. *See* Miller, *supra* note 2, at 3, 28-31, 34-37.
5   *Id.* at 3, 37.

39

also responds to Miller's fear of the coordination which such a policy would entail. Finally, Section III advances specific proposals for implementing an industrial policy in the United States.

I.   Miller's Erroneous View of Industrial Policy

A.   *A Definition of Industrial Policy*

Miller has obviously misunderstood the major proposals for a U.S. industrial policy. This misunderstanding may result in part from a failure to recognize the staggering number of microeconomic policy decisions which the federal government inevitably makes every year. For example, government agencies such as the Small Business Administration, the Export-Import Bank, and institutions within the Departments of Commerce and Agriculture annually dispense billions of dollars in loans and loan guarantees to a large number of industries.[6] Similarly, government agencies continually promulgate regulations that have a profound impact on the patterns of investment in, and the competitiveness of specific economic sectors. Unfortunately, rather than recognizing industrial policy as a means of coordinating these numerous microeconomic policy decisions, Miller views it as a monolithic system which, through central planning and with the cooperation of business and labor, would allocate resources and control prices, wages, and output.[7] Consequently, Miller believes that industrial policy "might impose unacceptable political and moral costs upon the nation's democratic processes."[8]

In my view, industrial policy is not such a monolith. Rather, it is a process of better organizing the microeconomic policy-making already being conducted by the federal government. It is not a blueprint imposed by government on the private sector, but a process of making microeconomic policies in a more sound way, with more involvement by the private sector. For example, the major industrial policy legislation introduced in Congress[9] by John LaFalce (D-N.Y.) and Stan Lundine (D-N.Y.) would create a Council on Industrial Competitiveness designed to aid the President in making microeconomic decisions.[10] The Council would not be empowered to plan the economy or to foster the types of anti-competitive

---

6.   The U.S. Government made $32.2 billion in new loan disbursements in fiscal year 1983. At the end of the fiscal year 1983, the U.S. Government had $227.4 billion in direct loans outstanding and an additional $387.0 billion in outstanding guaranteed loans. BUREAU OF THE CENSUS, U.S. DEPARTMENT OF COMMERCE, STATISTICAL ABSTRACT OF THE UNITED STATES: 1984, at 405 (104th ed. 1983) [hereinafter cited as STATISTICAL ABSTRACT OF THE UNITED STATES: 1984].

7.   *See* Miller, *supra* note 2, at 35-37.

8.   *Id.* at 37.

9.   Industrial Competitiveness Act, H.R. 4360, 98th Cong., 2d Sess. (1984).

10.   H.R. REP. NO. 697, 98th Cong., 2d Sess., pt. 1, 3-6 (1984).

40

industrial practices suggested by Miller. The Council would instead assist in the coordination of the government's microeconomic decision-making, just as the Council of Economic Advisers currently assists in the formulation of the government's macroeconomic policy.[11]

Contrary to Miller's assertion, moreover, the coordination of government's microeconomic policy decisions need not subject business to greater government intervention. In many industries such coordination may lead government to prescribe deregulation. The Carter Administration, which was more receptive to industrial policy than is Miller, deregulated the airline,[12] trucking,[13] and railroad[14] industries and began deregulating the banking[15] and telecommunications industries.[16] Japan, which has perhaps the most successful industrial policy, has employed deregulation as one component of its policy.[17] In some industries, such as our high-tech industries, government might decided to reduce trade barriers and provide permanent research and development tax credits but take no other action. Clearly, implementing an American industrial policy does not require the sacrifice of competition.

B. *Miller's Misleading Examples*

Miller reveals his misunderstanding of industrial policy through his discussion of the historical and contemporary examples which he believes are relevant to the current debate: the associationalist movement of the 1920's,[18] the National Recovery Administration of the 1930's,[19] the vari-

---

11. The Council of Economic Advisers established in the Executive Office by the Employment Act of 1946, Pub. L. No. 304, 60 Stat. 24, 15 U.S.C. 1023 (1942):

analyzes the national economy and its various segments; advises the President on economic developments; appraises the economic programs and policies of the Federal Government; recommends to the President policies for economic growth and stability; and assists in the preparation of the economic reports of the President to Congress.

OFFICE OF THE FEDERAL REGISTER, GSA, THE UNITED STATES GOVERNMENT MANUAL 1983/84, at 84 (1983) [hereinafter cited as U.S. GOVT. MANUAL].

12. *See, e.g.*, Airline Deregulation Act of 1978, Pub. L. No. 95-504, 92 Stat. 1705 (codified as amended in scattered sections of 49 U.S.C.) (partially deregulating airlines).

13. *See, e.g.*, Motor Carrier Act of 1980, Pub. L. No. 96-296, 94 Stat. 793 (codified as amended in scattered sections of 49 U.S.C.) (partially deregulating trucking).

14. *See, e.g.*, Staggers Rail Act of 1980, Pub. L. No. 94-448, 94 Stat. 1895 (codified as amended in scattered sections of 49 U.S.C.) (partially deregulating railroads).

15. *See, e.g.*, Depository Institutions and Monetary Control Act of 1980, Pub. L. No. 96-221, 94 Stat. 132 (codified as amended in scattered sections of 49 U.S.C.).

16. *See, e.g.*, Telecommunications Competition and Deregulation Act of 1979, S. 622, 96th Cong., 1st Sess., 125 CONG. REC. 4628-37. Although not enacted, this bill prepared the way for later deregulatory legislation.

17. *See generally*, Japan Economic Institute of America, Japan's Industrial Policies 27-28 (Apr. 1984) (discussing antitrust exemptions and permissible cooperative industry behavior).

18. *See* Miller, *supra* note 2, at 11-14.

19. *Id.* at 14-20.

41

ous French post-war economic plans,[20] and Japan's experience with industrial policy under the direction of the Ministry of International Trade and Industry.[21] None of these examples provides adequate support for Miller's assertion that implementing an industrial policy in the United States is undesirable. Indeed, only the Japanese example provides any insight into the real issue, that is, whether the United States could benefit from better coordination of its microeconomic decision-making.

Miller's first example of coordinated microeconomic policy-making is Hoover's associationalism, which Miller asserts was spawned by government leaders' experience with the War Industries Board of World War I.[22] It is obvious from Miller's own description, however, that associationalism did not involve government intervention in the economy, but rather was a policy of government acquiescence to the attempts of large corporations to limit competition through industry-sponsored codes which restricted output, undercut antitrust enforcement, and fixed prices.[23] The adverse consequences of associationalism described by Miller do not undermine the desirability of industrial policy. Rather, the associationalist experience illustrates what happens when the government abrogates its public responsibilities and permits unbridled private sector activity. A hallmark of the Reagan Administration is its hands-off attitude toward private sector regulation, consumer protection, and antitrust enforcement.[24] Hence, the Reagan Administration's policies arguably bear as much resemblance to Hoover's associationalism as any of the proposals for a coordinated industrial policy.

Two of Miller's examples, the National Recovery Administration and the French economic plans, involved a level of government control over wages, prices, and resources that no serious proponent of American industrial policy envisions today. Whatever the merits of these examples, they are not relevant to the debate over industrial policy proposals such as those now before Congress.[25] Moreover, these examples of government intervention were not the obvious disasters Miller portrays them to be. Miller concludes that the NRA "substantially impeded recovery from the Depression."[26] The basis for this conclusion is obscure, however, since the NRA was initiated in 1933, four years after the onset of the Depression,

20.   *Id.* at 23-25.
21.   *Id.* at 21-23.
22.   *Id.* at 11.
23.   *Id.* at 11-14.
24.   *See generally* G. EADS & M. FIX, RELIEF OR REFORM?: REAGAN'S REGULATORY DILEMMA (1984).
25.   *See supra* note 9.
26.   *See* Miller, *supra* note 2, at 18.

42

and lasted only two years before being declared unconstitutional.[27] There is no evidence that the NRA's demise accelerated the end of the Depression or that its brief tenure perpetuated it. Similarly, one cannot ascribe France's economic difficulties to its industrial policy programs. The French economy has performed poorly both with and without such programs.[28] Rather than reflecting a failure of industrial policy, current French economic woes reflect poor macroeconomic policy-making by the Mitterand government, which created more inflation than growth by following a "go-it-alone" stimulative policy at a time when other industrial nations were retrenching.

Although most of Miller's case histories are inapposite, he does discuss one genuine example of a modern industrial policy: Japan's Ministry of International Trade and Industry ("MITI").[29] Unfortunately, though, he draws misleading inferences from the Japanese experience. Based on the decline in employment experienced by the Japanese shipbuilding industry since 1977,[30] Miller concludes that "the once-touted examples of successful Japanese planning have come on hard times."[31] The decline, however, reflects the operation of the very marketplace that Miller extols, not the failure of industrial policy. It resulted from the Japanese shipbuilding industry's loss of sales to countries with lower labor costs, such as Korea, and from the substantial decline in the demand for oil tankers resulting from lower worldwide demand for oil.

Rather than causing the decline of Japan's shipbuilding industry, MITI's policies mitigated the adverse effects of that decline by permitting the industry to stabilize employment and return to profitability.[32] In addition, Japan's Depressed Industries Law[33] provided for the retraining of thousands of displaced workers who might otherwise have had difficulty finding new jobs. Contrary to Miller's assertions, developments in the Japanese shipbuilding industry do not undermine the desirability of industrial policy. Rather, they illustrate how industrial policy can be used not only to encourage an expanding sector of the economy, but also to streamline a contracting sector and make it competitive again.

In summary, it is disingenuous to cite Herbert Hoover's associationalism and Franklin Roosevelt's NRA as "dismal failures"[34] of our country's own experiments with tripartite cooperation. Similarly, one cannot label

---

27. *See* Schechter Poultry Corp. v. United States, 295 U.S. 495 (1935).
28. *See* N.Y. Times, Apr. 17, 1983, § 1, pt. 1, at 18, col. 3.
29. *See* Miller, *supra* note 2, at 21–23.
30. *Id.* at 22.
31. *Id.*
32. *See* ECONOMIST, Nov. 5, 1983, at 69.
33. Structurally Depressed Industries Law (1978) (revised and extended, June 1983).
34. Miller, *supra* note 2, at 10.

43

French or Japanese cooperative policies as failures without considering other factors that may be responsible for economic downturns in those countries. By using irrelevant and distorted examples, Miller has criticized a policy that no responsible American proponent of industrial policy would support. He thus has failed to support his claim that an American industrial policy is unnecessary and undesirable. As the following discussion shows, moreover, Miller has ignored several compelling reasons for implementing such a policy.

II.   The Need for an Industrial Policy

Since the assimilation of John Maynard Keynes' economic theories into the government's economic thinking, and particularly since the creation of the Council of Economic Advisers in 1946,[35] all our Presidents have recognized that macroeconomic policy must be coordinated to achieve national goals. The annual budget process within the Executive Branch, organized by the Office of Management and Budget, represents one effort to coordinate fiscal policy; that process institutionalizes government's efforts to set tax and spending levels to improve the performance of the economy.

I firmly believe that a well-managed fiscal and monetary policy can solve most of our economic ills. I am also convinced, however, that it cannot solve all of them. First, U.S. fiscal policy cannot coordinate the microeconomic functions of government to eliminate the contradictory and irrational effects of many government programs. Second, it cannot by itself reverse the ballooning American trade deficit which results, in part, from trade restrictions imposed by other countries. Finally, U.S. fiscal policy cannot restructure America's declining basic industries and retrain the workers in those industries. As this section demonstrates, an industrial policy can effectively address these three challenges facing the U.S. economy.

A.   Coordinating Government's Microeconomic Decisions

Miller views the primary issue in the debate over industrial policy as whether the government should "try more actively to guide and coordinate the decisions of business and labor, or should . . . rely primarily on decentralized competitive forces."[36] In reality, however, the debate is not over what level of government intervention is proper, but rather over how government can maximize the effectiveness of whatever intervention occurs. We must choose between a coordinated program for government in-

35. *See supra* note 11.
36. Miller, *supra* note 2, at 2.

44

tervention, which systematically takes into account all the diverse effects of such intervention, and a continuation of the current system of uncoordinated programs with its often contradictory effects. A number of common microeconomic decisions—particularly those relating to import relief—illustrate the need for a coordinated program.

Currently, no institutional mechanisms exist for coordinating microeconomic policy decisions. Government economic intervention accordingly is an amalgam of independent and often conflicting programs, resting upon no apparent unifying principles and affecting different industrial sectors in ways unrelated to national goals. For example, the effective tax rate on different industries varies widely, but not in accordance with any professed policy of treating certain industries more favorably.[37] Similarly, the federal government supports almost half the research and development undertaken in the United States,[38] but this research follows no clear priorities.[39] One need not favor increased government involvement in the economy to support improved coordination of the involvement which already occurs.

The deleterious consequences of this lack of coordination are most apparent in the U.S. "system" for deciding when and how to provide relief to industries adversely affected by import competition. The United States International Trade Commission[40] and, ultimately, the President are continually faced with petitions for trade relief.[41] Our trade laws, together with economic and political imperatives, assure that every president will grant some of these petitions and impose trade restraints on the "free market." Given the absence of a coherent industrial policy with established criteria for evaluating such claims, however, immediate political considerations often dictate the response to each petition. Moreover, the remedies granted are rarely, if ever, designed to assure that further relief will not be required at a later date.[42]

One excursion into *ad hoc* industrial policy-making, involving trade re-

---

37. See JOINT COMM. ON TAXATION, 98TH CONG., 1ST SESS., STUDY OF 1982 EFFECTIVE TAX RATES OF SELECTED LARGE U.S. CORPORATIONS 5-8 (Comm. Print 1983).

38. See STATISTICAL ABSTRACT OF THE UNITED STATES: 1984, *supra* note 6, at 592-93 (10th ed. 1983).

39. See Address by Senator Paul E. Tsongas, Research & Development: The Impact and Challenge, 5-7, before the American Academy for the Advancement of Science (June 23, 1982).

40. This independent agency furnishes studies, reports and recommendations involving international trade and tariffs to the President, the Congress, and other governmental agencies. It conducts a variety of investigations, public hearings and research projects pertaining to U.S. international policies. U.S. GOV'T MANUAL, *supra* note 11, at 631-41.

41. Upon petition by an industry representative, the Commission conducts investigations to determine whether an article is being imported in such increased quantities as to be a substantial threat to the domestic industry. If the Commission finds such a threat, the President has discretion to provide import relief. Trade Act of 1974, §§ 201-203, 19 USC §§ 2251-2253 (1982).

42. See Eizenstat, *A Quid Pro Quo for Steel*, N.Y. Times, Sept. 18, 1984, at A27, col. 1.

45

lief to the steel industry, illustrates the failure of government to maximize the public benefits of intervention in a particular sector of the economy. In 1980, a Presidential Steel Task Force submitted a relief program for the steel industry to President Carter.[43] The program called for implementation of a trigger pricing mechanism for import relief, extension of anti-pollution deadlines,[44] and institution of faster depreciation writeoffs for equipment.[45] While the steel industry was pleased with the program that eventually was adopted, the public did not get enough in return. The industry made no commitments to reduce excess capacity or modernize plants, and labor made no concessions on work rules or wages. Indeed, none was requested. The only concession obtained from the steel companies was a vague, eleventh-hour promise to reinvest the additional cash attributable to the relief program in modernizing plant and equipment.[46] As shown by U.S. Steel's subsequent purchase of Marathon Oil Company,[47] this promise was not enough. The lesson from this example is clear: Although government has no right to direct the pattern of U.S. Steel's investments, U.S. Steel should not be allowed to use federal relief for a purpose unrelated to that for which the relief was granted. Because no effective mechanism for coordinating microeconomic policy was in place, the effort to rescue the steel industry amounted to no more than an open-ended handout.

Although the steel incident occurred during the Carter Administration, each administration inevitably will grant some of the many requests for import relief it receives. The Reagan Administration, which professes a commitment to the free market, has established tariffs or quotas in the automobile,[48] textile,[49] specialty steel,[50] and motorcycle industries,[51] all without any coordinated policy or clearly defined objectives. In addition,

---

43. *See* Address by Senator Paul E. Tsongas, "Research & Development: The Impact and Challenge" 5-7, before the American Academy for the Advancement of Science (June 23, 1982).

44. *Id.*

45. *Id.*

46. *See* Eizenstat, *supra* note 47.

47. *See* N.Y. Times, Jan. 7, 1982, at A1, col. 5.

48. *See* Rowan, *Detroit: Hooked on Protection*, Wash. Post Nat'l Weekly Ed., Nov. 21, 1983, at 5, col. 1.

49. Exec Order No. 12475, *reprinted in* 1984 U.S. CODE CONG. & AD. NEWS B60.

50. Presidential Proclamation of Temporary Duty Increases and Quantitative Limitations on the Importation Into the United States of Certain Stainless Steel and Alloy Tool Steel, 1983 U.S. CODE CONG. & AD. NEWS A80 (July 19, 1983).

51. Message from the President of the United States Transmitting Notice of his Decision to Impose Incremental Tariffs on the Importation of Heavyweight Motorcycles, Pursuant to Section 203 of the Trade Act of 1974, H.R. Doc. No. 37, 98th Cong. 1st Sess., *reprinted in* 1983 U.S. CODE CONG. & AD. NEWS A49.

46

the Administration currently plans to negotiate bilateral restraints to reduce steel imports from 25% to 18.5% of the U.S. market.[52]

These practices demonstrate the need for an industrial policy, one
which could provide clear criteria for awarding relief and guidance on
designing that relief to ensure proper responses to the problems facing the
affected industries. Government could, for example, condition relief on
concessions from management and labor. Such concessions might include
reducing outmoded capacity, trimming labor costs, and revising outmoded
work practices. Those instances in which direct government assistance
worked best during the Carter Administration—Chrysler Corporation and
New York City—involved preconditioning the aid on the recipients' making concessions that would make the federal aid worthwhile. In short,
careful coordination based on established policy objectives would allow
government to get "the biggest bang for the buck," both in granting trade
relief and in making other microeconomic policy decisions.

Despite such compelling arguments for this type of industrial policy,
Miller dismisses as politically infeasible the suggestion that government
coordinate its microeconomic policy decisions. He argues that the American system of government, which encourages interest groups to lobby for
government action in their interests, will prevent formation of a consensus
about which actions should be taken.[53] In addition, Miller argues that
coordinating microeconomic policy decisions would lead to an undesirable
concentration of government decision-making power.[54]

Certainly, formulation of industrial policies will be subjected to the influence of parties seeking to further their own interests. But that is true of
the microeconomic and fiscal policies government already makes. America
is a democracy; industrial policy decisions, like other government decisions, cannot be made in isolation by a few wise men and women. Nevertheless, I see no reason why attempting to coordinate the inevitable government decisions on microeconomic matters would further politicize the
decision-making process. On the contrary, coordination would likely help
government identify situations in which an interest group has been able to
exercise excessive control over a particular facet of government
microeconomic decision-making. Similarly, industrial policy would not require granting the government greater control over microeconomic policy.
It would merely allow government to coordinate the decisions it is already
empowered to make. Obviously, eliciting input from labor and management will not insure that government decisions receive universal support.

---

52. *See* N.Y. Times, Sept. 20, 1984, at D1, col. 3.
53. *See* Miller, *supra* note 2, at 30–31.
54. *See id.* at 35–36.

47

Nevertheless, an industrial policy process can, at a minimum, provide the government with insight into the needs of business and labor and with a forum in which business and labor can be called on to make meaningful concessions.

B. *Enhancing Trade*

America also needs a sound industrial policy to enhance U.S. trade. American firms face foreign competitors who benefit from coherent industrial policies implemented on their behalf by their governments.[55] The idealized world of free international markets described by Adam Smith and relied on by Miller just does not exist. To make U.S. firms competitive, therefore, the government must respond to the trade programs of foreign governments with equal care and interest. American business needs carefully integrated federal programs to help open foreign markets, reduce artificial trade barriers, provide export financing, and assure that U.S. firms are able to compete to their full capacities. The current patchwork of programs is not sufficient.

C. *Mitigating Transitional Problems*

Problems of economic transition illustrate a third reason for implementing an industrial policy in the United States. The former U.S. industrial heartland cannot manage the difficult transition from a manufacturing economy to a service and information economy without consistent and coherent government support. Traditional market forces are inadequate to retrain the new class of structurally unemployed Americans for new jobs. Implementing a comprehensive set of training and relocation programs to aid these workers, however, is hardly the sort of "coordinated action" which Miller so fears and abhors.[56] To the contrary, such a program ultimately would strengthen the independence of the private sector by enhancing the productivity and competitiveness of American workers. The Japanese experience with job training programs shows the truth of this assertion.

In summary, the United States needs an industrial policy to coordinate and synthesize the microeconomic decisions which government already makes. Such coordination will, in turn, help enhance international competition and ameliorate the transitional problems of the changing U.S. economy. As shown below, moreover, improved coordination of government

---

55. Weil, *U.S. Industrial Policy: A Process in Need of a Federal Industrial Coordination Board*, 14 L. & INDUS. POL. INT'L BUS. 981, 993–1004 (1983).

56. *See* Miller, *supra* note 2, at 37.

48

microeconomic programs can be achieved without, as Miller fears, impeding competition and restricting freedom.

III. PROPOSAL

Effective coordination of government programs requires the free and efficient exchange of information and opinions between business, labor, and government. Without such an exchange, government will have a difficult time ascertaining the needs of particular industries and determining how these needs can be met in a way that will maximize public benefits. Unfortunately, no forum exists in the United States to facilitate cooperation or the exchange of information between business, government, and labor. In America, labor and management generally meet only over the collective bargaining table, as adversaries.[57] Only one regular forum exists in which top labor and business leaders can discuss their differences free of such belligerence: an informal group organized by former Labor Secretary John Dunlop.[58] The deliberations of this group, however, are not open to government.[59]

To help government coordinate its microeconomic programs to serve the public better, I favor the creation of a "Council on Industrial Competitiveness." This Council could aid administrations in promoting management-labor-government cooperation, reducing confrontation, and determining the amount and types of information necessary to formulate sound microeconomic policies. The Council could, for example, help the President evaluate petitions for trade relief; it also could help labor and management agree to changes on wages, work rules, managerial policy, and capacity which could make industries seeking governmental assistance more competitive. The Council would be a resource, similar to the Council of Economic Advisers,[60] upon which the President could draw when making decisions with microeconomic ramifications. To maximize the information flowing to the government, the Council would be composed of representatives from business, government, labor, and the general public. It would work closely with the White House domestic policy staff and the Office of Management and Budget to see that microeconomic decisions are better coordinated and synthesized. In short, the Council would be an ad-

---

57. By contrast, it is no accident that Japan's industrial surge coincided with a move away from the labor-management confrontations of the 1950's, or that West Germany's post-war economic miracle was built in part upon worker co-determination.

58. *The Industrial Competition Act: Hearings on H.R. 4360 before the Subcomm. on Commerce, Transportation, and Tourism of the House Comm. on Energy and Commerce*, 98th Cong., 2nd Sess. 15 (1984) (testimony of Stuart Eizenstat).

59. *Id.*

60. *See supra* note 11.

49

visory group to the President, not a decision-making body with power to direct the allocation of resources.

To aid the Council, I also favor the creation of a new "Bureau of Industrial Analysis" within the Department of Commerce. The Bureau could provide the Council with expertise in industry-by-industry analysis comparable to that now provided by the Bureau of Labor Statistics for macroeconomic policy-making.[61] Wise policies can only be fashioned on sound information. No agency, however, regularly gathers and publishes the information needed to formulate sound microeconomic policy.

In setting its agenda, the Council might concentrate first on economic problems that are particularly amenable to resolution through government action. For example, the Council might help the President evaluate a number of initiatives designed to help American industries compete with foreign companies. Such initiatives might include implementing reciprocity legislation[62] when necessary to open foreign markets, encouraging private sector research and development by changing the antitrust laws to allow coordinated industry efforts[63] and by offering favorable tax treatment of research and development expenses, and strengthening the Export-Import Bank[64] to make financing arrangements for the purchase of American goods more competitive with those for foreign products. The Council also could propose or review initiatives for easing the burden of the inevitable restructuring which is occuring in our declining industries. One such initative might involve shifting government resources away from assistance programs, such as trade adjustment assistance, and focusing them instead on retraining workers who have lost their jobs through industrial transition and foreign competition.

In summary, this Council would provide a mechanism for coordinating government decisions with microeconomic ramifications. Contrary to

---

61. *See* U.S. GOVT. MANUAL, *supra* note 11, at 379.

62. Legislation already passed authorizes retaliation against restrictive foreign trade practices when necessary to open foreign markets. *See* Tariff Treatment Act of 1984, Pub. L. No. 98-573 (1984).

63. A bill to modify the application of the antitrust laws with respect to joint R&D programs has been introduced into the House of Representatives by Cong. Lipinski. H.R. 5830, 98th Cong. 2d Sess., 130 CONG. REC. 5677 (1984).

64. The Export-Import Bank of the United States ("Eximbank"), an independent agency:
   facilitates and aids in financing exports of U.S. Goods and services. Eximbank has implemented a variety of programs to meet the needs of the U.S. exporting community, according to the size of the transaction. These programs take the form of loans or the issuance of guarantees and insurance, so that exporters and private banks can extend appropriate financing without taking undue risks. Eximbank's direct lending program is limited to larger sales of U.S. products and services around the world. The guarantees, insurance, and discount programs have been designed to assist exporters in smaller sales of products and services.
U.S. GOVT. MANUAL, *supra* note 11, at 486-88.

50

Reply

Miller's assertions, however, it is politically feasible and would not entail any additional centralization of government power.

Conclusion

Miller's article misses its mark because it fails to address the real issue posed by the debate over American industrial policy: Can better coordination enhance the effectiveness of government microeconomic policy-making? Instead of addressing this issue directly, Miller criticizes irrelevant or inaccurate models of centralized planning and argues that it is politically infeasible or undesirable to coordinate the microeconomic policy decisions that inevitably will be made. The true choice is not, as Miller argues, between competition or coordination in the economy, but rather between coordination and chaos in government's response to microeconomic problems. In my view, the answer is obvious. As evidenced here, the microeconomic decisions of government can be coordinated to provide effective responses to problems in the U.S. economy. This coordination, moreover, can be achieved without producing the kind of collectivist, anti- competitive results which Miller fears.

51

The Potential for Industrial Policy:
LESSONS FROM THE VERY HIGH SPEED INTEGRATED CIRCUIT PROGRAM

Glenn R. Fong

Abstract

A Pentagon program to advance semiconductor technology offers some important empirical evidence for the national debate over industrial policy. While not an explicit attempt at promoting international competitiveness, the Very High Speed Integrated Circuit (VHSIC) program does contain a whole series of industrial policy-like features, including joint government–industry planning, widespread industry participation, and multifirm collaboration. These striking features cannot be attributed solely to VHSIC's affiliation with the military. Instead, the sources of the program's industrial policy characteristics are to be found in the nature of the technologies selected for development, the incorporation of private sector advice, the mitigation of threats to proprietary interests, avoidance of redistributional issues, and the utilization of industry competition and networks of communication—all factors directly relevant to industrial policymaking generally.

While the debate over industrial policy may ebb and flow over time, the issue will remain on the national agenda for the foreseeable future.[1] The industrial challenge posed by foreign rivals is certainly not abating. As long as American industries face, stiff foreign competition, and especially if foreign competitors are backed by their governments, the controversy over U.S. industrial policies will continue. At stake is whether this country should adopt public policies—for instance, subsidies, credit schemes, tax measures, trade policies, antitrust regulations, and research and development programs—that are specifically designed to promote industrial adjustment and international competitiveness.[2]

While forcing a reexamination of fundamental government–business relations, discourse on industrial policy remains largely normative in character. Industrial policy advocates have focused

Journal of Policy Analysis and Management, Vol. 5, No. 2, 264–291 (1986)
© 1986 by the Association for Public Policy Analysis and Management
Published by John Wiley & Sons, Inc.   CCC 0276-8739/86/010264-28$04.00

on the question of "why the United States needs an industrial policy." America's current domestic and international economic problems are highlighted, including persistent recession, widespread layoffs and plant closings that amount to "deindustrialization," lagging productivity, mushrooming trade deficits, and a declining standard of living. Proponents of industrial policy point out that American firms are besieged by low-wage producers in the Third World and by more advanced neomerchantilist states "artificially" creating comparative advantage in strategic sectors. A purely private sector response is considered inadequate since many of the nation's competitive problems are seen as results of myopic management strategies and self-centered labor practices. Neither are conventional economic policies seen as a source of industrial renewal. Current policies toward industry amount to an ad hoc collection of loans, subsidies, tax breaks, regulations, and trade protection that contribute little to competitiveness at best, and more than likely undermine competitiveness by favoring the preservation of politically powerful established industries. Proponents believe a positive and essential government contribution can and must be made by systematically encouraging investment in new high-risk technologies and smoothing the social costs of transition out of declining sectors.

Critics point out that explicit industrial policies would profoundly violate American ideological values and political traditions regarding the primacy of the market mechanism and limited government. Once implemented, industrial policies would produce serious economic dislocations by, among other things, crowding out from capital markets those sectors not considered strategic, and magnifying if not "nationalizing" unsuccessful industrial ventures. Moreover, industrial policies are deemed unnecessary since there are overlooked signs of America's industrial vitality (for instance, substantial research and development expenditures and an expanding share of world exports of manufactures). While serious economic trouble spots are acknowledged, they can be adequately addressed by sound macroeconomic policies.

While both proponents and opponents have invested a great deal of energy into arguing over whether the U.S. needs and should have explicit industrial policies, relatively little attention has been given to the issue of whether or not this country can adopt such policies in practice.[3] Although normative questions are crucial to any policy debate, they must be informed by empirical considerations indicating what is possible and what is not. Indeed, negative empirical conclusions may render the entire normative debate moot.

The experience of a concrete industrial policy-like program in the U.S., the Very High Speed Integrated Circuit (VHSIC) program, offers some important empirical evidence for the policy debate. The VHSIC experience sheds light on whether the U.S. can effectively implement policies involving a direct government role in industry-level efforts to promote international competitiveness.

The VHSIC program was established by the Department of Defense in 1979 to infuse research and development funds into the electronics industry. While VHSIC is not an explicit attempt at industrial policy in the United States, the program shares many features with such policies. The program represents a concerted, long-range effort at advancing the state of the art in integrated circuitry by several years. Government officials consulted extensively with industry leaders in formulating the program, and some 25 companies ranging from major computer manufacturers to merchant semiconductor firms have been on the receiving end of VHSIC contracts. Industrial research has received constant guidance from government experts, and industry participants have teamed up with one another to coordinate their research efforts. The program is currently budgeted at $680 million over an eight-year period.

The combined features of the VHSIC program make it the closest contemporary American parallel to the collaborative government–industry programs in high technology that have been seen in Japan and Western Europe. Industrial policy is epitomized, in many respects, by such overseas programs as Japan's very large scale integration project (1976–1980) in which the Ministry of International Trade and Industry collaborated with the country's five major electronics firms to develop next-generation semiconductor technology.

There are two major reasons why an examination of the VHSIC program may be particularly instructive in shedding light on the debate over industrial policy. First, in involving the American microelectronics industry, the program may offer lessons in designing public policies promoting high-technology "sunrise" industries generally. Paralleling the heightened attention that corporations have given to advanced technology as a competitive tool, national governments have increasingly focused their efforts on fostering high-technology sectors. Even if VHSIC's lessons for designing policies for mature and declining industrial sectors prove limited, the "targeting" of high-technology industries by governments provides an important if not growing policy arena to which the VHSIC experience may be relevant.

Second, collaborative research and development programs such as VHSIC are among the most intensive and challenging forms of industrial policy. Arm's length relationships between public and private sectors are broken down in collaborative technology programs where government and industrial officials remain in close contact over an extended period of time. Broad consensus on program objectives must be achieved. Intimate working relationships and public–private communication links must be established. Research and development (R & D) projects may require much more detailed government–industry collaboration than the redrafting of tax legislation or the revision of antitrust regulations. Hence, an assessment of America's capabilities in the arena of collaborative R & D should shed much light on the potential for industrial policymaking in the U.S. generally.

It should be emphasized that VHSIC was *not* designed as an industrial policy program, and the focus here is not on whether the Pentagon initiative promotes international competitiveness. Indeed—while it may be unfair to evaluate a program according to criteria that it was never designed to meet—serious reservations can be raised about VHSIC's ultimate impact upon civilian integrated circuit technology and upon the commercial competitiveness of the American semiconductor industry.[4]

Other than examining VHSIC's technological or economic consequences, one might also investigate whether VHSIC can serve as a future model for the Department of Defense to contribute to industrial policy objectives.[5] In addition, one might be interested in deriving lessons from VHSIC for the design of other, future and purely military-oriented technology programs.

While all are worthy and fascinating angles on VHSIC, none are explicitly explored here. Instead, the key issue is whether some of VHSIC's industrial policy attributes might be transferable *outside* the Department of Defense. In particular, three select yet significant features of VHSIC's formative stages are examined: the program's joint planning by government and industry officials; the means by which VHSIC gained widespread industry support; and the encouragement of collaborative research among private firms.

Each of these VHSIC features critically reflects upon major reservations raised about the ability of the U.S. to implement industrial policies. One practical problem area concerns the lack of government competence in industry affairs.[6] Insufficient expertise and analytical capabilities as well as inaccessability to crucial industry information serve to hinder sound policy decisions. Another set of impediments to the implementation of industrial policy derives from traditional adversarial relations between public and private sectors.[7] While American business leaders enjoy easy access in the political process, they remain hostile to government interference. A third source of difficulty for industrial policymaking relates to the atomistic character of the American business community.[8] National business organizations are weak and trade associations fragmented. Whether because of Yankee individualism, their historical status as early industrializers, or simple fear of antitrust prosecution, U.S. firms manifest little of the collusive behavior exhibited by many foreign counterparts. Taken altogether, these adverse conditions should have crippled VHSIC's planning, circumscribed industry support, and delimited collaboration among companies.

An explanation of VHSIC's anomalous characteristics should help to define America's industrial policymaking capabilities.[9] VHSIC's potential for revealing America's general industrial policymaking capabilities, however, rests upon whether the program's three industrial policy-like features—government–industry planning, industrywide participation, and multifirm collaboration—were based upon its military affiliation. National security considerations may have imbued the program with such strategic importance so as to secure private sector cooperation. Long-standing links between the Pentagon and defense contractors may have provided the foundation for VHSIC's intensive government–industry collaboration. Other military attributes such as technical expertise and organizational discipline may have facilitated the program's planning and implementation. If military factors alone account for the industrial policy-like characteristics of this program, then VHSIC's relevance to the general industrial policy debate vastly diminishes.

Many features of the VHSIC program are, no doubt, attributable to its sponsorship by the Department of Defense. While the following analysis takes note of a number of VHSIC's *exceptional* features, it also establishes that the roots of the program's industrial policy qualities are not due to conditions necessarily *unique* to military technology programs.

VHSIC OBJECTIVES AND ORGANIZATION
The overall objective of the VHSIC program is the design and development of advanced integrated circuits highlighting specific military needs and the introduction of those circuits into military systems in a timely and affordable manner.[10] The technologies under development are comprehensive, ranging from the fundamental design of computers to the testing of finished electronic components. A major aim of the program is the development of high-speed integrated circuits with ultrafine micrometer and submicrometer features[11] and high-speed computational capabilities.

The program consists of four phases. Phase 0, completed in November 1980, was a study phase to define detailed approaches for achieving the ultimate objectives of the program and to prepare Phase I proposals. As listed in Table 1, 14 prime contract bids were submitted for Phase 0, and 9 contracts amounting to $10.3 million were awarded.

Phase I consisted of the development of 1.25 μm circuitry and initial efforts to extend technology to submicrometer geometries. The nine Phase 0 prime contractors submitted bids for Phase I, and six awards amounting to $167.8 million were made in May 1981. Phase I work was to be completed in 1984.

VHSIC Phase II is designed to enhance the yields of 1.25 μm technology; rapidly insert 1.25 μm circuits into military systems; standardize the computer languages developed by VHSIC contractors; and continue the Phase I effort to develop submicrometer technologies. With respect to this submicrometer work, nine study contracts (a'la Phase 0) were awarded in July 1983, and three finalists were selected in October 1984. At least $446.6 million is to be allocated for all Phase II efforts, and the work will run through 1988.

Phase III ran in parallel with the other phases and consisted of many smaller, shorter-term efforts in specific technology areas designed to support the main program. Fifty-nine Phase III contracts amounting to $35.8 million were awarded to some twenty-five companies and universities.

VHSIC is centrally managed by the Department of Defense rather than by the separate military services. The program is a

Table 1. VHSIC bidders and contractors.[a]

VHSIC status	Phase 0 1980	Phase I 1981–1984	Phase II[b] 1984–1988
CONTRACT WINNERS	GENERAL ELECTRIC 　Analog Devices 　Intersil 　Tektronix HONEYWELL 　3M HUGHES 　Burroughs 　Signetics IBM RAYTHEON 　Fairchild 　Varian ROCKWELL 　Perkin-Elmer 　Sanders TEXAS INSTRUMENTS TRW 　GCA 　Motorola 　Sperry WESTINGHOUSE 　Control Data 　National Semiconductor	HONEYWELL 　3M HUGHES 　Perkin-Elmer 　RCA 　Rockwell 　Union Carbide IBM TEXAS INSTRUMENTS TRW 　Motorola 　Sperry WESTINGHOUSE 　Control Data 　Harris 　National Semiconductor	HONEYWELL 　Motorola 　General Electric 　3M IBM TRW 　General Dynamics 　Motorola
LOSING BIDDERS	BOEING 　General Instrument HARRIS 　ERIM 　Perkin-Elmer SINGER 　American Microsystems 　Amheart Systems WESTERN ELECTRIC 　Bell Labs	GENERAL ELECTRIC 　Analog Devices 　Intersil 　Martin Marietta 　Tektronix RAYTHEON 　Fairchild 　Varian ROCKWELL 　Perkin-Elmer 　Sanders	HUGHES 　Perkin-Elmer TEXAS INSTRUMENTS WESTERN ELECTRIC 　Bell Labs 　E-Systems 　Raytheon WESTINGHOUSE 　Control Data 　National Semiconductor

[a] Prime contractors in upper case letters; subcontractors in lower case.
[b] Submicrometer development contractors and bidders only.

tri-service effort in which the military departments (Army, Navy, Air Force) monitor VHSIC contractors on a day-to-day basis. The VHSIC Program Office, located in the Office of the Undersecretary of Defense for Research and Engineering, has coordinated the three services, ensured technological commonality across the services, minimized duplicative efforts, and set technical priorities.

VHSIC'S MILITARY ORIGINS

While it will be argued that VHSIC's industrial policy features were not inordinately dependent upon factors unique to the military world, several national security concerns did in fact spur the Pentagon's initial thoughts on the program. First, the VHSIC program grew out of the "smart weapons" strategy initiated by the Department of Defense during the Carter Administration. High-performance, high-technology weaponry are to be utilized by American defense forces to offset the numerical advantages of the Soviet military. VHSIC is to provide the fundamental ingredient of advanced electronics for this countervailing strategy.[12]

A second national security motivation behind VHSIC was the need to reassert Pentagon influence over the development of semiconductor technology.[13] Between 1965 and 1979, the proportion of integrated circuit production that went to meet military demand plunged from 70 to 7%. Semiconductor developments came to be driven by industrial and consumer needs, and commercial products began to diverge from military requirements. The adaptation or customization of commercial circuits to meet military specifications not only entailed high cost but substantial delays of up to 12 years between the commercial availability of a chip and its utilization in defense systems. Currently, while the commercial industry has moved well into very large scale integration (VLSI), most military systems do not even utilize large-scale integrated circuitry.[14] VHSIC was designed, in part, to address this insertion problem.

A third national security consideration—the concern over Soviet advances, specifically in integrated circuitry—acted as the immediate stimulus for the planning of VHSIC.[15] In the autumn of 1977, the Pentagon's Office of Electronics and Physical Sciences turned up an intelligence report suggesting that the U.S. military (but not commercial) lead over the Soviets in microelectronics had diminished significantly. A brief note on these findings was submitted in a report to Secretary of Defense Harold Brown. The report was returned by Brown with a hand-written note inquiring to the effect: "What can we do about this?" With those few words, the Office of Electronics and Physical Sciences mobilized to plan in earnest for the program that would become VHSIC.

In exploring the motives for the Pentagon's initiation of VHSIC it is important to consider the role of foreign competition in semiconductors from Japan. It is a widespread assumption that VHSIC was a military response to—if not modeled after—Japan's very large scale integration project launched in 1976. However, officials have denied any such links both in private interviews and in the public press.

It is clear that as far as VHSIC planners in the Pentagon were concerned, VHSIC was not a reaction to any Japanese semiconductor thrust, but a response to the three military concerns cited above. Yet there is evidence that once the program was given the go-ahead, the Japanese experience did have an impact upon VHSIC planners. For instance, it has been acknowledged that the setting of VHSIC's initial budget at $140 million was gauged on the basis of the $200 million VLSI effort in Japan.[16] In their consultations with industry specialists, defense officials inquired as to "how soon any foreign country will arrive at 0.5 micron capabilities?"[17]

Pentagon officials recognized that VHSIC would aid U.S. industry in its response to the Japanese.[18] A revealing indicator of the extent of thought that was put to the Japan–VHSIC link was the fact that VHSIC planners agreed early on to be silent on the Japan issue. The fear was that the linkage would backfire politically, given the lack of Department of Defense jurisdiction in commercial matters.

GOVERNMENT– INDUSTRY PLANNING
To acknowledge that national security considerations initially spurred Pentagon thinking on VHSIC is not to say that such concerns were responsible for VHSIC's planning process or programmatic features. VHSIC's planners received little guidance from either the Secretary of Defense or Undersecretary for Research and Engineering William Perry, the architects of the smart weapons concept.[19] It would be difficult to link even the general outlines of the VHSIC program to concerns over the Soviet military threat. The insertion problem had been long-standing and was insufficient on its own to generate a concerted response.[20] The reported shrinking lead over the Soviets in military electronics was never substantiated, even after intensive study.[21] Only personal initiative and leadership can account for the transformation of abstract national security motivations into concrete policy action.

To begin with, Defense Secretary Brown's expressed interest in a remedy for the alleged Soviet microelectronics advances permitted VHSIC's planners to cut through a great deal of bureaucratic red tape. Instead of laboriously promoting the VHSIC case up through the ranks of the Pentagon, VHSIC planners immediately and directly briefed Brown and the top military brass on their proposal. At that briefing (formally, the January 1978 meeting of the Armed Forces Policy Council), Brown did more than just endorse the proposal. He responded that the program would be the most important technology initiative in the department and he asked the military services for their support. When the military leaders raised questions about the proposal, it was Brown—not VHSIC's organizers—who answered them.[22] That the Secretary of Defense, an official with responsibility for a defense budget of hundreds of billions of dollars, would commit himself so resolutely to a hundred million dollar initiative set VHSIC squarely on the right track politically and bureaucratically.

Initial planning for VHSIC was carried out during the spring

91

and summer of 1978 by a small handful of officials in the Office of Electronics and Physical Sciences.[23] Key program features established at this time included:

> funding the program at $100 million or more—setting VHSIC apart from all prior electron device programs typically funded at no more than $5 million each,

> establishing high-speed computational capability as the program's major technological objective,

> emphasizing lithography (the techniques by which circuit patterns are etched or implanted on semiconductor materials) advances to achieve micrometer and submicrometer features,

> investigating circuit design approaches that would minimize customization,

> requiring system demonstrations of VHSIC circuits,

> pursuing several competing integrated circuit technologies,

> setting off a diffuse technology support element (Phase III) from the mainstream industry effort, and

> determining that the program would be a triservice effort with central management in the Office of the Secretary of Defense.[24]

Another vital feature of VHSIC's formulation regards the willingness of Pentagon officials to seek out and incorporate industry advice.[25] VHSIC's planners and advocates[26] had widespread contacts in industry. Through 1978 the VHSIC office resembled a revolving door as company after company contributed their thoughts on how the program should be designed. VHSIC organizers also made several cross-country trips for advice and information gathering purposes.

The contacts of one official complemented those of the others. While one official might work closely with the commercial semiconductor industry, another would be particularly well connected with traditional defense contractors. More specialized officials consulted with company research directors and program managers while higher Pentagon officials met with top corporate executives.

Besides the aforementioned officials, other defense agencies served as contact points for companies interested in VHSIC, notably, the Defense Advanced Research Projects Agency, the Institute for Defense Analyses, and the three military services. Such multiple access points served VHSIC's planning well by promoting industry input. Indeed the breadth of industry consultation—one might call it "participatory consultation"—probably enhanced industry support for VHSIC by creating at least the perception of political efficacy among companies.

One critical institutional link between government and industry during VHSIC's planning was the consultative forum provided by the Advisory Group on Electron Devices (AGED). Sponsored by the Department of Defense, AGED is composed of preeminent industrial and academic specialists who evaluate all military research and development contracts in electronics. In September and November 1978, Pentagon officials organized two AGED conferences to aid in VHSIC's formulation. Specialists from 21 major academic and industrial institutions participated in these sessions.[27] In addition, representatives from 13 companies were invited to make formal presentations on prospective VHSIC research.[28]

The AGED meetings dramatically illustrate both the openness of VHSIC planning to private sector advice and the significant contribution made by industry to the structure and orientation of the program.[29] Industry input in general and AGED deliberations in particular contributed the following six major features of the VHSIC program.

Silicon v. gallium arsenide—In the earliest plans for VHSIC, the program was to include semiconductor work in both silicon (the primary semiconductor material presently in use) and gallium arsenide, a largely experimental material with greater speed than silicon. Because of the difficulty in working with gallium arsenide and because of budget constraints, VHSIC planners accepted the recommendation of AGED to drop the technology from the program.

1.25 μm interim objective— As originally conceived, VHSIC was to be a concerted push to achieve circuitry with submicrometer features. Through 1978, however, the Pentagon was counseled to adopt a less ambitious midterm milestone for the program. Industry specialists warned against pushing too hard, too fast.[30] Military service officials argued that achieving an intermediate objective midway through the program would result in quicker payoffs for military systems compared to an eight-year wait for submicrometer circuitry. The AGED reviews arrived at a broad consensus designating 1.25 μm as VHSIC's intermediate milestone after the first three years.

Computer-aided design (CAD)—Pentagon planners have acknowledged their neglect of computer-aided design (the use of specialized computer programs to design circuits) in their early VHSIC formulations. The CAD budget was first augmented after an April 1978 AGED meeting highlighted the importance of the technology. Due to continued industry pressure, CAD now accounts for 40–45% of VHSIC's budget.

Systems orientation—Until the AGED technology reviews, VHSIC was still a highly technology- and device-oriented program. Priority was placed on developing specific electronic components with the fastest speeds, smallest features, and least customization. It would come to the Pentagon's surprise that AGED participants—both industrial and academic, military contractors and commercial semiconductor makers—would unanimously recommend that VHSIC components be designed to meet the specific needs and requirements of computers and other electronic systems. While the end goal of the program had always been to enhance defense systems with advanced circuitry, the AGED deliberations revealed that system considerations would have to guide circuit design from the outset. The advisory group warned that developing circuits in isolation and then searching for systems applications at a later date would prove highly problematic.

Vertical integration—Through 1978 VHSIC planners considered fragmenting the program into as many as four separate technical efforts. Separate contractors would be awarded for computer-aided design; computer architecture and software; lithography; and semiconductor fabrication. By early 1979, however, VHSIC organizers had decided to require each prime contractor to address virtually all aspects of VHSIC technology from initial circuit design to system demonstration. Critical to this decision to vertically integrate the program was a suggestion in the AGED meetings that bidders for mainstream VHSIC contracts be "required to respond to the whole ball of wax."

Teaming—Along with fragmenting the program by technical area, VHSIC planners considered making awards to numerous individual contractors. These officials would later encourage companies to form contract teams, and again, AGED played a role in this policy change. The notion of multifirm teaming was first seriously discussed in the November AGED conference. Moreover, AGED recommendations that circuit design be system driven and that the program be vertically integrated implicitly required the formation of teams among manufacturers of defense systems, merchant semiconductor firms, and companies specializing in such areas as computer-aided design, lithography, packaging, and testing.

AGED is but one of many advisory boards linking the industrial and scientific communities to the Department of Defense.[31] VHSIC organizers were not, however, required to consult with the advisory group. Since AGED is chartered to review only those R & D contracts submitted to the Department of Defense by the military services, and since VHSIC originated not in the services but within the Department of Defense itself, there was no formal requirement for AGED evaluation of the VHSIC program. In a similar vein, projects conducted by the Defense Advanced Research Projects Agency and by in-house military labs are not reviewed by AGED.[32] The advisory group is not even consulted on many of the projects for which it is expressly responsible. A 1974 General Accounting Office report found that AGED reviewed only 56% of the contracts that fell under its jurisdiction.[33] In addition, AGED's practice of holding special conferences to review selected new technologies had begun only in the early 1970s.[34] Until the VHSIC sessions in late 1978, a special AGED technology review had not been held for at least three years. The organization of the VHSIC reviews represents, then, an important institutional innovation that cannot be assumed to be standard operating procedure in the military world. This point is underlined by the fact that, since VHSIC's establishment, the advisory group has not reviewed the program's progress on a regular basis. Indeed, concerns have been raised over the lack of AGED oversight for the VHSIC program.[35]

Consultative institutions such as AGED can be found outside the defense sector, as can government officials with widespread contacts in private industry. AGED consultants as well as other specialists serve on civilian advisory panels (for instance, those sponsored by the National Academy of Sciences), and AGED's military affiliation garners no more sense of responsibility than these civilian boards.[36] In sum, AGED's military affiliation neither ensured consultation with industry during VHSIC's formulation nor suggests that such consultation can only take place in the defense sector.

DUSTRY SUPPORT   In 1979, 32 electronics firms submitted bids for VHSIC contracts, defusing fears that the program would not be supported by industry. For many of these firms, however, interest in VHSIC came as no surprise. Foremost among such companies were traditional defense contractors that manufacture radar, electronic warfare, communications, and guidance systems for the military. These "systems houses" are always on the lookout for military contracts. Moreover, the VHSIC program was viewed as setting new ground rules for the procurement of defense electronics. Participation in the program and developing the capabilities to produce VHSIC circuits was deemed vital to the maintenance of their positions in the military market.[37]

Among those industries whose technologies are utilized in VHSIC, the reaction of commercial semiconductor producers to the program carries the greatest ramifications for government–industry relations and industrial policymaking in the U.S. Ten of the top fifteen manufacturers of semiconductors for the open market (that is, beyond in-house usage) have been involved with or sought involvement with VHSIC.[38] And unlike the case of the military systems houses, the warm reception that VHSIC received from the merchant semiconductor industry cannot be explained by close ties to the Department of Defense.

Semiconductor producers were once heavily dependent upon the Pentagon. During the 1950s and early 1960s, the military served as the primary market for semiconductors and as a major source of the industry's R&D funds.[39] By the late 1970s, this dependence drastically dissipated to the extent that only 7% of integrated circuit sales went to the military, and only 5% of the industry's R&D expenditures were financed via defense contracts.[40]

The poor state of relations between the industry and military was also reflected by the fact that the VHSIC program was stimulated, in part, by the lack of attention given to military needs by the merchant producers.[41] With the merchants' development and production efforts having become overwhelmingly oriented towards the industrial and consumer markets by the 1970s, certain military integrated circuit requirements were left wanting. (Most important, the industry focused on large-scale rather than high-speed processing.) The VHSIC program would not have been needed if the close ties between the military and the merchants of the 1950s and 1960s had been maintained.

The relative autonomy of the merchant semiconductor industry from the defense sector eliminates an important reason why companies might automatically flock to a military program such as VHSIC. Interviews with eight of the ten merchants who have sought VHSIC participation confirm that military-related factors played only a limited role in corporate motivations. Reflecting the nonmilitary nature of the decision to participate in VHSIC is the fact that semiconductor industry officials responsible for the decisions were not from the military or government divisions of the firms. Instead, key decision makers were senior corporate executives responsible for strategic business and technology initiatives. The VHSIC question was treated as an issue of corporate strategy rather than a strictly military matter.[42]

Rather than resting upon military factors, the dominant rationale for seeking VHSIC participation was the assessment of complementarity between VHSIC technology and mainstream commercial technology. The program's objectives were seen as matching those of in-house technology efforts and VHSIC participation was sought to accelerate those efforts.[43] This view of the convergence between VHSIC and commercial technology has been manifested in the organization of VHSIC activities by those merchant houses that have been awarded VHSIC contracts. Rather than relegating VHSIC to peripheral military divisions within companies, VHSIC activities have been integrated into mainstream commercial and technology efforts. For instance, everyday VHSIC activities at Texas Instruments, Motorola, and National Semiconductor have been directed by corporate vice presidents responsible for semiconductor research and development. At Motorola and National, VHSIC engineers were drawn from and work closely with the companies' advanced technology labs. These same engineers were part of larger company programs, in place well before VHSIC, to develop state-of-the-art very large scale integration technology. In this way, VHSIC work has been fused with and designed to intensify in-house commercial VLSI efforts. At Texas Instruments, a distinct VHSIC organization has not even been established. Instead, VHSIC activities were divided among and integrated with the broader responsibilities of the company's semiconductor, computer, and research divisions.[44]

It is no accident, of course, that VHSIC technology was seen as complementing mainstream commercial technology. Defense planners sought to ensure that VHSIC research would not radically deviate from industrial research. In an early planning document, VHSIC planners stipulated that:

> technologies employed [in the program] must be consistent with mainstream industry efforts. . . . Program goals must be consistent with the industry learning process.[45]

In the AGED sessions held in late 1978 to secure the advice of industry and academic specialists, defense officials acknowledged the rationale for this requirement: "If [VHSIC technology is] not in the mainstream of commercial work we're going to lose it eventually."[46]

Related to envisioned technological complementarity, VHSIC support was won by the prospect of commercial payoffs from participating in the Pentagon program. Commercial spinoffs are especially expected in areas of process technology such as lithography, circuit technology, design approaches, and computer-aided design.[47] For instance, the development of a CMOS (complementary metal oxide semiconductor) production line for VHSIC circuits should advance the process technology for other CMOS applications in the fields of microprocessors and telecommunications. Whereas many of the final VHSIC circuits will probably only have military applications, some may be directly transformed into commercial products (such as random access memories and gate arrays).[48]

Pentagon officials were, in fact, always mindful that the commercial payoffs from VHSIC would garner industry support for the program. During VHSIC's planning in 1978, Defense officials recognized that "one important side product of what DOD [Department of Defense] does should be to help U.S. industry."[49] Just as Pentagon planners sought to maintain complementarity between VHSIC and civilian technology, they were careful to explore the commercial spillovers from VHSIC technology that would be gained by industry participants.[50]

While always citing military necessity first, Pentagon officials highlighted commercial payoffs in seeking industry support for the program. In late 1978, the Pentagon's Director of Electronics and Physical Sciences stated:

> We judge that about three-fourths of the [VHSIC] program will proide direct and indirect fallout to the IC [integrated circuit] industry.[51]

The Secretary of Defense met with industry leaders in 1980 to ensure that an adequate response would be given to the bidding for VHSIC Phase I contracts. In arguing for industry support, he stressed first national interest and military necessity and then the commercial and competitive benefit that would derive from VHSIC participation.[52]

The ultimate achievement of technological complementarity and commercial spillovers is a highly debatable point. Indeed, one major semiconductor producer, Intel, vehemently opposed the defense initiative precisely on these issues. VHSIC technology was seen as a divergence from mainstream industrial efforts that would produce commercially unviable products. Moreover, the program was seen as draining scarce scientific and engineering talent towards military work and thereby crowding out commercial research and development.[53]

A resolution of this debate is, as indicated in the introduction, beyond the scope of this analysis. Yet if the final consequences of the program are yet to be determined, there is absolutely no doubt that the *prospects* of technological synergy and commercial benefits helped win support for VHSIC among most semiconductor producers. These companies looked well beyond the military market in deciding to participate in the program, and Pentagon planners sought to design a commercially appealing program. The intensive consultation between industry and government officials during VHSIC's planning helped establish these program attributes.

Besides favorable assessments of VHSIC's technology and spillover potential, two environmental pressures that emerged in the late 1970s helped condition semiconductor producers to be more receptive to VHSIC. First, the industry's capital requirements began to mount dramatically. Startup costs for a semiconductor facility have risen from under $1 million in the 1950s to $10 million in 1970 to $30–40 million in the late 1970s.[54] VHSIC was well timed in the sense that companies welcomed new sources of capital financing.[55]

Second, the program was well timed in aiding company responses to the Japanese competitive threat in semiconductors. While the Japanese threat played only a minimal role in the Pentagon's formulation of the program, the merchant semiconductor producers have cited the competitive pressure from Japan as a rationale for their VHSIC support. For these companies, participation in the military program has figured into their broader strategies to counter the competitive challenge from Japan.[56]

In sum, a government program successfully attracted the support of merchant semiconductor producers on the basis of nonmilitary, commercial factors. Some of those factors, namely, the environmental pressures of capital costs and international competition, were beyond the control of VHSIC planners. Still those pressures would have been insufficient in attracting support for the program if efforts were not made to make VHSIC compatible with mainstream technology.

MULTIFIRM COLLABORATION   Work conducted under each of the VHSIC prime contracts have been separate and competing efforts. Not only do prime contractors not work together, they work with different circuit technologies and design approaches, and develop circuits for different system applications. For instance, one prime contractor may design standard circuits for multiple applications, while another develops highly customized chips for specialized functions.

While the VHSIC program calls for little technical cooperation among the prime contractors, the program has entailed a significant degree of collaboration among companies within contract teams. Thirteen of the eighteen VHSIC prime contracts have gone out to teams of companies (see Table 1). In most of these cases, members of contract teams have avoided overlapping functions. One member may be responsible for chip fabrication, another for computer-aided design, and a third for system architecture. Teammates may also be responsible for different circuit technologies.

Despite the establishment of such complementary yet distinct divisions of labor, VHSIC teammates have displayed a significant degree of collaboration. Just the process of segmenting functions has required a great deal of team work to ensure systemwide compatibility. The definition of the Westinghouse standard chip set exemplifies this collaboration. Westinghouse and Control Data first analyzed a whole series of military systems (radar, electronic warfare, sonar, and fire control) in order to determine a common design architecture for a set of circuits. Once the chip set was outlined, National Semiconductor contributed its expertise in process technology to develop the individual circuits. The proposed module was then reanalyzed by Harris as well as Westinghouse and Control Data to test its applicability to specific military systems. Minor changes were found necessary and the chip set was redesigned accordingly. Such close working relations have been maintained as teammates have integrated their efforts in order to produce the final circuits.[57]

While many of the companies teamed together in VHSIC have been contract partners in other military work, those prior relationships have had little impact upon their degree of VHSIC collaboration. The VHSIC program is rather unique in the Department of Defense in that it has involved multifirm collaboration for technology development. Most military R & D contracts go out to single contractors. Where companies have worked together on other military contracts, that work has involved the production of military equipment or components for procurement rather than the development of new technologies. Hence, while the military equipment and military components divisions of companies have subcontracted with each other, research and development organizations—those organizations most centrally involved in VHSIC—in different firms have had little contact with one another. An indication of the new organizational relationships established in VHSIC is the widespread recognition that the program has dramatically improved communication between systems experts in one company with components expertise in another.[58]

To account for the degree of collaboration within VHSIC teams, one must turn to two nonmilitary factors: technological imperatives and industry competition. The technical areas to be pursued under VHSIC contracts are formidable and include: system architecture and design; computer-aided design; lithography; and circuit design, processing, fabrication, packaging, and testing. Not only is the program's agenda comprehensive, but Pentagon officials decided that instead of breaking up VHSIC tasks among a multitude of contractors, each bid for a mainstream VHSIC contract had to be responsive to the entire spectrum of VHSIC technology. This requirement has compelled companies to pool their efforts in order to adequately cover VHSIC's various technical requirements. In all but two cases, the breadth of the program's objectives outstrips the capabilities of any one firm.

Perhaps the major source for the coalescence of VHSIC teammates (and the industriousness of VHSIC contractors generally) has been the structuring of industry competition into the program. One of the purposes of the phasing of the program was to allow the Department of Defense to progressively select the strongest performers. The nine Phase 0 contractors were narrowed down to six in Phase I and to only three in Phase II.

The general effect of this progressive narrowing of the field was to promote a very competitive environment among the VHSIC contractors. Each company was well aware that fellow contractors were competitors for the next round of contracts. One manifestation of this competition is the fact that most VHSIC contractors have augmented their VHSIC efforts with internal company funds at least matching their official government contract money. Companies determined that in order to perform well enough to make the next "cut" they had to supplement VHSIC money with their own.[59]

The competitive environment has also strengthened the cohesiveness of the contract teams. Institutional barriers between companies were broken down as teams sought to win in the next round of contracting. For example, officials from each company in a team practically "camped out" with each other for as long as two weeks in order to make proposal deadlines.[60]

Pentagon officials were, of course, fully aware of the competitive pressures built into the VHSIC program. Indeed, the Pentagon has acknowledged the "successful employment of competition" as a means by which it "gains leverage" with (i.e., gets the most out of) the VHSIC contractors.[61]

IMPLICATIONS Within the Department of Defense, the VHSIC program has been seen as a successful model for other joint government–industry efforts in high technology. In October 1982, the Pentagon launched a seven-year $250 million software initiative to upgrade computer software technology.[62] In May 1983, the Department of Defense unveiled a $100 million program to develop integrated circuits made from gallium arsenide—the experimental material first considered and then dropped from the VHSIC program.[63] Most important, the Pentagon has embarked upon a $500–750 million "*N*th generation" computer project to develop next generation artificial intelligence, supercomputer architecture, and software.[64]

Yet the military's track record with technology programs is replete with cases of mismanagement, inefficiency, and commercial unviability. Even the most recent programs mentioned above have not been invulnerable to ill-conceived planning and management. The gallium arsenide program has not been well received by commercial firms because, in part, the military effort focuses not on high-speed circuitry but upon low-power consumption (and, thereby, low speed).[65] The software initiative has begun to founder *within* military circles because, among other things, its diffuse technological objectives lack clear end-product payoffs.[66]

In light of the military's checkered experience in technology development, this analysis has focused not on how well the Pentagon

Table 2. Implications of the VHSIC program for explicit industrial policy programs.

Objective	Policy questions
Strengthening Program Planning	• Are government officials able and willing to seek out and incorporate industry advice? • Can government–industry consultative forums be utilized or created? • Can government access to industry information be enhanced by focusing on generic, nonproprietary technologies and by taking advantage of industry norms of information exchange? • Can generic technologies be targeted to relieve government officials from having to pick "winners" and "losers"?
Gaining Industrywide Support	• Will efforts build upon mainstream industry technology? • Will commercially viable (at least in the long term) technologies be developed? • Can threats to proprietary interests be minimized by focusing on generic technologies? • Can redistributional, "fairness" issues be moderated in the context of dynamic growth sectors?
Fostering Multifirm Collaboration	• Are ambitious technological objectives beyond the capabilities of single firms to be established? • Can competition between teams of companies be designed to consolidate working relations among teammates? • Can proprietary concerns be lessened by avoiding the development of applied, product-specific technologies? • Do industry networks of communication exist?

might be able to enhance commercial competitiveness, but on what the VHSIC program can tell us about the capabilites of this country in pursuing industrial policy programs *outside* of the military area.

The foregoing analysis, as well as subsequent discussion, reveals that three aspects of the VHSIC experience—government–industry planning, industrywide support, and multifirm collaboration—have been as much if not more dependent upon generic, nonmilitary factors as upon purely military attributes. As indicated in Table 2, these generic factors may be relevant to the design and implementation of explicit industrial policy programs.

It has been acknowledged that national security concerns did, in fact, spur the Pentagon's initial planning of VHSIC and that defense-related factors can account for the support that the program received from traditional military contractors. More generally, VHSIC's military sponsorship provided both an aura of national security that helped reduce (but did not completely eliminate) congressional opposition, and a relatively lavish budget.

Yet none of these defense-related factors can fully account for any of the three VHSIC features considered here to take on industrial policy-like dimensions. None of the various national security concerns that initiated deliberations on the VHSIC program—the Soviet military threat, the insertion problem, and Soviet advances in microelectronics—provided concrete programmatic guidelines for defense planners. While Congress mandated that the program be centrally managed and required that VHSIC technology be licensed domestically while being subject to strict export controls,[67] Congress had no impact on the process by which the program was planned nor did it have impact upon the substance of the planning.

Intense and widespread government–industry consultation, a practice over which the Department of Defense has no natural monopoly, proved instrumental to VHSIC's successful planning. While VHSIC organizers were able to utilize a long-standing military consultative forum, namely, AGED, similar institutions exist or others could be created outside the military arena. Similar government–industry meeting grounds are to be found in the Department of Commerce, the U.S. Trade Representative's Office, and the National Academies of Science and Engineering.

The rather unsurprising conclusion regarding the importance of consultation with industry has too often been surprisingly overlooked in the design of other technology programs both within and outside the Department of Defense. With regard to the Pentagon's gallium arsenide program cited above, defense officials ignored company pleas to concentrate on high-speed technologies that would have great commercial value.[68] In 1978, the Department of Transportation launched—without the advice of the auto makers—the Cooperative Automobile Research Program, an effort to "reinvent the automobile." The absence of industry support effectively undermined the program before it was cancelled by the Reagan administration.[69]

Concern for national security failed to attract the support of the commercial semiconductor industry—the one industry whose VHSIC participation illustrates that government technology programs might be able to reach beyond the defense sector. Critical to the support of this industry were efforts by VHSIC planners to design technology objectives that coincided with civilian technology and that promised commercial payoffs. Such criteria for program objectives would seem to be a requisite of any viable industrial policy program; and the effort to arrive at appropriate technological goals in the VHSIC program depended in large part upon the close government–industry consultation discussed above. Private sector input during the planning stages helped increase the chances that the program would receive widespread industry support.

The designation of technologically ambitious and complex tasks compelled most VHSIC contractors to seek the collaboration of partners. Teamwork was ingeniously fostered by pitting VHSIC teams against one another in competition for future contracts. Utilization of a thoroughly American trait—industry competition—

helped produce within VHSIC teams an atypical American phenomenon: multifirm collaboration. Structured competition between corporate participants might be a distinctive and fruitful characteristic of American industrial policy programs.

Finally, the role of informed, competent government officials in consulting with industry, determining VHSIC objectives, winning industry support, and managing industry competition cannot be underestimated. It is to be acknowledged that the technical and managerial talent attracted to the government sector pales in comparison with private industry.[70] Yet a handful of such government personnel—and only a select few were necessary—proved sufficient to bring about the VHSIC program. Perhaps the difficulties in bringing together similar officials from within civilian ranks for commercial industrial policy programs might be equally solvable.

If military factors do not underlie the industrial policy characteristics of the VHSIC program, then these program features may be transferable outside the military arena. Before concluding, consideration should be given to the scope and limits of VHSIC's generalizability. The degree to which the VHSIC experience may be replicated in civilian sectors of government may be determined, if not by military factors, by the nature of VHSIC's work. In particular, certain characteristics of VHSIC's technology and of the microelectronics sector generally may have provided the necessary preconditions underlying the technical expertise of government personnel, the level of communication between public and private sector officials, the degree of industry support for the program, and the willingness of companies to collaborate in research. Three such necessary conditions stand out: the generic nature of VHSIC's semiconductor technology, the dynamic growth of the microelectronics industry, and networks of communication among semiconductor specialists.

Generic technology involves work that does not relate to the design or operational details of particular products or processes.[71] Instead, generic technology encompasses broad design concepts and general working principles of processes. Such technologies fall in between fundamental scientific research and the applied research and development of private firms. Many of the process technologies under investigation in VHSIC—circuit technology and design, lithography, computer-aided design, testing and packaging—have generic characteristics. Since generic technologies may be applicable to broad classes of products and processes, government programs in support of such research may be viewed as politically acceptable by private firms.

> Companies do not perceive such programs as posing sharp threats to their commercial positions, or the threats, if perceived, are seen as diffuse and not readily identifiable as dangerous to any particular portion of the industry.[72]

In VHSIC's case, commericial spinoffs from the contract work are at least several years off.

Because generic research seldom poses an immediate threat to the proprietary interests of firms, companies may be willing to collaborate in such research. For instance, aircraft producers were able to collaborate in research in the 1920s and 1930s under the auspices of the National Advisory Committee on Aeronautics, a government research organization and forerunner of the National Aeronautics and Space Administration.[73] The committee undertook experiments and studies relevant to aerodynamics and aeronautics in general rather than working on specific aircraft designs. The generic characteristics of VHSIC technology may similarly buttress the ability of contractors to collaborate within VHSIC teams.

Besides lowering barriers to collaborative research, generic technology programs also minimize some significant problems confronting government officials in managing technology programs. To begin with, in an environment where corporations are more likely to exchange information and collaborate in research, government officials may also have greater access to industry information. Perhaps more importantly, generic research programs reduce the need for such access to information or, at least, lower the demands placed upon limited government expertise. Since highly specific product technologies need not be defined in generic research, government officials need only determine general research objectives. Moreover, generic work allows—if not requires—the investigation of a multitude of technologies. In the VHSIC program, several alternative technologies are being pursued in each of the areas of circuit technology, chip design, lithography, and computer-aided design. Defense planners simply established broad performance targets (for example, speed and feature size) for VHSIC circuits and have given contractors the freedom to reach those targets by utilizing any of a number of technologies. The general and flexible nature of generic technology programs relieves government officials from having to make judgments regarding the commercial promise of any specific technology and, therefore, from the ire of having made poor judgments. Indeed, generic technology programs save government officials from one of the potential pitfalls most often cited by critics of industrial policy: the picking of "winner" technologies and industry segments for government support. Whether access to technical information is enhanced or the demands placed upon government expertise are lowered, generic technology reduces one of the major constraints hindering government industrial policymaking: insufficient information to guide policy decisions.

A second permissive condition underlying some of VHSIC's industrial policy attributes, and in particular, the legitimacy of a government role in technology development, relates to the dynamic growth characteristics of the American microelectronics industry. While sensitive to economic recessions, the semiconductor industry has enjoyed rapid growth over the past three decades. Driven by ever-increasing demand (domestic and foreign) for semiconductor products, U.S. semiconductor output rose from $600 million in 1960 to $9.5 billion in 1982—representing an annual growth rate of 14%.[74] Growth opportunities for individual semiconductor producers have been enhanced not only by the aggregate growth of the entire sector but also by the proliferation of semiconductor product types and product applications. Technological innovation has created hundreds of distinct and viable product offerings. Semiconductor markets have expanded from military applications to computer, broader industrial, consumer electronics, and automobile applications. Each product line and market niche is often able to sustain a different producer. Indeed, a new major semiconductor maker can emerge rapidly from nowhere by assuming a position of market leadership in a given line of products. Such opportunities for growth have proven inviting to successive waves of new entrants into the business.

Government intervention in a dynamic growth sector is less likely to confront another often cited obstacle to industrial policy: the problem of fairness.[75] Industries will oppose government programs that are viewed as helping one part of the industry at the expense of another. Threats to the status quo would be especially acute in industries characterized by stagnant or declining production where the competitive balance among major producers might be easily upset by government intervention. Industrial policy proposals might, therefore, be vigorously opposed by producers seeking to hold on to existing market shares. In contrast, the politics of government intervention in dynamic growth sectors takes on characteristics of a nonzero sum game. Private firms may be less concerned about the competitive impact of government programs under circumstances where virtually all parties are enjoying rapid growth. Moreover, government influence over an industry's competitive balance might be minimized or neutralized where there are a multitude of sources for corporate growth. The bases for competitive advantage in the semiconductor industry are many and range from technological excellence to low-cost manufacturing to quality control to marketing skills. Under such conditions, no one competitive factor—including government support— emerges as critical to a firm's market success. Since redistributional concerns, zero-sum concerns, and problems of fairness may be diminished, the legitimacy of government intervention may come under less challenge in dynamic growth sectors like the semiconductor industry.

A third and final facilitating feature of the VHSIC experience concerns the highly developed networks of communication among semiconductor industry officials and engineers. This community has been characterized as "an information system for the exchange of technical knowledge."[76] While knowledge is not pooled, information is rapidly disseminated throughout the industry. This transfer and diffusion of knowledge between semiconductor producers applies to the newest of technologies. The means for such technology transfer include such official mechanisms as published papers and conferences of professional societies. More importantly, substantial communication takes place through informal yet dense networks of regular contacts between individuals. This latter category includes discussions over drinks or on the golf course as well as over the telephone among friends who work for different companies.

The foundations for these networks of information exchange include the high levels of uncertainty entailed in semiconductor innovation and the competitive nature of the industry. Information is sought to cope with uncertainty and to keep abreast of competitors. Communication among firms is facilitated by the highly developed professional orientation among American scientists and engineers. The individuals concerned share common technical backgrounds and university training. Finally, communication is enhanced by high levels of interfirm mobility of semiconductor personnel. Very few engineers spend their careers with a single firm, and very many have worked for three or four companies within a decade. Annual employee turnover rates in this industry exceed 30%. Such high job mobility creates substantial linkages between firms.[77]

Such networks of communication and norms of information exchange certainly facilitated the collaboration manifested between VHSIC teammates. Such norms and practices were also extended by industry officials in their contacts with government. VHSIC organizers were, therefore, able to consult extensively with industry specialists. The lowered barriers to public–private communication, in turn, heightened the Department of Defense's access to information vital to VHSIC's sound planning. Limited government expertise was, as a result, applied more effectively.

Generic technology, dynamic industrial growth, and communication networks represent three necessary and nonmilitary conditions that facilitated the emergence of VHSIC's industrial policy characteristics. Such preconditions do not, however, sufficiently account for any features of VHSIC's planning process or programmatic content. The opportunities provided by the facilitating conditions required, as recounted above, exploitation by innovative political, organizational, and managerial initiatives.

Still, the three permissive conditions serve to delimit the generalizability of the VHSIC experience for potential arenas of industrial policy. Generic technology, dynamic growth, and networks of communication are not generally characteristic of most technologically mature or declining industries. Hence, the relevance of the VHSIC experience for such sectors as the textile, steel, and shipbuilding industries may be severely limited. Yet VHSIC's facilitating conditions are features of most high-technology, emerging industries. On this basis, the VHSIC case might be of relevance to the computer, telecommunications, aerospace, robotics, biotechnology, advanced materials, and alternative energy industries as well as to the semiconductor industry.

More generally, the VHSIC experience raises important questions to be explored in considering government initiatives in support of industrial competitiveness. The organizational principles upon which VHSIC was based and the underlying conditions fa-

vorable to the establishment of the program may highlight necessary requisites in the design of explicit industrial policy programs.

For their comments on earlier drafts of this article, I am grateful to Sidney Fong,
Stephan Haggard, Peter Katzenstein, Judith Reppy, Andy Ross, Raymond Vernon,
Tony Walters, David Yoffie, and Michael Yoshino.

*GLENN R. FONG is assistant professor of political science at the
University of Illinois at Chicago.*

NOTES 1. This research was sponsored by the Division of Research and the
Harvard Competitiveness Project, both at Harvard University Graduate School of Business Administration. Program-specific details reported here largely draw upon personal interviews with government
and industry officials conducted between November 1982 and February 1984.

2. As used in this paper, industrial policy (or explicit industrial policy)
refers to government initiatives designed for the express purpose of
developing and/or retrenching various industries to maintain global
competitiveness. Corporate strategies carried out in coordination
with government policies would be considered part of industrial policy, while public policies that have unintended consequences for industrial competitiveness and exclusively private-sector competitive
strategies would not.

For some of the industrial policy debate see: Allen, Christopher S.
and Rishikof, Harvey, "Tale Thrice Told: A Review of Industrial Policy Proposals," *Journal of Policy Analysis and Management*, 4(2) (Winter 1985); Bluestone, Barry and Harrison, Bennett, *The Deindustrialization of America* (New York: Basic Books, 1982); Diebold, William,
Jr., *Industrial Policy as an International Issue* (New York: McGraw-
Hill, 1980); Gresser, Julian, *High Technology & Japanese Industrial
Policy* (Washington, DC: U.S. Government Printing Office, 1980); *The
Industrial Policy Debate*, Chalmers Johnson, Ed., (San Francisco: Institute for Contemporary Studies, 1984); Krugman, Paul, "Targeted Industrial Policies" in *Industrial Change & Public Policy*, Federal Reserve Bank of Kansas City, (1983); Lawrence, Robert, *Can America
Compete?* (Washington, DC: The Brookings Institute, 1984); Magaziner, Ira, and Reich, Robert, *Minding America's Business* (New York:
Harcourt, 1982); Phillips, Kevin, *Staying on Top: The Business Case for
a National Industrial Strategy* (New York: Random House, 1984); Pinder, John et al., *Industrial Policy & the International Economy* (New
York: Trilateral Commission, 1979); *National Industrial Strategies &
the World Economy*, John Pinder, Ed. (Totowa, NJ: Rowman and Al-
lanheld, 1982); Reich, Robert, "Why the U.S. Needs an Industrial
Policy," *Harvard Business Review* (January–February 1982); Reich,
Robert, "Making Industrial Policy," *Foreign Affairs* (Spring 1982);
Royatyn, Feliz, "The Coming Emergency and What Can Be Done
About It?" *New York Review of Books* (December 4, 1980); Rohatyn,
Felix, "Reconstructing America," *New York Review of Books* (February
5, 1981); Scott, Bruce, "Can Industry Survive the Welfare State?"
Harvard Business Review (September–October 1982); Scott, Bruce,
"National Strategy for Stronger U.S. Competitiveness," *Harvard
Business Review* (March–April 1984); Thurow, Lester, "The Produc-
tivity Problem," *Technology Review* (November/December 1980);

Thurow, Lester, *The Zero-Sum Society: Distribution and the Possibilities for Economic Change* (New York: Basic Books, 1980); Vogel, Ezra, *Japan as Number One: Lessons for America* (New York: Harper and Row, 1979); *Toward a New U.S. Industrial Policy*, Michael Wachter and Susan Wachter, Eds. (Philadelphia: University of Pennsylvania Press, 1981); and Zysman, John, and Cohen, Stephen, "Double or Nothing: Open Trade & Competitive Industry," *Foreign Affairs* (Summer 1983).

3. A major exception is Badaracco, Joseph L. and Yoffie, David B., "Industrial Policy: It Can't Happen Here," *Harvard Business Review* (November–December 1983).

4. See Brueckner, Leslie with Michael Borrus, "Assessing the Commercial Impact of the VHSIC (Very High Speed Integrated Circuit) Program" (Berkeley Round Table on the International Economy, 1984).

5. See Ouchi, William G., *The M-Form Society: How American Teamwork Can Recapture the Competitive Edge* (Reading, MA: Addison-Wesley, 1984), ch. 6, on the VHSIC program. More generally, see *Commercializing Defense Related Technology*, Kuhn, Robert, Ed. (New York: Praeger, 1984).

6. Badarracco and Yoffie, *op. cit.*; and Schultze, Charles L., "Industrial Policy: A Dissent," *Brookings Review* (Fall 1983).

7. Shonfield, Andrew, *Modern Capitalism: The Changing Balance of Public and Private Power* (New York: Oxford University Press, 1965), ch. 13; Vogel, David, "Why Businessmen Distrust Their State: The Political Consciousness of American Corporate Executives," *British Journal of Political Science* (January 1978); and McCraw, Thomas K., "Business & Government: The Origins of the Adversary Relationship," *California Management Review* (Winter 1984).

8. Katzenstein, Peter, J., "Conclusion: Domestic Structures and Strategies of Foreign Economic Policy," in Peter J. Katzenstein, Ed., *Between Power and Plenty: Foreign Economic Policies of Advanced Industrial States* (Madison, WI: University of Wisconsin Press, 1978); Salisbury, Robert H., "Why No Corporatism in America?" in Phillippe C. Schmitter and Gerald Lehmbruch, Eds., *Trends Toward Corporatist Intermediation*, (Beverley Hills, CA: Sage, 1979).

9. In addition, a consideration of implementation issues can shed light on the economic and technological accomplishments of the VHSIC program and of industrial policy efforts generally. For instance, the policymaking process by which technological objectives are formulated may help determine the appropriateness of those objectives. Likewise, the modes of collaboration effected between government and industry and among different firms may determine whether progress is achieved and economic benefits gained or lost.

10. The following description is based upon: Committee on Assessment of the Impact of the DOD Very High Speed Integrated Circuit Program, *An Assessment of the Impact of the Department of Defense Very High Speed Integrated Circuit Program* (Washington, DC: National Academy Press, January 1982); Sumney, Larry W., "VHSIC Status and Issues," 1981 VHSIC Conference; and "The VHSIC Program: Review and Status," October 14, 1982 (prepared by the VHSIC Program Office).

11. The micrometer (or micron) is one-thousandth of a millimeter and is the industry's unit of measurement referring to the feature sizes of a circuit (e.g., line widths). A human hair is about 100 μm in diameter, and cigarette paper is about 25 μm thick.
Minimum feature sizes for integrated circuits have decreased from

1 mm in the late 1960s to 10 μm in the mid-1970s to 5 μm in 1978. Reduced dimensions are considered critical to increasing the complexity of IC's.

U.S. Department of Commerce, Industry and Trade Administration, *A Report on the U.S. Semiconductor Industry*, September 1979, pp. 111–112; Integrated Circuit Engineering Corporation, *Status 1983: A Report on the Integrated Circuit Industry*, 1983, p. 9; Dataquest, *Semiconductor Industry Service*, June 15, 1980, p. 1.5-4.

12. Interview materials.

13. This paragraph is based upon: Committee on Assessment; Preston, Glenn W., *Large Scale Integrated Circuits for Military Applications* (Arlington, VA: Institute for Defense Analyses, May 1977); and VHSIC documentation.

14. Up to 10 transistors per chip represents small-scale integration (SSI); 100 transistors per chip represents medium-scale integration (MSI), 1000 transistors per chip represents large-scale integration (LSI), and 100,000 transistors per chip represents very large scale integration (VLSI).

15. Interview materials.

16. Interview materials.

17. VHSIC documentation.

18. Interview materials.

19. Interview materials.

20. Committee on Assessment, pp. 6–7.

21. Interview materials.

22. Interview materials.

23. Primarily, Leonard Weisberg, Director of the Office of Electronics and Physical Sciences, and Larry Sumney, a staff specialist in E&PS and VHSIC's first program manager from 1978 to 1982.

24. Interview materials and VHSIC documentation.

25. The following discussion is based upon interview materials.

26. Key Pentagon supporters included Undersecretary for Research and Engineering William Perry and Deputy Undersecretary for Research and Advanced Technology Ruth Davis.

27. Bell Labs, California Institute of Technology, Carnegie Mellon, Clemson, Cornell, Fairchild, Hewlett-Packard, Institute for Defense Analyses, Jet Propulsion Labs, Johns Hopkins, Lincoln Labs, Massachusetts Institute of Technology, RCA, Research Triangle Institute, SRI, Stanford, Tektronix, Texas Instruments, TRW, University of California at Berkeley, and Westinghouse. (VHSIC documentation.)

28. Fairchild, General Electric, Hughes Aircraft, IBM, Motorola, National Semiconductor, Raytheon, RCA, Rockwell, Sandia, Texas Instruments, TRW, and Westinghouse. (VHSIC documentation.)

29. The following discussion is based upon interview materials and VHSIC documentation.

30. The 1978 state-of-the-art in terms of feature sizes for commercial circuits was 5 μm.

31. See Adams, Gordon, *The Politics of Defense Contracting: The Iron Triangle* (New Brunswick, NJ: Transaction Books, 1982), pp. 165–173.

32. U.S. General Accounting Office, *Review of the Operations of the Advisory Group on Electronic Devices Sponsored by the Department of Defense* (December 9, 1974).

33. *ibid.*
34. Other special AGED reviews have examined design automation, lasers, and fiber optics.
35. Interview materials.
36. Interview materials.
37. Interview materials.
38. The ten VHSIC contractors or bidders are: Texas Instruments (contractor, 1980–1984); Motorola (contractor, 1980–present); National Semiconductor (contractor, 1980–1984); Signetics (contractor; 1980); Fairchild (contractor, 1980); General Instruments (bidder, 1979), American Microsystems (bidder, 1979); Harris Semiconductor (second source, 1983–present); Analog Devices (contractor, 1980); and Intersil (contractor, 1980). The five companies that have not sought VHSIC contracts are Intel, Advanced Micro Devices, Mostek, RCA, and Synertek. Ranking in the top 15 based upon integrated circuit shipments in 1982 as reported by Integrated Circuit Engineering Corporation.
39. See Asher, Norman J. and Strom, Leland D., *The Role of the Department of Defense in the Development of Integrated Circuits* (Arlington, VA: Institute for Defense Analyses, May 1977); Utterback, James M., and Murray, Albert E., *The Influence of Defense Procurement and Sponsorship of Research and Development on the Development of the Civilian Electronics Industry* (MIT Center for Policy Alternatives, June 30, 1977); and Levin, Richard C., "The Semiconductor Industry," in *Government and Technical Progress: A Cross-Industry Analysis*, Richard R. Nelson, Ed. (New York: Pergamon, 1982); and Tilton, John E., *International Diffusion of Technology: The Case of Semiconductors* (Washington, DC: The Brookings Institute, 1971), p. 90.
40. Wilson, Robert W. et al., *Innovation, Competition, and Government Policy in the Semiconductor Industry* (Lexington, MA: Lexington, 1980); p. 146; Davis, Ruth, "The DOD Initiative in Integrated Circuits," *IEEE Computer* (July 1979); Committee on Assessment, *op. cit.*, p. 22; Semiconductor Industry Association estimates. These aggregate industry trends also apply, on an individual basis, to most major semiconductor producers.
41. Committee on Assessment, *op. cit.*, p. 6.
42. Interview materials.
43. Interview materials.
44. Interview materials.
45. VHSIC documentation.
46. VHSIC documentation.
47. Interview materials.
48. Interview materials; also Moore, David H. and Towle, William J., *The Industry Impact of the Very High Speed Integrated Circuit Program: A Preliminary Analysis* (Arlington, VA: The Analytic Sciences Corporation, August 15, 1980).
49. VHSIC documentation.
50. VHSIC documentation.
51. As quoted in *Business Week* (November 27, 1978).
52. Interview materials.
53. Interview materials.
54. Dataquest, *op. cit.*, p. 1.5–7; Wilson et al., *op. cit.*, p. 167.
55. Interview materials.

56. Interview materials.

57. Interview materials; also *Aviation Week* (February 16, 1981): 58, 61; *Military Electronics* (February 2, 1982): 84.

58. Interview materials.

59. Interview materials.

60. Interview materials.

61. Defense Science Board, *Report of the Task Force on Very High Speed Integrated Circuits (VHSIC) Program*, February 17, 1982, pp. 35–36.

62. Office of the Deputy Undersecretary of Defense for Research and Engineering (Research and Advanced Technology), "Strategy for a DOD Software Initiative," October 1, 1982; *Electronic News* (November 15, 1982): 39; *Electronic News*, (March 21, 1983); *Defense Week* (June 6, 1983).

63. *Electronic News* (May 16, 1983); *Electronics* (July 28, 1983).

64. *Electronic News* (February 7, 1983): 30; *Aviation Week* (April 18, 1983); *Electronics* (June 16, 1983); 50.

65. *Defense Week* (June 6, 1983); *Electronics* (July 28, 1983); interview materials.

66. Interview materials; *Defense Week* (June 6, 1983).

67. Interview materials; Committee on Assessment, *op. cit.*, p. 9; Defense Science Board, *op. cit.*

68. Interview materials.

69. White, Lawrence, J., "The Motor Vehicle Industry," in Richard R. Nelson, Ed., *op. cit.*

70. See Badaracco and Yoffie, *op. cit.*, p. 99.

71. This section draws upon Nelson, Richard R., "Government Stimulus of Technical Progress: Lessons from American Industry," in Richard R. Nelson, Ed., *op. cit.;* and Nelson, Richard R., "Government Support of Technical Progress: Lessons from History," *Journal of Policy Analysis and Management*, 2(4) (Summer 1983).

72. Nelson, Richard R., "Government Stimulus," *op. cit.*, p. 465.

73. Mowery, David and Rosenberg, Nathan, "The Commercial Aircraft Industry," in Richard R. Nelson, Ed., *op. cit.;* also Nelson, Richard R., "Government Stimulus," *op. cit.*

74. U.S. Congress, Office of Technology Assessment, *International Competitiveness in Electronics* (November 1983), p. 130.

75. Nelson, Richard R., "Government Stimulus," *op. cit.;* and Nelson, Richard R. and Winter, Sidney G., *An Evolutionary Theory of Economic Change* (Cambridge, MA: Harvard University Press, 1982), pp. 392–393.

76. Rogers, Everett, M., *Diffusion of Innovations*, 3rd ed. (New York: Free Press, 1983), p. 141.

77. Braun, Ernest and MacDonand, Stuart, *Revolution in Miniature: The History and Impact of Semiconductor Electronics*, 2nd ed. (Cambridge, England: Cambridge University Press, 1982), ch. 10; *Competitive Edge: The Semiconductor Industry in the U.S. and Japan*, Okimoto, Daniel I. et. al., Eds. (Stanford, CA: Stanford University Press, 1984), pp. 60–61; Rogers, Everett M., "Information Exchange and Technological Innovation," in *The Transfer and Utilization of Technical Knowledge*, Devendra Sahal, Ed. (Lexington, MA: Lexington, 1982); Tilton, John E., *op. cit.*, pp. 77–81.

THE SOUTHERN SPEECH COMMUNICATION JOURNAL
48 (FALL, 1982), 38-50

REGULATION OF
TELEVISION ADVERTISING TO CHILDREN:
THE POLICY DISPUTE
IN ITS SECOND DECADE

DAVID H. GOFF AND LINDA DYSART GOFF

1980 marked the beginning of the second decade of the policy dispute over television advertising to children. In the early 1970s regulatory steps by advertisers and broadcasters satisfied the regulatory concerns of the FCC. However the FTC retained its interest in this area and in 1978 began consideration of the "unfairness" of advertising any product to children too young to comprehend television advertising. Vigorous, coordinated lobbying by concerned industries led to the inclusion, in the FTC Improvements Act of 1980, of a provision prohibiting further FTC consideration of the unfairness of children's advertising. The restrictiveness of this law caused the FTC to abandon its rulemaking proceeding in 1981, thus ending the present phase of this twelve-year dispute. Regulatory agency ineffectiveness and a rapidly evolving regulatory environment suggest that concerned groups might have more impact on children's advertising policy by working outside the regulatory administrative process.

C ritics of television advertising claim commercials are unfair and inappropriate for many children. Preschoolers and others who lack the level of cognitive development needed to understand fully such messages are particular subjects of concern.[1] In January, 1970, the citizen group, Action for Children's Television (ACT), petitioned the Federal Communications Com-

---

David H. Goff (Ph.D., Massachusetts, 1975) is Associate Professor and Chairman of the Department of Radio, Television, and Film, and Linda Dysart Goff (Ph.D., Massachusetts, 1975) is Associate Professor of Speech Communication, Division of Communication, University of Southern Mississippi, Hattiesburg, Mississippi.

[1]Seymour Banks, "Public Policy on Ads to Chilren," *Journal of Advertising Research*, 15, No. 4 (1975), 7.

mission (FCC) with a rulemaking proposal designed to restructure commercial television for children. The profound changes in advertising policy sought by ACT initiated a controversy which is now in its thirteenth year and is still unresolved.

This report traces the children's television advertising policy dispute from 1970 to the termination of its most recent phase by the Federal Trade Commission (FTC) in 1981. For those with an interest in media regulation, the events described provide a classic case study of policy formation within the jurisdiction of older regulatory agencies like the FCC and FTC. The case takes on added significance when considered in the context of the deregulatory climate in government under the Reagan administration.

ACT's 1970 petition to the FCC made three proposals: 1) banning of sponsorship and commercials on children's programs; 2) prohibiting performer use or any other mention of products, services, or stores by brand name during such programs; 3) daily programming totaling fourteen hours per week (minimum) aimed at three specific children's age groups. The ACT proposal was handled cautiously by the FCC. The text was released in February, 1970 in a public notice inviting comments from interested parties. After reviewing these comments the commission voted to give more thorough consideration of ACT's proposal by adopting, in January, 1971, a *Notice of Inquiry and Proposed Rulemaking.*[2]

The commission's inquiry phase comprised nearly three years of panel discussions, reports, and filings considering all aspects of the rules proposed by ACT. While the so-called "kidvid" debate continued in the FCC's forum, the broadcasting and advertising industries began "a series of self-regulatory programs in attempt to divert, delay, or dilute possible public policy action."[3]

The Television Code of the National Association of Broadcasters was amended six times between 1970 and mid-1974. Chil-

---

[2]Federal Communications Commission, *Children's Television Programs: Report and Policy Statement,* 50 FCC 2d 1 (1974); Barry Cole and Mal Oettinger, *The Reluctant Regulators: The FCC and the Broadcast Audience* (Reading, Massachusetts: Addison-Wesley, 1978), 251; and Federal Communications Commission, *First Notice of Inquiry,* 28 FCC 2d, 368 (1971).

[3]William H. Melody and Wendy Ehrlich, "Children's TV Commercials: The Vanishing Policy Options," *Journal of Communication,* 24, No. 4 (1974), 122.

dren's program hosts and primary cartoon characters were forbidden to deliver commercial messages during or adjacent to children's programs. Vitamin and drug ads during such programs also were prohibited and the use of an audio/visual device to separate program from commercial content was required. Nonprogram time limitations were adopted in several phases. The result was that by January 1, 1976, only nine and one-half minutes of non-program time per hour were allowed during weekend children's shows, with twelve minutes allowed during weekday programs. Weekend program interruptions were cut from eight to four minutes per hour. (As late as 1972, the code allowed sixteen minutes of non-program time during children's programs while the prime time standard was nine and one-half minutes.)[4]

In October, 1974, the FCC took action on its 1971 notice with the adoption of its *Children's Television Programs: Report and Policy Statement.* This document established "policies and guidelines for children's programming and advertising," but left the manner of attaining compliance up to industry self-regulation.[5] Regarding specific commercial policy, recently adopted NAB Television Code guidelines for children's spots were described by the commission as satisfactory.[6] In keeping with a 1972 liason agreement, all concerns with the content of commercials were delegated to the Federal Trade Commission (FTC) for consideration.

The FCC did make it clear in its 1974 *Policy Statement* that industry compliance with its advertising and programming policies would be reviewed. A *Second Notice of Inquiry* was issued in 1978 to evaluate progress since 1974.[7] In October, 1979, the Children's Television Task Force of the FCC reported the industry had complied with the advertising, but not the programming guidelines of the 1974 *Policy Statement.* The industry was criticized for not increasing its overall amount of programming

---

[4]Cole and Oettinger, 263-77; and William Melody, *Children's Television: The Economics of Exploitation* (New Haven: Yale University Press, 1973), 91.

[5]Federal Communications Commission, *In the Matter of Children's Television Programming and Advertising Practices: Notice of Proposed Rulemaking,* 75 FCC 2d, 139-42 (1980).

[6]Cole and Oettinger, 276-77.

[7]Federal Communications Commission, *Children's Television Programming and Advertising Practices: Second Notice of Inquiry,* 68 FCC 2d, 1344 (1974).

for children. Also, efforts to increase levels of educational and informational programming and to target programs at both pre-schoolers and school-agers were found to be insufficient.[8] Subsequent to this report, on December 29, 1979, the FCC issued a new *Notice of Proposed Rulemaking* intended to reconsider programming concerns only.[9]

Following the FCC's 1974 decision to deal only with the level of commercialization and the separation of programming from non-programming content in children's programs, the Federal Trade Commission became the regulatory center of the children's television advertising dispute. As early as 1971, the FTC had conducted hearings into children's television advertising but with little result. The 1971 hearings investigated the manipulative aspects of commercials directed at youngsters in an effort to determine possible harmful effects of such practices.[10] These hearings roughly coincided with several FTC actions against firms accused of deceptive advertising practices. Ideal Toy Co., Mattel, Inc., and Topper Corp. were found guilty of conveying "specific misimpressions regarding toys," and ITT Continental Baking Co. was charged with deceptive and unfair practices regarding its Wonder Bread claims.[11] Vitamin commercials directed at children were investigated by the FTC in 1972, but following "voluntary" cessation of such practices by the vitamin industry the FTC dropped its probe.[12]

During 1973 and 1974, the FTC, like the FCC, favored a voluntary approach to improving children's television commercial practices and attempted to involve both industry and consumer groups in the development of a children's advertising code. In addition to the NAB Code revisions already cited, FTC and in-

---

[8]FCC, *Children's Television Programming and Advertising Practices*, 139-42.

[9]FCC, *Children's Television Programming and Advertising Practices*, 138.

[10]Linda Dysart Goff, "Television Advertising and Elementary School Children: A Study of Commercial Order Effects and Product Type as Variables Influencing Recall and Attitude," Diss. University of Massachusetts 1975, pp. 3-7.

[11]Federal Trade Commission, *FTC Staff Report on Television Advertising to Children* (Washington, D.C.: GPO, 1978), 326-28, 188.

[12]*FTC, Television Advertising*, 187.

dustry discussions led to a revision of self-regulation governed by the National Advertising Review Board (NARB).

The NARB examines truth and accuracy in advertising and is administered by a council representing the Council on Better Business Bureaus (CBBB), the American Advertising Federation (AAF), the Association of National Advertisers (ANA), and the American Association of Advertising Agencies (AAAA). Under the plan agreed to in 1974, the National Advertising Division (NAD) of the CBBB would include an NAD/NARB Children's Unit and a director of Children's Advertising Review to consider fairness, truth, and accuracy in children's commercials.[13]

Substantive FTC action in the area of children's television advertising began with a 1974 proposal to ban promotion of premiums to children under twelve years of age as an unfair trade practice. The proposal was rejected in 1977 after the FTC became convinced that the ban could not be supported by available research evidence.[14]

In April, 1977, two citizen groups, ACT and the Center for Science in the Public Interest (CSPI), petitioned the FTC to make a trade rule regulating television advertising of candy and other sugared products to children. (CSPI is described as a non-profit, Washington-based corporation "which works to improve domestic food policies.") Specifically, ACT requested a ban on candy advertising "(a) before 9:05 p.m.; or (b) where the dominant appeal of the advertising is to children; or (c) during any periods when children make up at least half the audience." CSPI requested that ads for "between-meal snacks which derive more than 10% of their calories from added sugar" be banned "during any periods when children make up at least half the audience." CSPI also wanted mandatory affirmative disclosure of the added sugar content of advertised foods and the dental health risks of eating such foods during the same periods.[15]

The response of the FTC to these petitions surprised observers of the regulatory scene and infuriated the broadcasting, advertis-

---

[13]Melody and Ehrlich, 123.

[14]Federal Trade Commission, *FTC Statement of Reasons for Rejecting the Proposed Guide on Television Advertising of Premiums to Children*, 42 FR, 15069 (1977).

[15]FTC, *Television Advertising*, 2-4.

ing, toy, cereal, and snack food industries. The commission's Division of Advertising Practices undertook "a broad inquiry into the full range of factual and legal issues raised by the petitions," and considered the appropriateness of promoting *any* product to children too young to understand or evaluate commercials.[16] A 346-page analysis of these issues was made public on February 27, 1978, in the *FTC Staff Report on Television Advertising to Children*. The report recommended that the FTC begin rulemaking proceedings under the 1975 Magnuson-Moss FTC Improvements Act to:

(a) Ban all televised advertising for any product which is directed to, or seen by, audiences composed of a significant proportion of children who are too young to understand the selling purpose of, or otherwise comprehend or evaluate, the advertising;

(b) Ban televised advertising directed to, or seen by, audiences composed of a significant proportion of older children for sugared products, the consumption of which poses the most serious dental risks;

(c) Require that televised advertising directed to, or seen by, audiences composed of a significant proportion of older children for sugared food products not included in paragraph (b) be balanced by nutritional and/or health disclosures funded by advertisers.[17]

Two months later the FTC voted to initiate the recommended rulemaking proceedings.[18] Industry response was predictably hostile, and perhaps unique in that this particular FTC action caused the uniting of several industries influenced by current or pending FTC actions.

In November, 1978, a coalition composed of the Kellogg Co., the Toy Manufacturers of America, and the ANA, AAF, and AAAA successfully brought suit to bar FTC Chairman Michael Pertschuk from participating in the children's adverstising proceedings. Pertschuk had been publically critical of these industry groups, and was barred by a Washington district court for his "emotional use of derogatory terms and characterizations about

---

[16]FTC, *Television Advertising*, 345.

[17]FTC, *Television Advertising*, 345-46.

[18]News Release, Federal Trade Commission, Office of Public Information, 20 June 1980, "Special Backgrounder on Children's Advertising Rulemaking."

children's advertising."[19] In December, 1979, an appeals court overturned the lower court's decision, but Pertschuk disqualified himself from further participation in the belief that "congressional review of the children's advertising rulemaking would be clouded by his continued involvement."[20] In a related move, the AAAA, AAF, and ANA jointly hired the public relations firm of Burson-Marsteller to handle public relations problems resulting from the children's advertising dispute.[21] However, the most significant activities undertaken were stepped-up lobbying efforts in Congress by representatives of a variety of businesses undergoing FTC scrutiny.

At this time the FTC was highly vulnerable to congressional involvement in its activities. Because of a dispute between the House and Senate, the commission had been operating without legislative authorization since 1977. Bills allowing a legislative veto and review of FTC rules had been introduced in Congress several times since 1974. However, the Senate supported a two-house veto plan while the House favored a veto which could be imposed by either the House or the Senate.[22]

Against this backdrop of lobbying and legislative activity, the FTC's children's advertising proceedings continued during 1979. FTC Administrative Law Judge Morton Needelman conducted hearings during January and March in San Francisco and Washington in which "more than 200 witnesses entered over one million words into the record."[23] Needelman reported his recommendations to the FTC in August, 1979, delineating three "disputed issues of fact" to be resolved in further hearings and four other issues to be dealt with in written submissions.[24] Needelman's seven questions for further study were:

---

[19]"Judge Gessell Bars FTC's Pertschuk from Kid's TV Case," *Advertising Age,* 6 November 1978, 1.

[20]"Pertschuk Pulls Out of Children's Ad Proceeding," *Advertising Age,* 14 January 1980, 86.

[21]"Jumping the Gun on Washington Children's Ad Proceedings," *Broadcasting,* 5 March 1979, 29.

[22]"Legislative Veto Gains Four A's Support," *Advertising Age,* 7 May 1979, 14.

[23]"FTC Law Judge Cites Three Issues for Further Study in Ad Ban Case," *Broadcasting,* 6 August 1979, 2.

[24]Richard L. Gordon, "Kid Ad Probe Down to Seven Questions," *Advertising Age,* 6 August 1979, 32.

1) To what extent can children between the ages of two and 11 distinguish between children's commercials and children's programs to the point that they comprehend the selling purpose of television advertising aimed at children?

2) To what extent can children between the ages of two and 11 defend against persuasive techniques used in commercials, such as fantasy or cartoon presenters, premiums, limited information, and various associative appeals?

3) What health effects, actual or potential, attach to any proven lack of understanding of selling intent or inability to defend against persuasive techniques?

4) Are there some broadcasters, perhaps uhf or vhf independent stations, who would face "drastic economic consequences" from an FTC ban on some or all tv advertising to children?

5) Is there any basis for concluding that a ban on some or all children's tv ads would diminish the current amount of children's tv programming?

6) How sound are assertions that an ad ban would raise the prices of products advertised to children?

7) To what extent can additional disclosures, particularly sugar content disclosures, remove whatever unfairness or deception that may exist in children's tv ads?[25]

FTC action in the children's advertising area subsequent to Needelman's recommendations was delayed while Congress considered authorization legislation for the commission. Such legislation finally cleared both houses of Congress, and the Federal Trade Commission Improvements Act of 1980 (Public Law 96-252) was signed by President Carter on May 28, 1980. The content of the law reflects the success of industry lobby efforts.

The new law provides for the two-house veto favored by the Senate. All final rules proposed by the FTC must be submitted for consideration to designated committees in the House and Senate on the same date and while Congress is in session. A rule of the FTC will take effect unless both houses of Congress adopt a concurrent resolution disapproving such a rule within ninety calendar days of continuous session.[26]

In addition to creating a congressional veto over FTC activities, the Improvements Act included sections which directly influenced not only children's advertising inquiry, but also com-

---

[25]Gordon, 2.

[26]Public Law 96-252, *Federal Trade Commission Improvements Act of 1980*, 94 Stat., 393 (28 May 1980).

mission proceedings involving agricultural cooperatives and the insurance and funeral industries. Specifically, the FTC was expressly forbidden "to promulgate any rule in the children's advertising proceeding . . . on the basis of a determination . . . that such advertising constitutes an unfair act or practice." The new law also restricts the commission from using appropriated funds to initiate any new rulemaking proceeding involving "unfair" advertising through the 1982 fiscal year. Another section restricts FTC compensation of persons or groups participating in rulemaking efforts thereby limiting the ability of such parties to maintain a strong presence during protracted rulemaking proceedings.[27]

While the "unfairness" criterion was taken away from the commission, its long-standing mandate to deal with deception in advertising remained intact. However, a continued children's advertising proceeding would have to be based upon a documented contention that such advertising is deceptive. On June 18, 1980, the FTC ordered its staff to determine if available evidence supported a deception theory.[28] To the surprise of few, the staff recommendations released on March 31, 1981, concluded "that no further rulemaking proceedings are warranted at this time" and recommended that the current children's advertising rulemaking be terminated.[29] Following analysis of public comment on this recommendation, the FTC announced the termination on September 30, 1981.[30]

The FTC reached this decision because it could not develop "viable solutions, which the Commission could implement through rulemaking, to the problems articulated during the proceeding."[31] The commission staff actually formulated specific conclusions about advertising to children aged six and under: "(1) They place indiscriminate trust in televised advertising messages; (2) They do not understand the persuasive bias in television advertising; and (3) The techniques, focus and themes

---

[27]FTC Improvements Act of 1980, 94 Stat., 375-92, *et passim.*

[28]News Release, FTC, 20 June 1980.

[29]Federal Trade Commission Staff Report, "FTC Final Staff Report and Recommendation," 31 March 1981, 95.

[30]Federal Trade Commission, *In the Matter of Children's Advertising,* 16 CFR 461 (30 September 1981).

[31]FTC, *Children's Advertising,* 8-9.

used in child-oriented television advertising enhance the appeal of the advertising and the advertised product." Only "a ban on all advertisements oriented toward young children" could resolve these concerns. Advertising appeals, like programs, are directed at children between the ages of two and eleven, or between six and eleven. No commercial programs are aimed at children aged two to six. Therefore, the commission found itself unable to define "advertisements oriented toward young children." Banning commercials in programs with "audiences composed of a majority or substantial share of young children" was rejected also. Only one network program (Captain Kangaroo) was determined to have a regular proportion of viewers aged six and under falling between thirty and fifty percent. If the cutoff for a ban were lowered to a twenty percent figure, more programs would be included, but "the use of such a low cutoff figure would affect the viewing of the 80% of the audience who were not young children and who do not have their cognitive limitations." Therefore, the staff rejected the idea of banning commercials based upon audience composition data.[32]

Concerns over candy and other sugared products were also addressed by the staff. However, the contradictory evidence "with respect to the effect of sugared product advertising on the nutritional attitudes of children under 12" was considered "inconclusive" by the staff. Further, the staff concluded that no valid and reliable methodology existed "for determining the cariogenicity of individual food products."[33] Since neither nutritional nor dental health issues could be resolved by the staff no further rulemaking on these issues could be justified.

The outcome of the children's television advertising policy dispute suggests a profound and alarming shift in power from a regulatory agency to the regulated industries. This is not the case, however. The literature on regulatory agencies and the administrative process cites many theories explaining the domination of regulators by the regulated. According to the popular "capture theory," "regulatory agencies are established for 'public interest' purposes, but subsequently they become the tools of the industry they regulate." Some proponents of this theory even suggest that

---

[32]FTC, "Final Staff Report and Recommendation," 2-46, *et passim*.
[33]FTC, *Children's Advertising*, 9.

"regulatory agencies are in fact *created* to serve the interests of the industry they regulate, as a direct response by congressmen to the demands of industry for cartel management." Owen and Braeutigam view the capture theory as "a framework in which the purpose of regulation is to redistribute incomes in favor of groups that will supply electoral rewards to the politicians who engineer the redistribution." These authors also suggest that the typical regulatory process can be used strategically by industry "to attenuate the rate at which market and technological forces impose changes on individual economic agents. . . . The result is to give individuals and firms some legal rights to the status quo."[34]

According to Owen and Braeutigam, the goal of regulated firms is to effectively use the quasi-judicial nature of the administrative process to delay and to create additional expense for other parties. Certainly such commonplace practices as agency lobbying and litigation can help achieve such a goal. Information and innovation can also be used as tools. By withholding information a firm can force an agency to sue for the desired material. The selective release of information by one or more parties can slow the progress of an agency proceeding. The subsequent availability of additional or new information, especially information about some innovation, "can moot a difficult issue," or can "change the terms of the debate . . . sufficiently to require the decision process to begin anew." Owen and Braeutigam even point out that "it is often useful to control access to information within the firm itself so that officials testifying for the company do not have knowledge of damaging facts." Delays can also be caused by the production of an abundance of often irrelevant information. Finally, when faced with damaging expert testimony, firms often present contradictory testimony from "independent experts" hired as consultants by the firms.[35]

While the duration of the children's television advertising dispute was noteworthy, the outcome was predictable according to analyses of the regulatory process. Melody and Ehrlich concluded in 1974 that the elimination of advertising from children's

---

[34]Bruce M. Owen and Ronald Braeutigam, *The Regulation Game: Strategic Use of the Administrative Process* (Cambridge, Massachusetts: Ballinger, 1978), 1-11, *et passim*.

[35]Owen and Braeutigam, 2-8.

programs would constitute a major change in the structure of the commercial broadcasting system. The authors pointed out that industry could not be expected to voluntarily adopt structural change because "economic incentives within the structure are simply too compelling." Melody and Ehrlich also observed that regulatory agencies are "reluctant to address policy issues that would require structural change."[36] While the Federal Trade Commission did actually consider banning some children's commercials, such a structural change was precluded by Congress. Once again, regulated firms had strategically manipulated the administrative process to maintain the status quo.

The children's television issue is not dead. Concerns raised by activist groups still exist. Some groups, like ACT, continue to work "within the system" to bring about change. ACT has indicated that it will try to "halt unfair and deceptive ads" on a case-by-case basis, while also attempting "to reduce the amount of children's advertising on television."[37] ACT also hopes to influence the emerging structure of cable television program services to provide non-commercial programs for children. However, the frustrations of working within the system may force others to apply at least the tactics of groups like the Coalition for Better Television. This association monitors programs for what it considers to be objectionable content and pressures sponsors of such programs to bring about change. The coalition is supported in its endeavors by the Moral Majority, a national organization which seeks to organize voters to support conservative political candidates and programs. The direct application of economic pressure upon firms and political pressure upon elected officials can have results. Such tactics may become even more attractive in the near future, because both the television industry and the regulation of television are undergoing rapid change.

New cable-delivered networks and program services are appearing to compete with broadcasters and the three commercial networks. Compared with network programs, these new cable sources are typically aimed at smaller, more well-defined audiences. News, sports, religion, performing arts and children's pro-

---

[36]Melody and Ehrlich, 113-16, 122.

[37]"FTC Calls Off Children's Ad Processing." *Broadcasting,* 5 October, 1981, 22.

grams are already available. As mentioned above, ACT is attempting to convince cable programming sources to provide a variety of children's programs commercial-free.

In the regulatory arena, the term "deregulation" is frequently heard today. The new FCC chairman, Mark S. Fowler, has "promised to declare war on every regulation in sight, [and] vowed to make the marketplace the only standard to measure performance" of broadcasters.[38] Certainly deregulation has already been experienced by the FTC and the participants in the children's television advertising dispute. While industries are jubilant about the spread of deregulation, some individuals and groups are concerned about potential abuses of the public interest by deregulated firms. Indeed, abuses may occur, but when firms are freed from the apparent onus of regulation, they lose the protection from marketplace forces (their "legal rights to the status quo") afforded by regulatory agencies. Activist citizens and groups finding it more difficult to contend issues before regulatory agencies may resort to other, more powerful "marketplace" tactics to accomplish their ends.

---

[38]"The First Fifty Years of Broadcasting: 1981," *Broadcasting*, 5 October, 1981, 53.

Reindustrialization, Liberal Democracy, and Corporatist Representation

ROBERT C. GRADY

For nearly a decade the role of the state in the economy has been controversial. Numerous public figures and scholars have challenged the adequacy of government's mid-century role as regulator of conditions for market competition or free enterprise. Their challenges have produced a debate over the reindustrialization of the American economy and the need for some form of industrial policy. At the center of this debate is the proposition that the state must be an active participant in, and guarantor of, specific types of investment and productivity decisions for specific firms or sectors of the economy.

Since the New Deal, the ground rules for the regulated but competitive economy have been virtually unquestioned.[1] Public consensus for the role of the state was explained by the pluralist or interest-group liberal theory of politics. Pluralism stressed that bargaining and accommodation among the various interests affected by public policy encouraged consensus and legitimated the role of the state. This explanation reached its peak of acceptability during the period immediately preceding the Great Society years. During those eras, potentially divisive issues of who pays, who benefits, and who represents whom in the pro-

---

[1] In certain respects the current controversy is similar to one during Roosevelt's first New Deal, but that one was set aside (or at least its significance obscured) by the second New Deal's shift from a "concert of interests" to the regulated but competitive economy. For an overview, see Arthur M. Schlesinger, Jr., *The Coming of the New Deal* (Boston, Mass.: Houghton Mifflin, 1959) and *The Politics of Upheaval* (Boston, Mass.: Houghton Mifflin, 1960); R. Jeffrey Lustig, *Corporate Liberalism* (Berkeley: University of California Press, 1982); and Thomas K. McCraw, ed., *Regulation in Perspective* (Cambridge, Mass.: Harvard University Press, 1981).

ROBERT C. GRADY is professor of political science at Eastern Michigan University. He is the author of articles on classical and contemporary liberalism and is completing a project on American theories of representation.

cess of sustaining economic productivity were muted because certain public-interest criteria concerning social welfare, equity, and group accommodation were sustained.[2]

The basis for consensus, however, has broken down in the past decade. The United States's economic leadership of the world has waned. Declining and emerging industries have scrambled for various governmental supports. Citizens have increasingly become disaffected because of unemployment, inflation, and taxes. In short, problems such as these have called into question the possibility of realizing both economic growth and equity. Productivity and equity are now divisive issues, not goals believed achievable within the regulated but competitive economy. The reindustrialization debate has emerged as the consensus has fallen apart.

Leading intellectual proponents of reindustrialization are self-described liberals. They range from people like Robert B. Reich, who urges a systematic national industrial policy guided by democratic planning, through Felix Rohatyn, who advocates resurrection of the Reconstruction Finance Corporation, to Lester C. Thurow, who proposes a mix of policies to encourage investment in new technologies and to mitigate the effects of declining industries — "sunrise" and "sunset."[3] Taken together, these liberals go beyond the consensual ground rules for the regulated but competitive economy. They believe that attempts by the state to adjust to or improve upon market limitations have proved to be inadequate. In place of the regulatory state they propose a general framework for a managed capitalist economy. At the same time, they claim that their values, or normative ideals, are consistent with the traditional normative assumptions of liberal democratic thought.

Socializing Risk and Corporatist Representation

This article assesses the liberal approach to reindustrialization and its implications for certain norms or requirements for liberal democracy. Specifically the paper is concerned with the problem of *representation*. The thesis is twofold: The liberal approach to reindustrialization provides for a managed capitalist economy in which the state assumes major responsibility for capital accumulation. That is, reindustrialization requires the socialization of risk. The approach necessitates some form of functional or corporatist representational arrangements, which are highly problematic given the ideal of popular representation articulated in traditional liberal democratic theory.

[2] Theodore J. Lowi, *The End of Liberalism*, 2nd ed. (New York: Norton, 1979).

[3] Reich, Rohatyn, and Thurow have published numerous articles and essays on the American economy. Most relevant are Robert B. Reich, *The Next American Frontier* (New York: Times Books, 1983); Felix Rohatyn, "The Coming Emergency and What Can Be Done About It," *The New York Review of Books*, 4 December 1980, 20–26; and Rohatyn, "Reconstructing America," *The New York Review of Books*, 5 March 1981, 16–20; Lester C. Thurow, *The Zero-Sum Society* (New York: Basic Books, 1980).

Two qualifications should be noted at the outset; the first, terminological, the second, substantive. First, to assert that the liberal approach to reindustrialization requires the socialization of risk is simply to supply a rubric that encompasses the various policy proposals of the approach. Socialization of risk refers to governmental assumption of responsibility for the continuation or the development of firms, sectors, or markets and for the success of decisions and policies that traditionally have been viewed as private-sector functions in an otherwise entrepreneurial society. The key referents are two: *governmental* — or *public* — *assumption of responsibility* and activities *traditionally believed to be* private sector.

Ordinarily the socialization of risk has pejorative connotations. For instance, Theodore J. Lowi, in his criticism of interest-group liberalism, argues that the liberal state is reduced to "buying" its legitimacy because policies that socialize risk indiscriminantly guarantee solvency to the highest bidders — to firms and organizations, such as unions, which have well-established political resources. Two conclusions follow. The state's pretensions to democratic legitimacy are eroded. And capitalism loses its moral capital: the entrepreneurial spirit is entrepreneurial no more.[4]

The socialization of risk can be used constructively, however. Lester Thurow's prescriptions in *The Zero-Sum Society* provide examples of this. The zero-sum society resembles the world of interest-group liberalism, and public policy makers do accede to the demands of the major political interests. The main problem, in Thurow's view, is that policy makers simply rely on double standards for economic productivity and for equity. He proposes to rectify the problem with a series of political-economic changes that make criteria for productivity and equity interdependent. His proposals include policies that socialize risk, and they allow the notion to be used without the usual critical connotations.[5]

An immediate, substantive objection to the second part of the thesis should be: Why corporatism? And, if so, so what? The assertion that reindustrialization of the American economy requires functional or corporatist representation may not appear to be particularly novel or even problematic. Well-known arguments by Lowi, Grant McConnell, and others regarding the delegation of legislative authority and the role of private governments demonstrate that, in practice, American liberals have accommodated themselves to functional representation as though it were merely a theoretical inconvenience.[6] There is, however, an

---

[4] Lowi, *End of Liberalism*, 271–294.

[5] On double standards, see the "doctrine of failure" in Thurow, *Zero-Sum*, 21–22, also 80–82. See also Reich, *American Frontier*, 176–200. On risk socialization, see Robert B. Reich, Lester C. Thurow, Gus Tyler, and Michael Harrington, " 'A Path for America': Three Comments on Michael Harrington's Article and His Reply," *Dissent* 30 (Winter 1983): 25–32; and the remarks of Thurow in *What Kind of Industrial Policy?* (Washington, D.C.: Democracy Project Reports — no. 2, 13 January 1982), 5–12.

[6] Lowi, *End of Liberalism*; Grant McConnell, *Private Power and American Democracy* (New York: Vintage Books, 1966).

enormous difference between acknowledging or tacitly accepting the consequences of contemporary practices and proclaiming the need for, and legitimacy of, functional representation arrangements. Affirmative proposals for socializing risk require formal or public recognition of corporatist representation. Such proposals change the terms under which traditional liberal democratic theories of representation have been developed. But in changing the terms for traditional discourse, they amount to a reformulation of legitimation requirements for liberal democracy.

Functional representation has not been a positive component of liberal democratic theory but, to the contrary, a problem for it, the problematic character of which is clearly enunciated in the notion of faction. Writers such as Lowi and McConnell have criticized contemporary political practices not simply because they distort the theory, but because no alternative justification for functional representation has been forthcoming.[7] To avoid this type of criticism, and thus the familiar charge that reindustrialization is simply a new installment in the corporation's battle with democracy, the liberal approach to reindustrialization must contain a justification for corporatist representation that supplements, but does not supplant, the liberal democratic ideal of popular representation.[8] The justification can make corporatism legitimate on grounds of expertise, efficiency, a public interest in economic growth, and so on. But in this reformulation of democratic legitimation requirements, these criteria must be reconciled with the criterion of popular representation.

None of the reindustrialists explicitily attempt to reformulate liberal democratic legitimation requirements and reconcile corporatist criteria with popular representation. This is an understandable shortcoming, since the reindustrialization debate is polemical and proposals are often designed for specific constituencies. An initial step toward overcoming this deficiency is to anchor liberal reindustrialization proposals in a theoretical analysis, which addresses the sorts of problems that must be confronted if corporatism is to be reconciled with democratic ideals. This type of analysis is provided by Charles E. Lindblom in *Politics and Markets.*[9] However, an assessment of his work in conjunction with reindustrialization proposals indicates that arguments for corporatism, at least in the context of American politics and economics, tend to supplant rather than complement popular representation.

By linking the proposals of Thurow in *The Zero-Sum Society* with Lindblom's theoretical analysis, implications of reindustrialization for liberal democracy can be assessed. The linkage does not produce perfect congruence between Thurow and Lindblom, and the Thurow-Lindblom position that results is necessarily

[7] See especially McConnell, *Private Power*; and also Charles W. Anderson, "Political Design and the Representation of Interests," *Comparative Political Studies* 10 (April 1977): 127–152; Lustig, *Corporate Liberalism.*

[8] The advantages for business are assessed in William E. Connolly, "The Politics of Reindustrialization," *Democracy* 1 (July 1981): 9–21; Maurice Zeitlin, "Democratic Investment," *Democracy* 2 (April 1982): 69–80.

[9] Charles E. Lindblom, *Politics and Markets* (New York: Basic Books, 1977).

somewhat artificial. It is the necessary, if less than satisfactory, consequence of linking practical proposals with theoretical analysis.[10] Thurow's proposals exemplify the sorts of concrete steps necessary to fill out a highly tentative recommendation put by Lindblom at the conclusion of his book: "Governments might take on the meticulous task of designing a highly discriminating mixture of financial inducement to business with governmental control over them."[11] Thurow and Lindblom differ in many respects. In general, however, they are troubled by the awkward relationship between democratic aspirations for popular control over public policy in a society in which business is, to them, disproportionately influential. They also are troubled with how this relationship between public and private power affects equity or distributive justice. A brief overview of their common concerns provides a useful introduction to the analysis in the remainder of this article.

Theoretically, everyone can be the long-term beneficiary of socializing risk, *if* it is developed properly. But politics operates in the short term, if for no other reason than the truism that the effects of today's decisions affect tomorrow's calculations. In the short term two basic points stand out: Citizens are the ultimate risk takers under policies that socialize risk; businesses and other actors immediately associated with them (for example, unions) are generally the immediate beneficiaries. Consequently, the likelihood of formulating risk-socializing policies in a manner that enhances popular control (let alone distributive justice) at the expense of disproportionate business influence is remote. It is, therefore, on no small paradox that Lindblom concludes *Politics and Markets*: "The large private corporation fits oddly into democratic theory and vision. Indeed, it does not fit."[12]

In one form or another, socializing risk always taps into the system of incentives that motivates businessmen. As Lindblom puts it, answering his rhetorical conjecture about inducements and echoing Adam Smith's view that businessmen normally gravitate to mercantilist protections: "They do so because it pays."[13] Thus if the payoffs or inducements are sufficient, businesses and their associated actors might allow both a measure of public influence over their activities and support equity goals, the approximation of which would make any measure of public influence that much more meaningful.

This overview of concerns held by Thurow and Lindblom is cursory but suggestive. In a sense they adopt a variant of the Marxist analysis of the capitalist

[10] Thurow is emphasized largely for reasons of convenience: his is the most systematically presented reindustrialization position; it is less given to conflicting interpretations than others'; and he is explicit in his commitments to democratic legitimacy and equity. For a useful overview, see James P. Young, "Political Economy & the Democratic Left," *Polity* 14 (Spring 1982): 519–522. Rohatyn's contributions to the reindustrialization debate have come more in the form of policy guidance than publication, and he is more frequently charged with promoting business conservatism than are the others. See, for example, Zeitlin, "Democratic Investment."

[11] Lindblom, *Politics and Markets*, 349.

[12] Ibid., 356.

[13] Ibid., 349.

state's "accumulation" and "legitimation" functions. Traditionally, Marxist analysis has held that the capitalist state attempts to balance two contradictory functions. It must sustain capital accumulation as an agent of the capitalist class. Simultaneously, it must maintain legitimacy before a public electorate by appearing to pursue the public interest and to give priority to the demands of citizens over those of special interests.[14] These democratic liberals, however, attempt to resolve the contradiction. They do this by arguing that the liberal democractic state can provide the context for capital accumulation *in return for* its legitimacy by linking economic growth (capital accumulation) to equity or redistributional goals (legitimacy). The conditions for attaining this resolution between capital accumulation and popular control or legitimacy, however, place substantial constraints upon liberal democratic theory.

The following section briefly summarizes relevant arguments and proposals put forth by Thurow. The next section examines in some detail Lindblom's position and its implications. The final section concludes by using the Thurow-Lindblom position to explore the plausible consequences of corporatist policy making for the liberal ideal of popular representation.

LEARNING TO LIVE WITH THE SOCIALIZATION OF RISK

The Zero-Sum Society contains proposals that flesh out the skeleton of Lindblom's tentative recommendation. Thurow's task is dual: to develop a case for equity and to develop the policy initiatives necessary for restoring U.S. economic productivity. The two arguments should be viewed as a piece. Thurow argues that the United States can establish internationally competitive productivity levels. He further argues that this can be accomplished while meeting domestic societal demands by moving toward a more acceptable range of equity, which itself is essential to worker productivity.

Thurow's major concern is that current economic policies discourage facing up to equity or redistributive issues and, in doing so, exacerbate the problem of attaining appropriate levels of growth. Current policies fail, and their failures are traceable in large part to the ideological predispositions of business and policy elites. They tend to assume that equity flows from productivity—to the extent that they consider equity at all. In effect, with his proposals Thurow asks these elites to repudiate the conventional wisdom.[15]

---

[14] James O'Connor, *The Fiscal Crisis of the State* (New York: St. Martin's Press, 1973), especially chap. 4; Claus Offe, "The Theory of the Capitalist State and the Problem of Policy Formation," in Leon N. Lindberg, Robert Alford, Colin Crouch, and Claus Offe, eds., *Stress and Contradiction in Modern Capitalism* (Lexington, Mass.: D.C. Heath, 1975), 125–144. Admittedly the point here overgeneralizes since it collapses the distinction between "instrumental" and "structural" Marxism.

[15] On the narrow vision of business elites and their failure to grasp the relationship between business concerns such as growth and productivity and other moral or social issues such as equity, see Leonard Silk and David Vogel, *Ethics and Profits* (New York: Simon and Schuster, 1976), chaps. 7–8, esp. 136–151, 189–197, 232–239; David Vogel, "The Inadequacy of Contemporary Opposition to Business," *Daedalus* 109 (Summer 1980): 47–58.

The failure of current policies to address equity and growth is nowhere better exemplified than in the prevailing opinion regarding tax policy. The favorable presumption toward growth helps justify tax slashes and accelerated depreciation to spur reinvestment while blinding elites to the interrelationship between growth and equity. Thurow puts the issue succinctly:

> To raise investment it is necessary to improve the characteristics of the labor market. . . . Simply raising the income of capitalists, with tax cuts that must be paid for with tax increases for workers, is unlikely to achieve either more investment or a higher growth of productivity. In generating more profitable investment opportunities, skill acquisition and a cooperative work force are as important as more funds to buy new equipment. Starting a class war is hardly the way to proceed.[16]

Echoing new familiar themes of Fred Hirsch and others, Thurow argues that the promise of economic growth has been a surrogate for addressing distributive justice, since it is widely believed that equity will flow from abundance. In a no growth or low growth economy, however, failure to address equity comes home to roost. Nonetheless, sustaining economic growth (increasing productivity) is essential to establishing economic equity, however defined. The problem is to develop policies that allow for real growth in which the equity demands of former losers (women and minorities) and the gains for former winners (white males) can be accommodated or reconciled.[17]

Thurow calls for a series of policies that are designed to utilize the market allocation system while tapping into the incentive system that informs the behavior of business and policy elites. His proposals for the productivity side of the equation include the establishment of a national investment committee, governmental funding for recapitalization and process research and development (R&D), investment guarantees to encourage moves from sunset to sunrise industries, a socialized sector of employment and a government-funded safety net for individuals. These place the burden of risk squarely upon the government; that is, risk is socialized among the taxpaying public. However, these proposals are designed to discriminate between investments that are productive and consistent with equity and those that are not.[18]

The goals of Thurow's proposals are straightforward. The policies do designate obvious beneficiaries, and that is precisely the point: they are not hidden. The beneficiaries of the policies are articulated in terms of the public purpose behind the policies (productivity and equity, for Thurow), not hidden behind a sentiment that amounts to a generality (maintaining or unleashing free enter-

[16] Thurow, *Zero-Sum*, 84. See also Thurow, "Getting Serious About Tax Reforms," *The Atlantic Monthly*, March 1981, 68–72; Robert B. Reich, "Beyond Reaganomics: How the Rage for Supply-Side Riches Is Impoverishing Our Politics," *The New Republic*, 18 November 1981, 19–25.

[17] Fred Hirsch and John H. Goldthorpe, eds., *The Political Economy of Inflation* (Cambridge, Mass.: Harvard University Press, 1978), esp. chap. 2; Fred Hirsch, *Social Limits to Growth* (Cambridge, Mass.: Harvard University Press, 1976), 9–12, 117–122, 173–190; Thurow, *Zero-Sum*, 16–24, 178–189, 194–208.

[18] See Thurow, *Zero-Sum*, 78–102, 145–153, 167–211.

prise, or invoking capitalist ideology as a smokescreen). The policies involve constraints or sanctions — they come with strings attached — to achieve the public ends. In Thurow's view, the adoption of the proposals would avoid the double standard of rescuing one interest at the expense of another or, as critics aver, of attempting to salvage major political interests simply because they control extensive capital investments, established labor pools, and the like.[19]

Thurow's insistence that public-policy goals and equity judgments guide the reindustrialization effort addresses the thrust of Lindblom's proposal in *Politics and Markets* to induce businesses to waive privileges, say by trading productivity guarantees for public controls. But how plausible or viable the proposals are in the context of prevailing economic wisdom — the ideology and incentives of policy elites — is another matter. For example, Thurow recognizes that his proposals threaten vested interests and in the case of the socialized employment program require a restructuring of the economy. His call for responsible political parties acknowledges that the major problem is political but also that his analysis fails to deal adequately with the roles and values of interest groups, particularly business, in policy making.[20] Lindblom's analysis illustrates both the limitations of Thurow's proposals and the sorts of incentives required by them.

THE "PAY-TO-WAIVE" STRATEGY

Politics and Markets delineates the basic constraints that interrelationships between state and market place on policy choices in a liberal democracy. As Lindblom analyzes these constraints, policy makers have a limited range of options, which require essentially that they calculate trade-offs between economic needs and political values in making their decisions.[21] Lindblom's recommendation to combine inducements for businesses with government controls over them is an example of one type of trade-off. It is also the central one in his book. The recommendation bears reiterating, this time in full:

> Clearly governments have not in the past carefully distinguished between two types of privilege: [1] those that directly assure profitability and [2] those that give the corporation autonomy to pursue profits with little constraint. Corporations have insisted on both, hardly distinguishing between the two. A policy based on a fundamental distinction between the two would seem a possibility worth examining.[22]

[19] In effect, Thurow proposes to make systematic the ad hoc policies criticized in Lowi, *End of Liberalism*, 271-294, and Reich, *American Frontier*, 176-186. For debate over Thurow's position, see Barry Bluestone, Harley Shaiken, and Lester Thurow, "Roundtable: Reindustrialization and Jobs," *Working Papers* 7 (November–December 1980): 47-59.

[20] Thurow, *Zero-Sum*, 203-207, 212-214; Young, "Political Economy and the Democratic Left," 520-521.

[21] Lindblom, *Politics and Markets*, 345-351. For Lindblom, the function of theoretical analysis is to enhance public choice, that is, to link theory with practice. See Charles W. Anderson, "The Political Economy of Charles E. Lindblom," *American Political Science Review* 72 (September 1978): 1012-1016; Stephen L. Elkin, "Market and Politics in Liberal Democracy," *Ethics* 92 (July 1982): 720-732.

[22] Lindblom, *Politics and Markets*, 350.

And he suggests, "The key strategy is, in effect, to pay businesses to waive some of their privileges."[23] Hereafter, Lindblom's strategy is termed the pay to waive strategy.

The pay-to-waive strategy is based on Lindblom's argument about "the privileged position of business." Business privilege derives from a dual system of public authority, which, he claims, characterizes liberal democracies. The institutions, practices, and traditions of liberal democratic governments ("polyarchies," in Lindblom's parlance) constitute one form of public authority. The activities of business and the role of the market constitute the other. Business competes with political authority and attempts to dominate democratic politics and its interest groups, parties, and elections. The result of the competition is "to restrict polyarchal rules and procedures to no more than a part of government and politics, and to challenge them even there."[24] Citizens, moreover, accept business values as their own. Certain "grand" issues, as Lindblom styles them, of capital control, the distribution of income and power, and the like, about which challenges to businesses and markets could be made, are sublimated. This civic learning process or indoctrination enables business to win victories on a political battlefield devoted to "secondary" issues of unemployment, welfare, and inflation, which are viewed by the public as functions of government spending and regulations.[25]

The net effect of these various phenomena — the dual system of authority, successful business competition against political authority, citizen acquiescence in business vlaues — is that business influence and success are disproportionately greater than the influence and successes of other political institutions and practices within liberal democracies. Indeed, Lindblom asserts before an American business audience that, since business long ago won the war over the grand issues, public officials simply must make concessions to businesses in order to gain approval for their policies.[26] Therefore, in view of business privilege, two obvious questions stand out regarding the pay-to-waive strategy: Why would business leaders have any incentives to waive any privileges and accede to any measure of popular control? If they did, in return for what?

It is commonplace that American business claims to be averse to government regulations. Research on the attitudes and values of business leaders indicates that American business people have a generalized psychological disposition against regulations, an aversion built around the presumed virtues of the free enterprise system. This disposition enables them as a matter of course to oppose regulations that appear to contravene their activities and strategies, even if such regulations may promise greater gains for them in the future. At the same time,

---

[23] Ibid., 349.

[24] Ibid., 190. On the dual system of authority and business privilege, see ibid., chaps. 10–14.

[25] Lindblom describes this process of indoctrination as "circularity"; ibid., chaps. 15–16.

[26] Charles E. Lindblom, "Why Government Must Cater to Business," *Business and Society Review* 27 (Fall 1978): 5–6 and fn. 15.

business people take for granted that the state should encourage productivity and its precondition, profitability.[27]

Business people can rationalize these seemingly contradictory attitudes about regulatory constraints and state-supported productivity because, in their minds, the free enterprise system is natural and integral to a free society. Thus they predict, and often produce, dire consequences both in the aftermath of regulations and in the absence of favorable dispensations. ("If spokesmen for businessmen predict that new investment will lag without tax relief, it is only one short step to corporate decisions that put off investment until tax relief is granted.")[28] Or, in individual cases, they accept or often support favorable regulations or dispensations, such as protections for sunset industries, since these are rationalized as exceptional cases. As David Vogel puts it:

> Industries may be embarrassed by protective regulations or subsidies, but they are not opposed to them. It is rather that they see these policies as exceptional. They do not understand that the American capitalist system requires a large degree of state intervention for its very survivial; they only want to support those policies and agencies that directly benefit their firm or industry.[29]

And they also find acceptable constraints imposed by the state that effectively reallocate responsibility and blame from the firm to the state—labor relations, unemployment compensation, employee drug use, civil rights, affirmative action.[30]

For the pay-to-waive strategy, much turns on the beliefs and perspectives of business people. Several of the reindustrialists criticize business attitudes and practices, claiming that business looks to the short-term (the annual report to stockholders as the measure of managerial success) rather than to the long-term productive status of their firms and industries. They recommend industrial policies that would provide incentives for business to take the longer view.[31] Lindblom suggests, however, that any incentives must be reconciled with the privileged position of business: "Businessmen ask for a great deal. They also

---

[27] For this and the next three paragraphs, see Silk and Vogel, *Ethics and Profits*, 162-177, 193-217; David Vogel, "Why Businessmen Distrust Their State: The Political Consciousness of American Corporate Executives," *British Journal of Political Science* 8 (January 1978): 45-78; Lindblom, *Politics and Markets*, 172-187, 190; Edward S. Herman, *Corporate Control, Corporate Power* (New York: Cambridge University Press, 1981), chap. 5, esp. 172-175; Thurow, *Zero-Sum*, 126-145. This disposition is not monolithic, however. See James O'Toole, "What's Ahead for the Business-Government Relationship," *Harvard Business Review* 57 (March-April 1979): 94-105.

[28] Lindblom, *Politics and Markets*, 185.

[29] Vogel, "Why Businessmen Distrust," 67-69, at 69. See also Herman, *Corporate Control*, 251-301.

[30] See the insightful comments on affirmative action by Barbara R. Bergmann, "An Affirmative Look at Hiring Quotas," *New York Times*, 10 January 1982. On business advantages under the new regulation, see Herman, *Corporate Control*, 182-184.

[31] In addition to Thurow, *Zero-Sum*, see Reich, *American Frontier*, 140-172.

routinely protest any proposal to reduce any of their privileges. They are not highly motivated to try to understand their own needs."[32]

How, then, is business to be induced or paid to waive any of its privileges, especially its autonomy? What incentives must government provide and what can be gained in return? The pay-to-waive strategy suggests inducements such as enhanced productivity and profitability in return for public controls. What is at stake, however, are not simply the terms and conditions of productivity, which, as Lindblom suggests, business is not highly motivated to understand. At stake are prerogatives or privileges in seeking these terms. Vogel provides a fair paraphrase of Lindblom:

> What is precious [to businessmen] about the American system is not so much its superior performance but rather the relative autonomy that its managers enjoy. . . . [T]he real relevant meaning of freedom for the American bourgeoise is the ability of those who own or control economic resources to allocate or appropriate them as they see fit — without interference from either labor unions or governmental officials.[33]

The main thing business values is managerial autonomy or, as Lindblom terms it, corporate discretion, and not simply greater productivity and profitability.

Reindustrialization proposals that are designed to improve economic productivity by socializing reinvestment risks are simply unrealistic if, in return for the benefits to business, public policy appears to constrain managerial autonomy. Lindblom emphasizes the practical limitations that business privilege places on the pay-to-waive strategy by outlining an idealized blueprint for the strategy. He suggests: "the hypothetical possibility of a hybrid form of popular control that combines market control over outputs with polyarchal control, weak as it is, over the delegated decisions on which market control is weak."[34] The hybrid helps illustrate how proposals such as Thurow's could be adopted by public officials and reconciled with business privilege. More importantly, it suggests that corporatist policy-making arrangements are necessitated by the pay-to-waive strategy.

First, a planner-sovereignty approach illustrates the market control side of the hybrid. Since business output decisions are determined in part by the market (how much of a good to produce at what price), the state could regulate demand, and thus indirectly production, by purchasing products. By regulating demand, such an approach would provide a general framework for implementing a version of Thurow's proposed shift from sunset to sunrise industries. The practical limitations to this approach are that it offers inducements but no real trade-offs in terms of government controls, and that it does not directly address the issue of managerial autonomy or corporate discretion. ("One of the great misconcep-

---

[32] Lindblom, *Politics and Markets*, 179.
[33] Vogel, "Why Businessmen Distrust," 54.
[34] Lindblom, *Politics and Markets*, 156.

tions of conventional economic theory is that businessmen are induced to perform their functions by purchases of their goods and services.")[35]

A second approach, for the other side of the hybrid, would require governmental (polyarchal) control over delegated decisions. This approach highlights the role of the pay-to-waive strategy more explicitly than the planner-sovereignty approach does. The market delegates decisions about resource allocation to businessmen—reinvestment, diversification, technological innovation, organization of the work force, plant location, and so on. These decisions shape the contours of the economy's industrial structure and of its abilities to save, invest, and consume; they effectively constrain market controls. In Lindblom's view, decisions about resource allocation are determined chiefly by corporate discretion. Business defends these discretionary decisions on the grounds that it must control all decisions in order to attain least-cost outcomes (efficiency pricing). However, business has little guidance in allocating resources, since market controls are weak and constrained; and at any rate, as Lindblom argues, there is in principle no single least-cost solution in the first place.[36] It follows, he concludes, that

> if enterprises cannot unerringly find least-cost decisions and if in any case there are alternative least-cost decisions depending on corporate strategy [regarding the various resource allocation options] , . . polyarchal regulation need not necessarily result in higher costs.[37]

Lindblom's argument about government controls makes a plausible case for socializing risk. Resource-allocation decisions always incur risk, which business wants to reduce. Policies that socialize risk (assuming that government decision making is no more error prone that that of business) can reduce potential corporate costs. Further, they can provide governmental sanction for such public-interest objectives as environmental quality and energy conservation, unemployment levels and employee retraining, and the like, which involve factors that are external to the firm. Thus Lindblom provides a framework of trade-offs—incentives for business and gains for public concerns—which support, for example, Thurow's proposals regarding reinvestment.

The practical limitations to the second approach are that, when risk is socialized, the trade-offs are limited by the needs of business:

> What, then, is the list of necessary inducements? They are whatever businessmen need as a condition for performing the tasks that fall to them in a market system: income and wealth, deference, prestige, influence, power, and authority, among others.[38]

---

[35] Ibid., 173; the approach is discussed at 98–103, 147–148. One of Lindblom's critics argues that planner sovereignty is the core of Lindblom's book: Aaron Wildavsky, "Changing Forward Versus Changing Back," *Yale Law Journal* 88 (November 1978): 217–234.

[36] Lindblom, *Politics and Markets*, 147–148, 152–157. Lindblom dismisses the view that corporate managers have developed a sense of social responsibility, which guides their delegated responsibilities; whatever their values, they exercise discretion: ibid., 155–156 fn.

[37] Ibid., 156–157, at 156.

[38] Ibid., 174.

The point, however, can be generalized to both approaches. Public officials need to maintain conditions necessary for adequate business performance — "whatever businessmen need" — because business performs functions that officials "regard as indispensable."[39] Policy makers may attempt to utilize the incentives that motivate businessmen, but at the same time they are constrained by them and by the general dispositions of business to maintain and enhance managerial autonomy in a free enterprise system. For their part, business leaders may claim that only exceptional circumstances require supportive public policies. But they consistently ask for and receive appropriate inducements and incentives from public officials. In short, public officials and business elites have shared and reciprocal interests in maintaining an "acceptable" level of economic performance.

When Lindblom's pay-to-waive strategy is examined from the perspective of business privilege and the attitudes of American business, the limitations and requirements of reindustrialization proposals such as Thurow's are clarified. Based on the assessment provided in this section, the limitations are not economic or policy limitations. In a technical sense, of course, such limitations are highly controversial and form part of the current reindustrialization debate. They are attitudinal or ideological — generalized business dispositions against government regulations. However, the assessment here indicates that these limitations can be overcome by two other factors: the interests of public officials in overseeing acceptable economic performance and the interests of business elites in the success of that enterprise. Because both policy and business elites have these shared and reciprocal interests, the pay-to-waive strategy provides a basis for functional representation in the policy process, or for a form of corporatist policy making. This conclusion is not an explicit part of Lindblom's analysis. It is an implication — and a problematic one for his liberal democratic commitments — drawn from his strategy, which demonstrates that the trade-offs for corporatism are both feasible and desirable for business and policy elites.[40]

LIBERAL DEMOCRACY AND CORPORATIST REPRESENTATION

Numerous scholars of comparative politics have claimed that corporatism provides an explanatory framework that is preferable to the traditional pluralist theory of interest-group bargaining and mutual adjustment. Pluralism, it is argued, gained popularity in the United States because it provides an understandable account of politics in an environment in which the state is comparatively weak, serving as a neutral arbiter or umpire for competing interests. Corporatism, by contrast, provides a fruitful approach for understanding the political process in advanced industrialized nations where patterns of interaction,

[39] Ibid., 175.

[40] Anderson, "Political Economy of Charles E. Lindblom"; Rune Premfors, "Review Article: Charles Lindblom and Aaron Wildavsky," *British Journal of Political Science* 11 (April 1981): 201–225.

cooperation, and accommodation between the state and key societal actors have emerged. Policy making is viewed as an interactive process between the state and its major functional organizations, which utilizes these organizations as "agencies of mobilization and social control for the state vis-à-vis their members." The corporatist approach can account for the roles of organized interests in public policy making and for the shared and reciprocal incentives that both government and societal elites must utilize for interactive policy making. Advocates of corporatism tend to stress the policy-making process and the mobilization of group members and resources in support of public policy.[41] For the pay-to-waive strategy, however, the emphasis on reciprocal incentives for mutually beneficial exchanges between government and societal elites is the more significant feature of corporatism.

Few scholars would argue that politics in the United States is comparable to the politics of a developed corporatist system, in which "the structured representation of functional interests in the process of policy-making" is formalized and considered to be legitimate.[42] But quite a few have argued that the pluralist theory no longer provides an adequate explanation of American politics. The role of the state in its interaction with major societal interests, especially business, has gone far beyond the idealized role of arbiter or umpire for countervailing interests. To their critics, pluralists do not seem to recognize the significance of reciprocal government-business values or the extent to which quasi-corporatist forms of policy making have come to be an acceptable norm for major areas of public policy. In the context of these criticisms, the pay-to-waive strategy is simply a constructive alternative to the pluralist explanation of politics.

More importantly, however, the pay-to-waive strategy provides the justification for a corporatist form of politics that is highly problematic for liberal democratic legitimation norms. The strategy provides an explicit rationale for recognizing and incorporating major interests such as business within the policy process. Thurow and Lindblom propose the sorts of mutually beneficial exchanges between the state and business that are central to the corporatist explanation of policy making. In effect, corporatist policy making can be claimed to resolve the contradiction between the state's need to sustain capital accumulation and growth for business while maintaining its legitimacy before the public. By examining some of the relevant incentives in contemporary politics for corporatist policy making, the implications and significance of the Thurow-Lindblom position for liberal democratic theory may be explored.

Business, as noted in the preceding section, regardless of its anti-government-

---

[41] Leo Panitch, "The Development of Corporatism in Liberal Democracies," *Comparative Political Studies* 10 (April 1977): 65–66, 74–82; Phillippe C. Schmitter, "Modes of Interest Intermediation and Models of Societal Change in Western Europe," *Comparative Political Studies* 10 (April 1977): 7–38. Panitch prefers the term "quasi-corporatism" for assessing real world cases because corporatist structures are just that, "quasi." Hereafter, references to corporatism have this qualification in mind.

[42] Anderson, "Political Design," 141.

intrusion sentiments within a free enterprise system, is adept at rationalizing supportive governmental sanctions and subsidies. And public officials, as Lindblom argues over and again, recognizing the need to maintain adequate business performance, give their support. One manifestation of this relationship is the so-called political business cycle in which public officials attempt to avoid blame at election time for poor economic performance (or receive credit for good performance).[43] State inducements to business in the context of electoral expectations cut two ways, however. By adapting to popular expectations, public officials pursue economic expansionist policies that simultaneously benefit business, and its need for an environment of growth, and constrain the autonomy of business elites, whose investment and marketing strategies must be undertaken within the context of policies keyed to electoral returns.

Business elites thus have two strong incentives for seeking corporatist representational and policy-making forums. First, corporatist policy making tends to be insulated from electoral pressure (corporate tax policy, hidden subsidies via regulatory policy, off-budget waivers and guarantees), particularly for the larger organizations and their associated actors. Second, the rhetoric of business may be anti-government, but for the prerogatives necessary to a free enterprise system between policy elites and popular demands, policy elites are the lesser of two evils, particularly as business elites respond to increasing popular distrust of business.[44] Thurow underscores the relevance of the second point in a somewhat different context of hidden benefits of regulatory legislation: "whatever the overt objective, the implicit objective is always the distribution of income and this is almost always the real reason for the existence of any regulation." The advantage of calling something regulatory when it is redistributive is obvious. The redistribution is hidden: "Voters will not put up with large direct subsidies, but large indirect subsidies can be hidden from the voter if rules and regulations are used."[45]

These two incentives, and especially the first, are reciprocated by policy elites, who conceivably could utilize the political business cycle to pursue a classic divide-and-conquer strategy among various sectors of the economy; but they do not consistently do so. The advantages of a corporatist form of policy making often outweigh such a strategy. Corporatism effectively reduces the scope of the electoral agenda. It tends to reduce pressures on elected officials to solve economic problems when these are transformed into technical problems to be dealt with by experts. Additionally it frees policy elites from bearing responsibility for

[43] Edward R. Tufte, *Political Control of the Economy* (Princeton, N.J.: Princeton University Press, 1978).

[44] On the first point, see Lester M. Salamon and John J. Siegfried, "Economic Power and Political Influence: The Impact of Industry Structure on Public Policy," *American Political Science Review* 71 (September 1977): 1026–1043; David R. Cameron, "The Expansion of the Public Economy: A Comparative Analysis," *American Political Science Review*, 72 (December 1978): 1243–1261. On the second, see Silk and Vogel, *Ethics and Profits*; Vogel, "Contemporary Opposition"; O'Toole, "Business-Government Relationship."

[45] Thurow, *Zero-Sum*, 123, 145.

adhering to public representation guidelines and for the use of government coercion or authority insofar as these functions are transferred to the domains of sectors or organizations responsible for performance.[46]

The preceding characterizations of business and policy elites and their reciprocal incentives for seeking the advantages of corporatist policy making should have familiar contours. They describe phenomena with a longstanding history in the literature critical of pluralism — the "delegation of authority" to "private governments," a process through which elective responsibility is increasingly subordinated to the domain of "symbolic politics."[47] Corporatist policy making does not displace key components of pluralism (legislative representation and interest-group lobbying), but it does seriously limit the significance of pluralist explanations for policy making in instances where functional representation is preferred by both business and policy elites. The advantage of a corporatist explanation is that it provides a basis for understanding mutually beneficial exchanges between business and policy elites as just that — initiated for mutual benefit — rather than as by-products of countervailing powers or of accommodations and compromises between contending interests. Moreover, since the explanation stresses the incentives of business and policy elites to reduce electoral constraints on their actions, it also raises a dilemma for democratic theory.

Charles W. Anderson argues that corporatism might account for the political roles of prevailing institutions, but that theories of corporatism have not reconciled the role of functional representation with a theory of legitimacy:

> It is extremely hard in democratic theory to find grounds for investing the interests of capital and labor with the authority to make what are in effect public decisions. This is the flaw in any corporate theory of representation. How can one legitimate the legislative authority of powerful and contending interests over popular consent?[48]

Anderson goes on to sketch the framework for an affirmative response to the question.

Anderson argues that the formal incorporation of powerful interests as actors in policy making presupposes that two criteria are met: First, interest representatives are included in policy making according to whether or not their *roles* are compatible with the stated purposes of public policy. Second, the actual *decisions* taken by corporate or functional representative bodies must be made legitimate on the basis of whether their decisions conform to the criteria of public

[46] On limits of a divide and conquer strategy, see Eric A. Nordlinger, *On the Autonomy of the Democratic State* (Cambridge, Mass.: Harvard University Press, 1981), 138-139. The main point of the paragraph is due to Frank Hearn; see his "The Corporatist Mood in the United States," *Telos* 56 (Summer 1983): 41-57. See also the observations of Panitch concerning the role of the Labour party and the Trade Union Congress in constraining union members to accede to business needs under the guise of the national interest (an incomes policy): Leo Panitch, *Social Democracy and Industrial Militancy* (New York: Cambridge University Press, 1976), 246-250.

[47] Lowi, *End of Liberalism*; McConnell, *Private Power*; E. E. Schattschneider, *The Semisovereign People* (New York: Holt, Rinehart and Winston, 1960). On the domain of symbolic politics, see Murray Edelman, *The Symbolic Uses of Politics* (Urbana: University of Illinois Press, 1964).

[48] Anderson, "Political Design," 143.

purpose informing the decision-making body and not simply on grounds that they meet the interests of the groups represented. The second criterion bears quoting:

> the decisions taken by bodies structured on functional lines are not rendered legitimate by virtue of the principle of representation on which they are based but by the conformity of their decisions to some substantive criterion of public actions. . . . [P]olicies are not legitimate because they are made by a certain kind of representative body but because they conform to an explicit standard of public decision.[49]

In other words, the legitimate role of the interests under the first criterion is not a sufficient test for public policy. The decisions taken must be conformable to generalized and formal procedures. Anderson cites, for example, Theodore Lowi's proposal for a "rule of law" criterion.

Anderson's criteria for reconciling functional representation with popular representation, like Lindblom's hybrid of popular and market controls, have analytic value but practical limitations. Both Thurow's and Lindblom's proposals approach Anderson's first criterion — especially Thurow's in his insistence that productivity be linked to equity. Thurow may be correct that issues of equity or distributive justice underlie the problem of attaining appropriate levels of productivity. And he forthrightly attempts to reconcile the two in his proposals. But meeting the second of Anderson's criteria is problematic. Recall that the acceptability of proposals such as Thurow's must be keyed to the sorts of trade-offs that Lindblom suggests for the pay-to-waive strategy. And that strategy is informed by a context of business privilege and a political agenda devoted to secondary issues. It is thus quite likely that the actual process of establishing criteria for decision making in the public interest — Anderson's second criterion of public purpose — would be undertaken in conjunction with the needs and aspirations of business. In other words, substantive procedural criteria upon which the decisions of representative bodies are to be grounded would be, roughly, business definitions. One should not expect enhanced public control of policy making to occur at the expense of business autonomy.

Business elites might meet public concerns about equity, however, in a way that constitutes a perverse variation of the pay-to-waive strategy (and which bypasses Anderson's second criterion and ostensibly meets his first one). Business elites might be induced to satisfy equity demands in return for socializing the risks of reinvestment. For example, affirmative action is a case in point of acceptable equity policy; and personal income tax reform, in exchange for investment incentives, is a plausible one (suggested by Thurow). The acceptance of equity demands in return for reinvestment assistance is compatible with the incentives of business and policy elites. The trade-off does not restrict managerial autonomy, and it permits policy elites to appear responsive to popular demands or to explicit public-interest criteria. Far from increasing public control, however, it is a perverse variation on the pay-to-waive strategy, since the equity

---

[49] Ibid., 143-145, 148-150, quoted from 148-149.

benefits may be provided with little constraint on business. The public's agenda remains circumscribed as an arena of secondary issues apart from the policy domains of business elites.

The pay-to-waive strategy for socializing risk is conceived with the best of intentions. But in the context informing it — the privileged position of business — it implies a substantially revised role for popular representation in liberal democracy. No one would seriously deny tht the American Founding Fathers were concerned with economic productivity; some might say that Alexander Hamilton was preoccupied with it. But no one would seriously claim either that they envisioned sectorial representation — interest representation — as permissible other than *through* popular representation and its geographic variant, not alongside it or in lieu of it.[50] Proposals to reindustrialize the American economy, however, rely on the reciprocal incentives of business and government elites to develop industrial policies for their mutual benefit. Evidence suggests that these incentives support a form of corporatist policy making that subordinates popular representation to an agenda of largely secondary or symbolic politics.

To incorporate business and its needs in the formulation of public policy is tantamount to making its public authority legitimate. The pay-to-waive strategy for socializing risk provides an explicit rationale for recognizing the reciprocal interests of business and policy elites to engage in quasi-corporatist forms of policy making. The value of the strategy is not that it provides an adequate reconciliation of functional and popular representation — it clearly does not. The value of it is that it articulates that major constraints on liberal democratic ideals that underlie the reindustrialization debate.

The arguments cited and utilized in this section are neither new nor exceptional. They are aspects of the long-standing critique of pluralism or interest-group liberalism. Pluralist theory may not recognize the privileged position of business, and it may have tacitly accepted functional representation, but it did not formally legitimize it. If it is, as critics contend, the "elitist theory of democracy," it is elitist by default, not by design. Given the conflicts between business privilege and popular representation, there may be no practical, let alone theoretical, way to reconcile the needs of functional interests with the requirements of popular representation. But the analysis of Thurow, Lindblom and others, who assess the reciprocal interests of business and policy elites, also make it clear that an appeal for a return to the regulated but competitive economy, as explained by pluralism, can no longer be understood as elitist by default, but by design.*

[50] Scarlett G. Graham, "Government and the Economy," in George J. Graham, Jr. and Scarlett G. Graham, eds., *Founding Principles of American Government* (Bloomington: Indiana University Press, 1977), 312–323; J.R. Pole, *Political Respresentation in England and the Origins of the American Republic* (New York: St. Martin's Press, 1966), 374–375.

*This paper originated in Eric Nordlinger's National Endowment for the Humanities seminar, Harvard University, 1981; it was presented at the 1982 annual meeting of the Midwest Political Science Association. The comments of Charles Anderson, Alfonso Damico, Richard Goff, Frank Hearn, and Lawrence Joseph are appreciated.

From Conservation to Environment: Environmental Politics in the United States Since World War Two

Samuel P. Hays
University of Pittsburgh

14

The historical significance of the rise of environmental affairs in the United States in recent decades lies in the changes which have taken place in American society since World War II. Important antecedants of those changes, to be sure, can be identified in earlier years as "background" conditions on the order of historical forerunners. But the intensity and force, and most of the substantive direction of the new environmental social and political phenomenon can be understood only through the massive changes which occurred after the end of the War - and not just in the United States but throughout advanced industrial societies.

Such is the argument of this article. I will identify a variety of ways in which one can distinguish the old from the new, the pre- from the post-War, and sequential changes within the decades of the

Environmental Era themselves. My argument will emphasize change rather than continuity. In historical analyses we are constantly forced to cope with the problem of sorting out the strands of continuous evolution from the discontinuities which mark new directions. When we are close to a broad social and political change, displaying elements of what we call social movements, we often depart from that task by a temptation to ferret out "roots" in order to give historical meaning and significance to them. So it is with the "environmental movement." Here I prefer a larger view, shaped by the overarching historical problem of identifying patterns of continuity and change. Where do environmental affairs fit in those larger patterns of evolution in 20th century American society and politics? In my view that "fit" lies in an emphasis on the massive changes in America after World War II and on the War itself as a historical dividing point.

The Conservation and Environmental Impulses

Prior to World War II, before the term "environment" was hardly used, the dominant theme in conservation emphasized physical resources, their more efficient use and development. The range of emphasis evolved from water and forests in the late 19th and early 20th centuries, to grass and soils and game in the 1930's. In all these fields of endeavor there was a common concern for the loss of physical productivity represented by waste. The threat to the future which that "misuse" implied could be corrected through "sound" or efficient management. Hence in each field there arose a management system which emphasized a balancing of immediate in favor of more long-run production, the coordination of factors of production under central management schemes for the greatest efficiency. All this is a chapter in the history of production rather than of consumption, and of the way in which managers organized production rather than the way in which consumers evolved ideas and action amid the general public.

Enough has already been written about the evolution of multiple-purpose river development and sustained-yield forestry to establish their role in this context of efficient management for commodity production.[1] But perhaps a few more words could be added for those resources which came to public attention after World War I. Amid the concern about soil erosion, from both rain and wind, the major stress lay in warnings about the loss of agricultural productivity. What had taken years to build up over geologic time now was threatened with destruction by short-term practices. The soil conservation program inaugurated in 1933 gave rise to a full-scale attack on erosion problems which was carried out amid almost inspired religious fervor.[2] In the Taylor Grazing Act of 1934 the nation's grazing lands in the West were singled out as a special case of deteriorating productivity; it set in motion a long-term drive to reduce stocking levels and thereby permit recovery of the range.[3] Also during the 1930's, scientific game management came into its own with the Pittman-Robertson Act of 1936 which provided funds.[4] This involved concepts much akin to those in forestry, in which production and consumption of game would be balanced in such a fashion so as not to outrun food resources and hence sustain a continuous yield.

Perhaps the most significant vantage point from which to observe the common processes at work in these varied resource affairs was the degree to which resource managers thought of themselves as engaged in a common venture. It was not difficult to bring into the overall concept of "natural resources" the management of forests and waters, of soils and grazing lands, and of game. State departments of "natural resources" emerged, such as in Michigan, Wisconsin and Minnesota, and some univer-

15

sity departments of forestry became departments of natural resources
-- all this as the new emphases on soils and game were added to the
older ones on forests and waters.[5] By the time of World War II a complex of professionals had come into being, with a strong focus on
management as their common task, on the organization of applied knowledge
about physical resources so as to sustain output for given investments of
input under centralized management direction. This entailed a common
conception of "conservation" and a common focus on "renewable resources,"
often within the rubric of advocating "wise use" under the direction of
professional experts.[6]

     During these years another and altogether different strand of
activity also drew upon the term "conservation" to clash with the thrust
of efficient commodity management. Today we frequently label it with
the term "preservation" as we seek to distinguish between the themes of
efficient development symbolized by Gifford Pinchot and natural environment management symbolized by John Muir. Those concerned with national
parks and the later wilderness activities often used the term "conservation" to describe what they were about. In the Sierra Club the "conservation committees" took up the organization's political action in
contrast with its outings. And those who formed the National Parks
Association and later the Wilderness Society could readily think of
themselves as conservationists, struggling to define the term quite
differently than did those in the realm of efficient management. Even
after the advent of the term "environment" these groups continued to
identify themselves as "conservationists" such as in the League of Conservation Voters, especially when they wished to draw together the
themes of natural environment lands and environmental protection. The
National Parks Association sought to have the best of both the old and
the new when it renamed its publication, *The National Parks and Conservation Magazine: The Environmental Journal.*[7]

     Prior to World War II the natural environment movement made some
significant gains. One thinks especially of the way in which Pinchot
was blocked from absorbing the national parks under his direction in
the first decade of the century and then, over his objections, advocates
of natural environment values succeeded in establishing the National
Park Service in 1916. Then there was the ensuing struggle of several
decades in which an aggressive Park Service was able to engage the
Forest Service in a contest for control of land and on many occasions
won. One of the best described of these events concerns the establishment of the Olympic National Park in 1937, a former national monument
under Forest Service jurisdiction until Franklin D. Roosevelt transferred
all the monuments to the Park Service in June of 1933; in 1937 it was
expanded by the addition of considerable acreage from the surrounding
national forest.[8] Despite all this, however, the theme of management
efficiency in physical resource development dominated the scene prior to
World War II and natural environment programs continued to play a subordinate role.

     After the War a massive turnabout of historical forces took place.
The complex of specialized fields of efficient management of physical
resources increasingly came under attack amid a new "environmental"
thrust. It contained varied components. One was the further elaboration
of the outdoor recreation and natural environment movements of pre-War,
as reflected in the Wilderness Act of 1964, the Wild and Scenic Rivers
Act of 1968, and the National Trails Act of the same year, and further
legislation and administrative action on through the 1970's. But there
were other strands even less rooted in the past. The most extensive was
the concern for environmental pollution, or "environmental protection"

16

as it came to be called in technical and managerial circles. While smoldering in varied and diverse ways in this or that setting from many years before, this concern burst forth to national prominence in the mid-1960's and especially in air and water pollution. And there was the decentralist thrust, the search for technologies of smaller and more human scale which complement rather than dwarf the more immediate human setting. One can find decentralist ideologies and even affirmations of smaller-scale technologies in earlier years, such as that inspired by Ralph Borsodi not long before World War II.[9] But the intensity and direction of the drive of the 1970's was of a vastly different order. The search for a "sense of place," for a context that is more manageable intellectually and emotionally amid the escalating pace of size and scale had not made its mark in earlier years as it did in the 1970's to shape broad patterns of human thought and action.

One of the most striking differences between these post-War environmental activities, in contrast with the earlier conservation affairs, was their social roots. Earlier one can find little in the way of broad popular support for the substantive objectives of conservation, little "movement" organization, and scanty evidence of broadly shared conservation values. The drive came from the top down, from technical and managerial leaders. In the 1930's one can detect a more extensive social base for soil conservation, and especially for new game management programs.

But, in sharp contrast, the Environmental Era displayed demands from the grass-roots, demands that are well charted by the innumerable citizen organizations and studies of public attitudes. One of the major themes of these later years, in fact, was the tension that evolved between the environmental public and the environmental managers, as impulses arising from the public clashed with impulses arising from management. This was not a new stage of public activity per se, but of new values as well. The widespread expression of social values in environmental action marks off the environmental era from the conservation years.

It is useful to think about this as the interaction between two sets of historical forces, one older that was associated with large-scale management and technology, and the other newer that reflected new types of public values and demands.[10] The term "environment" in contrast with the earlier term "conservation" reflects more precisely the innovations in values. The technologies with which those values clashed in the post-War years, however, were closely aligned in spirit and historical roots with earlier conservation tendencies, with new stages in the evolution from the earlier spirit of scientific management of which conservation had been an integral part. A significant element of the historical analysis, therefore, is to identify the points of tension in the Environmental Era between the new stages of conservation as efficient management, as it became more highly elaborated, and the newly evolving environmental concerns which displayed an altogether different thrust. Conflicts between older "conservation" and newer "environment" help to identify the nature of the change.

One set of episodes in this tension concerned the rejection of

17

multiple-purpose river structures in favor of free flowing rivers; here
was a direct case of irreconcilable objectives, one stemming from the
conservation era, and another inherent in the new environmental era.
There were cases galore. But perhaps the most dramatic one, which pin-
points the watershed between the old and the new, involved Hell's Canyon
on the Snake River in Idaho.[11] For many years that dispute had taken
the old and honorable shape of public versus private power. Should
there be one high dam, constructed with federal funds by the Bureau of
Reclamation, or three lower dams to be built by the Idaho Power Company?
These were the issues of the 1930's, the Truman years and the Eisenhower
administrations. But when the Supreme Court reviewed a ruling of the
Federal Power Commission on the issue in 1968, it pointed out in a
decision written by Justice Douglas that another option had not been
considered - no dam at all. Perhaps the river was more valuable as an
undeveloped, free flowing stream. The decision was unexpected both to
the immediate parties to the dispute, and also to "conservationists" in
Idaho and the Pacific Northwest. In fact, those conservationists had
to be persuaded to become environmentalists. But turn about they did.
The decision seemed to focus a perspective which had long lain dormant,
implicit in the circumstances but not yet articulated, and reflected a
rather profound transformation in values which had already taken place.

There were other realms of difference between the old and the new.
There was, for example, the changing public conception of the role and
meaning of forests.[12] The U.S. Forest Service, and the entire community
of professional foresters, continued to elaborate the details of scientific management of wood production; it took the form of increasing input
for higher yields, and came to emphasize especially even-aged management.
But an increasing number of Americans thought of forests as environments
for home, work and play, as an environmental rather than as a commodity
resource, and hence to be protected from incompatible crop-oriented
strategies. Many of them bought woodlands for their environmental

18

rather than their wood production potential. But the forestry profession
did not seem to be able to accept the new values. The Forest Service
was never able to "get on top" of the wilderness movement to incorporate
it in "leading edge" fashion into its own strategies. As the movement
evolved from stage to stage the Service seemed to be trapped by its own
internal value commitments and hence relegated to playing a rear-guard
role to protect wood production.[13] Many a study conducted by the Forest
Service experiment stations and other forest professionals made clear
that the great majority of small woodland owners thought of their hold-
ings as environments for wildlife and their own recreational and residential activities; yet the service forester program conducted by the
Forest Service continued to emphasize wood production rather than environmental amenities as the goal of woodland management. The diverging
trends became sharper with the steadily accumulating environmental
interest in amenity goals in harvesting strategies and the expanding
ecological emphases on more varied plant and animal life within the
forest.[14]

There were also divergent tendencies arising from the soil conservation arena. In the early 1950's, the opposition of farmers to the high-dam strategies of the U.S. Army Corps of Engineers led to a new program under the jurisdiction of the Soil Conservation Service, known as PL 566, which emphasized the construction of smaller headwater dams to "hold the water where it falls." This put the SCS in the business of rural land and water development, and it quickly took up the challenge of planning a host of such "multiple-use" projects which combined small flood control reservoirs with flat-water recreation and channelization with wetland drainage.[15] By the time this program came into operation, however, in the 1960's, a considerable interest had arisen in the natural habitats of headwater streams, for example for trout fishing, and wetlands for both fish and wildlife. A head-on collision on this score turned an agency which had long been thought of as riding the lead wave of conservation affairs into one which appeared to environmentalists to be no better than the Corps - development minded and at serious odds with newer natural environment objectives.[16]

There was one notable exception to these almost irreconcilable tensions between the old and the new in which a far smoother transition occurred - the realm of wildlife. In this case the old emphasis on game was faced with a new one on nature observation or what came to be called a "non-game" or "appreciative" use of wildlife.[17] Between these two impulses there were many potential arenas for deep controversy. But there was also common ground in their joint interest in wildlife habitat. The same forest which served as a place for hunting also served as a place for nature observation. In fact, as these different users began to be identified and counted it was found that even on lands acquired exclusively for game management the great majority of users were non-game observers. As a result of this shared interest in wildlife habitat it was relatively easy for many "game managers" to shift in their self-conceptions to become "wildlife managers." Many a state agency changed its name from "game" to "wildlife" and an earlier document, "American Game Policy, 1930," which guided the profession for many years, became "The North American Wildlife Policy, 1973."[18]

If we examine the values and ideas, then, the activities and programs, the directions of impulses in the political arena, we can observe a marked transition from the pre-World War II conservation themes of efficient management of physical resources, to the post-World War environmental themes of environmental amenities, environmental protection, and human scale technology. Something new was happening in American society, arising out of the social changes and transformation in human values in the post-War years. These were associated more with the advanced consumer society of those years than with the industrial manufacturing society of the late 19th and the first half of the 20th centuries. Let me now root these environmental values in these social and value changes.

19

The Roots of New Environmental Values

The most immediate image of the "environmental movement" consists of its "protests," its objections to the extent and manner of development and the shape of technology. From the media evidence one has a sense of environmentalists blocking "needed" energy projects, dams, highways and industrial plants, and of complaints of the environmental harm generated by pollution. Environmental action seems to be negative, a protest affair. This impression is also heavily shaped by the "environmental impact" mode of analysis which identifies the "adverse effects" of development and presumably seeks to avoid or mitigate them.

The question is one of how development can proceed with the "least" adverse effect to the "environment." From this context of thinking about environmental affairs one is tempted to formulate an environmental history based upon the way in which technology and development have created "problems" for society to be followed by ways in which action has been taken to cope with those problems.

This is superficial analysis. For environmental impulses are rooted in deep seated changes in recent America which should be understood primarily in terms of new positive directions. We are at a stage in history when new values and new ways of looking at ourselves have emerged to give rise to new preferences. These are characteristic of advanced industrial societies throughout the world, not just in the United States. They reflect two major and widespread social changes. One is associated with the search for standards of living beyond necessities and conveniences to include amenities made possible by considerable increases in personal and social "real income." The other arises from advancing levels of education which have generated values associated with personal creativity and self-development, involvement with natural environments, physical and mental fitness and wellness and political autonomy and efficacy. Environmental values and objectives are an integral part of these changes.

Extensive study of attitudes and values by public opinion analysts and sociologists chart these larger changes in social values in considerable detail.[19] Some have brought them together in comprehensive accounts They can be best observed in the market analyses which have been sponsored by the American business community since the 1920's which gave rise to the initial interest in attitude surveys. Such analyses have identified value changes in almost every sub-group in the American population, from different ages to ethnic and religious variations, to regional differences and rural-urban distinctions. Two of the most comprehensive and long-term studies are now in progress, financed by American business corporations, one the Values and Lifestyles Study (VALS) conducted by Arnold Johnson at Stanford Research Institute and the other, emphasizing content analysis of newspapers, being undertaken by John Naisbett, associated with the firm of Yankelovitch, Skelly and White in Washington, D.C.[20]

From these more general surveys, from studies specifically of environmental values, from analyses of recreational and leisure preferences undertaken by leisure research specialists, from surveys of the values expressed by those who purchase natural environment lands, and from the content of environmental action in innumerable grass-roots citizen cases one can identify the "environmental impulse" not as reactive but formative.[21] It reflects a desire for a better "quality of life" which is another phase of the continual search by the American people throughout their history for a higher standard of living. Environmental values are widespread in American society, extending throughout income and occupational levels, areas of the nation and racial groups, somewhat stronger in the middle sectors and a bit weaker in the very high and very low groupings.[22] There are identifiable "leading sectors" of change with which they are associated as well as "lagging sectors." They tend to be stronger with younger people and increasing levels of education and move into the larger society from those centers of innovation. They are also more associated with particular geographical regions such as New England, the Upper Lakes States, the Upper Rocky Mountain region and the Far West, while the South, the Plains States and the lower Rockies constitute "lagging" regions.[23] Hence one can argue that environmental values have expanded steadily in American society, associated with demographic sec-

20

tors which are growing rather than with those which are more stable or
declining.

Within this general context one can identify several distinctive
sets of environmental tendencies. One was the way in which an increasing
portion of the American people came to value natural environments as an
integral part of their rising standard of living. They sought out many
types of such places to experience, to explore, enjoy and protect:
high mountains and forests, wetlands, ocean shores, swamplands, wild and
scenic rivers, deserts, pine barrens, remnants of the original prairies,
places of relatively clean air and water, more limited "natural areas."[24]
Interest in such places was not a throwback to the primitive, but an
integral part of the modern standard of living as people sought to add
new "amenity" and "aesthetic" goals and desires to their earlier preoccupation with necessities and conveniences. These new consumer wants were
closely associated with many others of a similar kind such as in the
creative arts, recreation and leisure in general, crafts, indoor and
household decoration, hi-fi sets, the care of yards and gardens as living
space and amenity components of necessities and conveniences. Americans
experienced natural environments both emotionally and intellectually,
sought them out for direct personal experience in recreation, studied them
as objects of scientific and intellectual interest and desired to have
them within their community, their region and their nation as symbols of
a society with a high degree of civic consciousness and pride.[25]

A new view of health constituted an equally significant innovation
in environmental values, health less as freedom from illness and more as
physical and mental fitness, of feeling well, of optimal capability for
exercising one's physical and mental powers.[26] The control of infectious
diseases by antibiotics brought to the fore new types of health problems
associated with slow, cumulative changes in physical condition, symbolized most strikingly by cancer, but by the 1980's ranging into many
other conditions such as genetic and reproductive problems, degenerative
changes such as heart disease and deteriorating immune systems. All
this put more emphasis on the non-bacterial environmental causes of
illness but, more importantly, brought into health matters an emphasis
on the positive conditions of wellness and fitness. There was an
increasing tendency to adopt personal habits that promoted rather than
threatened health, to engage in physical exercise, to quit smoking, to
eat more nutritiously and to reduce environmental threats in the air
and water that might also weaken one's wellness. Some results of this
concern were the rapid increase in the business of health food stores,
reaching $1.5 billion in 1979,[27] the success of the Rodale enterprises
and their varied publications such as *Prevention* and *Organic Gardening*,
and the increasing emphasis on preventive medicine.[28]

These new aesthetic and health values constituted much of the roots
of environmental concern. They came into play in personal life and led
to new types of consumption in the private market, but they also led to
demands for public action both to enhance opportunities, such as to make
natural environments more available and to ward off threats to values.
The threats constituted some of the most celebrated environmental battles:
power and petrochemical plant siting, hardrock mining and strip mining,
chemicals in the workplace and in underground drinking water supplies,
energy transmission lines and pipelines.[29] Many a local community found
itself faced with a threat imposed from the outside and sought to protect
itself through "environmental action." But the incidence and intensity
of reaction against these threats arose at a particular time in history
because of the underlying changes in values and aspirations. People had
new preferences and new personal and family values which they did not

21

151

have before. Prior to World War II, the countryside, that area between the nation's cities and its wildlands, had been an area of rapid decline, a land much of which "nobody wanted," but in the years after the War it became increasingly occupied and hence defended.[30] Here was a major battleground for the contending environmental and developmental antagonists. Because of these new values developmental activities which earlier might have been accepted were now considered to be on balance more harmful than beneficial.

Still another concern began to play a more significant role in environmental affairs in the 1970's - an assertion of the desirability of more personal family and community autonomy in the face of the larger institutional world of corporate industry and government, an affirmation of smaller in the face of larger contexts of organization and power. This constituted a "self-help" movement. It was reflected in numerous publications about the possibilities of self-reliance in production of food and clothing, design and construction of homes, recreation and leisure, recycling of wastes and materials, and use of energy through such decentralized forms as wind and solar. These tendencies were far more widespread than institutional and thought leaders of the nation recognized since their world of perception and management was far removed from community and grass-roots ideas and action. The debate between "soft" and "hard" energy paths seemed to focus much of the controversy over the possibilities of decentralization.[31] But it should also be stressed that the American economy, while tending toward more centralized control and management, also generated products which made individual choices toward decentralized living more possible and hence stimulated this phase of environmental affairs. While radical change had produced large-scale systems of management it had also reinvigorated the more traditional Yankee tinkerer who now found a significant niche in the new environmental scheme of things.

Several significant historical tendencies are integral parts of these changes. One involves consumption and the role of environmental values as part of evolving consumer values.[32] At one time, perhaps as late as 1900, the primary focus in consumption was on necessities. By the 1920's a new stage had emerged which emphasized conveniences in which the emerging consumer durables, such as the automobile and household appliances were the most visible elements. This change meant that a larger portion of personal income, and hence of social income and production facilities were now being devoted to a new type of demand and supply. By the late 1940's a new stage in the history of consumption had come into view. Many began to find that both their necessities and conveniences had been met and an increasing share of their income could be devoted to amenities. The shorter work week and increasing availability of vacations provided opportunities for more leisure and recreation. Hence personal and family time and income could be spent on amenities. Economists were inclined to describe this as "discretionary income." The implications of this observation about the larger context of environmental values is that it is a part of the history of consumption rather than of production. That in itself involves a departure from traditional emphases in historical analysis.

Another way of looking at these historical changes is to observe the shift in focus in daily living from a preoccupation with work in earlier years to a greater role for home, family and leisure in the post-War period. Public opinion surveys indicate a persistent shift in which of these activities respondents felt were more important, a steady decline in a dominant emphasis on work and a steady rise in those activities associated with home, family and leisure. One of the most significant

22

aspects of this shift was a divorce in the physical location of work and home. For most people in the rapidly developing manufacturing cities of the 19th century the location of home was dictated by the location of work. But the widespread use of the automobile, beginning in the 1920's, enabled an increasing number of people, factory workers as well as white collar workers, to live in one place and to work in another. The environmental context of home, therefore, came to be an increasingly separate and distinctive focus for their choices. Much of the environmental movement arose from this physical separation of the environments of home and work.

One can identify in all this an historical shift in the wider realm of politics as well. Prior to World War II the most persistent larger context of national political debate involved the balance among sectors of production. From the late 19th century on the evolution of organized extra-party political activity, in the form of "interest groups", was overwhelmingly devoted to occupational affairs, and the persistent policy issues involved the balance of the shares of production which were to be received by business, agriculture and labor, and sub-sectors within them. Against this array of political forces consumer objectives were woefully weak. But the evolution of new types of consumption in recreation, leisure and amenities generated a quite different setting. By providing new focal points of organized activity in common leisure and recreational interest groups, and by emphasizing community organization to protect community environmental values against threats from external developmental pressures, consumer impulses went through a degree of mobilization and activity which they had not previously enjoyed. In many an instance they were able to confront developmentalists with considerable success. Hence environmental action reflects the emergence in American politics of a new effectiveness for consumer action not known in the years before the War.

One of the distinctive aspects of the history of consumption is the degree to which what once were luxuries, enjoyed by only a few, over the years became enjoyed by many - articles of mass consumption. In the censuses of the last half of the 19th century several occupations were identified as the "luxury trades," producing items such as watches and books which later became widely consumed. Many such items went through a similar process, arising initially as enjoyed only by a relative few and then later becoming far more widely diffused. These included such consumer items as the wringer washing machine and the gas stove, the carpet sweeper, indoor plumbing and the automobile. And so it was with environmental amenities. What only a few could enjoy in the 19th century came to be mass activities in the mid-20th, as many purchased homes with a higher level of amenities around them and could participate in outdoor recreation beyond the city. Amid the tendency for the more affluent to seek out and acquire as private property the more valued natural amenity sites, the public lands came to be places where the opportunity for such activities remained far more accessible to a wide segment of the social order. 23

A major element of the older, pre-World War II "conservation movement," efficiency in the use of resources, also became revived in the 1970's around the concern for energy supply. It led to a restatement of rather traditional options, as to whether or not natural resources were limited, and hence one had to emphasize efficiency and frugality, or whether or not they were unlimited and could be developed with unabated vigor. Environmentalists stressed the former. It was especially clear that the "natural environments" of air, water and land were finite, and that increasing demand for these amid a fixed supply led to considerable inflation in price for those that were bought and sold in the private market. Pressures of growing demand on limited supply of material resources appeared to most people initially in the form of inflation; this trend of affairs in energy was the major cause of inflation in the entire economy. The great energy debates of the 1970's gave special focus to a wide range of issues pertaining to the "limits to growth."[33] Environmentalists stressed the possibilities of "conservation supplies" through greater energy productivity and while energy producing companies objected to this as a major policy alternative, industrial consumers of energy joined with household consumers in taking up efficiency as the major alternative. In the short run the "least cost" option in energy supply in the private market enabled the nation greatly to reduce its energy use and carried out the environmental option.[34]

In accounting for the historical timing of the environmental movement one should emphasize changes in the "threats" as well as in the values. Much of the shape and timing of environmental debate arose from changes in the magnitude and form of these threats from modern technology. That technology was applied in increasing scale and scope, from enormous drag-lines in strip mining, to 1000-megawatt electric generating plants and "energy parks," to superports and large-scale petrochemical plants, to 765-kilovolt energy transmission lines. And there was the vast increase in the use and release into the environment of chemicals, relatively contained and generating a chemical "sea around us" which many people considered to be a long-run hazard that was out of control. The view of these technological changes as threats seemed to come primarily from their size and scale, the enormity of their range of impact, in contrast with the more human scale of daily affairs. New technologies appeared to constitute radical influences, disruptive of settled community and personal life, of a scope that was often beyond comprehension, and promoted and carried through by influences "out there" from the wider corporate and governmental world. All this brought to environmental issues the problem of "control," of how one could shape more limited personal and community circumstance in the face of large-scale and radical change impinging from afar upon daily life.[35]

Stages in the Evolution of Environmental Action

Emerging environmental values did not make themselves felt all in the same way or at the same time. Within the context of our concern here for patterns of historical change, therefore, it might be well to secure some sense of stages of development within the post-World War II years. The most prevalent notion is to identify Earth Day in 1970 as the dividing line. There are other candidate events, such as the publication of Rachel Carson's *Silent Spring* in 1962, and the Santa Barbara oil blowout in 1969.[36] But in any event definition of change in these matters seems to be inadequate. Earth Day was as much a result as a cause. It came after a decade or more of underlying evolution in attitudes and action without which it would not have been possible. Many environmental organizations, established earlier, experienced considerable growth in membership during the 1960's, reflecting an expanding concern.[37] The regulatory mechanisms and issues in such fields as air and water pollution were shaped then; for example the Clean Air Act of 1967 established the character of the air quality program more than did that of 1970. General public awareness and interest were expressed extensively in a variety of public forums and in the mass media. Evolving public values could be observed in the growth of the outdoor recreation movement which reached back into the 1950's and the search for amenities in quieter and more natural settings, in the increasing number of people who engaged in hiking and camping or purchased recreational lands and homes on the seashore, by lakes and in woodlands.

24

This is not to say that the entire scope of environmental concerns emerged
fully in the 1960's. It did not. But one can observe a gradual evolution
rather than a sudden outburst at the turn of the decade, a cumulative
social and political change that came to be expressed vigorously even long
before Earth Day.[38]

We might identify three distinct stages of evolution. Each stage
brought a new set of issues to the fore without eliminating the previous
ones, in a set of historical layers. Old issues persisted to be joined
by new ones, creating over the years an increasingly complex and varied
world of environmental controversy and debate. The initial complex of
issues which arrived on the scene of national politics emphasized natural
environment values in such matters as outdoor recreation, wildlands and
open space. These shaped debate between 1957 and 1965 and constituted the
initial thrust of environmental action. After World War II the American
people, with increased income and leisure time, sought out the nation's
forests and parks, its wildlife refuges, its state and federal public
lands, for recreation and enjoyment. Recognition of this growing
interest and the demands upon public policy which it generated, led
Congress in 1958 to establish the National Outdoor Recreation Review
Commission which completed its report in 1962.[39] Its recommendations
heavily influenced public policy during the Johnson administration, leading directly to the Land and Water Conservation Fund of 1964 which established, for the first time, a continuous source of revenue for acquisition
of state and federal outdoor recreation lands. It accelerated the drive
for the National Wilderness Act of 1964 and the Wild and Scenic Rivers and
National Trails Acts of 1968.

These laws reflected in only a limited way a much more widespread
interest in natural environment affairs which affected local, state and
federal policy. During the 1950's many in urban areas had developed a
concern for urban overdevelopment and the need for open space in their
communities. This usually did not receive national recognition because
it took place on a more local level. But demands for national assistance
for acquisition of urban open space led to legislation in 1960 which provided federal funds. The concern for open space extended to regional as
well as community projects, involving a host of natural environment areas
ranging from pine barrens to wetlands to swamps to creeks and streams to
remnants of the original prairies. Throughout the 1960's there were
attempts to add to the national park system which gave rise to new parks
such as Canyonlands in Utah, new national lakeshores and seashores and
new national recreation areas.

These matters set the dominant tone of the initial phase of environmental concern until the mid-1960's. They did not decline in importance,
but continued to shape administrative and legislative action as specific
proposals for wilderness, scenic rivers or other natural areas emerged
to be hotly debated. Such general measures as the Eastern Wilderness
Act of 1974, the Federal Land Planning and Management Act of 1976 and
the Alaska National Interest Lands Act of 1980 testified to the perennial
public concern for natural environment areas. So also did the persistent
evolution of indigenous western wilderness groups in almost every state
and the formation of a western umbrella organization, the Wilderness
Alliance, headquartered in Denver, in 1978.[40] One might argue that these
were the most enduring and fundamental environmental issues throughout
the two decades. While other citizen concerns might ebb and flow, interest in natural environment areas persisted steadily. That interest was
the dominant reason for membership growth in the largest environmental
organizations. The Nature Conservancy, a private group which emphasized
acquisition of natural environment lands, grew in activity in the latter

25

years of the 1970's and reached 100,000 members in 1981; this only
further emphasized the persistent and enduring public concern for natural environment areas as an integral and important element of American
life.[41]

Amid this initial stage of environmental politics there evolved a
new and different concern for the adverse impact of industrial development with a special focus on air and water pollution. This had long
evolved slowly on a local and piecemeal basis, but emerged with national
force only in the mid-1960's. In the early part of the decade air and
water pollution began to take on significance as national issues and by
1965 they had become highly visible. The first national public opinion
poll on such questions was taken in that year, and the President's annual
message in 1965 reflected, for the first time, a full fledged concern for
pollution problems. Throughout the rest of the decade and on into the
1970's these issues evolved continually. Federal legislation to stimulate remedial action was shaped over the course of these seven years,
from 1965 to 1972, a distinct period which constituted the second phase
in the evolution of environmental politics, taking its place alongside
the previously developing concern for natural environment areas.

The legislative results were manifold. Air pollution was the subject of new laws in 1967 and 1970; water pollution in 1965, 1970 and
1972.[42] The evolving concern about pesticides led to revision of the
existing law in the Pesticides Act of 1972.[43] The growing public interest in natural environment values in the coastal zone, and threats to
them by dredging and filling, industrial siting and offshore oil development first made its mark on Congress in 1965 and over the next few years
shaped the course of legislation which finally emerged in the Coastal
Zone Management Act of 1972. Earth Day in the spring of 1970 lay in the
middle of this phase of historical development, both a result of the previous half-decade of activity and concern and a new influence to accelerate action. The outline of these various phases of environmental activity,
however, can be observed only by evidence and actions far beyond the
events of Earth Day. Such more broad-based evidence identifies the years
1965 to 1972 as a well-defined phase of historical development in terms
of issues, emphasizing the reaction against the adverse effects of industrial growth as distinct from the earlier emergence of natural environment issues.

Yet this new phase was shaped heavily by the previous period in that
it gave primary emphasis to the harmful impact of pollution on ecological
systems rather than on human health - a concern which was to come later.
26   In the years between 1965 and 1972 the interest in "ecology" came to the
fore to indicate the intense public interest in potential harm to the
natural environment and in protection against disruptive threats. The

impacts of highway construction, electric power plants and industrial
siting on wildlife, on aquatic ecosystems and on natural environments in

156

general played a major role in the evolution of this concern. One of the
key elements of evolving public policy was the enhanced role of the U.S.
Fish and Wildlife Service in modifying decisions by developmental agencies
to reduce their harmful actions.[44] The effects of pesticides were thought
of then in terms of their impact on wildlife and ecological food chains,
rather than on human health. The major concern for the adverse effect of
nuclear energy generation in the late 1960's involved its potential disruption of aquatic ecosystems from thermal pollution rather than the effect
of radiation on people. The rapidly growing ecological concern was an
extension of the natural environment interests of the years 1957 to 1965
into the problem of the adverse impacts of industrial growth.[45, 46, 47]

     Beginning in the early 1970's still a third phase of environmental
politics arose which brought three other sets of issues into public debate: toxic chemicals, energy and the possibilities of social, economic
and political decentralization. These did not obliterate earlier issues,
but as some natural environment matters and concern over the adverse
effects of industrialization shifted from legislative to administrative
politics, and thus became less visible to the general public, these new
issues emerged often to dominate the scene. They were influenced heavily
by the seemingly endless series of toxic chemical episodes, from PBB's
in Michigan to kepone in Virginia to PCB's on the Hudson River, to the
discovery of abandoned chemical dumps at Love Canal and near Louisville,
Kentucky.[48] These events, however, were only the more sensational aspects of a more deep-seated new twist in public concern for human
health.[49] Interest in personal health and especially in preventive
health action took a major leap forward in the 1970's. It seemed to
focus especially on such matters as cancer and environmental pollutants
responsible for a variety of health problems, on food and diet on the one
hand and exercise on the other. From these interests arose a central concern for toxic threats in the workplace, in the air and water, and in
food and personal habits that came to shape some of the overriding issues
of the 1970's on the environmental front. It shifted the earlier emphasis
on the ecological effects of toxic pollutants to one more on human health
effects. Thus, while proceedings against DDT in the late 1960's had
emphasized adverse ecological impacts, similar proceedings in the 1970's
focused primarily on human health.

     The energy crisis of the winter of 1973-74 brought a new issue to   27
the fore. Not that energy matters had gone unnoticed earlier, but their
salience had been far more limited. After that winter they became more
central. They shaped environmental politics in at least two ways. First,
energy problems brought material shortages more forcefully into the
realm of substantive environmental concerns and emphasized more strongly
the problem of limits which these shortages imposed upon material
growth.[50] The physical shortages of energy sources such as oil in the
United States, the impact of shortages on rising prices, the continued
emphasis on the need for energy conservation all helped to etch into the
experience and thinking of Americans the "limits" to which human appetite
for consumption could go. Second, the intense demand for development of
new energy sources increased significantly the political influence of developmental advocates in governmental, corporate and technical institutions which had long chafed under both natural environment and pollution
control programs. This greatly overweighted the balance of political
forces so that environmental leaders had far greater difficulty in being
heard. In the face of energy issues environmental leaders formulated

their own energy proposals which they sought to inject into the debates, but not yet with overriding success amid an overwhelming emphasis on traditional approaches to increasing energy supply.

Lifestyle issues also injected a new dimension into environmental affairs during the course of the 1970's.[51] They became especially visible in the energy debates, as the contrast emerged between highly centralized technologies on the one hand, and decentralized systems on the other. Behind these debates lay the evolution of new ideas about organizing one's daily life, one's home, community and leisure activities and even work - all of which had grown out of the changing lifestyles of younger Americans. It placed considerable emphasis on more personal, family and community autonomy in the face of the forces of larger social, economic and political organization. The impact and role of this change was not always clear, but it emerged forcefully in the energy debate as decentralized solar systems and conservation seemed to be appropriate to decisions made personally and locally - on a more human scale - contrasting markedly with high-technology systems which leaders of technical, corporate and governmental institutions seemed to prefer. Issues pertaining to the centralization of political control played an increasing role in environmental politics as the 1970's came to a close.

To define stages in the evolution of environmental affairs in this manner helps to interweave those affairs with broader patterns of social change. One should be wary, perhaps, of the temptation to argue that by 1980 a "full-scale" set of environmental issues had emerged, bit by bit, to form a coherent whole. For there were many different strands which at times went off in different directions. Those whose environmental experience was confined to the urban context did not always share the perspective and interest in issues of those who were preoccupied with the wildlands. Yet it was rather striking the degree to which working relationships had developed amid the varied strands.[52] What was especially noticeable was the degree to which the challenge posed by the Reagan administration tended to mobilize latent values and strengthen cooperative tendencies.[53] From the beginning of that administration, the new governmental leaders made clear their conviction that the "environmental movement" had spent itself, was no longer viable, and could readily be dismissed and ignored. During the campaign the Reagan entourage had refused often to meet with citizen environmental groups, and in late November it made clear that it would not even accept the views of its own "transition team" which was made up of former Republican administration environmentalists who were thought to be far too extreme.[54] Hence environmentalists of all these varied hues faced a hostile government that was not prone to be evasive or deceptive about that hostility. Its anti-environmental views were expressed with enormous vigor and clarity.

28

We can well look upon that challenge as an historical experiment which tested the extent and permanence of the changes in social values which lay at the root of environmental interest. By its opposition the Reagan administration could be thought of as challenging citizen environmental activity to prove itself. And the response, in turn, indicated a degree of depth and persistence which makes clear that environmental affairs stem from the extensive and deep-seated changes we have been describing. Most striking perhaps have been the public opinion polls during 1981 pertaining to revision of the Clean Air Act. On two occasions, in April and in September the Harris poll found that some 80% of the American people favor at least maintaining that Act or making it stricter, levels of positive environmental opinion on air quality higher than for polls in the 1960's or 1970's.[55] One can also cite the rapid increases in membership which have occurred in many environmental organizations, most notably the Sierra Club, as well as financial contributions to them.[56] And the initial forays into electoral politics which environmentalists have recently undertaken seems to have tapped activist predispositions mobilized by the fear of the new administration.[57]

We might take this response to the Reagan administration challenge, therefore, as evidence of the degree to which we can assess the environmental activities of the past three decades as associated with fundamental and persistent change, not a temporary display of sentiment, which causes environmental values to be injected into public affairs continuously and even more vigorously in the face of political adversity. The most striking aspect of this for the historian lies in the way in which it identifies more sharply the social roots of environmental values, perception and action. Something is there, in a broad segment of the American people which shapes the course of public policy in these decades after World War II that was far different from the case earlier. One observes not rise and fall, but persistent evolution, changes rooted in personal circumstance which added up to broad social changes out of which "movements" and political action arise and are sustained.[58] Environmental affairs take on meaning as integral parts of a "new society" that is an integral element of the advanced consumer and industrial order of the last half of the 20th century.

The Environmental Economy and Environmental Ideology

There remain two larger modes of analysis which help to define the historical role of environmental affairs - one economic and the other ideological. In neither case can one associate environmental politics with either the pre-World War II economy or its ideology. In both cases we must look to innovations rooted in post-War changes.[59]

Environmental impulses served as a major influence in shaping the newer, more "modern," economy. They brought to the fore new demand factors which in turn generated new types of production to fill them; they placed increasing pressure on greater technological efficiency in production to reduce harmful residuals and resource waste. In many aspects of the economy one can distinguish between older and newer forms of demand and supply, institutions and modes of economic analysis. The transition represents a shift from the older manufacturing to the newer advanced consumer economy. In this transition environmental influences were an integral part of the emerging economy that was struggling for a larger role in America amid more established economic institutions. From this context of analysis we can establish further elements of the role of environmental affairs in long-run social change.

29

In public debate there was a tendency to set off the "economy" versus the "environment" as if the latter constituted a restraint on the former.[60] But environmental affairs were a part of the economy, that part which constituted new types of consumer demand, giving rise in turn to new modes of production to supply that demand, some in the private market and some in the public. The ensuing controversies were between older and newer types of demand, and the allocation of resources as between older and newer types of production as patterns of demand changed. It was difficult for the older manufacturing economy, with its emphasis on consumer necessities and conveniences and physical commodities to fill them, to accept the legitimacy of the newer economy which gave rise to newer consumer needs and types of production.[61] The tension between old and new was reminiscent of the similar tension in the 19th century between the older agricultural and the newer manufacturing economies.

Much of the American economy had moved beyond necessities and conveniences to encompass amenities. It is difficult to identify this change if one begins the analysis with the traditional focus on modes of production; it is more easily identified if one starts with changing patterns of consumption. The former approach lumps together many and varied changes as one "service economy," that beyond raw material extraction and manufacturing. The latter identifies varied new sectors associated with consumption such as the "recreation economy," the "leisure economy," "the health economy," the "creative arts economy," and the "environmental economy" each of which identifies a new direction of economic change. Much of this involves discretionary income, the allocation of expenditures not just to amenities but also to reshaped and restyled necessities and conveniences themselves to make them aesthetically more appealing, to add to them elements other than traditional characteristics of "utility."

The most serious question of resource allocation raised by the environmental economy lay in the appropriate balance which should be struck between natural and developed environments. The new environmental consumer society called for more of the former. This gave rise to massive debates over such issues as wilderness and other natural environment proposals. It was difficult, if not impossible, for those associated with the older developmental economy to accept the notion that natural environments should play a major role in modern economic affairs. Hence they tended to argue that in this matter a proper "balance" should involve only minimal allocation of air, land and water to natural environments. Often they maintained that such allocations should end. They might approve some role for natural environments in the modern economy but only if they were on sites which developers themselves did not want.[62] Hence, mining companies argued that wherever minerals were to be found they should be developed irrespective of their implication for the degradation of natural environments.

The environmental impulse also had major implications for the technology of production, serving as a force toward more rapid modernization of plant and equipment.[63] In any given segment of industry plants constituted a variable spectrum ranging from the most obsolete to the most modern. In the normal course of private market choices the more obsolete were discarded and the more modern added, giving rise to a general tendency for the entire industry toward modernization. But environmentalists felt that the pace of change was too slow. They were especially interested in the environmental efficiency of production, the degree to which it reduced the output of residuals per factor input; they believed that plants which were more obsolete in material product output were also more obsolete in environmental output. Hence they urged that the most modern plants, the "average of the best," should serve as examples against which the rest of the industry should be judged. In focusing on these "best technologies" as models for achievement by all, environmentalists served as a force for technological innovation.[64]

It was often difficult, however, for industry to move at the pace which environmentalists desired. Many corporate leaders were from sales and marketing origins, rather than engineering and production, and tended not to press continually for cost-reducing technologies but to maintain cost-increasing ones so long as they were profitable.[65] At the same time the corporate response to regulatory requirements often led to superficial changes to reduce the immediate burden of governmental decisions, such as legal action or limited "add on" pollution control technology, rather than to re-examine production technologies in order to seek combined efficiencies in both product and environmental output.[66] Those who took a leading role in that direction, such as Joseph Ling of the 3-M corporation were often thought of as "eccentrics," by their fellow executives. The internal politics of trade associations which spoke for business in the larger political scene often required that their public positions not be too "advanced," since their members included both the more obsolete and the more modern firms; in water pollution control, for example, they argued, that the median firm rather than the most efficient ten percent should serve as the model for the rest of the industry to follow. Corporate leaders often argued that regulation was a roadblock to greater production efficiencies, but when such a proposition was subject to empirical examination it was found, on the contrary, that if regulation was sufficiently firm it gave rise to more serious examination of manufacturing processes and resulted in innovation.

We might also profitably identify the environmental impulse more precisely in terms of its ideological component. What is the place of environmental ideas amid the political ideologies inherited from the recent past? These customarily divide political forces between the "liberal" and the "conservative." The corporate business community and critics of growth in government are thought of as "conservatives," while more subordinate sectors of society who look to government to aid them are thought of as "liberal." While these ideological patterns have roots deeper in history than the 1930's, they were given a new twist during the New Deal when controversies over public spending for social programs such as welfare and social security were added to those of earlier vintage which involved disputes among business, labor and agriculture over the distribution of the fruits of production.

Environmental issues and environmental ideas are difficult to classify in this way. If one raised the question as to whether or not environmentalists favored public or private enterprise in principle, one would have to observe that while they called for greater governmental initiatives in behalf of their objectives such as in public land management or environmental controls on private production, they were as skeptical of public as they were of private enterprise. The Tennessee Valley Authority, the major example of public ownership of the means of industrial production in recent times was roundly condemned when its actions with respect to air pollution, dam building and coal and uranium mining were environmentally detrimental and was applauded when it took up innovative energy measures during the Carter administration.[67] Was it associated with ideological traditions sustained by the politics of the industrial working class? Certainly not with socialist ideologies and with more reformist movements only partially. For while worker movements grew out of the struggle among producers for varied shares of the profits of production, environmental values were associated more with consumption which tended to draw lines of demarcation between environmentalists and producers as a whole. Only when it came to environmental health, which brought occupational and community health concerns together, did workers and environmentalists find common ground.[68]

Environmental values and ideas tended not to fit into traditional political ideologies, but to cut across them.[69] They tended to define corporate leaders as radicals, as responsible for massive, rapid and deep-seated transformations in modern society that threatened to destroy prized natural environments, that uprooted stable ways of life, and generated pervasive and persistent chemical threats. Corporate leaders were ever demanding that people change their lives markedly in order to accommodate developmental objectives, and to accept the risks of their proposals for rapid and far-reaching change. In response to these demands, environmentalists sought to slow up the pace of innovation, to restrain it. Hence they were conservative. It would not be accurate to describe them

31

as one industry leader did as "stone-age neanderthals," for environmentalists shared, with approval, the material benefits of modern production. But they were willing to argue that the pace of change in America in the 1960's and 1970's was far too rapid and should be slowed down so as not to destroy values important to a society of modern patterns of life.[70]

They were also often fiscal conservatives when the use of public funds was an important instrument of material development and engaged in many a political struggle to cut back public spending. The 1960's and 1970's were decades of rapid economic "growth" in which jobs and product increased dramatically and public programs with public funding played a major role in it: construction of dams and highways, rebuilding on flood plains after floods, channelization of streams and rivers, development of barrier islands, a host of "rural development" programs which had become extended from the "depressed" area of the Appalachians to the entire nation.[71] All these tended to encourage more rapid economic development. The most widely known cases of environmental action on this score pertained to funds for construction of public works in rivers and harbors under the auspices of the U.S. Army Corps of Engineers.[72] It was no wonder that in fashioning coalitions to scale back such expenditures environmentalists joined with the National Taxpayers Union and other "fiscal conservatives" in Congress who tended to give ideological support to reduced public spending.

At the same time, in social values environmentalists could be thought of as innovative rather than conservative. Their views about natural environments and human health were associated with newer rather than older ideas about human wants and needs; they had a larger association with other innovations in values such as the more autonomous role of women, more cosmopolitan rather than traditional ways of life, and "freer" ways of thinking that were associated with social modernization. Such value changes had taken place at a number of times in the nation's past and these historians understand by sorting out newer values from older, distinguishing those people who espoused the newer with enthusiasm from those who drew back in defense and fear against cultural change. In the mid-19th century, for example, the Republican party had been associated with innovations in cultural values and the Democratic party with a defense of older ones. But in the mid-20th century, the party roles were reversed, as the Democrats seemed to harbor cultural innovation and the Republicans spoke out in defense of older values. These patterns of cultural change tended to define what was "conservative" and what was "liberal" in terms different from the issues of economic controversy. And so it was with environmental values in which environmentalists both expressed the defense of daily life from technological radicalism and espoused innovations in cultural values.[73]

Within the context of these more "modern" and more innovative values, however, there was in environmental affairs a deeply conservative streak in a different sense that went far beyond the role of corporations and their defense to the larger ideology of conservatism - a search for wider human meaning. Environmentalists tended to work out their values amid a "sense of place" that provided roots to life's meaning much in the same way as "local" community values long had displayed. It was their involvement with the natural environments of given places that had engaged emotions and minds. It was the threat to that "place" of home, work and play from large-scale developments, from air and water pollution, and from toxic chemical contamination which aroused them to action. Environmentalists sought roots in the less developed and more natural world, and rapid change threatened those roots with impairment and destruction. Insofar as one could describe conservatism as more generally a search for roots, for stability and order amid the larger world of rapid change, then environmentalists shared that impulse.[74]

Summary

This article has constituted an attempt to place the environmental affairs of the past three decades in the perspective of historical evolution. I have sought not just to search for antecedants which would serve to link the more recent and the more remote pasts through some similarity of human activity. Instead I have sought to determine the degree to which a relatively full range of characteristics of environmental affairs, from values to political controversy to economic change and political ideology constitute merely an elaboration of earlier tendencies or something that was relatively new, a departure from the past. I have argued that these cannot be understood adequately unless they are associated with the newer society, the newer economy and the newer politics of the decades after World War II. Moreover, they can be understood only as an evolving phenomenon within those post-War decades, amid the patterns of change in the advanced consumer society as it steadily took shape. American society today is far different than it was in the 1930's. It can best be understood not as an implication of the New Deal years, but as a product of vast social and economic transformations which took place after World War II which brought many new values and impulses to the American political scene. And so it is with environmental affairs. While displaying some roots in earlier times they were shaped primarily by the rapidly changing society which came into being after the War which, in so many ways, constitutes a watershed in American history.

ENDNOTES

[1]For this theme see Samuel P. Hays, *Conservation and the Gospel of Efficiency* (Cambridge, 1958).

[2]A somewhat larger ecological context for analysis of the soil conservation movement is Donald Worster, *Nature's Economy* (San Francisco, 1977), pp. 189-253.

[3]For the Taylor Grazing Act and its implementation see Phillip O. Foss, *Politics and Grass; The Administration of Grazing on the Public Domain* (Seattle, 1960); Marian Clawson, *The Bureau of Land Management* (New York, 1971); William Voigt, Jr., *Public Grazing Lands: Use and Misuse by Industry and Government* (New Brunswick, N.J., 1976).

[4]See, especially, James B. Trefethen, *An American Crusade for Wildlife* (New York, 1975), esp. pp. 243-255.

[5]The University of Michigan School of Forestry, for example, became the School of Natural Resources when Sanuel Dana succeeded Filibert Roth, a protege of Gifford Pinchot, as Dean. One of Dana's major innovations was to bring wildlife more fully into the curriculum. Interview with Carl Holcomb, student at the School in the early 1930's and editor of its student magazine, *Michigan Forests*, in 1934.

[6]*Forests and Waters* was one of the titles of the magazine published by the American Forestry Association (now *American Forests*) in the early 20th century. It was also the name of the administering agency for

33

Pennsylvania resources, the Department of Forests and Waters until 1970 when it was changed to the Department of Environmental Resources.

[7]The National Parks Association added this new title to its publication in 1970. At the same time it revised its own name from National Parks Association to National Parks and Conservation Association.

[8]A brief statement of this competition between the Park Service and the Forest Service, and a detailed analysis of the Olympic case is Ben W. Twight, "The Tenacity of Value Commitment: The Forest Service and the Olympic National Park," PhD thesis, University of Washington, Seattle, 1971.

[9]See, for example, Ralph Borsodi, *Flight from the City: An Experiment in Creative Living on the Land* (New York and London, 1933), and a publication, edited by Mildred Loomis, which grew out of Borsodi's inspiration, *The Green Revolution*, 1962- , published in the 1960's at the School of Living, Freeland, Maryland.

[10]For a brief description of this social context see Samuel P. Hays, "The Structure of Environmental Politics Since World War II," in *Journal of Social History*, 14-4 (Summer, 1981), 719-738.

[11]See William Ashworth, Hells Canyon, *The Deepest Gorge on Earth* (New York, 1977); interview with Brock Evans (May 1980) who at the time of the Hells Canyon decision was Pacific Northwest representative of the Sierra Club.

[12]These developments are worked out more fully in Samuel P. Hays, "The Role of Forests in American History," paper presented at a conference on the Future of the American Forests, sponsored by the Conservation Foundation, Seattle, Washington, April 1979. See also Hays, "Gifford Pinchot and the American Conservation Movement," in Carroll W. Purcell, Jr., ed., *Technology in America; A History of Individuals and Ideas* (Cambridge, 1981), 151-162.

[13]This analysis of the relationship between the U.S. Forest Service and the wilderness movement is drawn from a variety of sources, including Twight (fn. 8); James Gilligan, "The Development of Policy and Administration of Forest Service Primitive and Wilderness Areas in the Western United States" (2v), PhD thesis, University of Michigan, 1953; articles in *The Living Wilderness* and the *Sierra Bulletin* from the mid-1930's onward; accounts of wilderness politics in state publications such as "Wild Oregon," "Wild Washington," "The Wilderness Record" (California); and the Sierra Club *National News Report*.

[14]For accounts of these divergent views see articles in *Forest Planning*, Forest Planning Clearinghouse, Eugene, Oregon, which began publication in April 1980.

[15]For a continuing treatment of issues arising from this program see the annual *Proceedings* of the National Watershed Congress, first held in 1953 and annually thereafter.

[16]The issues in stream channelization can be followed in Committee on Government Operations, U.S. House of Representatives, *Stream Channelization* (4 parts), 92nd Congress, 1st Session (Washington, D.C., 1971).

[17]For a survey of non-game wildlife issues, see Wildlife Management Institute, "Current Investments, Projected Needs & Potential New Sources

34

of Income for Nongame Fish & Wildlife Programs in the United States,"
(Washington, D.C., 1975).

[18]Wildlife Management Institute, "The North American Wildlife Policy,
1973," which includes a copy of the "American Game Policy, 1930."
(Washington, D.C., nd).

[19]For two recent compilations of value changes over the past several
decades see Joseph Veroff, Elizabeth Douvan and Richard A. Kulka, *The
Inner American: A Self-Portrait From 1957 to 1976* (New York, 1981);
Daniel Yankelovich, *New Rules: Searching for Self-Fulfillment in a World
Turned Upside Down* (New York, 1981).

[20]See Arnold Mitchell, "Social Change: Implications of Trends in
Values and Lifestyles," VALS Report No. 3, Stanford Research International,
Menlo Park, 1979; and John Naisbitt, "The New Economic and Political
Order of the 1980's," speech given to The Foresight Group, Stockholm
Sweden, Apr. 17, 1980, available from the Center for Policy Process, Wash-
ington D.C. For periodic coverage of work on value changes consult
Leading Edge Bulletin: Frontiers of Social Transformation, published by
Interface Press, Los Angeles, Calif.

[21]See, for example, Mary Keys Watson, "Behavioral and Environmental
Aspects of Recreational Land Sales," PhD thesis, Department of Geography,
Pennsylvania State University, 1975.

[22]A considerable number of public opinion polls by the Gallup, Harris
and Roper organizations indicate the range of expression of environmental
values. There are also numerous polls on specialized environmental subjects which reflect environmental values. Among them are: Stephen R.
Kellert, "American attitudes, knowledge and behaviors toward wildlife and
natural habitats," study funded by the U.S. Fish and Wildlife Service, of
which three of four phases were completed as of the end of 1980. The
titles of each of phases I, II and III were: "Public Attitudes Toward
Critical Wildlife and Natural Habitat Issues," "Activity of the American
Public Relating to Animals," and "Knowledge, Affection and Basic Attitudes
Toward Animals in American Society." See also The Gallup Organization,
"National Opinions Concerning the California Desert Conservation Area,"
study conducted for the Bureau of Land Management (Princeton, 1978); and
Opinion Research Corporation, "The Public's Participation in Outdoor
Activities and Attitudes Toward National Wilderness Areas," prepared for
the American Forest Institute (Princeton, 1977).

[23]This sectional analysis is derived from tabulation of environmental
votes in the U.S. House of Representatives, 1970-77, originally prepared
by the League of Conservation Voters, Washington, D.C. for each congressional session.

[24]One type of evidence which reflects these growing interests is the
"field guide," which grew rapidly in extent and circulation in the 1960's
and 1970's. The most traditional format was that represented by the
Peterson guide series which identified birds, plants and animals. But
there were an increasing number of hiking guides which included considerable information about the natural environment through which one hiked.
Often each new site around which public natural environment interest arose
led to a guide which enabled people to "find their way" and to appreciate
what they saw. In 1980 the Sierra Club began to publish a new series of
regional "naturalist guides" which provided similar assistance to seeking
out a wide range of natural environmental areas.

35

[25]One of the major expressions of this interest was nature photography. This cannot be pinned down quantitatively, but not wholly irrelevant was the rise in photography as a whole in American society. The 1980 edition of the survey of American participation in the arts indicated that the number of Americans engaged in photographic pursuits rose from 19% in 1975 to 44% in 1980. Westerners tended to be more active (56% participation in 1980) than those in other parts of the country. See American Council for the Arts, *Americans and the Arts* (New York, 1981), p.37.

[26]Two documents which reflect this emphasis at a governmental level are U.S. Senate, Select Committee on Nutrition and Human Needs, *Dietary Goals for the United States* (Washington, GPO, 1977); and U.S. Department of Health Education and Welfare, Public Health Service, *Healthy People; the Surgeon General's Report on Health Promotion and Disease Prevention* (Washington, GPO, 1979). See also, as a representative more popular statement, *Environmental Science and Technology*, Apr. 1970, 275-277, interview with Dr. Paul Kotin, director, National Institute for Environmental Health Sciences, including the statement, "Now people are interested not merely in not being very sick but in being very well."

[27]The economic role of the health food industry can be followed in its trade publication, *Whole Foods*, published in Santa Ana, California, beginning in January 1978. For data on the level of business see "First Annual Report on the Industry," in *Whole Foods: Natural Food Guide* (And/Or Press, Berkeley, California, 1979), 268-274.

[28]In late 1981 a new magazine, *American Health*, was announced, subtitled "Fitness of Body and Mind." The initial direct-mail test to establish the existence of potential readers brought a 7.2% response when 5% is considered to be very good. The initial subscription offer will go to readers of a variety of publications, such as *Runners' World, Psychology Today* and other science, health, class, food and self-help magazines, which, taken as a whole, reflect the varied dimensions of the value changes associated with new attitudes toward health. New York Times, Nov. 23, 1981.

[29]Some of these issues have now become "classic," the subject of book-length writing. See, for example, Allan R. Talbot, *Power Along the Hudson; The Storm King Case and the Birth of Environmentalism* (New York, 1972); Barry M. Casper and Paul David Wellstone, *Powerline; The First Battle of America's Energy War* (Amherst, Mass., 1981); Joyce Egginton, *The Poisoning of Michigan* (New York, 1980); Paul Brodeur, *Expendable Americans* (New York, 1973).

36

[30]For an analysis in this vein see William E. Shands and Robert G. Healy, *The Lands Nobody Wanted* (The Conservation Foundation, Washington, D.C., 1977).

[31]A classic expression of the environmental view in this debate is Amory B. Lovins, *Soft Energy Paths; Toward a Durable Peace* (Cambridge, Mass., 1977). An analysis of the values implicit in these contrasting positions is included in Avarham Shama and Ken Jacobs, *Social Values and Solar Energy Policy; The Policy Makers and the Advocates*, Solar Energy Research Institute, Oct. 1979, SERI-RR-51-329.

[32]See, for example, Susan Jay Kleinberg, "Technology's Step-Daughters; the Impact of Industrialization Upon Working Class Women, Pittsburgh, 1865-1890." University of Pittsburgh, PhD thesis, 1973.

[33]The most celebrated book in this debate was Donella H. Meadows and

Dennis L. Meadows, *The Limits to Growth* (New York, 1972). See also a reply by H. S. D. Cole, et al (eds), *Models of Doom; A Critique of the Limits to Growth* (New York, 1973). For one important item in the energy debate see Robert Stobaugh and Daniel Yergen, *Energy Futures* (New York, 1979).

[34]See Roger W. Sant, et al, *Eight Great Energy Myths; the Least-Cost Energy Strategy - 1978-2000*, Energy Productivity Report No. 4, The Energy Productivity Center, Mellon Institute, Arlington, Va., 1981.

[35]See items in fn 29; see also Hays, "The Structure of Environmental Politics Since World War II," fn 10.

[36]See, for example, Craig R. Humphrey and Frederick R. Buttel, *Environment, Energy and Society* (Belmont, Calif., 1982), which describes Rachel Carson as an "important catalyst for the environmental movement" and the Santa Barbara oil spill as a "pivotal event." (pp. 7 and 122). This book, the most comprehensive account yet from the perspective of "environmental sociology" gives heavy emphasis to the campus student movement of 1969-1970 as the source of environmental concern.

[37]The Sierra Club, for example, grew from 7000 in 1952 to 70,000 in 1969, and the Wilderness Society from 12,000 in 1960 to 54,063 in 1970.

[38]The relative significance of widely-shared social and economic changes on the one hand, and dramatic events on the other is a major set of alternatives in many historical analyses. The environmental scene is an especially striking case of the way in which preoccupation with the more publicized events has obscured the more fundamental changes.

[39]For hearings leading up to the appointment of the NORRRC see United States Senate, Committee on Interior and Insular Affairs, 85th Congress, 1st Session, Hearing, "Outdoor Recreation Resources Commission," May 15, 1957 (Washington, GPO, 1957). See accounts of the outdoor recreation situation, which reflect varied responses to it, in *American Forests*, Dec. 1960, pp. 58-59, and Nov. 1961, pp. 40-41 and 55-56; and in *Living Wilderness* in issues through 1959 to 1962, for example, Winter-Spring, 1962, pp. 3-9.

[40]For the American Wilderness Alliance see its publications, *Wild America* (1979-present) and "On the Wild Side" (1979-present). See also *Proceedings, 1980 Western Wilderness and Rivers Conference*, Denver, Colorado, Nov. 21-22, 1980, distributed and apparently published by the Alliance.

37

[41]The work of the Nature Conservancy can best be followed in its quarterly publication, *Nature Conservancy News* (Arlington, Va.), which began publication in 1951.

[42]For items on the air quality issue see John C. Esposito, *Vanishing Air* (New York, 1970) and Richard J. Tobin, *The Social Gamble* (Lexington, Mass., 1979). On water quality see David Zwick and Marcy Benstock, *Water Wasteland* (New York, 1971) and Harvey Lieber, *Federalism and Clean Waters* (Lexington, Mass., 1975).

[43]The pesticide controversy has produced several "tracts for the times", among them Frank Graham, Jr., *Since Silent Spring* (Boston 1970); Rita Gray Beatty, *The DDT Myth; Triumph of the Amateurs* (New York 1973); Georg Claus and Karen Bolander, *Ecological Sanity* (New York 1977); and Robert van den Bosch, *The Pesticide Conspiracy* (New York 1978).

[44]For the early stages of this issue see Committee on Merchant Marine and Fisheries, Subcommittee on Fisheries and Wildlife Conservation, 89th Congress, 2nd Session, Hearing, "Estuarine and Wetlands Legislation," June 16, 22-23, 1966. One can follow the issue as it developed leading up to the Coastal Zone Management Act of 1972. That Act was an important example of how a major environmental thrust, a proposal for a system of national estuarine areas to be managed by the National Park Service, much akin to the newly emerging concept of seashores and lakeshores, was almost completely turned back. It appeared in the 1972 Act in the very limited form of "estuarine research areas."

[45]One of the most significant backgrounds to the 1969 National Environmental Policy Act lay in the concern of the Fish and Wildlife Service about the failure of federal agencies to consider the impacts of development on fish and wildlife habitat, and especially their failure to "consult" with the agency under the Fish and Wildlife Coordination Act. One such issue was the dredge and fill practices of the U.S. Army Corps of Engineers who refused to consider "impacts" other than those on the maintenance of navigation channels. To rectify this problem, Rep. John Dingell of Michigan included in a proposed estuarine area act a section which would require the Fish and Wildlife Service to approve each permit granted by the Corps. See Committee on Merchant Marine and Fisheries, Subcommittee on Fisheries and Wildlife Conservation, 90th Congress, 1st Session, Hearing, "Estuarine Areas," (Washington, GOP, 1967); see especially testimony of Alfred B. Fitt, U.S. Army Corps of Engineers, pp. 119-207.

[46]One of the major thrusts leading up to NEPA took place in the Subcommittee on Fisheries and Wildlife under the leadership of Rep. Dingell. See its hearing, "Environmental Quality," 91st Congress, 1st Session, on HR 6750, a bill designed to amend the Fish and Wildlife Coordination Act (Washington, GOP, 1969).

[47]It should be emphasized that in its origins NEPA was an inter-agency review and not a public review process. It constituted a far more diluted response to the problem of inter-agency review than did the Dingell proposal for a "Veto" or "dual permit" procedure, since it gave agencies the authority only to comment and not to veto the actions of other agencies. Only under modifications by the Nixon administration and the courts did NEPA become an instrument of public review.

[48]Toxic chemical cases were numerous and have generated a considerable amount of writing. See, for example, Ralph Nader, Ronald Brownstein and John Richard, eds., *Who's Poisoning America; Corporate Polluters and Their Victims in the Chemical Age* (San Francisco, 1981); Michael H. Brown, *Laying Waste; the Poisoning of America by Toxic Chemicals* (New York, 1979)

[49]For some more recent events in these affairs see "Exposure," newsletter published by the Environmental Action Foundation (Washington, D.C.), Feb. 1980- ; and "The Waste Paper," published by the Sierra Club, Spring 1980- (Buffalo, New York).

[50]A brief, concise statement of environmental energy perspectives is in Gerald O. Barney, ed., *The Unfinished Agenda* (New York, 1977), pp. 50-68. The most eloquent speaker for the environmental energy view was Amory Lovins (fn. 31).

[51]A source which provides one of the most comprehensive views of this concern is the series of "whole earth" catalog publications. These include Stewart Brand (ed), *The Whole Earth Catalog* (Menlo Park, Calif., 1968); *The Last Whole Earth Catalog* (1971); *The Whole Earth Epilog* (1974),

38

and *The Next Whole Earth Catalog* (1980). The spirit of personal autonomy is expressed by a statement introducing the 1980 edition: "So far remotely done power and glory - as via government, big business, formal education, church - has succeeded to the point where gross defects obscure actual gains. In response to this dilemma and to these gains a realm of intimate, personal power is developing - the power of individuals to conduct their own education, find their own inspiration, shape their own environment, and share the adventure with whoever is interested. Tools that aid this process are sought and promoted by The Next Whole Earth Catalog." (p.2). See also *Mother Earth News*, (fn. 9) for a view of the range of facets in this perspective.

[52]On many and varied occasions there were expressions of cooperation and joint action. The most extensive occurred in 1981 when the Global Tomorrow Coalition was formed, by the end of the year comprising 53 environmental organizations, most of them formed during the environmental era. See its publication, *Interaction* (Washington, D.C.), the first issue of which appeared November/December 1981.

[53]See a varied set of newspaper clippings and articles, author file; also interviews with national leaders of the Sierra Club and the National Parks and Conservation Association concerning their varied efforts to maintain working liaison with Secretary of the Interior James Watt.

[54]See report, "Protecting the Environment: A Statement of Philosophy," drawn up by the 14-member Task Force on the Environment, co-chaired by Dan W. Lufkin and Henry L. Diamond; see also accounts of the Task Force, list of its members and a summary of its report in *Environment Reporter,* Oct. 17, 1980, p. 812, and Jan. 30, 1981, pp. 1855-1856. The Task Force report was rejected and its personnel replaced as lead administration advisers on environmental affairs by another group, quite divorced from earlier environmental activity, headed by Norman Livermore, a former administrator in California during the governorship of Ronald Reagan. See *Environment Reporter*, Jan. 12, 1980, p. 1226. For a brief account of this transition in advisers see *Wilderness Report*, Dec. 1980.

[55]See The Harris Survey, "Substantial Marjorities Indicate Support for Clean Air and Clean Water Acts," June 11, 1981, in the form of a news release.

[56]From Oct. 1, 1980 to Oct. 1, 1981 Sierra Club membership increased by 35%, and in October 1981 went over the 250,000 mark. Organizations less politically oriented grew in both membership and financial contributions, but less rapidly.

[57]See *Washington Post*, Nov. 15, 1981, Section L-1 for a brief account of the "green vote" in the 1981 elections; see also clippings (author file) from New Jersey newspapers concerning participation in electoral politics there during the summer primaries.

[58]This conclusion differs markedly from the views of environmental sociologists; see, for example, Humphrey and Buttel, *op. cit.*, 123-127, who speak of "rise and fall" rather than "persistent evolution" of environmental affairs. Their analysis seems to rest not on an examination of environmental values as social and political phenomena, but on their judgement as to the balance of political forces involved in a few selected "environmental problems."

[59]The following analysis is rarely made explicit in contemporary writings, but rests more on my own judgment about tendencies and implica-

39

tions inherent in environmental activity.

[60]A recent non-ideological analysis which assumes this approach is Jerry A. Kurtzweg and Christina Nelson Griffin, "Economic Development and Air Quality: Complementary Goals for Local Governments," in *Journal of the Air Pollution Control Association,* 31-11, Nov. 1981, pp. 1155-1162.

[61]Perhaps it is not coincidental that the environmental movement was distinctively weak, compared with regional levels of education and urbanization, in the old "factory belt" of the North - as measured by votes in the U.S. House of Representatives on environmental issues, and as concluded from an analysis of environmental affairs within those states.

[62]Hence, support from the corporate business community for "natural areas" programs, for example on the part of the Nature Conservancy, but opposition to wilderness which involved larger tracts of land on which conflicts with development were far more likely to occur.

[63]The close relationship between production efficiency and environmental efficiency is described in Michael G. Royston, *Pollution Prevention Pays* (Pergamon Press, New York, 1979).

[64]This setting for innovation was defined especially in the water quality program in which "technology standards" were adopted in the 1972 Clean Water Act and in which as a result the Environmental Protection Agency was required to analyze existing technologies to decide which was "the average of the best."

[65]For a view on one aspect of this problem see Hyman G. Rickover, "Getting the Job Done Right," *New York Times,* Nov. 25, 1981, op. ed. page.

[66]Nicholas A. Ashford and George R. Heaton, "The Effects of Health and Environmental Regulation on Technological Change in the Chemical Industry: Theory and Evidence," in Christopher T. Hill (ed), *Federal Regulation and Chemical Innovation* (American Chemical Society, Washington, D.C., 1979), 45-66.

[67]The classic case with respect to TVA was the controversy over the construction of Tellico Dam in the Little Tennessee River. But this was only one of many such issues. These can be followed in the monthly newsletter of the Tennessee Citizens for Wilderness Planning.

[68]The "OSHA/Environment Network" organized to defend both occupational and community environmental protection programs during the early years of the Reagan administration extended earlier more informal cooperation into a more formal organization. See author clipping file, and miscellaneous documents on activities of the Network during 1981 (author file).

[69]This is reflected in party and ideological analyses of environmental support. See "The public speaks again: A new environmental survey," *Resources,* Resources for the Future, Washington, D.C., No. 60, Sept.-Nov. 1978.

[70]This view seems to be implicit in a wide range of environmental issues, especially in the nation's countryside and wildlands.

[71]See the activities of the Environmental Policy Center, Washington, D.C., with respect to appropriations for the construction of dams; this was led throughout the 1970's by Brent Blackwelder of the Center. See

also "Alternative Budget Proposals for the Environment, Fiscal Years 1981 & 1982," drawn up by 9 national environmental organizations to suggest ways in which the Reagan administration could reduce federal expenditures.

41

ALLEN KAUFMAN
L. S. ZACHARIAS
ALFRED MARCUS

Managers United for Corporate Rivalry: A History of Managerial Collective Action

Students of American corporate political behavior have long asked whether or not the corporate sector acts collectively to influence the public policy process. Corporate concentration of wealth in the late nineteenth century first suggested particular business interests enjoyed a privileged political position.[1] After World War II American pluralists, while conceding that economic concentration posed a threat to democracy, noted that economic concentration could not be translated into political privilege without a high degree of corporate political unity.[2] In this respect, they reasoned that big business was unlikely to engage in collective action because of the divisive nature of economic competition. For a long while, this optimism about the market's policing powers assuaged most fears of corporate political domination, even though several scholars offered contrary evidence.[3] The recent corporate political mobilization, however, has renewed the debate on corporate political unity.[4]

Those debating corporate sector cohesion and fragmentation over the years have largely been responding to two sets of questions: The one is factual (Do corporate sector firms act collectively for political gain?), the other normative (Is corporate sector cohesion good or bad for American democracy?). Moreover, commentators reaching similar conclusions on the one set of questions frequently diverge on the others. A brief review of the literature illustrates the point.

Michael Useem, for instance, has suggested that corporate sector firms

We gratefully acknowledge the generous encouragement and expert advice of Edwin Epstein and William Becker. We are also indebted to Marvin Karson for the collegial role he has played in this and other research projects.

JOURNAL OF POLICY HISTORY, Vol. 2, No. 1, 1990.
Published by The Pennsylvania State University Press, University Park and London.

do act collectively and that their cohesion tends to undermine the democratic character of American politics. His argument depends on research
into the corporate sector's interorganizational network.[5] Although Useem
admits that no authoritative organization enforces coordination or collective action among firms in America's corporate sector, he insists that
recent trends in corporate concentration, diversification, intercorporate
ownership, and interlocking directorates have created an infrastructure
through which a unified corporate position can develop. In Useem's opinion, this "class-wide rationality" turns into political action through elite
business associations such as the Business Roundtable.

In contrast, Mancur Olson laments the lack of coordination among
American corporate sector firms, suggesting that their political fragmentation tends to undercut the possibility of a national industrial policy that is
sorely needed to shore up the American economy against its foreign rivals.[6]
Like Useem, Olson believes that particular interests may become general
when an encompassing organization has the authority to represent its members' interests in public policy debates. However, Olson does not agree with
Useem that the economic linkages among American corporations and the
weak business associations to which they belong are sufficient to weld a
general corporate will. He argues, further, that coordination will bolster
democracy by mitigating contentious, zero-sum, interest-group politics
that have so troubled modern democracies. In this respect, Olson joins a
growing number of political scientists who are questioning the efficacy of
conventional liberal pluralist democracy and who are recommending the
virtues of corporate collective action.[7]

The polarization of the normative debates is further underscored by the
conclusions of two earlier, highly influential writers on American pluralist
theory, E. E. Schattschneider and Charles Lindblom.[8] Schattschneider
and Lindblom agreed on a factual middle ground, namely, that "big business" coheres to a limited extent, but disagreed sharply on the overall
benefits of cohesion to American society. While Schattschneider claimed
that big business's privilege is the necessary means to keep big government
in check, Lindblom countered that, but for big business's control over
public policy, U.S. society would not be confronted today with so many
ultimately fatal problems (environmental destruction, energy shortages,
public health disasters) the government cannot appropriately address.

In this essay we offer an interpretive historical answer to *factual* questions
about American corporate political "solidarity." However, where others
have answered either yes or no to the question, Do corporate sector firms
act collectively on public policy? we argue that the answer is a consistent
yes *and* no. In what ways, then, does history provide insight into the

debate? We can note at the outset that social scientists have relied on the theory of collective action to understand why individuals coordinate their behavior. At the same time, the social scientific literature on collective action has itself acknowledged that the realization of potential patterns of collective behavior can be understood only in light of behavioral conventions that have developed over time.[9] Our aim is to describe the emergence and maintenance of conventions in U.S. business-government relations that have reinforced both political coordination and competition at a national level among corporate sector firms.

Social scientists have long relied on Mancur Olson's discussion of corporate collective action in reaching the conclusion that corporate political cohesion is highly unlikely.[10] In more recent years, however, Russell Hardin has pointed to a central flaw in Olson's logic, which, when corrected, suggests the usefulness of historical analysis.[11] Olson suggests that group behavior comprised of self-interested rationally maximizing actors is characterized by a paradox, namely, that individual rational maximizing behavior may result in a suboptimal provision of public goods.[12] Olson reasons that while citizens with a common political interest can be expected to organize to obtain that public good, the benefits from it will be shared by the group as a whole regardless of the contributions made by each member; consequently, the benefits to each member will decrease as the group's size increases. From this proposition, Olson concludes that collective action becomes less likely as group size increases because the rising cost/benefit ratio makes it rational for individual members to free-ride, that is, to defect from collective action while hoping that others will continue to cooperate. For these reasons, Olson doubts that the corporate sector as a whole can organize, even though small subgroups, for example, industry coalitions, may be politically effective.

Hardin begins his critique by noting that Olson's predictions rest on the assumption that public goods are not in "joint supply," that is, the benefits of the desired public good diminishes as the size of the group increases. However, Hardin reminds us that there are many public goods—in the case of the corporation, tax benefits or managerial authority—that may be shared without diminishing their benefit to group members. Thus an individual can expect full remuneration from actions taken to acquire a public good regardless of the group's size, and an attractive cost/benefit ratio will make it rational for individuals to act collectively even if others free-ride.

Although Hardin expects group action, particularly among large groups, when the desired public good is in joint supply, he admits to coordination problems. These arise because of the difficulties in negotiating a common strategy. Although each individual can collectively gain from collective action, the particular strategy employed will distribute these benefits differentially, breeding competition within the group. To sort out the preferences among interested parties and to assure adherence to a charted course of action, conventions arise, according to Hardin, that set expectations and penalties among the group's members. Thus, Hardin tells us that to understand a group's conventions one must understand its history.

Accordingly, in this article we draw on those business and public policy histories that have elaborated on the shared experiences of corporate sector firms in pursuing public goods in joint supply—that is, goods that promise benefits to the corporate sector as a whole, ranging from particular forms of corporate autonomy to particular arrangements for securing national economic prosperity. And we are singling out the managerial role in the firm, for that role has long drawn the focus of attention in the political theory and history of the modern corporation in America. For one, writers over the years have focused on the legitimacy of managerial autonomy as the central regulatory problem raised by the modern corporation.[13] In addition, writers have also noted that the common quest of large firm managers and federal political leaders for economic growth and stability on a national scale has led to mutually accommodating institutional arrangements and regulative structures.[14]

In sketching out the history our aim is to identify the shared values and group interests that have been at the heart of managerially directed corporate collective action.[15] It is useful to note that managers were competing for control with several distinct groups—the entrepreneurial families, bankers, workers, public administrators—and we can point to specific advantages that managers held in claiming authority. In part, management's victory came from their technical expertise in integrating mass production and distribution technologies and from the developed capital markets, which separated ownership from control and positioned managers to develop economic and political coalitions that furthered the corporate interest in conjunction with their personal interest.

And, in part, this victory came from management's ability to present its authority as a condition for constitutional rule. From the start, managers were aligned with the instrumental tradition of private property that dominated U.S. economic development, and they worked out the private systems of monitoring and accountancy that reinforced the values of privacy and market efficiency, even as the mass capital markets undermined familial control. As the overseers of America's largest firms, managers claimed to be mediators among private contracting groups—shareholders, creditors, employees and customers. When management succeeded in working out agreements with the firms' stakeholders privately, managers avoided regulation. When they were pushed into the political arena by their inability to reach agreement, as was the case in the 1930s and 1940s and again in the 1960s and 1970s, they sought to limit government intervention by structuring it in ways that preserved management's authority. A similar dynamic played itself out in management's efforts to find macroeconomic policy for reviving the troubled economy of the 1930s and for guiding it thereafter.

These interactions with government, and in particular the threat of intrusive regulation, forced managers to act collectively and fostered among them a constitutional language by which to present themselves both as stewards of America's productive resources and its democratic traditions. As the welfare state emerged, the private property rights of individuals no longer served to check the growth and abuse of public power as effectively as it had in the more classically liberal stages of national development. In this respect, then, corporate managers, through their extensive control of private resources, presented themselves as the central guardians of individual liberty in the liberal pluralist state. For if corporate managers could not cohere and resist appeals to the government over issues that went to the heart of constitutional regulation of the public and private spheres, it would be unlikely that any other private interest could successfully defend itself against the will of public officials.

At the same time, however, management noted that its collectivity rested on preserving management's authority over the firm's operations. Consequently, they could argue that managerial solidarity did not pose a threat to majoritarian rule. For in bonding together, managers sought to protect managerial autonomy and market competition, both of which perpetuated rivalries and hindered the development of coordinated action on a broad array of economic questions, such as tax reform, tariffs, and subsidies. For this reason, we conclude that corporate managers politically coalesce on matters that directly affect their authority, while they fragment over issues that differentially affect their firm's performance.

In describing this historically specific form of corporate collective action as a consistent yes and no, we are referring to a paradox in the political interests and activities of managers: Corporate managers will pursue economic policies collectively, but only insofar as those policies also preserve managerial autonomy and corporate rivalry.[16] Their very commitment to autonomy and "market" competition hinders the development of authoritative institutions and associations to coordinate political action or act on their behalf in the public policy arena. Nevertheless, as we shall see below, corporate sector firms did develop decentralized means for coordinating and expressing their collective interests; and so they were able to influence public policy and regulation in two areas of central concern to the managers of large firms—the conforming of managerial activities to stakeholder interests and social values in ways that would legitimate broad managerial discretion, and the institutionalization of policies that would stabilize competition and national economic growth.

Large-Scale Corporate Enterprise and Banker Control

In 1901, shortly after the formation of U.S. Steel as the nation's largest manufacturing concern, Chairman of the Board Elbert Gary warned J. P. Morgan, the financial creator of the new corporation, that the government would not allow so large an amalgamation to live, unless members of the board demonstrated to the public that their "intentions were good."[17] Quite in contrast to the financiers who ruled American industry near the turn of the century with attitudes that ranged from Commodore Vanderbilt's "the public be damned" to Morgan's simple insistence on "trust," Gary, an early prototype of the professional corporate sector manager, had a profound respect for public opinion and the government responses it could evoke.

While Gary himself identified the corporation with the interests of the investors, his recognition of a "public interest" in the operations of the firm gradually played itself out in subsequent generations of management. In reviewing the history of corporate sector political action up through the early years of the New Deal, we must ask how bankers and managers came to part ways with respect to the operations of the large firm and the proper role of government.

1. *Large Firms, Technology, and Consolidation.* Debates continue over the rise of the large, modern industrial corporation—the causes for its sudden growth and its relative advantages over more decentralized and socialized forms of business organization.[18] While some firms grew because they outperformed their competitors, adapting new technologies and achieving economies of scale, others grew out of the consolidations and financial reorganizations of firms worn down by competition, often on the brink of failure. In any case, the great American merger movement of 1897–1904, which absorbed as many as 1,800 entrepreneurial firms, deepened several tendencies in the development of American business; and these tendencies came to be reflected in the structure of business-government relations.[19]

The large vertically integrated firms that grew out of the merger movement and ultimately succeeded in competition did so, at least in part, by exploiting mass production and distribution technologies that ranged from railroads and industrial machinery to bureaucratic methods of organization and cost accounting.[20] These firms also provided outlets for the investment of capital funds centralized in New York, Boston, and Philadelphia banking syndicates.[21] They offered the framework for stable administrative solutions to the problems induced by cyclical economic expansion and contraction, in particular internecine price wars. And they did, in the main, come to be characterized by a configuration of social-class interests that laid both legal and moral claim to the firm.

Historians now generally agree that the mergers came about by strategic design as a means for containing the competitive price wars precipitated by the depression of 1893.[22] The price wars were the unintended by-products of investments in capital-intensive, mass-production equipment that enabled large-batch and continuous-process production methods. Entrepreneurs in industries that ranged from oil, sugar, fat, and alcohol refining, to cigarette, soap, match, and textile manufacturing, to grain milling invested heavily in fixed assets to take advantage of the large regional and national markets that had been realized by completion of a sea-to-sea railroad system and tariffs that fended off foreign competitors. Fixed capital investments, however, had rendered producers less flexible during recessions, forcing them to expand market shares and drive less efficient producers under. High debt payments, in effect, precluded firms in these capital-intensive industries from pursuing the sorts of price and production agreements, such as pools, trade associations, and cartels, that might typically have seen them through downturns in a mercantile economy.

2. *Role of the Banks.* America's financial community actively encouraged industrial mergers and vertical integration of the large firm.[23] The handsome promoters' profits that accompanied corporate consolidations and financial reorganizations no doubt weighted the advice of bankers heavily. Just as important, however, bankers looked to limit their risks and mitigate the sudden economic up- and downturns that characterized intense and chaotic competition. They saw consolidation as the most certain means of securing the stability they so cherished.

The New York investment banks, led by J. P. Morgan, had risen to prominence through the financing of the railroads, which from 1860 to 1890 had added 254,000 miles of track and multiplied their capitalization fourfold, from $2.5 to $10 billion.[24] Essentially, the bankers had served as intermediaries between American businesses and European capital markets; but their local resources also enabled them to underwrite new capital issues—that is, advance funds on a short-term basis and so dictate the financial terms of new securities—in ways that gave them special privileges, including directorships, in the emerging corporations.[25] In general, the banks and railroads had worked out cooperative relationships. Railroads humbled by recessions regularly turned to the banks for new loans, refinancing, reorganization, and ultimately consolidation. The banks, meanwhile, sought to extend this cooperative framework to manufacturing as a whole.[26]

Bankers, perhaps more than any other business interest, were extremely skeptical about governmental administration of private economic affairs.[27] In particular, they facilitated the growth and reallocation of industrial resources—that is, the liquidation of one form of property and the reinvestment of the proceeds in other properties. Accordingly, they resisted laws and regulations that empowered public officials to control the disposition and profitability of private property and so interfere with private valuation processes, including financial markets and banker appraisals. Meanwhile, banking interests found safe harbors in the courts, whose role it was to preserve constitutional prescriptions in favor of private property rights.[28]

We may see these banking interests reflected in a series of developments in regulation, both at the state and federal levels. Railroad corporations, for instance, chartered originally by state legislatures, came to be regulated in most states by railroad commissions.[29] The latter tended to be "sunshine" commissions, concerned more with monitoring corporate abuses and disseminating information about fares, safety conditions, and so forth than with public control. To some extent these commissions helped rationalize state rail networks, systems and fare structures, but in general such matters were left to be carried out by managers and the bankers who controlled the railroads' boards of directors and could organize traffic pools and private industry associations.

In time, however, regulation at the state level proved inadequate in resolving a host of conflicts over interstate commerce. Farmers, smaller-scale manufacturers who shipped and received goods, merchants, and various classes of consumers protested discriminatory and at times seemingly irrational rate structures; and Congress ultimately responded by establishing the Interstate Commerce Commission (ICC) in 1887.[30] Notwithstanding substantial efforts to reform and strengthen the ICC's powers over the next thirty years, the agency did not prove an administrative success. Throughout those years, but especially up to the passage of the Hepburn Act in 1906, which amended the original federal railroad legislation, the railroads successfully resorted to the federal courts to weaken the regulatory powers of the ICC.[31]

Similarly, the banks resisted the Sherman Antitrust Act up until its passage in 1890 and used the courts to weaken its effects.[32] Before 1890 the use of the corporate form to consolidate independent businesses into one unit had been regulated by state officials who had power to oversee and restrict the conditions and purposes of business incorporations in their respective states.[33] As manufacturing enterprises grew on a national scale, state law, with its jurisdictional limitations, became relatively weak. In 1883 New Jersey exploded state controls by enacting a corporation law that gave firms wide latitude in setting up their governance structures, issuing new stock and holding stock in other corporations for purposes of mergers, acquisitions, and consolidations. The New Jersey law invited numerous "foreign" firms to incorporate under its aegis and pay the relatively small corporate tax for the privilege. Indeed, the law firms that represented the New York banks were the principal promoters and drafters of the legislation. In the wake of the New Jersey law, the complaints of smaller businesses, farmers, shippers, and consumers intensified, and Congress responded by enacting the federal antitrust law in 1890.[34] Again bankers, railroad managers, and their allies resorted to the courts and defused the Sherman Act's potential for disrupting the pace of consolidation.

In some ways the federal government posed less of a threat to the banking interests than had state governments in the nineteenth century. Congress was limited by the U.S. Constitution in these matters to "regulating interstate and foreign commerce," while states retained "police powers" that enabled state officials to expropriate private property, at least to some degree.[36] Near the turn of the century, however, bankers and their allies won perhaps the most significant victory in the courts, namely, the reception of a "natural entity" doctrine that accorded private business corporations the constitutional rights of citizens.[37] Under that doctrine the corporation was considered not merely a legal fiction, through which the state granted incorporators certain powers to conduct their business, but the evolutionary outgrowth of voluntary association among rational men engaging in business ventures to maximize their own and so too, presumably, society's utilities. The natural-entity doctrine virtually precluded state governments from exerting any radical authority over the property of manufacturing concerns or, accordingly, interfering with consolidations among competitors. So long as the federal courts, then, continued to construe Congress's power to regulate commerce narrowly, the large corporation seemed to have little to fear from government.

The point is that bankers succeeded in keeping public officials' hands off corporate property. In so doing, they won for themselves a measure of freedom in consolidating industrial capital and controlling the resultant firms to stabilize prices and levels of production in industrial markets. The bankers' principal antagonists were industrial workers, farmers, and small businesses drowned in the wash of consolidation; by moving the locus of governmental industrial policy to the courts, banking interests managed by and large to ward off legislative attempts to mitigate the hardships that accompanied consolidation, not to mention attempts at redistribution.

Emergence of a Managerial Class

The initial mergers and consolidations of industrial capital around the turn of the century were designed to centralize control over production and so stabilize price competition. Once the large firms had come into being, however, they opened up new vistas on the relationship between market competition and bureaucratic design.

As noted earlier, managers came to recognize a professional interest of their own in the running of the large firm, namely, the establishment of "group ethics" that would harmonize the competing interests that laid claim to the firm and underscore managerial authority. Elbert Gary, for instance, has been singled out for developing a code of business practices that was at odds with the banking, proprietary, and entrepreneurial mentalities that ruled the corporation at the time. The financiers had treated the large corporation not as a consolidation that could achieve some greater good but as a cartel of competing interests combining for convenience and using the corporate form both to evade antitrust restrictions and to exploit the opportunities of the rapidly developing capital markets.[38]

Nevertheless, while the professionalization of management came to be widely recognized by the second decade of the century, the assertion of managerial authority developed more gradually, firm by firm, industry by industry. Management of the railroads, for example, had become highly professionalized by the turn of the century;[39] the younger automobile industry, in contrast, retained its entrepreneurial spirit until the 1920s.[40] Unlike the bankers, moreover, whose interlocking directorates, geographically centralized offices, and underwriting syndicates offered a shared overview of American industry, corporate managers looked out from their individual firms.[41] Unlike other groups of middle-class professionals, they formed no single central organization and had relatively little need to band together, except perhaps in industry groupings that circulated information and otherwise sought to stabilize competition in oligopolistic markets.[42] Only when economic irregularity itself undercut their ability to manage production and prices did managers have reason to contest the bankers' loose control over the system.

Managers were drawn from a wide variety of ranks active in corporate affairs, including financial analysts, lawyers, cost accountants, human-resources and "scientific" managers, production engineers, and conventional administrators.[43] What they had in common was the urgency of striking deals among the corporate stakeholders and developing moral climate that would legitimate their decisions among those stakeholders and so expedite the operations of the firm. In part, the managers' ascendancy was a by-product of the large firm's increasing dominance and management's unchallenged technical authority. With respect to the latter, the large firm had clearly established itself as the central organization within the economy of the 1920s.[44] Moreover, a number of the leading firms, such as General Motors (GM) and DuPont, had instituted a decentralized structure in which autonomous profit centers, "divisions," reported their earnings to central headquarters. These kinds of adjustments were at the root of managerial solutions to complex coordination problems that grew out of the need to reconcile unique labor, customer, geographic, and product markets.[45] Just as important, the managerial accounting procedures and standards that large firms spawned helped adapt the modern corporation to the private investment and commercial banking system and so reinforced the private nature of the economy.[46]

The emergence of decentralized structures also separated daily operations from long-term planning and so permitted top managers to concentrate their efforts on entrepreneurial activities.[47] Corporate headquarters functioned, in effect, as mini-capital markets, reallocating the firm's resources among profit centers based on long-range expectations about growing. As a result, corporate managers performed functions that had once been the sole domain of investment bankers.[48] Further, as increased corporate profits built up intracorporate capital funds in the form of retained earnings, managers gained in bargaining power vis-à-vis their own investment bankers and even pressed them to compete with others. Still, it was not until the Great Depression, when financial control of the economy proved itself generally inadequate, that the split between managerial and banking authority became complete.

As managers' skills in handling their firms' long-term planning requirements improved, as too did their ability to coordinate activity within their industries. Industry associations and individual firms, such as GM, engaged in data gathering that enabled them to project demand and prices and to forecast larger changes in the economy. Essentially, managers hoped that planning would avoid the ravages of overproduction and excessive competition.[49] For the most part, planning occurred in oligopolistic industries, but it was also supported by government-sponsored publications of useful statistics.[50] The federal government, for instance, began collecting and publishing extensive price and wage data during World War I and had earlier made available even more data for particular industries such as railroads, shipping, and commodities subject to tariffs.[51]

During the first two decades of the century, managers had played parts in loose, sometimes "progressive" organizations like the National Civic Federation, which promoted business interests in a general way.[52] As noted earlier, managers did not group together to promote shared interests distinct from those of the banking interests then in control of the corporate sector. Elbert Gary, for instance, though cognizant of a public interest in the large firm, remained the spokesman for the firm's investors, aiming to hold public officials at bay. Only as occasional economic downturns gradually demonstrated the bankers' inability to manage the economy did the independent shared interests of corporate sector managers materialize. American institutional economists, meanwhile, where quick to note the significance of these developments,[53] and Thorstein Veblen, above all, wrote with increasing alarm through the 1920s about the dire consequences of not getting the corporate "engineers" out from under the control of the financiers.[54]

One of the early institutional frameworks in which the managerial interest emerged was the War Industries Board (WIB), established during World War I to allocate and stabilize production.[55] A number of the WIB administrators were drawn from the managerial ranks of American industry; and through Bernard Baruch's able leadership, the WIB came to represent the benefits that could be gained through business-government cooperation. Ironically, the bulk of power in the WIB had rested in private hands, while the government's power largely derived from Baruch's persuasiveness on the virtues of cooperation. Managers seeing themselves as the technical experts on regulating production nevertheless valued the assistance of the WIB in rendering such regulation feasible. After the war, notwithstanding the liquidation of the WIB, managers continued to look to government for the sort of statesmanship that Baruch had personified.

To some degree they found support in Herbert Hoover's "associative" policies.[56] Yet, by and large, these policies worked in only two kinds of industries: in regulated utilities industries, because public administrators could exert legal control; and in oligopolistic industries, because dominant firms could exercise price and production "leadership" by threatening maverick competitors with economic retaliation. In other industries, the codes of corporate conduct that industry and trade associations elaborated proved ineffective without government enforcement. A part of the motivation for the Federal Trade Commission's establishment in 1914 had been to standardize enforceable methods of competition so that businessmen would have to stoop to the lowest common denominator. Indeed, this aspect of the legislation had won the support of corporate managers as well as small businesses and labor. In the ten years following, however, the FTC failed to develop a clear sense of its own mission; and when, during the Hoover Administration, the FTC began to use its enforcement powers in support of industry codes, the federal courts dismantled the agency's authority.[57]

Nonetheless, increasing corporate political activity throughout the period gave shape to managerial interests. The larger firms helped establish strong trade associations to promote their interests within the government.[58] In addition, large firms' operations gave rise to the field of public relations; and, during the 1920s, they adapted the field to their particular needs by instituting corporate public relations offices.[59] These offices, though they seemed early on to be mere novelties, eventually provided corporate staffs with useful information about public opinion, legislative activity, and regulatory actions and advice on securing the firm's political objectives.

In general, then, corporate sector managerial interests slowly defined themselves and took on institutional form during the first three decades of the century. Without doubt, the managers had to adjust corporate activities to the demands of the bankers, who had the power both to disinvest the firm's capital and in most instances to replace one group of managers or "management team," with another. The managers, while more sanguine than financiers about the capacity of public administrators to construct codes of conduct and otherwise shape market regulations, followed the financial community's lead in entrusting industrial policy to the courts and to a series of "rules of reason" that the courts developed in scrutinizing other government agencies' regulatory and enforcement actions.

Just as important, however, managers had to adjust their operations to the needs of small businesses that served the larger firms both as suppliers and distributors and competed viably with them in certain kinds of geographical and product markets,[60] to workers (and their alteregos, consumers),[61] and to the local, state, and federal public officials who would respond to demands for legislation and regulation whenever the large corporations played cavalierly with the interests of those individual citizens.[62]

The onset of the Great Depression signaled an end to the bankers' central role and gave managers an opening to assert control not only over their individual firms but over the larger economy.[63] As the banking industry and the economy in general fell apart, Hoover experimented with macroeconomic policy.[64] He outlined a deliberate economic recovery program that depended in large part on the cooperation of the banks and resisted the encroachment of public power upon private affairs. He refused, for instance, to run a federal deficit in fear that financial liquidity and, in particular, the bond markets would suffer; instead, he sought measures that would revitalize investment, secure commercial lending, and shore up wages. Yet, the banking community betrayed Hoover's expectations in favor of private opportunities and so undercut the program. By the time Hoover finally appreciated the need for more radical measures, he had lost the confidence of Congress. His Reconstruction Finance Corporation, which served as a lender of last resort to financial institutions and railroads, and in this respect was designed to stimulate the extension of new credit more generally, did little more during his administration than patch cracks in an economic infrastructure rent by earthquakes.

Once Roosevelt came into power, Congress began passing a series of measures that radically restructured the U.S. banking system and made it virtually impossible for investment bankers to reassert their former control over America's center industries.[65] Congress split the commercial banking functions away from the investment houses, imposed severe restrictions on various sorts of speculative leveraging devices, including the use of holding companies and low-margin-securities trading accounts, prohibited stock-trading practices that undermined confidence in securities markets, instituted procedures for disseminating nonpublic information that affected securities prices, empowered a new agency, the Securities and Exchange Commission, to oversee market procedures and investment bankers' practices, and beefed up the Federal Reserve Board's authority to set interest rates and control the currency supply.

Notwithstanding the resistance of the investment bankers and the leading private securities markets, in particular the New York Stock Exchange, the various acts passed quickly and government administrators, under the leadership of James M. Landis, soon gained the upper hand in regulating the industry.[66] Economic and political circumstances clearly contributed to the bankers' inability to resist or control the shape of the regulations; but the bankers, unused as they were to negotiating on equal terms with federal government administrators, cemented their own graves. Following the reforms, moreover, which fragmented the banking industry into quite different classes of interest, the bankers lost much of the potential clout they had had before. As one conservative student of the period put it, the reforms "transferred power from sophisticated bankers . . . and from Wall Street lawyers . . . to Akron tire-makers and rubber-makers, and to steel-makers in Gary and Birmingham."[67]

As the quote suggests, corporate sector managers were meanwhile seizing the opportunity to take charge and strengthen their relationships with government.[68] During the latter part of Hoover's administration, leading corporate managers, such as Gerard Swope of General Electric, had proposed to manage the economy centrally in a form that could replace private financial controls. The object of centralization was to regulate aggregate economic cycles over which individual managers had little control in running their own firms, however large those firms happened to be. The means of regulation would mirror the administrative procedures with which corporate sector executives had become both familiar and comfortable—namely, corporate boards, trade and industry associations, and intracorporate negotiations with several classes of interest, above all labor. Hoover had forcefully rejected Swope's plan, arguing that it would subject the American people to the control of monopolies bolstered by federal law.[69] When FDR came to power, however, Congress enacted a modified version of Swope's plan in the National Industrial Recovery Act (NIRA). FDR soon appointed Hugh Johnson to head up the National Recovery Administration and enforce the plan. As in the case of the WIB during WWI, the NRA drew a large share of its administrators from business management.

The NRA had power to write industry codes of conduct on practices that pertained to competition, consumers, and workers, and to stabilize wages and prices within industries.[70] While Johnson had the blessings of big business as well as FDR's radical planners, the experiment ultimately gave way to the fractiousness of particular interests.[71] In general, big business, small business, and labor in many industries could not reach consensus, nor did they have much basis on which to agree. When industries agreed on a code, the NRA itself tended to rubber-stamp it. By their nature, the codes tended to favor larger businesses, which depend on a more consistent competitive environment and can, with time, spread the cost of accommodating new rules over a greater volume of sales. Accordingly, smaller businesses had some incentive not to agree to a code in the first instance and, when the code was in fact adopted, not to conform to its terms. Since the enforcement of the codes under the NIRA depended to a large degree on voluntary compliance and the threat of consumer boycotts (businesses upholding the codes were permitted to post "blue eagles" as signals of compliance to customers), the NRA's prospects for long-term success in the harrowing economic climate of the Depression were dim.

In any case, the U.S. Supreme Court, troubled by the delegation of what was, in effect, law-making power to private interests, objected to enforcement of the codes and struck down the major part of the NIRA.[72] This decisive defeat of the managerial plan to bring the price and production system under control by extending corporate administrative methods to the operation of government led corporate sector managers to distance themselves from further proposals for business-government links.[73] The experience, however, was useful, for it taught managers to distinguish cooperative ventures among themselves, wholly private, from ventures that relied on public power, such as the NRA.[74] They learned, moreover, that the traditional liberal distinction of public from private authority was a double-edged sword, particularly where the corporate sector was concerned: For just as it protected private business interests from being overrun by public officials, so also it served to protect the public domain, ostensibly responsive to individual citizens, from domination by more powerful economic interests. This was, in effect, the wisdom of the Supreme Court's judgment on the NIRA. Finally, in looking out from under the wreckage, managers could begin to understand more clearly the extent of their autonomy within the firm and the interests they shared with managers of other large firms.

The Elaboration of a Managerial Collective Interest

In the years following the demise of the NRA, FDR devised a series of alternative proposals to achieve what the NIRA had not, namely, to stabilize labor and consumer markets, to safeguard individual workers and consumers from unfair business practices, and to preserve, at least within limits, smaller businesses and communities against the ravages of depression.[75] The proposals were many, touched on virtually all industries, and took a variety of forms that ranged from industry (and even firm) specific to very general interindustry sorts of regulation.

The corporate sector, for its part, was in political retreat during this "Second New Deal" and, by most accounts, had considerably less impact on the legislation than it had had during the earlier years when FDR's "Brain Trust" informed New Deal policies.[76] More important, the public image of corporate sector leaders had been tarnished, not just by the ineffectiveness of the NRA in stabilizing the economy and its eventual collapse but also by a series of studies—particularly Adolf Berle and Gardiner Means's *The Modern Corporation and Private Property*—that documented and simultaneously questioned the increasing concentration of

relatively unchecked economic power in the hands of corporate managers.[77] The latter part of the 1930s, then, was a period of retrenchment for
corporate sector managers. They sought to come to grips with the new era
and they scurried to react, in accordance with their firms' particular
interests, to the broad range of new laws, administrative rulings, and
court decisions that were affecting their business operations.

What follows is not an account of the postwar business-government
relations as a whole. It is simply a sketch of the large firms' shared history
and the corporate managerial perspective on business-government relations that materialized in the context of that history. In particular, we
focus on two aspects of the regulatory system that emerged: first, on the
stakeholder regulations that were designed to render managers account-
able to politically defined social interests and values; and, second, on the
industry and macroeconomic policies that were designed to promote but
at the same time stabilize the economic growth of the nation.

1. *Stakeholder Regulation.* As noted earlier, the central role of the manager in the large corporation was in negotiating agreements with groups of
stakeholders and in inscribing those agreements, through something like a
code, into the values, contracts, and rules of the firm. Those agreements
and rules, in turn, gave managers their authority—that is, the room to
mobilize their firm's resources in clear directions.[78] In any large corporation, the stakeholders included shareholders and creditors, workers, consumers (who bargained over the price and quality of the firm's products),
and in a vague sort of way the "community" (which ranged from local
interests to federal officials enforcing some "public interest").[79] Each of
these stakeholders could at once pursue conventional private processes of
negotiation that led to contracts—that is, through the market's or the
firm's internal processes—or try to elicit support through political processes that led to rules and rulings by public officials.[80]

When managers succeeded in working out agreements with stakeholders on a private basis, they could avoid government intervention.
When managers were pushed into the political arena by their inability to
reach agreement, their primary concern (along with preserving the economic health of their firm) was to limit government intervention so that
public officials could not restrict managers' capacity to negotiate contracts
privately later on. That is, the managers' authority depended on rules that
continually reinforced their own capacity to negotiate contracts with
their stakeholders.

From the perspective of federal public policymakers, however, the problem was one of keeping managerial autonomy in check without expressly
taking over the operations of the firms themselves—that is, leading the

nation down the path of socialism.[81] During the Second New Deal, Congress passed a series of laws to protect the interests of various groups of stakeholders vis-à-vis business across all industries. We have already described the federal laws that sought to restore investor confidence and develop the securities markets by modifying and stabilizing industry practices. In this instance, Congress had originally empowered the FTC to administer the new laws, but a year later created another independent agency, the SEC, to which it transferred the authority. In the case of workers, Congress created yet another agency, the National Labor Relations Board, in 1935 to protect workers from retribution and discrimination on the basis of their union-organizing and collective-bargaining activities. In 1938 Congress passed additional legislation, the Fair Labor Standards Act, to impose minimum-wage and maximum-hour restrictions on all labor contracts, regardless of whether the contract was bargained with workers collectively or individually. Finally, in 1938, Congress amended the FTC Act, expanding the FTC's powers to enable the prosecution of acts and practices that were unfair or deceptive to consumers as well as competitors. In this respect, the agency's mission was refocused, though somewhat ambivalently, from protecting mainly smaller and honest businesses against larger or less scrupulous competitors to protecting consumers directly.[82] The refocusing of the FTC's mission had nevertheless been rendered ambivalent by the earlier passage of the Robinson-Patman Act (1936). That act, while it empowered the FTC to protect consumers in less competitive regional and local markets from price gouging by larger firms, had also required the FTC to defend smaller middlemen and retailers against the market power of their larger competitors.

The laws establishing and empowering the independent regulatory agencies were open to a broad range of interpretations. Roughly speaking, the agency's mission in each case was to protect a particular class of corporate stakeholders against a vaguely defined set of managerial acts, such as misleading claims or unfair practices. What still had to be worked out through the regulatory process was a consistent theory of corporate regulation: That is, should public administrators represent the interests of the stakeholders directly by imposing fiduciary obligations on managers? Or, should they let stakeholders fend for themselves once corporate managers had been made to comply with process requirements and market standards, such as information disclosures or bargaining procedures? As we shall see below, investment regulation and consumer protection hardly threatened the initiative of large firm managers. In contrast, the unfolding of labor regulation during the New Deal and up through World War II did threaten managerial autonomy and impressed managers with the need for statesmanship that would reaffirm the legitimacy of both private corporate power and the corporate managerial role.

New Deal historians by and large have regarded the SEC's leadership as the ablest among independent federal agencies.[83] James M. Landis and Joseph P. Kennedy combined their talent and experience at the outset, and William O. Douglas continued their work before his appointment to the U.S. Supreme Court in 1938. Essentially, the SEC, by recognizing the self-interest of the institutions it sought to regulate—bankers, brokers, dealers, and investment specialists—won broad cooperation in its efforts to stabilize the various securities markets. While the SEC, in effect, retained power to license brokers and underwriting, it also relinquished two principal vehicles for investor protection, namely, market rules and corporate governance, to the self-regulation of the private exchanges (NYSE and ASE) in which corporate sector securities were traded and state corporation laws. Furthermore, the SEC, in establishing corporate- and underwriting disclosure requirements, relied on private independent accounting firms to facilitate and maintain disinterested but professional auditing procedures and financial reporting standards. Since the structural changes in the banking system tended to safeguard everyday depositors' savings from speculative risk, SEC officials were relatively sanguine in keeping only a light touch on the affairs of those private investors eager for higher, though also riskier, returns. Public officials aimed less to protect private individuals from dubious market practices directly and more to secure public confidence in investment markets generally.

With respect to consumers, federal policies were still ambivalent.[84] On the one hand, FTC officials sought to protect unsuspecting consumers from exploitation through advertising and associated deceptive practices that led to substantial consumer harm. In those cases, the FTC not only prosecuted offending businesses but also succeeded in developing far-reaching rules that constrained commercial advertising and marketing practices in general. On the other hand, the FTC did not seek to represent consumer interests more broadly, on matters ranging from product innovation, quality and design, to corporate pricing strategies. Insofar as FTC officials did seek to use antitrust laws, including the Robinson-Patman Act, to tie managers' hands in these matters, they were gradually repulsed by the federal courts, to whom corporate attorneys were able to appeal under the constitutional guidelines for administrative procedure.[85] Significantly, the larger firms, with their financial resources and capacity to draw on superior legal talent, were better able to resist the FTC's more radical policies through drawn-out administrative and court proceedings. That very capacity for resistance, moreover, led to the wider postwar appreciation of those firms as guardians of liberal democracy in America.[86]

Finally, with respect to workers, federal policies were of two kinds. First, Congress had sought to equalize the bargaining power of workers against large industrial firms.[87] Accordingly, the NLRA eased common-law property and contract prescriptions that had inhibited union organizing and collective bargaining, and it placed those activities under the administrative jurisdiction of the National Labor Relations Board. Second, Congress also set minimum-wage and maximum-hours standards to protect the majority of unorganized workers; under the Fair Labor Standards Act, the Department of Labor was designated the enforcer of those standards. Nevertheless, much as in the case of consumer protection, the federal policies on labor unions were ambivalent; and from the passage of the NLRA in 1935 to its amendment in the Taft-Hartley Act of 1947, corporate managers and labor leaders engaged in a vicious struggle for the soul of the NLRB.

The original version of the NLRA, the Wagner Act of 1935, supported two broad conceptions of the structure of labor relations and the role of federal administrators in the workplace.[88] The one, trade-union conception, saw workers as part of a larger labor market in which groups of workers could organize themselves according to the particular skills they offered. Unions served to match the skills of workers with the needs of individual firms; and in this context, unions served to represent the interests of those workers and could bargain with managers over the terms of employment. In general, the union gained its strength by monopolizing the available labor for particular skills, while the corporation gained its strength by monopolizing the available jobs. Federal administrators, for their part, could see to it that unions and managers attempted to monopolize skills and jobs "fairly." The Wagner Act empowered the NLRB in two principal ways: to balance the scales that the courts in their earlier rulings had tipped in favor of management; and to guard against coercive managerial tactics directed at individual workers engaging in proper union activities.

The other, industrial-union conception of labor relations, held workers to be relatively captive to the firms that employed them. The problem, within this conception, was how to render the internal labor markets of the giant industrial corporation more equitable from the workers' point of view. Proposals ranged from an essentially trade-union approach, in which the union would organize workers by industry into bargaining units, to more radical approaches. The latter included the appointment of public-bargaining agents or the selection by workers of competing private agents to represent the workers in individual firms. From the managerial point of view, the more radical proposals were unbearably intrusive, in effect placing managers and public officials in opposition to one another, severely limiting managerial initiatives to keep a firm's workers from organizing themselves, and finally threatening the extension of federal power into the workplace in ways that augured a socialized economy.

As the Wagner Act came to be interpreted, managers were able to ally with trade-union interests to root more radical proponents out of the NLRB and out of the labor movement itself.[89] Moreover, by resorting to the courts, managers were also able to bolster their own rights to resist union organizing and bargaining activities and so limit the extent to which the Wagner Act succeeded in empowering unions. In general, smaller manufacturers, through, for instance, the National Association of Manufacturers, continued to resist all federal intervention on behalf of unions; in contrast, industry leaders, including GM, Allis-Chalmers, Kaiser, U.S. Rubber, and General Foods, learned to accommodate the presence of unions in the workplace and through the special circumstances of World War II relied on the unions' authority to integrate and discipline their workers.[90] Finally, following the war, the business community as a whole pushed through the 1947 amendments to the NLRA to preclude further radical interpretations of the act and ensconce a relatively weak trade-union conception of worker protection in American labor law.

2. *Stabilization and Growth Policies.* The regulation of stakeholders, though it confronted issues surrounding managerial power and autonomy, did not address the overriding social and business problems of the Great Depression—the problems of economic stabilization and growth. Following the collapse of the NRA, business interests generally and, in large part, the managers of large firms as well withdrew from active participation in FDR's administration until the onset of World War II. Yet the deepening of the economic crisis in 1938 and the growing prospect of centralized government planning (along with the rise of industrial unions) impelled business leaders to develop decentralized regulatory alternatives that would preserve the private nature of the American economy.

In general, stabilization and growth strategies had to be worked out on two levels: industrywide and interindustry or macroeconomic. World War II offered managers not only the opportunity to explore regulatory alternatives that would keep the centralized planners at bay but also to develop an understanding of their own role as statesmen. It was during this period that the vision of American liberal pluralism cohered.[91] Corporate managers, meanwhile, with their own threatening power seemingly held in check by stakeholder regulation and by emergent corporate norms of social responsibility, were able to capitalize on the pluralist vision to begin persuading the American public of the large corporation's positive nature.[92] In this respect, the demands of political incumbency and managerial careers coincided along lines of stabilization and growth.

Still questions remained. How would corporate managers pursue public policies that secured general stability and growth while still competing with one another in the market? How would they avoid the pitfalls—Hoover's too weak associationism, FDR's excessive NRA—to which they had fallen prey following their successful experiences in World War I with the WIB? The answers are relatively well documented, both with respect to industrywide and macroeconomic regulation.

In general, FDR's administrations were the seedbeds of modern industrial regulation, fostering a haphazard array of rules, processes, agencies, and bureaus to which postwar political scientists sought to give order through what they termed "iron triangles."[93] Congress had enacted the regulations, industry by industry, during the 1930s and 1940s; it placed communications, trucking, and airlines under the jurisdiction of "independent regulatory agencies" (the FCC, ICC, and CAB), which in effect managed the industries as cartels; and it stimulated national security industries, including automobiles, aerospace, and computers, through federal research programs and spending contracts (e.g., the Highway Trust Funds, Defense contracts, and National Science Foundation programs).[94] Other industries, ranging from mining and energy to food and drug industries, had also become subject to a complex variety of institutionalized subsidies and strictures.

Yet notwithstanding the apparently haphazard development of industrial regulation, two consistent patterns gradually did emerge. First, the administrative process developed coherence that was finally given its form in the Administrative Procedure Act of 1946.[85] Second, a series of "iron triangles" emerged as loose tripartite arrangements that governed policy development and execution. The triangles comprised congressional committee staffs in charge of drafting legislation for particular industries, federal bureau or agency staffs vested with rule-making and enforcement powers over the industry, and industry or trade association staffs that represented the industry in its political affairs. In effect, then, congressional committees responsible for oversight and the bureaus responsible for administering these programs saw their legitimate role as public servants in catering to the private constituencies,[96] while specific private interests claimed "jurisdiction" over particular public policy programs.[97]

In general, the business community found in these "iron triangles" a political base for securing beneficial "industrial policies" and for defeating New Deal radicalism.[98] The oil industry, for example, allied with bureaucrats in the Department of the Interior to forestall the Interior Secretary's designs to develop a national oil company. The utility industry, meanwhile, blocked the government's entry into the lucrative power-distribution business. Usually trade associations were the principal business actors in this policy environment, although it was not unusual for firms in regulated industries to employ specialized personnel.

Nevertheless, the "iron triangles" required an expanding economy to work, and the Great Depression had instructed the nation that growth was not a self-sustaining phenomenon. Growth required careful management. Congress and the President monitored the regulatory activities of legislative and executive staffs, respectively. In contrast, the business community had not, since the weakening of investment bankers' control and the breakup of the NRA, developed the means for reconciling the narrow and often conflicting policy demands of representative industry and trade associations. For the major corporations no form existed in which top managers could collectively consider such broad issues or through which a consensus, if achieved, could be transmitted effectively to a now-fragmented policy arena.[99] Unlike other industrialized countries, American business had no "peak" association that legitimately represented, let alone ruled, the diversity of corporate interests. The United States' relatively isolated geography and enormous home market, its developed competitive capital markets, its antitrust tradition, its weak labor movement, its ongoing rivalry between small and big business, and its decentralized electoral politics combined to keep the political aims and interests of the business community as a whole fragmented.[100]

The Chamber of Commerce, for example, encompassed the interests of both big and small business; yet, in this respect, it represented the corporate sector imperfectly.[101] When in 1935 the Chamber's leadership, drawn mainly from big business, proposed new methods of business-government cooperation to stimulate growth, the majority of its members had responded negatively, for small businesses hated the New Deal's "radical" labor and social-welfare policies. Indeed, the membership had forced the Chamber to break all ties with the Roosevelt administration. At the time, however, more moderate members of the corporate sector felt that dialogue, not confrontation, would constrain the New Deal's excesses and reform the federal government in line with their own interests. Accordingly, they broke away from the Chamber in search of their own voice and in 1942 established the Commitee for Economic Development.[102]

The CED brought together three kinds of groups: selected top managers of large industrial firms, enlightened or "progressive" entrepreneurs, and intellectual policy analysts. Throughout the New Deal fiscal-policy enthusiasts, such as Marriner Eccles, had been advocating more liberal macro-economic policies.[103] Though the advice had fallen largely on deaf ears in government circles, those who came together under the aegis of the CED gradually recognized its worth. Macroeconomic policy, together with the stabilizing industry regulations that evolved out of the "iron triangles," came to represent the key to securing stable national growth.[104] The CED, in statements issued in 1944, 1945, and 1948, offered a number of policy proposals. By insisting that government use monetary and fiscal policies rather than direct investments or redistributive schemes, the CED fostered a commercial Keynesianism in which business could benefit from macroeconomic policy's benefits, while making sure that investment and income redistribution questions remained outside normal public policy discussions. These ideas could be seen to take hold, initially in the Employment Act of 1946 and then more generally in macroeconomic policy administration.[105] During the Eisenhower and Kennedy administrations this combination of interest-group pluralism (the "iron triangles") and elite macroeconomic policy positions became the crux of the public-private partnership that informed political and economic values.[106]

Even after formation of the CED, political conflict within the corporate sector persisted. Yet, these conflicts were largely over policy details and specific claims to government largesse, not over the ground rules for the new political order.[107] Through much of the 1960s, economic growth tended to confirm the wisdom of pragmatic and fragmented corporate politics. Under these circumstances, the business community held ideological and partisan support for congressional and presidential contestants unnecessary, so it took few steps toward reforming the government's intervention into the economy.[108]

The Managerial Response to Crisis

Toward the end of the 1960s a series of events and circumstances began undercutting the success of postwar federal policies. By the early 1970s the U.S. economy was beset by simultaneously rising inflation and unemployment; and as in 1938, stagflation pushed the corporate sector to reorganize itself politically and develop appropriate policies for reforming the public sector. Unlike the earlier period, however, big business did not retreat defensively. To the contrary, corporate sector leaders blamed labor and public-interest groups for the growing economic crisis and the misdirection of federal policy, in particular its unbridled social welfarism. Ironically, while the corporate leaders mustered a solid front against their perceived antagonists and so honed their electoral and bureaucratic political operations, they also fell to bickering over policy details in ways that slowed their capacity to win coherent economic and political reform. Nevertheless, the advocacy of organizations such as the CED and the Business Roundtable eventually developed reform policies around which corporate sector leaders were willing to rally.

A selective review of business and public policy leaders' perceptions about the causes of economic disorder will help put the corporate sector managerial responses in perspective.

The signs of economic malaise went from inflation during Lyndon Johnson's administration to spiraling inflation and unemployment during the 1970s. At first, business leaders ascribed the crisis to Johnson's fiscal irresponsibility or cowardly failure to raise sufficient taxes for his War on Poverty and the Vietnam War.[109] Increased government spending was the natural by-product of multiplying interest-group demands, a circumstance brought about by postwar pluralist politics in which governmental agencies were encouraged to give access to all readily definable groups. Ironically, business had been the principal beneficiary of the federal government's liberal orientation toward process rights, so long as the federal bureaucracy dealt largely with matters of industrial stabilization and growth. Accordingly, when a new breed of "public interest" groups, staffed by a highly educated middle class and resorting to grass-roots lobbying and electoral campaign strategies, won first political recognition and then a series of "social regulations" from Congress, business leaders were hard put to claim that public interest groups had not been deserving of their political success.[110]

At the same time, it became clear to business leaders and public policy analysts alike that the number of interest groups making discrete demands upon Congress were exhausting the public trough.[111] The social regulations ranged from gender, race and age discrimination laws, to environmental and occupational health safeguards, to consumer and public health regulations.[112] Moreover, Congress's haphazard organization made coordinated business attempts to influence economic policy impossible. For Congress, in effect, presided over an *ad hoc* budget, while its revenue projections and consequent taxation policies were based on turns in the business cycle *post hoc*.[113]

When Nixon took office, business leaders expected more responsible fiscal policies to bring inflation under control. Inflation, however, turned into stagflation. Accordingly, evaluations of the economic crisis shifted over the following years toward more fundamental concerns about the private economy, in particular declining rates of productivity and capital reinvestment, especially relative to the United States' economic competitors. Business association policy analysts and publicists, who had been labeling contemporary inflation as demand-driven, now began seeing it as a cost-driven process.[114] Corporate sector leaders turned their attention away from federal expenditures toward the trade unions, which, they said, were driving wage settlements beyond the limits of productivity gains. The CED, among others, advised Nixon to impose temporary wage and price controls to break the wage-price spiral.[115] Nixon, though reluctant at first, finally responded in August 1971, apparently to bolster his reelection prospects in the face of the waning economy. When Nixon imposed wage-price controls, he also removed the United States from the gold-exchange standard in an effort to correct yet another prospective fault in America's battered economy, namely, the growth of its trade deficits.[116]

Meanwhile, corporate sector leaders met with sharp resistance in Congress and the federal regulatory bureaucracy. Labor, both in alliances with public-interest groups and as an active participant in the administration of wage-price controls, was able to block serious threats to its negotiating power.[117] The new public-interest groups, moreover, not only articulated nonbusiness values in policy debates that earlier had been exclusively under business "jurisdiction,"[118] but they also succeeded in threatening managerial discretion within the corporation itself.[119] For one, they regularly exposed the private sanctity of the corporate boardroom to public scrutiny.[120] Moreover, they were advocating a broad variety of corporate governance reforms, including public-interest representation, worker participation, and shareholder democracy, to receptive federal and state officials.[121] In this respect, corporate sector managers saw both halves of the postwar regulative infrastructure collapsing at once: stabilization and growth policies at the industry and macroeconomic levels and stakeholder policies that legitimated managerial discretion in the large firm's day-to-day operations and longer-term investment decisions.

What the nation's most prestigious business associations described as cost-push inflation continued throughout the 1970s. Tripartite cooperative efforts to constrain wages and prices voluntarily and initiate productivity-enhancing programs during the Ford and Carter administrations failed, undermined in part by corporate sector managers' will to preserve their firms' independence and so weather the economy's volatility. To be sure, the Arab oil embargo contributed to the spiraling price escalation and demanded considerable attention from public policymakers, including the CED.[122]

As the 1980–82 global recession brought energy prices under control in the 1980s and broke labor's ability to win inflationary wage demands, the

CED still found that productivity lagged significantly. Above all, declining productivity growth, according to the CED, was responsible for America's failure to compete internationally. While government debt and the trade imbalance replaced inflation as the significant immediate economic problems, productivity remained in the opinion of corporate sector policy analysts the root cause of the nation's woes and the lever for restoring the nation's economic vitality.

Although not as dramatic as business' efforts under the NRA, the wage-price control debacle and subsequent tripartite failures once again demonstrated to the corporate sector that a centrally administered solution to America's economic decline was impractical.[123] Yet, the events of the 1970s have led to the most recent round of political strategic planning and public-affairs restructuring within the business community. For one, corporate sector firms cooperated in establishing the Business Round-table, both to educate top managers on policy issues and the positions favorable to the corporate sector as a whole and to draw on the political and analytical resources of individual firms in specific corporate sector policy, lobbying, and electoral initiatives.[124] In addition, corporate public-affairs offices have grown in scope and size to handle the issue networks in which large firms find themselves.[125] Notwithstanding the significance of these and other more recent developments, the CED has developed publicly the most coherent set of responses to the economic disorder external to the firms, while at the same time recognizing that corporate sector managers can best adapt to political structures and policies that reinforce managerial discretion and market rivalry. With this understanding, we can turn to the CED's proposals for reform.

1. *The CED's Plan.* Shortly after the wage-price controls' failure, the CED undertook a multiyear study to formulate a strategy for correcting the economy's decline.[126] Its final recommendations precluded a centralized administrative solution. Instead, it prescribed greater reliance on monetary policy and restructuring business government relations in a way that would not violate the "pluralistic" premises of American politics. Its reform proposals would strengthen the corporate sector's political position, because conflicting values and interests inside the policy process would be subordinated to the economy's demand for "efficiency." Whereas Europe seemed to be moving in a corporatist direction,[127] the United States, at least as the CED saw it, could retain the flexible decentralized policy arrangements that characterized postwar liberal pluralism so long as the coordination of fiscal and monetary could be improved and interest-group politics more effectively constrained by economic "logic."

For the CED, the central problem was the nation's decreasing productivity. Between 1945 and 1965, labor productivity grew at an annual rate of about 3.2 percent. During the slowdown of 1966–72, labor productivity advanced at a rate between 2.0 and 2.5 percent a year; thereafter productivity increased at an annual rate of less than one percent and came to a near standstill by the end of the 1970s.[128] During the decade, the CED consistently pointed to the nation's inadequate capital investments as the principal cause for the economy's lackluster performance. By the end of the decade, the CED noted that while gross capital investment had remained relatively stable since 1965, the net figures in new capital investment had declined dramatically from 64 percent to 49 percent of the gross in the 1970s.[129] Low productivity had contributed to inflation, and so, according to the CED, was to blame for management's hesitation to commit capital to new undertakings; inflation disrupted the capital markets, increased interest rates, and undermined the value of equities, all of which forced managers to concentrate their efforts on short-term projects that would pay off debts and maintain stock price to earnings ratios.

Throughout the period, moreover, corporate tax payments to the federal government increased with artificially surging profits. Standard accounting statements meanwhile had not adequately reflected the replacement costs for capital and inventories. To avoid these new costs, financial managers, according to the CED, misspent their energies, developing tax-saving schemes rather than capital projects that might substantially enhance their firms' productive capacity.[130] Thus, real profits and capital investments dwindled, and, the CED concluded, inflation and decreasing productivity had become mutually reinforcing phenomena.

To break this spiral the CED insisted on reforming macroeconomic policy. Ever since the CED's original support for modified Keynesian policies in the 1940s, it had rallied behind fiscal, not monetary, initiatives to engineer the economy. With the stagflation of the 1970s, the CED reasserted its basic support for fiscal policy and objected to the Federal Reserve Board's (FRB) erratic handling of the money supply, in particular, the FRB's flipflop from easy money policies in 1971–72 to tight ones in 1973–74. From those changing policies, the CED had inferred a belief on the FRB's part that restrictive monetary policy could, by itself, break the inflationary spiral. CED analysts felt such a course foolhardy, because the recession induced by restrictive monetary policy would inevitably render politicians more amenable to undesirable inflationary fiscal responses to mobilize the economy. In addition, high interest rates prompted by the FRB's desire to slow the economy would attract foreign capital to the United States and push the dollar's value up. A strong dollar—buoyed by the FRB's tight monetary policy—would open the

United States to foreign competition and cause even more unemployment. Good sense, according to the CED, demanded that monetary policy serve fiscal policy by avoiding extreme policies of expansion and contraction and by concentrating its efforts on sustaining an efficient capital market.[131]

Since the mid-1960s, the CED maintained, imprudent social spending had induced inflation: The federal government had been competing with industry for capital and so forcing interest rates up. To make matters worse, the federal budget directed capital investments in an economically unsound way, namely, through unchecked federal loan guarantee programs. In fact, in the CED's opinion, the enormous expansion of social-welfare spending after 1964 functioned as an alternative to the market for distributing wealth. Furthermore, the CED believed that the congressional budget process encouraged excess by simply adding up budget proposals instead of setting budgetary objectives consistent with economic trends. The CED characterized what had happened in broad ideological terms by arguing that the state's imprudence was the product of an excessive democracy that stymied individual freedom and economic efficiency.[132] In this respect, federal officials had disrupted the postwar pluralist design of business-government relations, along with its balance of public and private power.

To redress the situation, the CED advocated budgetary reforms to those already instituted in 1974 and a review of federal programs to make sure they conformed to strict market principles.[133] The proposed reforms, which the CED submitted in a 1979 report entitled *Redefining the Government's Role in the Market System*, suggested that conflicting policy demands should be reconciled on the basis of a single criterion—market efficiency. While the CED's report acknowledged that efficiency alone would not satisfy the demands for greater substantive equality, environmental protection, and improved public health, it nevertheless asserted that without a prosperous economy in the first instance, those demands could never be satisfied.[134]

Subsequently, the CED also advocated tax reform as part of its agenda for restructuring government's role in the economy. In general, reducing the effective tax rate on income generated from capital would shift tax burdens from productive to consumption expenditures.[135] Prominent among the CED's recommendations was a proposal for rapid capital depreciation rates. In addition, the CED recommended the elimination of the special tax breaks individual industries had secured through the "iron triangles" to allow for an across-the-board lowering of the corporate tax rate. The equalizing of tax rates across industries would serve to improve the market and contribute to sustained growth; firm profits would once more depend on economic rather than political dexterity, and managers would be forced to pay primary attention to business, not political affairs.[136]

Finally, at least for our purposes, the CED sought regulatory reform. In the hopes of improving productivity, it advocated a review of economic regulation that had long protected certain industries from market competition. Similarly, the CED believed that social regulation as it was constructed interfered with the managerial prerogative and so worked against sound economic decisions.[137] Accordingly, the CED proposed that social regulation be subjected to cost-benefit evaluations and that market incentives be incorporated into all regulatory designs. Of all these regulatory issues, the CED campaigned most passionately for an end to oil price controls.[138]

2. *The Continuing Struggle for Corporate Advantage.* Interestingly, the kind of coherence found in the CED's program has prompted some observers to conclude that big business can act with a single purpose.[139] To underscore that conclusion, they point to the Business Roundtable, which appeared in 1972 as the main lobbying and education group for big business.[140] In so doing, these writers neglect the centrality of managerial autonomy and firm independence as positive principles around which corporate sector firms rally. For otherwise the writers would note that, the need for economic stabilization policies notwithstanding, corporate sector managers will resist the formation of a strong encompassing organization that has the authority to forge a unified corporate political program and course of action. Indeed, both the CED and the Business Roundtable have looked to the firm for the political muscle to reform government and have consistently shied away from centralizing proposals, thus seriously undercutting big business's organizational capacity to act as a "class." Such a strategy conforms not only to the firm-oriented bias of the American economy but also to the bias favoring multiple trade and business associations that reproduce the business community's competitive fractures in their political initiatives.

The business community in the United States has remained seriously divided, with associations that reinforce the great divide between big and small business. The CED and the Business Roundtable, along with the Business Council, provide big business with its principal forums for reflecting on and intervening in public policies that affect the "business community." Small business, meanwhile, has its own champions—the National Federation of Independent Businesses (NFIB) and the U.S. Chamber of Commerce.[141] Although the NFIB denies membership to large firms, the Chamber embraces both big and small and, so, has attempted to mediate between them. But for the most part, policy differences between big and small are significant and frequently unresolved.

The business community's peak associations have no public authority, so even their own members are not bound to follow the organizations' recommendations. For example, the Business Roundtable's insistence that its corporate members institute public-affairs offices that are "class conscious" is moral rhetoric, for the Business Roundtable has no power to impose such a requirement on its corporate members. The Chamber of Commerce finds itself in similar circumstances: unable to negotiate between its members' differences effectively, it has usually shied away from taking stands on divisive issues.

True, reform has also occurred among business associations as we have seen in the CED's commitment to restructuring American "political economy" and in the formation of the Business Roundtable[142] None of them can overcome the basic factionalism of the business community, and none supports recommendations for hierarchical coordination of business' political activities. These business associations, for example, have resisted the call for an "industrial policy" that would serve to facilitate cooperation among competing business interests, labor, and government.[143] Perhaps the resistance to new "corporatist" solutions is also linked to earlier failures, including the NRA and Nixon's wage-price stabilization program. At the same time, the corporate sector has moved toward the perception that decentralized private-planning mechanisms constrained by the market offer greater efficiencies than public planning.[144]

Leadership in business politics largely comes from individual firms.[145] Before 1970, even firms with active policy programs had small public affairs offices with narrow responsibilities. Trade associations evolved to take up the slack and still constituted—together with peak associations—the focal points of business-sector political activity. After 1970, however, the large firm increased its range of political action, but to ward off the challenges of "public interest" reformers and to gain flexibility in an era of deteriorating public-private commitments. By the early 1980s, a large proportion of *Fortune* 500 firms (in industries as diverse as energy, insurance, chemicals, and telecommunications) had substantial public-affairs offices integrated into their daily and strategic operations.[146]

The transformation at the firm level was pervasive; if the central apparatus for corporate-sector political initiative had not been at the firm level before, by the 1980s it most certainly was. Trade associations—particularly for those industries hard hit by social regulation or economic decline—lost their leadership roles in formulating industry political strategies. In industries characterized by large firms, the firms internalized many lobbying costs and integrated them into their strategic policies; accordingly, they preferred to formulate strategies independently and resisted supporting industry lobbyists that duplicated efforts or sustained competitors' political interests.[147]

The dependence of business's political activity on the firm is manifested in a decentralized strategy to promote macroeconomic and industrial reform through *ad hoc* coalitions that include public-interest groups.[148] Corporations, in other words, are not trying to "redefine government" by establishing novel "tripartite commissions" or central planning boards; rather, they are hoping to accomplish that reformation through traditional pluralist means of *ad hoc* coalition building, even if these are somewhat broader than has previously been the case. To be sure, these coalitions have been used to secure competitive advantage. Nonetheless, these coalitions, assisted by business's financial and organizational resources, provide forums in which to foster corporate legitimacy on a much broader ideological basis.

As firm-centered coalitions, in the electoral as well as legislative and regulatory processes, become more effective and important, they force others to consider carefully their assumptions about the market's efficiency. Politicians, for example, are well aware that large corporations are now a more important source of campaign funds than labor; to access these new funds most candidates endorse legislation that makes use of economic incentives and is justified on grounds of market efficiency.[149] Even though increasing the firm's political abilities may foster business factionalism over specific policy revisions, sufficient unity has been achieved, particularly in opposition to labor and its allies, for the corporate sector to have played an important role in bringing about the recent bipartisan conservative shift in public policy.[150]

Corporate Cohesion, Corporate Fragmentation

The integration of the public-affairs function into the strategic-planning process has given the well-known claim of Adolf Berle and Gardiner Means in 1932,[151] that good management is in fact good statesmanship, an operationally specific meaning that even these two thinkers could not have foreseen. The consequent business mobilization, along with the far-ranging policy recommendations of peak associations such as the CED, has caused some writers to conclude that corporate collective action is not only possible but actual.[152]

At the same time, a number of writers have also highlighted the fractious consequences of decentralizing corporate political power. Studies covering a wide range of cross-industry public-policy issues, including deregulation, industrial policy, and environmental regulation,[153] lend support to earlier pluralists' assessment that corporate "solidarity" is implausible.[154]

The point of this essay has been to show that this apparently irreconcilable dichotomy—cohesion versus fragmentation—has a historically specific meaning. The peculiar forms of collective political action among corporate sector firms in the United States has functioned not just to legitimatize the role of the large firm in the American economy, but at least since the 1930s to reaffirm management's authority in arranging the contractual relationships among the firm's stakeholders. When management fails to keep its affairs private, the corporations typically lose bargaining power, particularly in relationship to organized labor. Thus, the threat of government scrutiny and, worse, regulatory intrusion into the bargaining process between management and the firm's various stakeholders and, through macroeconomic policies, into managerial authority over the firm's investments develops a need and a disciplinary force for coordinated political action among managers. Yet, this form of collectivity seeks to perpetuate managerial autonomy and so fosters competition among firms in their efforts to secure competitive advantages through industrial policies. That this combination has met with political success over the past half century can be attributed in large part to the political traditions and constitutional values particular to the United States. For these reasons, we contend that the corporate sector displays a dual pattern of solidarity and rivalry.

University of New Hampshire
University of Massachusetts, Amherst
University of Minnesota

Notes

1. Richard L. McCormick, "The Discovery that Business Corrupts Politics: A Reappraisal of the Origins of Progressivism." *American History Review* 86 (1981), 247–74.

2. Among the basic works on this topic are Raymond Bauer, Ithiel de Sola Pool, and Lewis Anthony Dexter, *American Business and Public Policy: The Politics of Foreign Trade* (New York, 1963); Arnold M. Rose, *The Power Structure: Political Process in American Society* (New York, 1967); and Edwin Epstein, *The Corporation in American Politics* (Englewood Cliffs, N.J., 1969).

3. C. Wright Mills, *The Power Elite* (New York, 1956) remains the classic dissenting work; also see G. William Domhoff, *Who Rules America?* (Englewood Cliffs, 1967).

4. Much of the recent debate has focused on corporate political-action committees.

See, for example, Dan Clawson, Alan Neudstadtl, and James Bearden, "The Logic of Business Unity: Corporate Contributions to 1980 Congressional Elections," *American Sociological Review* 51 (1988), 797–811; Allen Kaufman, Marvin Karson, and Jeffrey Sohl, "Corporate Factionalism and Corporate Solidarity in the 1980 and 1982 Congressional Elections," *Journal of Political and Military Sociology* 15 (1987), 171–85; Theodore J. Eismeier and Philip H. Pollock III, "The Retreat from Partisanship: Why the Dog Didn't Bark in the 1984 Election," in Alfred Marcus, Allen Kaufman, and David Beam, eds., *Business Strategy and Public Policy: Perspectives from Industry and Academic* (Westport, 1987); Ian Maitland, "Interest Group Politics and Economic Growth Rate," *Journal of Politics* 47 (1986), 44–58; Thomas Byrne Edsall, *The New Politics of Inequality: How Political Power Shapes Economic Policy* (New York, 1984); Theodore J. Eismeier and Philip H. Pollock, III, *Business, Money, and the Rise of Corporate PACs in American Politics* (New York, 1988).

5. Michael Useem, *The Inner Circle: Large Corporations and the Rise of Business Political Activity in the U.S. and U.K.* (New York, 1984); and Beth Mintz and Michael Schwartz, *The Power Structure of American Business* (Chicago, 1985).

6. Mancur Olson, Jr., *The Rise and Decline of Nations: Economic Growth, Stagflation, and Social Rigidities* (New Haven, 1982).

7. Suzanne Berger has assembled a collection of essays that challenge pluralist views in *Organizing Interests in Western Europe* (Cambridge, 1981).

8. E. E. Schattschneider, *The Semi-Sovereign People: A Realist's View of Democracy in America* (New York, 1960); and Charles E. Lindblom, *Politics and Markets: The World's Political Economic Systems* (New York, 1977).

9. The classic work is J. Von Neuman and O. Morgenstern, *The Theory of Games and Economic Behavior* (Princeton, 1944); for a summary of recent developments, see Martin Shubik, *Game Theory in the Social Sciences: Concepts and Solutions* (Cambridge, MA, 1982).

10. Mancur, Olson, Jr., *The Logic of Collective Action* (Cambridge, MA, 1965).

11. Russell Hardin, *Collective Action* (Baltimore, 1982).

12. Olson, *The Logic of Collective Action*, 9–16; and Olson, *The Rise and Decline of Nations*, chap. 2.

13. See, for example, Edward S. Mason, ed., *The Corporation in Modern Society* (Cambridge, MA, 1959); Arthur M. Schlesinger, Sr., "Biography of a Nation of Joiners," in *American Historical Review* 50 (1944), 1–25; and Adolf A. H. Berle, Jr., and Gardiner Means, *The Modern Corporation and Private Property* (New York, 1933).

14. Kim McQuaid, *Big Business and Presidential Power* (New York, 1982); Lindblom, *Politics and Markets*; John K. Galbraith, *The New Industrial State*, 2d ed. (Boston, 1971); and Grant McConnell, *Private Power and American Democracy* (New York, 1966).

15. Reinhard Bendix, *Work and Authority in Industry: Ideologies of Management in the Course of Industrialization* (Berkeley, 1974), provides a useful comparative study on this topic; Francis X. Sutton, Seymour E. Harris, Carl Kaysen, James Tobin, *The American Business Creed* (Cambridge, MA, 1956), documents the ideological unity that underlies American managerial political practice.

16. The essays in Alfred Marcus, Allen Kaufman, and David Beam, eds., *Business Strategy and Public Policy* explore this topic.

17. Ida M. Tarbell, *The Life of Elbert H. Gary: The Story of Steel* (New York, 1925), 137.

18. The relevant works are Alfred D. Chandler, Jr., *Strategy and Structure: Chapters in the History of the Industrial Enterprise* (Cambridge, MA, 1962); Alfred D. Chandler, Jr., *The Visible Hand: The Managerial Revolution in American Business* (Cambridge, MA, 1977); Naomi Lamoreaux, *The Great Merger Movement in American Business, 1895–1904* (Cambridge, 1985); Martin J. Sklar, *The Corporate Reconstruction of American Capitalism, 1890–1916: The Market, the Law, and Politics* (Cambridge and New York, 1988); and Ralph C. Nelson, *The Merger Movements in American Industry 1895–1956* (Princeton, 1959).

19. Sklar, *The Corporate Reconstruction of American Capitalism*, and William E. Nelson, *The Roots of American Bureaucracy, 1830–1900* (Cambridge, MA, 1982).

20. Chandler, *The Visible Hand*; in particular, see parts III and IV.

21. Vincent P. Carosso, *Investment Banking in America: A History* (Cambridge, MA, 1970), 29–32; and Vincent P. Carosso, *The Morgans: Private International Bankers, 1854–1913* (Cambridge, MA, 1987), 390–96 and chap. 13.

22. Lamoreaux, *The Great Merger Movement in American Business*, 1–5, 4–15, and chap. 3; and Thomas K. McGraw, "Rethinking the Trust Question," in Thomas K. McCraw, ed., *Regulation in Perspective: Historical Essays* (Boston, 1981), 2–6.

23. Carosso, *The Morgans*, 465–95.

24. Carosso, *The Morgans*, 219.

25. Carosso, *The Morgans*, 486–93; Edward S. Herman, *Corporate Control, Corporate Power* (Cambridge, 1981), 117–20; and David Kotz, *Bank Control of Large Corporations in the United States* (Berkeley, 1978), 31–38.

26. Carosso, *Investment Banking in America*, chap. 2; Carosso, *The Morgans*, chaps. 10 and 13.

27. Carosso, *The Morgans*, 364–65; and Richard Abrams, "Brandeis and the Ascendancy of Corporate Capitalism," in Louis Brandeis, *Other People's Money: And How the Bankers Use It* (New York, 1967), vii–xliv.

28. Arnold Paul, *Conservative Crisis and the Rule of Law: Attitudes of Bar and Bench, 1887–1895*, rev. ed. (New York, 1969), 185–237; Sklar, *The Corporate Reconstruction of American Capitalism*, 47–53; and Lamoreaux, *The Great Merger Movement*, 175–78.

29. Thomas K. McCraw, *Prophets of Regulation: Charles Francis Adams, Louis D. Brandeis, James M. Landis, Alfred E. Kahn* (Cambridge, MA, 1984), 7–40; and Gabriel Kolko, *Railroads and Regulation, 1877–1916* (Princeton, 1965), 7–29.

30. Nelson, *The Roots of American Bureaucracy*, 126–32; and Kolko, *Railroad and Regulation*, 30–44.

31. See generally, Albro Martin, *James J. Hill and the Opening of the Northwest* (New York, 1976); Albro Martin, *Enterprise Denied: Origins of the Decline of American Railroads, 1897–1917* (New York, 1971); and Kolko, *Railroads and Regulation*, 80–90, 135–43.

32. The relationships between the banks and antitrust litigation must be put together through the doctrinal and interest-group histories on the topic. For example, see Sklar, *The Corporate Reconstruction of American Capitalism*, 104–13; Lamoreaux, *The Great Merger Movement*, chap. 6; William Letwin, *Law and Economic Policy in America: The Evolution of the Sherman Antitrust Act* (New York, 1965), 100–237; Gabriel Kolko, *The Triumph of Conservatism: A Reinterpretation of American History, 1900–1916* (New York, 1963), 61–72; and Hans Thorelli, *The Federal Antitrust Policy: Origination of an American Tradition* (Baltimore, 1955), 235–556.

33. Morton Horowitz, "*Santa Clara* Revisited: The Development of Corporate Theory," *West Virginia Law Review* 88 (1985), 173–224; Charles W. McCurdy, "The Knight Sugar Decision of 1895 and the Modernization of American Corporate Law, 1869–1903," *Business History Review* 53 (1979), 304–42; and James Willard Hurst, *The Legitimacy of the Business Corporation in the Law of the United States, 1780–1970* (Charlottesville, 1970), 15–22.

34. Horowitz, "*Santa Clara.*"

35. See note 33.

36. Nelson, *The Roots of American Bureaucracy*, chaps. 4 and 5.

37. Horowitz, "*Santa Clara,*" and Hurst, *The Legitimacy of the Business Corporation*, 58–73.

38. Tarbell, *The Life of Elbert H. Gary*, 126–51. For the years prior to World War I, see Ida M. Tarbell, *New Ideals in Business* (New York, 1916); and Walter Lippmann, *Drift and Mastery: An Attempt to Diagnose the Current Unrest* (Englewood Cliffs, 1961).

39. Martin, *Enterprise Denied*, 51–95; and Chandler, *The Visible Hand*, chap. 3.

40. Alfred Chandler recounts the history of the auto industry in his *Strategy and Structure*, chap. 3. Also see Davis Dyer, Malcolm S. Salter, and Alan Webber, *Changing Alliances: The Harvard Business School Project on the Auto Industry and the American Economy* (Boston, 1987), 23–36.

41. John Moody, *The Truth About the Trusts: A Description and Analysis of the American Trust Movement* (New York, 1904), 490–93; Robert H. Wiebe, *Businessmen and Reform: A Study of the Progressive Movement* (Cambridge, MA, 1962), 21–41; and Mark Mizruchi, *The American Corporate Network: 1904–1974* (Beverly Hills, 1982), 100–109.

42. Wiebe, *Businessmen and Reform*, 179–224.

43. Chandler, *The Visible Hand*, 464–68; Neil Fligstein, "The Intraorganizational Power Struggle: Rise of Finance Personnel to Top Leadership in Large Corporations, 1919–1979," *American Sociological Review* 52 (1987), 44–58; and Edwin T. Layton, Jr., *The Revolt of the Engineers: Social Responsibility and the American Engineering Profession* (Baltimore, 1986), 10–13.

44. John Desmond Glover, *The Revolutionary Corporations: Engines of Plenty, Engines of Growth, Engines of Change* (Homewood, IL, 1980), 35–41.

45. Chandler, *Strategy and Structure*, 7–17.

46. H. Thomas Johnson and Robert S. Kaplan provide an excellent historical treatment of the accounting profession in their *Relevance Lost: The Rise and Fall of Management Accounting* (Boston, 1987); see also David F. Hawkins, "The Development of Modern Financial Reporting Practices Among American Manufacturing Corporations," *Business History Review* 37 (1963), 135–68.

47. Chandler, *Strategy and Structure*, 290–98.

48. Oliver Williamson, *The Economic Institutions of Capitalism: Firms, Markets, Relational Contracting* (New York, 1985), 287–88.

49. Louis Galambos and Joseph Pratt, *The Rise of the Corporate Commonwealth: U.S. Business and Public Policy in the Twentieth Century* (New York, 1988), 92–99.

50. William J. Barber, *From New Era to New Deal: Herbert Hoover, The Economists and American Economic Policy, 1921–1933* (Cambridge, 1985), 8–13; and Ellis Hawley, *The New Deal and the Problem of Monopoly: A Study in Economic Ambivalence* (Princeton, 1966), 7–13.

51. U. S. Department of Commerce, *Historical Statistics of the United States: Colonial Times to 1970* (Washington, D.C., 1975), 284; and Daniel Horowitz, *The Morality of Spending: Attitudes Toward the Consumer Society, 1875–1940* (Baltimore, 1985), 120–23.

52. Sklar, *The Corporate Reconstruction of American Capitalism*, 204–13; and James Weinstein, *The Corporate Ideal in the Liberal State: 1900–1918* (Boston, 1968), 6–39.

53. See Allan G. Gruchy, *Modern Economic Thought: The American Contribution* (New York, 1948).

54. John Patrick Diggins, *The Bard of Savagery: Thorstein Veblen and Modern Social Theory* (New York, 1978), 90–95.

55. For a thorough discussion of this topic, see Robert D. Cuff, *The War Industries Board: Business-Government Relations During World War I* (Baltimore, 1973).

56. Barber, *From New Era to New Deal*, chap. 1; Ellis Hawley, "Herbert Hoover, the Commerce Secretariat and the Vision of an 'Associative' State," *Journal of American History* 61 (1974), 116–40; and Ellis Hawley, "The Facets of Hooverian Associationalism: Lumber, Aviation, and Movies, 1921–1930," in Thomas McCraw, ed., *Regulation in Perspective: Historical Essays* (Boston, 1981), 95–123.

57. The principal histories of the period are G. Cullom Davis, "The Transformation of the Federal Trade Commission," *The Mississippi Valley Historical Review* 49 (1962), 437–55; Carl McFarland, *Judicial Control of the Federal Trade Commission and Interstate Commerce Commission, 1920–1930: A Comparative Study of the Relations of Courts to Administrative Commissions* (Cambridge, MA, 1933); and Thomas C. Blaisdell, *The Federal Trade Commission: An Experiment in the Control of Business* (New York, 1932). For an interpretive assessment, see Lawrence S. Zacharias, "Unfairness, Advertising Regulation and Corporate Legitimacy" (School of Management Working Paper Series, University of Massachusetts, Amherst, 1985).

58. Galambos and Pratt, *The Rise of the Corporate Commonwealth*, 92–99.

59. Richard S. Tedlow, *Keeping the Corporate Image: Public Relations and Business, 1900–1950* (Greenwich, 1979), 31–48.

60. McCraw, "Rethinking the Trust Question," 17–19; and Robert T. Averitt, *The Dual Economy: The Dynamics of American Industry Structure* (New York, 1968), 47–58.

61. See, for instance, Sanford M. Jacoby, *Employing Bureaucracy: Managers, Unions and the Transformation of Work in American Industry, 1900–1945* (New York, 1985); Sanford M. Jacoby, "The Development of Internal Labor Markets in American Manufacturing Firms," in P. Osterman, ed., *Internal Labor Markets* (Cambridge, MA, 1984); and Daniel Nelson, *Managers and Workers: Origins of the New Factory System in the United States, 1880–1920* (Madison, 1975).

62. Thomas C. Cochran, *Business in American Life: A History* (New York, 1972), 305–12.

63. Vincent P. Carosso, *Investment Banking in America*, chaps. 15–19.

64. Barber, *From New Era to New Deal*, chaps. 4–6.

65. McCraw, *Prophets of Regulation*, 169–81; and Michael E. Parrish, *Securities Regulation and the New Deal* (New Haven, 1970), 1–4.

66. McCraw, *Prophets of Regulation*, 181–200. For an excellent biography of Landis, see Donald A. Ritchie, *James M. Landis: Dean of the Regulators* (Cambridge, MA, 1980).

67. David Riesman in Louchheim, ed., *The Making of the New Deal: The Insiders Speak* (Cambridge, MA, 1983), 75–76.

68. Management pursued this opportunity through the National Recovery Administration. For a discussion of the NRA, see John Kennedy Ohl, *Hugh S. Johnson and the New Deal* (Dekalb, IL, 1985); and Bernard Bellush, *The Failure of the NRA* (New York, 1975).

69. Barber, *From New Era to New Deal*, 190–92.

70. Ohl, *Hugh S. Johnson and the New Deal*, chap. 7 details the codes in a number of industries, including coal, oil, autos, textiles, and lumber.

71. See especially Belush, *The Failure of the NRA*, 55–84, 176–79.

72. The antecedents of FDR's "court-packing" plan have been amply covered by Frank Friedel, "The Sick Chicken Case," in John Garraty, ed., *Quarrels That Have Shaped the Constitution* (New York, 1964).

73. Robert M. Collins, *The Business Response to Keynes, 1929–1964* (New York, 1981), 31–42; and Thomas C. Cochran, *The American Business System: A Historical Perspective, 1900–1955* (Cambridge, MA, 1957), 316–21.

74. Kim McQuaid, "Corporate Liberalism in the American Business Community, 1920–1940," *Business History Review* 52 (1978), 342–68.

75. William E. Leuchtenberg, *Franklin D. Roosevelt and the New Deal, 1932–1940* (New York, 1963), 146–166; and Arthur M. Schlesinger, Jr., *The Age of Roosevelt: The Politics of Upheaval, 1935–1936* (Boston, 1960), 316–21.

76. Schlesinger, *The Age of Roosevelt*, 291–342 and 385–423.

77. Jordan A. Schwartz, *Liberal: Adolf A. Berle and the Vision of an American Era* (New York, 1987), 50–68.

78. In general, the law defines management's relationship to the firm's stakeholders either in trustee or contract terms. See John C. Coffee, Jr., "Shareholders vs. Managers: The Strain in the Corporate Web," in John C. Coffee, Jr., Louis Lowenstein, and Susan Rose-Ackerman, eds., *Knights, Raiders, and Targets: The Impact of the Hostile Takeover* (New York, 1988), 110–13; and Allen M. Kaufman and Lawrence Zacharias, "The Problem of the Corporation and the Evolution of Social Values," presented at the Academy of Management Annual Meeting, New Orleans, 1987. For the purposes of this essay, we make use of the contractual approach. For example, see Coffee, "Shareholders vs. Managers," 77–110; Masahiko Aoki, *The Co-operative Game Theory of the Firm* (Oxford, 1984); and Eugene F. Fama and Michael C. Jensen, "Separation of Ownership and Control," *Journal of Law and Economics* 26 (1983), 301–25. Among these scholars two serious disagreements exist. First, there is a descriptive disagreement as to whether management has a distinctive interest; and second, there is a normative question as to whether management should function as a

referee, impartially negotiating among the stakeholders, or as an agent of the shareholders. Aoki, *The Co-operative Game Theory*, chaps. 2, 3, and pp. 61–63 summarizes these debates.

79. R. Edward Freeman, *Strategic Management: A Stakeholder Approach* (Boston, 1984), provides an excellent introduction to the idea of corporate stakeholders and corporate stakeholder management.

80. Kaufman and Zacharias, "The Problem of the Corporation."

81. Hawley, *The New Deal and the Problem of Monopoly*, 14–16.

82. Zacharias, "Unfairness, Advertising Regulation and Corporate Legitimacy," and Richard S. Tedlow, "From Competitor to Consumer: The Changing Focus of Federal Regulation of Advertising, 1914–1938," *Business History Review* 55 (1981), 35–58.

83. McCraw, *Prophets of Regulation*, 201–3.

84. Zacharias, "Unfairness, Advertising Regulation and Corporate Legitimacy," 14–32; and Robert H. Bork, *The Antitrust Paradox: A Policy at War with Itself* (New York, 1978).

85. Lowell Mason, *The Language of Dissent* (Cleveland, 1959), 31–44.

86. Mason, *The Language of Dissent*, 115–17, 274–78, 301–4; and Schattschneider, *The Semi-Sovereign People*, 47–61, 129–42.

87. Christopher L. Tomlins, *The State and the Unions: Labor Relations, Law and the Organized Labor Movement in America, 1880–1960* (Cambridge and New York, 1985), 100–138; and Howell John Harris, *The Right to Manage: Industrial Relations Policies of American Business in the 1940s* (Madison, 1982), 20–23.

88. Tomlins, *The State and the Unions*, 132–38.

89. Tomlins, *The State and the Unions*, 172–95, 216–39; and Bert Cochran, *Labor and Communism: The Conflict That Shaped American Unions* (Princeton, 1977), 248–71.

90. Harris, *The Right to Manage*, 154–56.

91. For an intellectual history of pluralism, see David M. Ricci, *The Tragedy of Political Science: Politics, Scholarship and Democracy* (New Haven, 1984); Carol Pateman, *Participation and Democratic Theory* (Cambridge, 1970); and Robert Fowler, *Believing Skeptics: American Intellectuals, 1945–1965* (Westport, 1978).

92. Robert Griffith, "Dwight D. Eisenhower and the Corporate Commonwealth," *American Historial Review* 87 (1982), 122.

93. Richard B. Stewart, "Regulation in a Liberal State: The Role of Non-Commodity Values," *Yale Law Journal* 92 (1983), 1537–90; J. Ronald Fox, *Managing Business-Government Relations: Cases and Notes on Business-Government Problems* (Homewood, IL, 1982), 137–38; McConnell, *Private Power and American Democracy*, 338–52.

94. Galambos and Pratt, *The Rise of the Corporate Commonwealth*, 131–54, 211–13.

95. Ernest Gelhorn and Barry B. Boyer, *Administrative Law in a Nutshell*, 2d ed. (St. Paul, 1981).

96. J. Leiper Freeman, *The Political Process: Executive Bureau-Legislative Committee Relations* (New York, 1955), 6–14; and Thomas L. Gais, Mark A. Peterson, and Jack L. Walker, "Interest Groups, Iron Triangles and Representative Institutions in American National Government," *British Journal of Political Science* 14 (1984), 161–63.

97. Theodore J. Lowi, *The End of Liberalism: The Second Republic of the United States*, 2d ed. (New York, 1979), 50–63.

98. Robert Griffith, "Forging America's Postwar Order: Politics and Political Economy in the Age of Truman," unpublished manuscript, 1984.

99. Graham Wilson, *Business and Politics: A Comparative Introduction* (Chatham, 1985), 8–13.

100. David Vogel, "Why Businessmen Distrust Their State: The Political Consciousness of American Corporate Executives," *British Journal of Political Science* 8 (1978), 45–78: Thomas K. McGraw, "Business and Government: The Origins of the Adversary Relationship," *California Management Review* 26 (1984), 33–52.

101. Collins, *The Business Response to Keynes*, 43–52.

102. Collins, *The Business Response to Keynes*, chaps. 3 and 4.

103. Jonathan R. T. Hughes, *The Vital Few: The Entrepreneur and American Economic Progress*, rev. ed. (New York, 1986), 517–47.

104. John K. Galbraith summarizes these ideas in *American Capitalism: The Concept of Countervailing Power*, 2d ed. (Boston, 1956) and *The New Industrial State*.

105. Herbert Stein, *Presidential Economics: The Making of Economic Policy from Roosevelt to Reagan and Beyond* (New York, 1984), chapter 3; Griffith, "Dwight D. Eisenhower and the Corporate Commonwealth;" and Collins, *The Business Response to Keynes*, chaps. 6 and 7.

106. See, for example, Collins, *The Business Response to Keynes;* Galbraith, *American Capitalism;* Robert Lekachman, *The Age of Keynes* (New York, 1966); McConnell, *Private Power and American Democracy;* and Galambos and Pratt, *The Rise of the Corporate Commonwealth*, 119–54.

107. Allen J. Matusow, *The Unraveling of America: A History of Liberalism in the 1960s* (New York, 1984), 32–59.

108. See Epstein, *The Corporation in American Politics*, chaps. 4 and 5.

109. Matusow, *The Unraveling of America*, chap. 6.

110. For an account of these developments, see Hugh Heclo, "Issue Networks and the Executive Establishment," in Anthony King, ed., *The New American Political System* (Washington, D.C., 1978); and Gais et al., "Interest Groups," 164–85. On public interest groups, see Andrew S. McFarland, *Public Interest Lobbies: Decision-Making on Energy* (Washington, D.C., 1976), for a useful introduction to public-interest groups. Also see Mark V. Nadel, *The Politics of Consumer Protection* (Indianapolis, 1971); Jeffrey M. Berry, *Lobbying for the People: The Political Behavior of Public Interest Groups* (Princeton, 1977); and Simon Lazarus, *The Genteel Populists* (New York, 1974).

111. Olson, *The Rise and Decline of Nations*, 69–73; Samuel P. Huntington, "The United States," in Michel J. Crozier, Samuel P. Huntington, and Joji Watanuki, *The Crisis of Democracy: Report on the Governability of Democracies to the Trilateral Commission* (New York, 1975), 59–118; and Committee for Economic Development, *Redefining Government's Role in the Market System* (New York, 1979), 13–15.

112. David Vogel, "The 'New' Social Regulation in Historical and Comparative Perspective," in Thomas K. McCraw, ed., *Regulation in Perspective: Historical Essays* (Cambridge, MA, 1981), 155–86.

113. Alfred C. Neal, *Business Power and Public Policy: Experiences of the Committee for Economic Development* (New York, 1981), 40–41; and Allen Schick, "The First Five Years of Congressional Budgeting," in Rudolph G. Penner, ed., *The Congressional Budget Process After Five Years* (Washington, D.C., 1981), 4–7.

114. McQuaid, *Big Business and Presidential Power*, 266–67.

115. Frank V. Fowlkes, "Washington Pressures: CED's Impact on Federal Policies Enhanced by Close Ties to Executive Branch," *National Journal* (27 June 1987), 1015–24; Hugh Rockoff, *Drastic Measures: A History of Wage and Price Controls in the United States* (New York, 1984), chap. 7; and Neil de Marchi, "The First Nixon Administration: Prelude to Controls," in Craufurd D. Goodwin, ed., *Exhortation and Controls: The Search for a Wage-Price Policy, 1945–1971* (Washington, D.C., 1975), 295–352.

116. Robert Gilpin, *The Political Economy of International Relations* (Princeton, 1987), 134–42; David P. Calleo, *The Imperious Economy* (Cambridge, MA, 1982), chap. 4; Stein, *Presidential Economics* (Princeton, 1982), 155–80; and Fred L. Block, *The Origins of International Economic Disorder: A Study of U.S. International Monetary Policy from World War II to the Present* (Berkeley, 1977), chaps. 6 and 7.

117. McQuaid, *Big Business and Presidential Power*, 270–81.

118. McFarland, *Public Interest Lobbies*, 4–12; and Vogel, "The New Social Regulation," 164–75.

119. Murray Weidenbaum, *Business, Government and the Public* (Englewood Cliffs, 1977), 372–74.

120. Ralph Nader and Mark J. Green, eds., *Corporate Power in America* (New York, 1973); and Vogel, *Lobbying the Corporation: Citizen Challenges to Business Authority* (New York, 1978), 11–18.

121. Christopher Stone, *Where the Law Ends: The Social Control of Corporate Behavior* (New York, 1975); and Robert Dahl, "Governing the Giant Corporation," in Nader and Green, eds., *Corporate Power*, 10–24.

122. For an excellent account of energy policy, see Richard K. Vietor, *Energy Policy in America Since 1945: A Study of Business-Government Relations* (Cambridge and New York, 1984). The Committee for Economic Development spelled out its policy recommendations in *Achieving Energy Independence* (New York, 1974).

123. On the importance of productivity, see Committee for Economic Development, *Productive Policy: Key to the Nation's Economic Future: A Statement* (New York, 1984). For the corporate sector's opposition to centralized solutions to America's economic ills, see Committee for Economic Development, *Strategy for Industrial Competitiveness: A Statement by the Research and Policy Committee of the Committee for Economic Development* (New York, 1984), 76–77; and Business Roundtable, "Analysis of the Issues in the National Industrial Policy Debate: Working Papers" (New York, 1984), 10–24.

124. McQuaid, *Big Business and Presidential Power*, 293–96; and Thomas K. McGraw, "The Business Roundtable (A)," Harvard Business School Case #9–379–118 (Boston, 1979).

125. Alfred Marcus and Allen Kaufman, "The Continued Expansion of the Corporate Public Affairs Function," *Business Horizons* 31 (1988), 58–62; and James E. Post, Edwin A. Murray, Jr., Robert Dickie, and John F. Mahon, "Managing Public Affairs: The Public Affairs Function," *California Management Review* 25 (1983), 135–50.

126. Neal, *Business Power and Public Policy*, 3–5.

127. See Suzanne Berger, "Introduction," in Berger, *Organizing Interests in Western Europe*, 1–26.

128. Committee for Economic Development, *Productivity Policy*, 12.

129. Neal, *Business Power and Public Policy*, 63–64.

130. On management's misinvestments, see Neal, *Business Power and Public Policy*, 67; for a discussion about the relationship between declining productivity and inflation, see Committee for Economic Development, *Productivity Policy*, 26. Douglas Hibbs, Jr., offers a somewhat more scholarly analysis of the effects of inflation and taxation on corporate capital expenditures in *The American Political Economy: Macroeconomics and Electoral Politics* (Cambridge, MA., 1987), 101–5.

131. These arguments are laid out in Committee for Economic Development, *Fighting Inflation and Promoting Growth: A Statement on National Policy* (New York, 1976); and *Fighting Inflation and Rebuilding a Sound Economy* (New York, 1980); see also Neal, *Business Power and Public Policy*, chap. 3.

132. Committee for Economic Development, *Redefining Government's Role*, 13–14, 29–31, 41–44.

133. Committee for Economic Development, *Redefining Government's Role*, 86–90 and chaps. 6 and 7.

134. Committee for Economic Development, *Redefining Government's Role*, 18–19.

135. Neal, *Business Power and Public Policy*, 69–76.

136. Committee for Economic Development, *Productivity Policy*, 54–57; and Committee for Economic Development, *Strategy for U.S. Industrial Competitiveness*, 36–37.

137. Committee for Economic Development, *Fighting Inflation and Promoting Growth*, 57–59; *Redefining Government's Role*, 56–78; and *Productivity Policy*, 65–68.

138. Committee for Economic Development, *Achieving Energy Independence; Key Elements of a National Energy Strategy: A Statement on National Policy* (Washington, D.C., 1977); and *Helping Ensure Our Energy Future: A Program for Developing Synthetic Fuel Plants Now* (Washington, D.C., 1979).

139. For example, see Useem, *The Inner Circle*, chap. 4; Thomas Byrne Edsall, *The New Politics of Inequality: How Political Power Shapes Economic Policy* (New York, 1984), chap. 3, and McQuaid, *Big Business and Presidential Power*, chap. 4.

140. Edsall, *The New Politics*, 120–23; and McQuaid, *Big Business and Presidential Power*, 289–96.

141. Sar A. Levitan and Martha R. Cooper, *Business Lobbies: The Public Good and the Bottom Line* (Baltimore, 1984), chaps. 2 and 3.

142. Richard I. Kirkland, "Fat Days for the Chamber of Commerce," *Fortune*, 21 September 1981, 144–58.

143. Committee for Economic Development, *Strategy for U.S. Industrial Competitiveness*, 9–18; and Business Roundtable, "Analysis of the Issues," 12–28.

144. Neal, *Business Power and Public Policy*, 26–35; and Committee for Economic Development, *Redefining Government's Role in the Market System*, 29–39.

145. For an introduction to public affairs management, see Marcus et al., *Business Strategy and Public Policy*.

146. See note 125.

147. Kay Lehman Scholzman and John T. Tierney describe the declining importance of the trade association for the business community in Washington in *Organized Interests and American Democracy* (New York, 1986), 81–82. Robert H. Miles describes the formation of the public affairs office in the tobacco industry in his *Coffin Nails and Corporate Strategies* (Englewood Cliffs, 1982) and offers a general theory in *Managing the Corporate Social Environment: A Grounded Theory* (Englewood Cliffs, 1987). Other studies that explore the interactions between the firm and trade association are John F. Mahon and James E. Post, "The Evolution of Political Strategies During the 1980 Superfund Debate," in Marcus et al., *Business Strategy and Public Policy*, 61–80; Martha Derthick and Paul J. Quirk, *The Politics of Deregulation* (Washington, D.C., 1985), 157–59; and Allen Kaufman, "Synthetic Fuels and Public Policy: Challenges for Business Solidarity," in Lee Preston, ed., *Research in Corporate Social Performance and Policy* (Greenwich, 1984), 187–212.

148. Stephen E. Littlejohn, "Competition and Cooperation: New Trends in Issue Identification and Management at Monsanto and Gulf," in Marcus et al., *Business Strategy and Public Policy*, 19–30, discusses the strategic criteria that inform corporate political coalition building. Joseph L. Bower extends the argument by providing examples of corporate/public-interest group coalitions—which Bower calls forums—that have helped shape public policy; see his *The Two Faces of Management: An American Approach to Leadership in Business and Management* (Boston, 1983), chap. 9. George C. Lodge provides a similar analysis in *The American Disease* (New York, 1984), 147–69, even if he argues for a more coherent industrial policy than the corporate sector has yet been willing to endorse.

149. Edsall, *The New Politics of Inequality*, 138–40.

150. Kaufman et al., "Corporate Factionalism and Corporate Solidarity." For an assessment of the conservative shift that occurred in 1980, see Walter Dean Burnham, "Into the 1980s with Ronald Reagan," in Walter Dean Burnham, *The Current Crisis in American Politics* (New York, 1982), 268–320; James L. Sundquist and Richard M. Scammon, "The 1980 Election: Profile and Historical Perspective," in Ellis Sandoz and Cecil V. Crabb, Jr., eds., *A Tide of Discontent: The 1980 Elections and Their Meaning* (Washington, D.C., 1981), 32–33; Thomas Byrne Edsall, "The Changing Shape of Power: A Realignment in Public Policy," in Steve Fraser and Gary Gerstle, eds., *The Rise and Fall of the New Deal Order, 1930–1980* (Princeton, 1989), 269–93; Hibbs, *The American Political Economy*, 191–208; and Stein, *Presidential Economics*, chap. 9.

151. Berle and Means, *The Modern Corporation*, 356–57.

152. See, for example, Edsall, *The New Politics of Inequality*; Levitan, *Business Lobbies*, 3–8; Useem, *The Inner Circle*; and Thomas Ferguson and Joel Rogers, "The Reagan Victory: Corporate Coalitions in the 1980 Campaign," in Joel Rogers and Thomas Ferguson,

eds., *The Hidden Election: Politics and Economics in the 1980 Presidential Campaign* (New York, 1981); and Clawson et al., "The Logic of Business Unity."

153. Derthick, *The Politics of Deregulation;* Mahon and Post, *Business Strategy and Public Policy;* and Alfred Marcus and Allen Kaufman, "Why It Is Difficult to Implement Industrial Policies: Lessons from the Synfuels Experience," *California Management Review* 28 (1986), 98–114.

154. Ian Maitland, "Self-Defeating Lobbying: How More Is Buying Less in Washington," *The Journal of Business Strategy* 7 (1986), 67–74; Ian Maitland, "Collective Versus Individual Lobbying: How Business Ends Up the Loser," in Marcus et al., *Business Strategy and Public Policy*, 95–104; and Eismeier and Pollock, III, "The Retreat from Partisanship."

The New Regulation of
Health And Safety

K. ROBERT KEISER

Regulation has been used to serve numerous ends: health and safety, consumer information, fair prices and wages, product quality, economic stability, and environmental protection. The construction of any empirically based general theory of regulation depends upon the creation of more knowledge about the regulatory process and its results for each of these ends. Health and safety regulation, for example, may be an area in which governmental controls are both more politically possible and more effective. Although the federal government has long sought to protect the health and safety of consumers and workers in certain sectors of the economy, such as the food and drug industries, the airlines, and the mining industry, a new wave of legislation was passed in the 1960s and 1970s to protect the public from injury and disease. In this article, evidence concerning the Food and Drug Administration (FDA), the National Highway Traffic Safety Administration, the Occupational Safety and Health Administration (OSHA), and the Consumer Product Safety Commission (CPSC) is used to elucidate how policy has been formulated and implemented in the regulation of health and safety. This analysis focuses on those factors that either promote or impede regulatory activism; little is said about the outcomes of regulation.

CAPTURE AND IMMOBILIZATION OF REGULATORY AGENCIES

The theory that regulated industries capture the agencies established to regulate them has long dominated thinking about regulation. Although the theory was originally devised to describe the behavior of independent regulatory commis-

K. ROBERT KEISER is assistant professor of political science at San Diego State University.

Political Science Quarterly   Volume 95   Number 3   Fall 1980

479

215

sions, similar tendencies have been observed in other types of regulators. What is important about the capture theory is not that it concludes that regulation is biased in favor of industry, but that it delineates a process that leads to such a policy result. The agency, possessing ambiguous statutory authority, isolated from executive and legislative leadership, and receiving little constituency support, tends to succumb to a dependent relationship with the industry.[1] While this dependent relationship is quite subtle, some obvious indicators point to its existence, such as when the agency heavily relies upon the regulated industries to supply its staff.

The Food and Drug Administration, the oldest of the regulators in the area of health and safety, reveals some of the behavioral patterns that are part of the process of capture. Consider the following exchange between Senator Thomas Eagleton and Richard A. Merrill, the chief counsel for the Food and Drug Administration:

> Mr. MERRILL. That is right. I was in the private practice of law for four years.
> Senator EAGLETON. What firm was that with?
> Mr. MERRILL. Covington and Burling.
> Senator EAGLETON. Who was your predecessor Chief Counsel?
> Mr. MERRILL. Peter Hutt.
> Senator EAGLETON. Where was he from when he came to the Food and Drug and where did he go when he left?
> Mr. MERRILL. He came from Covington and Burling and has since returned to that firm. . . .
> Senator EAGLETON. What were the larger companies they [Covington and Burling] represented in 1969 while you were there?
> Mr. MERRILL. They did work for Parke-Davis Co. They did work for Abbott Laboratories. They did work for Ames, that is, Miles Laboratories.[2]

The use of advisory committees provide another opportunity for linkages between the agency and the industry. In order to draw from the limited supply of expertise in the field, the agency has accepted the advice of chemists, pharmacologists, and physiologists who also are employed as consultants to the industry.[3] Although some observers asserted that these outside advisers were tougher on the industry than were the agency's own people, other reports contended that abuses had occurred. When the FDA staff determined some drugs to be unsafe, the agency delayed taking any action and waited for outside recommendations.[4]

[1] Marver Bernstein, *Regulating Business by Independent Commission* (Princeton, N.J.: Princeton University Press, 1955), pp. 74–90. Detailed investigations by political scientists have cast doubt on the capture theory. See Alan Stone, *Economic Regulation and the Public Interest* (Ithaca, N.Y.: Cornell University Press, 1977), pp. 56–64, and Erwin J. Krasnow and Lawrence D. Longley, *The Politics of Broadcast Regulation* (New York: St. Martin's Press, 1978), pp. 27–90.

[2] U. S., Congress, Senate, Committee on Appropriations, *Agriculture and Related Agencies Appropriations for Fiscal Year 1978*, Part 3, 95th Cong., 1st sess., 1977, pp. 1285–86.

[3] Milton Silverman and Philip R. Lee, *Pills, Profits, and Politics* (Berkeley: University of California Press, 1974), pp. 241–42.

[4] Morton Mintz, "FDA Hit on Use of Medical Advisory Committees," *Washington Post*, 26 January 1976.

Furthermore, employees who behaved in a more adversary manner toward the industry were subjected to systematic discipline involving involuntary transfers.[5]

The impetus toward capture remains incomplete, however, because it is somewhat checked by other institutional and political forces. The FDA's statutory authority is specific and firm enough to provide the justification for substantial regulation. The 1962 Kefauver-Harris amendments to the drug laws compel manufacturers to demonstrate that new drugs are both safe and effective. Although this requirement can be challenged on the grounds that no drug is safe under every circumstance, the double imperative that must be satisfied through "well-controlled investigations . . . by experts qualified by scientific training and experience" does provide a handle for stringent regulation.[6] Some critics, in fact, have argued that the regulation has been so tight it has served to hinder the development of new drugs.[7] A key point at issue in this public debate is whether or not the agency has failed to approve new drugs of therapeutic importance. What the evidence most clearly reveals is that the FDA has hardly behaved as a captured agency.

An increase in constituent support for more regulation has acted as another deterrent to industry domination. Even when no organized interest group of significance exists to mobilize support for health and safety measures, a political entrepreneur capable of monitoring bureaucratic activity and acting as a spokesman for a constituency can bolster an agency's regulatory efforts.[8] Sidney Wolfe, head of Ralph Nader's Health Research Group, Morton Mintz, journalist for the *Washington Post*, and a few members of Congress, including Senators Edward Kennedy and Gaylord Nelson and Representatives Paul Rogers and L. H. Fountain, have played this role in relation to the FDA.

The other health and safety agencies—the National Highway Traffic Safety Administration, the Occupational Safety and Health Administration, and the Consumer Product Safety Commission—have been even less subject to capture than has the FDA. While the major safety initiatives of the National Highway Traffic Safety Administration have been opposed by the automobile companies, the agency has gained some support from the insurance companies. Both the Occupational Safety and Health Administration and the Consumer Product Safety Commission were designed with certain institutional safeguards against capture: OSHA was placed within a supportive organizational environment, the Department of Labor with its ties to the trade unions; and the CPSC was established as a horizontal agency regulating several industries, which should make it less susceptible to the formation of a symbiotic relationship with the industries it regulates.

[5] U. S., Department of Health, Education, and Welfare, Review Panel on New Drug Regulation, *Final Report* (Washington, D.C.: Government Printing Office, 1977), p. 17.

[6] *Weinberger* v. *Hynson, Westcott, and Dunning*, 412 U.S. 609 (1973).

[7] Henry G. Grabowski, *Drug Regulation and Innovation* (Washington, D. C.: American Enterprise Institute for Public Policy Research, 1976), pp. 17–37.

[8] Paul Sabatier, "Social Movements and Regulatory Agencies," *Policy Sciences* 6 (Fall 1975): 318–20.

Yet these agencies have not been any more aggressive at regulation than the FDA, and most observers would agree that OSHA and the CPSC have been less effective. Although tendencies toward capture continue to exist, and thus can hamper regulation, the principal threat to health and safety regulation is immobilization, a phenomenon which does not render the agency completely motionless, but which constrains its freedom of action and reduces its pace of operation to a form of protracted incrementalism. An agency can be immobilized by a number of conditions, including insufficient authority, the failure to obtain adequate resources, the veto actions in other parts of the government, adverse publicity that seriously damages the agency's reputation, and the goal orientations of the agency leadership.

The reverses in National Highway Traffic Safety Administration's efforts to issue an air bag standard vividly illustrates how an agency can be frustrated by veto action. The chairman of the Ford Motor Company, Henry Ford II, visited the White House to complain that the cumulative impact of emissions and safety standards would double the price of its new subcompacts. In response, the White House ordered that the introduction of a passive restraint system be postponed in favor of an interlock system that attempted to compel drivers to fasten the seat belts.[9] OSHA and the CPSC, on the other hand, have even found it difficult to initiate major regulatory efforts. During its early years OSHA lacked not only technical and professional manpower but also a strong orientation toward the problems of occupational disease. It also suffered much adverse publicity because it attempted to enforce what many considered to be trivial rules concerning safety. The CPSC has been both resource-poor and burdened with standard-setting procedures conducive to delays; it initially appeared more determined to be an open agency than to be an effective one.

PROTRACTED INCREMENTALISM AND THE NEED FOR CHANGE

Health and safety regulation has been neither comprehensive nor large scale, but rather mostly a series of marginal adjustments to an expanding number of threatening situations. An incrementalist strategy is not necessarily a conservative approach to problem solving; as Braybrooke and Lindblom point out, "the strategy specifies nothing about the speed with which change is to be carried on."[10] While conservatives may use an incrementalist strategy to move slowly, progressives may quicken the pace and advance toward their own objectives. Yet since the health and safety agencies have adopted a strategy of small steps as a result of immobilization, the incrementalist pattern they have followed has been more protracted than progressive.

Whatever the virtues of incrementalism, it is not equally suited to all public

[9] U. S., Congress, House, Committee on Interstate and Foreign Commerce, Subcommittee on Oversight and Investigations, *Federal Regulation and Regulatory Reform*, 94th Cong., 2d sess., 1976, pp. 187–88.

[10] David Braybrooke and Charles E. Lindblom, *A Strategy of Decision* (New York: Free Press, 1963), p. 109.

policies, and certain problems in health and safety are less amenable to incre-mentalist tinkering. Some health problems, for one thing, are more likely to involve long-term consequences.[11] A trial-and-error approach can be too late in the detection of error; applied to toxic substances with long latency periods and sleeper effects, it can lead to disaster. There is also the problem of irreversible effects. Incrementalist strategy assumes that marginal measures will avoid a devastating mistake that cannot be repaired. In matters of health and safety, however, irreversible effects are more likely to be produced by too little rather than too much governmental action. When piecemeal measures fail to safeguard public health, curative medicine has been unable to treat the malignant damage that carcinogens and mutagens cause.

The incrementalist tactics that the health and safety agencies have used include remediality, seriality, and bottleneck breaking.[12] OSHA's standard-setting process, responding to tragedies that have resulted from the use of such toxic substances as asbestos, vinyl chloride, bischloromethyl, and kepone, has concentrated on remedial efforts to ameliorate obvious wrongs rather than developing a more comprehensive program to promote occupational health. OSHA also has focused on the training of more health compliance officers to try to break a significant bottleneck in health protection. The FDA has altered its previously lax policy toward food and additives and has proceeded step by step against cyclamates, red dye #2, and saccharin. The pace of this sequence of actions has hardly been rapid; the ban on red dye #2 finally was decreed after some fifteen extensions that allowed for provisional use of the substance.[13]

On other occasions the regulators have neglected to seize the opportunity to employ incrementalist tactics. One example is remediality. The FDA, caught in some confusion about statutory interpretation, has been reluctant to rely on its "imminent hazard" authority to remove unsafe drugs from the marketplace once those drugs have been approved.[14] After fifteen fatalities were reported at the Bridesburg, Pennsylvania, plant of Rohm and Hass Company, OSHA fol-lowed up on the matter but failed to investigate the deaths or assign a team to inspect the plant.[15] OSHA also missed an opportunity to employ another incre-mentalist tactic—that is, the revision of marginal reforms in response to feed-back—when it maintained its asbestos standard despite the fact that the National Institute for Occupational Safety and Health reported new informa-tion revealing that the level of allowable exposure was excessive.[16]

[11] Robert Goodwin and Ilmar Waldmer, "Thinking Big, Thinking Small, and Not Thinking At All," *Public Policy* 27 (Winter 1975): 1–24.

[12] For a discussion of incrementalist tactics, see Charles E. Lindblom, *The Policy Making Process* (New York: Prentice-Hall, Inc., 1968), pp. 24–27.

[13] P. M. Boffey, "Death of a Dye," *New York Times Magazine*, 29 February 1976, p. 48.

[14] House Subcommittee on Oversight and Investigations, *Federal Regulation and Regulatory Reform*, pp. 292–94.

[15] William S. Randall and Stephen D. Solomon, *Building 6* (Boston, Mass.: Little, Brown and Co., 1977), pp. 202–7.

[16] Samuel S. Epstein, *The Politics of Cancer* (San Francisco, Calif.: Sierra Club Books, 1978), pp. 91–92.

Two alternatives to incremental politics are technical decision making, which is marked by high understanding and small change, and wars, revolutions, crises, and "grand opportunities," which are characterized by low understanding and large change.[17] Technical decision making is more likely to occur at the lower levels of the bureaucracy and is delegated to a specialized group such as engineers, economists, or physicians. The decisions that instigate large change are sometimes induced by extenuating circumstances and on other occasions are risk-taking ventures in the face of limited understanding. Since many wars, much of the decision making in response to economic instability and human disasters, and some revolutions are reactions to threatening situations, it is more likely that such attempts to leap forward are "grand defensives" rather than "grand opportunities." For health and safety regulation to become a less protracted process, it must take on some of the aspects of both technical decision making and "grand defensive" politics. Such matters as the protection of occupational health and the construction of safer automobiles require the advancement of knowledge and the use of scientific and professional expertise. But the enlargement of technical understanding and the resolution of conflict among values and interests would necessitate some risk-taking behavior on behalf of greater health and safety. These alterations in policymaking depend upon an increase in the professionalization of reform and an acceleration in the public demand for increased regulatory activism.

The Professionalization of Reform

An increasingly professionalized society, it has been suggested, should lead to a society more oriented toward reform.[18] An enlargement of the knowledge sector strengthens the societal capacity to perform the function of problem identification. In turn, the government, better guided by technical expertise, can more effectively respond to the problems that are discovered and defined. In addition, an increase in the number of relatively autonomous and economically secure occupational roles provides the opportunity for greater commitment to reform. And the rise of philanthropic foundations has provided financial support for the work of the professionals.

To some extent, the advancement of health and safety regulation has resulted from the professionalization of reform. The promotion of automobile safety, for example, was not the product of a mass movement, but rather began with the efforts of a few specialists who conducted crash tests at Cornell University and the University of California at Los Angeles.[19] Harvey Wiley, chief of the Bureau of Chemistry in the Department of Agriculture, crusaded for the original food and drug law, and Francis Kelsey's persistent resistance to an

[17] Braybrooke and Lindblom, *Strategy of Decision*, pp. 66–71.

[18] Daniel P. Moynihan, *Maximum Feasible Misunderstanding* (New York: Free Press, 1969), pp. 21–36.

[19] Charles McCarry, *Citizen Nader* (New York: Signet, 1972), pp. 63–74.

application to market thalidomide contributed to more reform. Irving Selikoff, head of the Division of Environmental Medicine at the Mount Sinai School of Medicine of the City University of New York, persevered without cooperation from the asbestos industry and without support from the Public Health Service to demonstrate that occupational exposure to asbestos was related to cancer and to press for protective measures.[20]

Nevertheless, several constraining factors have attenuated the relationship between professionalism and regulatory activism. The rudimentary level of health and safety knowledge, the deficiencies in education and training, the blockages in the occupational communications network, the sources of financial support, the biases in the sense of professional mission, and the lack of institutional support have hindered the professionalization of reform. More than anything else, the large degree of uncertainty and ignorance diminishes the amount of influence health and safety professionals can exert on public policy. For example, an insufficient data base generated from experiments on animals exists for estimating the extent of the risk of carcinogens on humans.[21] Little is also known about such potential problems as the effects of occupational noise on levels of stress.[22] And it is difficult to determine whether stricter safety regulations or changes in the levels of income, in the ratio of younger to older drivers, and in accident costs have caused a decline in highway fatality rates.[23] Visits to hospital emergency rooms have yielded quantitative information that reveals which consumer products are more often associated with accidents, but data analysis has been less certain about how products can be improved to prevent injury.[24]

Even when more knowledge has been gained, it has not always spread to many members of the professional community. Occupational diseases have been diagnosed as bronchitis or emphysema and attributed to cigarette smoking. Physicians have not been well trained to handle such cases because the subject of occupational health has been crowded out of the medical school curriculum.[25] The professional communications network used to disseminate innovations has also been insensitive to precautionary measures. A closed-circuit

[20] Paul Brodeur, *Expendable Americans* (New York: Viking Press, 1974), pp. 7-17.

[21] U. S., Congress, Office of Technology Assessment, *Cancer Testing Technology and Saccharin* (Washington, D.C.: Government Printing Office, 1977), pp. 23-24.

[22] U. S., Department of Health, Education, and Welfare, National Institute for Occupational Safety and Health, *Criteria for a Recommended Standard . . . Occupational Exposure to Noise* (Washington, D.C.: Government Printing Office, 1972), vol. IV, pp. 10-11.

[23] Sam Peltzman, "The Effects of Automobile Safety Regulation," *Journal of Political Economy* 83 (August 1975): 677-725; and U. S., Congress, House, Committee on Appropriations, Subcommittee on the Department of Transportation and Related Agencies, *Appropriations for the Department of Transportation and Related Agencies, 1977*, 94th Cong., 2d sess., 1976, pp. 369-82.

[24] Paul Bosch, "A Review and Critical Evaluation of the Consumer Product Safety Commission," *Journal of Marketing* 40 (October 1976): 48.

[25] U. S., Congress, House, Committee on Education and Labor, Subcommittee on Manpower, Compensation, and Health and Safety, *Oversight Hearings on the Occupational Safety and Health Act*, Part 2, 94th Cong., 2d sess., 1976, pp. 370-72.

television symposium, accredited by the American Medical Association but paid for by a pharmaceutical company, was criticized for neglecting to emphasize the cardiovascular effects of oral diabetic pills.[26]

Financial support from industry for scientific research and professional activities is also related to the lack of professional endorsement of regulatory activism. The National Academy of Science's food protection committee has received much of its budget from the food industry, and it has not shown much enthusiasm for strict regulation of food additives.[27] Whatever the effects of material incentives, the normative orientations of the professional community have not always been conducive to activities beneficial to health and safety protection. The biomedical scientists' preference for basic research and the medical profession's partiality for curative medicine have had negative consequences for research related to preventative health measures. Although the National Cancer Institute has been heavily subsidized, only a small portion of those funds has been directed toward research on chemical carcinogenesis and methods of cancer prevention.[28]

The efforts of professionals to improve regulatory action on behalf of health and safety depend upon some kind of institutional support. Selikoff received the cooperation of the International Association of Heat and Frost Insulators and Asbestos Workers so that he could proceed with his research on the hazards of exposure to asbestos. Wilhelm Hueper, a pioneer in the study of carcinogenesis who served as chief of the Environmental Cancer Section of the National Cancer Institute, was labeled a "troublemaker" and instructed to discontinue his epidemiological research.[29]

Public Demands for Increased Activism

Anthony Downs has asserted that all bureaucracies are subject to a law of increasing conservatism. As an agency grows older, it is likely to become dominated by conservers who are chiefly interested in convenience and security rather than by climbers who seek more power and status or by advocates and zealots who are motivated to pursue policy goals.[30] Older agencies also develop more elaborate rule systems that contribute to bureaucratic inertia. If the principal threat to health and safety regulation is immobilization, Downs's hypothesis suggests that the agencies' capacity for resistance will only diminish with the passage of time. On the other hand, while certain processes inside bureaucracy might bring about more conservatism, other dynamics, especially changing con-

[26] Morton Mintz, "Drug Makers' Influence on Doctors Is Criticized," *Washington Post*, 29 April 1976.

[27] Boffey, "Death of a Dye," p. 49.

[28] Richard A. Rettig, *Cancer Crusade* (Princeton, N.J.: Princeton University Press, 1977), pp. 305-6.

[29] Larry Agran, *The Cancer Connection* (Boston, Mass.: Houghton-Mifflin Co., 1977), pp. 27-28.

[30] Anthony Downs, *Inside Bureaucracy* (Boston, Mass.: Little, Brown and Co., 1967), pp. 18-21.

ditions outside bureaucracy, can foster more activism. Even Downs states that aging will not be associated with conservatism when an agency experiences rapid growth. The FDA, the oldest of the health and safety regulators, had its budget augmented from $3 million in 1945 to $66 million in 1968. During the same period, the number of its personnel increased from 850 to 6,200.[31] If the younger agencies experience similar growth in the future, they should be subject to less rather than more immobilization.

Budgeting tends to be incremental, a phenomenon which limits an agency's capacity for action during its early years. In its formative years, a relatively young agency such as OSHA thus possesses too little resources to make much headway in either standards development or rule enforcement. After five years of operation, for example, the agency employed less than ten health professionals in its Office of Standards Development and had introduced very few health standards.[32] It was able to employ only about one-third of the number of compliance officers envisaged in its ultimate staffing model.[33] One estimate calculated it would take the agency more than fifty years to inspect every workplace under its jurisdiction.[34] In addition, the quality of inspections suffered. Even after the situation improved, OSHA could only slowly cross-train safety inspectors in industrial hygiene and far too little equipment existed for the laboratory analysis of worksite samples.[35]

Agencies must not only accumulate resources; they must also learn from experience what tactics make for more effective policy. This repertoire of techniques includes both general prescripts useful to all agencies and specific tactics applicable to the agency's particular task. Numerous clearance points within the decision-making process can delay and obstruct any agency's efforts to implement policy.[36] OSHA, for example, has developed joint priority listings with the National Institute for Occupational Safety and Health to try to quicken the pace of the process of standards development. In a matter more peculiar to the agency's responsibilities, OSHA discovered after it had issued a strict regulation concerning vinyl chloride that the chemical industry, despite its predictions to the contrary, was able to comply with the directive without severe economic hardship.[37] Although this example demonstrates that a technology-forcing tac-

[31] Morton Mintz, "FDA—Protection Without a Sword," *Washington Post*, 3 July 1976.

[32] U. S., Congress, Senate, Committee on Appropriations, *Departments of Labor and Health, Education, and Welfare and Related Agencies Appropriations for Fiscal Year 1976*, Part 1, 94th Cong., 1st sess., 1975, p. 330.

[33] U. S., Congress, House, Committee on Appropriations, Subcommittee on the Departments of Labor and Health, Education, and Welfare, *Departments of Labor and Health, Education, and Welfare Appropriations for 1976*, Part 5, 94th Cong., 1st sess., 1975, p. 615.

[34] Ralph Nader, Mark Green, and Joel Seligman, *Taming the Giant Corporation* (New York: W.W. Norton, 1976), p. 147.

[35] U. S., Congress, House, Committee on Appropriations, Subcommittee on the Departments of Labor and Health, Education, and Welfare, *Departments of Labor and Health, Education, and Welfare Appropriations for 1979*, Part 1, 95th Cong., 2d sess., 1978, pp. 627–34.

[36] Jeffrey L. Pressman and Aaron Wildavsky, *Implementation* (Berkeley: University of California Press, 1973), pp. 143–46.

[37] Steven Rattner, "Did Industry Cry Wolf?" *New York Times*, 28 December 1975.

tic can produce results, some observers have advised that it would not work so successfully if it were applied to a less technologically advanced and economically viable industry.[38] It will take time and experience for the agency to learn what tactics work in which situations.

It has already been stated that an increase in constituent support for the health and safety regulators has helped to deter their capture by industry. The passage of new legislation and the creation of new agencies have been symbolic events, but rather than lulling members of the public into quiescence, they have contributed to an arousal of more interest in the protection of health and safety. The creation of OSHA has stimulated more labor union activity on behalf of health and safety. The Oil, Chemical, and Atomic Worker's Union has conducted a series of conferences to enhance awareness concerning the problems of occupational disease, and the number of unions insisting on more protection for their members has increased.[39] The Insurance Institute for Highway Safety, directed by the former head of the National Highway Traffic Safety Administration, and Allstate Insurance Company have strongly supported the agency in its attempt to introduce mandatory air bags for automobiles.[40] Political entrepreneurs, especially in the Congress, have been another source of constituency support for activism. Although it has been frequently asserted that Congress lacks the resources to conduct oversight, the monitoring of the bureaucracy does occur when legislators are motivated.[41] In 1973 FDA officials appeared before thirty-three committee hearings, a number which has become the norm for that agency.[42]

Although the political support for health and safety regulation is relatively weak in intensity and organization, it is periodically activated in response to recurrent calamitous events and threats of calamity. After oral contraceptives were found to have caused thromboembolism, Senator Gaylord Nelson held committee hearings concerning the problem. The FDA, in turn, ordered mandatory "patient package inserts" warning women about the risks they might incur, a decision which departed from the standard procedures for dispensing prescription drugs.[43] Subsequently, "patient package inserts" were required for other drugs. The discovery that Aldactazide, a medication G. C. Searle introduced for the treatment of high blood pressure, increased the risks of breast cancer led to inquiries concerning the validity and reliability of the testing for the approval of

[38] Herbert R. Northrup, Richard L. Rowan, and Charles R. Perry, *The Impact of OSHA* (Philadelphia: University of Pennsylvania, 1978), pp. 417–18.

[39] Samuel S. Epstein, *Politics of Cancer*, pp. 405–11 and Nicholas A. Ashford, *Crisis in the Workplace* (Cambridge, Mass.: MIT Press, 1976), pp. 199–200.

[40] Morton Mintz, "3 Stunt Drivers Cite Air Bag Safety, Call Delay on Air Bags 'Criminal,' " *Washington Post*, 3 August 1976.

[41] Morris S. Ogul, *Congress Oversees the Bureaucracy* (Pittsburgh, Pa.: University of Pittsburgh Press, 1976), pp. 181–86.

[42] Rita Ricardo Campbell, *Drug Lag* (Stanford, Calif.: Hoover Institution Press, 1976), p. 32.

[43] Silverman and Lee, *Pills, Profits, and Politics*, pp. 101–3.

new drugs.[44] Senator Edward Kennedy accordingly conducted hearings, and the FDA established a bioresearch monitoring program to improve testing procedures.[45] An investigation of the Hopewell, Virginia, disaster, in which the workers at a kepone manufacturing plant suffered severe damage to their central nervous systems, revealed that a former employee had filed a complaint to OSHA ten months before the tragedy was discovered.[46] OSHA has since revised its policy to require that any worker complaint that may constitute an imminent hazard must be investigated within twenty-four hours, and any complaint about a serious hazard must be followed up within three working days.[47]

These governmental responses to calamitous events have been more than mere symbolic acts of reassurance: a political breakthrough regarding entitlements to life and health occurred during the 1960s and early 1970s. Federal regulation was significantly expanded; the Kefauver-Harris amendments strengthened the drug laws in 1962, and the National Highway Traffic Safety Administration was created in 1966, OSHA in 1970, and the CPSC in 1972. Coming during and after the civil rights movement, the political climate of this period was particularly sensitive to issues of human rights. Protective regulations were not the only actions taken on behalf of life and health. Medicare and Medicaid were enacted, and greater action was focused on the reduction in infant mortalities.[48]

CONCLUSION

Important matters of disagreement remain to be more fully resolved in the aftermath of this political breakthrough. One dispute concerns the degree to which the protection of health and safety should be an individual responsibility or a societal responsibility. An OSHA official can still place the blame for health hazards on workers who "like their chewing tobacco" and fail to wear their respirators.[49] Part of the underlying philosophy of health and safety regulation, however, is that collective measures are more apt to save lives than are methods

[44] Morton Mintz, "FDA Evaluates Link Between Cancer, Drug," *Washington Post*, 12 July 1975.

[45] U. S., Congress, Senate, Committee on Human Resources, Subcommittee on Health and Scientific Research, *Preclinical and Clinical Testing by the Pharmaceutical Industry, 1977*, Part IV, 95th Cong., 1st. sess., 1977, pp. 26–51.

[46] House Subcommittee on Manpower, Compensation, and Health and Safety, *Oversight Hearings on the Occupational Safety and Health Act*, Part 2, pp.135–48.

[47] U. S., Congress, Senate, Committee on Human Resources, Subcommittee on Labor, *Oversight on the Administration of the Occupational Safety and Health Act*, 95th Cong., 2d sess., 1978, p. 37. This calamity-and-response behavior is more serial and less volatile than the "issue attention cycle" Downs has outlined. Health and safety regulation never rose as high as environmental protection on the public agenda nor did it experience a similar dropoff in support. See Anthony Downs, "Up and Down with Ecology—the 'Issue Attention Cycle'," *Public Interest* 28 (Summer 1972): 38–50.

[48] Karen Davis and Cathy Schoen, *Health and the War on Poverty* (Washington, D. C.: Brookings Institution, 1978), pp. 148–53.

[49] Brodeur, *Expendable Americans*, p. 78.

that require repeated individual decisions. As one public health advocate pointedly remarked, "Pasteurization is more simple than each person boiling his own milk."[50] The first chairman of the CPSC believed he was even obligated to protect the public from "some foolishness" because the commission's enabling legislation called for it to review the "reasonably foreseeable misuse" of products when it developed safety standards.[51]

The monetary cost of regulations is another issue of contention. Although the Congress instructed the National Highway Traffic Safety Administration to include economic factors in its decision-making process, the House of Representatives rejected an amendment that would have mandated that costs and benefits be equivalent. The Senate report for the legislation stipulated that safety should be the "overriding consideration."[52] The only legislative instructions to OSHA related to costs required that regulations be "feasible." The U.S. Court of Appeals for the District of Columbia declared that an entire industry could not be severely dislocated in the interests of health and safety, but profit margins could be reduced and laggard companies could be put out of business.[53]

Nothing like a "revolution in rising entitlements" has taken place;[54] what has occurred is a satisficing breakthrough committing the government to the reduction of injuries and fatalities to a more tolerable level. The availability of alternative sets of cognitive assumptions regarding the causes of accidents and injuries allow for ambivalent and contradictory public responses to regulatory issues.[55] More regulation is supported, but the ideology of individual responsibility remains embedded enough in public rhetoric to evoke protests against certain regulatory initiatives. And the greater commitment to life and health tends to waver when economic analysis projects the costs of regulations.

Immobilization, not capture, poses a major threat to health and safety regulation. To some extent, immobilization will be overcome as the numbers and expertise of the health and safety professionals are enhanced. Nevertheless, the professional community is not likely to provide the primary impetus for regulatory activism. Numerous constraints impede the professionalization of reform. Even when the levels of knowledge have increased, what will result is

[50] U. S., Congress, House, Committee on Interstate and Foreign Commerce, Subcommittee on Consumer Protection and Finance, *Installation of Passive Restraints in Automobiles*, 95th Cong., 1st sess., 1977, p. 139.

[51] U. S., Congress, House, Committee on Appropriations, Subcommittee on Department of Housing and Urban Development—Independent Agencies, *Department of Housing and Urban Development—Independent Agencies Appropriations for 1977*, Part 1, 94th Cong., 2d sess., 1976, p. 37.

[52] House Subcommittee on Oversight and Investigations, *Federal Regulation and Regulatory Reform*, p. 175.

[53] *Industrial Union Department* v. *Hodgson*, 499 F. 2nd. 467, 478 (1974).

[54] See Daniel Bell, *The Cultural Contradictions of Capitalism* (New York: Basic Books, 1976), pp. 232-35.

[55] For a discussion of alternative cognitive assumptions, see Murray Edelman, *Political Language* (New York: Academic Press, 1977), pp. 5-12.

the transformation of ignorance into uncertainty. This uncertainty will partially undermine any attempt on the part of the professionals to become spokesmen for reform, and it will encourage opposition from groups that would be adversely affected by more regulation. Furthermore, historical studies have indicated that the main thrust of organized professionals has been the pursuit of monopolization on behalf of their own interests rather than the alleviation of mass suffering or injustice.[56]

Political entrepreneurs and organized interest groups have mobilized more constituency support for regulatory activism, and a satisficing breakthrough in protective entitlements has been achieved. The scope and intensity of these public demands could be escalated because the American public, as well as the rest of the world population, places great value on good health as a personal aspiration.[57] Any increase in the recurrence of calamitous events or in perceptions of threats of calamity would contribute to the escalation of these public demands. On the other hand, the public also hopes for an improved standard of living, and any regulatory efforts that appeared to jeopardize these economic aspirations would encounter much opposition. In short, while regulatory activism has been increasing, there is little evidence to forecast a full-scale "grand defensive" against injuries and fatalities.

[56] Jeffrey Lionel Berlant, *Profession and Monopoly* (Berkeley: University of California Press, 1975); and Gerald S. Auerbach, *Unequal Justice* (New York: Oxford University Press, 1976).
[57] Hadley Cantril, *The Pattern of Human Concerns* (New Brunswick, N. J.: Rutgers University Press, 1965), pp. 34–36.

Irwin M. Marcus

THE DEINDUSTRIALIZATION OF AMERICA: HOMESTEAD, A CASE STUDY, 1959-1984

In less than two decades the United States has suffered a serious erosion of its international trade position, its heavy industry and its technological standing. The two decades after World War II witnessed the virtually uncontested international economic supremacy of the United States. However, this special era ended in the wake of the effects of the Vietnam War, the energy crisis and stagflation. Management responded to this growing peril by seeking government aid and retrenching its mainstream operations rather than increasing productivity by accelerating technological innovation. In its search for higher profits companies in heavy industry disinvested by more internationalizing and conglomerating. These developments hurt the steel workers especially in Youngstown and the Mon Valley with their almost total dependence on the industry for economic viability. By the late 1970's plant closings and job cutbacks produced massive unemployment in both areas. Its effects transcended the damage inflicted on the displaced and their families and caused serious problems for their towns. The immensity of the crisis spurred cooperation among workers, local unions and community groups. In Homestead, Local 1397 of the United Steelworkers of America took the initiative and received reinforcement from community groups especially the Tri-State Conference on Steel, the Mon Valley Unemployed Committee and the Denominational Mission Strategy. These groups devised and implemented survival programs and developed plans to improve economic conditions in the Homestead area. Their plans, although currently focused on the Mon Valley, can exert a wider influence. If this decentralized democratic alternative proves feasible it can provide a viable alternative for other areas suffering from deindustrialization which desire to maintain their heavy industry base and existing community framework.

World War II opened a new era as the depression ended and the federal government helped to engineer growing prosperity by dispensing defense contracts, building factories, and planning the economy. While the economic position of the United States improved, the war undermined the competitiveness of the Soviet Union, Western Europe and Japan especially in the decade following 1945. This combination of events set the stage for a brief period of global hegemony in which the military and political might of the United States reinforced its economic power. The end of the war provided new investment opportunities for United States businessmen abroad and at home. Rebuilding the damaged economies of Western Europe and Japan and the unleashing of vast effective demand in the United States created huge markets. Consumers scrambled for expensive durable goods and the auto, steel and appliance industries responded. Suburbanization spurred economic growth as residential, commercial and manufacturing construction shifted to new areas to accompany changing population patterns. This new prosperity provided the foundation for a more cooperative relationship between big business and major unions. While executives remained adamant about the inviolability of management rights, they proved more willing to share the growing economic surplus of their companies. They accepted union demands for improvements in wages and fringe benefits especially when they could link those concessions with agreements for joint efforts to increase productivity and counter the increasing influx of imports.

The growing tide of imports reflected the widening and deepening cracks in the structure of American global hegemony. By the late 1960's the industrial plants of Germany and Japan, built with state of the art technology, exported products to regions formerly dominated by the United States, including our domestic market. Developments in the Third World contributed to the global realignment. The ascendancy of Fidel Castro in Cuba and his symbolization of revolution in Latin America provided an alternative and a challenge to the United States. The Vietnam War exacted a higher direct price from the United States with the loss of thousands of lives, the erosion of international standing and declining economic viability. In the aftermath of this setback, American leaders undertook a military buildup. This expansion, which peaked in the Reagan Administration, channeled resources from the civilian sector, placed a premium on wasteful means of production and accelerated inflation. Other inflationary pressures in the 1970's came from the rising cost of necessities including fuel, food, housing and medical care. Productivity gains slowed as large companies increased the number of management layers, failed to utilize the latest technology and purchased existing companies rather than constructing new facilities in the United States. By the mid 1970's the American economy faced the combined pressures of increasing imports and intensifying stagflation. To protect themselves, corporate grants sought government aid and concessions from workers. The federal government responded with import restrictions, tax relief, and flexibility in the enforcement of environmental and safety regulations. In the auto and steel industries management received concessions from labor during the severe recession of the early 1980's. Union leaders granted work rule changes, wage cuts and reductions in fringe benefits.

Developments in the steel industry paralleled many of the trends in the general economy and the heavy industry sector. The coming of World War II reversed the pattern of curtailed output and profits and reduced employment and wages of the Depression Era. The conflict triggered a federal government program, implemented by the War Assets Administration, which spent over seven hundred million dollars on steel mills. These expenditures produced four new integrated steel mills, a clear contrast to the single major greenfield mill constructed by private enterprise in the two decades prior to the war. The government built many additions to existing steel plants with the major steel companies deriving the primary benefits of these activities. U.S. Steel purchased the giant Geneva, Utah plant at a bargain price and bought the Homestead mill for one-half of its reported cost. The latter purchase provided a substantial addition to the company's flat-rolled capacity as it obtained slab and plate mills, two new blast furnaces, a new open-hearth unit, electric furnaces and facilities for armor forging, heat treating and alloy heat-treating. The profits of steel companies grew during the war and steel workers made gains with improved employment opportunities, higher wages and abundant overtime work. Union leaders shared in the benefits as the National Labor Relations Board sanctioned a dues checkoff system, which alleviated the chronic financial problems of the United Steelworkers of America, as a type of repayment for their signatures on a no-strike pledge. This system buffered them from pressures applied by members and accelerated the shift toward the bureaucratization of the union. The large industrial unions dispatched many of their best representatives to the capital where they acquired the legal and political skills necessary to negotiate and administer collective bargaining contracts. Leaders accelerated centralization tendencies within the union by pushing for industrywide bargaining and the union shop. These mechanisms promoted more stability in labor-management relations and undermined rank-and-file militancy and decentralization-ist tendencies.[1]

After World War II the steel industry experienced heavy demand for its products. Auto manufacturers, appliance producers and home builders responded to consumer demands. Industrialists needed steel for machine tools, pipelines and power plants. Steel companies responded to these opportunities by expanding their output aided by the production from newly installed open hearth furnaces. Their increased profits also financed high dividends and substantial salaries and bonuses to top executives. Steel workers struck frequently between 1946–59 and won wage increases and improved fringe benefits. In exchange for these benefits and job security for its members the union accepted management rights in the tradeoff which comprised the informal social contract. The "broker state" undergirded this economic growth coalition by providing a "good business climate" for the companies and Keynesianism and some welfare state measures for the steel workers. The virtual disappearance of foreign competition in an expansionist period provided the setting for these arrangements.[2]

Below the glittering facade of international leadership a fundamental change in steel technology signaled the inauguration of a crucial shift in the standings of steel producing nations. For more than fifty years the major steel companies of the United States had been indifferent to new technology. However, distance and lack of fundamental change forestalled financial retribution. In the late 1950's the absence of a competitive attitude became important as foreign producers developed and installed modern equipment, particularly the basic oxygen furnace. An examination of the diverse responses to the introduction of this process helps to explain the changes in the international standing of steel producing nations. An Austrian firm began large scale commercial production in 1952 and many other European companies implemented the technology within a few years. United States Steel and Bethlehem Steel waited until 1964 before they installed the process. The basic oxygen process involved both low capital costs and savings in operating costs which more than overbalanced any benefits from continuing to use existing equipment. Top officials of the leading steel companies had many opportunities to obtain information about the success of the new technology. Numerous visitors reported on the Austrian firm and the McLouth Steel Company in the United States, which installed the process in 1954, and technical and trade journals publicized the Austrian invention. Steel specialists in the United States and Europe praised the new development. The Kefauver Committee of the U.S.

Senate asked steel company executives about their failure to emulate the Europeans, but U.S. Steel and the other major steel companies remained unmoved by the challenge. Walter Adams, an economist at Michigan State University, argued that a complete substitution could have been achieved by 1961 with limited difficulty and great financial benefit for the large, integrated steel companies.[3]

The responses of these companies to continuous casting, which revolutionized steel making along with the basic oxygen furnace, illustrated the costs of its limited expenditures on research and development and its conservatism in adopting technological breakthroughs. Continuous casting displayed many advantages including energy savings, the potential for higher labor productivity, better quality steel, reduced pollution and lower capital costs. Despite these advantages the United States lagged far behind Japan and West Germany in adopting this technology. In 1978 Japan continuously cast 50% of its steel production, West Germany stood at 38% and the United States achieved 15%. An explanation of this outcome must take account of modes of business operation and changes in transportation costs and the availability and costs of raw materials. Many steel executives devoted little investment to research and development and preferred to purchase proven technologies rather than undertake the risks of innovation. They paid relatively little attention to long range strategic planning and technological planning and failed to project the long term economic advantages of the new technology. Faced with limited amounts of discretionary income by the mid 1960's they used their money for short term capital projects rather than plunging into giant, state of the art steel complexes. Steel companies introduced continuous casting capacity gradually and often suffered from equipment at different levels of sophistication because the country constructed only two integrated "greenfield" plants after World War II, the Fairless Works and Burns Harbor. The availability of new sources of iron ore and coke eliminated a competitive advantage of the United States and the development of lower cost bulk carriers to transport these raw materials gave Japan an important cost advantage in the 1960's. The Japanese exploited these opportunities by building huge new mills accessible to these ships. By the late 1960's the smaller, older, less productive United States plants fell far behind their Japanese and West German counterparts.[4]

Labor-management relations provided the other major center of attention in the late 1950's and the 1960's. Since 1946 intermittent strikes characterized the industry culminating in the lengthy strike of 1959. In its aftermath steel company executives and leaders of the

United Steelworkers of America began a period unmarked by a major strike in the next quarter of a century. Their informal bargain provided wage increases and fringe benefit gains for the steel workers along with recognition for the labor leadership. In return for these advances the workers and the union accepted management rights, acted jointly with management to increase productivity and limit imports and accepted "broker state" capitalism. This arrangement gave management some sense of predictability and offered union leaders a record of tangible gains for their members to which they pointed when challenged by dissident workers and dissatisfied local leaders. This informal pact received more formal recognition in the Experimental Negotiating Agreement of 1973 which forbade strikes in exchange for a bonus and a system of cost of living allowances. However, changing conditions in the late 1970's would jeopardize the agreement and produce a more confrontational climate.

In the period of labor peace of the 1960's steel company executives partially shifted their attention from labor-management relations to a concern about the profitability of their industry compared with domestic manufacturing industry in general. An examination of this picture revealed lower profits and a pattern of decline in relative standing which worried top management. In the 1950's steel companies earned a 10.7% return on equity, 95% of domestic manufacturing in general. For the 1960's the return fell to 7.8%, only 70% of the profitability of domestic manufacturing industry. Both profit level and standing compared with other manufacturing industries continued to drop between 1970–1978. They paid less attention to another statistic which showed the profit rate of the steel industry in the United States exceeded other steel industries except Canada. Their diagnosis of the problem emphasized rising costs as an explanation of their growing plight and they pinpointed energy prices, compliance with environmental guidelines and labor costs as the chief culprits. Raw material prices rose in the 1970's especially energy costs as OPEC and the major oil companies exploited their opportunities. Environmental groups and politicians targeted the steel industry as a major polluter and the Environmental Protection Agency pressured steel companies to conform to its regulations. Compliance with these regulations absorbed 17% of the capital investments of steel companies according to an estimate by the Office of Technology Assessment. These expenditures placed a burden on the industry but its competitors faced comparable conditions. The Japanese spent more for pollution abatement per ton of steel produced than the United States. In explaining their declining international competitiveness company representatives emphasized excessive labor costs while their critics saw high wages as desirable, wage rates for industrial workers as roughly comparable in other advanced nations and inefficient management as a key factor in the distress of the steel industry. Steel executives characterized the late 1970's as a period of galloping labor costs with fringe benefit expenses and cost of living allowances in the 1974 and 1977 settlements as the major causes. J. Bruce Johnston, Vice President for Labor Relations of the U.S. Steel Company, described labor costs as far out of line at more than 100% greater than the average for all manufacturing in the United States and at even greater variance compared with steel workers in other nations. Ann Markusen, Department of Urban Planning of the University of California at Berkeley, offered an alternative perspective and called for higher wages for other workers and viewed the wages of steel workers as a reflection of company profits. Barry Bluestone, Department of Economics at Boston College, agreed with Professor Markusen and noted that European unions won comparable benefits for their members but their industries competed more effectively in the international market than ours. He rejected a reduction in the standard of living of American workers as unjust and ineffective in promoting international competitiveness and productivity. Professor Bluestone explained the cause of the problem as inefficient management which failed to develop and implement new technologies.[5]

Management disputed this interpretation and turned to lobbying for changes in government policy, diversification and concessions from workers. Companies demanded and received a variety of benefits from the federal government in international trade, taxation and environmental policy. Trigger price mechanisms, quotas and voluntary agreements provided protection against imports. A reduced corporate income tax, an accelerated depreciation allowance and an investment tax credit left the companies with more disposable income and the Carter administration added a loan program for the steel industry. Government flexibility in the pollution control area resulted in extensions and modifications of regulations. In the case of open hearths of the Homestead mill, US Steel closed the facility after it received government concessions. These benefits failed to make the integrated mills internationally competitive nor satisfy some steel company executives about the responsiveness of the federal government to their increasing plight. Bruce Johnston criticized the government for raising company costs by granting the rights of collective bargaining and striking to the labor force, pursuing inflationary energy and monetary policies and taxing the industry while other nations subsidized their steel industries.[6]

Dissatisfied with the results of their efforts to gain redress of their grievances from the federal government, steel companies turned to changes in business practices and labor policies. As profits in the steel industry continued to decline more companies practiced diversification rather than modernization. U.S. Steel invested in the chemical industry and real estate and spent over six billion dollars to acquire Marathon Oil. After this major acquisition in the early 1980's its steel operations comprised less than 30% of the company's total investments. Earlier, steel companies sought to increase their profits by cutting the size and growth of labor costs. An influx of young, women and black workers changed the character of the heavy industry labor force in the late 1960's. These better educated and more independent employees resented dictatorial methods on the shop floor and exhibited less commitment to the work ethic prized by employers. Steel company executives responded to their assertiveness by hiring more supervisors to apply pressure and increase productivity.

The new employees sought changes in management practices and union leadership. Pockets of dissidents began to surface particularly in the Chicago, Baltimore and Pittsburgh regions. These activists met at a conference in Chicago in July 1974 and formed a loose network to institute a court fight against the Experimental Negotiating Agreement. They scored a major victory in 1974 when Ed Sadlowski became director of District 31, the Chicago area district with the largest membership in the union. This triumph provided him with a base to challenge Lloyd McBride in the 1977 presidential election. He founded Steelworkers Fight Back as his organizational mechanism and conducted a strong, but unsuccessful, campaign focused on the union democracy issue and his dynamic personality. Unfortunately for the dissidents the Sadlowski struggle, although successful in the basic steel industry, left a limited tangible legacy. It did provide the growing rank-and-file groups with opportunity for interaction, but the domination of Sadlowski's Chicago area supporters and the emphasis on personality rather than program left a limited foundation for constructing a decentralized democratic alternative.[7]

Some locals, such as 1397 in Homestead, continued to struggle for change in the aftermath of the Sadlowski setback. Michele McMills and John Ingersoll headed a small core of active dissidents who turned from campaigning for Sadlowski to democratizing their local. Some members of the local expressed dissatisfaction with the leadership of 1397 for its inability to win grievances, its lack of financial accountability and its long term of office holding. The dissidents realized that this dissatisfaction seldom led members to attend meetings of the local except at contract time. Therefore, democratization required outreach to members using innovative methods to arouse their interest. Dissidents responded to this challenge by meeting at people's homes and at bars where they planned raffles and other fund raisers, prepared leaflets and decided to start a newspaper. Socializing and working together gave the participants an opportunity to get to know each other and to develop a sense of solidarity. Holding or attending demonstrations around issues got people to put their "bodies on the line" and reinforced this feeling of unity as well as generated press coverage. Participation in demonstrations offered members of local 1397 an opportunity to meet other steel workers and show solidarity with them, particularly in the rallies protesting the closing of the mills in Youngstown. By this time their sense of group consciousness had been strengthened by their joint efforts in publishing their newspaper for several years.[8]

The election of delegates to the convention of the United Steelworkers of America in 1976 provided dissidents with a test of their popularity. Local 1397 gave them an endorsement by electing McMills and Ingersoll as well as Ron Weisen. Weisen supported Sadlowski the following year and helped him carry local 1397, but he concentrated most of his attention on unseating the incumbent leadership of the local. His campaign produced a victory in 1979 when he won the presidency and John Ingersoll became vice-president. The new administration faced local difficulties and more general problems as the steel companies responded to pressure on their profits with cost cutting measures. In Homestead the company took a strong stand against absenteeism which they attributed to the atrophied work ethic of young, black and women workers. Youngstown steel workers faced more pressing problems, which would soon pervade other older steel mills, as the major steel companies closed their mills in the late 1970's and created mass unemployment in the city.[9]

The Youngstown struggle signaled the start of a new era which continues to plague steel workers and their communities today. In September 1977 Youngstown Sheet and Tube laid off more than 4,000 workers at the Campbell Works. This decision undermined the economic base of the Mahoning Valley and threatened the viability of Youngstown as a community of ethnic, single-family-house neighborhoods. Shortly after the closing, a coalition of steel workers, local business people and community organizations, operating under clerical leadership, proposed a reopening of the plant with ownership vested in a new, locally based corporation. They argued that Lykes, an absentee conglomerate, closed the plant because it failed to earn the highest possible profit, but Youngstown citizens would accept a lower return if they could maintain the economic stability of the city. "Save our Valley" pledges raised millions of dollars and consultants designed a modernization plan which steel industry experts considered feasible. However, the opposition of U.S. Steel and the denial of a request for federal loan guarantees doomed the project.[10]

The next major battle resulted from Jones and Laughlin closing its Brier Hill mill and U.S. Steel shutting the Ohio and McDonald Works in December 1979. These decisions cost 5,000 jobs and started a pattern for other older steel centers which left steel workers and their families vulnerable. They responded to this threat to their way of life by judicial action and direct action. Several steelworker locals retained attorney Staughton Lynd to sue U.S. Steel for violating an oral agreement with the union to keep plants open as long as they earned a profit. Judge Thomas Lambros, who upheld the right of U.S. Steel to close the plants, described the issue in the case as balancing the protection of the free enterprise system and the interests of the community which built itself around the steel mills and thereby developed some property rights in their continuation. Steelworkers from Ohio and Pennsylvania, including several hundred from local 1397 in Homestead, occupied the U.S. Steel headquarters in Youngstown and secured a meeting with company officials to discuss the future of the plants but the mills remained closed.[11]

The Youngstown struggle catalyzed a series of actions designed to prevent the spread of the contagion of plant closings from Youngstown to the Mon Valley. The Tri-State Conference on Steel, organized in 1979 as a coalition of union, clergy and community activists, supported the efforts of the Youngstown steelworkers to save their mills and jobs. They realized that the outcome of the battle would set a precedent for the Mon Valley. Local 1397 participated in court actions to defend the interests of steelworkers in older mills as they joined a diverse group of litigants who hired Staughton Lynd to challenge the environmental permits granted to U.S. Steel to construct a huge steel complex in Conneaut, Ohio. Homestead steelworkers and local union leaders feared that this "greenfield" plant would destroy thousands of jobs in the Pittsburgh area and transform their ethnic communities into "ghost towns." They acted as an intervenor in a consent decree proceeding in 1979 between the Environmental Protection Agency and U.S. Steel by filing a motion to delete paragraph 40. This section permits a company to comply with its obligations under the Clean Air Act by installing pollution control equipment or closing the facility. According to local 1397 the latter option would violate the intent of Congress in the Steel Industry Compliance Extention Act of 1981 which sought to achieve clean air and jobs. Staughton Lynd captured the symbolism of the closing of open hearth no. 5 of the Homestead Works for the Mon Valley when he noted that this decision would end steel making at U.S. Steel's largest and most historic mill in the Mon Valley and reduce the facility to a finishing mill. However, his plea went unheeded and Homestead lost its standing as an integrated mill.[12]

Youngstown lost its uniqueness in the early 1980's as a severe recession aggravated the structural problems plaguing the steel industry and produced massive problems and unemployment. Slackened production in the auto, construction and energy industries undermined the steel industry's major markets and it faced competition from plastics and aluminum as well as imports. Third World nations, such as Brazil and South Korea, joined Japan and West Germany as efficient steel producers and exporters to the United States. The intensified pressure on profits led to more determined efforts to lobby the federal government for trade legislation to put a cap on imports and limit shipments from the Third World as well as the European Community and Japan. Conglomeration and internationalization grew as U.S. Steel negotiated with British Steel and purchased Marathon Oil. Mergers gained popularity with Jones and Laughlin and Republic Steel obtaining government approval and U.S. Steel and National Steel suffering a rebuff.

However, most steel company executives targeted excessive wage costs as the key problem and devised methods to lower them. Using Youngstown as a precedent they closed plants and curtailed production particularly in aging facilities. In the four-country Western Pennsylvania area around Pittsburgh, nearly 65,000 of 90,000 basic steelworkers remained on indefinite layoff in the summer of 1983. Employment in U.S. Steel's six integrated mills in the Mon Valley declined from 28,000 in 1980 to 8,000 by 1983 with the labor force in the Homestead Works falling from 8,000 to 2,500. The employed didn't escape unscathed as cutbacks effected shop floor conditions and pay envelopes. Companies attempted to squeeze more work out of fewer workers with U.S. Steel reducing the amount of maintenance and demanding obedience from employees who faced the threat of dismissal for disobedience. In spite of these economy moves company losses mounted in the early 1980's culminating in a record $1.16 billion loss for 1983 including a $983 million deficit for the fourth quarter. That year David Roderick, chairman of the board, received a salary increase of $49,562 and the company demanded and received a concessions contract from the United Steelworkers of America. The 41-month contract temporarily cut wages by $1.25 an hour, about 9%, and reduced benefits. It eliminated cost-of-living adjustment payments in the first year and cancelled one week's annual vacation for the first year of the contract. In exchange the company promised to invest the savings in modernizing its steel operations. Responses to this settlement varied with the company supportive, union leadership accepting and rank-and-file sentiment more critical. J. Bruce Johnston, chief management contract negotiator, described it as "a step in the right direction" which will provide "a little bit of cash recovery" but "a far cry from solving the labor costs premium disadvantage that the steel industry has accrued over the years . . ." James Smith, Acting Research Director of the United Steelworkers of America, hoped that the agreement would make it easier for American steel companies to compete with imports and help get some older plants operating sooner and remain in operation longer. Mike Stout, a grievanceman at local 1397 in Homestead, worried about the effect of the wage reduction on his ability to meet the mortgage payments on his house.[13]

Homestead shares many of the characteristics of Youngstown and other steel communities as residents worry about the effects of massive, prolonged unemployment on the stability and future of the town. The community has experienced high levels of residential stability, a strong sense of neighborhood, close family and friendship ties, a stress on ethnicity and the centrality of the church. The town played a special role in the Mon Valley as a center of four or five boroughs which attracted former residents for church and shopping. On Saturday night it brought together shoppers, walkers and movie goers. The Leona Theater, which operated from 1925–73, featured vaudeville, films and marathon dancing and drew large audiences. Today a 24-hour restaurant, a convenience store and a gasoline station occupy the site. Eighth Avenue, the borough's main thoroughfare, suffers from many vacant storefronts, potholed streets and the threat of crime. The police force shrank as reduced municipal revenue curtailed public services.

Nevertheless, Homestead retains resiliency and vibrancy based on the strength of its people and their way of life. Few people move in and out of Homestead and Munhall. The majority of families in Reverend Von Dreele's parish count three or four generations of residence and many relatives in the community. However, the rising tide of unemployment threatens this way of life. The high school graduates expect fewer jobs in the area than earlier and see the Army as a last resort if they can't afford to go to college. Families face severe problems with lack of money causing mounting anger and frustration which can produce excessive drinking, drug use and sexual activity by the young.[14]

Homestead lacks an in depth study of the effects of its unemployment but partial research and well-regarded general studies offer a basis for projecting some trends. Dr. Ruth Kane, a psychiatrist at the St. Francis General Hospital in Pittsburgh, conducted an informal study at a Health-O-Rama held in Homestead in April 1982. Her examination of the effects of unemployment on 250 Pittsburgh workers and their families revealed that they suffered from higher blood pressure levels, higher cholesterol levels and more marital discord. Speakers addressing a conference held at the hospital reinforced these findings. For example Ann Mooney, a sociologist at the University of Delaware, reported a heavy toll in self-confidence and physical illness, including cardiovascular disorders and more deaths from cirrhosis. Other researchers have related higher unemployment rates to increases in child abuse and rising rates of juvenile delinquency. M. Harvey Brenner, a professor of operations research at Johns Hopkins University, discovered connections, with appropriate lags, between the level of unemployment and the rates for suicide, infant mortality, homicide and heart disease mortality. His latest research led him to conclude that the depression of the early 1980's would undermine the overall health of Americans.[15]

As the crisis mounted for Homestead residents they looked first to their churches. The churches responded to these requests with Reverend Von Dreele developing a program to match the unemployed and homeowners seeking assistance with repairs. The project created odd jobs for two score men and women but the limited resources of the churches couldn't cope with massive unemployment. Government agencies lacked the resources or commitment and U.S. Steel and the national leaders of the United Steelworkers of America offered limited assistance. Many unemployed workers turned to local 1397 and several, newly formed dynamic community groups.

Local 1397 responded to the emergency with a series of their own activities, cooperation with steel locals and other unions and alliances with community organizations. *1397 Rank & File,* the local's newspaper, publicized its activities and maintained worker morale and solidarity. Its pages contained articles with a strong grassroots flavor as the authors posed questions about the availability of canteens and vending machines in specific departments, criticized job elimination and job combining and documented numerous unreported accidents. Steel company executives received criticism and the paper reported on instances of mismanagement. Union members read admonitions to remember their pledge of solidarity when the company offered them an opportunity for overtime. The local started the first food bank in the United States and conducted fund raisers to meet the costs of operation. In 1981 Pittsburgh rock groups held a benefit concert for the 1397 food bank and a year later many of the city's leading jazz musicians teamed up for a concert which raised money for the 1397 and Mon Valley food banks. A Christmas special in 1982 featured the distribution of 1,000 turkeys, toys and bags of groceries to the accompaniment of band music. The local undertook programs to stop mortgage foreclosures and to extend unemployment benefits. It hosted a meeting of the presidents of steelworker locals to protest the proposed arrangement between U.S. Steel and British Steel. PATCO and Greyhound strikers received their support and many members participated in the anti-Reagan demonstration in Pittsburgh and other demonstrations in the area. Leaders of the local followed a three pronged strategy: meeting the immediate needs of the unemployed, using the legal system and politics to forward social change and educating people about the need for fundamental change. In pursuit of these purposes some of them campaigned for Jesse Jackson who won the Democratic primary in Homestead in 1984. To forward their goals of raising consciousness and pursuing fundamental change the local collaborated with community groups which stressed the need for a basic steel industry, described the underlying causes of the crisis and formulated a program for basic change.

The Denominational Mission Strategy, a Protestant ministerial group,[16] worked to achieve these purposes often in cooperation with local 1397. Its initial purpose focused on training clergy to develop their leadership and organizational skills. The trainers took the problems affecting people's lives and turned them into issues and discussed what could be done to deal with these issues. The ministers, led by Reverend James Von Dreele of St. Matthew's Episcopal Church in Homestead, also developed a more broad based strategy. They investigated the legal code and discovered a 1978 state law which allowed a disaster emergency to be declared when conditions threatened the safety, health or welfare of a substantial number of the citizens of the state. Citing the massive unemployment in the Mon Valley as an emergency they requested job retraining, restoration of municipal services and support for new municipal services. However, the governor's office declared that the law didn't apply and they couldn't respond to these requests. The movement held a rally to plan strategy in light of this rejection and the participants decided to turn to the corporations and convince them to request the politicians to obtain relief for the Mon Valley. By this time a variety of Protestant churches and local unions had joined the campaign. In 1983 they began to hold weekly meetings and undertake intensive research which revealed the key role of banks, particularly Mellon Bank, in the disinvestment and plant closing process. This bank had foreign loans of several billion dollars including investments in Brazilian, Japanese and Taiwanese steel mills. To counter this disinvestment process the Network to Save the Mon Valley, the name of the organization handling the campaign, held mass meetings and launched a "Pledge Card Campaign." The initiators of this strategy wanted to educate the public about the role of banks and engage people directly in the campaign. The bank boycott led to the withdrawal of checking and savings accounts which provided the cash flow for overseas investments. The campaign failed to undermine the financial position of Mellon Bank and left unrealized the hope that bank executives would begin serious negotiations about their participation in the future of the community. Nevertheless, it produced much publicity and educated the public about international business connections and the role of banks. Mellon Bank suffered a damaged reputation which undermined its self-proclaimed good neighbor slogan.[17]

The Mon Valley Unemployed Committee, formed in 1982, became a champion of the unemployed and a provider of services to them. By the following year the organization reached more than 1,500 dues paying members, mostly laid-off steelworkers. It operated food banks, supplied "walk-in" counseling and provided a "hot line" which offered information about solving housing, welfare and health care problems. However, more direct political action formed the main thrust of its organizational activities. Mortgage foreclosures became its focus as the organization picketed banks, secured injunctions and met with bankers and government officials in behalf of the unemployed. The committee brought people to sheriff's sales to protest foreclosures and displayed cardboard vultures swooping down over the heads of prosecution attorneys. The pressure and publicity generated by these activities induced Sheriff Coon and Judge Papadakas to place a moratorium on foreclosures and persuaded the state legislature to consider and eventually enact ameliorative legislation. The organizers sought to broaden their base by direct actions and creating national linkages. Members lobbied state legislators, testified at hearings and traveled to other cities to build a network of unemployed organizations. In March 1983 they participated in a mass lobby day and rally in Washington and the following month organized a demonstration against President Reagan when he visited Pittsburgh. The focus of the Mon Valley Unemployed Committee shifted in June as it helped to establish the first national conference of unemployed groups. The 250 activists, who gathered for the conference, formed the National Unemployed Network and formulated a program for action with the achievement of a decent standard of living for all as its general objective. More specifically, the delegates demanded a change in the government's budget priorities from money for war to money for jobs and called for a struggle against the disproportionate effect of unemployment on women, minorities and handicapped workers. To secure these aims the organization tried to build a unified force of all workers, employed and unemployed, around common interests. The national network published the *National Unemployed News* and stimulated the birth and growth of local committees.[18]

The Tri-State Conference on Steel, another community organization, took a somewhat different approach by formulating strategy and tactics to take over and operate steel mills in behalf of the workers and their communities. It found the legal basis for its plan in section 306 of the Municipal Authorities Act of 1945 which granted borough councils the power to establish a "public authority" to acquire and develop existing industries by using the power of eminent domain. Eminent domain, the right of public agencies to acquire private property when necessary for public safety, health, interest or convenience has a long history. However, most often powerful corporations derived the benefits as they did in Pittsburgh with Renaissance I and the forcible eviction of residents of the Hazlewood section so Jones and Laughlin Steel Company could use the land. In late 1981 and early 1982 the Tri-State Conference on Steel concentrated on an educational campaign to inform the public and the politicians about eminent domain and its possibilities in condemning and using local steel mills. At the same time researchers for the organization investigated the sources of just compensation embodied in the eminent domain strategy. They discovered that municipal authorities could issue bonds, an interested buyer could supply the capital and the pension funds of workers could be used. Their initial opportunity to use eminent domain came in the summer of 1982 when Crucible Steel Company in Midland, PA announced its closing. Several factors favored the use of eminent domain including the existence of a municipal authority, the presence of a company interested in operating the facility and a relatively new mill. However, local leaders rejected the idea because residents viewed the Tri-State Conference on Steel as an outsider and the organization lacked the time to develop support among local steel workers. The organization also introduced the eminent domain approach in the struggles to save the Nabisco Plant in Pittsburgh and the Mesta Machine Company in West Homestead. In the former case the threat of eminent domain contributed to the company's decision to keep the plant open, but the Save Mesta Committee failed to achieve its objective although it publicized the approach and generated support in the West Homestead Borough Council.[19]

By the middle of 1983 most of the efforts of the Tri-State Conference on Steel focused on putting together a comprehensive program for saving and revitalizing the steel and related industries in the area. Its proposal rested on the assumption of the need for steel in a modern society based on economic growth and full employment. The steel industry still provides the economic base of the region but it requires immediate revitalization in order to continue to play this role. The capital costs of modernizing the Pittsburgh area facilities, an investment of several billion dollars, far exceeds the amount available under current levels of profit in private capital markets. Government and labor concessions to steel companies don't produce modernization as recent events demonstrate. Therefore, action by the federal government, using an authority such as TVA or Conrail use, offers the most promising path. The plan envisions a Federal Steel Authority operating the facility with an enhanced role for workers in the collective bargaining and production processes. A federal government program to undertake an industrial rebuilding and infrastructure reconstruction would provide a major market for the products of this new complex. This massive reconstruction program would dovetail with the specialization of the new facilities in the production of plate and structural steel. The scenario envisioned by the authors of the Tri-State Plan received reinforcement from the conclusions of other researchers who reported on the serious deficiencies of basic public works. Their findings included revelations of obsolete and decaying bridges, crumbling highways, deteriorated rail facilities and leaky water and sewer mains. A modernized, reconstructed steel industry would provide many jobs which fit the needs of area residents and pay a reasonable wage. However, a modernized industry would employ fewer workers than at the peak employment level. Therefore, the drafters of the plan advocated special support for workers adversely effected by the new character of the industry. Their recommendation included consideration of work sharing as an element of the transitional phase, job retraining linked to redevelopment programs for the younger workers and a guaranteed annual income to workers too old to retrain but too young to retire.[20]

The United States has entered a new economic era in which current policies fall short of effectiveness and the widely discussed alternatives such as industrial policy and targeting winners suffers from major flaws. The social contract based on economic growth which responded to some of the needs of workers in the primary labor sector has been replaced by demands for concessions, anti-union employer activities and reductions in the social safety net. The economy has failed to solve the central problem of how to combine full employment, stable prices and rising real income. The realization of these objectives requires the use of planning as a key mechanism to rejuvenate the sluggish economy and redistribute income. Some critics of current policy such as Gar Alperovitz, David Gordon, Barry Bluestone and Bennett Harrison advocate democratic reindustrialization to revitalize heavy industry, which remains the core of our national economic vitality. Their common agenda links national planning with a community orientation including a public balance sheet, a strengthened local planning capacity and democratized economic institutions. National planning would discourage the growing obesity of the American corporate bureaucracy and encourage measures supportive of justice such as restrictions on capital mobility, assurance of access to the basic necessities of life and economic conversion from a war economy to the production of products which serve human needs. Elements of the program include passage of effective plant closing legislation, the widespread availability of food, fuel, health care and shelter and the encouragement of alternative production strategies such as the Lucas Aerospace Plan. The foundation for this new direction would be a deep commitment to certain values especially fairness and community. Job security and wage growth would be accorded high priority. Union and worker participation in the decision making process would replace the current brute-force strategy of most managements. Experiments in community and worker ownership would be encouraged especially in heavy industry. Public policy would foster greater workers' control on the shop floor thereby enhancing the contribution and participation of workers.[21]

Implementation of this program requires a new political alliance to replace the coalition composing the Democratic party, which relied on industrial workers and more liberal capitalists who support the welfare state and the informal social contract with economic growth induced by the federal government as its foundation. Today, however, industrial workers, blacks and women find their limited share of the bounty jeopardized and face an economic future comprised of low wage jobs and the threat of unemployment. The effects of the current structural changes in the economy open new political opportunities. A program emphasizing productivity, and the reduction of waste, civilian and military, provides a basis for forming a popular coalition for progressive change. A leading element of the transformation would involve a determined organizing effort among the working poor, administrative workers and workers in new scientifically based technologies. A revitalized labor movement in combination with minorities, underclasses and women provides another fundamental building block of the new coalition. In the 1930's and 1940's in some industrial cities class consciousness emerged out of linkages between workers and neighborhoods. Some towns and cities preserved those forms of community and can build on them, while other places must construct new forms. In some cases the two types of communities can be brought together by one area drawing on the experience of another region such as the Mon Valley. Recently, officials in New Bedford, Massachusetts decided to investigate the use of eminent domain as a means of preserving Morse Cutting Tools, Inc. as a resource to provide jobs for residents.[22]

The steel industry contributed to the economic success of the United States immediately after World War II and later played a role in deindustrialization and our declining international trade position. Employers responded to the shift with demands for government aid and labor concessions based on the rationale that their difficulties stemmed from government policies and excessive labor costs rather than managerial miscalculation and technological backwardness as their critics alleged. In the Mon Valley steel workers and their communities paid the price in job cutbacks and received little relief from the government and the steel companies. In their distress they turned to local unions and community groups who offered emergency aid and the prospect of new directions. Their programs met some immediate needs and offered an alternative. In combination with national planning, the democratic decentralization offered by these groups provides a viable alternative to current government, business and national union policies.

NOTES

1. Interview with Ann Markusen, Professor of Urban Planning, University of California, Berkeley, April 28, 1983; John M. Blair, *Economic Concentration* (New York, 1972), 381–83; Nelson Lichtenstein, *Labor's War at Home: The CIO in World War II* (Cambridge, England, 1982), 81–82.

2. Markusen Interview; U.S. Congress, Senate, Subcommittee on Antitrust and Monopoly of the Committee on the Judiciary, *Administered Prices,* 85th Congress, 1st Session, 1957, XVII, 562, 580.

3. Walter Adams and Joel B. Dirlam, "Big Steel, Invention and Innovation." *Quarterly Journal of Economics,* 80 (May 1966), 174–86, *Administered Prices,* 711.

4. David Ault, "The Continued Deterioration of the Competitive Ability of the U.S. Steel Industry: The Development of Continuous Casting, *Western Economic Journal* (March 1973), 89–90, 95; U.S. Congress, Office of Technology Assessment, *Technology and Steel Industry Competitiveness,* 1980, 8, 10–11; Robert W. Crandall, *The U.S. Steel Industry in Recurrent Crisis* (Washington, 1981), 18–20.

5. Office of Technology Assessment, *Technology and Steel Industry Competitiveness,* 20, 22; Interview with J. Bruce Johnston, Vice-President for Labor Relations, U.S. Steel, April 6, 1983; Markusen interview; Interview with Barry Bluestone, Professor of Economics, Boston College, May 19, 1983; Crandall, *U.S. Steel Industry,* 22–23.

6. Johnston Interview.

7. Interview with Michele McMills, worker, activist and journalist, October 26, 1982; Philip W. Nyden, *Steelworkers Rank-and-File: The Political Economy of a Union Reform Movement* (South Hadley, Ma. 1984), 55–90.

8. Interview with McMills.

9. Interview with Ron Weisen, President of Local 1397 USWA, November 15, 1982.

10. Staughton Lynd, *The Fight Against Shutdowns* (San Pedro, Ca. 1982), 32–48.

11. *Ibid.,* 160–89.

12. Transcript of Press Conference, Closing of Open Hearth, June 2, 1982.

13. Johnston Interview; Interview with James Smith, Acting Research Director of the USWA, April 8, 1982; Interview with Mike Stout, Grievanceman Local 1397 USWA, April 29, 1983; Mike Stout, "Eminent Domain v. Bank Boycotts; The Tri-State Strategy in Pittsburgh," *Labor Research Review,* (Summer 1983), 7.

14. Interview with Reverend James Von Dreele, Homestead clergyman, February 8, 1983.

15. *Ibid.,* Henry W. Pierce, "Woes of all kinds grow in hard times," *Pittsburgh Post-Gazette,* May 18, 1982; Henry W. Pierce, "Joblessness, inflation take health toll," *Pittsburgh Post-Gazette,* June 18, 1982; U.S. Congress, Joint Economic Committee Congress of the United States, Estimating the Effects of Economic Change on *National Health and Social Well-Being,* 98th Congress, 2nd Session, 1984, 64–65.

16. Interview with Mike Stout; Manning Marable, "Beyond the Rainbow," *New Statesman,* July 6, 1984, 17–18.

17. Vita Christy, "A campaign from the heartland," *Multinational Monitor* 4 (June 1983), 10–11; Stout, "Eminent Domain," 14–17.

18. Dianne Feeley, "Unemployment Grows, A New Movement Stirs." *Monthly Review,* 35 (December 1983), 20–25; Cynthia Deitch, "Unemployed Protest and Organizing in the 1980's: The Movement in the Pittsburgh Area." Paper presented at the 1984 American Sociological Association.

19. Mike Stout, "Eminent Domain," 12–13, 17–19; Presentation by Jay Hornack, attorney specializing in eminent domain litigation, The Industrial North Conference, Indiana University of Pennsylvania, October 1982.

20. Tri-State Conference on Steel, "Steel Valley Authority: A Community Plan To Save Pittsburgh's Steel Industry." 1984, 1–11; John Herbers, "Alarm Rises Over Decay in U.S. Public Works." *New York Times,* July 18, 1982.

21. Barry Bluestone and Bennett Harrison, *The Deindustrialization of America: Plant Closings, Community Abandonment and the Dismantling of Basic Industry* (New York, 1982), 231-64; Gar Alperovitz and Jeff Faux, *Rebuilding America: A Blueprint for the New Economy* (New York, 1984), 271-82; David M. Gordon, "To Get Workers Working." *New York Times,* July 11, 1984.

22. Stanley Aronowitz, Working Class Hero: *A New Strategy for Labor* (New York, 1983), 199-207; Bennett Harrison and Barry Bluestone, "More Jobs, Lower Wages." *New York Times,* June 19, 1984.

BRAVE NEW CORPORATE WORLD: AN ASSESSMENT OF INDUSTRIAL POLICY

BY RICHARD McINTYRE AND MICHAEL HILLARD

Public concern with the dangers of corporate power reached a feverish pitch in the early 1970s. Bills designed to control perceived abuses were passed by Congress, establishing the Environmental Protection Agency (EPA) and the Occupational Safety and Health Agency (OSHA) and curbing the widespread practice of overseas bribery. This antimonopoly fervor peaked with the attempt to nationalize the oil industry, and with Congressional consideration of the Hart Deconcentration Act. Though these efforts failed, they placed the monopoly problem at the center of the liberal agenda.

Ten years later, worrying about monopoly seems quaint. The political ascendance of corporate reaction, combined with corporate "hired guns" from the University of Chicago and the American Enterprise Institute, have all but extinguished the antitrust movement. Nevertheless the basic tenet of twentieth-century liberalism—that capitalism can be reformed by wise state intervention—survives in the current school of industrial policy advocates. These neoliberals, an eclectic mix of lawyers, political scientists, labor and international trade economists, and a handful of politically active bankers and industrial capitalists, are providing the ideological bridge between academics and politicians for a new round of state intervention, much as an earlier group of intellectuals legitimized the macroeconomic fine-tuning advocated by American Keynesianism in the 1960s.

Conceding the debate on monopoly power to the right,

The authors are graduate students in economics at the University of Massachusetts/Amherst.

14

industrial policy advocates tend to focus on the international economy. They emphasize the need to reorganize corporate management in the United States, with a view to enabling U.S.-based corporations to accommodate rationally to the changing structure of international trade. They argue that macroeconomic demand management is insufficient unless accompanied by mechanisms for dealing with change in industries, firms, and regions. The disturbing employment, profit, and growth statistics of the past fifteen years are seen as the consequence of corporate management's emphasis on short-run profits rather than long-run growth. For a variety of cultural and historical reasons, U.S. capitalism is said to be stuck with tax experts and "go-go" finance wizards at the economy's helm. Only prudent state intervention into the detailed functioning of the economy will prevent collapse under the weight of Japanese and third world imports.

Industrial policy appeals to many on the left as a sophisticated, activist response to reaction and economic crisis. At the end of the 1970s economists such as MIT's Lester Thurow and businessmen such as investment banker Felix Rohatyn began calling for state-led economic restructuring. While the views of these earlier advocates were criticized as being anti-democratic, more recent proponents of industrial policy—in particular Ira Magaziner and Robert Reich—have adopted a more democratic orientation.

After Reagan's anti-"big government" election swept many major Democratic politicans out of office and reduced the power of those who remained, the Democrats became a party "in search of ideas." One of those ideas has been industrial policy. Robert Reich, Lester Thurow, and others were admitted to the inner circles of the Hart and Mondale campaigns. Indeed, the *New York Times* reported that, after reading Reich's *The Next American Frontier*, Mondale proclaimed: "This should do it for the Democrats in 1984."

If the Democrats should succeed in deposing Reagan this year, a change in economic policy as sweeping as supply-side economics or the "New Economics" of the Kennedy-Johnson years may follow. Should the left applaud this? Should it "jump on the bandwagon"? Are there important criticisms to be mounted against this new version of liberalism?

Thurow's popular 1980 book, *The Zero Sum Society*, was the first coherent statement of the industrial-policy position. Like Robert Reich and others after him, Thurow put forward the thesis that the principal obstacles facing the United States in restructuring its economy are political, not economic. He pointed to the extensive degree of state intervention in the economy, both here and abroad. Inevitably, this intervention favors some industries over others. For Thurow, the main task is to adopt government policies that promote growth sectors, a process currently blocked by entrenched business and labor interests. New state policies are required to impose sacrifices on losers, assist winners, and end-run the zero-sum logic of current politics by redistributing some of the gains of winners to the losers.

Productivity is the key concept in Thurow's analysis. He claims that investment as well as research and development in high-productivity industries are the essential forces behind productivity increases. The main constraints on the operation of these forces are barriers to the movement of capital and labor out of less productive areas. Thus, healthy growth requires the decline of some sectors and, in turn, the decline of someone's income. This creates a political constraint on an otherwise felicitous process of disinvestment. In Thurow's words, "Economic pains . . . are endemic whenever disinvestment occurs. Someone is worse off because of those disinvestments, and they have every incentive to appeal for government to stop or slow down the process of disinvestment." (*The Zero Sum Society*, p. 82)

Thurow points to three ways to improve the situation. First, he argues that a less adversarial, more flexible workplace will improve productivity. Second, risky R&D projects, particularly in new production techniques, should be subsidized by the federal government. Finally, state measures are needed to bolster capital formation and investment. According to Thurow, the tax structure and the financial sector conspire to favor older industries, representing perhaps the greatest constraint on disinvestment. Long time-horizons and patient investors are needed to produce winners in world markets and productivity increases at home. He argues that the government should run a budget surplus and use it to finance a national investment program.

Following Thurow, Robert Reich of Harvard's Kennedy School of Government has argued for industrial policy. His two books—*Minding America's Business,* coauthored with business consultant Ira Magaziner, and *The Next American Frontier*— have tried to answer many of the criticisms of Thurow's work. In addition to the increasing social irrationality of investment, Reich stresses industrial democracy and the importance of the changing international economy.

In *Minding America's Business,* Reich and Magaziner claim that the failure of macroeconomic policy in the 1970s was due to the increasing integration of the United States into the world economy. Whereas the sum of the value of exports and imports is now nearly 25 percent of the gross national product, it was less than 12 percent in 1969. This growing integration has exposed the inefficiency of many domestic capitalists vis-à-vis their foreign rivals. In turn, these rivals have captured a growing share of U.S. markets in steel, auto, and other industries, causing permanent layoffs in the core of high-wage industrial blue-collar occupations. Magaziner and Reich attribute these results to the inability of U.S. firms to improve productivity. Only such productivity improvements will deliver higher quality products at lower prices than rivals in other industrialized countries, while at the same time allowing for high-wage employment domestically.

Conservatives argue that capital shortages are the root cause of productivity problems in the United States. They claim that government tax and regulatory policies blunt incentives to save and invest and thereby lower the rate of capital formation. In fact, as Magaziner and Reich point out, U.S. aggregate investment has been at historically high rates over the past decade.

Period	Non-Residential Fixed Investment as Percent of GNP
1949-53	9.04
1954-57	9.58
1958-69	9.84
1970-73	10.42
1975-79	10.42

Source: U.S. Department of Commerce.

Magaziner and Reich argue that the trouble lies in the *patterns* rather than the *rates* of investment, i.e., current corporate and government policies make investment patterns socially irrational. On the corporate side, managers are being sent the wrong signals for evaluating investment opportunities. Short-run gains are emphasized and cheap labor is valued more than improved productivity. In the public sector, policies affecting the economy are uncoordinated. In this view, the alternatives facing state policymakers are not intervention versus *laissez-faire,* but coordination versus anarchy. A conscious industrial policy is necessary to ease adjustment to change, equitably distribute losses, and deal with situations (infrastructure, research and development, and key "feeder" industries such as steel) where the public return on investment exceeds the private return.

Whereas *Minding America's Business* develops Reich's analysis of current economic problems, *The Next American Frontier* explores the historical roots of the dilemma facing today's policymakers. The first two decades of the twentieth century are seen as a period of crisis, as early social relationships between management and labor broke down under the strain of rapid economic growth and technological change. The social and institutional structure was transformed; the result was the rise of managerialism as philosophy, science, and metaphor. Reich believes that scientific management and its kin eventually pervaded all aspects of social life: "The logic of routine large-scale manufacturing first shaped its original business environment and then permeated the larger social environment." (p. 49)

Managerialism saw *all* problems, economic, political, and social, as amenable to technical solution. This system of privately coordinated economic planning culminated in the permanent mobilization that began during the Second World War. Business committees, organized along industry lines, were set up in each of the major government departments. The structure of strategic planning now operated in the firm, in industries as a whole, and in government itself.

Managerialism found its greatest success in standardized, high-volume production in capital-intensive manufuacturing. Insulated from foreign competition, and with stable markets and market shares, managers could focus on achieving economies of scale. Thus, the premise of managerialism's success in this era was a stable environment.

Reich attributes the current crisis in the U.S. economy to the increasing irrationality of managerialism in a new era of rapid technological change and international competition. The standard explanations of the crisis (over-regulation, deficits, capital shortages, oil shocks, declining R&D expenditures, entrance of women and minorities into the labor force) are wrong because they "fail to take into account the worldwide reorganization of production and America's failure to adapt to it." (p. 121)

Reich describes in detail the changes in transportation, communications, and international financial markets which, along with uneven wage levels, have created the two outstanding characteristics of the new international division of labor: the declining competitiveness of basic industry in advanced countries and the physical fragmentation of production. In such a world, high-volume, standardized production using semi-skilled labor is no longer an option for the United States.

Reich claims that such countries as Japan, France, and West Germany have adjusted to the new regime by shifting their industrial bases. These countries have moved into custom and technology-intensive products that rely on skilled labor (usually working in teams). Formerly separate business functions have been merged into integrated systems for quick response to changing conditions. Reich emphasizes the link between cooperation, flexibility, and productivity growth.

Reich refers to this as the "flexible system" of production. The strong commitment to managerialism in the United States has prevented the adoption of the "flexible system." Instead, managers have adopted the strategy of "paper entrepreneurialism," i.e., practices that merely redistribute, rather than create, wealth. He cites the rise of lawyers, financiers, and accountants over production managers within the corporate hierarchy as evidence of the growing speculative orientation of U.S. business. Conglomerate expansion, unfriendly takeovers, and "creative" accounting are typical paper entrepreneurial strategies. The collapse of the conditions supporting managerialism as a production-oriented culture has released finance and law from their once close association with production.

The challenge of the new international order has also been evaded by the political system. Like Thurow, Reich claims that government protection has not been tied to economic restructuring programs. Declining industries and regions wield disproportionate political power, encouraging preservation rather than adjustment. In addition, the United States has little in the way of labor training programs outside of the military, and public assistance programs reinforce racism by characterizing welfare as charity rather than as an investment in human development.

What can be done? Reich recommends altering the mix of tax incentives and subsidies to discourage paper entrepreneurialism; explicit quid pro quos for any government assistance to business; reverse depreciation of human capital to encourage policies that improve productivity rather than seeking low-wage labor; and risk-based unemployment insurance payments for employers to discourage frequent lay-offs. But in the final analysis, Reich pins his hopes on a brave new corporatist world to resolve the problems of the U.S. economy:

> Business enterprises ... will largely replace geographic jurisdictions as conduits of governmental support for economic and human development. ... As a result, economic development programs and social services will be closely linked. ... [All] citizens (and their dependents) will become employee/members of some business enterprise. ... The work community will replace the geographic community as the most tangible American social setting. (pp. 248-49, 251)

In this new order, capitalists are assumed to adopt non-hierarchical relationships with their employees. To legitimize control, managers will offer substantial social services, lifetime employment, and educational and training benefits to their "citizen-members." Given a real stake in the success of the firm, workers will respond by promoting adaptability, innovation, and productivity, the necessary components of competitiveness in the new international economy. Meanwhile, corporations will invest in new skill-intensive processes, while farming out standardized production to the periphery. U.S. workers, third world workers, and U.S. firms will all prosper.

Reich tells us in effect that capitalism can and will work if firms treat workers well and innovation is encouraged. The attraction of this vision is that it replaces the traditional altruistic ground held by liberals when arguing for more "welfare" and better treatment of the working class: social programs should be supported not because they are "humane" but because they promote economic growth. Development of human capital and civic virtue go hand in hand, in this best of all possible liberal worlds.

Much of the industrial policy position is very old wine in shiny new, high-tech bottles. Underneath the veneer of trendy policy language lie old liberal dogs that the left should let sleep rather than kick around yet one more time.

Reich's work would not be so objectionable if his policy recommendations were consistent with the body of analysis he presents. He shows that during the 1970s corporations stepped up union-busting, shifted production to the third world where repressive governments guaranteed low wages, increasingly engaged in speculation rather than production, and enlisted the federal government in self-serving protectionist and bail-out programs. Ironically, after blaming corporate mismanagement for economic decline, Reich proceeds to propose an expansion of the social role of private corporations. In the end, he is as trapped by his liberal assumptions as the corporate managers are in their "short-run" outlook.

Further, if flexible-system production were really profitable, why haven't U.S. corporations already made the transition? Reich blames the stupidity of managerialism, but in fact many U.S. corporations have *maintained* profitability precisely through paper strategies and capital flight.

Reich is looking for a connection between social welfare and capitalist efficiency of a kind that economists have posited ever since Adam Smith. But all these welfare/efficiency claims are at best based on deceptive half-truths. As Marx noted, capitalism does have progressive dimensions, but to argue that capitalism's positive aspects are inherent while treating exploitation, unemployment, crises, and extremes of wealth and poverty as aberrations is to indulge in the shallowest kind of liberal apologetics. It is just such an apologetic evasion of reality that lies at the heart of industrial policy.

That this is indeed the case is most clearly illustrated in Reich's discussion of multinationals. He defines two categories: "pure" and "national." The latter are progressive, pursuing policies which institute flexible systems domestically. They maintain profitability in mature lines by moving them offshore, and use the resulting profits for domestic investment. These "national" multinationals live up to the true spirit of flexible systems:

> Flexible-system enterprises exist in large part for the people who work within them. Of course, if the enterprise is successful, they also enrich their customers, suppliers, and stockholders. But one of their central missions is to enhance the lives of their employees. In a real sense they are a political community whose leaders are accountable to their members. (p. 257)

On the other hand, "pure" multinationals act only to benefit stockholders and managers, fleeing from one country to the next in pursuit of profitable branches, subsidiaries, and joint ventures without regard for the effects of capital mobility on workers. In contrast to "national" multinationals, they are neither formally nor informally bound to promote the living standards of any nation. U.S. multinationals are, of course, of the "pure" variety: thus they fail to live up to their role as the agents of *their* society. This is reflected in their investment strategy. The "pure" multinational attempts to preserve market shares in existing product lines by locating overseas, rather than concentration on improving skills and techniques in production and moving into new product areas, thereby preserving domestic, high-wage employment.

The implication is that the U.S. government should step in to prevent U.S. multinationals from pillaging the domestic economy. In effect, Reich is calling for the government to act as labor's representative. Basically, this recommendation stems from a totally distorted view of the success of other nations in regulating multinational corporate behavior. For example, German corporations play the *Länder* (provinces) off against each other to obtain tax breaks, just as U.S. corporations extract concessions from states and localities. The Japanese lifetime employment system applies to a small minority of workers and is purchased at the expense of poor working conditions and cyclical unemployment for the majority.

Reich calls for popular participation in his new corporatist world, as if workplace democracy were the inevitable result of economic development. He praises progressive multinationals in other countries as if they represented a higher order of development brought about by efficient managers, wise government leaders, and superior local culture. What is clearly missing in his analysis is any sense of the way capitalism really works, of the class basis of power, and of the role of struggle in determining policy.

With the fate of all workers in the hands of corporations, one might at least ask what the prospects would be for realizing full employment through industrial policy. Yet Reich makes absolutely no attempt to demonstrate empirically the prospects for employment growth in the sector of "flexible-systems" enterprises. We are left with a sneaking suspicion that the benefits of the new order can only be bought by the maintenance of a permanent underclass, as is the case in Japan.

Despite the current "economic recovery" (which still leaves millions of unemployed, many of whom once held high-paying industrial jobs, with little prospect for decent jobs in the future), the matter of industrial policy is a leading issue in this election year, and perhaps beyond. In judging its eventual fate, we should perhaps take a lesson from the experience of Keynesian economics. While Keynes's critique of capitalism was in some respects quite radical, he ultimately believed that if the right people were in possession of the right ideas, capitalism could be made to work for the betterment of all. Yet in practice only those policies that reinforced capitalist social relations survived in the peculiar economic theory and practice of U.S. Keynesianism. We suspect that industrial policy will face the same fate. As long as the country's basic power structure remains what it is, even the best of ideas will be twisted to benefit its beneficiaries.

Industrial Policy: Reindustrialization Through Competition or Coordinated Action?*

James C. Miller III†

Thomas F. Walton††

William E. Kovacic†††

Jeremy A. Rabkin††††

The American economy is just now recovering from its most difficult period since the Great Depression. In the eight years following the 1973 oil embargo by the Organization of Petroleum Exporting Countries (OPEC), the average annual rate of growth in industrial production fell by nearly sixty percent, while the rate of growth in labor productivity fell by approximately seventy percent relative to the average rates of the preceding twenty five years.[1] By 1980 the annual rate of inflation, as measured by the Consumer Price Index, had reached 13.5 percent, the highest rate since 1947 and more than twice the rate in 1970;[2] and by 1982 the rate of unemployment had reached 9.7 percent, the highest rate since 1941

* All views expressed are strictly the authors' own and not necessarily those of the institutions with which they are affiliated. The present paper relies heavily on five addresses by Chairman Miller: "Reindustrialization Policy: Atari Mercantilism?," *Policy Report* (Cato, July 1983); "Industrial Policy: Panacea or Pandora's Box?," presented to the Commonwealth Club of California (San Francisco, Sept. 30, 1983); *Reindustrialization Through the Free Market*, 53 ANTITRUST L.J. 121 (1984); "The Case Against 'Industrial Policy,' " presented to the Cato Institute Policy Conference (Washington, Apr. 27, 1984), forthcoming in 4 CATO JOURNAL (Fall 1984); and "Why Is There No 'Industrial Policy' in America?," presented to the Kansai Federation of Economic Organizations (Osaka, Japan, May 21, 1984). We are grateful for suggestions and comments on earlier drafts by John Hilke of the Federal Trade Commission and by the Journal's editors. Any errors remain our own.
† Chairman, Federal Trade Commission.
†† Director of Microeconomic and Strategic Studies, General Motors Corp., and recently Special Advisor for Regulatory Affairs, Federal Trade Commission.
††† Attorney, Washington, D.C., and recently Attorney Advisor to Commissioner George W. Douglas, Federal Trade Commission.
†††† Professor of Political Science, Cornell University.
1. COUNCIL OF ECONOMIC ADVISERS, ECONOMIC REPORT OF THE PRESIDENT 266, 269 (1984).
2. *Id.* at 282-83; BUREAU OF THE CENSUS, U.S. DEP'T OF COMMERCE, HISTORICAL STATISTICS OF THE U.S., COLONIAL TIMES TO 1970, BICENTENNIAL EDITION, PART 1, at 135 (1975).

1

and nearly double the rate in 1970.[3] In the six years following the OPEC embargo the nation's view of its economic future changed from one of seemingly boundless optimism to one of great concern. The new mood was perhaps best captured by President Carter in his famous 1979 speech on "malaise" in America.[4]

Out of these experiences came the realization that new government policies might be necessary to revive the nation's industrial base and restore the economy to its post-World War II trend of steady growth with minimal inflation and low unemployment. Very few people dispute that government should play some role in promoting industrial and economic growth; discussion today centers on the nature of government's role in formulating and implementing industrial policy. Simply stated, should it try more actively to guide and coordinate the decisions of business and labor, or should it rely primarily on decentralized competitive forces?

Advocates of a more centralized approach argue that a host of market imperfections badly distort the American economy.[5] In their view, industrial policy is not a preference for central planning over some idealized model of laissez-faire, but rather a means of making the best of an unavoidably imperfect marketplace. Given certain inevitable distortions, government, business, and labor should participate in a cooperative effort to rationalize the distortions and bring order from chaos. Robert Reich, whose writings have played a major part in stimulating and shaping debate on industrial policy, has called for "a political forum capable of generating large-scale compromise and adaptation" which would "enable government, business, and labor to fashion explicit agreements to restructure American industry."[6] Such spokesmen often urge the U.S. govern-

---

3. BUREAU OF THE CENSUS, U.S. DEP'T OF COMMERCE, STATISTICAL ABSTRACT OF THE UNITED STATES: 1984, at 405 (104th ed. 1983).

4. N.Y. Times, July 16, 1979, at A10, col. 1, 2 ("The symptoms of this crisis of the American spirit are all around us.").

5. *See, e.g.,* Kuttner, *Commentary on Paul Krugman's "Targeted Industrial Policies: Theory and Evidence,"* in INDUSTRIAL CHANGE AND PUBLIC POLICY 169-76 (1983) (a symposium sponsored by the Federal Reserve Bank of Kansas City). "Microeconomically, we know that investors often strive for short-run profit-maximization that often fails to serve long-run industrial well being. . . ." *Id.* at 169.

6. Reich, *The Next American Frontier,* ATL. MONTHLY, Apr. 1983, at 98, 107. *See also* R. REICH, THE NEXT AMERICAN FRONTIER (1983); I. MAGAZINER & R. REICH, MINDING AMERICA'S BUSINESS (1982); Eizenstat, *Reindustrialization Through Government-Business-Labor Alliance,* 53 ANTITRUST L.J. 105 (1984); *Do Modern Times Call for an Industrial Policy? A Conversation with Herbert Stein and Lester Thurow,* PUBLIC OPINION, Aug.-Sept. 1983, at 2-9, 58-59; Kuttner, *supra* note 5, at 169, 171, 176; *Hearings on a U.S. Industrial Policy Before the Subcomm. on Economic Stabilization of the House Comm. on Banking, Finance, and Urban Affairs,* 98th Cong., 1st Sess., 340-41 (1983) (statement of Owen Bieber, President, United Automobile, Aerospace and Agricultural Implement Workers of America). Other prominent supporters of some form of tripartite cooperation and planning include AFL-CIO chairman Lane Kirkland, investment banker Felix Rohatyn, and former DuPont chairman Irving S. Shapiro. Messrs. Kirkland, Rohatyn, and Shapiro have proposed a National Industrial Policy Board consisting of leaders from business, government and labor under

2

ment to emulate the allegedly more cooperative, tripartite microeconomic policies of such growth-oriented nations as Japan.

Advocates of a more prominent role for decentralized market forces acknowledge that the government has an important responsibility to promote economic growth through sound macroeconomic and microeconomic policies.[7] They fear, however, that any comprehensive effort to coordinate the decisions of private entrepreneurs and laborers would be dominated by special interests and do more harm than good.[8] They believe that, despite its imperfections, competition is the best coordinator of business, labor, and consumer decisions—especially in a complex industrial economy.[9] They question how successful West European and Far Eastern governments have been in fostering economic growth through programs emphasizing coordinated action.[10] Finally, many advocates of the market-based approach worry about the implications of a coordinated business, labor, and government strategy for fairness, individual liberty, and the nation's political institutions.

These opposing positions, however, are not polar extremes. Cooperative or group action can sometimes coincide with intense competition. For example, there is widespread agreement that research joint ventures among otherwise independent firms can contribute to the nation's technological progress.[11] The nation's space exploration program illustrates how the government can achieve discrete, well-defined objectives through a centrally-coordinated mix of competition and cooperation. The Alaska pipeline provides an example of a highly successful joint venture of independent

the supervision of Congress. Various bills have been introduced to create tripartite coordination mechanisms. Congressman LaFalce, for example, has conducted extensive hearings in which he invited testimony from a wide cross section of both proponents and opponents of such plans. *See, e.g.,* HOUSE COMM. ON BANKING, FINANCE, AND URBAN AFFAIRS, 98TH CONG., 1ST SESS., FORGING AN INDUSTRIAL COMPETITIVENESS STRATEGY 61-73 (Comm. Print 1983).

7. Representative statements of this view include Schultze, *Industrial Policy: A Solution in Search of a Problem,* CAL. MGMT. REV., Summer 1983, at 4, 13 [hereinafter cited as *A Solution in Search of a Problem*]; Schultze, *Industrial Policy: A Dissent,* 2 BROOKINGS REV. 3 , 11 (1983) [hereinafter cited as *A Dissent*]; R. LAWRENCE, CAN AMERICA COMPETE? 112-15 (1984); Krugman, *Targeted Industrial Policies: Theory and Evidence,* in INDUSTRIAL CHANGE AND PUBLIC POLICY 123-55 (1983).

8. *See A Dissent, supra* note 7, at 9-10; Eads, *Commentary on Paul Krugman's "Targeted Industrial Policies: Theory and Evidence,"* in INDUSTRIAL CHANGE AND PUBLIC POLICY 157-67 (1983).

9. *See, e.g., A Solution in Search of a Problem, supra* note 7, at 11, 15; *A Dissent, supra* note 7, at 12.

10. *See, e.g., A Dissent, supra* note 7, at 6-7.

11. *See, e.g.,* SENATE COMM. ON THE JUDICIARY, THE NATIONAL PRODUCTIVITY AND INNOVATION ACT (S. 1841), S. REP. NO. 427, 98th Cong., 2d Sess., 1-4 (1984); HOUSE COMM. ON THE JUDICIARY, JOINT RESEARCH AND DEVELOPMENT ACT OF 1984 (H.R. 5041), H.R. REP. NO. 656, 98th Cong., 2d Sess. (1984); HOUSE COMM. ON SCIENCE AND TECHNOLOGY, RESEARCH AND DEVELOPMENT JOINT VENTURE ACT OF 1983, H.R. REP. NO. 571, 98th Cong., 1st Sess. pt. 1, 8-11 (1983). *See also* J. Miller III, Research Joint Ventures, Antitrust, and Industrial Innovation, Address before the Berlin Cartel Conference (July 2, 1984).

3

corporations.[12] But each such program has been justified as a special exception in which substantial benefits existed beyond those which could have been captured through ordinary marketplace competition. From the time the country was founded, the U.S. economy has been organized largely according to the principle encompassed in its antitrust laws: Vigorous competition should be the predominant means for promoting a strong industrial base and stimulating long-term economic growth.

In this Article, we first discuss the historical origins of the debate over industrial policy. This discussion comprises the classical economists' critique of mercantilism, as well as the early tension in the United States between antitrust and regulatory policies, which culminated in the differing policy prescriptions of Theodore Roosevelt and Woodrow Wilson. Next, we examine the National Recovery Administration, the only comprehensive and centralized peacetime industrial policy in the history of the United States. We then consider current international experiences with "indicative planning" policies—policies that rely heavily on government guidance and industry cooperation. Finally, we assess the feasibility of adopting such policies within the unique framework of the American political system, and the implications of such a program for U.S. political institutions.

I. The Origins of the Debate Over Industrial Policy

A. *The Challenge Posed by the Classical Economists*

The first systematic, empirical studies of a centralized program of industrial policy were presented by Adam Smith and David Hume. Smith and Hume demonstrated that government attempts to coordinate the efforts of entrepreneurs almost invariably discouraged economic growth and reduced economic well-being.[13]

In particular, Smith devoted much of his classic treatise, *The Wealth of Nations*,[14] to an empirical assessment of the system that he and Hume called mercantilism. This system:

> endeavours, either, by extraordinary encouragements, to draw towards a particular species of industry a greater share of the capital of the society than what would naturally go to it; or, by extraordi-

---

12. *See generally*, U.S. GOV'T ACCT. OFF., LESSONS LEARNED FROM CONSTRUCTING THE TRANS-ALASKA PIPELINE (1978) (report to Congress by the U.S. Comptroller General).

13. *See* A. SMITH, THE WEALTH OF NATIONS (Canaan ed. 1937) (1st ed. 1776); Rotwein, *Introduction* to DAVID HUME—WRITINGS ON ECONOMICS at lxxviii-lxxxi (E. Rotwein ed. 1955) (on Hume's condemnation of domestic market-restrictions in his HISTORY OF ENGLAND).

14. *See, e.g.*, A. SMITH, *supra* note 13, at 627-53.

4

nary restraints, to force from a particular species of industry some share of the capital which would otherwise be employed in it . . . .[15]

Smith concluded that mercantilism "retards, instead of accelerating, the progress of the society towards real wealth and greatness; and diminishes, instead of increasing, the real value of the annual produce of its land and labour."[16]

Smith found two basic reasons for the failure of the industrial policies of his day: a tendency of special interests to turn government programs to their own narrow advantages,[17] and a tendency of joint business efforts to result in collusion to reduce output and raise prices, especially when government willingly permits such collusion.[18] According to Smith:

> People of the same trade seldom meet together, even for merriment and diversion, but the conversation ends in a conspiracy against the public, or in some contrivance to raise prices. It is impossible indeed to prevent such meetings, by any law which either could be executed, or would be consistent with liberty and justice. But though the law cannot hinder people of the same trade from sometimes assembling together, it ought to do nothing to facilitate such assemblies; much less to render them necessary.[19]

The first comprehensive experiment with the alternative, competitive approach to industrial policy—the founding of the American state—began in 1776, the year that Smith's treatise was first published. Milton and Rose Friedman have observed that, from the American Revolution until about 1929, the nation enjoyed substantial economic growth and prosperity, as well as unparallelled advances of human freedoms.[20] Of course, government coordination and business cooperation played a role in fostering U.S. economic development—as is demonstrated by the experience with railroad land grants, agricultural research programs, and the building of canals and turnpikes.[21] Each of these programs involved substantial

---

15. *Id.* at 650.

16. *Id.* at 651; *see also* Rotwein, *supra* note 13.

17. Smith, for example, spoke of the ability of manufacturing interests to "intimidate the legislature" and specifically to block the restoration of free trade in Britain. *Id.* at 437-38. These "[m]erchants and manufacturers are the people who derive the greatest advantage from this monopoly of the home-market." *Id.* at 426.

18. *Id.* at 60-62.

19. *Id.* at 128.

20. M. FRIEDMAN & R. FRIEDMAN, FREE TO CHOOSE: A PERSONAL STATEMENT 35-37 (1980).

21. *See* D. NORTH, ECONOMIC GROWTH OF THE UNITED STATES 1790-1860, at 143 (1966); L. DAVIS, AMERICAN ECONOMIC GROWTH 391-93, 475-85, 495-97, 648-50 (1972); W. BROWNLEE, DYNAMICS OF ASCENT 228-31 (1974).

5

external benefits for the entire economy, however, and was thus consistent with Adam Smith's public works rationale for government intervention.[22]

B. The First Proposals for a Centrally Coordinated U.S. Policy

The term "industrial policy" is a recent addition to the lexicon of American public affairs but, as shown by Adam Smith's discussion of mercantilism, it embraces fundamental economic issues with significant, long-lived antecedents. In several important periods in American history, moreover, the basic questions of whether government should shape industrial activity directly and how it might do so have commanded the attention of public officials, business leaders, and scholars.[23] A brief examination of the origins of the country's experience with centrally coordinated industrial policies illuminates the current debate.

Although it is possible to identify other actions of the U.S. government which foreshadowed modern industrial policy, two efforts with special significance for the present debate were begun roughly a century ago. In 1887, Congress passed the Interstate Commerce Act,[24] which forbade certain forms of price discrimination in rail transportation and established the Interstate Commerce Commission (ICC) with authority to regulate and oversee many aspects of the railroad industry.[25] As its powers were expanded over subsequent decades, the ICC eventually assumed responsibility for coordinating business activity (including the setting of rates and control of entry and exit) in several transportation sectors—first rail, and later motor carrier and water transportation.[26] Only three years after the

22. A. SMITH, *supra* note 13, at 681–768. According to Smith's public works rationale, government must erect and maintain certain public institutions and public works which are advantageous to society, but which would not generate enough revenue to make it profitable for an individual or small number of individuals to maintain them. Such institutions and works include those necessary for education, defense, administering justice, and facilitating commerce.

23. *See, e.g.,* REGULATION IN PERSPECTIVE (T. McCraw ed. 1981) (collection of essays discussing the history of U.S. economic regulation); OFFICE OF SPECIAL PROJECTS, BUREAU OF COMPETITION, FEDERAL TRADE COMM'N, NATIONAL COMPETITION POLICY: HISTORIANS' PERSPECTIVES OF ANTITRUST AND GOVERNMENT-BUSINESS RELATIONSHIPS IN THE UNITED STATES (1981); Kovacic, *The Federal Trade Commission and Congressional Oversight of Antitrust Enforcement,* 17 TULSA L.J. 587, 602–11 (1982).

24. Interstate Commerce Act, ch. 104, 24 Stat. 379 (1887) (codified as amended in scattered sections of 49 U.S.C.).

25. Interstate Commerce Act, ch. 104, §§ 2–6, 11, 24 Stat. 379, 379–83 (1887) (codified as amended in scattered sections of 49 U.S.C.). For discussions of the origins and aims of the Interstate Commerce Act, see 1 L. SHARFMAN, THE INTERSTATE COMMERCE COMMISSION 17–90 (1931); P. MACAVOY, THE ECONOMIC EFFECTS OF REGULATION: THE TRUNKLINE RAILROAD CARTELS AND THE INTERSTATE COMMERCE COMMISSION BEFORE 1900, at 111–13 (1965); Hilton, *The Consistency of the Interstate Commerce Act,* 9 J. L. & ECON. 87 (1966).

26. Congress reiterated and expanded the ICC's authority to regulate railroads through the Elkins Act of 1903, Pub. L. No. 57–103, 32 Stat. 847, the Hepburn Act amendments of 1906, Pub. L. No. 59–337, 34 Stat. 584, and the Mann-Elkins Act of 1910, Pub. L. No. 61–218, 36 Stat. 539 (these acts are codified as amended in scattered sections of 49 U.S.C.). Collectively these measures strengthened

6

ICC's creation, Congress passed the Sherman Act of 1890,[27] which embraced what would prove to be a largely different approach toward the government's role in the market. Although they embodied a wide range of congressional and public aspirations, the Sherman Act and its antitrust progeny[28] rested upon a preference for market forces as a means of organizing the nation's economic life.[29] Thus, in a brief but important period, Congress enacted two contending models for the government's role in the economy.

Neither the Sherman Act nor the Interstate Commerce Act was the final word on industrial policy. The issue of government's proper role in shaping business behavior commanded widespread attention in the presidential election campaign of 1912. The platform of Theodore Roosevelt's Progressive Party urged that the federal government's power be used to force private industry to serve broad public goals.[30] Roosevelt contem-

the existing ban in the Interstate Commerce Act against rebating and price discrimination, expressly granted the Commission power to prescribe maximum rates and control rate increases, and enlarged its enforcement powers. Congress extended the ICC's regulatory authority to interstate motor and water transportation through, respectively, the Motor Carrier Act of 1935, Pub. L. No. 74-255, 49 Stat. 543 (codified as amended in scattered sections of 49 U.S.C.), and the Transportation Act of 1940, Pub. L. No. 76-785, 54 Stat. 898 (codified as amended in scattered sections of 49 U.S.C.).

27. Sherman Antitrust Act, ch. 647, §§ 1-6, 8, 26 Stat. 209-10 (1890) (current version at 15 U.S.C. §§ 1-7 (1982)).

28. The Sherman Act's progeny include the Clayton Act, ch. 323, §§ 1-10, 38 Stat. 730-34 (1914) (current version at 15 U.S.C. §§ 12-20 (1982)); and the Federal Trade Commission Act, ch. 311, §§ 1-11, 38 Stat. 717-19 (1914) (current version at 15 U.S.C. §§ 41-58 (1982)). For a further discussion of the FTC Act, see *infra* text accompanying notes 57 to 73.

29. For a recent discussion of the goals of the Sherman Act and a summary of the literature analyzing the objectives of American antitrust legislation, see Lande, *Wealth Transfers as the Original and Primary Concern of Antitrust: The Efficiency Interpretation Challenged*, 34 HASTINGS L.J. 65 (1982). The public mood that spurred congressional moves in the late 19th and early 20th centuries to redress monopoly is discussed in R. HOFSTADTER, THE AGE OF REFORM 213-69 (1955); H. THORELLI, THE FEDERAL ANTITRUST POLICY 54-163, 235-368 (1955); S. HAYS, THE RESPONSE TO INDUSTRIALISM 1885-1914, at 4-93 (1957); R. WIEBE, THE SEARCH FOR ORDER 1877-1920, at 1-163 (1967).

30. A. LINK, WOODROW WILSON AND THE PROGRESSIVE ERA 18-21 (1954); R. HOFSTADTER, *supra* note 29, at 249-54. Two major works helped develop Roosevelt's thinking on these issues. The first was H. CROLY, THE PROMISE OF AMERICAN LIFE (1909). On Croly's significance to Roosevelt's thinking, see A. LINK, *supra* at 18-19, and E. GOLDMAN, RENDEVOUS WITH DESTINY 146-65 (1955). Regarded by many historians as the philosophical foundation for the early 20th century progressive movement, Croly's book sought to overcome the historical perception that equated a Hamiltonian policy of government intervention with aristocracy and special privilege. This attitude, he argued, had inhibited the creation of national policies to achieve Jeffersonian, or democratic, ends. To reach these goals, the country needed a "new nationalism" in which the federal government would assume an active role in changing economic and social conditions.

The second publication was C. VAN HISE, CONCENTRATION AND CONTROL: A SOLUTION OF THE TRUST PROBLEM IN THE UNITED STATES (1912). Van Hise believed economic concentration was predetermined by the evolution of modern business. In his view, strategies designed to arrest this process through antitrust enforcement were either futile or counterproductive. Nonetheless, he believed administrative control of the products of this evolutionary trend was essential: "[I]f we allow concentration and cooperation, there must be control in order to protect the people, and adequate control is only possible through the administrative commission." *Id.* at 278. On Roosevelt's reliance on Van Hise's view, see A. SCHLESINGER, THE CRISIS OF THE OLD ORDER 1919-1933, at 22 (1957).

7

plated creating a federal agency with authority to regulate virtually all major aspects of corporate activity. Such a body would have established hours, wages, and other conditions of labor, set maximum prices for goods produced by firms with "dominant" positions in their industries, compelled the publication of company accounts, controlled the issuance of securities, and investigated business activity in general.[31] His system would have tolerated the level of corporate growth needed to achieve the benefits of large-scale production, but would have ensured that industry serve specific public ends.

To his Democratic Party opponent, Woodrow Wilson, Roosevelt's program seemed perilous. Wilson reasoned that if government began to tell business leaders how to run their businesses, business interests would "capture the government, in order not to be restrained too much by it."[32] Rather than accept what he called an "avowed partnership between the government and the trusts,"[33] Wilson proposed a reduction in tariffs and greater reliance upon antitrust enforcement to secure competition.[34] This competition would in turn stimulate superior performance. The prevention of monopoly, Wilson argued, would guarantee that "the limitations on private enterprise shall be removed, so that the next generation of youngsters, as they come along, will not have to become protégés of benevolent trusts, but will be free to go about making [of] their own lives what they will . . . ."[35]

To many observers, the contending views of Wilson and Roosevelt reflected a sharp philosophical split over government's proper role in influencing economic activity.[36] Historian George Mowry has noted that "one school cherished the competitive system with its individual values and

31. Roosevelt, *The Trusts, the People, and the Square Deal*, 99 THE OUTLOOK 649 (1911). During his presidency Theodore Roosevelt had acquired a reputation as a "trustbuster" because of several major Sherman Act prosecutions, including his Administration's successful effort to dissolve the Northern Securities Company, a holding company for three of the country's larger railroads. *See* Northern Securities Co. v. United States, 193 U.S. 197 (1904). Over time, however, Roosevelt became increasingly disenchanted with the Sherman Act as a tool for government economic regulation. By the time of America's entry into World War I, he publicly had turned against the statute. *See* T. ROOSEVELT, THE FOES OF OUR OWN HOUSEHOLD 122 (1917).

32. W. WILSON: THE NEW FREEDOM 201–02 (1913). Wilson's economic thinking drew heavily upon the views of Louis Brandeis, whom Wilson first met in August 1912. "[I]t was Brandeis," Link writes, "who clarified Wilson's thought and led him to believe the most vital question confronting the American people was preservation of economic freedom in the United States. Brandeis taught, and Wilson agreed and reiterated in his speeches, that the main task ahead was to provide the means by which business could be set free from the shackles of monopoly and special privilege." A. LINK, *supra* note 30, at 20–21.

33. W. WILSON, *supra* note 32, at 202.

34. *See*, A. LINK, WILSON: THE NEW FREEDOM 178, 241 (1956).

35. W. WILSON, *supra* note 32, at 222.

36. *See, e.g.*, G. MOWRY, THE ERA OF THEODORE ROOSEVELT 1900–1912, at 57 (1958); A. LINK, *supra* note 30, at 18–21 (1954); J. BLUM, WOODROW WILSON AND THE POLITICS OF MORALITY 59–62 (1956).

8

feared the powerful state; the other welcomed concentrated power whether in industry or politics, looked to a paternalistic state staffed by an educated elite for leadership, and depreciated individualism."[37]

After his victory in the general election, Wilson swiftly moved to implement the chief elements of his economic program. In 1913 he secured congressional approval of the Underwood Tariff Act,[38] which produced the first substantial tariff reductions since the Civil War. In 1914 Wilson asked Congress to augment the Sherman Act's broad provisions with a roster of specific illegal practices and to establish a new trade commission with advisory, investigatory, and prosecutorial powers in the antitrust field.[39] Congress ultimately approved Wilson's two antitrust initiatives as the Clayton and Federal Trade Commission Acts, but engaged in extensive debate about the new Commission's policymaking function. In particular, the legislators debated whether the agency should promote competition or, alternatively, should become the engine for comprehensive regulation envisioned by Roosevelt and his supporters in the 1912 campaign.[40]

Congress endorsed the former of these two models in establishing the Federal Trade Commission.[41] The agency's new "regulatory" role would be narrow. The Commission would investigate, publicize, and remedy market failures that hindered the competitive process.[42] It would not, however, perform the comprehensive oversight urged in some of Roosevelt's proposals for federal regulation.

Notwithstanding its considerable legislative success, Wilson's "New Freedom" economic program drew a harsh assessment from observers

37. G. MOWRY, *supra* note 36, at 57.

38. Pub. L. No. 63-16, ch. 16, 38 Stat. 114 (1913) (current version at 19 U.S.C. §§ 128, 130, 131 (1982)). The battle for tariff reductions provided a stern test of Wilson's market-oriented convictions. Congressional consideration of the Underwood bill stimulated an unprecedented lobbying campaign, as representatives of interests shielded by the tariff crowded the nation's capital. The spectacle outraged Wilson, who said Washington was so besieged by lobbyists that "a brick couldn't be thrown without hitting one of them." A. LINK, *supra* note 30, at 41. "It is of serious interest to the country," Wilson declared soon afterwards, "that the people at large should have no lobby and be voiceless in these matters, while great bodies of astute men seek to create an artificial opinion and to overcome the interests of the public for their private profit." N.Y. Times, May 27, 1913, at 1, col. 1, *quoted in* A. LINK, *supra* note 30, at 41.

39. *See,* A. LINK, *supra* note 30, at 436-42.

40. *See, e.g.,* 51 CONG. REC. H9538-611 (1914) (debates over the Clayton Act); 51 CONG. REC. S11,870-876 (debates over bill to establish the Federal Trade Commission). *See also* A. LINK, *supra* note 30, at 68-73 (describing the opposition of various groups in Congress to the Clayton and Federal Trade Commission bills.)

41. S. REP. NO. 597, 63d Cong., 2d Sess. 10 (1914); *see also* T. BLAISDELL, THE FEDERAL TRADE COMMISSION 1-2 (1932).

42. Federal Trade Commission Act, ch. 311, §§ 5-16, 38 Stat. 717, 719 (1914) (current version at 15 U.S.C. §§ 45-56 (1982)).

9

such as Walter Lippmann. Antitrust enforcement and other competitive policies, Lippmann wrote, foolishly obstructed modern industrial progress:

> If the anti-trust people really grasped the full meaning of what they said, and if they really had the power or the courage to do what they propose, they would be engaged in one of the most destructive agitations that America has known. They would be breaking up the beginning of a collective organization, thwarting the possibility of co-öperation, and insisting upon submitting industry to the wasteful, the planless scramble of little profiteers. They would make impossible any deliberate and constructive use of our natural resources, they would thwart any effort to form the great industries into coordinated services, they would preserve commercialism as the undisputed master of our lives, they would lay a premium on the strategy of industrial war,—they would, if they could.[43]

The crucial failing of these "anti-trust people," Lippmann concluded, was that they never saw "the possibilities of organized industries."[44]

II. The First American Experiments

Lippmann's caustic evaluation of competition as the core principle of economic organization accompanied his recommendation that business and government join in a cooperative venture to direct the economy.[45] During the next two decades, the federal government tried three major experiments with such cooperative programs: the War Industries Board, the "associationalist" policies of Herbert Hoover, and the National Recovery Administration. Viewed from the standpoint of consumer welfare, the two peacetime experiments were dismal failures.

A. The War Industries Board

America's entry into World War I in 1917 presented the first opportunity to pursue a cooperative policy of the type proposed by Lippmann. Central planning and coordination strategies received unprecedented attention during the American war mobilization effort.[46] Through the War Industries Board (WIB), the federal government exercised sweeping

43. W. LIPPMANN, DRIFT AND MASTERY 124 (1914).
44. *Id.*
45. *Id.* at 138–41. Lippmann notes that the men of the new generation "have the vast opportunity of introducing order and purpose into the business world, of devising administrative methods by which the great resources of the country can be operated on some thought-out plan." *Id.* at 141.
46. *See* Himmelberg, *The War Industries Board and the Antitrust Question in November 1918*, 52 J. AM. HIST. 59 (1965) [hereinafter cited as "Himmelberg, *The War Industries Board*"]; Cuff, *Business, the State, and World War I: The American Experience*, in THE ORDEAL OF TWENTIETH-CENTURY AMERICA, INTERPRETIVE READINGS 48 (J. Schwartz ed. 1974).

10

power over the nation's economy, controlling production priorities, resource allocation, and pricing.[47] The WIB sanctioned and promoted cooperative business efforts that during peacetime could have resulted in criminal violations of the Sherman Act.[48]

The war mobilization effort produced the country's first major experiment in comprehensive government economic planning. As historian Eric Goldman describes it, this experiment convinced many leaders in business, government, and academia that the WIB model of government-business cooperation deserved a trial in peacetime as well:

> Many of the dollar-a-year men went back to their fifty-thousand-dollar-a-year jobs with an idea buzzing in their heads. Perhaps their decades-old battle for "free competition" and against "government in business" had not been wise. They had been given striking proof that federal activity need not be anti-business, and they had seen the advantages that could come from joint operations under federal aegis.[49]

To Bernard Baruch, who headed the WIB, the experience with central control had shown antitrust law to be an anachronism.[50] The WIB, he noted, had enabled businessmen to enjoy "the tremendous advantages, both to themselves and to the general public, of combination, of cooperation and common action with their natural competitors."[51]

B. Hoover's Associationalism

At the war's conclusion, many WIB veterans sought to apply the lessons of the mobilization effort to the peacetime economy.[52] Some business leaders tried, without success, to obtain a continuing, formal relaxation of antitrust enforcement.[53] In addition, much effort went into the develop-

---

47. W. LEUCHTENBURG, THE PERILS OF PROSPERITY 1914-1932, at 39-40 (1958); A. SCHLESINGER, supra note 30, at 37-38. See generally B. BARUCH, AMERICAN INDUSTRY IN THE WAR (1941) (a compilation on industrial mobilization for war including Baruch's 1921 Report of the War Industries Board).

48. Himmelberg, The War Industries Board, supra note 46, at 60-62.

49. E. GOLDMAN, supra note 30, at 237. This feeling was especially pronounced among adherents to the Rooseveltian brand of progressivism. Donald Richberg, who worked in Roosevelt's 1912 campaign and who would become head of the National Recovery Administration in the 1930's, observed: "The truth is that no man of any political intelligence and economic vision has been able to defend the existing economic order since the World War laid bare its utter inadequacy and its insane consequences." D. RICHBERG, TENTS OF THE MIGHTY 81-82 (1930).

50. B. BARUCH, supra note 47, at 104-07. Baruch called the antitrust laws "a moderately ambitious effort to reduce by Government interference the processes of business so as to make them conform to the simpler principles sufficient for the conditions of a bygone day." Id. at 104.

51. Id. at 105.

52. Himmelberg, The War Industries Board, supra note 46, at 60-62.

53. See id. at 62-63. See generally R. HIMMELBERG, THE ORIGINS OF THE NATIONAL RECOVERY

11

ment of trade associations and other devices for industry self-regulation.[54] The principal patron of this "associationalist" movement was Herbert Hoover, who, as Secretary of Commerce and President, encouraged the formation of trade associations and professional societies.[55] A Hoover admirer, Jean Monnet, later renamed the Hoover philosophy "indicative planning" and "made it the basis both for France's post-war planning system and for the European Economic Community."[56]

Hoover's associationalist values strongly influenced the activities of government agencies whose charters nominally committed them to promote competition.[57] The Federal Trade Commission's 1928 *Annual Report*, for example, reveals the impact of associationalist values on that agency's work:

> Never in the history of American business has there been a time when self-regulation has received more intensive consideration . . . . If an industry is capable of self-regulation the trade practice conference procedure of the Federal Trade Commission affords the most effective method yet devised to accomplish this end . . . . Trade associations, "institutes," the United States Chamber of Commerce, and business organizations in other forms have done, and are doing, excellent work in this respect . . . .[58]

The trade practice conference, discussed in the above quotation, was the most important manifestation of associational attitudes in the 1920's.[59]

ADMINISTRATION: BUSINESS, GOVERNMENT, AND THE TRADE ASSOCIATION ISSUE, 1921-1933 (1976).

54. Himmelberg, *The War Industries Board, supra* note 46, at 60-61. *See also* U.S. DEP'T OF COMMERCE, TRADE ASSOCIATION ACTIVITIES (1927); FEDERAL TRADE COMM'N, OPEN PRICE ASSOCIATIONS (1929); *Trade Associations: Cooperation or Restraint of Trade,* 12 PROC. ACAD. POL. SCI. 3-99 (1926); Hawley, *Herbert Hoover, the Commerce Secretariat, and the Vision of an "Associative State," 1921-1928,* 56 J. AM. HIST. 116, 139 (1974). Hawley estimates that the number of major national associations grew from approximately 700 in 1919 to more than 2,000 in 1929. The number of lesser statewide or regional bodies may have been much larger. *See* C. WILCOX, COMPETITION AND MONOPOLY IN AMERICAN INDUSTRY 225 (1940) (T.N.E.C. Monogram No. 21).

55. Hawley, *supra* note 54; A. SCHLESINGER, *supra* note 30, at 84-89; J. HICKS, REPUBLICAN ASCENDANCY 1921-1933, at 12 (1960). Although Hoover supported certain forms of intra-industry coordination, he generally opposed attempts to push such coordination activities beyond the limits established by prevailing Supreme Court antitrust decisions and beyond "the point at which competition and cooperation could be reconciled ideologically." R. HIMMELBERG, *supra* note 53, at 220. Hoover would later denounce the National Recovery Administration's voluntary industry codes as "totalitarian" for their use of government compulsion. P. JOHNSON, MODERN TIMES 256 (1983).

56. P. JOHNSON, *supra* note 55, at 243.

57. FEDERAL TRADE COMM'N, ANNUAL REPORT 5 (1928) (showing the impact of associationalist values on the Federal Trade Commission); Hawley, *supra* note 54, at 136 (showing the impact of associationalist values on the Department of Justice). *See also* T. COCHRAN & W. MILLER, THE AGE OF ENTERPRISE 345-46 (1942).

58. FEDERAL TRADE COMM'N, *supra* note 57, at 5.

59. The trade practice conference, which began in 1919, went by the name of "trade practice submittal" until 1925. *See generally* Kittelle & Mostow, *A Review of the Trade Practice Conferences of the Federal Trade Commission,* 8 GEO. WASH. L. REV. 427 (1940).

12

Outwardly designed to suppress "unfair" or "unscrupulous" forms of business behavior, the conferences in practice acted to curb legitimate means of competition. The FTC initiated the conferences by inviting all firms in an industry to meet in the presence of a commissioner and members of the commissioner's staff to discuss disputed practices within the trade.[60] When a majority of the conferees opposed some business tactic, the conferees approved resolutions calling for a ban on the suspect practices.[61] If the FTC endorsed the conferees' views, it could classify the resolutions as either "Group I" or "Group II" rules.[62] The Commission treated violations of Group I rules as *prima facie* violations of the FTC Act and sought cease and desist orders to halt them.[63] For violations of Group II rules, however, the FTC based its decision to prosecute on the circumstances of each claimed infraction.[64]

The trade conference mechanism gradually grew from several meetings per year in the early 1920's to become one of the Commission's chief enforcement activities by the end of that decade.[65] Approximately sixty conferences were held between July 1927 and November 1929.[66]

For some observers, the FTC's reliance on the conferences displayed a healthy inclination to replace competition-preserving enforcement with cooperation-based policies.[67] From a consumer welfare perspective, however, the effect of the conferences hinged mainly on whether the rules the Commission endorsed were actually sanctioning or fostering collusion. In this important respect, the Commission failed to protect consumer interests. By the end of the 1920's, the Commission routinely endorsed codes that tended to restrict output. Arthur Schlesinger's history of the period states: "Though dedicated to the elimination of 'unfair' trade practices, the codes

---

60. *See* FEDERAL TRADE COMM'N, TRADE PRACTICE SUBMITTALS 1919 TO 1923 (1923); McCarty, *Trade Practice Conferences*, 2 CORP. PRAC. REV. 19 (1930).

61. For a general discussion of the trade practice conference procedures, see Kittelle & Mostow, *supra* note 59. *See also* A. BURNS, THE DECLINE OF COMPETITION 69-73 (1936); T. BLAISDELL, *supra* note 41, at 93-98.

62. Kittelle & Mostow, *supra* note 59, at 428.

63. *Id.*

64. *Id.*, at 428-29.

65. T. BLAISDELL, *supra* note 64, at 91-94.

66. *Id.* at 94.

67. In 1930, one former Commission official applauded this shift in emphasis:
The trade practice conference marks the beginning of systematic cooperative effort between various progressive industries and the government to establish and enforce intelligent rules of business conduct. It permits industries to become self-governing through responsible trade organizations whose activities are supervised in the public interest by the Federal Trade Commission . . . . It creates among businessmen a more enlightened sense of their responsibility to the public, and it creates . . . in the public a similar sense of its responsibility to permit business interests . . . to conduct business on sound economic principles of cooperative effort as distinguished from destructive competition.
McCarty, *supra* note 60, at 29.

13

gradually began to spill over into such questions as price-cutting and, in some cases, provided fronts behind which businessmen fraternally conspired to evade the antitrust law."[68] Many trade agreements were "essentially smoke screens to permit price fixing."[69] Some codes so alarmed the Justice Department that the Antitrust Division in 1930 called for the FTC to condemn trade agreements that seemed to violate Section 1 of the Sherman Act.[70] This effort was successful.[71]

Once the Great Depression persisted through 1932, however, there emerged substantial pressure for reinstating the authority of the FTC to permit trade groups to fix prices, allocate production, and consummate mergers and acquisitions that were "prohibited or which might be considered prohibited by the Anti-Trust Acts."[72] The supporters of cooperation between industry and government were concerned that destructive competition was severely inhibiting economic recovery.[73]

C. The National Recovery Administration

The World War I mobilization and the associationalist experiments of the 1920's had given the planners and cooperation advocates important, if limited, tests of their theories. The economic collapse of 1929, however, spurred the ideological descendants of Theodore Roosevelt to promote cooperation-based policies that might have displaced the competition model permanently. Leading War Industries Board members such as Bernard Baruch and Gerard Swope asked that the federal government suspend antitrust laws to permit business self-regulation.[74] A younger group of academicians and public administrators, including Rexford G. Tugwell, A.

---

68. A. SCHLESINGER, *supra* note 30, at 65. *See also* Kittelle & Mostow, *supra* note 59, at 436–38; W. LEUCHTENBURG, *supra* note 47; E. GOLDMAN, *supra* note 30, at 237; T. BLAISDELL, *supra* note 41, at 95–96; T. COCHRAN & W. MILLER, *supra* note 57, at 346, 348; J. CLARK, THE FEDERAL TRUST POLICY 231–32 (1931). Clark observed that, in the late 1920's, "[t]he industrialists persisted . . . in their effort to exploit the opportunity they found in the trade practice conference to temper the warfare of industrial competition and they were successful in devising euphemisms for trade-restraining agreements which escaped the attention of the commission . . . ." *Id.*

69. C. ROOS, NRA ECONOMIC PLANNING 16 (1937). Roos served as Director of Research for the NRA during its two-year existence.

70. *Id.* at 16; E. HERRING, PUBLIC ADMINISTRATION AND THE PUBLIC INTEREST 132 (1936); R. HIMMELBERG, *supra* note 53, at 93–98.

71. C. ROOS, *supra* note 69, at 16.

72. *Id.* at 17.

73. E. HAWLEY, THE NEW DEAL AND THE PROBLEM OF MONOPOLY 27, 40–41 (1966).

74. *See* Baruch, *A Plan for the Regulation of Production,* in A PHILOSOPHY OF PRODUCTION 93, 101–03 (J. Frederick ed. 1930). Gerard Swope, president of General Electric Corp., proposed the use of trade associations to coordinate industry-wide production and stabilize prices. A government economic council would oversee the associations. Swope was one of several industrialists, including Walter Teagle of Standard Oil of New Jersey and Myron Taylor of U.S. Steel, who wanted government action to adjust production to demand. *See also* A. SCHLESINGER, *supra* note 30, at 181–82; B. BELLUSH, THE FAILURE OF THE NRA 3 (1975).

14

A. Berle, and Gardner Means, supplied the theoretical foundation for policies that would permit government to coordinate economic activity on the basis of plans proposed by each industry.[75] Finally, the inauguration of Franklin D. Roosevelt in 1933 brought into office a "new Administration, skeptical of the individualism of the past, expressing confidence in a greater degree of collective action, and heralding a 'New Deal'."[76]

The early New Deal drew upon the country's war mobilization and associationalist experiences in its efforts to stimulate economic recovery.[77] The country embarked upon an unprecedented program of peacetime economic planning in June 1933 with passage of the National Industrial Recovery Act (NIRA).[78] The statute created the National Recovery Administration (NRA),[79] which promptly set about procuring trade agreements or "codes" for individual industries covering output, prices, wages, working conditions, investment, and trade practices such as advertising. Within a year the NRA had produced 450 codes covering 5 million employers and 23 million workers.[80]

75. *See* A. BERLE & G. MEANS, THE MODERN CORPORATION AND PRIVATE PROPERTY (1932); R. TUGWELL, THE INDUSTRIAL DISCIPLINE AND THE GOVERNMENTAL ARTS (1933). For a discussion of the influence of these works upon the evolution of business-government cooperation theories in the early 1930's, see W. LEUCHTENBURG, FRANKLIN D. ROOSEVELT AND THE NEW DEAL, 34-35 (1963); A. SCHLESINGER, *supra* note 30, at 190-97.

76. L. LYON, P. HOMAN, G. TERBORGH, L. LORWIN, C. DEARING & L. MARSHALL, THE NATIONAL RECOVERY ADMINISTRATION 3 (1935) [hereinafter cited as L. LYON].

77. A. SCHLESINGER, THE COMING OF THE NEW DEAL 87-94 (1959) R. HIMMELBERG, *supra* note 53, at 181-82; W. LEUCHTENBURG, *supra* note 47, at 41-42; B. BELLUSH, *supra* note 74, at 14, 16, 45; L. GALAMBOS, COMPETITION AND COOPERATION: THE EMERGENCE OF A NATIONAL TRADE ASSOCIATION, 201-02 (1966). *See generally* E. HAWLEY, *supra* note 73.

78. Act of June 16, 1933, Pub. L. No. 67, ch. 90, 48 Stat. 195 (1933). "It is hereby declared to be the policy of Congress to . . . provide for the general welfare by promoting the organization of industry for the purpose of cooperative action among trade groups, to induce and maintain united action of labor and management under adequate governmental sanctions and supervision, to eliminate unfair competitive practices, to promote the fullest possible utilization of the present productive capacity of industries, to avoid undue restriction of production (except as may be temporarily required), to increase the consumption of industrial and agricultural products by increasing purchasing power, to reduce and relieve unemployment, to improve standards of labor, and otherwise to rehabilitate industry and to conserve natural resources."

The Reconstruction Finance Corporation (RFC) was another New Deal program with implications for the present industrial policy debate; however, it was not involved in the tripartite microeconomic planning with which this article is concerned. The RFC began operations in January 1932 under the Hoover Administration. The program operated both as a source of funds to aid failing banks and as an investment bank to stimulate business, particularly small business. Although it apparently helped preserve many struggling banks, the RFC "failed" many small businesses "in their hour of need." C. ROOS, *supra* note 69, at 393. The RFC program played only a small role as an investment bank in the 1930's; it had little or no impact on economic recovery.

79. The NIRA authorized President Roosevelt to establish "such agencies . . . as he may find necessary" to effectuate the policies of the Act. Act of June 16, 1933, Pub. L. No. 67, ch. 90, 48 Stat. 195 (1933). The NRA was established by executive order pursuant to Title I of the NIRA. Exec. Order No. 6173 (1933); Exec. Order No. 6205-A (1933).

80. C. ROOS, *supra* note 69, at ix. The NRA appears to have modelled its code program on the FTC's trade practice conference procedure. *See* A. BURNS, THE DECLINE OF COMPETITION 463 (1936); *see generally*, R. HIMMELBERG, *supra* note 53.

15

In promoting the bill, President Roosevelt stressed the importance of joint business and government efforts to restore prosperity. For example, on May 4, 1933, six weeks before the NIRA was passed, he told an approving audience at the United States Chamber of Commerce:

> You and I acknowledge the existence of unfair methods of competition, of cutthroat prices and of general chaos. You and I agree that this condition must be rectified and that order must be restored. The attainment of that objective depends on your willingness to co-operate with one another to that end, and also your willingness to co-operate with your Government.[81]

In signing the legislation President Roosevelt urged businesses to "band themselves faithfully in . . . modern guilds" and to unite in a "great spontaneous co-operation to put millions of men back to work in their regular jobs."[82] The President said: "We are relaxing some of the safeguards of the antitrust laws. . . . [W]e are putting in place of old principles of unchecked competition some new government controls . . . ."[83]

Reaction on Wall Street to the introduction of the recovery legislation generally had been bullish.[84] To many in the business community, industry-wide codes designed to bar price-cutting and increase profits would be a *quid pro quo* exchanged for labor's right to boost wages through collective bargaining.[85] The bill had enjoyed broad support from what a 1935 Brookings Institution study called "[a] curious combination of . . . reform

---

81.   Address by President Roosevelt to the U.S. Chamber of Commerce (May 4, 1933), *quoted in* C. ROOS, *supra* note 69, at 41.

82.   F. ROOSEVELT, STATE OF POLICY ON INDUSTRIAL RECOVERY ACT (June 16, 1933) *quoted in* C. ROOS, *supra* note 69, at 53. The theme of "cooperation" soon emerged throughout what Hawley called a "whole set of favorable collectivist symbols" to herald the ascendency of coordination strategies over competition-oriented policies. Hawley observed:

> New Deal and business spokesmen wrought a virtual revolution in popular symbolism. "Competition" became "economic cannibalism" and "rugged individualists" became "industrial pirates." Conservative industrialists, veteran antitrusters, and classical economists were all lumped together and branded "social Neanderthalers," "Old Dealers," and "Corporals of Disaster." The time-honored practice of reducing prices to gain a larger share of the market became "cut-throat and monopolistic price slashing," and those that engaged in this dastardly activity became "chiselers." Conversely, monopolistic collusion, price agreements, proration, and cartelization became "cooperative" or "associational" activities—and devices that were chiefly designed to eliminate competition bore the euphemistic title, "Codes of Fair Competition."

E. HAWLEY, *supra* note 73, at 54.

83.   F. ROOSEVELT, STATE OF POLICY ON INDUSTRIAL RECOVERY ACT (June 16, 1933), *quoted in* C. ROOS, *supra* note 69, at 53.

84.   C. ROOS, *supra* note 69, at 43-45; E. HAWLEY, *supra* note 73, at 26-28.

85.   C. ROOS, *supra* note 69, at 234; B. BELLUSH, *supra* note 74, at 16-17, 28. Within the business community there was opposition to the NRA from smaller firms seeking to enter or expand in selected industries and from firms whose operations had been largely profitable. R. HIMMELBERG, *supra* note 53, at 221-22; L. GALAMBOS, *supra* note 77, at 226.

16

groups, business groups, and labor groups, each seeing in the developing bill an opportunity to promote ends of its own."[86]

The NRA allowed participation of three principal groups in its code-making deliberations: In addition to the Administrator and his deputies, the NRA had a Consumer Advisory Board, a Labor Advisory Board, and an Industrial Advisory Board. In theory, each industry's "code" was to be set in a "forum of cooperation" in which the NRA planner would steer "unselfish" group interests toward mutually satisfactory agreements.[87] In practice, this "idealized version" yielded to the "realities of an out and out bargaining process, in which selfish interests were played against one another."[88]

The dominant members of the tripartite coalitions were the trade associations. An NRA release noted that the new law's relaxation of antitrust strictures had given the associations a new importance. It said, "They are almost a part of the government and they can do and agree to many more things than they could do before."[89] A Brookings study described the new efforts of the associations to free their members from the hostile forces of competition:

[C]ommittees of business men were crowding into Washington and staying for weeks and months for the privilege of increasing their costs by raising wages and reducing hours of work. For the most part, they were there to secure a sufficient *quid pro quo*, hoping (as against official pronouncements) that the *quid* would sufficiently outweigh the *quo* to make the effort worthwhile in terms of profits. The imaginations of groups of business men were fired by the prospect of removing or mitigating the competitive handicaps to which they so largely attributed the unhappy absence of profits.[90]

Indeed, the "central motivating force" of the trade associations was the

---

86. L. LYON, *supra* note 76, at 7. *See also* E. HAWLEY, *supra* note 73, at 33 ("Within the confines of a single measure, . . . the formulators of the National Industrial Recovery Act had appealed to the hopes of a number of conflicting pressure groups").

Not everyone, however, embraced the new legislation. "Opposition to the proposal," Hawley wrote, "came from antitrusters and small business liberals, men who stressed the evils of monopoly and were reluctant to abandon the competitive tradition." *Id.* at 29. Among the leading intellectual opponents of the bill were architects of and successors to Woodrow Wilson's New Freedom program. Justice Louis Brandeis, whom Wilson had appointed to the Supreme Court, attacked in his correspondence the proposed bill because of "the impossibility of enforcement, the dangers to the small industries, the inefficiency of the big unit, be it governmental or private." N. DAWSON, LOUIS D. BRANDEIS, FELIX FRANKFURTER, AND THE NEW DEAL 66 (1980).

87. L. LYON, *supra* note 76, at 83-85.

88. *Id.* at 85.

89. *Id.* at 89, n.7, (quoting NRA Release No. 11, June 25, 1933); *see also*, E. HAWLEY, *supra* note 73, at 55-62; B. BELLUSH, *supra* note 74, at 45; R. HIMMELBERG, *supra* note 53, at 211.

90. L. LYON, *supra* note 76, at 91-92.

17

desire to improve prices and profits by "collective action."[91] Labor groups, too, were pleased to secure a *quid pro quo* in the form of higher wages, and government administrators no doubt enjoyed their newly found power over commerce and trade.

These gains to business, labor, and government interests, however, frequently came at the expense of consumers. The government planners, "hungrily seeking new fields to conquer, seized upon any reason for extending their domain."[92] For example, the NRA granted monopolies to the copper and petroleum industries in the name of environmental preservation as well as national defense.[93] In addition to the deliberate creation of monopolies, moreover, NRA administrators readily acquiesced in numerous code provisions that facilitated "monopolistic or semi-monopolistic prices."[94] Some codes fostered extensive and explicit collusion among bidders for state, local, and federal government contracts, thereby raising profits for the favored firms.[95] Others facilitated clandestine price-fixing[96] and restricted interregional product shipments.[97] The glass container industry received an especially strong code as a reward for helping the government enforce the liquor revenue laws.[98] And restrictions on timber production guaranteed prices equal to several times the replacement value of the timber.[99] The codes of the timber, copper, and glass container industries all "had their origin in pre-code price-fixing activities of the groups concerned."[100]

All such practices led to "consumer gouging."[101] They also harmed smaller firms because the larger firms dominated the code-making deliberations.[102] Moreover, although NRA activities successfully raised profits and wages for many of the favored firms and their employees, the agency substantially impeded recovery from the Depression.[103] In 1935, when the

91. *Id.* at 94. *See also* E. HAWLEY, *supra* note 73, at 56-62.

92. C. ROOS, *supra* note 69, at 360.

93. *Id.* at 354-58, 359.

94. *Id.* at 373.

95. *Id.* at 323.

96. *Id.* at 289; E. HAWLEY, *supra* note 73, at 57-61.

97. C. ROOS, *supra* note 69, at 372-73.

98. *Id.* at 360.

99. *Id.* at 250.

100. *Id.* at 360; *see also* L. GALAMBOS, *supra* note 77, at 201-02 (discussing the application of the NRA codes to the cotton textile industry).

101. C. ROOS, *supra* note 69, at 467.

102. *Id.* at 416; L. LYON, *supra* note 76, at 745; W. LEUCHTENBURG, *supra* note 47, at 69.

103. C. ROOS, *supra* note 69, at 415-16; L. LYON, *supra* note 76, at 873-76; N. DAWSON, *supra* note 86, at 65, 73 (concluding that the NRA "retarded" recovery). *See also* E. HAWLEY, *supra* note 73, at 131-32; A. SCHLESINGER, *supra* note 77, at 172-76; B. BELLUSH, *supra* note 74, at 61-64, 70-71, 80-82, 140, 144, 149-50, 161, 165-67. Bellush records criticism of the NRA's output restricting effects by Brookings Economist George Terborgh and John Maynard Keynes. B. BELLUSH, *supra* note 74, at 63-64, 144. Bellush writes that Keynes, who argued that the NRA had been put across too

18

NRA was effectively abolished by a Supreme Court decision,[104] the unemployment rate stood at 20 percent.[105] This figure was less than the rate inherited by the Roosevelt Administration, but was more than six times the rate in 1929.[106] In the words of Charles F. Roos, who had served as the NRA's Director of Research, the Court's action had "destroyed the monstrosity, that during 1934 and 1935 had kept business in a churn, prevented reemployment, and consequently retarded economic development."[107]

The lesson for future students of industrial policy was clear: Attempts at economic planning would deteriorate into nothing more than bargaining between economic groups. Monopolistic advantages would be exchanged for labor concessions, with the choicest gains flowing to the groups exhibiting the greatest political power. As Roos concluded two years after the NRA's demise: "To trust the economic order to such 'planners' would be rash indeed; there would be a greater chance that they would reduce it to chaos than that a baby handed a watch and hammer would smash the watch."[108]

Although the NRA was the most far-reaching industrial policy pursued in the 1930's, it was not the only such policy. The economic collapse gave rise to a wide range of programs designed to rescue various industries from the effects of "cutthroat" competition. In the natural resource and transportation fields, Congress enacted legislation which effectively converted otherwise competitive industries into highly regulated, cartelized, and often inefficient industries.[109] In the transportation field, the jurisdiction of the Interstate Commerce Commission was extended to trucking,[110] and the Civil Aeronautics Board was established[111] to employ government-sponsored cooperation in awarding routes and setting prices. A large

hastily "in the false guise of being part of the technique of recovery," criticized the NRA's attempt to raise prices "by deliberately increasing prime costs or by restricting output. . ." B. BELLUSH, *supra* note 74, at 63–64.

104.   On May 27, 1935, the Supreme Court struck down the NIRA on the ground that the statute was an unconstitutionally broad delegation of legislative power. Schechter Poultry Corp. v. United States, 295 U.S. 495 (1935). Only months earlier, the Court had invalidated the NRA's "hot oil" provisions on similar grounds. *See* Panama Refining Co. v. Ryan, 293 U.S. 388 (1935). On the day of the *Schechter* decision, Justice Brandeis told newspaper reporters that May 27, 1935, was "the most important day in the history of the Court and the most beneficent." Thomas Corcoran, one of President Roosevelt's advisors, later noted that, following *Schechter*, Brandeis said, "This is the end of this business of centralization, and I want you to go back and tell the President that we're not going to let this government centralize everything." N. DAWSON, *supra* note 86, at 129.

105.   *See* BUREAU OF THE CENSUS, *supra* note 2, at 135.

106.   *See id.*

107.   C. ROOS, *supra* note 69, at 472.

108.   *Id.* at 467.

109.   *See, e.g.,* E. HAWLEY, *supra* note 73, at 205–80.

110.   *See supra* note 26.

111.   Civil Aeronautics Act of 1938, Pub. L. No. 75-706, 52 Stat. 973.

19

body of literature has demonstrated that many of these cooperative ventures produced tremendous social costs in the form of higher prices and resource misallocation.[112] Indeed, only within the past decade have some of the chief regulatory measures of the 1930's been repealed or substantially modified to permit greater reliance on market forces.[113] These reforms have produced substantial gains for the general public.[114]

III.   Contemporary Industrial Policies

At the heart of the current industrial policy debate is the assertion that, through tripartite (business, labor, and government) cooperation, government can "guide" leading industries to successful growth opportunities.[115] Proponents of industrial policy point to "indicative planning" policies in other leading industrial nations, including France, West Germany, and Japan as evidence of the benefits of coordinated action.[116] The experiences of these countries, however, like U.S. experience with the NRA,[117] provide little support for more centralized coordination.

A.   Indicative Planning Policies of Japan

The "miracle" of "Japan, Inc."[118] is frequently offered as an example of the benefits of coordinated policies.[119] Japan's Ministry of International

---

112.   *See, e.g.*, G. DOUGLAS & J. MILLER III, ECONOMIC REGULATION OF DOMESTIC AIR TRANSPORT: THEORY AND POLICY (1974); Eads, *Competition in the Domestic Trunk Airline Industry: Too Much or Too Little?* in PROMOTING COMPETITION IN REGULATED MARKETS 13 (A. Phillips ed. 1975); Moore, *Deregulating Surface Freight Transportation*, in PROMOTING COMPETITION IN REGULATED MARKETS 55 (A. Phillips ed. 1975); S. BREYER, REGULATION AND ITS REFORM (1982).

113.   *See, e.g.*, Staggers Rail Act of 1980, Pub. L. No. 96-448, 94 Stat. 1895 (partially deregulating railroads); Natural Gas Policy Act of 1978, Pub. L. No. 95-621, 92 Stat. 3350 (partially deregulating natural gas producers); Airline Deregulation Act of 1978, Pub. L. No. 95-504, 92 Stat. 1705 (partially deregulating airlines); and Motor Carrier Act of 1980, Pub. L. No. 96-296, 94 Stat. 793 (partially deregulating trucking).

114.   *See, e.g.*, OFFICE OF ECONOMIC ANALYSIS, CIVIL AERONAUTICS BOARD STAFF REPORT, COMPETITION AND THE AIRLINES: AN EVALUATION OF DEREGULATION (authored by D. Graham & D. Kaplan, 1982); OFFICE OF TRANSPORTATION ANALYSIS, INTERSTATE COMMERCE COMMISSION, THE INTERCITY BUS INDUSTRY (1984); Babcock, *Efficiency and Adjustment: The Impact of Rail Deregulation*, 33 CATO INSTITUTE POLICY ANALYSIS (1984); Moore, *Rail and Truck Reform—The Record So Far*, REGULATION, Nov.-Dec. 1983, at 33, 36.

115.   *See, e.g.*, I. MAGAZINER & R. REICH, *supra* note 6, at 377.

116.   *See, e.g.*, Weil, *U.S. Industrial Policy: A Process in Need of a Federal Industrial Coordination Board*, 14 LAW & POLICY IN INT'L BUS. 981, 1004-06 (1983); Krauss, *"Europeanizing" the U.S. Economy: The Enduring Appeal of the Corporatist State*, in THE INDUSTRIAL POLICY DEBATE 71-90 (C. Johnson ed. 1984).

117.   *See supra* text accompanying notes 74-114.

118.   "Japan, Inc." is a phrase commonly used by writers on Japan to denote the close ties between Japanese companies and their government. *See, e.g.*, Ohmae, *Japan vs. Japan: Only the Strong Survive*, Wall St. J., Jan. 26, 1981, at 20, col. 1. For a critique of "Japan, Inc." see T. SAKIYA, HONDA MOTOR: THE MEN, THE MANAGEMENT, THE MACHINES 137-38 (1982).

119.   *See, e.g.*, C. JOHNSON, MITI AND THE JAPANESE MIRACLE: THE GROWTH OF INDUSTRIAL POLICY, 1925-1975 at 30-32, 305-24 (1982); Weil, *supra* note 116, at 1004, 1033-38.

20

Trade and Industry (MITI) and the Bank of Japan have sought to facilitate coordinated activities among competing Japanese firms.[120] As a major element of its coordination efforts, MITI has sought to "cartelize and rationalize" several industries, sharing with them its "visions" of their competitive futures and providing them for a time with substantial import protection from foreign competition.[121]

However, it is hardly clear that policies emphasizing cooperation and joint planning have played a significant role in promoting Japan's phenomenal economic growth.[122] Indeed, there is considerable evidence that Japan's efforts to concentrate Japanese industry and coordinate firms' strategic behavior have frequently failed or produced unintended results. For example, in a seven-year period during which MITI attempted to concentrate Japan's cotton spinning industry, the 10-firm concentration ratio fell from 89 to 50 percent.[123] In spite of MITI's efforts to consolidate Japan's emerging auto industry, the number of significant firms grew from three to nine.[124] And MITI's effort to concentrate the Japanese computer industry's six firms into a single firm the equivalent of IBM never got off the ground.[125]

Many of the most successful Japanese industries, both concentrated and 'unconcentrated, have consisted of vigorously independent firms. For example, as mentioned above, Japanese auto companies successfully opposed MITI's merger efforts[126] and refused to heed the government's early advice to forego export sales;[127] they also resisted MITI's efforts to allocate sales and limit their export production to a "people's car."[128] When the government sought to ban certain forms of non-price competition in the pharmaceutical industry, fierce price competition erupted.[129] Sony resisted

---

120. To quote two leading authorities on Japanese industrial policies:

An important if fluid role in coordinating the actions of rival sellers has been played by agencies of the Japanese government, particularly the Ministry of International Trade and Industry. In a number of industries MITI has taken an active hand to promote coordination directly through "administrative guidance." The practice is without explicit statutory authority or legalistic procedure—it would be unthinkable in the United States, and is at least somewhat controversial in Japan's less legalistic political system.

R. CAVES & M. UEKUSA, INDUSTRIAL ORGANIZATION IN JAPAN 53-54 (1976).

121. E. KAPLAN, U.S. DEP'T OF COMMERCE, JAPAN: THE GOVERNMENT-BUSINESS RELATIONSHIP 16, 39, 85 (1972).

122. See Trezise, Industrial Policy is Not the Major Reason for Japan's Success, 2 BROOKINGS REV. 13-18 (Spring 1983); Sakoh, Industrial Policy: The Super Myth of Japan's Super Success, HERITAGE FOUND. (July 13, 1983).

123. R. CAVES & M. UEKUSA, supra note 120, at 55.

124. E. KAPLAN, supra note 121, at 108, 128; see also T. SAKIYA, supra note 118 at 134-137.

125. ECONOMIST, July 18, 1981, at 13.

126. R. CAVES & M. UEKUSA, supra note 120, at 151; Sakoh, supra note 122, at 12.

127. W. DUNCAN, U.S.-JAPAN AUTOMOBILE DIPLOMACY: A STUDY IN ECONOMIC CONFRONTATION 73-74 (1973); Etzioni, The Mitization of America?, PUB. INTEREST, Summer 1983, at 46.

128. ETZIONI, supra note 127, at 46; E. KAPLAN, supra note 121, at 121.

129. R. CAVES & M. UEKUSA, supra note 120, at 50.

21

MITI's efforts to prevent it from bringing transistor technology into Japan.[130] Indeed, analysts have speculated that MITI's efforts to discourage firms from entering certain industries may have acted on firms as an artificial incentive to enter those industries and share in the expected cartel profits.[131] In short, intense domestic competition has been the primary factor in many of the major Japanese industrial successes. The manufacturers have succeeded in spite of MITI's efforts to guide and coordinate their decisions, not because of those efforts.

Moreover, even if the planning and cooperation model had some relevance in the early post-war period, its current value is questionable. Jiro Tokuyama, dean of the Nomura School of Advanced Management in Tokyo, recently stated:

> Coordination is all right if you're building a steel and car industry on the model of other people. But now we're in an era of rapid change, of integrated circuits and microprocessors. . . . I don't think our large organizations can move quickly enough to make the changes. We must find our model among the entrepreneurs like [those] in your Silicon Valley.[132]

One indication that the planning model may be losing its relevance is that some once-touted examples of successful Japanese planning have come on hard times. Between 1977 and 1982, the Japanese shipbuilding industry lost 46,000 jobs.[133] Between 1976 and 1981, imports' share of domestic aluminum sales rose from 24 percent to 56 percent.[134] Even in steel, where the Japanese supposedly have achieved great success, there is substantial excess capacity. Japanese firms have been calling for the application of Japan's never-used laws prohibiting below-cost sales—"dumping"—by foreign firms.[135] Today, MITI is actively seeking to reduce overcapacity in many of the very industries it is credited with having created.[136]

In sum, the Japanese government does rely on a greater degree of consensus-building than does the United States government. Much can be learned from this greater degree of harmony among business, labor and government. Nevertheless, the Japanese success story arguably occurred de-

---

130. Henderson, *The Myth of MITI*, FORTUNE, Aug. 8, 1983, at 113; *A Rising Tide of Protectionism*, NEWSWEEK, May 30, 1983, at 28.

131. R. CAVES & M. UEKUSA, *supra* note 120, at 56.

132. Wash. Post, Apr. 29, 1984, at B1, col. 1.

133. Boyer, *How Japan Manages Declining Industries*, FORTUNE, Jan. 10, 1983, at 60.

134. *Id.* at 62.

135. For example, Japanese petrochemical manufacturers have complained about dumping by U.S. and Canadian firms. *See* ECONOMIST, Sept. 25, 1982, at 89.

136. *See generally* Boyer, *supra* note 133.

22

spite any policies of planning and cooperation, not because of them. The strongest Japanese industries are precisely those in which competition is most vigorous.[137] Hence the policy implications of the Japanese experience are ambiguous at best.

B. *Indicative Planning Policies of Western Europe*

Like the myth of "Japan, Inc.," popular accounts of the success of indicative planning policies in Western Europe are little more than folk stories. Both in France and in West Germany, attempts at comprehensive planning and coordination have been largely unsuccessful.

The roots of French indicative planning, at least at a theoretical level, reach back to the 18th century mercantilists, whose policies were criticized by Smith and Hume.[138] This interventionist philosophy proposed that government substitute "cooperation for conflict and competition,"[139] and that the state be "an active, initiating partner, not a distant policeman. Its role [was] to create the structures of cooperation and through them to guide the economy toward expansion and modernization."[140]

In this tradition, the objective of recent French indicative planning policies was "to increase the scale and efficiency of French industrial production"[141] and to "construct a series of national champions which would carry the French flag into battle against the foreign giants."[142] To the French planners a "fundamental harmony of interest [existed] between big business and the state."[143] The paradigmatic French mechanism for achieving industrial growth, therefore, consisted mainly in assembling an elite corps of civil servants insulated from political pressures and sensitive mainly to the desire of "industry to regulate competitive forces."[144] This forum for formulating French industrial policy would exclude "trade un-

---

137. Ken Ohmae, a leading Japanese executive has stated: "[T]he Japanese government has rarely been able to protect Japanese companies from *other Japanese companies*. And in almost every industry where Japanese companies have done well in export markets, they have honed their teeth in fierce domestic competition." Ohmae, *supra* note 118, at 20, col. 3.

138. One such French mercantilist was Colbert. For a discussion of Colbert's view of mercantilism, see C. COLE, COLBERT AND A CENTURY OF FRENCH MERCANTILISM 335–55 (2d ed. 1964). Adam Smith noted that "Mr. Colbert, the famous minister of Lewis XIV . . . had unfortunately embraced all the prejudices of the mercantile system. . . ." A. SMITH, *supra* note 13, at 627. According to Smith, Colbert favored urban industry at the expense of agricultural industry. *Id.* at 628.

139. STAFF OF SUBCOMM. ON ECONOMIC GROWTH AND STABILIZATION OF THE JOINT ECONOMIC COMM., 95TH CONG., 1ST SESS., RECENT DEVELOPMENTS IN FRENCH PLANNING: SOME LESSONS FOR THE UNITED STATES 6 (Comm. Print 1977) (authored by S. Cohen) [hereinafter referred to as S. COHEN].

140. *Id.*

141. *Id.* at 20.

142. *Id.* at 21.

143. *Id.* at 6.

144. *Id.* at 6, 7, 21.

23

ions, consumer groups, small business groups, peasant [agricultural] organizations and [even] Parliament,"[145] although "places [could] be kept at
the conference tables for the 'responsible' trade unionists [that] the
planned industrial evolution [was] supposed to produce."[146]

At first, this approach to industrial policy was nothing more than ideology and had little or no impact on French industry. The first four postwar
French "plans" were never taken seriously.[147] However, like the other
West European economies, the French economy experienced rapid growth
in the postwar period.[148] Many people associated the mythical indicative
planning policies with that growth.

The first real test of French planning came with the Fifth Plan, which
began in 1966. This Plan included a comprehensive program of "general
resource allocation," as well as an incomes policy for labor and a set of
targeted investments for business.[149] The plan "failed dramatically"[150]
and was aborted in May 1968, midway through its scheduled duration.[151]
The Sixth Plan, begun in 1970, had the "same basic structure"[152] as its
immediate predecessor and quickly met the same fate. The French government killed off the "comprehensive planning" elements of both programs well before it issued the official obituaries.[153] The reason was simple: No group was willing to cooperate—to give up its *quid pro
quo*—"not business, not the middle classes, not the unions, and not the
Government."[154]

Subsequent to the Sixth Plan, French efforts to spur industrial growth
and create a class of international champions have been limited to a case-

---

145.   *Id.* at 7.

146.   *Id.*

147.   Herbert Stein, as research director for the Committee for Economic Development, was sent
to France by President Kennedy in 1962 to "investigate the possibility of improving the performance
of the American economy by emulating French planning." Stein recalls that:

> Many people were infatuated with French planning at the time. The combination of intellec-
> tual rigor, as suggested by the word "planning," and romance, as suggested by the word
> "French," was extremely tempting. So a group of us went to Paris. We met with officials of
> the Commissariat du Plan, with French businessmen, and with economists. By the time we
> returned I had concluded, in a line that I could not get out of my mind: "*Le Plan Francais, il
> n'existe pas.*" The French government had forecasts about the economy, it made certain inter-
> ventions in the economy—but it had no plan. It had no blueprint for the desired course of the
> economy in specific and detailed terms and no machinery for bringing a blueprint into reality
> if one had existed. The French "plan" was soon enough forgotten by everyone.

Stein, *Don't Fall for Industrial Policy*, FORTUNE, Nov. 14, 1983, at 64.

148.   *See* J.-J. CARRÉ, P. DUBOIS & E. MALINVAUD, FRENCH ECONOMIC GROWTH 24–34 (1975).

149.   S. COHEN, *supra* note 139, at 13–16.

150.   *Id.* at 14.

151.   *Id.*

152.   *Id.* at 13–14.

153.   *Id.* at 14.

154.   *Id.* at 14–15.

24

by-case approach.[155] As in Japan, however, such policies have not been notably successful. The joint British and French Concorde, as well as the French government's attempt to encourage the development of its domestic computer industry, are illustrative examples.[156]

The attempts of other West European governments to guide and coordinate the activities of specific industries have not met with any greater success. The West Germans, like their French counterparts, had relied mainly on market forces until the latter 1960's.[157] In the 1970's, however, the West German government attempted to coordinate plans for its computer and nuclear power industries; these efforts have not been successful.[158] In addition, West Germany's once-heralded industrial policy successes in steel, coal mining, and shipbuilding have gone the way of their Japanese counterparts.[159] Overall, in the words of economist Michael Wachter, the West European experience with indicative planning "has just been terrible."[160]

Europe's comparatively poor economic performance over the past decade reinforces the suggestion that activist industrial planning policies were not the key to European industrial growth. In general, as the West European economies came to rely more on centralized industrial policies in the 1970's, their economic performance declined both absolutely and relative to the United States.[161] Since 1973, industrial growth has risen more rap-

---

155. *Id.* at 25.
156. *See* Kahn, *The Relevance of Industrial Organization*, in INDUSTRIAL ORGANIZATION, ANTI-TRUST, AND PUBLIC POLICY 16 (J. Craven ed. 1983).
157. Schmidt, *West Germany, Another Industrial Policy Victim*, HERITAGE FOUND. INT'L BRIEF-ING, Mar. 7, 1984, at 1.
158. *Id.* at 4.
159. *Id.* 5–7.
160. BUS. WK., July 4, 1983, at 61.
161. Chart I shows the absolute and relative 1983 levels of GDP per capita among the major industrial nations. It shows that the U.S. citizen still is substantially better off than citizens of any other major industrialized nation:

Chart I

GDP Per Capita of Leading
Industrial Nations,* 1983

Country	GDP/Capita	Percent US level = 100
United States	$13,106	100
Canada	12,104	92
Sweden	11,907	91
West Germany	10,691	82
France	9,961	76
Japan	8,966	68
United Kingdom	8,523	65
Italy	6,133	47

SOURCE: THE OECD OBSERVER, Mar. 1984, at 22-23.

*As defined in COMMITTEE FOR ECONOMIC DEVELOPMENT, PRODUCTIVITY POLICY: KEY TO THE NATION'S ECONOMIC FUTURE (April 1983).

25

idly in the United States than in any major industrialized West European nation. Of course, other factors such as the OPEC oil embargo undoubtedly impeded European economic growth during this period; we do not claim that increased reliance on planning and cooperation was necessarily the major problem. Nonetheless, there is little or no empirical evidence that industrial planning has led to significant economic growth in Western Europe. Indeed, West European leaders now seem to be retreating from the planning and cooperation model. As Bernard Attali, a socialist intellectual and adviser to French President Mitterand, recently conceded:

It might be argued that the United States would fare considerably worse if, say, 1980 exchange rates had been used to convert other nations' GDPs into U.S. dollars. However, the OECD ranking remains unchanged when conversions are made on the basis of "purchasing power parities," as opposed to the limited items entering into foreign trade. (Sweden and Canada were not included in the OECD study.) In the latter comparison, the U.S. level exceeds that of second-place Germany by $2,226. This second method results in the same rankings for 1980, when the U.S. dollar was not as valuable in foreign exchange. In that year, U.S. per capita GDP exceeded that of Germany by $1,936 in terms of "purchasing power parities." *See* OECD OBSERVER, Mar. 1982, at 31–32.

Consider as well the growth in industrial production from 1973 to 1983 for each of the eight nations depicted in Chart II. The countries are listed in the same order as in Chart I: that is, according to size of GDP per capita. The U.S. industrial growth rate is exceeded only by that of Japan. In short, since the OPEC embargo in 1973, the U.S. industrial base, as measured by its index of industrial output, has grown more rapidly than that of any of the major European nations.

Chart II

Percent Growth in Index of Industrial Production
for Eight Leading Industrial Nations, 1973-1983

Country	Growth %
United States	13.7
Canada	8.7
Sweden	5.1
West Germany	3.3
France	7.8
Japan	24.0
United Kingdom	-1.8
Italy	9.6

SOURCE: Based on INTERNATIONAL MONETARY FUND, 37 INTERNATIONAL FINANCIAL STATISTICS (Sept. 1984); INTERNATIONAL FINANCIAL STATISTICS, 1983 YEARBOOK.

The most telling indication of European economic performance is its failure to match the record of the U.S. economy in generating more than 20 million new jobs in the 1970's. In that period total employment in the European economy rose by approximately 3%, as opposed to a nearly 33% gain for the U.S. economy. In addition, nine out of ten new entrants were able to find jobs in the rapidly expanding U.S. labor force of the 1970's; only three of ten new entrants could find jobs in the European labor force during the same period. *See* Ostry, *The World Economy in 1983: Marking Time*, 62 FOREIGN AFF. 537 n.6 (1984).

Even as the U.S. rate of unemployment fell from 9.7% in 1982 to 8.2% in 1983, European unemployment rates were continuing their steady rise to 11%—more than three times their rate in 1973. Approximately 18.5 million Europeans were out of work, of which an estimated 33% to 50% were long-term, hard-core unemployed. Only 5% to 8% of the U.S. and Canadian labor force fell into that category. *Id.* at 536. *See also* Whitman, *Persistent Unemployment: Economic Policy Perspectives in the United States and Western Europe*, in UNEMPLOYMENT AND GROWTH IN THE WESTERN ECONOMIES 14 (A. Pierre, ed. 1984).

26

We know perfectly well that the growth we want depends on the entrepreneurial spirit. . . . Only entrepreneurs create jobs and new opportunities. The world is changing and we are all entering an era of profound decentralization and the entrepreneur. We are now interested in helping people go out there and help themselves.[162]

In summary, any argument that the U.S. government should rely more on policies of planning and coordination cannot draw strong support from the economic successes of Japan and the other Far Eastern free market economies.[163] That argument, moreover, is substantially weakened by the failure of West European experiments with indicative planning. Obviously, the U.S. government still should strive to promote economic development through sound macroeconomic and microeconomic policies. The government can play a useful role in reconciling seemingly contradictory policies and regulations. Nevertheless, the United States should pursue these objectives without relying upon the centralized industrial policies that have been tried elsewhere. To quote U.S. venture capitalist Peter Brooke: "It's incredible that some Americans are going to heavy state planning when I'm being asked to go to Europe to help them disband theirs. . . . We shouldn't follow their mistakes. Hell, we're the ones with the answers."[164]

IV. Political Feasibility of a Centralized Industrial Policy

Even if centralized industrial policies such as those discussed in the previous section had helped other nations, it would not follow that the United States ought to embrace such a policy. As the experience with the NRA suggests, attempts to implement a workable centralized industrial policy would affront some of the most ingrained characteristics of the American political system.[165] Moreover, "success" in overcoming the political obstacles to effective economic planning might impose substantial costs upon the nation's democratic processes and run counter to its tradition of individual liberty.

A. *Political Obstacles*

Advocates of an activist American industrial policy quickly dismiss any suggestion that their proposals would require a serious overhaul of Amer-

---

162. Wash. Post, Apr. 29, 1984, at B4, col. 5.
163. For an account of the successes of other Far Eastern market economies, see COMM. FOR ECONOMIC DEVELOPMENT, PRODUCTIVITY POLICY: KEY TO THE NATION'S ECONOMIC FUTURE 95–106 (1983).
164. Wash. Post, Apr. 29, 1984, at B4, col. 5.
165. *See supra* text accompanying notes 74–114.

27

ican government.[166] Many of them observe that the basic elements of such a system are already buried in the interstices of tax codes and tariff policies, and scattered about in individual subsidy schemes and regulatory measures. They believe that only a centralized decisionmaking structure needs to be added to transform this existing patchwork into an effective overall strategy.[167]

This argument, however, ignores a major fact about the place of centralization in American government. Although unified efforts to achieve clearly defined national goals are essential in times of war, centralized peacetime policymaking is just what the American political system was designed to prevent. Of course it is possible to overdo the argument for "American exceptionalism,"[168] thereby exaggerating the distinctiveness of American patterns. Political obstacles to effective government coordination and guidance of industry plans may exist to some degree in all democratic countries—as the Mitterand government in France has been discovering. Nevertheless, the political and institutional obstacles to a coherent industrial policy in this country are derived from some of the most pronounced and deep-rooted features of the American political system. Together they make it even less likely that the U.S. government could implement a successful industrial policy based largely on central planning and tripartite coordination.

Four related characteristics of the American political system would impede the success of any such policy: the extraordinary range and diversity of organized interest groups in the United States, the unusually accessible character of American political institutions, the absence of a well- established administrative elite, and the activist role of American courts.

1. *Profusion of Interest Groups*

The extraordinary profusion of interest groups in the United States is not a recent development or a chance phenomenon, but reflects the unusually diverse backgrounds of the American population and the dynamic character of American society. The proliferation of discrete interest groups can be traced back to the writings of the Founders. *The Federalist* argued that political debate could rarely be expected to rise above the clash of selfish factions and praised the federal union precisely for embracing numerous factions, thus diluting the strength of any particular interest: "Ex-

---

166. *See, e.g.*, I. MAGAZINER & R. REICH, *supra* note 6, at 379–80.
167. *See, e.g.*, I. MAGAZINER & R. REICH, *supra* note 6, at 235, 243–44; *Do Modern Times Call For an Industrial Policy?: A Conversation with Herbert Stein and Lester Thurow, supra* note 6, at 6.
168. "American exceptionalism" is a term applied by some historians to the development of values and institutions in the United States. *See* N. LEVIN, WOODROW WILSON AND WORLD POLITICS 3 (1968); L. HARTZ, THE LIBERAL TRADITION IN AMERICA (1955).

28

tend the sphere and you take in a greater variety of parties and interests; you make it less probable that a majority of the whole will have a common motive to invade the rights of other citizens."[169]

In the 1830's, Alexis de Tocqueville marveled at the alacrity with which Americans formed political associations to take up passing causes, noting that "this powerful instrument of action has been applied to more varied aims in America than anywhere else in the world."[170] Foreign observers are still struck by the organizing energy of Americans. Most Western countries, for example, have solicitations for several medical charities. In the United States, however, fundraising campaigns exist for hundreds of diseases, while some even have distinct lobbies for government assistance.

As observers of regulatory policymaking in Washington will recognize, this American passion for political organizing has serious ramifications for industrial policy. Proponents of a "coordinated" industrial policy invariably stress the advantages of government-sponsored consensus between "business" and "labor"[171]—as if these abstract entities could confer around an intimate little table. In Western Europe, a few powerful union leaders or trade association spokesmen might be accepted as authentic representatives of vast industrial constituencies. In the United States, however, one who claims to speak for "business" or "labor" often finds intense opposition from others in the same group who seek contrary objectives. The Federal Trade Commission, for example, is often confronted with pleas by one business organization, frequently supported by its employees, challenging a merger or marketing policy of another. Small businesses, which unlike their larger competitors frequently employ unorganized labor, often oppose the positions of larger businesses in the same trade. Within the same industry, businesses and their employees who stand to gain from a particular government program are opposed by those businesses and workers who stand to lose from the program. Opposition also can come from other industries that might be adversely affected.

In sum, the United States teems with entrepreneurial talent and ambition, both in politics and in business. This babble of competing voices simply cannot be orchestrated into the kind of harmony required for a coherent, consistent industrial policy. It is highly doubtful that Americans would accept the degree of subordination to "larger" interests which would be necessary to make such a policy successful.

169. THE FEDERALIST NO. 10, at 83 (J. Madison) (C. Rossiter ed. 1961).
170. A. DE TOCQUEVILLE, DEMOCRACY IN AMERICA 174 (G. Lawrence trans. 1966).
171. *See, e.g.,* R. REICH, *supra* note 6, at 276.

29

2. *Accessibility of Political Institutions*

This fragmentation of interests is exacerbated by the second characteristic of the American political system: the unusual accessibility of our governing institutions to factional pressures. State and local governments provide promotional platforms and mechanisms for obstruction that have few counterparts in the centralized systems of Western Europe.[172] Local and regional interests strain both major parties, neither of which has the capacity to impose much discipline, even within their congressional delegations.[173] Power in Congress is diffused among numerous rival committees and, in recent years, has been further diffused among even more numerous subcommittees.[174]

Moreover, the separation of powers mandated by the Constitution ensures a continual tension between the executive and legislative branches, a tension which produces additional accessibility. In contrast to the parliamentary systems of Western Europe and Japan, the American system affords little assurance that the legislative proposals of the Executive Branch actually will be enacted and virtually guarantees that they will not be enacted without considerable compromise and modification.[175] The system also ensures that once a measure is enacted by Congress, its implementation by the executive will be subject to continuous pressures by an array of oversight and appropriations committees, each with its own set of concerns.[176] Within the Executive Branch itself, agencies with related responsibilities are pulled in varying directions by their constituencies and their champions and critics in Congress.[177] The White House and the Office of Management and Budget (OMB) find that "coordinating" policy among different agencies is not always in their interest and is often beyond their

---

172. *See* D. HAIDER, WHEN GOVERNMENTS COME TO WASHINGTON 1–45 (1974).

173. *See* Ranney, *The Political Parties: Reform and Decline*, in THE NEW AMERICAN POLITICAL SYSTEM 223–24 (A. King ed. 1978); Ranney, *The President and His Party*, in BOTH ENDS OF THE AVENUE: THE PRESIDENCY, THE EXECUTIVE BRANCH AND CONGRESS IN THE 1980S 131–53 (A. King ed. 1983) [hereinafter cited as BOTH ENDS OF THE AVENUE].

174. L. DODD & R. SCHOTT, CONGRESS AND THE ADMINISTRATIVE STATE 111 (1979); Davidson, *Subcommittee Government: New Channels for Policy Making*, in THE NEW CONGRESS 99–133 (T. Mann & N. Ornstein eds. 1981).

175. *See* Ornstein, *The Open Congress Meets the President*, in BOTH ENDS OF THE AVENUE, *supra* note 173, at 185–211; Jones, *Presidential Negotiation with Congress*, in BOTH ENDS OF THE AVENUE, *supra* note 173, at 96–130.

176. *See* Schick, *Politics Through Law: Congressional Limitations on Executive Discretion*, in BOTH ENDS OF THE AVENUE, *supra* note 173, at 154–84.

177. *See* Nadel, *Making Regulatory Policy*, in MAKING ECONOMIC POLICY IN CONGRESS 240–43 (A. Schick ed. 1983); *see also* R. NOLL & B. OWEN, THE POLITICAL ECONOMY OF DEREGULATION: INTEREST GROUPS IN THE REGULATORY PROCESS 155–62 (1983).

30

capacity.[178] Merely establishing an interagency coordinating mechanism can trigger crippling administrative jockeying and political dispute.[179]

The significance of this political accessibility for any attempt to guide and coordinate industry plans should be obvious to anyone who has followed a few policy battles in Washington. Advocacy groups often make their pitches to several different agencies and then appeal unfavorable responses to the White House or OMB, all the while attempting to secure support in Congress. With so many points of entry into the policymaking process, even a distinctly bad idea will keep bouncing back to life, and a good idea will have a hard time preserving enough integrity to affect policy.[180] The chaos in the federal budget process,[181] more than sixty years after the institution of "centralized" budgeting controls in the Executive Branch[182] and ten years after the institution of a "centralized" budget committee in Congress,[183] provides sufficient testimony against the likelihood that a coherent, coordinated industrial policy will emerge.

3.   Absence of an Administrative Elite

Champions of a centralized policy frequently respond that past experience simply underscores America's need for a trusted, non-partisan coordinating mechanism to guide national industrial policy.[184] This argument fails, however, because of the third distinctive characteristic of the American political system: the absence of a well-established administrative elite. One wonders where the impartial industrial policy directors would come from in America and why anyone—especially Congress—would give them sufficient trust and deference.

There are two related reasons for the absence of a prestigious corps of American administrators. The first is the sweeping power of an American

---

178. *See* H. SEIDMAN, POLITICS, POSITION, AND POWER: THE DYNAMICS OF FEDERAL ORGANIZATION 200-31 (3d ed. 1980).

179. *See* Heclo, *One Executive Branch or Many?*, in BOTH ENDS OF THE AVENUE, *supra* note 173, at 26-58.

180. *See, e.g.*, Miller, Shughart & Tollison, *A Note on Centralized Regulatory Review*, 43 PUB. CHOICE 83 (1984) (decentralized administration will increase the ability of concentrated interests to influence policy outcomes).

181. *See generally* THE CONGRESSIONAL BUDGET PROCESS AFTER FIVE YEARS (R. Penner ed. 1981) (a collection of essays on the current state of the budget process); *see also* Schick, *The Three Ring Budget Process*, in THE NEW CONGRESS, *supra* note 174, at 288-328.

182. Budget and Accounting Act of 1921, ch. 18, 42 Stat. 20; *see also* J. HICKS, *supra* note 55, at 51 (discussing the Budget and Accounting Act of 1921).

183. Congressional Budget and Impoundment Control Act of 1974, Pub. L. No. 93-344, 88 Stat. 297 (1974) (codified in scattered sections of 2 U.S.C. and 31 U.S.C.); *see also* Caiden, *The Politics of Subtraction*, in MAKING ECONOMIC POLICY IN CONGRESS, *supra* note 177, at 100, 110-14; Schick, *The First Five Years of Congressional Budgeting*, in THE CONGRESSIONAL BUDGET PROCESS AFTER FIVE YEARS, *supra* note 181, at 3, 4-7.

184. *See, e.g.*, I. MAGAZINER & R. REICH, *supra* note 6, at 377-78.

31

president over administrative appointments. American government agencies have tremendous turnover in top personnel with each new administration, especially compared with Western Europe. A new American president controls several thousand immediate appointments,[185] while only a few dozen administrative posts change with the advent of a new cabinet in West European countries.[186] This "revolving door" at high levels in the bureaucracy virtually assures the existence of informed and experienced figures outside the U.S. government at any given time. Critics of prevailing or emerging policies in this country thus find it relatively easy to recruit "expert witnesses" to bolster their critiques of government policies; this tends to inhibit formation of the consensus among government administrators necessary for a successful coordinated policy.

The second reason for the absence of an administrative elite is the political difficulty of detachment and neutrality in administrative decisionmaking. Even the distinguished members of the Council of Economic Advisers and the Federal Reserve Board rarely have been immune from criticism, and still more rarely have they been free from powerful political pressures. Top officials in Washington almost invariably earned their prestige from past achievements in academe, business or politics, but rarely in careers devoted exclusively to administrative service. Their power typically derives not from their personal reputations for wisdom and experience but from their perceived support in the White House, Congress, or the press. Proximity to these power centers often is enough in itself to provoke partisan suspicion.

Indeed, available evidence suggests that American bureaucrats are more partisan than those in some other countries. For example, surveys of government administrators in Western Europe and the United States found that the U.S. officials reflected a much wider range of ideological orientations.[187] The American bureaucrats met far more often with private interest groups and had far more contact with legislators than did their European counterparts.[188] Detached, neutral administration is not what the American political system encourages, nor, by and large, what it delivers.[189]

---

185. *See* Nathan, *The Reagan Presidency in Domestic Affairs*, in THE REAGAN PRESIDENCY, AN EARLY ASSESSMENT 48, 71-72 (F. Greenstein ed. 1983); H. HECLO, A GOVERNMENT OF STRANGERS 36-41 (1977).

186. *See* B. PETERS, THE POLITICS OF BUREAUCRACY: A COMPARATIVE PERSPECTIVE 222-23 (1978).

187. J. ABERBACH, R. PUTNAM & B. ROCKMAN, BUREAUCRATS AND POLITICIANS IN WESTERN DEMOCRACIES 169 (1981).

188. *Id.* at 228-36.

189. *Id.*

32

One cannot, moreover, comfortably assume that an American industrial policy apparatus would somehow lend independent prestige to its political chiefs. Joseph Schumpeter has observed: "A good bureaucracy is a slow growth and cannot be created at will."[190] The prestigious and self-confident bureaucracies in Western Europe and Japan became established before the advent of full parliamentary politics.[191] In the United States, by contrast, democratic politics appeared first. Politicians in the United States thus do not stand in awe of the new bureaucracies they have created and nurtured in recent decades.

Largely for want of a respected corps of impartial administrators, therefore, administration of this nation's industrial policy likely would face some of the same political problems encountered in existing programs. Politicians could not be expected to keep their hands off the new industrial policy bureaucracy, given the vast economic stakes involved and the enormous array of conveniently divisible decisions directly affecting so many diverse constituencies. In this regard, the NRA experience discussed earlier provides little reassurance. A more recent experience with coordinated planning—defense procurement—also does not inspire confidence.[192] Although defense procurement is vital to the national interest and has been entrusted largely to an elite group of military officials, decisions on weapons systems and military supplies often are plainly and powerfully influenced by the interests of particular congressmen in securing financial benefits for their home states or districts.[193] Such Congressional involvement in the day-to-day implementation of industrial policy would seriously jeopardize the independence and neutrality of the responsible executive entity.

4. Activist Courts

The courts provide yet another source of fragmentation in the American system and, hence, another potential impediment to the success of any American industrial policy. Judges and lawyers play a far more active role in government policymaking in the United States than in any other country in the world. In part, this pattern reflects the fragmented and

---

190. J. SCHUMPETER, CAPITALISM, SOCIALISM AND DEMOCRACY 390 n.14 (3d ed. 1975).

191. For a discussion of the emergence of bureaucracies in Western Europe, see A. DE TOC-QUEVILLE, THE ANCIEN REGIME AND THE REVOLUTION 32-41 (S. Gilbert trans. 1955); F. HAYEK, THE CONSTITUTION OF LIBERTY 193-204 (1972); A. HEIDENHEIMER, THE GOVERNMENTS OF GERMANY 7, 68, 90-91 (1966). For a discussion of the origins of Japan's bureaucracy, see E. REISCHAUER & J. FAIRBANK, EAST ASIA, THE GREAT TRADITION 611-13 (1960).

192. The B-1 bomber program is one recent experience which shows that considerations not limited to national security can affect the development of an arms system. See, e.g., U.S. NEWS & WORLD REPORT, July 11, 1983, at 34-35.

193. J. FOX, ARMING AMERICA: HOW THE U.S. BUYS WEAPONS 83-84 (1974).

33

highly competitive character of U.S. politics and the tenuous standing of the administrative organs discussed above. These conditions encourage losers of policy battles to seek another round of struggle in the courts, and often prompt judges to cast a suspicious eye on the winners. The tradition of the American judiciary as a constitutional champion of minorities also encourages this enlarged role of courts and formal proceedings in American policymaking. The result is plain: To an extent unknown in Western Europe or Japan, American administrators must specify precise standards, articulate their policy rationales, supply detailed evidence justifying their decisions, and observe the elaborate niceties of correct procedure.[194] This system may give American lawyers and their clients more confidence in the fairness of resulting adminstrative decisions. However, it does not promote efficient or flexible, much less "coordinated," administrative decisionmaking.

In short, the American system of government is itself responsible for a number of market distortions that reduce industrial competitiveness and retard economic growth. Efforts to "reform" that system through reliance on comprehensive planning and cooperation, however, would probably fall victim to the very forces that created those distortions. As the NRA and West European programs of industrial planning have shown, such efforts diminish industrial competitiveness and retard economic growth.

B. Implications for Democratic Institutions

Even if the political obstacles to an effective, centralized industrial policy could be overcome, however, the potential political and moral costs of this achievement are sobering. These obstacles—and hence the costs of overcoming them—are especially serious because centralized industrial policy would have an extraordinarily broad scope. To overcome the political obstacles, the government, at a minimum, would have to: (1) create a broad-based, enduring perception of national peril, (2) delegate vast governmental powers to groups of private firms or other special interests, and (3) concentrate an extraordinary amount of power in a small group of government officials. These actions might entail unacceptable costs to the American political system.

The political and moral costs of a centralized industrial policy are directly related to the obstacles which it must surmount. To illustrate the severity of these obstacles, it is useful to contrast industrial policy with some recent issues addressed by presidential commissions. Bipartisan pres-

---

194. The requirements of correct administrative practice are set forth in the Adminstrative Procedure Act, 5 U.S.C. §§ 551–559 (1982). Judicial review of decisions reached by administrative agencies is also provided. See 5 U.S.C. §§ 701–706 (1982).

34

idential commissions, established on various occasions to resolve vexing political stalemates, can sometimes formulate widely accepted "package" solutions. President Reagan's recent commission on the social security financing crisis[195] is an example. However, these commissions are most successful in dealing with discrete, well-defined, and relatively short-term controversies. Commissions that have taken on larger and more open-ended policy controversies, such as the Kissinger Commission on Central America,[196] have had less success in forging political consensus.[197] Industrial policy, by contrast, involves precisely such long-term, open-ended issues. Hence the occasional special commission is not an appropriate model for the political management of industrial policy. A longer-term model, such as the planning experiences of the early New Deal,[198] must be studied instead.

Judging from these precedents, the first requirement for a successful industrial policy is a broad perception of national peril, a perception which would inspire a patriotic spirit of self- sacrifice among diverse economic interests. Even at the depths of the Great Depression, however, such a spirit could not be maintained very long. This failure is one reason why the NRA, after an enthusiastic reception, soon fell prey to bitter and vehement attack.[199] Perhaps only during the world wars was such a spirit maintained for any considerable length of time. But even in wartime the government reinforced the public's evident perception of external peril with a continual blare of patriotic propaganda. The government would have difficulty promoting such a self-sacrificing spirit in a prosperous peacetime period, because critics of industrial policy could plausibly argue that even the partial, short-term sacrifices imposed by such a policy were not really necessary. Almost inevitably, the managers of industrial policy would require a continuous din of supporting propaganda sufficient to intimidate the critics and silence the skeptics.

The second political requisite of successful industrial policy is a sub-

195. The National Commission on Social Security Reform was established by President Reagan on December 16, 1981. Exec. Order No. 12,335, 46 Fed. Reg. 61,633.

196. The National Bipartisan Commission on Central America was established by President Reagan on July 19, 1983. Exec. Order No. 12,433, 48 Fed. Reg. 33,227.

197. *See, e.g.*, N.Y. Times, Jan. 12, 1984, at A20, col. 1.

198. *See infra* text accompanying notes 199 to 206.

199. *See* E. HAWLEY, *supra* note 73, at 135–36. Hawley wrote:

Initially the NRA had appealed to a variety of conflicting economic and ideological groups, each bent upon implementing its own theory of recovery and its own vision of the good society. . . . Success in achieving all [of the groups'] goals was impossible; but in the beginning, the conflicts could be and were glossed over by a high-pressure propaganda campaign. The difficulty came when the propaganda wore off, the sense of impending national disaster passed, and the great cooperative effort disintegrated into the original welter of conflicting and quarreling groups.

Id.

35

stantial delegation of governmental power to well-established groups of private firms or special interests. The NRA codes, for example, although presented as the product of broad-based consultation, actually were promulgated by the established firms and labor organizations in each industry.[200] The industry codes, whose promulgation the larger firms typically controlled, tended to discriminate against smaller businesses.[201] The codes "retarded recovery, injured the wage earner, and interfered with President Roosevelt's efforts to eliminate unemployment."[202] They also hampered competition.[203]

These effects were not the result of corruption, but an inevitable consequence of the need to secure quick agreements. The easiest means of achieving agreement was to accommodate those with the most economic and political power. During World War I, under more exigent circumstances, the government proceded in similar ways.[204] Price levels, wage rates and cost-plus contract terms were set in agreement with established firms and labor organizations.[205]

The final requisite of a successful industrial policy is an extraordinary concentration of power in the hands of a small group of government administrators. Such concentration is the only way of maintaining coherence and continuity in a policy that must adapt to many changing particulars. The NRA was administered precisely with such extraordinary and open-ended power, allocated to a central administrative organization without any real guidance from Congress or any real possibility of control by the courts. Justice Cardozo characterized such a system as "delegation run riot" in the Supreme Court decision striking down the NRA.[206]

Even if these three conditions were satisfied, industrial policy would have a dubious chance of success. It is equally doubtful, moreover, that many Americans concerned about traditional democratic values would wish to see the policy succeed on such terms. Thomas Jefferson provided an emphatic warning about the threat of centralized government to individual liberty:

---

200. C. ROOS, *supra* note 69, at 68 ("[U]nder the NRA, . . . labor and industry jousted with each other to divide the spoils—the consumer's purchasing power."). *See supra* text accompanying notes 89-91.

201. L. LYON, *supra* note 76, at 745; B. BELLUSH, *supra* note 74, at 140, 149.

202. B. BELLUSH, *supra* note 74, at 144, 166; C. ROOS, *supra* note 69, at 149-51, 472. *See generally, supra* note 103, on the ill effects of the NRA.

203. The 1935 Brookings study described the codes in the following manner: "[S]o far as making competition more fair is concerned, the results were negative rather than positive." L. LYON, *supra* note 76, at 743.

204. *See supra* text accompanying notes 46-49.

205. *Id.*

206. Schechter Poultry Corp. v. United States, 295 U.S. 495, 553 (1935) (Cardozo, J., concurring); *see also* B. BELLUSH, *supra* note 74, at 236.

36

No, my friend, the way to have good and safe government, is not to trust it all to one, but to divide it among the many, distributing to every one exactly the function he is competent to. . . . It is by dividing and subdividing [the powers of government] from the great national one down through all its subordinations, until it ends in the administration of every man's farm by himself; by placing under every one what his own eye may superintend, that all will be done for the best. What has destroyed liberty and the rights of man in every government which has ever existed under the sun? The generalizing and concentrating all cares and powers into one body . . . .[207]

Conclusion

Efforts to strengthen the U.S. economy by creating a central administrative body to plan and coordinate a national industrial policy promise to be either ineffective or a cure worse than the perceived disease. Such an approach likely would make U.S. industry less competitive both at home and abroad; it would reduce the nation's standard of living. Even if the centralized approach did foster economic growth in other nations, moreover, it could not succeed in the American political system. The profusion of interest groups, the accessibility of the legislative and executive branches, the lack of an adminstrative elite, and the activist role of the judicial system in this country would thwart any comprehensive program of coordinated strategic planning. Moreover, any attempt to transplant such an industrial policy to American soil might impose unacceptable costs upon the nation's democratic processes. If the United States is to continue its long-term economic growth while preserving its democratic values, it must look to the principles of economic and political liberalism which the Founders embraced and which have made their American experiment the most successful economic system in history.

---

207. Letter from Thomas Jefferson to Joseph C. Cabell (Feb. 2, 1816), *reprinted in* THE LIFE AND SELECTED WRITINGS OF THOMAS JEFFERSON 660–61 (A. Koch & W. Peden eds. 1944). The following passage from *The Wealth of Nations* is also pertinent:

The statesman, who should attempt to direct private people in what manner they ought to employ their capitals, would not only load himself with a most unnecessary attention, but assume an authority which could safely be trusted, not only to no single person, but to no council or senate whatever, and which would nowhere be so dangerous as in the hands of a man who had folly and presumption enough to fancy himself fit to exercise it.

A. SMITH, *supra* note 13, at 423.

37

Journal of Economic Literature
Vol. XXIV (March 1986), pp. 1–40

Industrial Policy and American Renewal

By R. D. Norton
Bryant College

Thanks go to William Branson, Joseph Ellis, K. C. Fung, Carol Heim, Charles Kindleberger, Steven Marglin, Mancur Olson, and anonymous referees. Special thanks are owed to Robert Heilbroner.

INDUSTRIAL POLICY has turned out to be an idea with a brief career. In the summer of 1984, after Rhode Island's electorate voted 4–1 against a bond issue to give the state its own industrial policy, Robert Reich observed that "industrial policy is one of those rare ideas that has moved swiftly from obscurity to meaninglessness without any intervening period of coherence" (Reich 1984, p. 32). This from perhaps its chief advocate. In the fall, the Reagan reelection sealed the issue, ruling out a U.S. industrial policy for years to come.

Still, the industrial policy debate raised two central questions about economic change. (1) Why do older industries tend to show a retardation in output and employment growth? (2) Has industry aging eroded American competitiveness, so that the U.S. is in some sense "losing the economic race"? (Lester Thurow 1984).

To get at answers to the two questions, this paper offers a review of what economists have had to say about industry aging, economic maturity, and market-generated renewal. Because the subject matter is so vast, it will prove useful to begin with a guide to the territory, a roadmap.

I. Preliminaries

The first question, on industry aging, was explored systematically in the 1930s literature on the retardation thesis, later generalized in a *law of industrial growth* (Evan B. Alderfer and H. E. Michl 1942, pp. 14–17). To wit: Industries mature when major technology gains come to an end, slowing cost reductions, market expansion, and sales growth and leaving older industries vulnerable to the competition of younger rivals with faster productivity growth (Figure 1). Simon Kuznets (1930), Walther Hoffmann (1931), Arthur Burns (1934), Joseph Schumpeter (1939), and Alvin Hansen (1939) thus concluded that long-term growth entails the eclipse of older by younger industries.

The point seems obvious today, when newspapers are full of references to high-tech and smokestack industries. Yet it was largely forgotten after 1945 with the Keynesian revolution and the long (1948–1973) global expansion, which damped the decline of older industries. The corollary is Schumpeter's Creative Destruction, so different from demand-side con-

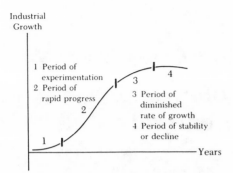

Figure 1. The Law of Industrial Growth

Source: Reproduced from E. B. Alderfer and H. E. Michl (1942, p. 14).

notations of continuous and manageable change. In Schumpeter's view, progress occurs via structural change, which tends to inflict pain.

The second issue, declining industrial competitiveness in the U.S. (and, for that matter, Europe) involves the more recent literature on the *product cycle*. Edgar M. Hoover (1948) and his co-worker, Raymond Vernon (1966), argued that industry maturity makes production increasingly footloose, free to migrate to low-wage, politically receptive locations at home and abroad.

Just as Vernon's pathbreaking 1966 article appeared, "the international economy began to turn on its head" (W. Arthur Lewis 1978a, p. 35). The advanced industrial countries (AICs) of the West experienced rising trade competition from a select group of less developed countries (LDCs), a group therefore dubbed newly industrializing countries (NICs).

The NICs' export-led growth reflected their comparative advantage (from low labor costs) in mature, standardized goods in a world economy newly unified by breakthroughs in transport and communications. The correlate was a loss of manufacturing employment, notably in mature

industries, in the U.S. North (Figure 2) and Europe after 1969.

So much can be described in terms of product aging alone, as in the dictum, "Regions don't grow old; products do" (John Hekman 1979). But a more general approach is the *maturity hypothesis* long advanced by Charles P. Kindleberger (1953, 1961, 1962, 1974, 1978, 1980) in a variation on Schumpeter's older theme, and developed independently in recent years by Mancur Olson (1977, 1982, 1983).

In early 1973, even before OPEC, Kindleberger warned of "the dynamic failure of the economy to produce new exports to replace those now being eroded by the product cycle." He considered whether the origins of this failure might lie in

a slowing down of American economic vitality and elan—a climacteric in the life of the economy and perhaps society, such as Britain experienced [after 1870] when it was overtaken by Germany and the United States as we are now being overtaken by Japan. (Kindleberger 1973)

The laggard U.S. adjustment to the first oil price shock led other economists to agree. Some came to view declining supply elasticities and rising core inflation rates as symptoms of a kind of institutional sclerosis (Tibor Scitovsky 1980). The crowning blow was the second (1979) oil price shock, which redirected U.S. demand toward smaller (Japanese) cars. Japan's triumph and Detroit's humiliation seemed to confirm America's industrial decline. Kindleberger's fears seemed to be borne out.

This, then, was the setting for the industrial policy debate of the early 1980s. Although the debate has come and gone, the question of American decline remains. As Moses Abramovitz asked in a presidential address to the American Economic Association in 1980: "Can we mount a more energetic and successful response to the challenge of newly rising foreign competitors after 1970 than Britain did after 1870?" (Abramovitz 1981, p. 10).

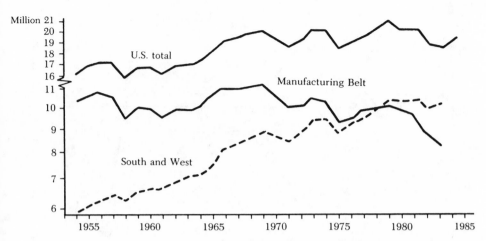

Figure 2. United States Manufacturing Employment, by Region, 1955–1984

Source: U.S. Department of Labor, Bureau of Labor Statistics, *Employment and Earnings*, various issues. *Note:* The Manufacturing Belt is approximated by data for the New England, Middle Atlantic, and East North Central divisions. The South and West consist of the other six divisions.

Countering the pessimists (Kindleberger, Reich and Thurow), optimists such as William Branson, Robert Lawrence, and C. Fred Bergsten would reply in the affirmative: that the case for continued U.S. competitiveness and vitality—in a word, renewal—is strong. The optimists point out that the U.S. accomplished major adjustments during the 1970s, even as Europe faltered. As Bergsten says, "it would be extremely difficult to conclude that the United States faces any fundamental problem of international competitiveness" (Bergsten 1983, p. 314).

Here analysis is made immensely more difficult by the course of exchange rates. During the 1970s, the dollar exchange rate fell by enough to restore a surplus on the U.S. trade balance for goods and services. Under the Reagan administration, the trade balance has plummeted into a deficit, in lockstep with the dollar's rise (Figure 3). By this reading the trade problem has macroeconomic origins—notably the federal budget deficit, acting through high interest rates to attract foreign capital flows to the U.S., driving up the dollar, and making U.S. exports more expensive and imports more attractive.

Paradoxically, then, a 15-year perspective poses not so much the question of where the U.S. went wrong, but *why the United States' adaptation to the new world economy has been more effective than Europe's*. In particular, how has the U.S. added some 30 million new jobs since 1970, when Europe's job count has been flat?

A suggestion advanced in this paper is that *U.S. regional diversity has enforced a painful but therapeutic adjustment* of a kind missing in Victorian Britain or contemporary Europe. But that comes later. In the meantime, section II sums up economists' criticisms of industrial policy, a treatment supplemented in an appendix. Section III recalls the literature of the 1930s. Then we turn to the product cycle (section IV), deindustrialization (section V), and the maturity hypothesis (section

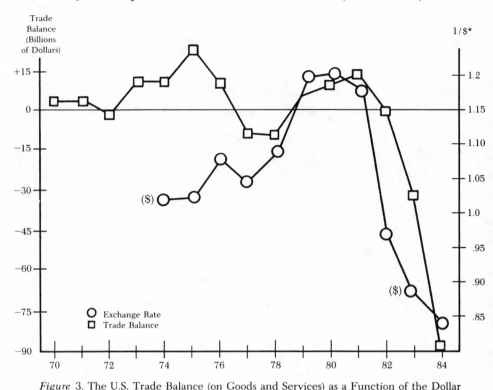

Figure 3. The U.S. Trade Balance (on Goods and Services) as a Function of the Dollar

Sources: Economic Indicators, March 1985, p. 36, for trade balance; *Economic Report of the President: 1984,* p. 331, for the exchange rate.
* Reciprocal of the "real" trade-weighted price of the dollar, lagged one year. As the dollar appreciates, this reciprocal therefore decreases.

VI). Sketches comparing the United States and Europe (section VII) and the United States and Japan (section VIII) are followed by some conjectures on the future (section IX).

II. *Industrial Policy: A Postmortem*

An appendix to this paper provides an account of the industrial policy debate as it flared up and died down in the years 1980–1984. The appendix reflects the following points:

1. A dichotomy marked industrial policy's goals. "Modernizers" wanted

to boost international competitiveness; "preservationists" were more concerned with saving jobs in industries that were losing out in international competition.

2. On either count, most economists rejected the arguments for an industry-specific or targeted industrial policy (Paul Krugman 1983).

3. The modernizers notwithstanding, there was no general decline in U.S. trade competitiveness in the 1970s; the exchange rate fell by enough to maintain it (William Branson 1981).

4. When the exchange rate rose sharply

under the Reagan administration, the "deindustrialization" that resulted had macroeconomic causes; industrial policy was beside the point (Robert Lawrence 1984).

5. Insofar as industrial policy proposals fronted for regional relief, much of the debate ran at cross purposes; economists rejected "preservation" as inefficient, whereas advocates made their case in terms of equity (George Eads 1983).

In sum, the economic arguments against an American industrial policy are persuasive. The national-security case for a program of sectoral intervention is weak, as Branson shows. The microeconomic or market-failure rationale fails also; Krugman's analysis is especially telling.

Beyond questions of theory, economists doubt the feasibility of implementing an industrial policy. In light of aggregate gains in U.S. manufacturing employment in the 1970s, some also doubt the very existence of a U.S. industrial problem.

Second Thoughts

Still, the one-sidedness of the debate may be deceptive. Criticizing industrial policy, Lawrence Summers questions as an "undocumented premise—the existence of industrial problems which go beyond those that could be expected to result from current macroeconomic policies" (Summers 1983, p. 82). In other words, if not for macroeconomic policy, industrial change would present no problem.

This view reflects a tendency for critics of industrial policy to discount structural change. Behind the veil of macroeconomic aggregates, however, has been a regional revolution, marked by the decline and fall of America's industrial heartland during the 1970s.

The danger in such overaggregation is that it

conceals . . . all the drama of the events—the rise and fall of products, technologies, and industries, and the accompanying transformation of the spatial and occupational distribution of the population. (William Nordhaus and James Tobin 1972, p. 2; quoted in J. J. Van Duijn 1983, p. 93)

The alternative, Nordhaus and Tobin add in their next sentence, is "Schumpeter's vision of capitalist development."

III. *Déjà Vu*

Two questions survive the industrial policy debate: (1) Why and how do industries mature? and (2) What does industry aging mean for a local, regional, or national economy? These questions were broached in the 1930s, in a literature temporarily eclipsed by the Keynesian revolution. Ironically, one of Keynes' chief American apostles may have been spurred by the fear that industry aging had triggered macroeconomic stagnation.

In a famous presidential address to the American Economic Association in December 1938, Alvin Hansen concluded that a decline in investment opportunities had brought an era of secular stagnation. His apocalyptic rhetoric seems oddly familiar:

The economic order of the western world is undergoing in this generation a structural change no less basic and profound in character than . . . "the Industrial Revolution." We are passing . . . over a divide which separates the great era of growth and expansion of the nineteenth century from an era which no man . . . can as yet characterize with clarity or precision. We are moving swiftly out of the order in which those of our generation were brought up, into no one knows what. (Hansen 1939, p. 1)

As if in reply, Schumpeter rejected any and all inherently economic reasons for the vanishing of investment opportunity (Schumpeter 1942, ch. 10). In general, he said, the capitalist growth system may be jeopardized by three factors. (1) The rise of big business may result in "petrified capitalism." (2) Affluence may erode the

TABLE 1
SCHUMPETER ON THE KONDRATIEFF CYCLE

Prosperity	Recession	Depression	Revival
I. Industrial Revolution (1787–1842): cotton textiles, iron, steam power			
1787–1800	1801–1813	1814–1827	1828–1842
II. The Bourgeois Kondratieff (1842–1897): railroadization			
1843–1857	1858–1869	1870–1885	1886–1897
III. The Neo-Mercantilist Kondratieff (1897–1939): electricity, automobile			
1898–1911	1912–1925	1925–1939	—

Source: Adapted from a table in Simon Kuznets, "Schumpeter's Business Cycles" (*Amer. Econ. Rev.*, June 1940, *30*(2), p. 257); reprinted in Kuznets (1953, p. 105).

legitimacy of capitalism's values and core institutions. (3) Investment opportunities might diminish.

As Schumpeter put it (p. 113), "The main reasons for holding that opportunities for private enterprise and investment are vanishing are these:"

- the saturation of human wants,
- the slowing of population growth,
- land and resource constraints,
- the waning of technological innovation, and
- a shift in investment projects toward public goods.

Schumpeter rejected each of these possible sources of stagnation, as would most economists today. There is no inherent limit to profit opportunities, he wrote, and thus none to continued private investment, or to continued growth. Further, he rejected the rise of big business as a source of stagnation, saying that in concentrated industries, competition continued, especially via technological innovation.

To Schumpeter, what appeared to be a vanishing of investment opportunity was actually the trough of the 50–55 year Kondratieff cycle, or "long wave" (Table 1). With a brutal optimism, Schumpeter saw the Great Depression as necessary to

purge the economy of outworn practices and to restore efficiency. In the end such creative destruction would set the stage for the rise of new industries. New industries would spur the next long upswing, assuring capitalism's unique achievement: the doubling of living standards every 50 years. There were no *economic* limits to growth.

Instead, the limits Schumpeter foresaw were political and cultural. He predicted that the reaction to creative destruction itself and a disenchantment with capitalism's core values would eventually usher in a planned regime not unlike socialism. A mature economy would be more regulated and less flexible, so that in the political long run, the growth system would come to an end.

Secular Stagnation, from the Supply Side

Hansen shared Schumpeter's belief in long waves, but ardently opposed his laissez-faire maxims. In a little-noted passage, he asserted not so much the permanent vanishing of investment opportunity, but its uneven clustering over time. Describing industrial change as occurring by "gigantic leaps and bounds," Hansen provided a distinctly Schumpeterian account of the Depression's sources. In particular, he posited a kind of natural law of industry aging:

> when a revolutionary new industry like the railroad or the automobile, after having in its youth a powerful upward surge of investment activity, reaches maturity and ceases to grow, as all industries finally must, the whole economy must experience a profound stagnation. . . . And when giant new industries have spent their force, it may take a long time before something else of equal magnitude emerges. (Hansen 1939, pp. 10–11)

This is a far cry from the stagnation thesis that has found its way into textbook footnotes about declining average propensities to consume. Instead, it is an industry-specific vision of economic decline, and as such, it foreshadows the industrial upheaval of the 1970s, and predates contemporary references to "old-line," "basic," or "smokestack" industries. So while Hansen is remembered as a pessimistic Keynesian, he might also be linked with Schumpeter in a fear of episodic but protracted retardation from industrial aging.

The Retardation Thesis

Simon Kuznets had dealt with the same problem in 1930 in the course of a more general study of secular movements in production and prices. In a chapter entitled "Retardation of Industrial Growth," Kuznets argued that the Industrial Revolution had set off a seemingly unlimited process of economic growth. Individual industries and nations had risen and then been eclipsed. Among nations, he wrote, "Great Britain has relinquished the lead . . . overtaken by rapidly developing Germany and the United States." A concomitant of such national shifts was one from older to younger industries. "The textile industries which had so spectacular a rise . . . ceded first place to pig iron, then to steel, while in turn the electrical industries assumed the leadership in the '80s and '90s" (Kuznets 1930, pp. 3–4).

To test the hypothesis of retardation in industry growth, Kuznets fitted Gompertz and logistic curves to time-series data for value-added in a large number of industries. He found that most series did indeed conform to the retardation thesis.

Hence the question: "Why is there an abatement in the growth of old industries?" (p. 5). His answer: a narrowing over time in the scope for technological breakthroughs, cost reductions, and further sales growth. In a searching historical account of the tendency toward the exhaustion of technological breakthroughs in specific industries, Kuznets drew on earlier work by the German economist Julius Wolf.

In 1912, Wolf had posited four "laws of retardation of progress." One in particular (tagged "Wolff's Law" [sic] in Freeman et al. 1982, p. 70), Wolf defined as follows:

> Every technical improvement, by lowering costs and by perfecting the utilization of raw materials and of power, bars the way to further progress. There is less left to improve, and this narrowing of possibilities results in a slackening or complete cessation of technical development.

Kuznets' work and similar findings were generalized in a 1934 NBER study by Arthur Burns. As Burns put it, "Following writers on biology and population, some economic statisticians have come in recent years to speak of a 'law of growth' in industries and to give this 'law' mathematical expression in the form of 'growth curves' " (Burns 1934, pp. 169–70). By this law, Burns meant only "that the percentage rates of growth of individual industries tend to decline as their age increases." In contrast to Hansen, Burns viewed industry aging not as a problem, but only as a normal part of the growth process.[1]

---

[1] Whereas Kuznets focused more on technology, Burns stressed the rise of new industries as a reason for the decline of old. As Burns put it, "The introduction of new industries has tended to retard the development of old industries through the channels of

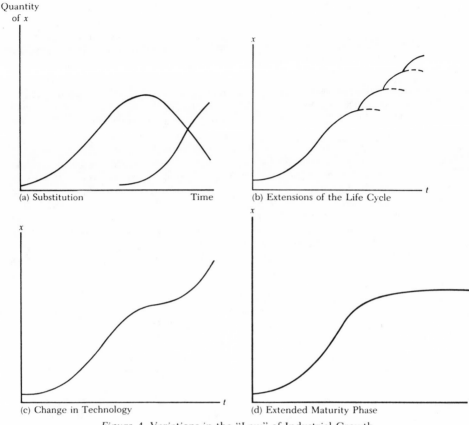

Figure 4. Variations in the "Law" of Industrial Growth

Source: Adapted from Van Duijn (1983, p. 24).

By the early 1940s, this law of industrial growth had found its way into textbooks on industrial economics. One text described the law as the tendency for industries to pass through "a period of experimentation, a period of rapid growth, a

competition for production, as well as through the channel of competition for custom [i.e., consumer spending]" (1934, p. 134). That is, new industries brought competition for capital, labor, and raw materials, and diverted expenditures away from existing (older) products. Burns' emphasis thus ties in directly with Schumpeter's notion of creative destruction: The rise of new industries occurs in part at the expense of older ones.

period of diminished growth, and a period of stability or decline" (Alderfer and Michl 1942, p. 14). In Europe, Walter Hoffmann would apply the same law to the British economy, and Fernand Braudel (in discussing examples of its operation in Europe before 1776) referred to the sequence as "Hoffmann's law" (Hoffman [1931] 1955; Braudel 1982, pp. 344–49).

The Retardation Thesis: So What?

After 1945, of course, the retardation thesis was soon forgotten in the United

States, as the focus of policy concern shifted fairly quickly to inflation. More generally, growing awareness of aggregate demand's role redirected attention away from industry trajectories. At the same time, the long global upswing in demand dampened any tendency toward growth reduction in mature industries.

In a systematic updating of Burns' study, for example, Bela Gold (1964) traced growth patterns in 35 industries over the period 1930–1955, and found the S-shaped curve generally irrelevant to industry trajectories. He therefore declared the whole approach useless. But Gold's benchmark years were ill suited to the task of measuring long-term trends. Any tendencies toward S-shaped output curves were swamped by the sustained rapid global expansion that marked the years 1948–1973.

The model's value was reaffirmed when J. J. Van Duijn updated Burns' and Gold's work and examined patterns covering the century 1873–1973. He found "an S-shaped growth pattern up to the maturity phase of an industry, with various possible patterns thereafter." As Figure 4 illustrates, and as Burns had emphasized in his 1934 study, "What actually happens to a commodity once it has reached its maturity phase" is thus not determinate, but varies with conditions specific to the industry (Van Duijn 1983, p. 29).

As for the links between the demand and supply sides, Kuznets himself may have summed it up best. Integrating his own earlier work with that of Burns, Kuznets wrote that sustained economic growth requires the spawning of

> new industries whose high rates of growth compensate for the inevitable slowing down in the rate of invention and innovation, and upon the economic effects of each, which retard the rates of growth of the older industries. A high rate of over-all growth in an economy is thus necessarily accompanied by considerable shifting in relative importance among industries, as the old decline and the new increase. (Kuznets 1959, p. 33)

This de facto rebuttal of the preservationist case has been so fully absorbed into the mainstream of economic thought that it is taken for granted. But Kuznets had also posed another question, about industry aging and comparative advantage.

IV. *The Product Cycle and World Development*

Kuznets had pointed out that "an industry in one country may be retarded by the competition of the same industry in a younger country" (1930, p. 10). How is the competitive position of a region or nation reshaped by the aging of its industries?[2]

A surprisingly complete answer appeared in 1948. Working outside the tradition of the retardation school, Edgar M. Hoover used much of the same language

[2] As a preface to the product-cycle discussion in the text, there is another familiar and logically antecedent process that also hastens the dispersion of older industries away from initial centers. It is a direct result of the rise of new industries.

Suppose an economy has an average growth rate of labor productivity of three percent per annum. Wages will tend to rise at three percent, and this will be uniform across industries. (Workers of equal skill tend to be paid the same no matter in what industry they work.) Then, if productivity growth is not uniform across industries, relative prices must rise in those industries in which productivity growth is laggard.

The ordinary workings of comparative advantage will then cause the laggard industry to be extruded from the country or region in question. It will gravitate to another country or region where the relation between wages and productivity is more favorable. The kinds of industries that will tend to fit this description are older ones, in which productivity growth has slowed as technical gains are exhausted in accordance with the retardation theory.

In short, as growth in an initial center occurs through the addition of new industries, older industries will tend to be squeezed out, driven to lower-wage sites. Although this may be hard on workers in older industries, the dislocations involved are due directly to growth per se. There are thus clear benefits for the country as a whole in that productivity and living standards rise.

All of this logically precedes the product cycle, which is based on standardization of technique—and whose dislocations are *not* automatically compensated by new growth.

to describe the geography of industry aging (Hoover 1948, ch. 10):

> The locational histories of individual industries have very often—one may almost say "typically"—involved an early stage of increasing [spatial] concentration followed by a later stage of redispersion. (p. 175)

> Ultimately the industry and its main production center "mature," in the sense that the rate of growth of market has slackened off, the fundamental questions of product design have been settled, and the necessary specialized machinery has been devised. It is then that a dispersion phase sets in. (p. 175)

The key to this process was labor. A high skill requirement makes for "a concentrated and rather stable pattern, clustering at points where such a labor supply has gradually developed" (p. 174). Over time, as technical advances typically sever this tie, an industry's processes eventually become routine. Then

> ordinary labor without special training can be used. The normal result is that the industry spreads or moves to other areas, its dispersion from the original centers . . . sped by the relatively high wages and inflexible conditions that have become established there by the skilled elite. (p. 174)

Nevertheless, the exodus of mature industries is by no means the death knell for the initial production centers. If they can spawn new activities, industry aging can be countered:

> This common association of decentralization with maturity does not by any means imply, however, that industry as a whole will or should progressively decentralize. New industries are continually being born. (p. 175)

This idea of renewal via technological innovation also figured in Raymond Vernon's 1966 essay, "International Investment and International Trade in the Product Cycle." Vernon transposed Hoover's argument to the scale of the world economy. Now the U.S. became the initial center, one fated to lose its mature industries to foreign competitors (Figure 5).

Vernon assigned each of three stylized stages of product development a different global location. In stage one, the typical new product would tend to be developed and produced in large American cities, near technical talent and customers. Such initial centers would then export the new product to domestic markets and abroad.

Stage two is precipitated in part by the fear that foreign producers (notably in Europe) will manage to capture part of their home markets for the product. This fear, Vernon says, spurs U.S. firms to place branches in Europe. They are likely to be aided in this attempt by a progressive reduction of uncertainty, as least-cost production technologies are found and standardized. Stage two is thus marked by a reduction in U.S. exports of the product abroad.

In stage three, that of maturity, the product can be produced anywhere, and the advantage of low labor costs in LDCs may become paramount. In practice, this will prove most feasible for such footloose activities as textiles, consumer electronics, and other high-value-to-weight items. By this stage, the U.S. tends to have become a net importer of the product.

The assignment of standardized or mature products to nations with low-cost labor has now become a conventional part of trade theory. Trade goods are now typically described as (1) Ricardian, (2) Heckscher-Ohlin, (3) or product-cycle goods. The first are resource tied (wine or oil), the second are mature or standardized commodities, and the third are new goods, not far removed from innovation. Under this scheme, the comparative advantage in some Heckscher-Ohlin goods has shifted to the NICs, while the advantage in product-cycle goods remains in advanced economies.

By 1980, Stephen Magee had generalized the product-cycle theory into a product-age theorem, which adds raw

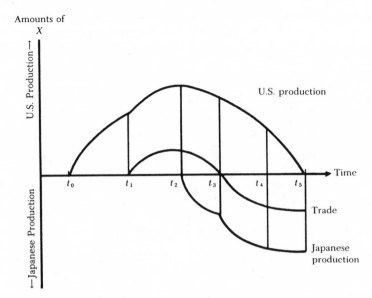

Figure 5. Production and Trade over the Product Cycle

Source: Adapted from John Adams (1979, p. 92).
Note: On the vertical axis, Japanese production and export of good X increase with distance below the origin. For example, Japan begins to run a trade surplus in good X at point t_3.

materials to the equation. In his words, "knowledge of production location requires only knowledge of product age, whether it is a manufactured good or a raw material." That is,

> Young manufactured products are produced in developed countries, while old manufacturing products are produced in developing countries; young raw materials [i.e., natural resources] are produced in developing countries, while older [i.e., synthetic] raw materials are produced in developed countries. (1980, p. xv)

The New International Division of Labor

Thus the logic of a new international division of labor, and of a new stage of world development emerges, as industrial capitalism moves south and east. Between 1963 and 1977, the share of world output of manufactures produced by a group of 10 NICs increased from 5.4 to about 9 per-

cent. Over this same interval, the share produced by Hong Kong, Singapore, South Korea, and Taiwan tripled, from 0.4 to 1.4 percent (Branson 1981, p. 386).

After 1973, when the growth of manufacturing exports from AICs (including Japan) was cut from ten to five percent a year, the LDCs as a group continued to increase their exports at 10 percent annually (Figure 6). The result, says Michael Beenstock, is a world economy in transition:

> The changing balance of world economic power . . . has moved in favour of developing countries. Economic expansion in the Third World has threatened the existing economic structures in the OECD countries, which in turn have been slow to adjust to these new circumstances. The origins of the slowdown are therefore structural, in the sense that market forces have changed and economic restructuring is necessary. (1984, p. 12)

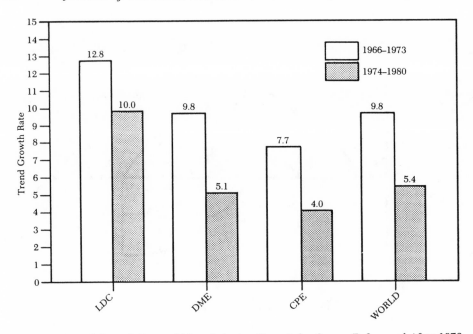

Figure 6. Trend Growth Rates of Manufacturing Exports by Group: Before and After 1973

Source: Reproduced from Chad Leechor, Harinder S. Kohli, and Sujin Hur (1983, p. 10).
Note: LDC refers to less developed countries, DME to developed market economies, and CPE to centrally planned economies.

The "sudden spurt in LDC industrialization" after 1965 created a supply shock in the world market for manufactures (p. 14). Goods prices fell relative to the prices of raw materials. "The rise in the relative price of raw materials that began toward the end of the 1960s was brought about by supply shocks in the market for manufactures . . . as much as . . . in the market for raw materials" (p. 15). The result is a "deindustrialization effect." Resources are shifted out of OECD manufactures and into other sectors (and to LDCs themselves, via capital flows). "Deindustrialization" in turn creates a "mismatch" problem, the symptom of which is increased unemployment in OECD countries.

V. *Deindustrialization?*

Beenstock's definition of deindustrialization does not fit the U.S. record, however. As Table 2 shows, U.S. manufacturing output was about the same share of GNP in 1979, before the dollar appreciated, as in 1969 or 1959: 25 percent.

"Postindustrialism" is equally debatable as a label for the U.S. economy—except in terms of employment shares. As Lawrence observes, "the United States could not be characterized as a service economy in 1980 any more than it was in 1960" (Lawrence 1984, p. 19). His comment refers to the fact that when measured at constant prices, goods output as a share of GNP held steady in 1960, 1970, and 1980, at just over 45 percent.[3]

Is there some other index that shows that the American economy has been suffering from deindustrialization? Not the job count in manufacturing, at least until the dollar's rise. As we saw at the outset (Figure 2), the number of U.S. manufacturing workers reached an all-time high of about 21 million in 1979. In the recession year of 1980, the count was higher than in the cyclically comparable year, 1970. Even the count for production workers was about the same, at 14 million, in 1980 as in 1970.

The American Manufacturing Belt—and Europe—did show large absolute losses in manufacturing employment for the decade, however. The Manufacturing Belt, the nation's northeast quadrant, lost about 1 million manufacturing jobs in the 1970s. In Europe, the net losses were also substantial.

Thus we have an introductory frame of reference. By the standard of the manufacturing job count, the U.S. has not been deindustrialized—but the U.S. North and Europe may have been.

Deindustrialization as Creative Destruction

Using a third indicator, gross job losses, Barry Bluestone and Bennett Harrison define deindustrialization as the destructive

TABLE 2

SECTORAL OUTPUT SHARES OF GNP IN THE UNITED STATES*
(PERCENT)

	1979	1969	1959
Total	100.0	100.0	100.0
Manufacturing	24.8	25.5	23.8
Trade	16.7	16.0	16.0
Finance, Insurance, Real Estate	15.3	14.1	13.7
Services	12.0	11.4	11.2
Government	11.8	14.0	14.4
Construction	3.9	5.1	6.3
Transportation	3.8	4.0	4.2
Communications	3.4	2.2	1.6
Agriculture, Forestry, Fisheries	2.7	3.0	4.3
Utilities	2.4	2.3	1.9
Mining	1.4	1.7	1.8

Source: *Survey of Current Business*, July 1981, as reported in *U.S. Industrial Outlook: 1982*, p. 425.
* Constant-dollar gross product originating in each sector.

side of creative destruction.[4] To appreciate their argument, it helps to note the irony of its timing. Their book, *The Deindustrialization of America*, appeared in late 1982, in the economy's third straight year of falling manufacturing employment, after a cumulative loss of almost 3 million jobs. But such net job losses were incidental to the book's message.

---

[3] How can public perceptions of a postindustrial or services economy, based on employment trends, be reconciled with these data? One answer concerns the importance of "producer services" as an input to the goods-producing sector.

Edward F. Denison (1973, esp. pp. 30–33) shows that much employment growth in services industries reflects the contracting out of work that had been done within "goods-producing" industries to those classified as "services." Hence the production of goods can proceed apace, and the goods-share of GNP can remain unchanged, while employment gains are ascribed to the services sector. See also footnotes 5 and 6 below.

[4] "Gross" job losses are all jobs lost, regardless of whether they are compensated by new jobs from other sources. Suppose that 35 million jobs were lost in plant shutdowns, contractions, and locational changes in the U.S. during the 1970s. These were gross losses. But the economy showed a (net) increase in total jobs of about 20 million. Thus some 55 million new jobs must have been created to replace the gross losses and generate the net increase of 20 million.

What matter to the authors are gross job losses, notably in mature or smoke-stack industries. The book's decisive number is their estimate that "between 32 and 38 million jobs were lost during the 1970s as the direct result of private disinvestment in American business" (p. 9). This process, which the authors trace to corporate flight, is said to erode higher-paying blue-collar jobs and to work via plant and, in effect, community shutdowns.

The book provides valuable evidence of the human costs of economic change. But Bluestone and Harrison's premises are open to question. (1) Is corporate strategy the cause (or only the callous agent) of economic change? (2) Concerning the "creative" side of creative destruction, more jobs were created within the manufacturing sector in the 1970s than were destroyed. (3) Because some jobs are going out of existence always and everywhere, the indicator Bluestone and Harrison use makes deindustrialization a universal outcome.

Five Sources of Structural Change

More generally, the structural change Bluestone and Harrison decry stems not just from corporate flight abroad but from a variety of sources. As Lawrence points out, "International trade is neither the sole nor the most important source of structural change. . . . At least five factors have had important effects on the U.S. industrial base" (Lawrence 1984, p. 4).

Edited and relabeled, here is Lawrence's list:

1. Postindustrial effects (a): "The share of manufacturing products in consumer spending has declined secularly because of the pattern of demand associated with rising U.S. income levels" (Lawrence 1964, p. 4).[5]

---

[5] For the record, this first postindustrial effect takes a back seat to the second, the lag in productivity growth in the services sector.

2. Postindustrial effects (b): Faster aggregate productivity growth in manufacturing than in other sectors reduces manufacturing's share of total employment.[6]

3. Cyclical effects: Slow growth in aggregate demand hits goods harder than it does services.

4. Trade effects (a): Competitiveness may suffer in the short run because of differences between the U.S. and other countries in the timing of their cyclical expansions and contractions or differing monetary policies.

5. Trade effects (b): Comparative advantage may shift over the long run, as

---

Victor Fuchs found that only about one-fourth of the differential 1948–1978 increase in services-sector employment reflected a higher income elasticity of demand for services than for the output of the sector he labeled "industry" (mining, construction, transportation, communications, and public utilities, in addition to manufacturing). Between 1948 and 1978, U.S. services job growth exceeded that of industry by 1.55 percentage points per year. Of this spread, 1.15 can be laid to faster growth in output per worker in industry, and only the remaining .40 point to differences in output growth (Fuchs 1981, p. 232). So about three-fourths of the differential reflected a productivity lag in services relative to industry.

This result accords with Denison's argument in footnote 3 above. See also Eckstein, et al. (1984, chart 6.1, p. 77), which shows no increase in output per worker in the economy's nonmanufacturing sector between 1965 and 1980, when output per worker in manufacturing rose by more than 50 percent.

[6] The postindustrial progression is strikingly uniform across AICs. Figure 7 illustrates the pattern. Reproduced from Fuchs' 1981 article, it suggests that sectoral employment shares are a function of income levels.

Fuchs regressed sectoral output shares on per capita GDP for the U.S. over time (1870–1978) and cross-sectionally for 23 OECD economies. He found the share for industry (defined as in footnote 5 above) to peak when earnings reach an average level between $3,000 and $3,500 (1972 U.S. dollars). This held for both the U.S. and for the OECD cross-sections. Moreover, for 10 of the 11 OECD economies with per capita GDP below $3,250 in 1970, industry's employment share did in fact rise between 1960 and 1976.

A notable anomaly was Britain, which alone among the lower-income OECD nations failed to show a rise in industry's employment share. In this context it looks less postindustrial than deindustrializing (Ajit Singh 1977; Frank Blackaby 1979).

when mature products migrate to LDCs.

Lawrence's lucidly reasoned 1984 book asks, *Can America Compete?* Lawrence links the dislocations of the 1970s to the third item in the list, slow growth in aggregate demand, a result in turn of supply shocks and stop-go attempts to combat inflation. The net job losses since 1979 are laid to item 4, short-run trade effects stemming from macroeconomic sources. In his view, manufacturing job losses since 1979 do not deserve the term deindustrialization. They do not reflect a long-term decline in U.S. competitiveness, Lawrence says, and they can be remedied by appropriate monetary and fiscal policies.

The same argument applies to the burgeoning U.S. trade deficits in the balance of payments accounts. At this point, having addressed the preservationist fear (deindustrialization) Lawrence confronts the modernizers, notably Thurow.

The Dollar and the Trade Deficit

U.S. trade competitiveness, in Lawrence's view, is mainly a function of the exchange rate for the dollar. In the 1970s, the relative prices of U.S. exports fell by 13.5 percent, and the relative prices of U.S. imports rose by 22.0 percent, partly as a consequence of the dollar's depreciation (Lawrence 1984, p. 48). As a result, between 1973 and 1980, trade's net effect on U.S. manufacturing employment (while small) was positive.

After 1980, in "a change that has resulted primarily from the large government deficits" (Lawrence 1984, p. 50), this process was reversed. U.S. interest rates rose relative to those elsewhere, triggering large capital inflows and driving the dollar up by more than 50 percent. Also, after 1982, the U.S. recovery led Europe's, raising U.S. import demand. A rising merchandise trade deficit, in this view, has been a predictable macroeconomic out-

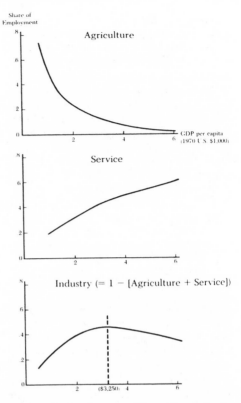

Figure 7. Employment Shares Versus Real GDP per Capita

Source: Victor Fuchs (1981, p. 229).
Note: Curves rendered here are fitted to U.S. time-series (1870–1978) data. Curves for cross-sectional OECD data are indistinguishable from these.

come. After 1980, Lawrence estimates, trade did in fact contribute to large net job losses in manufacturing.

Two kinds of objections to this overvalued-dollar view might be noted. One is that it is too simple: Many other signs testify to a deterioration in U.S. competitiveness. This is the general theme of the *DRI Report on U.S. Manufacturing Industries* (Otto Eckstein et al. 1984) and also of *Global Competition: The New Reality* (1985), a report by the U.S. President's

Commission on Industrial Competitiveness. The commission explicitly rejects the dollar argument (p. 31) and advocates 32 individual remedial policy measures (pp. 251–76).

Nevertheless, Lawrence's argument is persuasive. As Lawrence sees it, exchange rate adjustment can make up for a multitude of sins, including low productivity growth and adverse movements in unit labor costs. He reports equations, for example, that

> imply annual growth of export and import volumes of 6.0 and 6.5 percent, respectively. Starting from a position of balanced trade, the manufactured goods trade balance will decline secularly [if the exchange rate does not change]. However, an improvement of less than 0.25 percent per year in relative U.S. prices would suffice to ensure balanced trade in manufactured products (p. 48).

This result is suggestive. It signals a slight secular deterioration in the U.S. manufacturing sector's competitiveness, which can be offset by relatively small exchange-rate movements.[7] The dollar's depreciation in the 1970s served that end. By the same token, the dollar's spectacular rise in the first half of the 1980s made large trade deficits inevitable.

A second, deeper objection to the overvalued-dollar view is that a depreciating dollar is a sign of decline, and the U.S. should not have to rely on dollar depreciation to improve its trade position. This idea has been put most forcefully, perhaps, by Thurow, as the basis for his view the U.S. is "losing the economic race" (1984). He contends that a depreciating dollar worsens the terms of trade and to that extent reduces U.S. living standards. Still, it seems unrealistic to expect export-

[7] Such a currency depreciation would also, of course, raise the price of imports, worsen the terms of trade, and reduce real wages. For this reason, it is significant that the exchange-rate movement Lawrence found to be necessary to maintain the manufacturing sector's competitiveness was relatively small.

TABLE 3

PERCENTAGE CHANGES IN STANDARD METROPOLITAN STATISTICAL AREA EMPLOYMENT, 1970–1980, BY REGION
(UNWEIGHTED MEANS)

	Total	Manufacturing
64 SMSAs	32.0	9.8
North (30)	10.2	−9.1
South (14)	42.2	15.7
West (20)	57.7	33.9
F-value*	41.8	23.2

Source: U.S. Department of Labor, Bureau of Labor Statistics, *Employment and Earnings,* various issues.
* The F-value refers to the ratio of variation between regions to variation within regions.

ers to surmount the burden of $200 billion federal budget deficits. Also, what makes the recent exchange rate for the dollar the "right" one, against which any depreciation is viewed as a sign of national decline?

Region Shock

We have surveyed four indexes of deindustrialization:

1. manufacturing output as a share of GNP,
2. net changes in manufacturing employment,
3. gross changes in manufacturing employment, and
4. a growing U.S. trade deficit.

Lawrence says that if deindustrialization is to refer to worker dislocation, then item 2 is a good index because, "an absolute decline in industrial employment entails . . . adjustment difficulties" (1984, p. 17). By this measure, the U.S. has not been deindustrialized, not at least until dollar's rise in the 1980s. On the other hand, the same indicator suggests that urban and regional deindustrialization did occur in the 1970s. The mature metropolis (SMSA) of

TABLE 4

EMPLOYMENT RATES FOR BLACK MEN IN 20 LARGE SMSAs (1980)

SMSA	Employment Rate	Differential (White-Black Rate)	1970–1980 Job Growth Rank in Manufacturing
San Jose	.78	.04	1
Houston	.78	.08	2
Boston	.77	.04	7
Miami	.77	.05	4
Atlanta	.76	.05	8
District of Columbia	.76	.07	5
Dallas-Fort Worth	.74	.12	3
Los Angeles	.71	.08	6
Baltimore	.71	.08	18
Milwaukee	.67	.12	9
San Francisco-Oakland	.67	.11	10
Kansas City	.65	.14	13
Cincinnati	.64	.13	12
New York	.64	.07	20
Chicago	.64	.15	15
St. Louis	.63	.14	16
Philadelphia	.60	.16	19
Indianapolis	.59	.17	11
Cleveland	.59	.18	17
Detroit	.52	.21	14

Source: U.S. Department of Labor, Bureau of Labor Statistics (1982, Table 13, Table 1).
Note: The "employment rate" is the proportion of men 20 years and older who are employed.

the North averaged 9 percent losses in its manufacturing employment in the 1970s, and had total job growth less than half the U.S. average (Table 3). In contrast, SMSAs in the South did much better, while Western SMSAs industrialized rap-

idly, adding total jobs at an average rate of 58 percent.

In turn, manufacturing job losses have hit black men with a ferocity that has not been fully recognized (Table 4). In SMSAs losing manufacturing employment, the population share of black men over age 20 with jobs averaged little more than 60 percent in 1980. In Detroit, the employment rate was a stark 52 percent: Only half the black men over age 20 had legitimate jobs. By contrast, in San Jose (Silicon Valley), Dallas, and reindustrial Boston, the rate was above 75 percent.

All this points up the prior issue. What caused the North's industrial decline? More rudely put, "What is the Rust Belt's problem?" (Murray L. Weidenbaum and Michael J. Athey 1984). One answer is that the decline of the North was a fast-history replay of Britain's decline over the past century, a descent some historians trace to a British "climacteric."

VI. *Climacterics and Divides*

From the 1870s on, the British economy faced new competition from Germany, the USA, and other countries. The growth of its older industries suffered, and new industries failed to compensate. By recent estimates, its total factor productivity growth came to a dead stop between 1873 and 1913 (Table 5). Britain's recent decline in the relative per capita output standings of the AICs thus has roots before 1900 (Table 6). Historians refer to this episode as the *British Climacteric*, and some trace it to institutional and social features of Britain's landscape.

"All the strategies available to her were blocked off in one way or another," says Arthur Lewis, by "ideological traps."

She could not lower costs by cutting wages because of the unions, or switch to American-type technology because of the slower pace of British workers. . . . She could not pioneer in developing new commodities because this now

TABLE 5

THE HALT IN BRITAIN'S TOTAL FACTOR PRO-
DUCTIVITY GROWTH: 1873–1913

Growth Rates (percent per year)

Peacetime Phase	Gross Output	Total Factor Input, with Labor Quality Included	Total Factor Productivity
1856–1873	2.2	1.6	0.6
1873–1913	1.8	1.8	0.0
1924–1937	2.2	2.0	0.2
1951–1972	2.8	1.0	1.8

Source: R. C. O. Matthews, C. H. Feinstein and
J. C. Odling-Smee (1982, Tables 7.2 and 7.4, p. 208
and 211).

required a scientific base which did not accord
with her humanistic snobbery. So instead she
invested her savings abroad, the economy de-
celerated, the average level of unemployment
increased, and her young people emigrated.
(Lewis 1978b, p. 133)

Some observers see a parallel between
Britain's climacteric, or change of life, and
the U.S. and Europe today. This maturity
hypothesis dovetails with Schumpeter's
prediction of an eventual slowdown in advanced, affluent, inflexible economies.
Others, particularly on the left, see not
a climacteric but an epochal "divide" like
the one Alvin Hansen noted in 1938. They
regard the U.S. as poised between an obsolete commitment to a mass-production
system, and a new order, yet to emerge.

Kindleberger's Maturity Hypothesis

Figure 8 shows an economy-wide S-
shaped growth curve, as rendered in the
first edition of Kindleberger's international economics text (1953). Kindleberger's thesis was that output growth per
capita tends to accelerate in the early
stages of growth, then slow down as an
economy reaches a stage of economic maturity.

TABLE 6

BRITAIN'S DECLINE IN RELATIVE PER CAPITA
OUTPUT: 1950–1981

(INDICES OF GROSS DOMESTIC PRODUCT PER HEAD,
U.S. PRICES)

Country	1950	1981
United States	156	156
United Kingdom	100	100
Belgium	93	114
Denmark	93	120
Netherlands	90	113
France	85	120
Germany	65	124
Austria	55	112
Italy	48	95
Japan	30	115

Source: Wilfred Beckerman, "Economic Policy and
Performance in Britain Since World War II," in Arnold C. Harberger, ed. (1984, Table 1, p. 17).

In contrast, there is no such connotation
of a slowdown at the top in Walt Whitman
Rostow's *The Stages of Economic Growth*
(1960). In Rostow's subjective chronology,
maturity is the stage that follows the
"takeoff" into sustained economic growth
and in turn gives way to an open-ended
stage of "high mass consumption." Nevertheless, Rostow's typology does provide a
quick reference as to AIC industrial "age."
Using either his takeoff or his maturity
stage as a base date, Britain qualifies as
the oldest industrial power, followed by
France, the U.S., and Germany.

In this context, consider Kenneth
Boulding's life-cycle metaphor for the U.S.
economy:

From about 1880 to 1930 . . . was the period
of adolescent growth. The period after 1930
corresponds to young adulthood, when growth
shifts away from the physical into the intellectual domain. [Today] . . . we must accept the
fact that we are an increasingly mature society.
We are not going to expand much in population
or in wealth. (1980, p. 7)

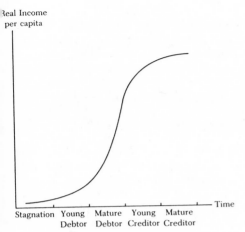

Figure 8. A Gompertz Curve of Growth Applied to Development

Source: Kindleberger (1953, p. 375).

This is grim stuff, in that Boulding defines maturity as "the realization and eventual exhaustion of potential" (p. 6).

But the question is whether to take the idea seriously. Indeed, some dismiss the maturity hypothesis as Spenglerian nonsense. Why should maturity matter?

Institutional Sclerosis?

In its early version, Kindleberger's maturity hypothesis was implicitly aggregative in character. It referred neither to the product cycle nor to S-shaped growth for specific industries. Here maturity reflects rising capital-output ratios, or a reduction in the rate of saving, or both. Maturity may thus imply an affluent society in which consumption is enjoyed at the expense of investment—as in the recent warnings by Thurow, Amitai Etzioni, and others.

By 1973, of course, Kindleberger had recast the argument in terms of (1) the product cycle and (2) the climacteric.

The product cycle dictated a shift to new industries, but some form of socioeconomic fatigue, in his view, eroded adaptive capacity.

As Kindleberger defined it, "Capacity to transform is capacity to react to change, originating at home or abroad, by adapting the structure of foreign trade to the new situation in an economic fashion" (1962, p. 99). Over time this capacity falls. "At some stage in the growth process it reaches a peak, and then there seems to be some diminution in it" (1962, p. 102).

Similarly, in "The Aging Economy" (1978), Kindleberger referred to the urgent "need to adapt to the diffusion of world technology" (p. 416). In his view, adaptive capacity was threatened in the U.S. by a "social arteriosclerosis," whose symptoms were interest-group politics, anachronistic practices by both labor and management, and a tendency for mature industries to have more political sway than growing ones.

Assar Lindbeck generalizes this diagnosis to Europe's AICs in "Can the Rich Countries Adapt?" (1981). Lindbeck makes five points: (1) There is now an urgent need for restructuring within Europe's AICs. (2) As a group, the AICs "show a reduced ability to carry out this reallocation smoothly" (p. 6). (3) In theory, governments can help via better macroeconomic and microeconomic policies. (4) This seems unlikely, however, "since political decisions are to a great extent responsible for the lessened allocative efficiency of our economies" (p. 9). (5) As a result, living standards may fall.

Is there an antidote? In his 1978 essay, Kindleberger concluded that the only remedy was a "sociological equivalent of defeat." To free an aging economy from obsolete practices and institutions, as Germany and Japan had been purged and modernized after World War II, the treatment needed was shock therapy.

The Olson Thesis

The maturity hypothesis provides a useful general framework. More specific questions of economic causality remain. Why should political cultures differ among countries and regions? How do political contrasts react upon economic growth?

Answers to such questions are suggested in Mancur Olson's pathbreaking work on "polyarchy," or government by interest-group pressure (Olson 1977, 1982, 1983). As Olson puts it, "The theory begins with organizations or groups that lobby for favorable legislation and administrative rulings or act cartelistically to influence prices or wages" (1983, p. 917). Such coalitions can organize more easily, the smaller the group and the better defined its object. Because of the free-rider problem, larger or more general-purpose groups like consumers or the poor require more time to get going, if they can manage to do so at all.

By relating interest-group formation to historical time, the theory provides one explanation for the rise and decline of nations, and regions (Olson 1982). Because it takes time for such groups to gather strength, interest-group formation will vary with a society's period of stability. Distributional coalitions will thus place politically long-stable societies at a disadvantage in their competition with younger economies. Institutionally purged societies like Germany and Japan (or the American South), or repressive ones like Korea or Taiwan, will grow faster than stable and long-settled areas like Britain and the American North.

The Olson thesis provides a consistent and detailed version of the economic-aging argument. For our purposes, three points about the thesis might be mentioned here.

First, it addresses the political side of economic maturity. It refers only in passing to industry aging and not at all to the

product cycle (Olson 1982, ch. 4). In this respect, the thesis sheds light on one of the two main elements in Kindleberger's climacteric argument, but less on the mobility of mature industries or changes in comparative advantage over time.

Second, historical time includes other things besides the coalescence of interest groups. Granting that *something* about continuous historical development cuts a system's flexibility, how do we know that it is polyarchy? The way maturity is measured means that other growth-retarding effects may be ascribed to the interest-group variable. For example, as Olson notes, the benefits of "youth" are likely to include catch-up gains via the absorption of technologies generated by mature leaders (Abramovitz 1983; Olson 1982, ch. 4).

A third, related issue is how to gauge maturity. What is the Big Bang or decisive event from which to measure "age"? The events Olson uses are mainly constitutional or formal in character (e.g., years since statehood—or since total defeat). Perhaps an equally useful criterion is the timing of the beginnings of industrialization. That is, industrial takeoffs (in Manchester in 1844, the North after the Civil War, Texas since 1945, or the Pacific Rim economies today) are presided over by industrialists and their champions. Subsequent political development restores a balance between industrialists, on the one hand, and everybody else: labor, farmers, environmentalists, consumers. The more ancient the industrial origins, the more time the political pendulum has in a democracy to swing back to favor other interests and so to generate an antibusiness environment or climate.

Business Climates

The Olson thesis hypothesizes a link between an American region's industrial maturity and its business climate. Suppose we measure maturity by the timing of industrialization. An index that can be used for this purpose is the share of a region's population holding manufacturing jobs in 1909, on the eve of World War I (Norton 1981, p. 257).

Maturity, business climates, and manufacturing job growth align as predicted by the thesis (Table 7). For example, the three youngest regions by this measure have probusiness policy environments and ranked highest in 1966–1979 manufacturing job growth. Conversely, the three "oldest" divisions, which together make up the Manufacturing Belt, had unfavorable business climates. Because each division lost manufacturing jobs over the period, they also have the three lowest growth ranks.

Correlations, of course, do not establish causality. What does seem clear is that U.S. industrial production is shifting to areas that manufacturers themselves regard as more probusiness. So the economic environment may become harsher or less humane—and at the same time more open to changes initiated by firms.

Among the many influences on the business climate, Olson assigns unions a key role in the U.S. regional drama. "The emphasis in any study of regional growth and decline within a country with free mobility of factors should . . . be particularly on the cartelization of the labor force" (Olson 1983, pp. 919–20). In both his general emphasis on the business climate and in singling out unions for particular attention, Olson is joined from the left by the proponents of the divide thesis.

Divides (1): Social Structures of Accumulation

In a "life-cycle hypothesis," David M. Gordon, Richard Edwards, and Michael Reich contend that the American labor movement today is under increasing pressure because the social accord dating from 1945 has come apart since about 1970 (Gordon et al. 1982, p. 11). Historically,

TABLE 7

MATURITY, BUSINESS CLIMATES, AND REGIONAL INDUSTRIAL GROWTH

Regional Maturity, as Ranked by Population Share in Manufacturing Jobs in 1909 Rank	Age Rank	Business Climate Rank, from Unweighted Averages of 1980 State Scores (Grant Index)	Growth Rank, from Percentage Change in Manufacturing Employment, 1967–1979
New England	9	8	8
Middle Atlantic	8	9	9
Upper Midwest	7	6	7
Pacific	6	7	4
South Atlantic	5	5	5
Plains	4	1	6
Southeast	3	3	3
Mountain	2	3	1
Southwest	1	2	2

Sources: Alexander Grant (1982); U.S. Department of Labor, Bureau of Labor Statistics, *Employment and Earnings,* various issues; U.S. Department of Commerce, Bureau of Economic Analysis (1973, p. 72).

in this view, each long swing or Kondratieff cycle has been matched by a distinctive environment regulating the terms of labor's struggle with capital. Now, in the declining phase of the fourth long wave,

> American capitalism is experiencing a prolonged economic crisis, different in form but as intractable and profound as the Depression of the 1930s. (p. 1) . . . we are currently witnessing the throes of a fourth structural transformation, another qualitatively new system shaping work and labor markets in the United States. (p. 17)

That is, each long wave is featured by a kind of nationwide business climate shaping labor's role. This the authors term a social structure of accumulation (SSA), "the specific institutional environment within which the capitalist accumulation process is organized" (p. 9). The institutional arrangements that make up an SSA serve as the basis for the long expansion, or Kondratieff upswing. Eventually, "the boom begins to fade when the profitable opportunities inherent within the existing [SSA] begin to dry up" (p. 10).

Thus, in contrast to Schumpeter, Gordon et al. explain long waves less as reflections of technological innovation and decay, than as outcomes of a class struggle over wages and profits, and over control of the conditions of work and production. The most recent SSA, marked by the "segmentation" of labor, hinged on "the successful integration of the strong national industrial unions of the 1930s into a cooperative collective bargaining system, limiting the further impact of the union movement and initiating a period of labor peace between employers and workers" (pp. 11–13).

As U.S. hegemony within the world economy ended after 1970, the post-1945 accord crumbled.

> As growth slowed, employers increasingly directed investment to regions, countries, and industries where the terms of the postwar accord did not obtain. The great Northeast-Midwest industrial belt, heartland of the postwar boom, showed the greatest decline. (p. 241)

This casual regional reference is a notable exception to the rest of the book, which tends to treat the U.S. as a geographical unity.

Indeed, the argument generally ignores the geography of U.S. industrial evolution since the mid-1960s. Externally, it slights the rise of Japan and the NICs, which are given little if any role in the breakup of the current SSA. Domestically, little mention is made of the diversity in business climates across regions within the U.S.

So on the one hand, the SSA concept seems relevant for interpreting cycles of growth and decline (Bruce Norton 1984). But the argument may be valid mainly for a mature region within the U.S., rather than the nation as a whole. Thus the authors note in the passage quoted above that U.S. investment shifted to regions where "the postwar accord did not obtain."

Divides (2): Unions and Restructuring

By contrast, in "American Labor and the Industrial Crisis" (1982), Michael Piore links the crisis for organized labor to unification of the world economy. (See also Piore and Charles Sabel 1984.) Piore observes that as mass-produced or standardized goods gravitate to LDCs, U.S. comparative advantage shifts to small-batch or flexible-design production runs. But as U.S. comparative advantage shifts from mature to product-cycle goods, the need for increased flexibility may place unions in a bind.

The problem is that American unions learned to deal with management via the institution of fixed *workrules*, which originated with the mass-production methods perfected in Henry Ford's assembly line in 1913. Only after 1935 and the Wagner Act were unions granted full bargaining powers, permitting union membership to soar. By then, Frederick Taylor's system of "scientific management" dominated the organization of the workplace. And it prescribed a rigidly codified division of labor on the shopfloor, a system that unions accepted as given and codified in workrules (Reich 1983, ch. 4).

In other words, what Piore terms the *regulatory system* pivoted on the institutions of mass production, Taylorism, and codified workrules in older American industries. From this regime in turn stemmed a de facto social contract between management and labor—and a welfare state in which the legitimacy of unions was taken for granted.

By the same token, the new management-union tension is about rigidity: Taylorist workrules, legacies of the era of standardized mass production. As stan-

Figure 9. The Clustering of "Right-To-Work" States in the South and West

Source: Barry Bluestone and Bennett Harrison (1972, p. 137).

dardized manufacturing migrates abroad, the need for flexibility requires more fluid work arrangements. Thus production-line managers turn militant, while unions fight to retain their shopfloor say.

Continental Divide

Piore's argument, like Olson's, suggests that the decline of the U.S. North reflects a flight from unions. But in Piore's framework, the redirection of investment is less a flight from high union wages than an attempt to escape rigid workrules. In other words, managers shift plants to less unionized sites to regain control of production and introduce new methods.

What makes this argument suggestive is that the U.S. displays sharp regional contrasts in the role that unions play. In particular, "right-to-work" laws (outlawing union shops) are found in 20 states—and

every one of them lies outside the Manufacturing Belt (Figure 9). In this light, U.S. regional contrasts provide a bridge between one institutional setting and another.

VII. *Renewal*

Most countries are roughly comparable to a region of the United States. . . .
William Shepherd 1979, p. 212

Continental scale makes the U.S. a network of diverse, country-sized regions—some long developed, some only recently industrialized. On both this count and in its decentralized political structure, the U.S. differs from Europe's smaller-scale, centralized AICs. As a result, the U.S. may be open to a political transformation that "dematures" its institutional framework.

By the same token, the climacteric Kindleberger perceived for the U.S. may have had only regional validity. As observers put it in 1983, "We saw the regions of America reacting quite differently to radically changed economic futures, depending on their particular cultures." As for adaptive capacity,

> the most resistant to change were the Midwestern states where even in the depression of the '80s many leaders in both management and labor seemed to imagine they could continue their old adversarial ways and regain their lost prosperity without fundamental adjustments. (Neil Peirce and Jerry Hagstrom 1983, p. 17)

Another observer compares this same "Foundry" to Britain, but says renewal is occurring anyway, on a continental scale:

> The error, as this continent matures, is in . . . equating the inevitable decline in the Foundry's dominance with an inevitable decline in the world position of the United States or Canada. What's happening in the Foundry today is perhaps comparable to the wrenching realizations Europeans were subjected to . . . not only does the sun not revolve around the earth; the earth does not revolve around London. Yet, somehow, Western civilization survives—even prospers. (Joel Garreau 1981, p. 65)

Europe's Jobless Growth

Under a regime of market-generated renewal the U.S. has added some 30 million jobs since 1970, whereas AIC Europe has added virtually none. Job losses between 1973 and 1980 were large enough that for eight European AICs combined, there was no employment growth between 1960 and 1980 (Lawrence 1984, p. 28).

In a valuable essay on Western European responses to the rise of the NICs, N. Plessz observes, "The real question is why . . . 'positive' responses have played a lesser role in Western Europe than in North America" (Plessz 1981, p. 228). As he observes,

> while labour-shedding continued, or sometimes accelerated, in the 'declining' industries, the absorption of labour by 'growth' industries has slowed down dramatically. In other words,

> the adjustment mechanism was blocked, at least within the manufacturing sector. (p. 231)

Compounding the problem was slow growth in services jobs. Rapid productivity growth permitted job reductions in manufacturing, but the job-creation side of "postindustrialism" was missing.

Contributing to Europe's jobless growth was real wage rigidity. Whatever the precise explanation, there are two obvious points of contrast with the U.S. One is that the initial employment shocks after 1973 could be absorbed by guest workers. As a result, employment could fall without placing as much downward pressure on real wages.

But the other point of contrast is the welfare-state phenomenon: subsidies and benefits that may approximate reservation wages. Unlike U.S. arrangements, most European welfare systems are true "entitlement" systems, free of the stigma that attaches to needs-based transfer programs here. And benefit levels are often generous.

This problem of incentives is compounded by the centralized governmental structures of the European welfare states. National uniformity, which may be desirable in itself, becomes a barrier to adjustment when transfer payments exceed reservation wages. More generally, employment policies geared to temporary relief in specific localities tend to become national, thwarting adjustment.

In addition, European workers' job rights make it much harder to fire workers than in the U.S. As a result, employers may become increasingly wary of hiring new workers—and in effect granting them "tenure."

Market-Generated Adjustment

Some writers argue that the choice facing the U.S. is between (1) protection and (2) rational, coordinated adjustment, as illustrated by Europe's human resource policies (Reich 1983; Robert Kuttner

1984). But as Robert Lawrence notes, a third approach is the "ad hoc and laissez-faire policies of the United States" (Lawrence 1984, p. 23). Such market-based adjustment in the U.S. has had a distinctive geographical matrix.

For better or worse, the diversity of state-administered welfare systems—and the low benefit levels in some rapidly growing states—offer a sharp contrast to the adequacy and uniformity of benefits in more centralized European systems. The result may be to neutralize the kind of work incentives problems that arise in Europe. To be sure, the American system is perverse in that high benefits levels in slowly growing states discourage mobility of the poor. But from a national standpoint, the other side of this coin finds superior work incentives in low-benefit, rapid-growth states.

In addition, a second source of wage flexibility is the replacement of unionized by nonunion workers, as production jobs in manufacturing change in makeup and location. The decline of the upper Midwest is also a blow to blue-collar unions. New England's high-tech reindustrialization replaces unionized older industries with growing nonunionized ones. Whatever the impact on work conditions, one result will be greater wage flexibility.

As with business climates, wage flexibility is a political lightning rod. Some will see it as a matter of better working conditions and more humane social legislation, on the one hand, versus the more primitive practices of an earlier historical era, on the other. Others will see job growth as the sine qua non of social opportunity, more important than productivity, per capita incomes, and even worker participation.

The point here is a different one. Regional competition has the effect of breaking up established structures and practices. To that extent, regional diversity enhances U.S. adaptive capacity.

Cowboy Capitalism

Similarly, Carol Heim (1984) shows that American continentality provides three sources of renewal absent from Britain. In a comparison of the geography of industrial modernization in the two countries, she finds American advantages in (1) lower factor costs in the more extensive U.S. periphery, (2) a city-building dynamic in the South and West that generates abundant profit opportunities to capitalists, and (3) a geographical and political diversity that offers ample opportunities for the kind of industrial restructuring now imperative in the AICs. The U.S. may thus derive a unique capacity for structural renewal from its own internal frontier. Both a recent and a more classical conception of the economic frontier are worth noting.

In "The Economics of the Frontier," Guido di Tella asks why a frontier stage led to subsequent rounds of development in the U.S. and Canada, but not, for example, in Argentina. He introduces the idea of *the frontier as a disequilibrium state,* "bursting with business opportunities with big profits and economic excitement, evidence of the existence of rent at the frontier" (di Tella 1982, p. 215). The scramble for rents and quasirents generates a powerful stimulus to investment—and to innovative behavior.

The setting for U.S. industrial change from about 1960 on was a disequilibrium between suppliers and their markets. Like Britain in 1870 and the northern European economies in 1970, the U.S. North was "hyperindustrialized" in 1950. The technological changes that weakened the North's industrial role created a profit-generating disequilibrium in the South and especially the West.

The deindustrialization of the North since the late 1960s has thus reflected *import substitution* in the South and West, as goods formerly imported from the North were increasingly produced locally.

TABLE 8

The Equalization of the Manufacturing-Population Ratio by Region
(1940–1979)

Area	Percentage Shares of U.S. Manufacturing Employment			Percentage Share of U.S. Population			Ratio of Manufacturing Share to Population Share			Change in Ratio		
	1979	1967	1939	1979	1967	1940	1979	1967	1940	1967–1979	1940–1967	1940–1979
Core	49.0	56.8	69.0	41.3	44.4	47.3	1.19	1.28	1.46	−.09	−.18	−.27
New England	7.1	8.0	11.8	5.6	5.7	6.4	1.27	1.40	1.84	−.13	−.44	−.57
Middle Atlantic	17.5	22.3	28.9	16.8	18.7	20.3	1.04	1.19	1.39	−.15	−.20	−.35
East North Central	24.4	26.5	28.3	18.9	20.0	20.1	1.29	1.32	1.41	−.03	−.09	−.12
Periphery	51.0	43.2	31.0	58.7	55.6	52.7	.87	.78	.59	.09	.19	.28

Sources: U.S. Department of Commerce, Bureau of Economic Analysis (1973); U.S. Department of Labor, Bureau of Labor Statistics, *Employment and Earnings;* U.S. Department of Commerce, Bureau of the Census, *Current Population Reports,* Series P-25.

The loss of the North's traditional export markets was hastened by the filling in, diversification, and catching-up of formerly less developed areas (Leonard Wheat 1973; Benjamin Stevens and George Treyz 1983). Table 8 depicts this leveling over time; it shows that regional shares of U.S. manufacturing employment are approaching regional population shares, such that the ratios of the two shares are everywhere converging to unity.

In turn, such import-substitution can provide a stimulus to innovative behavior that yields benefits for the national economy as a whole. This is the central point of Jane Jacobs' recent book, *Cities and the Wealth of Nations* (1984). It provides a natural complement to di Tella's frontier theory.

As a quick check on how far the market-as-magnet and restructuring influences go to explain manufacturing realignments in the 1970s, we can run a naive regression. It turns out that four influences can ac-

count for 80 percent of the variation in the 1970–1980 rates of state manufacturing job growth. These are market potential (MKT), the 1970–1980 change in a state's relative labor costs (DLC), the presence of a "right-to-work" (anti-union shop) law (NON-U), and a measure of other effects associated with distance from the old industrial core (PITT).

Denoting the percentage change in a state's manufacturing job count between 1970 and 1980 as DJOBS,

$$\text{DJOBS} = -14.1 + 16.6 \, \text{NON-U} - 1.8 \, \text{DLC}$$
$$\phantom{\text{DJOBS} = -14.1 +} (4.2) \phantom{\text{NON-U} -} (3.4)$$

$$+ \, 0.8 \, \text{MKT} + 15.4 \, \text{PITT},$$
$$ (5.2) \phantom{\text{MKT} +} (5.1)$$

$$R^2 = .80,$$
$$N = 48,$$

where the parenthesized values are t-ratios and where
NON-U = 1 in the 20 right-to-work states, 0 elsewhere;

DLC = the percentage change in a state's relative labor costs;

MKT = population/manufacturing employment for a state in 1970;

PITT = distance (1000 m) of a state's largest city from Pittsburgh.

The regression says that "right-to work" law states had 17 percent faster job growth in manufacturing over the decade. It suggests that a state whose labor costs fell by 1 percent relative to the U.S. average had a growth rate about two points higher than a state in which labor costs matched the U.S. trend. (But the identification problem rules out a causal interpretation here.) As for the market magnet, the latter two variables bear out the idea of decentralized filling-in. Thus the larger the initial ratio of population to manufacturing employment (MKT), and the farther the state from the industrial core (PITT), the faster the state's manufacturing job growth.

Turner on Renewal

A second, more classical, conception of a functional frontier is the Turner thesis. Frederick Jackson Turner's famous 1893 essay announced the closing of the literal American frontier, but it is the spirit of his thesis, not the letter, that is of interest here.

That much said, consider Turner on regional diversity as a source of change:

> American development has exhibited not merely advance along a single line, but a return to primitive conditions on a continually advancing frontier line, and a new development for that area. American social development has been continually beginning over again on the frontier. This perennial rebirth, this fluidity of American life, this expansion westward with its new opportunities . . . furnish the forces dominating American character. (Turner, in George Rogers Taylor 1949, pp. 1–2)

The paradox of renewal is that people, firms, and societies change only reluctantly, because change is often painful. "Market forces rarely work in a textbook fashion and smoothly re-allocate resources in response to the changing environment. Much social, economic and political pain is associated with the restructuring process and this fact is likely to represent a powerful force to slow it down" (Alan R. Roe 1984, p. xv).

As Roy Hattersley, a British Labour party official puts it, "The facts, though unpalatable, are undeniable. The world has changed, and with it the economic culture, based on mass production factories, in which the unions thrived" (1985). In this new context, the frontier factor may give the U.S. a decisive impetus to change.

VIII. *Who's Number 1?*

To sum up, regional diversity has enforced a rapid adjustment in the U.S. over the past 15 years. America's transition has been perhaps more painful but surely more effective than in Europe. The result has been rapid U.S. job growth over the period, during a time when new entrants flooded the American labor market. Before 1980, the process was aided by a depreciating dollar, improving U.S. export competitiveness. This stimulated the industrialization of younger regions and the reindustrialization of New England, in a continental restructuring.

The version of the renewal story just sketched emphasizes job creation. That puts it at odds with the modernizers, who focus instead on productivity growth. Some of the modernizers also contend that the U.S. has lost the lead in per capita output and living standards—and in technology. Can the two views be reconciled?

Convergence

As the distant leader, the U.S. was certain to be overtaken by other developed countries after 1950. In Rostow's phrase, the rebuilding economies could exploit the "backlog of technologies" from the U.S. So much was inevitable, and with it, falling U.S. shares of world industrial output and exports.

The logic—even desirability—of this convergence comes through clearly in Branson's comment in 1979, after the fact:

> The U.S. produced approximately 60 percent of the world output of manufactures in 1950. . . . This was obviously a transitory situation. During the 1950s the European economies recovered and rebuilt capacity. . . . Japan entered the competition in a major way in the 1960s, and in the 1970s [so did the NICs]. (Branson 1980, p. 185)

As a result, "gradually, over thirty-five years, the other industrial countries have caught up with the United States, restoring a kind of economic balance to the world picture" (p. 185).

The Catch-up Hypothesis

As for productivity growth, the U.S., at the frontier of knowledge, had to advance that frontier itself, rather than borrow from others. Thus Thorkil Kristensen comments that "the current rate of growth of knowledge . . . determines the slope of the S-curve at the highest income levels" (Kristensen 1974, p. 29, quoted in Rostow 1980, p. 362).

U.S. productivity was double that of other AICs, on the average, just after World War II. Moses Abramovitz has shown that average productivities in ten less advanced industrial countries (LACs) were only about 50 percent of U.S. levels in 1950, 60 percent in 1960, and 70 percent in 1970 (Abramovitz 1979, p. 8). Lacking an external source of new technologies to absorb, the U.S. could have been expected to grow more slowly.

The catch-up hypothesis, then, is that the larger the gap between an LAC's initial productivity level and that of the leader, the faster the LAC's subsequent productivity growth. To test this proposition, Abramovitz compared 1950 relative productivity levels and 1950–1970 growth rates in eleven countries. For three separate series on labor productivity growth,

the rank correlations came out virtually the same, at −.89 to −.91. The lower the level of a country's productivity in 1950, the faster its 1950–1970 growth rate (Abramovitz 1979, p. 11).

By 1980, the productivity gap had narrowed further, but by A. D. Roy's estimates, the U.S. retained the lead in output per employed worker (Roy 1982, p. 19). Moreover, this was true despite much faster 1970s job growth in the U.S. than in Europe.

The Disputed U.S. Lead in per Capita Output

But such findings point up another question. As recently as 1980 average LAC productivity levels remained well below U.S. levels. Then what are we to make of widely publicized claims that the U.S. had fallen behind in living standards by 1980?

In 1980, Thurow took the loss of the lead as a fait accompli. Contending that Japan had caught up to the point of a per capita GNP only 7 percent below the U.S. level, he wrote that ". . . we stood fifth among the nations of the world in per capita GNP in 1978, having been surpassed by Switzerland, Denmark, West Germany, and Sweden" (Thurow 1980, pp. 3–4).

The trouble with this ranking is that it used unadjusted currency values to measure comparative incomes. Nor was that approach unusual. *The New York Times* (1982), for example, reported such figures as a sign of U.S. decline. The fallacy here is dramatically illustrated in the appreciation of the dollar by more than 50 percent since 1980. Linking U.S. living standards to unadjusted currency values would lead us to believe that living standards had gone up apace, by 50 percent or more between 1980 and 1985.

The second and more accurate measure shows a completely different outcome. This adjusted measure uses purchasing-

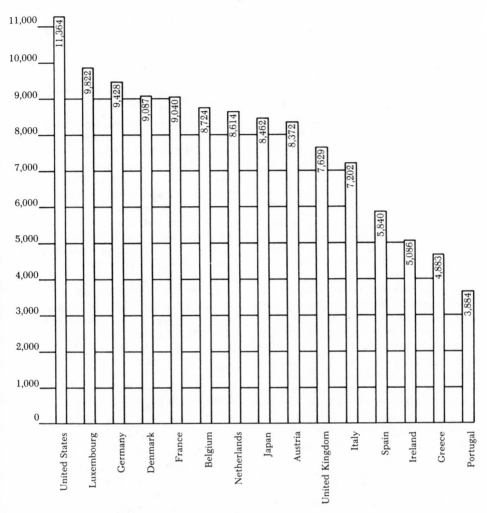

Figure 10. Gross Domestic Product per Head, 1980
(current prices in U.S. dollars converted by purchasing power parities)

Source: Reproduced from "Comparing Real Standards of Living," *OECD Observer* (Mar. 1982, p. 31).

power-parity indexes compiled by Irving Kravis and his co-workers (Kravis 1984). By this measure, as Figure 10 shows, in 1980 the U.S. retained the highest living standard of any AIC. So much is consistent with the evidence that U.S. productivity levels remain the world's highest.

A Technological Life Cycle?

Yet even before the dollar's appreciation and the widening of the U.S. trade deficit in the 1980s, these various indicators were valid only as snapshots of a moment in time. What counts in the long run is U.S. technological performance. Is it true that the U.S. has been hit by a "precipitous decline in its technological preeminence"? (Robert Solo 1984, p. 713).

If so, it would hardly be the first instance of a technological leader being overtaken and surpassed. Kindleberger suggests that over the very long run, economies follow a cycle that culminates in a loss of technological prowess:

> The British stole industrial secrets from Italy. . . . Then Germany stole British industrial secrets, as did the United States. . . . The Japanese copied American patents and copyrights and stole industrial secrets. . . . In each case, stealing technology was an interlude on the way to positive innovation. There is a cycle: imitation, innovation (including adaptation), invention, and then slowdown. (Kindleberger, letter to the author, 1984)

Why should there be a slowdown? Some possible answers are suggested in the literature on "early-start" thesis. This holds that as the cradle of the industrial revolution, Britain was somehow handicapped in its later capacity to innovate. The debate concerns how and why Britain was overtaken by the U.S. and Germany before 1914. One early landmark here was Ernest Edwin Williams' *Made in Germany* (1896). Another was Thorstein Veblen's 1915 essay on the advantages of borrowing and the handicap of an early lead.

Leon Trotsky perceived in the episode a Law of Combined Development. As he put it in 1926, "The fact that Germany and the United States have now economically outstripped England was made possible by the very backwardness of their capitalist development" (Baruch Knei-Paz 1978, pp. 91–92).

As if in reply, Edward Ames and Nathan Rosenberg point out in "Changing Technological Leadership and Industrial Growth" (1963) that the early-start thesis has three variants. In their words:

- The weak thesis asserts that the late comers will pass through any sequence of development more rapidly than early starters.
- The moderate thesis asserts that late comers will ultimately reach higher levels of development than early starters, even though the latter do not cease developing.
- The strong thesis states that late comers will surpass early starters, partly because the latter will cease to develop. (Ames and Rosenberg 1963, pp. 29–30)

The catch-up scenario is consistent with the first case. Ames and Rosenberg point out that it rests on the premise that followers can avoid the mistakes of the leader. The second makes the stronger assumption that the leader will be uniquely subject to some form of growth retardation. The third and strongest variant assumes that "the cost of moving from a lower to a higher technology is an increasing function of the level of technology already reached . . . [and] is based on transition costs" (p. 30). Which matches the British case they see as an empirical question.

The same can be said for the American case. That is, now that it has gone so far to catch up, can Japan wrest the lead from the U.S.?

U.S. Failure: Process Technology in Mature Industries

In a statement damning in its simplicity, *Consumer Reports* concludes, "No domestic [U.S.] car approaches the high quality and reliability of most Japanese imports" (1984, p. 333). The Japanese automotive triumph appears to be symptomatic of a more general management failure in mature U.S. industries (Paul Lawrence and Davis Dyer 1983).

With electronics in mind, Regis McKenna contends that the U.S. problem is production and marketing of mature products. In his view, "maturity, or a slow rate of innovation, is not an intrinsic competitive disadvantage" (McKenna 1984, p. 155). But as between the U.S. and Japan, it turns out to be:

> Mature markets are those that give advantages to our Japanese competitors because of the

latter's greater skills in, and attention to, marketing and manufacturing. Product standardization, process innovation, high-quality production, and incremental improvements are all Japanese strengths. (p. 155)

More specifically, Japan's daring and initiative on production methods come together in the "just-in-time" approach to inventory control. This Kandan (or semaphoric card) system has the revolutionary effect of putting the factory on a perpetual alert, drawing workers into every step of the production process (Richard Schonberger 1982).

Robert Lawrence notes more specific evidence of Japan's lead in several mature industries. He points out the estimates of Roy (1982) that "1980 output per employed worker-year in United States manufacturing was about 16 percent higher than in Japan" But in steel, general machinery, electrical machinery, transportation equipment, and precision machinery and equipment, the lead has gone to Japan (Lawrence 1983, p. 47).

The Japanese government has compared the U.S. and Japan in 190 technologies (81 of them process, 108 product). It concludes that Japan is superior in 20 percent of the product technologies, but in more than 40 percent of the process technologies. This information, so far as it goes, is consistent with the idea of Japanese superiority in manufacturing techniques.

The U.S. as the World's Technological Seedbed

But fundamental innovation may be a different story. Can Japan move through the stylized sequence Kindleberger outlined: from imitation and innovation (including adaptation) to invention? Putting it differently, catch-up gains and improvements are one thing, taking the lead is another.

The Japanese are now embarked on the celebrated "fifth-generation" computer mission to wrest the lead in this industry from the U.S. In a sense, however, the daring of the project only underscores how novel its realization would be. A sharp distinction has to be made, in other words, between methods of manufacturing, in which the Japanese may lead, and more basic breakthroughs.

A 1984 poll of managers in European high-tech firms finds that in nine high-tech industries, the U.S. trails Japan only in metals and robotics, while leading outright in engineering, chemicals, telecommunications, biotechnology, and computing (Table 9). While hardly definitive, this sort of polling of the competition offers a useful sightline on who defines the world's technological frontier.

In sum, "other nations, including the Japanese, have yet to demonstrate the innovative ability shown by Americans" (McKenna 1984, p. 155). But why, then, is the U.S. manufacturing sector depressed, even in the nation's fastest growing regions?

IX. Open Questions

The effect of the overvalued dollar is to truncate the renewal process by speeding up the product cycle, depriving U.S. locations of the initial employment benefits of innovation. To put the issue in perspective, consider "the two American economies"—the one within U.S. borders, and the worldwide American-owned "global factory." In a recent NBER working paper, Robert Lipsey and Irving Kravis report that the export performance of U.S. multinational firms was sufficiently strong through the late 1970s that the combined (domestic and foreign) U.S. export shares of world totals fell by much less than the U.S.-sited share. Lipsey and Kravis therefore conclude that

the search for causes of the changed U.S. position should be directed not to deficiencies in American industrial or technological leader-

TABLE 9

RANKING IN HIGH TECHNOLOGY: AN ASSESSMENT BY CHIEF EXECUTIVES OF MORE THAN
200 EUROPEAN FIRMS

	United States	Japan	Germany	Scandinavia	United Kingdom	France
Computing	1	2	3	4–5	6	4–5
Electronics	1–2	1–2	3	4	6–7	6–7
Telecommunications	1	2	3	4	5–6	5–6
Biotechnology	1	2	3	4	5	n.a.
Chemicals	1	2	3	4	5	6–7
Metals/Alloys	2	1	3	4	5–6	5–6
Engineering	1	2	3	4	5	6
Manufacturing	1–2	1–2	3	4	5	6
Robotics	2	1	3	4	6	5
Mean Rank	1.3	1.7	3.0	4.2	5.4	5.8

Source: John Marcum, "High Technology and the Economy" (*OECD Observer*, Nov. 1984, *131*, p. 5).
n.a. = not available.

ship but to other price- and cost-determining influences, such as productivity, wage setting, taxation, domestic inflation, and exchange rates. (*NBER Digest* 1985, p. 30)

By the same token, the effect of the dollar's appreciation since 1980 has been to deprive American workers of jobs in new, or product-cycle goods. As a recent bank letter puts it,

New England entrepreneurs in high tech industries are increasingly of the view that exchange-rate appreciation is analogous to production cost increases in any growing business: the only way in which these de facto cost increases can be combatted is through seeking more cost effective sites abroad in their expanding markets. (Diane Fulman 1985)

One result of this speedup in the product cycle, Fulman writes, is that U.S.-spawned technology will be more rapidly diffused abroad. Another will be to "rob U.S. technology centers of the local employment benefits of their industries." Pressure for more protection has spread accordingly from the declining heartland to the South and West, giving rise to argu-

ments for import tariffs to counter the exchange rate's effects.

The question that is still to be answered is whether the present difficulties of our manufacturing sector stem mainly from our macroeconomic policies or lie deeper. As the Federal budget deficit narrows in future years, we should get a clearer answer to this question.

Was Schumpeter Wrong?

A second open question concerns Schumpeter's version of what we have termed the *maturity hypothesis*. In Schumpeter's view, creative destruction supersedes class conflict as an agent of change. In a different context, this contrast has been pinpointed also by Jane Jacobs:

Marx thought that the principal conflict to be found in . . . industrialized countries, was the deep disparity of interests between owners and employees, but this is a secondary kind of conflict. . . . The primary economic conflict, I think, is between people whose interests are with already-established economic activities, and those whose interests are with the emergence of new economic activities. This is a conflict that can never be put to rest except by economic stagnation. (Jacobs 1969, pp. 248–49)

Yet, in a famous paradox, Schumpeter agreed with Marx on the outcome. Schumpeter predicted that capitalism's transition to socialism would occur not with a bang, but with a whimper—as a by-product of industrial capitalism's success. As Schumpeter put it, "capitalism is being killed by its achievements" (1942, p. xiv). To the question "Can capitalism survive?" Schumpeter answered, "No." That is, "My final conclusion does not differ . . . from that of all Marxists" (1942, p. 61).

Was Schumpeter wrong? Maturity and affluence did carry with them an antibusiness spirit, an attempt to right the wrongs of an earlier era. Yet competition from less developed capitalist economies, both within the U.S. and worldwide, has rocked the foundations of mature economies, forcing them to retreat to the more competitive, probusiness policies of the past.

Thus the mood surrounding the rise of younger nations and regions as driving forces in world development has been revised to take account of capitalism's open possibilities:

We are likely to see successful capitalisms and unsuccessful ones. We will have to wait and see whether the United States can overcome its present laggard condition to become, once again, an adaptive and creative variant of a system whose time within world history does not yet seem to have run its course. (Robert Heilbroner and Aaron Singer 1984, p. 353)

APPENDIX

A READER'S GUIDE TO INDUSTRIAL POLICY

The summer of 1980 saw various manifestos urging America's "reindustrialization." Such proposals preceded the idea of a targeted industrial policy for the U.S. They centered on more general tax and regulatory reforms to restore the nation's competitive vigor and rebuild its decaying infrastructure (and, in some versions, to mend its decadent values). Among the most influential advocates were Lester Thurow, *Business Week* magazine, and Amitai Etzioni.

Thurow's *The Zero-Sum Society* introduced a neoliberal theme of what might be termed *productive justice*. Central to his call for a freeze on consumption levels so as to boost investment and productivity growth was an emphasis on equal sacrifice, or shared austerity. The zero-sum reference was to the nation's apparent political impasse. Because of declining productivity growth, the de facto U.S. approach to inequality (rising standards of living, but with constant shares of the income pie) had broken down. In turn, the deadlock over shares barred any major new political initiatives that might help break the society out of its underinvestment mode (Thurow 1980).

The solution? Abolish the corporation income tax (i.e., integrate it with the personal income tax), thus boosting after-tax rates of return and stimulating investment. In a variant, Thurow would later propose a consumption tax as an alternative to the administration's individual income-tax cuts; the latter, he said, would favor consumption at the expense of investment. A value-added tax of 10 percent, he contended, could replace the corporation income and social security taxes, and spur incentives to work and to save (Thurow 1981; Barry Bosworth 1983).

All this sparked an enthusiastic review in *Business Week*, which soon devoted a full issue to "The Reindustrialization of America" (1980). The message reinforced Thurow's, while lending it the mantle of centrist corporate respectability. Management, labor, government, and affluence—all were to blame for American economic decline. Accordingly, what was needed was a new "social contract," which in the book version (1982) was replaced by the phrase "new social consensus." The goals: to allocate sacrifice fairly as steps were taken to (1) raise investment's GNP share; (2) stimulate work, saving, innovation, and export performance; and (3) rebuild the social infrastructure.

Meantime, Amitai Etzioni (a sociologist and policy planner in the Carter Administration) had written a series of articles that would eventually be published as *An Immodest Agenda: Rebuilding America Before the Twenty-first Century* (1983). Etzioni likened the U.S. to a "mature and aging" community in need of an infusion of capital for new infrastructure. His thesis was that over the period 1950–1980, "overconsumption—public and private—and underinvestment have created a maintenance gap, and an adaptation lag, due to insufficiently innovative response to changes in the outside world" (p. 191).

Etzioni saw three distinct policy strategies as possible:

1. On the right, supply-side economics was insufficiently targeted, and would spur consumption, not investment.
2. On the left was a targeted industrial policy, which to Etzioni connoted unwanted bureaucracy.
3. The third option was "semitargeted" reindustrialization.

In the last, preferred option, the idea was to "release resources to the private sector, but channel them to the infrastructure and capital goods sectors, away from public and private consumption" (p. 315).

What actually happened, of course, was option 1, the Reagan tax program. In turn, passage of the Reagan program in mid-1981 was greeted with numerous counterproposals for option 2, a targeted industrial policy, typically along the lines suggested by Japan's Ministry of International Trade and Investment (MITI).

THE PRESERVATIONISTS VERSUS THE MODERNIZERS

Thurow had not used the term *industrial policy.* But in that direction, and as a means of raising productivity growth, he did call for an updated version of the Reconstruction Finance Corporation. Contending that "disinvestment is what our economy does worst" (p. 77), he saw a role for "the national equivalent of a corporate investment committee to redirect investment flows from our 'sunset' industries to our 'sunrise' industries" (p. 95). In this view, the problem was that market forces failed to shift capital to growing industries fast enough.

In contrast, *Business Week* would soon call for targeted sectoral policies to counter—not to accelerate—market forces. In another special issue on America's restructured economy, (*Business Week* 1981), the case was made that the U.S. economy had "evolved into five separate economies [old-line and high-tech manufacturing, energy, agriculture, and services] that no longer act as one" (p. 56). This approach to the economy's evolving structure seemed mystifying, at least until the policy punchline.

The policy problem, in this view, was that without targeted sectoral policies, "the market will continue to steer all funds" to the energy and high-tech sectors of the South and West, thus further weakening the old-line manufacturing sector and the North. Therefore "government policies will have to be carefully targeted to meet special needs. . . . The government needs a new set of fiscal policies aimed at bringing out capital and channeling it in the right directions" (p. 100). So market forces work to hurt the basic industries of the North—and should be countered.

This dichotomy would prove characteristic of proposals for targeted industrial policies. On the one hand, the modernizers like Thurow (and Reich and Frank Weil) argued that without an industrial policy, the American economy would suffer a further relative decline within the world economy. Meantime, others argued for the restoration or at least support of declining industries and places—a preservationist strategy.

The distinction between modernizers and preservationists is highlighted by General Electric's marketing maxim, "Automate, emigrate, or evaporate." It arises also when an OECD report refers to "the two strategies of the mature industrial countries," that is, switching to automated methods or abandoning basic industries to LDCs (OECD 1980, p. 83). Productivity growth via robotic processes and other labor-saving innovations (or by abandoning older industries) may be lauded by modernizers, but not by job-oriented preservationists. The latter are more likely to be troubled by the specter of "jobless growth" (Colin Norman 1980, p. 35) and to turn to a third strategy, protectionism, to maintain jobs.

A key preservationist is Felix Rohatyn, the investment banker who presided over the Municipal Assistance Corporation which arranged New York's fiscal reorganization. His premise is that "market forces are destroying our basic industries, possibly permanently, but these market forces are by no means free" (Rohatyn 1983, p. 14). Hence they should be resisted.

Arguing for a "continuing institutionalized response" to the policies of other governments, Rohatyn advocates the kind of mandated cooperation among labor, business, and government that proved workable in New York. To this end, a new Reconstruction Finance Corporation "would be able to provide (or withhold) capital in exchange for concessions (from management, labor, banks, suppliers, local governments)" (p. 15). In sum, intervention is required to counter the tactics of other governments.

Perhaps the most fully developed rationale for an industrial policy comes from Reich—in the main, a modernizer. Having set forth a well-documented indictment of American management with Ira Magaziner in a 1982 book, Reich went on to write *The Next American Frontier,* renowned in part for its appeal to Walter Mondale as a blueprint for the Democratic party electoral campaign (Reich 1983).

Reich posits a divergence between two distinct cultures in the U.S.: the managerial (in which efficiency is the dominant value) and the civic (which values community and harmony). In nations forced to rebuild after World War II, economic nationalism reconciled these two strands. "These societies almost naturally connect economic development with social change" (p. 16). As a result, he contends, "since 1970 many of these other nations have been more successful . . . in adjusting to the new realities of international competition" (p. 17). Hence the book's title. "Adaptation is America's challenge. It is America's next frontier" (p. 21).

In Reich's view, "American producers have not fared well in [the] new contest" for world markets since roughly 1965 (p. 121). Japan, France, and Germany, he contends, have recognized that their comparative advantage in the new world economy lies in activities requiring skilled labor, such as precision, custom, and technology-intensive products. Such commodities "are relatively secure against low-wage competition because they depend on high-level skills" (p. 128). In contrast, American management, labor, and government have clung to arrangements left over from a bygone era of mass production.

The reasons he advances for failure to adjust lie in what he sees as the extreme hierarchy or separation of managers from workers in Britain and the U.S. In particular, "the radical distinction heretofore drawn between those who plan work and those who execute it is inappropriate to flexible-system production," the system required in the new international competition (p. 135). Instead of adjusting, the U.S. suffers from maladies that Reich terms (1) paper entrepreneurialism, (2) historic preservation (protection), and (3) a dead end for many American workers.

What is needed, as spelled out earlier in a 1982 article, "Industrial Policy: Ten Concrete Practical Steps . . . ," are policies to speed the shift of capital and labor into high value-added activities. (In this respect, Reich's program harmonizes with Thurow's sunset-sunrise investment policy.) Examples of such policy innovations are employment vouchers, a human-capital tax credit, regional development banks, and, to monitor government influences on capital allocation, a national industrial board.

Reich's larger—and more persuasive—message is that an industrial policy already exists in piecemeal form, through tax, regulatory, and protectionist policies. Accordingly, he contends that the relevant question is not whether to have an industrial policy. Instead, it is whether to monitor, coordinate, and improve upon the de facto industrial policy the U.S. already has.

THE REBUTTAL

Economists have replied to proposals for industrial policy with telling criticisms on three divergent counts. (1) As a matter of *theory*, the critics question the assumption of market failure implicit in calls for government intervention. (2) As a matter of *practice*, they argue that an undesirable bureaucratic layer would be required to administer a targeted program—and that such a program would inevitably revert to protectionism (or, in a radical variant, that it would become a captive of big business). (3) As a matter of *evidence*, some economists reject the notion of a fundamental decline in U.S. trade competitiveness.

1. The Problem in Theory (Branson and Krugman)

National security is sometimes invoked (especially by preservationists) as a reason to sustain industries like steel through some form of industrial policy. Branson assays this proposition in terms of two separate tests:

First, supply interruption must be plausible. It is not enough to note that effective defense requires chromium, or basic steel, or automotive products. It should also be plausible that the United States could be cut off from supply, implying that there are few enough sellers, concentrated in a hostile or potentially inaccessible area. Second, if the supply cut-off test is passed, the question remains whether to protect the domestic industry or to stockpile. (1981, p. 397)

While stockpiling may make sense for some raw materials (platinum, chromium, and manganese), the manufacturing industries sometimes cited as candidates for protection (autos and steel) do not pass the first test. The reason is the extreme improbability of an effective supply cut-off in either industry, given the present dispersion of worldwide capacity.

A separate issue arises in Marina Whitman's case for temporary protection of Detroit. In our terms, Whitman offers a modernizer's rationale for the preservationist position. By the same token, Branson

questions whether "assembled autos are high on the list of skill and technology-intensive components of industry that are the future growth sector in the United States" (Branson 1981, pp. 400–401; Whitman 1981). In his view, then, neither defense nor growth potential provides a persuasive rationale for the quotas the U.S. would impose on Japan.

In "Targeted Industrial Policies: Theory and Evidence" (1983), Paul Krugman also criticizes the concept and feasibility of targeting industries for government support. The key tactical question is which industries to support; that is, what criteria should be used to select them? The paper lists popular and more technical criteria for picking industries to target. Krugman rejects the first set of guidelines but is ambivalent about the second. His reasoning is worth recounting.

Among the popular criteria for targeting, various writers have suggested the following types of industries for support:

(A) *High value-added per worker.* Magaziner and Reich (1982) propose accelerating the shift of labor and capital to high-value-added industries. The result, they believe, would be to raise productivity and incomes.

Krugman counters this proposal by pointing out that what makes some jobs high in value-added is a combination of acquired skills and large capital backups. Shifting capital to such sectors (i.e., with high capital-output and capital-labor ratios) when market signals do not warrant it would actually reduce output and especially job growth.

(B) *Linkage industries.* Other writers urge support for such basic industries as steel because steel is an input for many other industries (Elinor Hadley 1983). Krugman replies that only if there is market failure would there be a case for promoting home production of a widely used intermediate good. Otherwise the inputs should be purchased at home or abroad, whichever offers the lower price, as usual.

(C) *Future competitiveness.* A number of writers have made the infant-industry case that the capacity to earn future export earnings is a good test of whether an industry merits current support (John Diebold 1980; F. Gerard Adams 1983). One criticism here is that with sufficient help, some industries may indeed succeed in world markets—but still fail a cost-benefit test for the assistance. If so, "eventual competitiveness is not a useful guide to selecting targets" (Krugman, p. 132). The standard caveats for aiding infant industries might also be mentioned: the problem of picking the right industry, and that of turning off the aid once the industry is on its feet.

(D) *Fighting fire with fire.* Rohatyn and others say the U.S. must target industry assistance to counter foreign subsidies. In practice, and as the examples of wheat and steel illustrate, this is likely to lead to subsidies for industries that already suffer from excess capacity worldwide, not a promising approach.

On the other hand, Krugman adds, *some types of deviation from the competitive model may make targeting defensible,* though here the problem is one of adequate information for policy makers.

(E) *Duopoly with steep experience curves.* In the presence of learning by doing, and with only two serious competitors, say one American and one Japanese, the firm that can demonstrate its willingness to incur current losses to gain market share and move down its experience curve may be able to drive the other firm out of the world industry. A temporary government subsidy may then help the U.S. firm move down the curve, winning the market. The assumption here is that government would be more willing to underwrite temporary losses than the market would be.

(F) *External economies and R&D appropriability.* Where the full benefits of R&D are spread beyond the firm paying for the research, there is a textbook justification for government support of industrial research. But Krugman questions whether government could act competently and also whether firms do indeed underinvest in R&D (cf. Thurow 1980, pp. 94–95; Richard Nelson 1982; Bosworth 1983; Edwin Mansfield 1983).

(G) *Offsetting other government policies.* In general, where specific government policies have created inappropriate incentives, the corrective should be general, not industry specific. If, as seems likely, tax provisions combined with inflation to favor housing investment over plant and equipment during the 1970s, then the response should be tax reform, not industrial targeting.

In sum, "If we must have a targeted industrial policy, it would probably be best to target the high technology industries, which have both important dynamic scale economies [i.e., steep experience curves] and important externalities. But we have no assurance that this is actually the right policy" (p. 138).

2. The Problem in Practice: More Planning, More Politics

In an attack on the whole idea of industrial policy as a new task for government, Charles Schultze (chairman of the CEA in the Carter Administration) charges that such proposals would needlessly add a new layer of bureaucracy to the federal government (Schultze 1983). From a different perspective, Samuel Bowles, David M. Gordon, and Thomas E. Weisskopf share Schultze's unease as regards industrial policy in practice. They charge that Rohatyn's plan amounts to a kind of "corporatism" that would elevate the interests of business over those of consumers, labor, and others (Bowles et al. 1983, ch. 9).

Reich summarizes such misgivings in his comments on Rhode Island's defeated bond issue (1984, p. 32):

Americans don't like central planning, they don't like complicated plans, and they especially don't trust business-government-and-labor elites to do the planning. These biases are as populist as apple pie, running clear across the political spectrum and rooted deep in our political history.

The political lesson: A U.S. adjustment plan should be fashioned within the existing institutional framework, free from the kind of tripartite administrative apparatus used in Japan and Europe.

3. Evidence: What Decline?

Schultze's wide-ranging attack contends that industrial policy proposals rest on four premises:

- that the U.S. economy was deindustrialized in the 1970s,
- that MITI enabled Japan to avoid a similar fate,
- that government here is capable of picking winners, and
- that it could then politically impose its choices.

Schultze rejects all four premises as invalid. His reasoning on the latter two points parallels that of Krugman, while reflecting the administrative experience he had as head of the CEA. As for MITI, Schultze contends that it is as much a symptom as a cause of Japan's cultural capacity for pursuing a catch-up strategy. Finally, his rejection of deindustrialization reflects the arguments outlined in the body of this paper.

This review brings us into the mid-1980s, when the debate shifts toward the dollar's role—and to the question of whether a currency's depreciation is too great a price to pay for restored competitiveness (Thurow 1984).

REFERENCES

ABERNATHY, WILLIAM J.; CLARK, KIM B. AND KANTROW, ALAN M. *Industrial renaissance: Producing a competitive future for America.* NY: Basic Books, 1983.

ABRAMOVITZ, MOSES. "Rapid Growth Potential and Its Realization: The Experience of Capitalist Economies in the Postwar Period," in *Economic growth and resources.* Vol. 1. *The major issues.* Ed.: EDMOND MALINVAUD. NY: The Macmillan Press, Ltd., 1979, pp. 1–51.

_____. "Welfare Quandaries and Productivity Concerns," *Amer. Econ. Rev.,* Mar. 1981, *71*(1), pp. 1–17.

_____. "Notes on International Differences in Productivity Growth Rates," in *The political economy of growth.* Ed.: DENNIS MUELLER. New Haven: Yale U. Press, 1983, pp. 79–89.

ADAMS, F. GERARD. "Criteria for U.S. Industrial Policy Strategies," in F. GERARD ADAMS AND LAWRENCE R. KLEIN, 1983, pp. 393–420.

_____ AND KLEIN, LAWRENCE R. *Industrial policies for growth and competitiveness.* Lexington, MA: D. C. Heath, 1983.

ADAMS, JOHN. *International economics: A self-teaching introduction to the basic concepts.* 2nd ed. NY: St. Martin's Press, 1979.

ALDERFER, EVAN AND MICHL, H. E. *Economics of American industry.* NY: McGraw-Hill, 1942.

ALEXANDER GRANT & COMPANY. *The third study of general manufacturing business climates of the forty-eight contiguous states of America: 1981.* Chicago, 1982.

AMES, EDWARD AND ROSENBERG, NATHAN. "Changing Technological Leadership and Industrial Growth," *Econ. J.*, Mar. 1963, *73*(289), pp. 13–31.

BALASSA, BELA. "A Stages Approach to Comparative Advantage," in *Economic growth and resources.* Ed.: Irma Adelman. London: Macmillan, 1979, pp. 121–56.

BEENSTOCK, MICHAEL. *The world economy in transition.* London & Boston: Allen & Unwin, 1984.

BELL, DANIEL. *The coming of post-industrial society.* NY: Basic Books, 1973.

BELL, MICHAEL E. AND LANDE, PAUL S., eds. *Regional dimensions of industrial policy.* Lexington, MA: Lexington Books, 1982.

BERGSTEN, C. FRED. "Commentary," in FEDERAL RESERVE BANK OF KANSAS CITY, 1983, pp. 312–20.

BLACKABY, FRANK, ed. *De-industrialisation.* London: Heinemann Educational Books, 1979.

BLUESTONE, BARRY AND HARRISON, BENNETT. *The deindustrialization of America.* NY: Basic Books, 1982.

BOLLING, RICHARD AND BOWLES, JOHN. *America's competitive edge.* NY: McGraw-Hill, 1981.

BORTS, GEORGE AND STEIN, JEROME. *Economic growth in a free market.* NY: Columbia U. Press, 1964.

BOSWORTH, BARRY. "Capital Formation, Technology, and Economic Policy," in FEDERAL RESERVE BANK OF KANSAS CITY, 1983, pp. 231–59.

BOULDING, KENNETH. "The Ripening Society," *Technology Rev.*, June/July 1980, pp. 6–7.

BOWLES, SAMUEL; GORDON, DAVID M. AND WEISSKOPF, THOMAS E. *Beyond the waste land: A democratic alternative to economic decline.* Garden City, NY: Anchor Press/Doubleday, 1983.

BRANSON, WILLIAM H. "Trends in United States International Trade and Investment Since World War II," in *The American economy in transition.* Ed.: MARTIN FELDSTEIN. Chicago: U. of Chicago Press, 1980, pp. 183–257.

———. "Industrial Policy and U.S. International Trade." In MICHAEL L. WACHTER AND SUSAN M. WACHTER, 1981, pp. 378–408.

BRAUDEL, FERNAND. *Civilization and capitalism: 15th–18th century.* Vol. II. *The wheels of commerce.* Translated by Siân Reynolds. NY: Harper & Row, [French, 1979] 1982.

BRITTAN, SAMUEL. "How British Is the British Sickness?" *J. Law Econ.*, Oct. 1978, *21*(2), pp. 245–68.

BURNS, ARTHUR. *Production trends in the United States since 1870.* NY: NBER, 1934.

Business Week. The reindustrialization of America. NY: McGraw-Hill, 1982 (Based on a special issue of *Business Week*, 30 June 1980, pp. 55–146).

———. *America's restructured economy.* Special issue. 1 June 1981, pp. 55–100.

CARNOY, MARTIN; SHEARER, DEREK AND RUMBERGER, RUSSELL. *A new social contract: The economy and government after Reagan.* NY: Harper & Row, 1983.

CIPOLLA, CARLO M., ed. *The economic decline of empires.* London: Methuen, 1970.

Consumer Reports. "Five Small Japanese Imports." June 1984, pp. 327–33.

CORNWALL, JOHN. *Modern capitalism: Its growth and transformation.* NY: St. Martin's Press, 1977.

DAHRENDORF, RALF, ed. *Europe's economy in crisis.* NY: Holmes & Meier, [German: Trendwende, 1981] 1982.

DEAN, JAMES W. "Polyarchy and Economic Growth," in DENNIS MUELLER, ed., 1983, pp. 231–57.

DENISON, EDWARD F. "The Shift to Services and the Rate of Productivity Change," *Surv. Curr. Bus.*, Oct. 1973, *53*(10), pp. 20–35.

DIEBOLD, JOHN. *Industrial policy as an international issue.* NY: McGraw-Hill, 1980.

DORNBUSCH, RUDIGER; FISCHER, STANLEY AND SAMUELSON, PAUL. "Comparative Advantage, Trade, and Payments in a Ricardian Model with a Continuum of Goods," *Amer. Econ. Rev.*, Dec. 1977, *67*(5), pp. 823–39.

EADS, GEORGE C. "Commentary," in FEDERAL RESERVE BANK OF KANSAS CITY, 1983, pp. 157–67.

ECKSTEIN, OTTO; CATON, CHRISTOPHER; BRINNER, ROGER AND DUPREY, PETER. *The DRI report on U.S. manufacturing industries.* NY: McGraw-Hill, 1984.

ETZIONI, AMITAI. *An immodest agenda: Rebuilding America before the twenty-first century.* NY: New Press, 1983.

FEDERAL RESERVE BANK OF KANSAS CITY. *Industrial change and public policy: A symposium sponsored by the Federal Reserve Bank of Kansas City.* Kansas City, 1983.

FREEMAN, CHRISTOPHER; CLARK, JOHN AND SOETE, LUC. *Unemployment and technical innovation: A study of long waves and economic development.* Westport, CT: Greenwood Press, 1982.

FUCHS, VICTOR. "Economic Growth and the Rise of Service Employment," in *Towards an explanation of economic growth: Symposium 1980.* Ed.: HERBERT GIERSCH. Tübingen: J.C.B. Mohr, 1981, pp. 221–42.

FULMAN, DIANE. "Do Deficits Matter?" *Bank of Boston Economic Review*, Spring 1985.

GARREAU, JOEL. *The nine nations of North America.* NY: Houghton Mifflin, 1981.

GIERSCH, HERBERT. "Aspects of Growth, Structural Change, and Employment—A Schumpeterian Perspective," *Weltwirtsch. Archiv*, 1979, *115*(4), pp. 629–52.

GILPIN, ROBERT. *U.S. power and the multinational corporation.* NY: Basic Books, 1975.

———. *War and change in world politics.* Cambridge: Cambridge U. Press, 1981.

GOLD, BELA. "Industry Growth Patterns: Theory and Empirical Results," *J. Ind. Econ.*, Nov. 1964, *13*, pp. 53–73.

GORDON, DAVID M.; EDWARDS, RICHARD AND REICH, MICHAEL. *Segmented work, divided workers: The historical transformation of labor in the United States.* NY: Cambridge U. Press, 1982.

HADLEY, ELINOR M. "The Secret of Japan's Success," *Challenge*, May/June 1983, *26*(2), pp. 4–10.

HALE, DAVID. "U.S. as Debtor: A Threat to World Trade," *The New York Times,* 22 Sept. 1985.

HANSEN, ALVIN H. "Economic Progress and Declining Population Growth," *Amer. Econ. Rev.,* Mar. 1939, *29*(1), pp. 1–15.

HARBERGER, ARNOLD, ed. *World economic growth: Case studies of developed and developing nations.* San Francisco: ICS Press, 1984.

HEILBRONER, ROBERT L. "Does Capitalism Have a Future?" *The New York Times Magazine,* 15 Aug. 1982, pp. 20ff.

———— AND SINGER, AARON. *The economic transformation of America: 1600 to the present.* 2nd ed. NY: Harcourt Brace Jovanovich, 1984.

CAROL HEIM. "Decline and Renewal in Britain and the United States: The Role of Less Developed Areas Within Mature Economies." Unpub. 1984.

HEKMAN, JOHN. "Regions Don't Grow Old; Products Do," *The New York Times,* Nov. 4, 1979.

HIRSCH, SEEV. *Location of industry and international competitiveness.* NY: Oxford U. Press, 1967.

HOFFMANN, WALTHER G. *British industry, 1700–1950.* NY: Augustus M. Kelley, [1931] 1955.

HOOVER, EDGAR M. *The location of economic activity.* NY: McGraw-Hill, 1948.

JACOBS, JANE. *The economy of cities.* NY: Random House, 1969.

————. *Cities and the wealth of nations.* NY: Random House, 1984.

JOHNSON, CHALMERS, ed. *The industrial policy debate.* San Francisco: ICS Press, 1984.

KAHN, HERMAN. *World economic development: 1979 and beyond.* NY: Morrow Quill Paperbacks, 1979.

KALDOR, NICHOLAS. "Capitalism and Industrial Development: Some Lessons from Britain's Experience," *Cambridge J. Econ.,* June 1977, *1*(2), pp. 193–204.

KATONA, GEORGE AND STRUMPEL, BURKHARD. *A new economic era.* NY: Elsevier, 1978.

KINDLEBERGER, CHARLES P. *International economics.* Homewood, IL: Richard D. Irwin, 1953.

————. "Obsolescence and Technical Change," *Bull. Oxford Univ. Inst. Econ. Statist.,* Aug. 1961, *23,* pp. 281–97.

————. *Foreign trade and the national economy.* New Haven, CT: Yale U. Press, 1962.

————. *The New York Times,* letter, 1 Mar. 1973.

————. "An American Economic Climacteric?" *Challenge,* Jan./Feb. 1974, *16*(6), pp. 35–44.

————. "The Aging Economy," *Weltwirtsch. Archiv,* 1978, *114*(3), pp. 407–21.

————. "The Economic Aging of America," *Challenge,* Jan./Feb. 1980, *22*(6) pp. 48–49.

————. [review of Olson] *International Studies Quarterly,* 1983, 1:1.

KLEIN, BURTON. *Dynamic economics.* Cambridge: Harvard U. Press, 1977.

KLEIN, LAWRENCE R. "International Aspects of Industrial Policy," in MICHAEL L. WACHTER AND SUSAN M. WACHTER, 1981, pp. 361–77.

————. "Identifying the Effects of Structural Change," in FEDERAL RESERVE BANK OF KANSAS CITY, 1983, pp. 1–19.

KNEI-PAZ, BARUCH, ed. *The social and political thought of Leon Trotsky.* NY: Oxford U. Press (Clarendon Press), 1978.

KRAVIS, IRVING B. "Comparative Studies of National Incomes and Prices," *J. Econ. Lit.,* Mar. 1984, *22*(1), pp. 1–39.

————; HESTON, ALAN AND SUMMERS, ROBERT. "New Insights into the Structure of the World Economy," *Rev. Income Wealth,* Dec. 1981, *27*(4), pp. 339–55.

KRISTENSEN, THORKIL. *Development in rich and poor countries.* NY: Praeger, 1974.

KRUGMAN, PAUL R. "Targeted Industrial Policies: Theory and Evidence," in FEDERAL RESERVE BANK OF KANSAS CITY, 1983, pp. 123–55.

KURTH, JAMES. "The Political Consequences of the Product Cycle," *Int. Organ.,* 1979, *33*(1), pp. 1–34.

KUTTNER, ROBERT. *The economic illusion.* Boston: Houghton Mifflin, 1984.

KUZNETS, SIMON. *Secular movements in production and prices—Their nature and their bearing upon cyclical fluctuations.* Boston: Houghton Mifflin, 1930.

————. *Economic change—Selected essays in business cycles, national income, and economic growth.* NY: W. W. Norton, 1953.

————. *Six lectures on economic growth.* Glencoe, IL: The Free Press, 1959.

————. *Economic growth of nations: Total output and production structure.* Cambridge: Belknap Press of Harvard U. Press, 1971.

LAWRENCE, PAUL R. AND DYER, DAVIS. *Renewing American industry.* NY: The Free Press, 1983.

LAWRENCE, ROBERT Z. "Is Trade Deindustrializing America? A Medium Term Perspective," *Brookings Pap. Econ. Act.,* 1983:1, pp. 129–71.

————. *Can America compete?* Washington, DC: Brookings Institution, 1984.

LEECHOR, CHAD; KOHLI, HARINDAR S. AND HUR, SUJIN. *Structural changes in world industry: A quantitative analysis of recent developments.* Washington, DC: The World Bank, 1983.

LEWIS, W. ARTHUR. *The evolution of the international economic order.* Princeton, NJ: Princeton U. Press, 1978a.

————. *Growth and fluctuations 1879–1913.* London: George Allen & Unwin, 1978b.

LINDBECK, ASSAR. "Can the Rich Countries Adapt? Needs and Difficulties," *OECD Observer,* Jan. 1981, *108,* pp. 6–9.

MAGAZINER, IRA C. AND REICH, ROBERT B. *Minding America's business: The decline and rise of the American economy.* NY: Harcourt Brace Jovanovich, 1982.

MAGEE, STEPHEN P. *International trade.* Reading, MA: Addison-Wesley, 1980.

MANSFIELD, EDWIN. "Commentary," in FEDERAL RESERVE BANK OF KANSAS CITY, 1983, pp. 261–65.

MATTHEWS, R. C. O.; FEINSTEIN, C. H. AND ODLING-SMEE, J. C. *British economic growth, 1856–1973.* Stanford, CA: Stanford U. Press, 1982.

MCKENNA, REGIS. "Sustaining the Innovation Process in America," in CHALMERS JOHNSON, ed., 1984, pp. 133–55.

MENSCH, GERHARD. *Stalemate in technology—Innovations overcome the depression.* Cambridge, MA: Ballinger Pub. Co., 1979.

MUELLER, DENNIS, ed. *The political economy of growth.* New Haven and London: Yale U. Press, 1983.

NBER Digest. Abstract of Robert E. Lipsey and Irving B. Kravis, "The International Competitiveness of U.S. Firms." NBER Working Paper No. 1557, June 1985.

NELSON, RICHARD R., ed. *Government and technical progress: A cross-industry analysis.* NY: Pergamon Press, 1982.

The New York Times. "The Ailing Economy—Diagnoses and Prescriptions," Apr. 4, 1982.

NORDHAUS, WILLIAM D. AND TOBIN, JAMES. "Is Growth Obsolete?" in *Economic research: Retrospect and prospect—economic growth.* Ed.: ROBERT J. GORDON. NY: NBER, 1972, pp. 1–80.

NORMAN, COLIN. *Microelectronics at work: Productivity and jobs in the world economy.* Washington, DC: Worldwatch Institute, 1980.

NORTON, BRUCE. "Marxian Stagnation and Long Wave Theories: A Review." Unpub., 1984.

NORTON, R. D. *City life-cycles and American urban policy.* NY: Academic Press, 1979.

——. "Regional Life-Cycles and U.S. Industrial Rejuvenation," in *Towards an explanation of economic growth. Symposium 1980.* Ed.: HERBERT GIERSCH. Tübingen: J.C.B. Mohr, 1981, pp. 253–80.

——. "Deindustrialization and SMSA Job Growth in the 1970s." Unpub., 1984.

—— AND REES, JOHN. "The Product Cycle and the Spatial Decentralization of American Manufacturing," *Reg. Stud.,* Aug. 1979, *13*(2), pp. 141–51.

OLSON, MANCUR. *The causes and quality of southern growth.* Research Triangle Park, NC: Southern Growth Policies Board, 1977.

——. *The rise and decline of nations: Economic growth, stagflation, and social rigidities.* New Haven: Yale U. Press, 1982.

——. "The South Will Fall Again: The South as Leader and Laggard in Economic Growth," *Southern Econ. J.,* Apr. 1983, *49*(4), pp. 917–32.

ORGANIZATION FOR ECONOMIC COOPERATION AND DEVELOPMENT (OECD). *Technical change and economic policy: Science and technology in the new economic and social context.* Paris: OECD, 1980.

PEIRCE, NEIL R. AND HAGSTROM, JERRY. *The book of America: Inside 50 states today.* NY: W. W. Norton, 1983.

PIORE, MICHAEL. "American Labor and the Industrial Crisis," *Challenge,* Mar./Apr. 1982, *25*(1), pp 5–11.

—— AND SABEL, CHARLES. *The second industrial divide.* NY: Basic Books, 1984.

PLESSZ, N. "Western Europe," in *The political economy of new and old industrial countries.* Ed.:

CHRISTOPHER SAUNDERS. London: Butterworth & Co., Ltd., 1981, pp. 217–39.

REICH, ROBERT B. "Industrial Policy: Ten Concrete, Practical Steps to Building a Dynamic, Growing and Fair American Economy," *The New Republic,* Mar. 31, 1982, *186,* pp. 28–31.

——. *The next American frontier.* NY: Penguin Books, 1983.

——. "Small State, Big Lesson," *The Boston Observer,* July 1984, *3*(7), p. 32.

ROHATYN, FELIX. *The twenty-year century: Essays on economics and public finance.* NY: Random House, 1983.

ROSENBERG, NATHAN. "History and Perspective," in *Regional conflict and national policy.* Ed.: KENT PRICE. Washington, DC: Resources for the Future, 1982a, pp. 18–33.

——. "The International Transfer of Technology: Implications for the Industrialized Countries" in *Inside the black box: Technology and economics.* NY: Cambridge U. Press, 1982b, pp. 245–79.

——. "U.S. Technological Leadership and Foreign Competition: De Te Fabula Narratur?" in *Inside the black box: Technology and economics.* NY: Cambridge U. Press, 1982c, pp. 280–91.

ROSTOW, WALT WHITMAN. *The stages of economic growth.* Cambridge, England: Cambridge U. Press, 1960.

——. *Why the poor get richer and the rich slow down: Essays in the Marshallian long period.* Austin: U. of Texas Press, 1980.

ROTHSCHILD, EMMA. *Paradise lost: The decline of the autoindustrial age.* NY: Random House, 1973.

ROY, A. D. "Labor Productivity in 1980: An International Comparison," *Nat. Inst. Econ. Rev.,* Aug. 1982, *101,* pp. 26–37.

SCHONBERGER, RICHARD J. *Japanese manufacturing techniques: Nine hidden lessons in simplicity.* NY: The Free Press, 1982.

SCHULTZE, CHARLES L. "Industrial Policy: A Dissent," *Brookings Review,* Fall 1983, *2*(1), pp. 3–12.

SCHUMPETER, JOSEPH. *Business cycles: A theoretical, historical and statistical analysis of the capitalist process.* Two vols. NY: McGraw-Hill, 1939.

——. *Capitalism, socialism, and democracy.* NY: Harper & Row, [1942] 1962.

SCITOVSKY, TIBOR. "Can Capitalism Survive? An Old Question in a New Setting," *Amer. Econ. Rev.,* May 1980, *70*(2), pp. 1–9.

SCOTT, BRUCE. "U.S. Competitiveness: Concepts, Performance, and Implications," in *U.S. competitiveness in the world economy.* Eds.: BRUCE R. SCOTT AND GEORGE C. LODGE. Boston: Harvard Business School Press, 1985, pp. 13–70.

SHEPHERD, WILLIAM G. *The economics of industrial organization.* Englewood Cliffs, NJ: Prentice-Hall, 1979.

SILVER, MORRIS. *Affluence, altruism, and atrophy.* NY: NYU Press, 1980.

SINGH, AJIT. "UK Industry and the World Economy: A Case of De-industrialisation?" *Cambridge J. Econ.,* Mar. 1977, *1*(2), pp. 113–36.

SOLO, ROBERT. "Industrial Policy," *J. Econ. Issues,* Sept. 1984, *18*(3), pp. 697–714.

STEINDL, JOSEF. *Maturity and stagnation in American capitalism.* Oxford: Basil Blackwell, 1952.

STEVENS, BENJAMIN H. AND TREYZ, GEORGE I. "Trends in Regional Industrial Diversification and Self-Sufficiency and Their Implications for Growth." Processed. 1983.

SUMMERS, LAWRENCE. "Commentary," in FEDERAL RESERVE BANK OF KANSAS CITY, 1983, pp. 79–83.

SVENNILSON, INGVAR. *Growth and stagnation in the European economy.* Geneva: UN Economic Commission for Europe, 1954.

TAYLOR, GEORGE ROGERS. *The Turner thesis concerning the role of the frontier in American history.* Boston: D.C. Heath, 1949.

DI TELLA, GUIDO. "The Economics of the Frontier," in *Economics in the long view.* Vol. 1. Eds.: CHARLES P. KINDLEBERGER AND GUIDO DI TELLA. NY: NYU Press, 1982, pp. 210–27.

THUROW, LESTER. *The zero-sum society.* NY: Basic Books, 1980.

———. "Getting Serious About Tax Reform," *The Atlantic,* Mar. 1981, *247,* pp. 68–72.

———. "Losing the Economic Race," *New York Review of Books,* Sept. 27, 1984, pp. 29–31.

U.S. CONGRESS, OFFICE OF TECHNOLOGY ASSESSMENT. *U.S. industrial competitiveness: A comparison of steel, electronics, and automobiles.* Washington, DC: U.S. GPO, 1981.

U.S. DEPARTMENT OF COMMERCE, BUREAU OF THE CENSUS. *Current population reports.* Series P-25.

U.S. DEPARTMENT OF COMMERCE, BUREAU OF ECONOMIC ANALYSIS. *Long term economic growth, 1860–1970.* Washington, DC: U.S. GPO, 1973.

U.S. DEPARTMENT OF LABOR, BUREAU OF LABOR STATISTICS. *Geographic profile of employment and unemployment: 1980.* Washington, DC: U.S. GPO, 1982.

———. *Employment and earnings.* Washington, DC: U.S. GPO, various issues.

U.S. PRESIDENT'S COMMISSION ON INDUSTRIAL COMPETITIVENESS. *Global competition: The new reality.* Washington, DC: U.S. GPO, 1985.

VAN DUIJN, J. J. *The long wave in economic life.* London: George Allen & Unwin, 1983.

VEBLEN, THORSTEIN. *Imperial Germany and the industrial revolution.* NY: Viking Press, [1915] 1939.

VERNON, RAYMOND. "International Investment and International Trade in the Product Cycle," *Quart. J. Econ.,* May 1966, *80,* pp. 190–207.

WACHTER, MICHAEL L. AND WACHTER, SUSAN M., eds. *Toward a new U.S. industrial policy?* Philadelphia: U. of Pennsylvania Press, 1981.

WEIDENBAUM, MURRAY AND ATHEY, MICHAEL J. "What Is the Rust Belt's Problem?" in CHALMERS JOHNSON, ed., 1984, pp. 117–32.

WEIL, FRANK A. "The U.S. Needs an Industrial Policy," *Fortune,* March 24, 1980, *101,* pp. 149–52.

WHEAT, LEONARD. *Regional growth and industrial location: An empirical viewpoint.* Lexington, MA: D.C. Heath, 1973.

WHITMAN, MARINA V. N. "International Trade and Investment: Two Perspectives." Graham Memorial Lecture, Princeton U., Princeton, NJ, Mar. 1981.

WILLIAMS, ERNEST EDWIN. *Made in Germany.* London: W. Heinemann, 1896.

WOLF, JULIUS. *Die Volkswirtschaft der Gegenwart und Zukunft.* Leipzig: A. Deichertsche Verlags., 1912.

ZYSMAN, JOHN AND TYSON, LAURA, eds. *American industry in international competition: Government policies and corporate strategies.* Ithaca: Cornell U. Press, 1983.

Price and Wage Controls in Four Wartime Periods

HUGH ROCKOFF

The debate over wage and price controls has taken a highly stylized form. Advocates of controls stress the direct effect on the obvious problem, inflation, whereas critics stress the side effects. This paper measures and compares the effects of controls during the four periods when controls have been used in the United States in the twentieth century. Although tentative conclusions are drawn concerning the price effects, the size of the administrative bureaucracies, and so forth, the clearest lesson, as usual, is that the issue warrants further investigation by economic historians because it is important, and because the historical record is surprisingly rich.

COMPREHENSIVE wage and price controls have been used four times in this century to stem inflation: during the two World Wars, during the Korean War, and toward the end of the Vietnam War. Both the advocates and critics of controls have made extensive claims about how well controls worked on these occasions, but with only a few exceptions economic historians have ignored these episodes. In this paper I hope to generate additional interest in wartime controls by showing that several of the crucial issues will yield to historical research. I concentrate primarily on the issues raised by the critics of wartime controls. I do so because the case for controls, as it is usually presented, is rather simple. Advocates of controls have tended to argue simply that price increases can be moderated by the force of law and that the test of controls is the stability of an appropriately chosen index. Table 1 shows that judged by this criterion controls were a success, at least in the first three cases. In the two World Wars and in the Korean War measured inflation was reduced from the extremely high rates that prevailed in the period immediately preceding the initiation of controls.

It is not self-evident that controls passed such a test, but that they did so

Journal of Economic History, Vol. XLI, No. 2 (June 1981). © The Economic History Association. All rights reserved. ISSN 0022-0507.

The author is Associate Professor of Economics at Rutgers College, New Brunswick, New Jersey 08903. He would like to thank Michael Edelstein, Stanley Engerman, Geoffrey Mills, Maury Randall, Joe Reid Jr., and the participants in a seminar at Virginia Polytechnic Institute, and a referee from this JOURNAL for helpful comments on an earlier version, and Robert Gallman and Louis Galambos for helpful comments on a longer, related manuscript. The usual caveat applies. He would also like to thank the Rutgers University Bureau of Economic Research for financial assistance. The similarity between the title and that of Milton Friedman's "Prices, Income and Monetary Changes in Three Wartime Periods," *American Economic Review,* 42 (May 1952), 612–25 is deliberate. As he pointed out, ignoring wartime periods because they are unusual is a mistake. The extreme changes that mark wartime periods test economic ideas in a way that the smaller and smoother changes that ordinarily characterize peacetime do not.

TABLE 1

INFLATION IN FOUR PERIODS OF WARTIME CONTROLS

Period[b]	Annual Rate of Inflation[a]		
	Six Months Before Controls	During Controls	Six Months After Controls
World War I (8/17–11/18)	34.7	7.1	−1.0
World War II (4/42–6/46)	10.3	3.5	28.0
Korea (1/51–2/53)	10.8	2.1	2.8
Vietnam (8/71–4/74)	4.6	6.2	12.1

[a] The consumer price index is used, except for World War I when the wholesale price index is used because the former is not available on a monthly basis.

[b] Dates when controls were imposed and removed are shown in parentheses. In some cases the dating is somewhat arbitrary. In World War II, for example, selective controls had been imposed before the "freeze" of April 1942.

Sources: The consumer price index is from various issues of the *Monthly Labor Review.* Wholesale Prices for World War I are from George F. Warren and Frank A. Pearson, *Prices* (New York, 1933), p. 13.

is not surprising. Critics of controls, on the other hand, have called attention to a number of indirect effects that are considered separately below. The first section examines the claim that controls only postponed inflation. The second examines the claim that controls required "huge bureaucracies" to administer them. The third examines the claim that controls reduced aggregate economic efficiency, and the fourth examines the claim that controls created an extensive black market. Finally, the last section recapitulates the main findings. Thus, the first four sections describe the impact of controls on what might be thought of as the arguments in a societal objective function. Clarifying the form of that function, and hence a definitive weighing up of the costs and benefits of controls, is beyond the reach of economic history; it lies within the realm of ethics. Clarifying the impact of controls on the arguments of that function, however, can lead to agreement by those historians who share a common set of values.

Generally, I have not cited sources for specific claims about controls. My intention has been to deal with a set of influential historical claims that only occasionally filter through to academic discussions. Also I have confined myself primarily to quantitative evidence, not because there is not much to be learned from an examination of qualitative evidence, but rather because the most important reason for the imprecise and exaggerated nature of the debate over controls has been the tendency to make quantitative claims on the basis of anecdotal evidence.

POSTPONEMENT OF INFLATION

Both Keynesian and monetarist models could serve as bases for the assertion that controls only suppress inflation, but the most careful statement has been from the standpoint of the monetarist model. I therefore will confine my discussion to this framework, and even more narrowly to a significant weakness in the monetarist argument. The argument that the price level will eventually return to an equilibrium dictated by the stock of money once controls are removed is not a new one. Attempts were made to control prices during the Revolutionary War, and John Adams in a letter to Abigail stated the monetarist case succinctly:

> The attempt of New England to regulate prices is extremely popular in Congress, who will recommend an imitation of it to the other States: For my own Part I expect only a partial and a temporary Relief from it. And I fear that, after a Time, the Evils will break out with greater Violence. The Water will flow with greater Rapidity for having been dammed up for a Time. The only radical Cure will be to stop the emission of more Paper, and to draw in some that is already out, and devise Means effectually to support the credit of the Rest.[1]

The best modern statements of the monetarist case appear in Milton Friedman's paper "Prices, Income, and Monetary Changes in Three Wartime Periods," and in Chapter 10 of Friedman and Anna Schwartz's *A Monetary History of the United States, 1867–1960.* Indeed, the difference between Adams on the one hand, and Friedman and Schwartz on the other, is not so much on the theoretical side, as on the empirical. Friedman and Schwartz are able to provide strong empirical support for their argument by bringing their important monetary series to bear.

The full logic underlying the monetarist case can be stated simply. The increase in prices between a pre-control equilibrium and a post-control equilibrium will be determined by three factors: the increase in the money supply, the increase in real income, and the increase in velocity. None of these, runs the monetarist argument, will be influenced by the temporary imposition of controls. The increase in the money supply is at the discretion of the monetary authority, the increase in real income will be determined by the stocks of real resources available to the economy, and the increase in velocity will be determined by such things as the changes in real income and interest rates or other determinants of the demand for money between the uncontrolled equilibria. Thus, the long-run increase of prices is independent of any short-term suppression. Price increases suppressed during the war would contribute to a post war bulge in inflation of the sort that can be seen after World War II in Table 1.

The evidence that Friedman presents involves comparisons among the

---

[1] L. H. Butterfield, ed., *Adams Family Correspondence,* vol. 2 (Cambridge, MA, 1963), p. 153.

Civil War, World War I, and World War II. The ratio of wholesale prices
at the postwar peak to prices at the outbreak of the war was 2.32 in the
Civil War, 2.32 in World War I, and 2.13 in World War II. Thus, a theory
that relies solely on the existence of controls to explain price performance
could predict the somewhat better performance in World War II than in
World War I, since controls were tighter in the latter war. But it could not
predict the common magnitude of the price increases in the Civil War and
World War I, since controls were used in the latter war but were absent in
the former. The absence of data on real income prevented Friedman from
applying the monetary theory to the Civil War. But a comparison of
World War I and World War II could be made. Controls, if they were to
have an effect, would have had to reduce velocity permanently. But, although they may have had a strong effect during World War II, by the
time of the postwar price peak their effect had disappeared. The ratio of
velocity at the price peak to velocity at the outbreak of the war was 1.16 in
World War I and 1.14 in World War II. Thus, velocity and—implicitly—
controls could not explain the superior price performance in World War
II. On the other hand, the ratio of money per unit of real output at the
price peak to money per unit of real output at the outbreak of war was
1.98 in World War I and 1.86 in World War II. Monetary factors could
explain the superior performance in World War II. The conclusion then,
to quote Friedman, is that "direct controls can be rejected as a factor affecting the ultimate magnitude of the price rise."[2]

The fly in the ointment here is that if controls reduce velocity, even
temporarily, they will reduce the total amount of money the government
needs to create to capture a given volume of real resources. Intuitively, the
explanation for this is that velocity is an index of how rapidly people are
spending the existing stocks of money. It follows that the more rapidly
money is spent in the private sector, the more money government must
print to compete effectively for resources. Thus, the total price rise determined by the ratio of money to real output will be less with temporary
controls than it would be in their absence, even if the comparison is made
between the uncontrolled equilibria. To pursue this point further we need
to examine whether, in fact, controls reduced velocity, and whether the reduction was a substantial one.

Ordinarily, determining whether a particular policy influenced velocity
would require that inferences be made from an econometric model. But
since it is possible to construct good proxies for velocity on a monthly
basis, and since across-the-board controls typically came in a sudden and
dramatic way, it is possible to get a nearly experimental view of the economy's initial reaction to the imposition of controls. This is shown in Table
2, which gives the rate of change of velocity from year earlier dates,
monthly, for the six months before and the six months after the imposi-

[2] Milton Friedman, "Prices, Income, and Monetary Changes," p. 617.

TABLE 2

RATE OF CHANGE OF VELOCITY BEFORE AND AFTER IMPOSITION OF ACROSS-THE-
BROAD CONTROLS, FOUR WARTIME PERIODS

(percent per year, from year earlier dates)

Month[a]	World War I	World War II	Korean War	Vietnam War
−6	6.6	10.0	4.9	−3.5
−5	9.6	10.8	5.5	−4.3
−4	22.4	13.7	6.2	−6.3
−3	28.8	13.0	9.6	−5.8
−2	27.3	13.7	9.5	−3.8
−1	28.3	14.9	11.2	−5.1
0	23.0	14.7	9.2	−4.5
+1	21.5	14.0	8.6	−4.4
+2	19.7	12.3	7.8	−3.6
+3	12.5	12.4	11.9	−3.0
+4	6.3	10.3	12.6	−2.5
+5	−2.3	9.8	11.2	−2.7
+6	3.9	9.1	9.8	−1.1

[a] The "zero" month is the one in which across-the-board controls were imposed. See Table 1 for the dates.

Sources and Methods: World War I: The proxy for velocity change was the rate of change of whole-sale prices (Paul Willard Garrett, *Government Control Over Prices* [Washington, D.C., 1920], pp. 427–28) plus the rate of change of industrial production (Geoffrey H. Moore, *Production of Industrial Materials in World Wars I and II,* NBER Occasional Paper 18 [New York, 1944], p. 9) less the rate of change of M_2 (Milton Friedman and Anna J. Schwartz, *Monetary Statistics of the United States* [New York, 1970], Table 2, col. 9). Later wars: The proxy was the rate of change of personal income (various issues of the *Survey of Current Business*) less the rate of change of M_2 (Friedman and Schwartz, *Monetary Statistics,* and various issues of the *Federal Reserve Bulletin*).

tion of controls. It is in effect a fever chart of the monetary system. In the two World Wars velocity was rising prior to controls and falling afterwards. Clearly, across-the-board controls appear to have calmed the inflationary fever in these two cases. In the Korean War, however, although controls arrested the acceleration of velocity, they do not seem to have produced an actual decline. In the Vietnam War little impact can be detected; if anything, velocity fell at a slower rate after controls were imposed.

Timing evidence alone, of course, cannot prove that controls were the cause of the coincident changes in velocity. But there are three reasons for thinking that controls were in fact the cause of the abatement of increases in velocity. First, the scenario makes sense. Velocity undoubtedly is a function of the expected rate of inflation. If in the early days of a war people expected high rates of inflation (as they would if they believed that heavy government spending would cause inflation), we would expect a rapid rise in velocity. If the government then declared that it would preserve purchasing power through a system of wage and price controls, and if people trusted their government, we would expect a sharp decline in velocity. This is what we observe in the first two cases.

Second, the circumstances surrounding the imposition of controls strongly suggest that they were imposed as a last resort because nothing else seemed to provide any hope of slowing inflation. In World War I, I have dated the imposition of controls (the "zero hour" in Table 2) as August 1917 when the Lever Food and Fuel Act was passed. This act clearly was a response to rising consumer prices, and Wilson's appointment of the widely respected Herbert Hoover to administer retail margins on food prices was an attempt to generate maximum public confidence in the program. There does not seem to have been any other event that could account for the sudden change in velocity. The imposition of across-the-board controls in World War II was dated from the General Maximum Price Regulation issued in April 1942. This regulation was a response to the failure of selective controls to contain inflation. Friedman and Schwartz acknowledge that controls may have pushed velocity toward the level reached in 1940; velocity and prices had been relatively stable from 1938 to 1940. They argue, however, that controls could not explain the decline below that level, or even all of the fall to it, because velocity probably had not adjusted fully to inflation by 1942. Their first point can be accepted, but their second point appears dubious. It is based on the observation that in peacetime the adjustment of velocity to inflation appears to have been "slow and tardy."

This may be because in peacetime moneyholders have few additional pieces of information from which to project rates of inflation. In wartime they are likely to be aware of the massive government deficits and looming shortages that presage inflation. Imposition of controls during the Korean War came in January 1951. Here the case is not as clear, since a variety of measures were adopted at this time to prevent inflation. Friedman and Schwartz point to the Treasury-Federal Reserve Accord of March 1951 as a factor that might have altered inflationary expectations.[3] Is it more likely, however, that the public's expectations were altered by its understanding of the implications of a shift in the means by which monetary policy was conducted, or by the freezing of prices throughout the economy? Finally, across-the-board controls were imposed by President Nixon in August 1971. This use of controls left the smallest imprint on velocity. This would be consistent if these controls were regarded as a temporary election-year ploy, rather than a serious attempt to stabilize the long-run rate of inflation.

Third, we can illuminate part of the chain connecting the imposition of controls with velocity by using public opinion polls. This form of evidence is available for World War II and later years. Although it must be used judiciously, it provides a unique view of the reaction to controls. It is clear, first of all, that in World War II there was a dramatic reduction in

---

[3] The discussions of velocity by Friedman and Schwartz are in *A Monetary History of the United States, 1867–1960* (Princeton, 1963), p. 218 (WW I), p. 559 (WW II), and p. 598 (Korean War).

expected inflation at the time when across-the-board controls were imposed. In January 1942 a National Opinion Research Center survey showed that 70 percent of the public expected "prices on most things" would be higher "next year"; by August, after controls, this percentage had fallen to 55. A Gallup poll showed a similar change. The polls, moreover, strongly suggest that controls accounted for the change in expected inflation. In September 1942 a National Opinion Research Center survey showed that 65 percent of the public believed that government would be able to control prices, and a *Fortune* survey of business executives, also reported in September, showed that 33.6 percent thought that price ceilings would prevent any increases, while another 50.1 percent felt that increases could be held under 20 percent. A poll taken by the National Opinion Research Center in December 1943 is even more to the point. Seventy percent of the public said they were better off under controls, and most of those who believed this (about one half of the total sample) thought that controls kept prices down. These results, it should be noted, also show that it is unlikely that so much economic activity moved underground when controls were initiated that the official statistics immediately became misleading. By way of contrast, the polls show that other measures that economists might think would reduce inflation did not appear to be potent anti-inflation weapons to the public. In June 1944, for example, a National Opinion Research Center poll showed that only 19 percent of the public thought that high wartime taxes decreased prices, whereas 45 percent thought they had the opposite effect.

During the Asian wars, however, the public reacted skeptically to the imposition of controls, a fact consistent with the "fever charts" in Table 2. In March 1951, three months after the imposition of controls, a Gallup poll showed that 65 percent of the public expected prices to be higher six months later. And, by June 1951, only 31 percent of the public was willing to say that controls had worked well. It was similar during the Vietnamese War. A Gallup poll taken in October 1971, just two months after the freeze, showed that 63 percent of the public expected higher prices six months later; by January 1972 this percentage had risen to 72. The Harris poll asked a more direct question immediately after the freeze: Will the new economic policy keep inflation in check? Only 46 percent answered yes, 29 percent answered no, and 25 percent were uncertain.[4]

In summary, the principle of Occam's Razor suggests that until a convincing alternative explanation for the coincidence of the imposition of controls and the peaks in the rate of growth of velocity can be found, we should adopt the hypothesis that controls were the causative factor.

[4] For World War II the polls cited are from Hadley Cantril, *Public Opinion: 1935-1946* (Princeton, 1946), pp. 665, 655, 659, and 669. For the Korean War the polls cited are from George H. Gallup, *The Gallup Poll: 1949-1958* vol. 2 (New York, 1972), pp. 974, 992. For the Vietnamese War the polls cited are from Gallup, *The Gallup Poll: 1949-1958*, vol. 3, p. 2328; Gallup, *The Gallup Poll: Public Opinion 1972-1977*, vol. 1 (Wilmington, DE, 1978), p. 6; and Louis Harris and Associates, Inc., *The Harris Survey Yearbook of Public Opinion, 1971* (New York, 1975), p. 190.

A model of wartime finance is needed to estimate the potential magnitude of the long-run effect of controls on the price level.[5] First, to see the effect of velocity on the amount of money created we can examine the identity

$$\left(\frac{\Delta M}{M}\right)_i = \left(\frac{\Delta M}{Y}\right)_i V_i, \tag{1}$$

where ΔM_i is the change in the stock of money in year i, Y is nominal income, and V is velocity as ordinarily defined. This identity is obvious when it is remembered that the traditional quantity theory of money is written as

$$MV = Y \tag{2}$$

and hence, that velocity is simply defined as the ratio of nominal income to money. If controls reduce expected inflation and hence velocity, they will reduce $(\Delta M/M)$ provided $(\Delta M/Y)$ is determined by an independent set of forces. To examine the latter point in greater detail, we can write the identity

$$\left(\frac{\Delta M}{Y}\right)_i = \left(\frac{W}{Y}\right)_i \left(\frac{\Delta H}{W}\right)_i \left(\frac{\Delta M}{\Delta H}\right)_i, \tag{3}$$

where W is what the government intends to spend on the war effort and civilian services, and ΔH is the increase in high-powered money. The fraction of nominal income allocated to the war effort, $(W/Y)_i$, was determined, at least in the major wars, by military considerations. The fraction of government spending financed by creating high-powered money, $(\Delta H/W)_i$, is less clearly independent. Without controls, the government might have decided to reduce $(\Delta H/W)_i$, and rely on taxes or borrowing. In an analysis of one policy, however, it is appropriate to regard other policies, at least initially, as fixed. Moreover, given the difficulty the Roosevelt administration encountered in trying to raise taxes during World War II,[6] and given also the attempt to finance the war in Vietnam without tax increases, it is by no means clear that taxes would have been increased in the absence of controls. The ratio $(\Delta M/\Delta H)_i$ can be regarded as determined largely by the habits of the banking system and the public. By creating expectations of price stability, controls, if they had any effect, would tend to raise the banking system's reserve-deposit ratio and the public's currency-deposit ratio. Both effects would tend to reduce $(\Delta M/\Delta H)_i$. Thus, the ratio $(\Delta M/Y)_i$ was largely independent of controls, and if anything might have been reduced by them. Holding $(\Delta M/Y)_i$ constant in

[5] This model is implicit in some of the calculations made by Friedman, "Prices, Income, and Monetary Changes."

[6] Roland Young, *Congressional Politics in the Second World War* (New York, 1956), ch. 5.

the calculations below leads to an underestimation of the long-run impact of controls.

Equation (1) can be used to calculate what the increase in the money stock would have been if controls had not been imposed. To make this calculation, assume that in the absence of controls velocity would have continued to increase annually at the rate it was increasing when controls were imposed but that ($\Delta M/Y$) would have been the same. This gives the following results. In World War I, the actual ratio of the money stock in 1919 to the money stock in 1916 was 1.49, but had the increase in velocity not been arrested, the ratio would have been 1.60. In the World War II period, the actual ratio of 1946 to 1940 was 2.51; had the increase in velocity not been arrested the ratio would have been considerably higher, 3.75. The same calculation cannot be carried out for the Asian wars because the arrest of velocity is problematical, as is the assumption that the increase in high-powered money was determined predominantly by the exigencies of war. What the calculations do show is that accepting the general framework of the monetarist analysis leads to the conclusion that during the World Wars the temporary imposition of controls reduced the amount of money created and thus had a more than temporary impact on the rate of inflation. In the case of the Asian wars, the monetarist claim is on firmer ground since the impact on velocity is less clear.

SIZE OF THE BUREAUCRACY

The argument examined in the preceding section is concerned with what happened after controls were removed, but the critics also claim that controls were costly even while they were in place. The most obvious cost is the "huge bureaucracy" needed to administer controls. Behind this concern lies an important vision of the role of prices in a market economy. If the market is regarded as a kind of giant computer that amasses and processes information to produce an array of efficient prices, then it is clear that the bureaucracy that seeks to produce a similar set of relative prices would have to make use of an enormous volume of resources.[7]

To interpret this claim one must have some standard with which to compare the wartime bureaucracies. Table 3, which shows the size of the bureaucracies administering controls in each war, uses the postal service as a basis of comparison. The postal service is the largest civilian bureaucracy. It is one of the few, moreover, for which nearly everyone has an in-

---

[7] This conception of the market, and the necessity for central planners to imitate its function, was the basis for the criticism of central planning made by Hayek, Mises, and others. See F. A. von Hayek, *Collectivist Economic Planning* (London, 1935); Ludwig von Mises, *Bureaucracy* (New Haven, 1944); and "The Defenses of Socialist Planning" in B. Lippincott, ed., *On the Economic Theory of Socialism* (Minneapolis, 1938).

TABLE 3
SIZE OF THE BUREAUCRACIES THAT ADMINISTERED WAGE AND PRICE CONTROLS IN FOUR WARTIME PERIODS

Period (fiscal years)	(1) Expenditures by the Agency with Primary Responsibility[a] (million dollars)	(2) Expenditures by Both Primary and Related Agencies[b] (million dollars)	(3) Expenditures by the Postal Service (million dollars)	(4) Column (1) Divided by Column (3) (percent)	(5) Column (2) Divided by Column (3) (percent)
World War I					
1918	5.3	n.a.	324.8	1.6	n.a.
1919	17.6	20.6	362.5	4.9	5.7
World War II					
1942	4.5	5.9	874.0	.5	.7
1943	111.0	152.8	952.5	11.6	15.9
1944	171.4	375.6	1,069.0	15.9	34.9
1945	183.5	389.1	1,145.0	15.9	33.8
1946	156.1	247.1	1,353.7	11.4	18.0
Korean War					
1951	91.0	97.5	2,341.4	3.9	4.2
1952	64.4	71.2	2,666.9	2.4	2.7
1953	1.5	2.0	2,742.1	.1	.1
Vietnam War					
Phase 2	n.a.	107.6	9,710.5	n.a.	1.1
Phase 3	n.a.	78.4	9,926.0	n.a.	.8
Phase 4	n.a.	99.9	11,295.0	n.a.	.9

[a] The primary agencies were: World War I, Food and Fuel Administrations; World War II, the Office of Price Administration; Korean War, Economic Stabilization Agency; Vietnam War, Price Commission.
[b] Related agencies were other agencies that played important roles in controlling prices or allocating resources such as the various boards that set wages and allocated supplies.
Sources: Control Agencies. World War I: U.S. Treasury, *Annual Report 1919*, pp. 191, 194–95. World War II and the Korean War: U.S. Treasury, *Combined Statement of Receipts, Expenditures and Balances of the United States Government*, passim. Vietnam War: John T. Dunlop, "Statement Before the Subcommittee on Production and Stabilization of the Senate Banking, Housing and Urban Affairs Committee on the Economic Stabilization Act" (Washington, D.C., 1974), Appendix O, p. A-105. Some figures are on a check-issued basis, whereas others are on a liability-incurred basis. Postal Service: U.S. Bureau of the Census, *Historical Statistics of the United States, Colonial Times to 1957* (Washington, D.C., 1960), series R141, p. 496; Vietnam War: *Statistical Abstract of the United States: 1979* (Washington, D.C., 1979), col. 3, p. 578.

tuitive grasp of size and ubiquity. Column (1) of the table shows the expenditures of only those agencies identified in the public mind with price control, such as the Office of Price Administration in World War II. Column (2) attempts to add the expenditures of all of those additional agencies that performed price-setting or rationing functions ordinarily performed by the price system. In World War II this column includes the expenditures of such agencies as the War Production Board and the Petroleum Administrator for War. The conclusion I would draw from the table is that although the bureaucracy required was indeed a large one, amounting to nearly 35 percent of the postal service in World War II, its cost was bearable. Would anyone seriously contend that an expansion of the postal system by this percentage over a period of several years would be an unreasonable price to pay for temporary price stability and some reduction of long-term inflation?

This finding is subject to two potential qualifications. The first is that during the major wars the administration of controls was greatly aided by volunteers whose services are not included in the government expenditures recorded above. World War II ration boards are the most familiar examples. This qualification, however, turns out to be relatively unimportant. For World War II a survey of the hours worked by volunteers is available. This survey, moreover, probably overstates hours worked because of the natural human tendency to overstate one's sacrifices for others. The survey shows that in the month preceding July 23, 1945, approximately 107,806 volunteers for the Office of Price Administration worked an estimated 1,067,812 hours.[8] Allowing 160 hours per month per full-time equivalent (4 weeks at 40 hours per week) means that the volunteer services were the equivalent of approximately 6,674 full-time workers. Since the average number of workers at the Office of Price Administration in 1945 was 64,517, it follows that the volunteers increased the strength of the Office of Price Administration by only a bit more than 10 percent. To be sure, the volunteers added an element of community participation that cannot be measured in labor-hours. On the other side, however, they could not be expected to have worked with the efficiency of full-time workers.

A more important qualification of Table 3 is that it ignores the less visible, but nonetheless real, bureaucracy created within the business sector to deal with the government's regulations. A single bureaucrat could request information that literally tens of thousands of businesses would be forced to supply. Several surveys of business costs are available for World War II and the Vietnam period, but only one, a survey taken by the Internal Revenue Service during the Vietnam episode, inspires confidence. The other surveys were taken by business groups that had obvious incentives to overstate costs. Even the study by Internal Revenue Service is likely to

---

[8] Imogene H. Putnam, *Volunteers in OPA*, General Publication No. 14, *Historical Reports on War Administration: Office of Price Administration* (Washington, D.C., 1947), p. 166.

be biased upward because of the tendency of respondents to overstate their burdens. This survey shows that costs to business on an annual basis during the Vietnam era probably fell in the range of $721 million to $2,024 million, or to use the same basis of comparison as previously used, from 8 percent to 22 percent of postal service expenditures in 1971.[9] It should be remembered, moreover, that the Nixon administration was especially concerned with minimizing the administrative costs of controls. In earlier episodes, particularly in World War II, the costs on the business side probably were greater. Thus, taking business costs into consideration would substantially qualify the quantitative picture drawn in Table 2. The full costs of administration were higher at the World War II peak than shown in Table 3, conceivably twice as high. Nevertheless, the overall impression of high but sustainable administrative burden is not changed. Even allowing for volunteers and business costs equal to government costs would leave the total administrative burden equal to about .8 percent of total federal expenditures at the World War II peak.

EFFECT ON AGGREGATE EFFICIENCY

If we return to the vision of the market developed above, a giant computer amassing information and computing relative prices, a second criticism of controls follows.[10] No matter how diligent the controllers, they are bound to make mistakes setting relative prices. Some prices will be too low, causing shortages; others will be too high, causing surpluses. Such effects can be shown easily by examples drawn from wartime periods. The shortages of meat that arose at the end of World War II are one example. But examples, even dozens of examples, cannot tell us much about the aggregate costs of inefficiency. Mistakes frequently occur in market economies as well as in controlled economies. Automobile manufacturers, for example, might fail to foresee the shift toward smaller vehicles. Only an aggregate measure of efficiency can, in principle, tell us whether the controllers made more or fewer mistakes than did the market system that they replaced, and more importantly, give us some idea of how significant the overall impact on efficiency really was.

How large a drop in efficiency the critics of controls expect is not clear. Here I shall be concerned with whether there is evidence of a dramatic decrease in the overall level of efficiency. The three most frequently used measures of efficiency are shown in Table 4: labor productivity and the

---

[9] John T. Dunlop, *Statement Before the Subcommittee on Production and Stabilization of the Senate Banking, Housing and Urban Affairs Committee on the Economic Stabilization Act,* Appendix P (Washington, D.C., 1974), p. A-109.

[10] The discussion that follows is concerned with efficiency in the private sector. Gordon Tullock pointed out to me that controls may have led to a misallocation of resources by the military, since the relative prices faced by military decision makers were distorted. As he also pointed out, however, in the absence of controls other measures might have been adopted to isolate military strategists from concern with mere "monetary" costs.

TABLE 4
PRODUCTIVITY CHANGE IN FOUR PERIODS OF WARTIME CONTROLS

Years	Real Output per Labor-Hour	Total Factor Productivity (Kendrick)	Total Factor Productivity (Denison)
World War I			
1917–1918	5.72	6.13	6.65
1918–1919	3.64	2.29	5.18
World War II			
1940–1941	6.27	3.82	5.10
1941–1942	.86	.42	1.58
1942–1943	2.34	1.10	−.37
1943–1944	6.51	6.23	3.91
1944–1945	4.05	4.40	2.38
1945–1946	−3.46	−3.63	−2.47
Korean War			
1950–1951	2.97	2.77	1.42
1951–1952	1.93	2.55	.27
1952–1953	4.06	3.21	2.13
Vietnam War			
1970–1971	3.2	2.21	2.01
1971–1972	2.8	3.18	4.04
1972–1973	1.7	2.01	1.53
1973–1974	−2.8	−2.93	−4.82

Sources and Methods: World War I and World War II: Col. 1, U.S. Bureau of Economic Analysis, *Long Term Economic Growth, 1960–1970,* Series A 168, p. 211; col. 2, *Long Term Economic Growth 1860–1970,* Series A 161, p. 209; col. 3, Series A 162, p. 209. Korean War and Vietnam War: Col. 1, Series A 168, p. 211, and various issues of the *Monthly Labor Review;* col. 2, John W. Kendrick and Elliot S. Grossman, *Productivity in the United States* (Baltimore, 1980); col. 5, p. 114; col. 3, Edward F. Denison, *Accounting for Slower Economic Growth: The United States in the 1970's* (Washington, D.C., 1979), Table 5–1, col. 1, p. 65.

Kendrick and Denison measures of total factor productivity. On theoretical grounds, the Kendrick and Denison measures are preferable because they consider all inputs in the production process, not just labor. The striking feature of Table 4 is that measured productivity rose in every full year under wage and price controls with only one exception in one index. A first look at the historical record gives no support to the claim that controls severely damaged aggregate efficiency. In the major wars, moreover, the productivity increases were large by historical standards. For example, between 1943 and 1945, the hold-the-line period in World War II when controls were strongest and the patriotic impulse was beginning to wane, all three indexes show extremely large increases. Even in the postwar period measured productivity increases under controls were substantial although not as great as in uncontrolled years. For the uncontrolled years in the 1948 to 1977 period the average increase in Kendrick's measure was 2.43 percent. During the controlled years the average was lower, 1.86 percent. This difference, however, given the large standard deviations in year-to-year percentage changes, 1.81 percent and 2.16 percent, is not sta-

351

tistically significant at conventional levels. If Denison's estimates are used, the results are similar. The difference in mean increases is somewhat greater, 1.96 in the uncontrolled years in the period 1948 to 1976 compared with .94 percent in the controlled years. But again, the large standard deviations, 2.37 percent and 2.78 percent, mean that the difference is not statistically significant.

To be sure, a number of factors make comparison of wartime productivity increases with peacetime increases treacherous. Here I shall briefly consider the possible impact of three factors that could have biased the comparisons just made in favor of controls: understatements in the price indexes, the impact of high aggregate demand, and changes in the mix of final output. But not all wartime changes favored productivity. For example, the replacement of experienced workers who were entering the armed forces with less experienced workers must have reduced efficiency.

To the extent that price increases were concealed, and the price indexes understate the true increases, the measures of real output that constitute the numerators of the productivity indexes will be overstated. This was especially a problem in World War II when black markets and rationing were most severe. What I believe to be a reasonable range for the total understatement in the consumer price index that accumulated over the years 1941 to 1946 would be 4.8 to 7.3 percent.[11] This can be compared with the total percentage changes of 10.6 in real output per labor hour, 8.5 in Kendrick's index, and 5.0 in Denison's index. Thus, allowing for a high estimate of unmeasured price increases still leaves evidence of increases in labor productivity and Kendrick's productivity measure. Moreover, Denison's newest estimates show a total increase of 8.7 percent for the period 1941 to 1947, compared to 3.6 percent in his earlier estimates. So, it is likely that if his earlier estimates were fully revised they would show increases in excess of my maximum estimate of the understatement in the consumer price index.[12] It should also be remembered that prices enter the denominators of the Kendrick and Denison series as deflators of the capital stock. If these prices as well as the prices of final products were understated, the error in the price index for the capital stock would partially offset the error in the index for final output.

The control periods were periods of high aggregate demand, a condition that normally produces productivity gains. It is probably true that the World Wars were so unique that the full impact of aggregate demand on productivity cannot be deduced by comparison with peacetime periods of

[11] Hugh Rockoff, "Indirect Price Increases and Real Wage Change in World War II," *Explorations in Economic History,* 15 (Oct. 1978), 417.

[12] In 1969, Robert J. Gordon pointed out that capital created by the government in World War II and on other occasions that had been transferred to the private sector had not been properly counted in the capital stock estimates. See Gordon, "$45 Billion of U.S. Private Investment Has Been Mislaid," *American Economic Review,* 59 (June 1969), 221. Adjustment for this problem did lead to upward revisions of the rate of growth of this input, but this effect appears to have been offset by revisions of the output data for World War II.

high aggregate demand. This was especially true in World War II because it was believed that the economy would return to a depressed state after the war. In such circumstances the correct decision would be to run down resources of capital and entrepreneurial energy while those resources yield the highest returns, to "make hay while the sun shines." Thus, the productivity gains recorded during the World Wars may have been bought at the expense of slower growth in later periods. After World War II, however, comparisons between controlled and uncontrolled years are more plausible. Such comparisons suggest that high aggregate demand was not obscuring severe damage to aggregate efficiency.

One piece of evidence is from Denison's analysis of productivity gains by source. In this analysis he partitions the productivity gain in a particular year into the amounts that can be attributed to various causes such as economies of scale, fluctuations in the intensity of demand, work stoppages, and so forth. The appropriate experiment for our purpose is to add the contributions to growth of those Denisonian categories likely to be affected by controls: "gains from the reallocation of resources" and "advances in knowledge and miscellaneous" (the famous residual). Presumably the sum of these categories would be negative if controls damaged productivity, even if other factors such as high aggregate demand offset them. In the postwar period, however, the period in which Denison's partition is available, these categories made positive contributions during control years. During the Korean War (1950–1951, 1951–1952, 1952–1953) the gains from these categories were 1.68 percent, 2.18 percent, and 1.84 percent. During the War in Vietnam (1970–1971, 1971–1972, 1972–1973, 1973–1974) the gains were 1.44 percent, 2.98 percent, 1.43 percent, and −0.8 percent.[13] The average contribution from these categories in the postwar period (1947–1976) was 1.41 percent, so most of the control years compare favorably with the average. To put the matter simply, abstracting from the effects of aggregate demand and other extraneous factors strengthens the picture of productivity growth under controls in the postwar period.

Kendrick does not provide a breakdown of productivity growth by source. But for the post-World War II period, Kendrick and Grossman do estimate total factor productivity by quarter. This makes it possible to compare the growth of productivity under controls with its growth in similar phases of the business cycle in the absence of controls. During the Korean War Kendrick's measure of productivity rose at 3.2 percent per year. This episode occurred entirely within the expansion phase of the business cycle, so it is appropriate to compare this rate to the median growth rate in postwar expansions, 2.8 percent. Most of the Vietnam episode fell within the expansion phase of the cycle, but a cyclical peak was reached

---

[13] Edward F. Denison, *Accounting for Slower Economic Growth: The United States in the 1970's* (Washington, D.C., 1979), Table 5–1, Cols. (2), (3), and (12), p. 65.

before the technical end of controls. From the beginning of controls in the third quarter of 1971 to the cyclical peak in the fourth quarter of 1973, productivity increased at an annual rate of 1.4 percent which, although positive, is substantially below the postwar median for expansion phases.[14] But the latter standard may be misleading if a secular retardation of productivity growth that some argue is the real cause of the recent slowdown (rather than temporary shocks such as the oil crisis) already had begun. On the whole, then, Kendrick's data tend to reconfirm the impression drawn from Denison's that there was no marked retardation of productivity growth due to controls, even if the role of aggregate demand is kept in mind.

Perhaps the most fundamental problem with the aggregate measures of productivity is that the mix of goods produced by the economy is different in war. War goods might have been easier to produce because mass production techniques could be employed more readily. This suggests that one might look separately at those industries that produced primarily for the war sector and at those that produced for the homefront. The critical case would be World War II when emphasis on war production was greatest. The evidence seems to be that there was some stagnation (although no decline) in labor productivity in manufacturing industries producing for the civilian sector, but substantial increases in labor productivity in other "civilian" sectors such as electric light and power and agriculture.[15] At the other end of the spectrum, during the Vietnam period when there was less disruption of the civilian economy sectoral developments appear to have been more favorable to the hypothesis that controls did not damage aggregate productivity.[16]

In sum, there appears to be little evidence that controls severely damaged productivity. Although the biases in the data prevent a definitive statement, the burden of proof clearly falls upon the critics of wartime controls.

EXTENT OF THE BLACK MARKET

Under price controls there may be numerous markets in which the official ceiling price is below the market clearing price. Whether this occurs because of mistakes by the controllers in setting relative prices, or because aggregate demand is increased to the point where excess demand characterizes most markets, or both, is not important here. It is possible to imag-

---

[14] John W. Kendrick and Elliot S. Grossman, *Productivity in the United States: Trends and Cycles* (Baltimore, 1980), pp. 83, 85, 115, and 117.

[15] Celia Star Gody and Allan D. Searle, "Productivity Changes Since 1939," *Monthly Labor Review*, 63 (Dec. 1946), 893–917.

[16] J. Randolph Norsworthy and Lawrence J. Fulco, "Productivity and Costs in Perspective," *Monthly Labor Review*, 98 (Nov. 1975), 44–52; Marvin H. Kosters, *Controls and Inflation: The Economic Stabilization Program in Retrospect* (Washington, D.C., 1975), pp. 91–100 draws a similar conclusion from qualitative evidence.

ine several kinds of socially desirable responses, in effect, voluntary or government-imposed rationing. But it is also possible to imagine evasion of controls, even black markets. The reason is simple. In any market characterized by excess demand there are buyers who are willing to pay more than the ceiling price, and sellers who would profit by selling to them. That buyers and sellers would find some way of getting together—in open black markets, through acquiescence in quality deterioration, and so on— would not be surprising. The crucial issue is how extensive was the evasion of controls. Did the black markets that developed during periods of wartime controls constitute serious drawbacks to the stabilization programs?

The discussion of black markets tends to be dominated by examples. For the case of World War II, dramatic examples can be given, ranging from an open black market in meat to rather subtle forms of evasion such as the elimination of lower priced lines of clothing.[17] As with the issues examined above, a list of examples, whatever its heuristic value, cannot support the claim that the black market was extensive. Such a claim by its very nature requires a quantitative measure and a comparison with the volume of illegal activity that constantly arises in a free market. The appropriate measure, however, is not readily apparent. The proportion of GNP traded in the black market, the measure that occurs first to an economist, is not available, and even if it were, it is not clear that it closely corresponds to the social costs of a black market. These costs lie mainly in the damage to the moral fabric of the community when evasion of the law is widespread. A measure of the black market that corresponds more to the social costs, and which is available, is the number of cases brought before the courts. To be sure, the number of cases will reflect a variety of factors besides the underlying volume of illegal activity: the volume of resources devoted to enforcement, the attitude of the courts, the structure of the legislation, and so forth.[18] Nevertheless, the case load appears to be the best measure available, and it can be used for making comparisons if one is willing to assume that the probability of a price control violation giving rise to a court case was similar to the probability of a violation under other legislation giving rise to a court case.

Table 5 shows the number of cases of price violators brought to the federal courts during the last three episodes, and compares the price violation cases with the total number of cases in the courts. This table extends the one given by Clinard and Mansfield to the two most recent episodes.[19]

---

[17] See Marshall Barron Clinard, *The Black Market: A Study of White Collar Crime* (New York, 1952), for a discussion of the many forms taken by evasion during World War II.

[18] See Ruth Duhl, "Enforcement History" (Typescript, Spring 1947), Harvard University Libraries, for a complete description of the enforcement effort during the war. Substantial enforcement efforts were made which would appear to be comparable to enforcement efforts in other areas.

[19] Clinard, *The Black Market*, p. 38; Harvey C. Mansfield and associates, *A Short History of OPA*, General Publication No. 15, *Historical Reports on War Administration: Office of Price Administration* (Washington, D.C., 1947), p. 271.

TABLE 5
CIVIL CASES COMMENCED IN U.S. DISTRICT COURTS IN THREE PERIODS OF
WARTIME CONTROLS

Year (Fiscal)	Price Control Cases	Total	Percentage
World War II			
1942[a]	42	29,592	.1
1943[a]	2,219	28,166	7.9
1944	6,980	38,499	18.1
1945	28,926	60,965	47.4
1946	32,209	67,835	47.5
1947	16,298	58,956	27.6
Korean War			
1951	4,322	51,600	8.4
1952	5,941	58,428	10.2
1953	4,303	64,001	6.7
1954	351	59,461	0.6
Vietnam War			
1972	376	96,173	0.4
1973	283	98,560	0.3
1974	175	103,530	0.2

[a] Excludes all cases from the District of Columbia and the Territories from both totals, and in addition excludes private cases from the price control cases.
Sources: U.S. Administrative Office of the Courts, *Annual Report of the Director*, various years, Table C_2. Data for 1942 and 1943 are from the *1946 Annual Report*, p. 56.

Not all of the court activity generated by controls is reflected in the table. In World War II, for example, a number of constitutional cases were brought before the Emergency Court of Appeals, a significant number of price violators were brought to court under criminal charges, and a number of cases reached state and local courts under laws passed in support of the federal legislation. Nevertheless, the table reflects the main form of legal activity generated by conventional violations of the price control laws.

It is clear that the black market, understanding the term in a broad sense, generated a substantial case load. At the World War II peak, the price control statutes generated nearly as many civil cases as the rest of the federal statutes combined. The similarity of the proportion of cases in fiscal 1945 and fiscal 1946 suggests that an equilibrium was reached. Or, to put the matter another way, it suggests that even though a large black market developed, its ultimate size was limited. The limit was probably determined by the amount of excess demand. Illegal activity grew with excess demand pressures in 1943, 1944, and 1945, and subsided quickly in the Korean War when monetary policy, in the wake of the Treasury-Federal Reserve Accord, followed a restrictive course. Thus, although the black market may have reached a temporary equilibrium because of temporary stability in the growth of excess demand, it is possible that the black market would have become even larger had the margin of excess demand grown even larger.[20]

No data for World War I are presented in Table 4 in part because the method for enforcing controls was somewhat different. Businesses were licensed and enforcement was achieved by revoking or threatening to revoke the license of a firm that violated the controls. Some violators were pursued in criminal cases, but the courts were not a major channel for enforcing controls. The total amount of enforcement activity, however, was relatively small, probably because the war ended soon after controls were imposed. The Food Administration, perhaps the major agency likely to encounter black market violations, revoked the licenses, either for all trading or with reference to particular commodities, of 436 firms. The total number of sanctions imposed, many of a minor character, was 8,603. This can be compared with a business population of some 140,000 firms monitored by the Food Administration. Thus, about 6.1 percent of the firms under observation—making the extreme assumption that multiple sanctions never had to be used—were disciplined by the Food Administration.[21]

The case load generated by the Vietnam controls is, to a lesser extent, also not directly comparable to the World War II and Korean cases. The control philosophy, for the most part, was to observe closely only the largest firms, and to rely as far as possible on voluntary compliance. The cases that did go to court were aimed as much at setting precedents and establishing the general threat of enforcement activity as at seeking compliance in individual cases. Perhaps a better basis of comparison for the Vietnam controls would be the volume of antitrust activity where a similar philosophy prevailed. Using this basis, the volume of enforcement activity in the Vietnam War period seems more substantial. The ratio of price control cases to antitrust cases was .27 in 1972, .24 in 1973, and .14 in 1974.[22]

In addition to the various forms of evasion that could be disciplined by the price controllers, and that would generate the case statistics discussed above, there were two important forms of evasion with which they could not cope so easily. First, in concentrated industries, managements used labor disputes to win concessions from the controllers by permitting strikes and refusing to settle unless substantial price increases were granted. Dur-

---

[20] The notion that the amount of excess demand played a crucial role in the functioning of the wartime system of wage and price controls was first pointed out by John Kenneth Galbraith, *A Theory of Price Control* (Cambridge, MA, 1952), who dubbed the amount of excess demand consistent with successful functioning of the system the "margin of tolerance."

[21] Sanctions are from William Clinton Mullendore, *History of the United States Food Administration, 1917-1919* (Stanford, 1941), p. 334. The number of firms under observation is from Paul Willard Garrett assisted by Isadore Lubin, *Government Control Over Prices*, Bulletin No. 3, *History of Prices During the War*, edited by Wesley C. Mitchell (Washington, D.C., 1920), p. 145.

[22] The sources are the same as for Table 5.

ing World War II, this tactic was muted by the no-strike and no-lock out agreements, and by the willingness of the government to seize firms when strikes threatened the stabilization effort. After VJ day and during the later episodes, however, this tactic could be used to great effect.[23] A second method of overcoming the stabilization authority was to appeal directly to Congress for special legislation exempting a particular industry. Again, this tactic was relatively ineffective during the heyday of controls in World War II. It played a crucial role, however, in weakening the stabilization agencies when it came to the final renewal of the legislation during World War II, and when it came to renewing the legislation in the Korean War.

The extent to which actors in the private sectors could overcome decisions by the price controllers perhaps provides an important clue to the relatively high rates of productivity growth observed under controls. In a free market in which the initial price is too low, market forces will quickly raise it to a level that will bring supply and demand into equilibrium, and will, in the process, attract additional resources into the market. In a controlled market if the initial price is set too low the adjustment process may not be as efficient as in a free market, but it is wrong to think that it will not occur. Black market transactions, quality deterioration, and the elimination of sales are all ways, albeit costly ways, of raising price, and such indirect increases will serve the same functions, although less efficiently, of allocating resources to their most productive ends. The market where price is too low, moreover, may generate strikes leading to wage and price increases, or political pressures leading to subsidies or outright exemption. These more roundabout means of evasion, as well as the more familiar kind, will substitute for correct decisions by the controllers. Thus, what at first glance appears to be a contradiction between the positive rates of productivity change observed during the war years, and the evidence of extensive evasion, may not be a contradiction at all. Indirect price increases may have substituted for direct increases, and may have prevented mistakes made by the controllers from seriously injuring aggregate productivity.

CONCLUSIONS

Despite the fact that all of the experiences examined here have occurred within the twentieth century, they have given rise to myths of which only some stand up under close scrutiny. In part this has resulted from the tendency to deduce quantitative conclusions from a limited number of examples. In summary then, I would offer the following conclusions, which appear to me to be better grounded in the quantitative evidence.

[23] See John L. Blackman, Jr., *Presidential Seizure in Labor Disputes* (Cambridge, MA, 1967), Appendix A, pp. 257–311, for the list of firms seized in labor disputes arising from conflicts with the stabilization agencies.

1. The monetarist contention that controls only postponed inflation must be qualified, especially for the World Wars. There is evidence for those periods that controls reduced monetary velocity. This made it possible to finance the same level of real spending out of newly created money while reducing the absolute amount of money created. In short, controls made the job of monetary policy easier by facilitating the transfer of resources to the government sector. This is, to be sure, a second-best argument. A financial policy that did not rely extensively on the creation of new money might have been ideal. But the contribution of controls, given what was politically feasible, should not be overlooked.

2. The contention that controls required "huge" bureaucracies to administer them is true only if the word "huge" is understood in the mundane sense of similarity to other large federal bureaucracies. The claim that the bureaucracies were "huge" does not stand up if huge is taken to mean a substantial fraction of the government's resources.

3. The contention that controls severely damaged the economy's allocative machinery is not supported by an examination of the standard measures of aggregate efficiency. The potential biases in these measures, however, preclude a definitive statement. A more subtle argument might be made that controls held productivity growth below what it otherwise would have been, but the uncertainty surrounding the estimates makes it extremely difficult to test this formulation.

4. The contention that controls produced "extensive" evasion appears to be true if "extensive" is taken to mean in comparison with the existing body of federal law. During World War II price controls led to a virtual doubling of the cases being filed in federal courts. The extent of evasion both through conventional and unconventional means may explain the productivity record. Severe mistakes by the controllers in setting relative prices may have been overcome by indirect price increases, or by concessions on prices won through political channels.

Can industry survive the welfare state?

To maintain worldwide competitiveness, the West must adopt strategies to achieve a balance between productivity and welfare goals

Bruce R. Scott

The recession dogging the U.S. economy is only symptomatic of the long-term decline suffered by many of our industries since the beginning of the 1970s. The evidence is everywhere, from sagging profitability — and even bankruptcy — of once-dynamic companies to chronic unemployment that reaches far beyond the 10% level for certain areas of the country and population segments. Furthermore, the same symptoms afflict all the other major economies of the North Atlantic area.

In this article, Bruce Scott argues that despite the degree of decline, no government has proposed a substantive or workable plan to reverse it. Using comparative economic analysis, he shows how the newly industrialized nations of East Asia have prospered just as the industrialized West has declined. Then he explains how the United States can begin the often-painful process of revitalization — not simply by implementing an industrial policy but by adopting a new way of thinking about a country's economic strategy in much the same way a company thinks about its strategy. The idea is revolutionary because, to make it work, government and labor will have to concede certain ground gained in the welfare reforms promulgated since the Great Depression. And for their part, corporations will have to take back some of the responsibility for the rights and security of their employees.

Mr. Scott is Paul Whiton Cherington Professor of Business Administration at the Harvard Business School. For the last eight years he has been involved in research, course development, and teaching of the required course, Business, Government, and the International Economy. This is his fourth article for HBR; the most recent is "OPEC, the American Scapegoat" (January-February 1981).

Illustration by Karen Watson.

Stagflation has affected the North Atlantic area for almost ten years. We may be able to explain continuous inflation at historically high levels in the face of slack demand in terms of successive oil price shocks, wage settlements that far outpace productivity gains, and excessive money creation (particularly U.S. dollars).

But what about economic stagnation? The "oil tax" levied by OPEC is part of the explanation. A slowdown in technological innovation may also be a contributing cause. But in addition to these exogenous or noncontrollable developments, it may be that the economic policies of the industrial countries themselves bear a major responsibility. We cannot ignore the growing tax take of the welfare state, particularly when the state uses those revenues for social welfare programs and transfer payments that are "entitlements" unconnected to any productive contribution to society. Deficit financing of these programs makes government an increasingly important competitor for public savings, crowding out more directly productive investments.

Despite the possibility that government policy may have been a major cause of the stagflation problem, a growing sense exists that governments can and should "solve" it. And it is no coincidence that, since 1976, voters have rejected all major Western governments except that of Chancellor Schmidt. New governments are experimenting with radically different programs from supply-side economics in the United States and the United Kingdom to more socialism in France. Each can look to its share of economic experts for support. Consensus on the diagnosis seems almost as elusive as on the most appropriate remedies.

Author's note: Much of my thinking in the area of corporate governance has been greatly influenced by the writings of Professor George C. Lodge, a colleague.

Editor's note: All references are listed at the end of the article.

Understandably, much of the attention thus far has focused on the obvious symptoms of unemployment and inflation. But it is time the policymakers of the major countries in the North Atlantic area turned their attention to the more fundamental problems of: (1) weakened industrial performance (declines in the growth of investments, productivity, jobs, and trade balances), (2) the shifting distribution of income that preceded it (toward wages and away from profits), and (3) the increasing vulnerability of the traditional industrial countries to the unprecedented challenge from Japan and the four "new Japans" of East Asia – Hong Kong, Korea, Singapore, and Taiwan.

One important aspect of the new competition is the speed with which it has developed. Japan started to industrialize little more than 100 years ago, while the others began only 30 years ago. But more significant, none of the newcomers has a base of natural resources on which to build an industrial society, and Japan is the only one with a large home market. They have succeeded by mobilizing human and financial resources through different policies and institutions.

While the North Atlantic countries have viewed economic growth in terms of exploitation of natural resources enhanced by trade, the East Asians have created a model that does not require any significant endowment of natural resources. Unwilling to accept the conventional Western idea that their role is to specialize in goods based on cheap labor (their major resource), the East Asians have forged a dynamic theory of comparative advantage that allows them to allocate human and financial resources toward jobs with high value added in growing industries and, for example, to succeed in steel despite a lack of both coal and iron.

This new industrial competition is the most important challenge facing the entire North Atlantic area. Whether economic growth recovers somewhat in the 1980s, the traditional industrial nations will continue to lose industrial competitiveness and industrial jobs unless they respond to it. A successful response will include policy changes to promote increased investment, more rapid adaptation by industry, and increased mobility of labor. These changes will require recognition of the disincentives to work, save, and invest that have become the hallmarks of the welfare state. And in the United States, we must address a special set of problems ascribed to an "adversarial relationship" between business and government.

None of these changes will come easily. Nor should the challenge be a pretext for turning the economic clock back to nineteenth-century private enterprise capitalism. Just as we need to rethink the goals and policies of the welfare state we need also to rethink the governance process of the corporation. If we expect government to revive its commitment to the value of work, saving, and investment, business must recognize investments made by employees as well as shareholders and accept a governance process that effectively reflects the essential rights of both.

Strategies of economic growth

Before accepting this "gloomy" or "challenging" diagnosis, we should review comparative performance data to check the severity of the alleged symptoms. The ruled insert details the economic reality. In terms of rising incomes and an improvement in distribution of wealth on a worldwide basis, the rapid rise of the East Asians is a positive development. Stagnation in the North Atlantic area, on the other hand, is not, particularly as we witness unemployment rates at levels unheard of since the 1930s. Continued weakness in the industrial sector threatens the loss not only of vital exports but also of highly productive jobs in mass production industries.

Some observers seem to regard industrial decline as a step forward toward a service-based "postindustrial" society. While it is important to recognize the growing importance of the service sector, the vision of a postindustrial society may well turn out to have been an elegant rationalization for failure to maintain a competitive industrial base. Before accepting industrial decline as an inevitable sign of sophistication and progress, we should reexamine how it has happened and the extent to which it may have been caused by differences in economic strategies among countries rather than by inevitable historical forces.

Classical economics has long taught that economic growth was built on the rational use of resources, with each country building on comparative advantage through trade. Worked out by Ricardo in the early 1800s, when competitive advantages were based on natural resources, the theory was essentially static. The advantages were "given"; there was little room or need for a strategy.

This static notion of comparative advantage has had a profound influence on economic thought throughout the North Atlantic area. Americans, in particular, are not used to thinking of government as needing an explicit economic strategy. The American economy became the most productive in the world without one. Blessed with the world's first "common market" and some of its richest resources, the United States grew by conquering the frontier via private enterprise, without an active government strategy. At least that is what we think. We should not forget that one of the critical elements of success was the

Interstate Commerce Clause of the Constitution that prohibited trade barriers among the states; another was the use of land grants to speed the opening of the West via the transcontinental railroads. Even the United States had a strategy of sorts.

Today, however, the static notion of comparative advantage is no longer relevant. The United States still has rich and abundant farmland and is the world's number one exporter of agricultural goods. But the United States no longer has an advantage in the size of its market. Europe has a market of roughly the same size, and Japan's is almost half as large. Raw materials have been found around the globe, and for many applications it is cheaper to import foreign ores than to exploit domestic ones. As a result, most of the natural advantages that were the sources of American economic strength are no longer of critical importance. Increasingly the vital resources are those we create through the organized exploitation of various technologies.

American experts misperceived postwar Japan's potential in large part because of the notion of static comparative advantage. In the 1950s it led Edwin Reischauer to conclude that "Japan's situation is basically similar to England's, but infinitely worse. She is far less richly endowed with the vital resources of coal and iron....She is far less highly industrialized. She has no overseas empire to aid her...and she has almost twice the population of Great Britain to support on her more meager resources."[1]

In the 30 years since Reischauer made this assessment, Japan has grown at a rate roughly triple that of the United Kingdom. Economists now recognize that Japan's greatest resource is its population; yet that largely misses the point. India and China have larger populations but have not generated economic performance that is remotely comparable. The Japanese have created a strategy and a set of institutional relationships to implement it. Mobility of capital has been one key, labor mobility another. By promoting savings and investing in the most modern technologies, Japan and the other countries of East Asia have shown that countries can create comparative advantages in almost any industry they choose. Their capacity to abandon older industries as they create new ones shows that a trained, disciplined, and relatively mobile labor force can be a nation's most important real resource.

In contrast, labor mobility and discipline of the older industrial states are declining. Unemployment benefits and various forms of adjustment assistance, however meritorious on other grounds, give added support to individuals who refuse to relocate, while increasingly generous health insurance plans—particularly in Europe—allow employees to be absent from work at almost no cost to themselves. Meanwhile, a variety of subsidies, such as "safe harbor

leasing," help prop up losing ventures. Taxes to finance these programs become an added burden on all companies located in these countries and another competitive disadvantage. As growth industries, such as electronics, become more knowledge intensive and as companies transfer technology anywhere on the globe, a nation's economic success hinges on the way it manages its human and financial resources. Under these circumstances, where the key to successful performance is mobility of capital and labor, Ricardo's theory no longer provides much of a framework for formulating public policy.

Recent experience in Korea, Taiwan, Hong Kong, and Singapore demonstrates that Japan is not unique. Without significant natural resources, these countries have achieved rapid growth by developing efficient, specialized manufacturing organizations backed by a system of social and economic incentives designed to promote work, saving, risk taking, investment, and labor mobility. Like Japan, they have built success by organizing human and financial resources and by not banking on the good fortune of natural resources. Their rapid industrialization has grown out of an economic strategy designed to promote productivity while sharply limiting the development of the welfare state.

Welfare vs. productivity strategies

Like companies, countries have strategies, or goals and policies, to orient the actions of their respective "managers." Some strategies are more explicit, some more coherent, some more effective. Because the United States is an extreme example of an implicit rather than explicit strategy and at times has a political rhetoric that proclaims the virtues of a government with no economic strategy at all, it may help to use the Japanese example as a starting point.

The goal of the Japanese has long been to catch and then surpass all others in economic performance. To achieve that goal, they have created a strategy to generate rising incomes by using the latest technology and equipment and employing mass production and marketing techniques to reach world markets. The Japanese strategy requires a high level of investment, hence access to a high level of savings. Rejecting Western advice about borrowing heavily or inviting foreign capital, they have chosen to finance their investment from domestic savings. For some years the Japanese have saved roughly 20% of personal disposable income (the current American rate is 5%). They save not because of high interest rates on bank deposits; indeed, when adjusted for inflation the rates have been negative through most of the 1970s. The Japanese save because they must if they are to make major purchases and provide for old age. The government restricts consumer credit. And pensions are only a fraction of American levels. The Japanese receive greater deductions for interest income than Americans, but they receive no tax deductions for interest payments. Japanese banks receive the savings, and because they cannot easily lend to consumers, they must lend to industry if they are to grow.

The Japanese have shaped their policies in housing, banking, and social welfare to support a strategy of raising the standard of living by raising savings, investment, and productivity. Labor policy is part of the strategy. Lifetime employment in large companies means employees share the productivity gains rather than being displaced by them.

'No strategy is good strategy'

The problem in the United States is that our strategy is largely implicit and forged in reaction to economic misfortunes. Until the Great Depression, the goal was a rising standard of living based on the Yankee virtues of work, saving, and investment. The government allowed companies a reasonable chance to compete and refereed the competition as it unfolded. Americans raised their standard of living both as producers and as consumers of goods and services delivered at reasonable prices in a competitive system.

The Depression led not only to a new economics of demand management based on Keynes's ideas but also to a gradual, steady shift in the economic strategies of all the North Atlantic countries.

The priorities shifted toward short-term consumer welfare. Productivity was downgraded, however implicitly. The Employment Act of 1946 committed the U.S. government to use its powers to stimulate demand to ensure a high level of employment. Subsequent legislation established penalty taxes on interest and dividends to help redistribute income from the rich to the poor. Taxes on consumption (sales or excise taxes) were rejected as regressive, and the federal government was financed largely by personal and corporate income taxes and social security contributions.

Although a nominal amount of interest and dividend income went tax free, interest payments on homes, consumer durables, and even credit card purchases became tax deductible. In this way, the United States promoted a higher standard of living through subsidies to consumption. Progressive income taxes designed in part to redistribute the income eroded traditional incentives to work, save, and invest. Ever-increasing levels of entitlements support short-

term consumer welfare at the expense of those who work and pay taxes. The result is a system that takes productivity for granted and tries to promote rising levels of consumption.

We can compare the welfare strategies of the North Atlantic area with the productivity strategies found in East Asia using a simple matrix (see *Exhibit I*). The East Asians place high priority on productivity and deliberately limit the growth of the welfare state. The North Atlantic countries have done the reverse. Many of the less-developed countries have done little of either, so they are positioned at the lower right.

The box at the upper left, though blank, suggests a strategy promoting both productivity and welfare. Until recently, Germany would be one country in the upper left box. After World War II, Germany exempted overtime earnings from taxation and gave tax exemptions both for savings and for interest income. On the other hand, it began creating a welfare state under Bismarck. With the victory of the Social Democrats in 1969, the Germans shifted in favor of the welfare state and now belong in the lower left-hand box, even if they are less firmly entrenched there than in Belgium, Holland, the Scandinavian countries, or the United Kingdom.

Worldwide prospects

If you use this conceptual scheme both to compare economic strategies and to think about the prospects for industries throughout the world, the implications are not reassuring. Unless strategies change, the welfare states of the North Atlantic are likely to be increasingly less competitive with the productivity-oriented countries of East Asia. They will suffer from lower levels of saving and investment and from a variety of disincentives to work. Entitlements, progressive income taxes, and subsidies for consumption will make them increasingly less competitive as locations for any industries where product values allow international trade. The problem is not so much with themselves as with the newly industrialized countries (NICs).

More important, today's NICs will not be alone for long. Since the continuing success of the East Asians does *not* require any natural resources, or even a large home market, other less-developed countries can copy it. Indeed, Malaysia and Thailand appear to be moving toward similar strategies, and a related process has brought rapid progress to Brazil.

A dynamic theory of comparative advantage

The implications of the world economic picture are clear. In industrial terms, the star performers of the last 30 years are a group of countries whose critical resources are not land or minerals but rather people and savings – and the policies and institutions to mobilize and periodically redirect both.

To be able to direct our own economic strategy in the United States, we need to construct a way of thinking that will foster this mobility. It will help to postulate that countries, like companies, have "portfolios" of businesses or industries. They can influence not only the mix in the portfolio at any time but also the rate of new business development, the redeployment of human and capital resources to growth sectors, and the withdrawal of those same resources from declining sectors. In fact, dynamic industrial policy should promote all three.

Several schemes have been developed for corporations looking at their portfolios of businesses. The Boston Consulting Group pioneered in this field, and I think governments would find a variant of its growth-share matrix useful (see *Exhibit II*). Based on industry growth rate and corporate market share, the original matrix related high market share to increased output, cumulative experience, and lower costs. For comparable products, lower costs mean higher margins.

The lower left-hand corner of the matrix symbolizes high share in a slow-growth industry that should generate high returns; low growth should not require high levels of investment. Businesses in the lower left should generate cash, while those in the upper left grow so rapidly that they require additional cash despite their presumably high profit margins. New ventures in the upper right may need additional cash to support fast growth on low margins.

If we think of a given portfolio of businesses, the scheme highlights the "mix" in terms of prospective growth, profitability, and cash flow. Of greater interest, however, is its dynamic aspect. A new product or business ideally moves from upper right to upper left to lower left over its life cycle. Cash from businesses in the lower left finances new entries in the upper right and likewise battles for market share and a hoped-for position in the upper left. Theoretically, a company balances the businesses in its portfolio by building some in the upper half, avoiding excess investment in the lower left, and considering disinvestment in the lower right (see *Exhibit III*).

Obviously, the growth-share concept has limits. First, strategies of technical and/or service

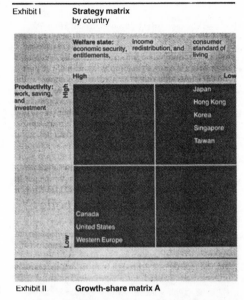

Exhibit I   **Strategy matrix** by country

Welfare state: economic security, entitlements,   income redistribution, and   consumer standard of living

Productivity: work, saving, and investment   High ... Low

High
Japan
Hong Kong
Korea
Singapore
Taiwan

Canada
United States
Western Europe

Low

Exhibit II   **Growth-share matrix A**

Growth rate

Market share   High ... Low

High

Low

Source:
Boston Consulting Group.

differentiation do not fit in well. Second, low cost and rising share correlate, but the correlation may be either circular or even the reverse of the original hypothesis.[2] Third, there is a great deal more to running a business than managing a portfolio – that is, there are people, products, technologies, and so forth. Finally, a corporate strategy is more than simply the sum of the portfolio decisions affecting separate business ends; corporate strategy refers to the corporation as a whole.[3] If we keep these limitations in mind, however, we can use the growth-share matrix as a comprehensive way to think about industry dynamics and as a more appropriate framework for forging an industrial policy.

How should we think about industrial policy?

Industrial policy is only one element, however important, of a country's total economic strategy. A government must formulate and implement industrial policy through institutions that are competent, committed, and able to wield political clout. Otherwise the risk is high that the process will yield a narrow technical exercise in portfolio analysis or, worse still, a new rationale for liberal bureaucrats to apply their noncompetitive values and theories.

With these caveats, let's look at a more general framework for industrial policy (see *Exhibit IV*), which would focus attention on opportunities to: (1) promote new undertakings in the upper right, (2) foster successful transitions in the upper left, (3) avoid excessive investment in the lower half (particularly the lower right quadrant), and (4) abandon businesses in the lower right unless special circumstances allow profitable operation. On the other hand, industrial policy should not attempt to do what it cannot: plan output and/or investment by sector.

1   Promoting innovation

Government can promote innovation both by subsidizing R&D costs and by increasing the rewards for successful entrepreneurship. The Japanese give tax credits for *increases* in R&D, coupled with a limit on the total amount of credit. The French have used a variety of subsidies, some reimbursable if the project is commercially successful.

The capital gains tax affects the risk-reward ratio for the scientist or entrepreneur as well as the mobility of risk capital. A high tax reduces the rewards for those who succeed and forces an investor

Exhibit III   **Growth-share matrix B**

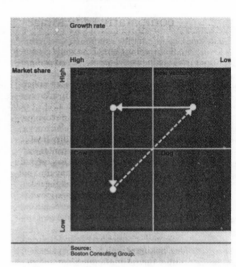

Source:
Boston Consulting Group.

Exhibit IV   **Competitive position matrix**

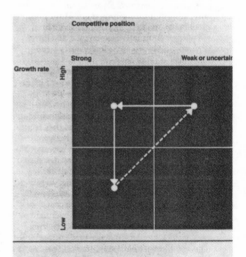

with a large capital gain in one venture to pay a severe penalty for transferring those funds to another venture. The Japanese have no capital gains tax. The Germans, however, tax capital gains as ordinary income. The French are particularly backward; a French inventor who receives stock in a new venture in recognition of the innovation must pay a tax on its nominal value at the time the stock is received rather than when the capital gains are realized.

The impact of the capital gains tax rate on the formation of new ventures in the United States has been analyzed in *America's Competitive Edge*.[4] The authors describe the decline in new ventures and in amounts of venture capital raised following the 1969 increases in the maximum rate on capital gains from 25% to 40%. They also note the dramatic increase in venture capital raised once the maximum rate was reduced to 25% in 1978.

Industrial policy can also promote new technologies within existing companies. While U.S. antitrust laws usually preclude joint ventures, the Japanese encourage them within an industry to solve major technical problems or to accelerate the development of prototypes. In numerous cases, the Japanese have made investment subsidies contingent on the formation of the joint venture. The participants are free to use the technological fruits of the venture in competition with one another as well as with foreign companies.

---

2 Encouraging 'winners'

With an adequate portfolio of new ventures and business development in established companies, government can help promote the growth of strong industries through foreign trade and investment policies. Japan, for example, restricted foreign imports and generally limited or prohibited foreign investment in new industries until Japanese entrants were established. While opening up its market in the 1970s, Japan has restricted the roles of foreign companies in those industries targeted for growth in the 1980s and 1990s, such as telecommunications, integrated circuits, and computers.

The European Common Market countries do not have this option. There is no European Community policy on restricting foreign investment, and internal trade restrictions are prohibited. The most a member country can do is discourage foreign takeovers and subsidize *selected* industries or companies. When the French tried to be quite restrictive, investors went to Belgium or Germany and exported to France.

The French government uses export subsidies to foster sales of capital equipment and weapons. Aiming to supply 20% of its energy needs by 1985 (compared with the 3% to 5% proportion of its neighbors), it also promotes the development of atomic power. But since the state, through the electricity monopoly, is the only buyer, this is not a model for the competitive sector.

In high-technology industries such as computers and space, the French have been less successful. The Plan Calcul was a costly failure, yet the takeover of Honeywell-Bull, plus subsidies for smaller companies, gives France a significant entry in mainframes and minis. Sponsorship by PTT (the French telephone company) of a "program télématique" based on subscriber telephones may give France a strong position, if not the lead, in a sector of telecommunications. Automobiles have been a consistently strong point among French exports, but both state-owned Renault and privately owned Peugeot have operated like private-sector companies. Unless the EC follows the French and Italian lead in imposing quotas on auto imports, France's auto sector is vulnerable to Japanese competition and also to the French tendency to maintain an overvalued exchange rate. France has a decidedly mixed record in building its new state-sponsored projects into strong, competitive activities.

Germany has enjoyed remarkable industrial strength for the past 30 years, but it is concentrated in chemicals, metalworking, and mechanical equipment. Its position is not nearly as strong in electronics, computers, or telecommunications. Indeed, several careful observers point out that Germany not only lags behind the United States, Japan, and France in these growth areas but also has not launched a program to catch up. If Germany permits the renewal of its industrial portfolio to lag, it will have less capacity to carry the costs of its increasingly generous welfare state in the late 1980s and 1990s.

The United States has the world's largest economy and industrial portfolio, mostly the result of natural competitive development. Public policy has focused on the U.S. market and prevention of cooperation among participants in an industry. Until very recently, international competition has been ignored. It is as if our market were so large and our companies so strong that the government need not be concerned with promoting their performance. Neither the regulators nor the courts have given much weight to the impact of regulation on either domestic economic performance or international competition. Recent decisions by the Reagan administration and the Federal Trade Commission to dismiss the antitrust suits against IBM and the cereal manufacturers represent an important and promising policy reversal. And the proposed settlement of the AT&T case should liberate one of the most important sources of U.S. technical strength to compete both internationally and domestically.

Industrial performance— Is there a problem?

How severe are our alleged symptoms? In the last decade, we have become aware that a rising standard of living depends primarily on increasing productivity and secondarily on growth in the labor force. Table A shows productivity trends for selected countries in the 1970s: while all countries grew less rapidly than in the 1960s, U.S. productivity grew the slowest; that of the East Asians, the fastest.

Turning to employment, and particularly to industrial employment, the Europeans come in last (see Table B). In each major European country, industrial employment peaked around 1970, well before the first oil crisis. The United States, Japan, and Canada have been able to create or maintain jobs in manufacturing. Europe lost manufacturing jobs, and Japan saw employment concentration shift from manufacturing to services—while always maintaining full employment.

In Europe, investment stagnated in the 1970s, in dramatic contrast to the situation in East Asia (Table C). The breakdown of industrial investment in Germany is especially illuminating. By 1976, investment in capacity expansion had almost disappeared, while capital to rationalize operations and so reduce the labor force increased. With a rising exchange rate, companies found investment in Germany less attractive but put in capital to reduce wage costs through labor-saving equipment.

Small differences in growth rates make a big difference if they persist. While in 1960 the industrial countries had a higher share of per-capita GNP invested than the East Asians, by 1979 they were outstripped by the Japanese, who were investing more per capita in absolute terms.

A shift in income distribution preceded the stagnation of investment. Between 1965 and 1975 the share of income going to employees went up (see Table D), that to property and entrepreneurship down. The achievement of full employment in the 1960s increased the power of organized labor, and wage demands far exceeded productivity gains. Eventually corporate balance sheets deteriorated and companies had to trim their rates of investment. By 1973 even the communist leadership in Italy wanted to moderate wage demands in order to reestablish more normal profit margins, new investment, and, finally, new jobs. While data on East Asia are fragmentary, trends of income distribution seem quite different, with only Japan showing a higher share of income for employees.

Rising labor costs are only part of the problem, of course. The East Asians benefited from trade negotiations that opened the world economy, shipping costs that declined relative to product values, and licensing agreements that made most technologies available on easy terms. Under these circumstances more and more investment has moved offshore, and the East Asians have gained in relative position as the older industrial societies have declined.

*New data series.
†1963 to 1970.

‡Column 2: the years are 1972-1973 for West Germany and Norway, 1971-1973 for South Korea. Column 4: the years are 1975-1977 for the Netherlands, 1976-1978 for Japan.

Sources: United Nations, Monthly Bulletin of Statistics, March 1981, table 66; International Labour Office, Yearbook of Labour Studies, 1980, table 3.

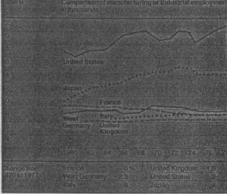

Source: OECD data, courtesy of Data Resources Corporation.

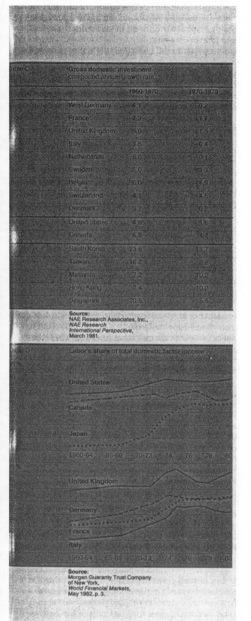

3 Limiting investment in low-growth sectors

The economic case for limiting investment in low-growth sectors is obvious; countries, like companies, should try to redeploy their resources where the prospects are brighter. In most cases, however, governments do not intervene but rely on market forces. How well the market works depends on the strategy and structure of individual companies. Single-business companies in low-growth industries will continue to invest despite low returns because they know only one product or industry. Diversified companies can invest in higher-growth sectors within the organization.[5]

Government may implicitly encourage investment in low-growth areas by distorting prices or providing loan guarantees. Trade barriers foster higher prices and profits in protected sectors. Domestic subsidies also lead to overinvestment. For example, the U.S. government protected small banks by fixing prices on savings accounts; at the same time, it provided low-cost mortgage money that increased jobs in the building trades. Coupled with tax deductions for interest payments on home mortgages and massive spending on freeways, the government subsidized the development of suburbs and drew capital away from industry and into unnecessarily large, single-family dwellings.

The negative impact of tariffs and subsidies is well known and the subject of continuing attention by the public and government. But less well understood is the effect of wage and price controls, which may be worse. By setting uniform criteria for all industries, they implicitly favor the older, slow-growth industries. But controls work against high-growth industries, which generally have the most rapid productivity increases and the opportunity to reduce prices while giving above-average wage increases. In fact, higher wages are necessary to attract enough new employees to *sustain* productivity. A wage and price control system allows no credit for price cuts by high-tech companies and, at the same time, forbids them to use rising wages to bid for new employees.

4 Abandoning losers

Political logic in a democracy works against accelerated abandonment of low-growth, low-profit industries. Winning, high-profit companies – and the new jobs they create – seldom get the headlines generated by potential job losses in declining industries. A job lost is more important politically than a job not created, as any government official knows. In most

of the North Atlantic countries, government, not business, takes responsibility for unemployment. Government must choose to keep a losing company solvent or
pay unemployment compensation and the other costs
of a decline or shutdown. The Chrysler saga points up
that continued operation, even with losses, may be less
costly – at least in the short run.

Operating in private and without formal
responsibility for job security, companies abandon losing ventures more rapidly than government does.
Democratic governments, naturally concerned with
jobs and votes, have a long record of retarding rather
than facilitating the process. In the same way, private
capital markets are more flexible and less politicized
than public funding over the long run. When it comes
to capital allocation, democratic governments will do
worse than the market mechanism and much worse
than well-managed diversified companies. If enacted,
proposals to revive the Reconstruction Finance Corporation are likely to give government a more adroit
mechanism for retarding rather than accelerating disinvestment – or, simply put, a better way of doing the
wrong thing. The problem lies not so much with the
concept as with the social and political context.

On the other hand, large private compa-
nies that take little or no responsibility for employment are a major cause of the government's active
involvement in ill-advised rescue attempts. To the
extent that senior executives think business leadership
is the management of assets that are bought and sold
to promote a higher share price for stockholders with
little regard for the "investments" made by long-term
employees, they abdicate a responsibility they should
shoulder. The root of the problem lies in a shortsighted
sense of business responsibility backed by equally narrow academic theories of corporate finance that force
government to compensate. The recent contract revisions between Ford Motor Company and the United
Auto Workers, with their emphasis on employment
security and changes in corporate governance, point in
a very positive direction. Unfortunately, it is unlikely
that the concessions were nearly enough for industry
to regain a sound competitive position in the near
future.

5   Investment & output planning

Several governments have tried to plan
investments and output. The most extensive experience was in France, where a process begun in 1945 was
much heralded in the 1960s and abandoned in the
1970s – for pragmatic rather than ideological reasons.
Bluntly put, it failed. Conceived in a closed economy
where the choice was either to make or do without and
where it worked well, the plan did not adapt to an open

economy with imports, exports, and the critical
choices of make or buy. Its focus remained domestic,
leading France to overinvest in industries sheltered
from foreign competition.[6]

In the 1950s and 1960s, the Japanese had
a similar approach but abandoned it as their economy
opened to world trade. At present only the Communist
countries, in circumstances reminiscent of the closed
economies of the 1950s, attempt to plan output and
investments.

There is an obvious theoretical attraction to the involvement of government in planning;
some economists note that because big business plans,
government should do no less. However, they overlook
the critical difference: business plans in private, while
government – in a democratic society – inevitably
plans in a quasi-public setting. Forcing a company to
do its planning in public would yield a public relations
document, not a plan. In the same way, the French government's industrial plans were essentially public relations documents by the 1960s and consequently of
little value to either business or government.

A cautionary note

Sound industrial policy could aid the
performance of all the industrial countries. But it is not
a panacea and does not exist in a vacuum. By itself it
cannot overcome the excessive costs and other competitive handicaps imposed by the welfare state, any
more than it can offset the impact of a consistently
overvalued currency.

In fact, much of the current enthusiasm
for the notion of industrial policy hinges on the premise that better "portfolio management" by government
is both necessary and sufficient to ease the growing
industrial malaise.[7] This position has obvious attractions for liberal economists with a strong ideological
commitment to the welfare state because it allows
some of them to dismiss as unimportant the inadequate levels of corporate profitability and investment
of recent years.

Exaggerated claims for industrial policy
could lead to the same kind of unrealistic expectations
as did the "fine tuning" of aggregate demand espoused
by liberal economists in the 1960s. The claims could
blind us to reforms needed to reverse the inadequate
corporate profitability found in all the North Atlantic
countries.

The idea of politicians and bureaucrats
guiding business toward a better industrial portfolio is
more or less reassuring depending on your view of
their values, business savvy, and professional competence. Those who draw inspiration from Japanese experience overlook not only the productivity-oriented

nature of the Japanese strategy but also the staffing of key ministries (MITI and Finance) by career civil servants of very high quality. The U.S. bureaucracy, conversely, is characterized by rapid turnover, uneven quality, and – at least historically – little understanding of or concern for the essentials of a productive, competitive industrial sector. These bureaucrats do not have the same capacity or motivation to take a sound, long-term view of business opportunities as do American business executives. And the adversary nature of U.S. business-government relations adds an additional hazard, for it is through this relationship that proposals would eventually be formulated and implemented.

Business-government relations

The four largest market economies have different records in this area. The French and Japanese promote industries most actively; the United States, least. In Germany the government has been less interventionist than in France or Japan, and Chancellor Schmidt's more activist ministers of science and technology offset free-market advocates in the ministry of economics. Despite their differences, France, Germany, and Japan believe that government is the senior member of the business-government partnership – in short, that it guides without enacting new laws or regulations. When the chips are down, business doesn't take government to court (as it does in the United States) but rather follows its advice.

In fact, we take for granted that business and government are natural adversaries in the United States. But it has not always been so. Alfred Chandler calls the 1890s the turning point for business-government relations here. While businessmen had always been active civic leaders prior to the Civil War, the public – through government – began to attack them before the end of the century. The reason was that big companies, particularly the railroads, came before big government. As Chandler notes, "In 1890 at least a dozen railroads employed over 100,000 workers, [while] the civilian working force in Washington numbered just over 20,000."[8]

The railroads enjoyed not only great size but near monopolies in many inland areas, with the power to make or break businesses or even towns by their rates. They also opened the way for national consumer-goods companies, such as the meat-packers or A&P, that displaced many small businesses – nearly 50% of the wholesalers between 1889 and 1929. Small business, not farmers or consumer groups, mounted the initial attack on big business and helped limit its powers.

In Europe and Japan, the national markets were much smaller and big government developed before big business. In addition, consumer-goods producers used wholesalers rather than displacing them through forward integration. Some of the largest companies were manufacturers of industrial goods and interested in export sales. Government was a natural ally; it was more of a senior partner to business than an adversary and sanctioned business federation as a practical mechanism for organized dialogue.

In each of these countries, business has developed a "peak federation" that serves not only as a legitimate interlocutor for business with government but also as a way of molding business consensus toward certain general, as opposed to company- or industry-specific, goals. While the United States has an established federation for labor, it has several for business – but not one that enjoys comparable standing to those in other industrial countries.

Lack of institutional mechanisms on the business side matches weak institutional links in the U.S. government. The Commerce Department, as spokesman for business interests, is still organized as a service bureau responsible for the census and weights and measures and not for an important policymaking role. Its voice has been fourth or fifth in economic policymaking, after the Treasury, State, and Justice departments, and the Council of Economic Advisers. Commerce has had very little power; the recent transfer of customs from Treasury to Commerce came not so much from a desire to give the department more power as from congressional frustration and anger that the Treasury could so easily flout legislative intent in the enforcement of antidumping statutes.

Adversary business-government relations, coupled with a consumer-oriented economic strategy, produce bizarre policy in the executive branch. For example, the government long considered imports of cheaper manufactured goods beneficial because they reduced costs for the consumer. That some imports might be favorably priced due to dumping – with the potential for destroying an American industry within a few years – concerned only those most directly affected, not the executive branch. Japanese television exports illustrate the problem. While Japanese companies cut prices and raised market share in the United States in the 1970s, their domestic market remained closed. Imports of color televisions into Japan from *all* foreign sources remained less than 0.5%.

First, the American television industry's claims of Japanese dumping produced four years of inaction, then a customs investigation that showed that dumping approached 20% of invoice prices. The Treasury Department attempted to squelch the investigation, but Congress intervened on behalf of the industry. Finally, after most American companies were either forced or bought out, the importers pleaded no contest and paid $77 million in fines for dumping and filing fraudulent invoices. Of course, the $77 million went to the Treasury Department, not to the injured companies. By settling for no-contest pleas, the executive branch acceded to Japanese requests that there be no public record of the behavior of the exporters, importers, or their respective governments.[9] A recently released study of the machine tool industry indicates that the television case is not an isolated example.

High officials of the U.S. government describe the process as one where Treasury, State, Justice, and the CEA will take the consumer point of view and support foreign companies against a hopelessly outgunned Commerce Department. Departed officials of the Carter administration not only point to the low priority accorded the role of healthy, productive companies in building the U.S. standard of living but also describe how high officials of the Justice Department threatened other government officials with personal criminal prosecution if efforts to help American companies were viewed as restraint of trade.

Our economic strategy is half a strategy, to foster short-term consumer welfare. It is not the strategy that built our industrial base in earlier decades nor is it the one used by the Japanese to overtake us in the last 30 years. Both of those relied on investing in the future to build a rising standard of living through rising productivity. Passing the benefits along to consumers in the form of lower prices was part of the story, but only part.

This "half" strategy has also allowed big business to escape responsibility for the economic security of its employees. When Japanese companies shoulder that responsibility, employees have a long-term stake in the company, its products, and their own productivity. Americans have increasingly looked to the federal government for their economic security; product quality and productivity suffer as economic security becomes an entitlement rather than something the employee and the company produce together.

Implications for the United States

To the extent that damage to our economy is self-inflicted, we can correct it through an appropriate change in economic policy. A good example is the U.S. capital gains tax. Its increase in 1969 resulted in declining investment in new ventures, while its reduction in 1978 quickly brought on a surge of new investment. Recent acceleration of depreciation

schedules will pump up cash flows and investment when the U.S. economy recovers. While helpful, the changes do not directly address the critical problem.

We cannot achieve long-term economic recovery as long as U.S. policy focuses on short-term consumer welfare and on the entitlements and subsidies of a welfare state. This policy has steadily shifted American economic incentives away from work, saving, and investment. Until the United States rebalances its priorities, its incentives, and its rhetoric, there is little chance we will become competitive with the productivity-oriented societies of East Asia.

The Europeans do not pose a similar competitive threat. If anything, they are in a weaker position than the United States because their priorities have become even more lopsided than our own.

Recently there has been much discussion of industrial policy and reindustrialization as well as a quickening of interest in improving the business-government relationship. While constructive steps can and should be taken, even the most favorable scenario for change does not nearly address the seriousness of the problem. For example, it is fantasy to hope that government aid in reallocating an inadequate level of saving and investment will turn the economy around.[10] In addition, real respect and constructive dialogue in business-government relations will require that both government and business see the need to balance short-term consumer welfare with the imperatives of investing to build long-term productivity.

The United States has few significant natural advantages to count on, except in agriculture. Our comparative advantage will depend more and more on the goals, policies, and institutions through which the American economy is organized. Over time, the United States and all the other welfare states of the North Atlantic area will be less competitive with the productivity-oriented societies. When we tinker with small issues, we overlook or deny the challenge. To address this fundamental problem, we must recognize that government, in assuming greatly increased responsibility for the economic security of the individual, has relieved the individual and the large business enterprise of that responsibility. The various security programs result in a double cost on business, first by taxing to finance welfare and economic security programs and second by reducing the responsibility, motivation, and mobility of labor. We cannot expect industrial performance to fundamentally improve until we reduce these costs.

What it will take

Industrial performance will improve when employees gain economic security through long-term commitments to productive, profitable companies. In turn, business must recognize this commitment and must adapt its strategies, organization, and personnel policies accordingly. Companies can no longer equate management with manipulation of the balance sheet, where divisions are bought and sold or plants closed and opened with little or no reference to the rights of those who work there. Management must adopt a measure of performance a good deal broader than the highly regarded "impact on the price per share." Unless management defines its role more broadly, government can hardly relinquish its responsibility for employment.

If business assumes more responsibility and government less, the two could then work toward a different kind of industrial policy. Achieving a better working relationship requires government to have a more knowledgeable, competent, and credible focal point for its contact with business. Antitrust laws that subject both business and government leaders to the threat of criminal prosecution should be substantially revised.

A new federal charter

To encourage big companies to accept greater responsibility for the interests of their employees, Congress should enact a new federal charter of incorporation, not to supersede state charters but to serve as an alternative. Incorporation under the new federal statute would require a formal commitment to the interests of both employees and shareholders. Specifically, companies would guarantee employment security for all employees with at least 10 years' service, subject to safeguards in case of gross negligence or misbehavior. In addition, companies would consult employees through their elected representatives, at various levels, including the shop floor, the plant or product division, and the corporate board of directors. While such a new law would allow companies to tailor their schemes of governance, the law would set certain standards and subject charters to challenge and adjudication in the courts. Charters would last for a finite term (say, 50 years) and would require periodic renewal.

As an incentive for management to accept these new responsibilities, a takeover of a federally chartered company would require an affirmative vote by employees as well as stockholders. In addition, the law would exempt the company from the treble-damage provision of the antitrust laws.

As an incentive for shareholders, the federal charter would permit creation of a reserve fund for employment stability. Annual payments would be tax deductible, and the fund would finance investments designed to enhance job security. Its use would require approval of employees as well as management. This special reserve for job security would enhance cash flows and strengthen the balance sheets of companies electing to adopt the new charter and thus enhance shareholder interests along with those of employees.

A new mission for the Commerce Department

The government should make the Commerce Department the focal point for industrial policy, broaden its powers, and change its name. At present, the U.S. government has no such clear focal point. Trade policy, for example, is the mandate of the special trade representative (STR) in the White House. I suggest the merger of STR with the Commerce Department into a new Department of Industry, Trade, and Commerce (ITC). ITC should have primary responsibility for promotion of U.S. exports and the power to authorize joint ventures to promote research or accelerate the development of a new technology, ventures that would be exempt from the antitrust laws.

Since the business community is highly fragmented and has no central organization, the ITC should work with business to establish a more legitimate form of dialogue to identify and evaluate industrial problems of general interest to business. The secretary of the ITC should have statutory powers to protect both corporate and government participants in this dialogue from criminal antitrust liability. Congress should grant immunity from the sunshine provisions of the Advisory Committee Act, as it has for the committees that now advise the STR.

Review of antitrust laws

Antitrust laws should reflect the realities of international competition and the need for a less hostile relationship between business and government. Recent decisions, such as the dropping of the case against IBM, are important steps in the right direction. They do not, however, go far enough. It will be difficult for business and government to work toward a more rational economic strategy as long as the Justice

Department has the legal basis to threaten either side with criminal prosecution whenever they discuss basic questions of economic strategy. In addition, American business needs some form of relief from the ever-increasing use of antitrust suits as a way to hold companies up for ransom. Such suits, when launched by lawyers working on a contingency-fee basis, have become a new frontier for entrepreneurially oriented lawyers, who know that it is usually cheaper to settle than to fight, even if the allegations are without merit. Provisions of the alternative charter provide one remedy; in its absence another is needed.

Industry probably *can* coexist with the welfare state. The reforms outlined here would enhance its chances of survival in the United States. By themselves they are not enough. Basic reform of the welfare state is also required.

References

1 Edwin O. Reischauer,
The United States and Japan. 3d ed.
(New York: Viking, 1964);
(original edition,
Cambridge, Mass..
Harvard University Press, 1950).

2 Richard G. Hamermesh,
"Administrative Issues Posed by
Contemporary Approaches
to Strategic Planning:
The Case of the Dexter Corporation,"
Harvard Business School Working Paper
(HBS 79-53, 1979).

3 Richard J. Rumelt and Robin C. Wemsley,
"In Search of the Market Share Effect,"
University of California at Los Angeles
Working Paper (MGL-63,
revised May 1, 1981).

4 Richard Bolling and John Bowles,
America's Competitive Edge
(New York: McGraw-Hill, 1982).

5 See my article,
"The Industrial State:
Old Myths and New Realities,"
HBR March-April 1973, p. 133.

6 See my article,
"How Practical Is National
Economic Planning?"
HBR March-April 1978, p. 131.

7 See Ira Magaziner and Robert Reich,
Minding America's Business
(New York:
Harcourt Brace Jovanovich, 1982),
and the Boston Consulting Group,
*A Framework for Swedish
Industrial Policy*
(Uberforlag, Sweden, 1978)
for examples of sound analysis of
industry coupled with a failure to
analyze the impact of the welfare state
on the competitive position of industry.

8 For a contrary view see Robert B. Reich,
"Why the U.S. Needs an Industrial Policy,"
HBR January-February 1982, p. 74.

9 Alfred D. Chandler, Jr.,
"Government versus Business:
An American Phenomenon,"
Business and Public Policy.
ed. John T. Dunlop
(Boston: Division of Research,
Graduate School of
Business Administration,
Harvard University,
1980), p. 3.

10 See "Zenith v. U.S.A.,"
nos. 4-379-054 and 4-379-067,
distributed by HBS Case Services,
Soldiers Field,
Boston, Mass. 02163;
and John J. Nevin,
"Can U.S. Business Survive
Our Japanese Trade Policy?"
HBR September-October 1978, p. 165.

Common cause

During the 1930s when the social contract, binding business to society, was being extensively rewritten, the business community resisted innovation and wound up with some unpalatable reforms and a blemished reputation. Now with the social contract again up for revision, new social and environmental problems are generating increasing pressure for further modification and regulation of business. By acting promptly, business can assure itself a voice in deciding the form and content of the new social contract. By taking the initiative, it can contribute technical competence, rational analysis and imaginative innovations to the process of adjusting our system – but it must recognize that some adjustments are inevitable.

In certain areas, there may have to be new laws to force consideration of the quality-of-life dimension so that the more socially responsive firms will not suffer a competitive disadvantage at the hands of others who refuse to aid voluntarily....

In view of the emerging demands for revision of the social contract, a passive response on the part of the business community could be dangerous. Any adaptation of our system to the changing environment is far more likely to be workable if those who understand the system's problems share in designing the solutions. So it is up to businessmen to make common cause with other reformers – whether in government or on the campus or wherever – to prevent the unwise adoption of extreme and emotional remedies, but on the contrary to initiate necessary reforms that will make it possible for business to continue to function in a new climate as a constructive force in our society.

From
a speech presented by
David Rockefeller
to the Advertising Council
Dinner in New York,
quoted in the *Wall Street Journal*
December 21, 1971.

JeI *JOURNAL OF ECONOMIC ISSUES*
Vol. XVIII   No. 3   September 1984

Industrial Policy

Robert Solo

Antitrust policy came into being during the last two decades of the nineteenth century, when the ideology of laissez faire liberalism, with its vision of self-equilibrating utility-optimizing markets, was absolutely dominant, with all good liberals commited to "eternal vigilance" against the poison of public intervention. It was a time when the Supreme Court interpreted the Constitution so as to rule virtually any government action upon the economy to be beyond the pale, with the antitrust laws as the unique exception, having as their objective not to countermand the salutory forces of market competition but to save and restore them.

Those laws, declaring monopoly and monopolizing, all combinations, conspiracies, and contracts in restraint of trade, and other specified anticompetitive practices to be illegal and punishable under the civil and criminal codes, are enforced by the Department of Justice, by the Federal Trade Commission, and by triple damage suits on private accounts.

Under the aegis of the Court, the paradigm of antitrust enforcement took its essential form in the period between 1890 and 1940. The Court permitted rigorous enforcement when it carried no threat to the integrity of operating organizations or to technology, as for example in disallowing price-fixing agreements between independent companies. Where the impact on organization and operation was uncertain and equivocal, as for example in eliminating the "open price systems" practiced through trade associations, the Court's enforcement was equivocal and uncertain as well. But when there was a clear presumption that to enforce the law would disrupt the integrity of established organization and operating technologies,

---

The author is Professor of Economics, Michigan State University.

the Court ruled out enforcement entirely, thus safeguarding the "good trusts" of the corporate organizational sector from antitrust attack. The monopoly power, as a function of market share exercised in a demonstrated ability significantly to influence price, was immunized from prosecution.

With the Great Depression and the New Deal came a critical and irreversible turning in the outlook of the Supreme Court. As it accepted the need for a strong and self-responsible state, it correspondingly lifted the old constitutional constraints on government intervention in the economy, yielding to the judgment of public agencies as to the appropriateness of such action. Thus was removed the tight leash on the agencies of antitrust enforcement, and a path was opened for a general attack on the market power of large corporate organizations. The Justice Department and the Federal Trade Commission plunged down that path.

Still the old tension remained between the potential benefits to competition through the rigorous enforcement of the letter of the law and the dangers of technological and organizational disruption following such enforcement. Given the reluctance of the Supreme Court to draw the line, thenceforth constraints on the agencies of antitrust enforcement would come from Congress (under pressure of affected interests), from the administration, from within the agencies of enforcement themselves (which perforce were obliged to apply their own rule of reason), and from their peers in academia or before the bar.

For a century the antitrust laws have been the United States' one coherent and continuing policy designed to upgrade the performance of industry—our only industrial policy. It is time to ask these questions: Do the antitrust laws suffice for that purpose? Do they make sense at all as a policy designed to upgrade industrial performance? And if we are to make that judgment, by what criterion can we evaluate antitrust as industrial policy? We cannot in that regard judge it by reference to its success in increasing competition (no matter how we might choose to measure the degree of competitiveness) since what is at issue is the value of a policy that takes the enforcement of competition as its objective. Competition is not an end in itself; it too needs to be justified by its real impact on industrial performance.

If what we want of industry is that it provide us with the material wherewithall of well-being, then the objective of industrial performance is in its capacity to provide more of that wherewithall of well-being, that is, a net increase in real income per capita. That being so, the first criterion of industrial performance is *productivity* as a measure of industry's capacity to produce a greater output (or a preferred set of outputs with the same input of resources). Higher productivity is presumably a function of greater efficiency, organizational effectiveness, or technological advance, and is reflected in lower prices and/or higher wages, and profits. Beyond productivity there are other measures, not so much of industrial but of overall economic performance in the capacity to utilize available resources, fully to employ labor, to keep prices stable, and to distribute income justly. Beyond the economic there are measures of social performance in the wise and compassionate use of resources and in a beneficent evolution of the patterns of work, life, and leisure. Here however our concern will be only with industrial performance, which is a foundation for the rest.

We return then to our question. Does American antitrust policy generate innovation? Accelerate technological advance? Support the transformations of industrial structure, or promote whatever it is that leads to higher productivity, to increased output, to new job and career opportunities, hence to greater real income? Whether or not we have the answer, has the question itself been asked? Has it been or is it being asked by the agencies of antitrust enforcement? Is it being or has it been asked by the courts that guide and control the enforcement of the law? The answer, alas, is that these questions concerning the impact of antitrust on industrial performance have not been and are not being asked by anyone in the system. There is no place in the system for asking them. No one looks back to find out, What happened then? There is no place, no effort to test the theory behind the law, to question its value or measure its impact as industrial policy. Those barriers to competition were broken down: what happened to industrial performance then? These anticompetitive practices were eliminated: what happened to industrial performance then? That monopoly was smashed, the company was fragmented: what happened to industrial performance then?

That this form of industrial policy ploughs ahead with its purpose obscured and its consequences unquestioned is in part because it is rationalized by, and operates under, the benediction of neo-classical ideologues whose vision of pure competition, with its self-equilibrating, utility-optimizing, price-directed markets as the essence of industrial reality, remains unshaken; and whose commitment to that vision as the policy norm, and whose belief in the salutory force of competition as the elixir of good tidings, is a matter of absolute faith. In part the failure to question the consequences of this industrial policy is a consequence of its mode of formation and enforcement under the aegis of the courts. The judicial system simply does not look back to take into account the consequences of its acts; nor does an evaluation of industrial performance fall within the competence, inclination, motivation, or mores of lawyer or of judge. Such evaluation is not what they are trained to do. It is not expected of them, nor do they expect it of themselves. It is their task to represent interests, to settle disputes, and to punish crimes. As one case is settled, one crime punished, they move on to the next case, to the next crime, with no time for looking back. After the antitrust blow has been delivered, they are not responsible for what happens then. No one is. Consequences are not their concern. Nor are they anyone's.

It is not quite true that no one has ever asked and tried to find answers to the question: What happened then? What happened when barriers to competition were eliminated, when anti-competitive practices were abolished, when a monopoly was smashed or a company fragmented? I asked those questions, and used what information I could find to discover what happened to productivity, production, employment, prices, technological innovation, and organizational integrity in the aftermath of antitrust enforcement. I thought I was alone in that quest until Joel Dirlam referred me to Simon N. Whitney, who had earlier asked the same questions.[2] Both of us, alas, quite independently found the same answer. What happened then was not good. By the evidence we could find, the general consequence of the application of antitrust policy to the corporate organizational sector was a deterioration in industrial performance.

Given the growing margin of the disillusioned among my fellow economists, one may hope that some of them, after the latest great antitrust victory in the breakup of AT&T, and the fragmenting of Bell Labs (which had been the most productive industry-oriented research center in the world) will pause to ask and find an answer to the question: What happened then?

The corporate organizational sector, for all its weaknesses and failures —and it has many—is nevertheless the strong heart of the modern industrial economy. Nor is there the faintest possibility that the sector can be battered and fragmented by antitrust policy into even a distant approximation of the neo-classical model of pure competition; nor has the antitruster any other workable model, or blueprint, for the industrial economy.

The inadequacy and contradiction of antitrust as industrial policy (and if it is not industrial policy it is nothing) is further demonstrated by its total unconcern with the weak, the static, the stagnant, the backward, the laggard, the failed, the failing firms or industries. By its nature antitrust has nought to do with the problem children of industry; and this at a time when the United States' loss of technological preeminance is more precipitous than ever before witnessed in history, at a time when great industries like steel, at the core of the industrial economy, are near collapse. Antitrust strikes only at the winners, selecting among these for ritual sacrifices to the gods of competition. It pursued A&P when that company was the world's most innovative marketer, and Alcoa, and Dupont, and United Shoe Machinery, and the U.S. movie industry at the time it dominated the world market, and IBM, and AT&T, forever dragging the goose that lays the golden egg to the antitrust chopping block. But if antitrust should be rejected, what should replace it as our industrial policy? To that question a different answer; a different policy is appropriate for the small business sector than for that of the corporate organizational giants.

The Corporate Organizational Sector

To comprehend the corporate organizational sector, at the heart of the U.S. industrial system, we must discard two popular illusions: that of the Chicago School and its allies, which consider the operations of this sector "to approximate," "to have as its essence," "for practical purposes to be regarded as the same as" the neoclassical model of pure competition; and that of the antitruster in hot pursuit of ravaging, price gouging, consumer-squeezing, inherently inefficient, necessarily exploitative monopolists/ oligopolists/monopsanists, with nothing for it but to cut down and slice up the wicked giants.

What we are in fact dealing with are autonomous power centers and communities of such power centers (industries), where each (corporate) center is a quasi-political entity operating through a variety of systems of decision and control, where sets of rights, responsibilities, and prerogatives attach to the divers components of the system. A case can be made that this corporate organizational sector enables the maximum technical flexibility and individual discretion compatible with the economies of large-scale production and with moderately long-range planning.

The entities of the sector, however, are not held to the straight and narrow by the forces of competition as they might be in decentralized price-directed markets. Nor are these power centers answerable to those who feel the consequences and suffer the impact of their actions, as public agencies are answerable, by way of Congress, to the electorate. Their power, in that sense, is *arbitrary*.

Nor is there any necessary relationship between the social interest (or for that matter, even between the corporate or trade union interest) in survival and prosperity and the motivation, choice, and actions of those who exercise authority or who influence or affect the policy of those entities. Effective policy objectives and internal arrangements for the maintenance and exercise of power are variable, and the implications of these for equity, efficiency, and technological progress are equivocal. By way of illustration consider the following.

The "media," that is, radio, television, newspapers, and magazines, operating under corporate management and the advertiser's influence and serving as gatekeepers to public information, exercise an enormous, indeed an immeasurable power in shaping our values, our attitudes, our ideologies, our sensibilities, our culture, our cognitive capacity, our political orientation, our public choice. For all its critical powers, the media is in no sense answerable for the consequences of what it is and what it does, nor are those consequences taken into account in the formation of its policies, nor has it any purpose exogenous to the variable interests of the components of this corporate organizational power center, nor does the force of "competition" hold the exercise of its great power to some straight and narrow path of the public weal. This is not to accuse it of wickedness nor to designate the consequences of its actions as pernicious, though certainly they may be. It is only to say that its exercise of power is arbitrary, and that which drives, orients, and motivates the media is equivocal. Nor is there anything in the system itself to prevent it from straying far from the path of the public weal!

The equivocal character and potential dangers in the spontaneous formation of arrangements internal to the corporate organizational entity, especially with respect to its locus of power and its exercise of choice, are exemplified by the conglomeration of U.S. enterprise after World War II. With passage of the Celler-Kefauver Act of 1950, amending Section 7 of the Clayton Act, and with all the leeway granted by the Supreme Court to the agencies of antitrust enforcement, those agencies imposed formidable barriers to horizonal mergers, vertical mergers, and to product-extension mergers. This is to say that mergers that *might* have some value for economies of scale (and hence might be sought by those elements of the corporate entity with an interest in them), for greater operating efficiency, for more effective marketing, for organizational streamlining, for the reduction of transaction costs, for the introduction of more encompassing technological systems, or for obtaining monopoly power in particular markets, were all effectively tabooed. Nevertheless merging did not cease. Rather its pace accelerated—though now as a consequence of the mindless antitrust policy there was a basic change in the character of mergers. By 1958, 90 percent of mergers were of conglomerates, bringing together a hodge-podge of operations without technical linkage, without organizational commensurability, without market ties. What could motivate, what reason could there be for mergers with no possible technological, operational, marketing, or organizational value, or relevance for market control? What interest within the corporate complex would be served by mergers such as these? With the former potentials of merging cleared away, what skills would now be emphasized, what new path for ambition would be opened within the corporate complex? The new form of mergers could have as its objective tax evasion, or stock promotion, or asset manipulation, generating industrial monstrosities without organizational or technological rationale. Thus a species of industrial leadership came to the fore consisting of financial wheeler-dealers and asset reshufflers without interest in or knowledge of the turning kaleidoscope of technologies that fell in and out of the compass of their control; they were quite unable, given the skills for which they are selected, their role, and the jumbles in which they deal, to innovate or evaluate technological innovation, to restructure operations, or to plan development, or to comprehend and activate transformations at the techno-operational level. The power over the nation's industrial future fell into the hands of those who are, in the nature of the case, inherently incompetent and incapable in exactly the areas that are all-critical for the strength and survivability of U.S. industry. Thus again the exercise of *arbitrary power* and its deviations from the public weal, the equivocal character of its motivation, and the pernicious internal arrangements and structures for the exercise of power that were its consequence. Occasionally, under the pressure of crisis or of grassroots outrage, the American state has acted to offset a deleterious exercise of this arbitrary power. For generations the media actively, aggressively encouraged the smoking of cigarettes, until finally, faced with overwhelming evidence that this was a major cause of lung cancer and heart disease, the state banned such advertising on television. In the face of grassroots "liberation" movements and black rioting in the cities, the state acted to constrain racial bias in corporate hiring and even promoted "affirmative action." In response to popular outrage at our poisoned earth and polluted waters, as the "chemical revolution" came home to roost, came the Environmental Protection Agency and the Environmental Impact Statement. Faced with the dire consequences of its collapse, the state funded Chrysler's rehabilitation. Such occasional offsets do not constitute an industrial policy. What should industrial policy be, then, for the corporate industrial sector?

An Industrial Policy for the Corporate Organizational Sector

Last of the greats from the golden age of economics in the 1930s, Abba Lerner told of a debate on "capitalism vs. socialism" in which he participated. In the days of his youth he was a socialist, and he took the socialist side. "I took the position," he said, "that the control of the economy should be left to the planning authority of the state, except of course where the market would do things better. My opponent took the position that the control of the economy should be left to the market, except of course where the planning authority of the state could do things better. And so, as it turned out, there was not much we had to debate about."

A charming story. Would that it were so easy to agree on what it is that the market and what it is that the state do best. That would nevertheless be our criterion for the development of an industrial policy, for we would envisage a system of dual industrial management, occasionally conflictual but basically symbiotic, one level geared to the operation of the firm with profitability as a key criterion, and the other representing the political authority, committed to the survival and growth of industry and the economy, to the expansion of career and employment opportunities, to price stability, to equity in income distribution, to environmental quality and other social values—and with each, corporate management and state management, enabled to do what it does best.

What is it, then, that corporate management does best? To control and to stand responsible for the internal organization and operation of the firm, for the formation and implementation of competitive strategies, for recruitment, hiring, and promotion, for planning and organizing procurement, R&D, production, marketing, product and process innovation, capital investments, and the intra-enterprise distribution of income would be the task of corporate management.

It would be for public management to do what can be done best, or can only be done at all, through an agency of the state. This would include targeting, supporting, and coordinating multi-firm, multi-faceted transformations of industry, establishing and spearheading new industrial beachheads. To achieve these objectives it would undertake explorative and enabling R&D and the development of an appropriate infrastructure.

It would co-participate with corporate management in the formation of some corporate policy, and in particular instances impose constraints and parameters on corporate choice, when and inasmuch as significant social effects and objectives were involved, including environmental quality, price stability, employment opportunity, and such corporate investment in other countries as might establish competitive operations or operations to replace those in the United States, or wherever important social effects are excluded from consideration in profit and loss accounts.

Public management would stand responsible, not to shareholders, whose interests are of quite another order, but to the nation at large for the survival and sustained growth of U.S. industry, for its long-range technological preeminence and rising productivity. On that account it would be obliged to monitor industrial performance industry by industry, great firm by great firm, and be able in the face of malperformance and failure to require the replacement of management and also to require and financially to support organizational restructuring and the upgrading of technology among the failing and the laggard. Demonstrably in the great industries of the corporate industrial sector, as in the case of U.S. railroads or steel, there is no spontaneous replacement of an incompetent or inadequate management nor reform of internal organization nor redesign and replacement of plant among the failing and the laggard through the operation of the market. Instead there are decades or generations of decline, malaise, and even regional catastrophe.

There are also requisites for an effective public management. First, an effective public management absolutely requires a dedicated corps of very competent civil servants, sensitized to the table of social values, skilled in the processes of policy formation and of policy implementation through the political system, and with a knowledge of technology and the context of industrial operations at least as great as that of the best of their industrial counterparts. The values, skills, and outlook required here are not those inculcated and selected through success at the corporate game. No effective public management team can be staffed with or led by borrowed businessmen. It must consist, top and bottom, of career professionals, systematically recruited, trained through their working lifetimes, and selectively rising to high responsibilities and positions of leadership.

Second, public management must possess considerable autonomy, for independent initiatives and for the formation and implementation of long-term planning and strategies. For this they must be insulated on two fronts—from the power and pressure of corporate ownership and management abetted by the force of mammon, and from the vagaries of partisan politics. Legal constraints that would prevent the career professionals of the public management corps from taking any position with or from accepting any support or favor from corporate management on the one hand, and the capacity of the corps to speak directly to the electorate and to create a constituency within it on the other, would militate against those dangers.

Third, while a public management corps must operate under rules, it must also possess independent power, preferably not to issue directives but in generalizable capacities to exercise leverage, for example, through making investable funds, R&D, and infrastructural supports available, and in the power to impose constraints, for example, on pricing policy and on investment.

Lest the reader suppose that what is proposed belongs to the realm of mere fantasy, being hence unworthy of consideration as impractical and unreal, what has been described and proposed is precisely the relationship of public management, via the Ministry of International Trade and Industry, with the corporate organizational sector in Japan. What would weigh most in favor of the success of such a scheme is that a dedicated and highly competent public management corps and an honest, capable corporate management interested in the technological viability and long-run survival and growth of the firm would be extremely useful to each other. Public management, answerable to the nation for industrial performance and growth, needs and must support well-managed firms. Its plans and strategies cannot succeed without them. For the firm it is of the utmost importance that social demands and public policies be filtered through an agency deeply knowledgeable of the circumstances and requisites of its operations, and that there exist such an agency able to represent its needs in the political arena. Survival and profitability of the firm in international competition may well require the targeting, coordinating, and long-range planning functions of the agency of public management.

Industrial Policy for the Small Enterprise Sector

John Kenneth Galbraith, I think, coined the phrase, "Administered prices are the easiest to administer," confessing that public controls operate far more easily in the regions controlled through the power of corporate management. Certainly a policy operating through direct or participatory public planning is more amenable by far to the circumstances of the corporate organizational industry than to the small enterprise sector. For that reason perhaps there has yet to emerge any effective corrective measure for the many weak and laggard areas in that sector, or any coherent policy to promote the development of small enterprise.

Its problems are brought to a head in a crisis of one of its healthiest parts: that of the thousands of tool and die makers, machine shops, parts manufacturers, contractors, and subcontractors, some comparatively large, many very small, who have in the midwest, and particularly in the state of Michigan, serviced and supplied automobile manufacturers. For generations the auto maker has been their hub, their production outlet, their design center, their financial base. Now auto makers can no longer play that role, certainly not as they once did. Their output has declined and will never regain earlier levels. Their loci of production have scattered.

They look abroad for supplies and parts. What then will become of the small enterprise mass for so long geared to, but no longer sustainable by, the demands of automobile production?

It is important for the nation's economic health that this small enterprise sector be salvaged, supported, developed, and helped to grow. It constitutes a great pool of self-replicable skills capable of being reoriented quickly and easily, hence constituting an element of technological flexibility. It springs from the vanishing domain of the highly skilled American craftsman with a grassroots command of technology that, as such, constitutes the prime potential source for mechanical invention, and a seedbed for technological innovation. Events have demonstrated that the fixed technologies of traditional mass production industries, wherein relatively low-skilled labor operates complex but inflexible machine lines, can be quickly replicated and activated in foreign countries such as Korea or Brazil, where workers are paid very low wages, undercutting U.S. products in world and domestic markets. The aforementioned skill-based small enterprise sector offers the basis for an alternative industrial structure that would remain indigenous, made up of flexible, specialized production lines generating a continuum of new outputs.

We will propose fragments at least of an industrial policy appropriate to this part of the small enterprise sector. It would support and promote coalitions of firms, with an independent capacity to group and re-group as needed to produce a variety of outputs, embodying innovative technologies, for diverse markets. An extraordinary industrial development in the central Italian province of Emilia-Romagna, dating from the end of the 1960s, provides something of a model. Charles Sabel has described this development; the following is exerpted from his work:

> There are small towns near Bologna, along the Adriatic coast near Ancona and Venice, where the number of officially registered factories or artisans' workshops almost equals the number of inhabitants. . . . Each district specializes . . . in Emilia-Romagna, knitwear is made at Capri, ceramic tiles at Sassuolo, motorcycles and automatic machines at Bologna, farm machinery at Reggio Emilia. . . .
>
> Some recall turn-of-the-century sweatshops. . . . But many of the others are spotless; the workers extremely skilled and the distinction between them and their supervisors almost imperceptible; the tools the most advanced numerically controlled equipment of its type; the products, designed in the shop, sophisticated and distinctive enough to capture monopolies in world markets. . . .
>
> The emergence of high-technology cottage industry in Italy is the result . . . [of] the industrial conflicts of the 1960s and 1970s . . . and [of] the general changes in market conditions. . . .
>
> As the union's power over wages, hours, work conditions, and employment levels in the large factories increased, managers tried to regain con-

trol by subcontracting work to small producers. Craftsmen, unsettled by the compression of wage and skill hierarchies, began to look for work in small shops. . . .

The upshot was that by the mid-1970s there were in Italy innumerable small firms specializing in virtually every phase of the production of textiles, automatic machines, machine tools, automobiles, buses, and agricultural equipment. . . . [Many] paid wages higher than those in the large factories . . . and had equipment identical to that used in the most modern factories to perform equivalent operations. . . . They bought modern, high-output machines, aggregated orders from different customers, and prorated the fixed costs of operation among them. . . .

A dramatic proof of the area's new riches is the ascent of Modena, regarded as the capital of the small-firm economy in the league tables of provincial wealth: Ranked by per capita income, it was the seventeenth richest province in 1970, the second richest (after a center of luxury tourism) in 1979.

. . . During the years immediately following 1969, even the larger and more advanced subcontractors were still subordinate to the big factories. Often the client delivered the blueprints and tools needed to manufacture the part: Like the emergent industrial countries, the subcontractors were dependent on someone else's know-how. . . . the subcontractors were still hostage to their customers' good will and prosperity.

To understand how this dependence was broken in the course of the 1970s, and a new system of production created, imagine a small factory producing transmissions for a large manufacturer of tractors. Ambition, the joy of invention, or fear that he and his clients will be devastated by an economic downturn lead the artisan who owns the shop to modify the design of the tractor transmission to suit the needs of a small manufacturer of high-quality seeders. To do this he draws on experiences acquired during years spent in West German factories, when he was unable to find work at home; or perhaps he consults with the young engineers working for his prospective client. But once the new transmission is designed, he discovers that to make it he needs precision parts not easily available on the market. If he cannot modify his own machines to make these parts, he turns to a friend with a special lathe, who like himself fears being too closely tied to a few large manufacturers of a single product. Soon more and more artisans with different machines and skills are collaborating to make more diverse products.

The result is a system of high-technology cottage industry that does in a decentralized way what large innovative companies like the Thyssen specialty steel division do within the framework of huge organizations. . . . Where the subcontractor's original customers arrive with a blueprint to execute, his new ones arrive with a problem to solve. They need, for example, a gearshift for a new small tractor, a pump for spreading a new insecticide that must be finely vaporized, or an elaborate container for mounting the cables of a nuclear power station. Even if the customer has a blueprint for his part, it is much more likely to serve as a guide to posing his problem than as a solution to it.

Typically, the small firm's solution will involve modifications of existing technology, which taken one at a time are marginally significant. For example, a conventional automatic packing machine is redesigned to fit the available space in a particular assembly line; a machine that injects one type of plastic into molds is modified to inject another, cheaper plastic; a membrane pump used in automobiles is modified to suit agricultural machinery; a standard loom or cloth-cutting machine is adjusted to work efficiently with particularly fine threads.

The innovative capacity of this type of firm depends on its flexible use of technology; its close relations with other, similarly innovative firms in the same and adjacent sectors; and above all on the close collaboration of workers with different kinds of expertise. . . .

No good comes of proposing a solution if the small firm cannot supply the proposed product at an affordable price. Hence the design of the new product is inextricably connected to discussion of its production; and the final blueprint can be drawn only after consultation among technicians of several kinds and production workers of several levels.

. . . An innovative artisan with a numerically controlled lathe or grinding machine is just as likely to tinker with it—inventing new tools, finding new ways to cut odd-shaped pieces—as an artisan with traditional equipment.

This tinkering, furthermore, constantly spurs and jostles suppliers of machine tools to improve their products. . . . In this way Italy has become a leading manufacturer of wood-cutting, ceramic, and metal-cutting machinery.

. . . Each firm is jealous of its autonomy, overly proud of its capacities, but fully conscious that its success and its very survival are linked to the collective efforts of the community to which it belongs and whose prosperity it must defend. . . .

The more the system of related, innovative small firms expands and prospers, pressing against its original limits, the more explicit the collective character of the activity becomes. . . . to expand business they must increase the sophistication and range of their products; and the only means to that end is to increase the range of sophistication of their capital equipment. But investment in exotic equipment is risky. No one is likely to undertake it unless he is confident that his friends will help him utilize the new machine by passing along orders even when there is no immediate profit to them from doing so. . . .

This sense of mutual dependence is further reinforced by an appreciation of economies of scale that can sometimes be achieved by explicit collaboration. For most aspects of production, the small firms are not at a disadvantage because of their size; they have found that economies of scale exist at the level of one or a very few machines, not whole factories. Three lathes in each of three shops are at least as efficient as nine lathes under one roof. But firms can seldom maintain white-collar staffs to handle marketing, accounting, or even technical services. An obvious solution frequently adopted in Italy is to pool resources and form an association of artisans or small employers who provide the services collectively. Similarly, consortia of small employers can purchase raw materials or secure bank loans at better prices than single firms. . . . collective provision of accounting services, advice on new marketing possibilities, and the applicability of new technologies to local needs could all encourage the new firms to grow through innovation.[3]

Though we are left with the impression that the state, at the level of regional Italian governments, contributed significantly to this industrial development, Sabel does not describe the character of that contribution. Nor does he offer any prospectus for an industrial policy that would promote and support collaborative activities and innovative technology in a small enterprise sector, save for such inferences as these:

> In Emilia-Romàgna, for instance, the innovative proprietors, the unions, and the regional government are already so intertwined by common political ideas that the creation of such collective services seems possible . . . in turn reinforced by the extensive aid the town and regional agencies under the Left's control give to small employers. . . . The region advises small firms on market strategy and the use of technology. The success of agricultural and industrial producers' cooperatives, owing in some measure to the government's willingness to place orders with local artisans determined to defend their independence against large firms, has popularized the idea of collectively owned enterprise while drawing the state and the labor movement still closer together.[4]

Clearly there exists the potential for a similar development among the midwestern small enterprise cluster hitherto geared to serving the automobile manufacturers. Thousands of independent firms there, possessing a great diversity of high quality skills and production capacities and capabilities, have known the grip of crisis and sense the threat to their survival. With a regional culture of neighborliness, they have the capacity to associate and a readiness to collaborate. They are quite aware of the need to search for alternative production outlets. Some will find such outlets. Spontaneous adjustments are, indeed, occurring. Experience suggests, however, that the required overall transformation of a small enterprise sector so pressured and so endowed will not occur spontaneously: witness the impoverished generations of British Midlands industry or of the New England mill towns. Such transformation could occur more easily in an urban context where many markets intermingle rather than with regionally isolated, specialized small enterprise clusters without proximity to alternative markets. Latent marketing opportunities may be real and rewarding but for the small entrepreneur tucked away in the regional cluster, those opportunities are unknown and even unknowable. The actual risks of reorientation may be low, but the uncertainties that confront the small firm undertaking that reorientation on its own are ineradicable and profound.

One finds an analogy to all this in the basic transformation of U.S. agriculture that came via the New Deal and rural electrification. That critical change could not and did not come spontaneously through the piecemeal exercise of individual demands. Electrical companies would not string out their power lines to meet the possible needs of farm families in their spatial isolation. It required that the state, through the Rural Electrification Administration, promote and support the formation of farm cooperatives, that is, collaborative action by sets of potential consumers, and that it extend credit to those cooperatives to build their own power lines into rural areas. Thus the process of rural electrification was set in motion. Once the state had pushed that transformation over the hump to fully demonstrated profitability, private electric power companies rushed in and speedily completed rural electrification. The industrial policy we are recommending here would be designed to push another innovationary transformation over the hump: reorienting the production capability of the midwestern (or other) metalworking clusters by forging linkages with new markets for diverse products.

Two critical supports, like pillars upholding the span of a bridge that would carry the flow of energies and resources in another direction to a different shore, are required for that transformation to occur. The first of these is an institutionalized capacity to search for market outlets and develop market opportunities, and to specify the marketable products that can effectively link the existing or latent production potentials of the metalworking small enterprise cluster to those outlets and opportunities. The second would be an institution with the capacity, the competence, and the commitment to finance such collaborative production for new markets.

It is notable that the Japanese have built their sets of rounded industrial communities, the Zaibatsu, and their remarkable industrial development on these twin foundations. At the heart of each of the Zaibatsu are (1) a mother bank geared to the needs and plans of the enterprise of that industrial community, constituting the primary source for the financing of all its industrial transformations, and (2) a trading company that operates as the marketing linkage between the existing or latent production potentials of that Zaibatsu and existing or latent sales opportunities throughout the world. To supply further intelligence concerning marketing opportunities and hence to facilitate exports, Japan has established the Japanese External Trade Organization, with operations in fifty-five countries.

A trading intermediary designed to serve the interests and collaborative efforts of the numerous small firms of the sector, or of different marketing intermediaries, each serving one of what would evolve as the specialized sets within the sector, will not develop spontaneously through the piecemeal striving of individual producers, but would require some enabling action by the state. One option (for example) would be to establish marketing cooperatives initially financed at least in part by the state but ultimately owned by sets of producers. These cooperatives would operate under the umbrella of a state agency that would: (1) explore for the cooperatives marketing opportunities in foreign markets and facilitate export linkages, (2) provide specialized services and expert counsel to the cooperatives, (3) by way of the marketing cooperatives, tie collaborative small enterprise production into target industries and long-range planning in the corporate organizational sector, and (4) provide political muscle in gaining the cooperatives entry into the processes of governmental procurement.

Similarly, given the innate conservatism of commercial banks and other private financial institutions and their very limited competence in evaluating innovative organizational and technological arrangements, private sector financing of collaborative small enterprise production will not spring forth spontaneously. As with the Rural Electrification Administration, a public agency committed to the program and able to give a hard-headed, competent evaluation of repayment prospects would be required, at least until the feasibility and profitability of the transformation has been demonstrated.

There are other supplementary public supports that would accelerate the sector's development. It would seem that the first impulse of government intent on promoting such development is to rally the efforts of the universities and to pour money into R&D institutes. These then engage in whatever high technology research is currently the fashion—today robotics, electronics, and genetic engineering. Lacking is a strong connection between such R&D and the producers for whom support is intended, especially connection with the firms of the small enterprise sector that might incorporate new technologies into their products or processes. There are various possible strategies for making those connections. The marketing cooperative would be useful here in searching out, in consultation with these research centers, potential products and processes commensurate with the skills and interests of their membership. In the decades after World War II the TNO (the Netherlands Organization for Applied Research) demonstrated the value of another relevant strategy, that of setting up and renting out pilot plants in new technology to small enterprises for their technological education and experimentation. It was in this way that the plastics industry took root there. Today such pilot operations (in, say, cryogenics) besides offering the firm the opportunity to learn the technology and to experiment within its frame, would serve as a locus of interaction among the R&D scientist and the university specialist and the operators of interested firms.

It would also be possible, and possibly very helpful, to establish centers where very heavy tools for molding, shaping, pressing, and metal cutting (tools which these days can be obtained from military installations for no more than the cost of transporting them) are brought together and made available to small enterprise for occasional special use.

Upgrading and extending training and education could fortify and deepen the potentials of the sector: for example, (1) vocational training that led directly to job opportunities, with loans and guidance made available to star performers so that they might set up independent operations, and (2) life-long engineering education designed not for the college-trained science graduate but intended to open new avenues of development for skilled workers possessed of talent and creativity.

Conclusion

Faced with a precipitous decline in its technological preeminence, with even basic industries in seeming danger of collapse, the United States needs a policy and the capacity to upgrade its industrial performance. All it has ever had for this purpose are the antitrust laws. Operating through lawyers and judges not competent in this regard, as part of a system that cannot look back to test the consequences of its actions, incapable of dealing with the sick and laggard industries but perennially dragging winners to butchery on the chopping block, the antitrust laws cannot do the job. Nor would any single industrial policy be appropriate for the diverse sectors of the U.S. industrial economy.

Foreign experience is suggestive. It cannot be overlooked, and our proposals take such experience as a reference base. The Japanese example suggests a dual system where the public and private sectors collaborate on corporate industrial policy as well as co-manage that part of the economy, with the former focussing on infrastructural development, on targeting and coordinating industrial growth and transformation, on overall employment and on the environment, and the latter concentrating on operations. Such a system would require the development of new competencies within the state, and the establishment of public agencies with considerable autonomy and leverage over industry.

Recent Italian experience illustrates further possibilities and offers guidance in upgrading technology and re-orienting production in that part of the small enterprise sector hitherto geared to servicing and supplying parts for a corporate industrial hub, for example, the great auto companies. That technological upgrading and re-orientation might turn on the axis of (1) cooperative, initially state-supported market instruments, serving coalitions of small enterprises, with (2) financing agencies, initially state-supported, interested in and able to evaluate the ventures at issue. Also important would be development of intermediary instruments that would channel information and help between esoteric, publicly supported high-tech R&D and the shop-level craft skills of small independent enterprise.

Notes

1. Robert Solo, *The Political Authority and the Market System* (Cincinnati: Southwestern, 1974).
2. Simon N. Whitney, *Antitrust Policies* (New York: Twentieth Century Fund, 1958).
3. Charles Sabel, *Work and Politics* (Cambridge: Cambridge University Press, 1982), pp. 220-21.
4. Ibid.

SOCIAL PROBLEMS, Vol. 32, No. 2, December 1984

INDUSTRIAL RESISTANCE TO OCCUPATIONAL SAFETY AND HEALTH LEGISLATION: 1971–1981*

ANDREW SZASZ
Rutgers University

Federal government intervention in the U.S. economy dramatically increased in 1970 with the creation of a series of "social" regulations to protect the public from the unintended health consequences of industrial production. By the early 1980s, a mere decade later, these same regulations had come under sustained attack and were being systematically curtailed by the government. This paper explores the role played by industry in the evolution of one of these new regulations, the Occupational Safety and Health Administration. I find that industry initially reacted defensively and developed containment strategies to minimize the impact of the new agency. They took the initiative in mid-decade, when growing economic malaise altered the political and ideological climate in their favor.

Rapid industrialization in the 19th century transformed the United States into an economic powerhouse, but the change was not without social costs. Industrial workers were largely unprotected against health and safety hazards on the job, and thousands died or suffered from injuries and illnesses. The toll continues to be very high. The National Safety Council and the Public Health Service have estimated that in the 1970s 14,000 workers died of industrial injuries and perhaps 100,000 more died of occupationally caused illnesses every year. In addition, there were over two million disabling injuries and 400,000 new occupational illnesses every year (Ashford, 1976:84,92). This direct and ongoing cost in illness, injury, and premature death was neglected by government, industry, and labor until the late 1960s, when a combination of events created sufficient pressure for federal action. In 1970 the Occupational Safety and Health Administration (OSHA) was born.

OSHA was one of a number of agencies created by the federal government in 1970 to protect citizens from the unintended health consequences of industrial production; others included the Mining Enforcement and Safety Administration (MESA), the National Highway Traffic Safety Administration (NHTSA), and the Environmental Protection Agency (EPA). These new "social" regulations differed from the more traditional form of "economic" regulations, such as the Securities and Exchange Commission (SEC) and the Interstate Commerce Commission (ICC), which govern competitive relations between firms (Lilley and Miller, 1977).

Economic regulations have been studied extensively by political scientists and economists (Bernstein, 1955; Mitnick, 1980; Owen and Braeutigam, 1978; Stigler, 1975). These studies have consistently shown that the political strategies of regulated industries have molded the evolution of these policies. This paper examines the role which industry has played in the evolution of one of the newer, social regulations, the Occupational Safety and Health Administration. Berman (1978), Brodeur (1973), Davidson (1970), and Page and O'Brien (1973) have written extensively about the history of health and safety prior to the formation of OSHA. Ashford (1976), Donnelly (1982), Mendeloff (1978), Page and O'Brien (1973), and Rothstein (1978) have analyzed the period leading up to the enactment of OSHA in 1970. The fate of OSHA after the election of President Ronald Reagan in 1980 has been examined by Calavita (1983), Grozuczak (1982), and Simon (1983). This paper focuses on the years 1971 to 1981: from the formation of OSHA to the election

* An earlier version of this paper was presented at the annual meetings of the American Sociological Association, Detroit, August 31 to September 3, 1983. The author thanks David Popenoe, Allan Schnaiberg, Joseph Schneider, Wendy Strimling, and the *Social Problems* editors and reviewers for their comments. Correspondence to: Department of Sociology, Rutgers University, New Brunswick, NJ 08903.

of Reagan. I show that industry strategies played a critical role in the evolution of OSHA in the 1970s. First, I review the historical background of industry resistance to effective action on health and safety before 1969. Second, I discuss my source of data and method of analysis. Third, I show how industry changed from defensive action in the first half of the 1970s to offensive action in the second half of the decade. Fourth I show how the election of President Reagan in 1980 signalled a victory for industry in the long battle against OSHA. I conclude by discussing differences in the evolution of social and economic regulation and the necessary antagonism between industry and the goals of social regulation.

HISTORICAL BACKGROUND

The damage to human health caused by rapid industrialization was abundantly visible by the early 19th century, especially in Great Britain, the cradle of industrial capitalism. Workers suffered from physical exhaustion caused by a long workday (Marx, 1967:253). Occupationally related illnesses such as potters' asthma, sulphur matchmakers' lockjaw, and chimney sweeps' scrotal cancer were already recognized (Denton, 1978:53; Marx, 1967:245). The British Parliament began to regulate the health effects of industrial production in 1833, when it passed the first Factory Act limiting the length of the workday for child laborers. Progress in protective legislation, however, has been slow. In the United States, it took massive demonstrations and occasionally bloody strikes to shorten the workday to eight hours (Boyer and Morais, 1955:32, 87, 142, 190). States formed factory investigating commissions only after major industrial catastrophes, such as the Triangle Shirtwaist fire which killed 145 women in New York City in 1911 (Berman, 1978:9). The federal government did not declare its intention to provide comprehensive protection for industrial workers until 1970.

To a large degree, federal inaction in the United States was due to the mobilization of a variety of industrial strategies aimed at keeping the issue of worker safety and health off the policy agenda and out of the public eye. Industry restricted knowledge of the scope of the problem by controlling information: records were poorly kept and little research was done on the potential hazards of industrial processes (Ashford, 1976:92, 102; Berman, 1978:38). Information showing the hazards of certain substances was actively suppressed, as in the cases of asbestos (Brodeur, 1973; *Progressive*, 1979), beryllium, cotton dust, PCBs, and Kepone (Berman, 1978:82, 91). Industrial management supported the ideology of accident proneness which blamed workers for their injuries (Szasz, 1984).

Management also created and funded a network of organizations through which they sought to control how society dealt with and thought about occupational safety and health. They influenced workmen's compensation through the National Council for Compensation Insurance (created in 1923); research and standard-setting through the American National Standards Institute (1926) and the Industrial Health Foundation (1935); company doctors and other industrial health professionals through the American Occupational Medical Association (1915), the American Industrial Hygiene Association (1939), and the American Conference of Government Industrial Hygienists (1938); and general public debate through the National Safety Council (1913). When directly challenged, industry asserted that working conditions were solely the prerogative of management. Industrial inactivity on the health and safety issue was compounded by the ineffectiveness of state regulatory laws (Ashford, 1976:47) and the absence of adequate action by labor unions (Bureau of National Affairs, 1973:5; Page and O'Brien, 1973:123).

In the late 1960s, a number of conditions and events coincided to stimulate federal regulatory activity. The U.S. economy was healthy, inflation was modest, and unemployment was low. According to Labor Department statistics, the annual rate of inflation was below 2 percent between 1960 and 1965 and rose no higher than 5 percent by 1969, while unemployment fell from a high of 6 percent in 1961 to a steady 3 percent in the latter half of the decade. Favorable economic conditions allowed workers to become concerned with non-economic issues at a time when injury rates were rising: the rate of industrial accidents rose 29 percent between 1961 and 1970. Meanwhile, researchers and some unions began to produce solid evidence about the causes of occupational illnesses (Ashford, 1976:3, 46). The work of Dr. Irving Selikoff on asbestosis and asbestos-induced cancer was an example of this new contribution from the scientific community (Berman, 1978:86). Rank-and-file movements in several industrial unions (Weir, 1970) brought in new leaders, notably I. W. Abel of the United Steelworkers as well as new leaders in the United Rubber Workers and the Oil, Chemical and Atomic Workers who were also conscious of the health and safety issue and aware of its potential as a focal point for rank-and-file discontent. These new union officials later led the labor movement in lobbying for federal intervention (Mendeloff, 1978:15). These conditions within the labor movement helped stimulate policy formation (Donnelly, 1982), but they were insufficient in themselves. When President Lyndon Johnson and Congressional Democrats first proposed new health and safety legislation in 1968, organized labor was tepid in its support (Page and O'Brien, 1973:143) and the effort died when Johnson declined to seek re-election.

However, when the Democrats reintroduced the legislation in 1969, chances for passage of an OSHA Act had improved. On November 20, 1968, an explosion at the Consolidated Coal Company's mine at Farmington, West Virginia, killed 78 miners. This disaster triggered both union and Congressional action, the former by strengthening a rank-and-file movement within the United Mine Workers which had arisen earlier in opposition to the union's leader, Tony Boyle. Miners responded to the accident with widespread wildcat strikes in West Virginia and thousands of miners marched on the West Virginia statehouse to demand protection (Mendeloff, 1978:17). The reaction impressed the leaders of other unions with the potential of the health and safety issue for rank-and-file disaffection and contributed to their growing interest in federal action. Meanwhile, Congress responded to the Farmington disaster with hearings into the mining industry and the Coal Mine Health and Safety Act, which it quickly passed. The hearings "served as a constant reminder of the larger, unsolved problem of job safety and health conditions" (Page and O'Brien, 1973:144) and helped generate "Congressional momentum" (Ashford, 1976:46) for the passage of the OSHA act.

The final step came in August, 1969, when newly-elected President Richard Nixon and the Republicans in Congress introduced their own version of an occupational safety and health bill. This was Nixon's way of attempting to limit the extent of federal intervention in the face of near-certain action from Congress, while giving the impression that the Republicans were willing to do something for workers. Both parties had bills pending in Congress. Labor leaders, motivated by the Farmington disaster and aghast at the possibility of the weak Republican version passing and thus preempting federal action for years, made passage of a strong occupational safety bill their top legislative priority. The strategies that industry had historically employed to keep the issue of safety and health off the policy agenda had failed. And, once they failed, industrial lobbyists could not force the genie back into the bottle.[1] Sufficient political momentum finally existed to ensure passage of some kind of regulatory law.

As Congress debated the various versions of the legislation, industry's strategic options narrowed, leaving it with only two feasible goals: (1) to try to work with the Republicans to limit the future regulatory agency's powers; and (2) to lobby for the creation of procedures in the legislation which would allow industry to contain the agency's impact later. In support of the first goal, industry supported Republican efforts to create an agency which would not do its own research and set its own standards but which would, instead, depend on research by the American

---

1. Wilson (1974:166) is right when he says that "control over the public agenda" is "the decisive stage" in the social conflict over policy.

National Standards Institute, the Industrial Health Foundation, and other industry-funded organizations. Industry also supported wording of the legislation which would have split enforcement authority between the Secretary of Labor and two independent commissions, thereby weakening OSHA's enforcement powers. And it lobbied against "worker rights" language in the legislation. In support of the second goal, industry fought for procedures which would force OSHA to go through many drafts, hearings, and discussions before establishing a safety or health standard. Industry also fought for procedural safeguards in the enforcement process, so that violations of standards could be appealed both to an independent board and to the federal courts.

The OSHA Act passed by Congress on December 16, 1970, was closer in language to the Democratic version supported by organized labor than to Nixon's version which was preferred by industry. However, Congress compromised on some issues and met some industrial demands. Although the Department of Labor would eventually write its own standards based on its own research, OSHA would start off by borrowing existing, "consensus" standards written by industry. The Labor Department would do all the inspecting and fining, but an independent review commission would hear appeals against OSHA citations. Industry was successful in its strategy to introduce procedural safeguards, but it won relatively little on substantive policy during the Congressional struggle. Despite these modest accomplishments, all was not lost. The new OSHA Act would be implemented by a president who was hostile, or at best indifferent, to its goals. The stage was set for a decade of serious social struggles on the issue of occupational safety and health.

DATA AND METHOD

I consulted 515 consecutive weekly issues of the *Occupational Safety and Health Reporter* (henceforth referred to as the *Reporter*): Volume 1, number 1, to Volume 10, number 47, from 1971 to 1981. The *Reporter* is an excellent source of data because it is both neutral in orientation and exhaustive in content. It is published by the Bureau of National Affairs, Inc., which also produces several other trade journals about different facets of federal activity. The bureau is funded exclusively by subscriptions to its trade publications and strives for journalistic neutrality in its coverage. The *Reporter* is subscribed to, and used by, all parties who have a continuing interest in occupational safety and health policy, including government officials, labor and industry lobbyists, lawyers, corporate health and safety departments, and occupational physicians. Every week the *Reporter* summarizes all major events relevant to occupational safety, including all debates and proceedings in Congress, decisions by the federal courts, actions and statements of the president and his staff, actions of labor and industry, major speeches and conferences, health and safety statistics, reports of research on hazards, and the actions of OSHA itself.

I analyzed the *Reporters* in three steps. First, I read the *Reporters* issue by issue and recorded the actions of both the federal government and organized social forces on the issues of OSHA standards, enforcement, worker rights, and general OSHA policy. Second, I identified categories of major actors, actions, and arenas of action, and organized my notes according to these categories in parallel lines, from 1971 to 1981. Third, I analyzed this data to discover trends in the strategy of major actors. Although I recorded data for both government and non-government actors, this paper used that part of the data which dealt with the policy goals of industrial actors and the strategies they used in an attempt to achieve these goals.

FINDINGS

Industrial reaction to the passage of OSHA can be divided into three stages, the first one very short and the last two roughly equal in length. First, just after the passage of the OSHA act, industrial actors tried to affect the Nixon Administration's initial implementation. Second, from mid-1971 to about 1974, industrial strategies were mainly defensive and aimed at containing the agency's effects. Third, from roughly 1975 to 1981, industry went on the offensive with an aggressive deregulatory campaign.

1971: Initial Strategies

After Congress passes a bill, considerable latitude remains in how the new law will actually function. The OSHA Act gave the Executive Branch four months to establish a new agency. Appointments had to be made; budgets written; offices and equipment procurred; initial standards adopted; enforcement rules promulgated; and compliance officers hired and trained. During the implementation period, industrial lobbying aimed at limiting OSHA's powers and establishing procedures which would allow future resistance. Industry focused on advising the Nixon Administration on ways to limit OSHA's enforcement powers. Large firms and business trade associations sent their lobbyists to advise that management be given advance notice of inspections, that management be allowed to refuse entry to OSHA inspectors, that management be allowed to limit inspections in the name of protecting trade secrets, and that inspection results be kept secret by OSHA. Industry asked for rules limiting the access of OSHA inspectors to company health data and establishing the right of management to legal counsel during inspections. Lobbyists also demanded that enforcement be applied to employees as well as management, so that employees would be equally liable for health practices and would be penalized for false complaints to OSHA. And industry continued to emphasize due process safeguards in both enforcement and standard-setting.[2]

The Nixon Administration agreed to protect trade secrets, but rejected other suggestions that would have overtly gutted OSHA's enforcement capability. Nonetheless, the Administration was openly sympathetic to industry concerns and found other ways to accommodate them. Nixon proposed an OSHA start-up budget of $25 million for fiscal year 1972, its first full year of operation — a meager amount considering OSHA's mandate and its need for data, equipment, and trained personnel. George C. Guenther, appointed to head the new agency, stressed fairness to business during his Senate confirmation hearings (Page and O'Brien, 1973:192). His actions in office reflected this orientation. Under Guenther's leadership (from 1971 to late 1972), OSHA stressed minor safety violations and imposed modest fines, a policy that his successor, John Stender, continued until 1974.[3] OSHA under Guenther adopted only one new health standard, for asbestos, and the worker rights clause in the OSHA Act was not implemented in any serious way. Guenther's attitude toward OSHA came to light later during the 1973 Watergate investigation which eventually led to Nixon's resignation. Investigators found a secret memo from Guenther to Nixon's re-election committee proposing that non-implementation of OSHA standards be promised to industry in exchange for corporate campaign contributions (Ashford, 1976:543).

1971-1974: Defense and Containment Strategies

Despite all efforts to blunt the new regulatory program, the OSHA machinery began to function in May, 1971. OSHA inspectors began visiting worksites to enforce a massive number of "consensus" standards that had been adopted *en masse*. The number of inspections grew rapidly. In its second year, for example, OSHA made 48,400 inspections and cited 155,800 violations. Though most of the violations were "minor" and resulted in an average fine of less than $30, the

---

2. Industry's many individual suggestions to Guenther's OSHA on the enforcement issue may be found scattered throughout the *Reporter*, Volume 1, numbers 5 through 9.

3. OSHA enforcement figures show that from fiscal years 1972 to 1975, 94.6 to 96.2 percent of the violations it cited were safety violations, 97.9 to 98.6 percent were for non-serious violations, and the average fine per violation was $25.40 (Szasz, 1982:362).

enforcement and inspection affected thousands of angry factory owners and managers. Although OSHA adopted only three new health standards in its first three years — for asbestos, vinyl chloride, and a package standard for 14 carcinogens — work started on a number of health standards with a potentially great impact.[4] Industrial actors began to develop strategies to cope with the threat.

Given the political conditions of the early 1970s, industrial actors could do no more than react defensively to contain the effects of the agency. There was widespread support in the United States for environmental regulation. Organized labor and its Congressional allies were on the offensive as they sought fuller implementation of the OSHA Act. Industrial actors had no coherent ideological position, no single rallying cry or policy slogan around which to unite. They professed to support the goals of safety and health,[5] but their actions showed that they had begun to work to contain the potential effects of the new regulatory agency. In reacting to OSHA, industry divided into two distinct sectors. One sector consisted of large firms and corporations at the heart of the U.S. economy — auto, steel, chemicals, plastics, textiles, oil, and rubber. The other was the self-defined "small business" sector. These two sectors had different fears about OSHA's potential impact, vastly different political resources, and, as a result, different strategic responses to OSHA.

Small Businesses: The majority of the four million workplaces covered by the OSHA Act are small firms. Over 90 percent of them employ 25 or fewer workers. Small firms typically had no safety program of any kind and, unlike the large corporations, they had no part in writing the consensus standards initially adopted by OSHA. Most small businesses first confronted OSHA when an inspector arrived unannounced at the door, armed with a thick book of regulations and the power to enter, inspect, and fine. OSHA, in fact, focused much of its enforcement apparatus in this period on firms with less than 50 employees.[6] Not surprisingly, small businesses wanted relief from enforcement. They sought total exemption for all firms with fewer than a certain number of employees. Failing that, they wanted penalty-free consultation in place of "punitive" enforcement, or advance notice of inspection, or no fines on first inspection.

This sector of industry had limited organizational resources and capacities. They lacked the large managerial structures, powerful Washington law firms, and wealthy trade associations which large corporations use to lobby the federal government. Thus, small businesses concentrated on lobbying their Congressional representatives. Members of the Congress reported being flooded by mail soon after OSHA inspections began in 1971. There was a "tremendous outcry of objection by the nation's small businessmen," according to Representative William Hungate (D–MO) (*Reporter* 2[3]:52). In response to the pressure the House Subcommittee on Environmental Problems Affecting Small Business scheduled hearings in June, 1972, so that small owners and their organizations (the National Federation of Independent Business, the National Association of Home Builders, and the American Retail Federation) could vent their rage. Small business and its allies also testified at hearings held by both House and Senate Labor Subcommittees, where they declared that OSHA inspectors were running "roughshod over thousands of struggling small enterprises . . . in the name of safety," according to Senator Carl Curtis (R–NE) (*Reporter*

4. Work commenced on over 50 standards, including such potentially serious ones as coke oven emissions, noise, heat stress, cotton dust, lead, pesticides, benzene, and arsenic (*Reporter*, 4[30]:867).
5. A study by Rickson (1977) supports my finding that industry approved of OSHA goals during this period. Rickson's interviews with corporate managers between 1972 and 1974 show that they tended to agree that government had a legitimate right to regulate waste and water pollution.
6. OSHA enforcement statistics show that during fiscal year 1973, 52.6 percent of inspections were carried out at firms with fewer than 50 workers; during 1974, 63.3 percent; during 1975, 70.3 percent (Szasz, 1982:362).

2[3]:52). A second round of these hearings were held in 1974, by both Labor Subcommittees and the Oversight Subcommittee on Government Regulations of the Senate Select Committee on Small Business. Members of Congress amplified the pressure brought to bear through such hearings by proposing numerous amendments to the OSHA Act. By June 1974, 82 amendments had been introduced in Congress, 66 of them calling for various forms of enforcement relief for small businesses. However, OSHA's Congressional friends on the Labor Subcommittees managed to bottle up all such amendments during this period.

Elements of the small business community also pursued enforcement relief through the federal court system. Several firms challenged the constitutionality of OSHA's power to inspect and fine firms. They lost their cases in the lower courts but pursued some all the way to the Supreme Court. (*Atlas Roofing v. Occupational Safety and Health Review Commission*, 1977; *Frank Irey v. Occupational Safety and Health Review Commission*, 1977). The Supreme Court refused a blanket condemnation of OSHA's enforcement powers in these cases, but subsequently ruled in favor of significant limits to these powers (*Marshall v. Barlow's*, 1978).

Large Corporations: Most large corporations had at least some safety program in place and were at least familiar with the consensus standards initially adopted by OSHA. Moreover, OSHA inspectors were concentrating their efforts on small businesses. So, while individual large corporations resisted enforcement and appealed citations and fines, as a sector they were generally unconcerned with enforcement. Instead, they focused on the implications of the OSHA Act for labor relations and the prospect that OSHA might someday adopt more stringent health standards.

The corporations worried that certain OSHA rules would give new power to workers: a worker's right to accompany OSHA inspectors might permit union organizers into unorganized shops; a worker's right to request inspection might be used to shut down plants during a strike; a worker's right to abandon imminently hazardous sites might be used to legitimize wildcat walkouts. Managers warned each other that "This law should be treated as gingerly as the NLRA [National Labor Relations Act]" (*Reporter* 1[56]:1230). However, the threat was only a potential one in this period, as neither Guenther nor Stender showed much enthusiasm for using the Act to extend worker rights. Thus, the corporations could deal with this threat by simply codifying a low level of worker rights through the collective bargaining process. Before OSHA, management had refused to negotiate health and safety issues with their unions; by 1973, 65 percent of all new contracts contained health and safety clauses, though the wording of these clauses was vague and gave workers few specific rights (Bureau of National Affairs, 1973). When, in the next period, OSHA intensified its efforts to implement worker rights, corporations switched to a more aggressive strategy of litigation in the federal courts.

Guenther and Stender did not aggressively promulgate strict health standards, either. Nonetheless, work was slowly progressing on issues such as coke oven emissions, noise, heat stress, cotton dust, lead, pesticides, and arsenic, which, if ever regulated, would have a major impact on the relevant industries. Faced with the prospect of eventually having to comply with stricter health standards, the corporations mobilized a combination of strategies: information control, delay, organizational cooptation, and legal action.

Resistance began with the withholding of vital information. The first step in developing a new standard is the collection of data on the exposure levels of workers to potentially hazardous substances and the analysis of employee health records. Most of this data, if it existed at all, was held by the corporations themselves. Both OSHA and its adjunct, the National Institute of Occupational Safety and Health (NIOSH)[7] reported that industrial groups and individual firms

---

7. The National Institute of Occupational Safety and Health was created by the OSHA Act and mandated to be the scientific research arm of the new regulatory agency. NIOSH gathered data and forwarded recommendations to OSHA when it felt that enough was known about a substance to say that it was hazardous.

consistently failed to cooperate with requests for basic data on toxicity and exposure. (When, in the subsequent period, OSHA aggressively asserted its right to industry data, major firms vigorously, but unsuccessfully, challenged this claim in the courts. *E. I. duPont de Nemours v. Finklea* (1977) was a key case.)

Withholding data created delay and made work on new standards difficult, but OSHA still moved forward on a number of health hazards. Whenever OSHA announced that it was beginning work on a new health standard, corporate representatives moved to control and coopt the process, under the name of "participation." In actual practice, "participation" meant a variety of actions, depending on the particular stage of the standard-setting process. At the first stage, when OSHA formed an advisory committee to gather scientific data and to formulate a proposal, industrial representatives on the advisory committee spoke consistently for delay, caution, and weak standards. Firms from the relevant industry also "participated" by suddenly funding research into the substance to be regulated and requesting that OSHA wait for their findings. This created delays of several years and industry-funded research inevitably supported standards weaker than those recommended by NIOSH, independent scientists, or organized labor.

When OSHA determined that a standard was warranted — based on the work of the advisory committee, NIOSH, or in response to pressure from unions — it published the proposed standard in the *Federal Register*, a daily publication of the federal government listing all agency rulings, announcements of hearings, and notices from the executive branch. Included with the published proposal was a call for comments from interested parties. "Participation" at this stage meant making full use of these discussion periods to mobilize economic, scientific, technical, and managerial experts to argue that the proposals were too stringent, were based on inadequate data, were economically harmful, and were technologically infeasible. Industry consistently supported higher levels of worker exposure to hazardous substances and compliance through the use of personal protective equipment — face masks, ear plugs — rather than through engineering controls.

"Participation" reduced the number of standards created by OSHA and weakened those that were adopted. For the few standards which OSHA actually adopted, industry had a final recourse — legal challenge in the federal courts. These strategies were all developed from 1971 to 1974, although they were used more intensively later in the decade. Two examples demonstrate how the strategies worked.

The United Steelworkers (USW) first requested a standard for coke oven emissions in September, 1971. NIOSH sent its recommendation to OSHA in March, 1973. After intense pressure from the USW, OSHA formed an advisory committee in October, 1974. Industry representatives on the committee claimed repeatedly that there was insufficient data for a standard and that compliance was technologically feasible only through face masks, not changes in factory equipment. The advisory committee forwarded its recommendation to OSHA in May, 1975. OSHA published a proposal in July. Industry officials repeatedly attacked it during the discussion period, arguing that the standard was economically and technologically infeasible. This argument was repeated until 1980 when the American Iron and Steel Institute and six steel companies withdrew their legal challenges to the standard and admitted that, in the intervening years, most of the industry had come into compliance with the standard (Szasz, 1982:395).

The AFL-CIO labor federation asked for a noise standard in September, 1971. NIOSH produced its recommendation in July, 1972, and OSHA formed an advisory committee in January, 1973. Industry argued that the NIOSH proposal was based on inadequate data and that compliance should be through ear plugs, not engineering controls. OSHA published its proposed standard in October, 1974. In four months OSHA received over 700 comments from industries pleading economic hardship and arguing for a weak standard (90 decibels instead of the 85 recommended by unions and hearing experts) and compliance through use of ear plugs. In 1976 the Inter-Industry Noise Study (IINS) was launched and industry requested OSHA to wait for its findings. The IINS proposed a standard of 92 decibels, in September, 1977, but continued research into 1980 and requested that OSHA wait for its findings. Although OSHA failed to produce a firm noise standard, a "hearing conservation amendment" was issued in January, 1981. It was immediately challenged in the courts and deferred by the Reagan Administration pending review (Szasz, 1982:398).

1975-1981: Offensive Strategies

While industry appeared to use the same strategies in the second half of the decade as it had during the first, a real, qualitative change had occurred. Reaction to OSHA changed from containment to counterattack. In part, this shift was made necessary by the fact that OSHA was intensifying its activities. More critically, it was made possible by the growing economic crisis of the 1970s, which altered the political balance among the parties interested in health and safety policies, and compromised general public support for regulation. This shift in the balance of forces allowed industry to unite its disparate strategies into a coherent and offensive campaign.

OSHA intensified its work under Dr. Morton Corn, head of OSHA during Gerald Ford's presidency, and Dr. Eula Bingham under Jimmy Carter's administration. Enforcement increasingly targeted larger firms and more serious health hazards; average fines were also increased.[8] But progress was especially notable in the areas of worker rights and health standards. OSHA promoted the right of workers to be paid to accompany OSHA inspectors, to abandon a hazardous site without penalty, to know the substances they handle, and to have access to company medical records. OSHA also issued health standards at a faster rate. Bingham issued standards for cotton dust, lead, hearing conservation, arsenic, benzene, acrylonitrile (AN), and DBCP, and promoted the so-called "generic carcinogen standard," a mechanism for accelerating the standard-setting process. Industrial actors responded with litigation in the federal courts. The right to abandon hazardous worksites was challenged both by the construction industry (*Marshall v. Daniel Construction*, 1977; *Usery v. Babcock and Wilcox*, 1976) and other corporations (*Whirlpool v. Marshall*, 1980). The right to be paid for accompanying OSHA inspectors was challenged by large and small firms (*Chamber of Commerce v. OSHA*, 1978, 1980; *Leone v. Mobil Oil*, 1975). The right to medical records was challenged in *Louisiana Chemical Association v. Eula Bingham* (1981). Virtually all of the new health standards were challenged in court, but the central issue at stake in these cases — the role of economic factors and cost/benefit analysis in standard-setting — was decided in the chemical industry's challenge to the benzene standard (*Industrial Union Department, AFL-CIO v. American Petroleum Institute*, 1980). Thus, industry responded to improvements in OSHA implementation by intensifying its resistance, but this only partially and inadequately describes the nature of the period. Traditional resistence strategies were transformed by an altered political and ideological context.

Economic downturn alters the political configuration: The recession of 1974-75 cast a pall over the latter half of the decade and altered the political balance of forces in the debate over occupational safety and health. The gross national product fell in 1974 and 1975; the unemployment rate rose to 8.5 percent in 1975, up from 4.9 percent in 1973; and the rate of inflation reached 9.1 percent in 1975 (U.S. Bureau of the Census, 1980:407, 438, 477). The recession and the growing national economic crisis weakened organized labor and compromised public concern over environmental issues. Workers were weakened both economically and politically. The unemployment rate was slow in falling; by 1979 it was still 5.8 percent (1980:407). Take-home earnings fell

---

8. OSHA enforcement statistics show that from 1975 to 1979 health inspections rose from 6.8 percent of all inspections to 19.3 percent; citation of serious violations increased from 1.3 percent to 29.5 percent; total proposed fines went from $8.15 million to $23.1 million (Szasz, 1982:362).

5 percent from 1973 to 1975 and stagnated for the rest of the decade (1980:422). Organizational weakness followed economic weakness. Unions lost members (1980:429). Strikes declined, from 2.42 million workers (3 percent of the labor force) on strike in 1976 to 1.37 million workers (1.5 percent) on strike in 1980 (1982:410). Organized labor's political influence with the federal government waned (*Nation*, 1981; Shabecoff, 1981). Organized labor continued to support full implementation of OSHA, but it lost the power to effectively resist industry's counterattack. The economic crisis also undermined public support for regulations by inducing fear of economic turmoil. Opinion surveys (Gallup, 1972, 1978, 1979, 1980, 1981) show that social issues were the first concern of the U.S. public until the recession of 1974–75; thereafter, concern about the economy rose rapidly and eclipsed all other public worries for the rest of the decade. The economic crisis thus weakened the political power and resolve of OSHA supporters. It also provided fertile ground for an ideological campaign to build public support for deregulation.

The ideological campaign: Industry's diverse strategies were given coherence by the ideology of deregulation. The theoretical basis for this campaign had been developed previously by economists with close ties to conservative foundations (Stone, 1980), but it only became a national movement when an ailing economy provided a fearful, receptive audience. The ideology of deregulation asserted that overregulation was a cause of rising prices, stagnating productivity, plant closings, and other economic problems. It proposed that national economic well-being could only be restored by giving the business world significant relief from regulation. And it called for the application of economic, cost/benefit criteria to regulatory decision-making.

Deregulatory ideology was introduced into public discourse through many channels. Books were written for the educated audience (MacAvoy, 1979; Smith, 1976; Weidenbaum, 1979). The argument was tirelessly repeated by corporate leaders and economists in speeches and articles.[9] Some of the largest corporations spread the word in privately produced glossy magazines and in advertising.[10] By the late 1970s, variants of the message could also be heard from both Republican President Ford and Democratic President Carter, their economic advisors, and from candidates seeking office. The message pervaded public debate. As a result, polls conducted between 1975 and 1980 by the Advertising Council, Cambridge Reports, Louis Harris, and CBS/New York Times showed that the U.S. public was increasingly likely to agree that overregulation had been harming the economy (Szasz, 1982:340, 353).

Politically on the offensive and increasingly victorious: Deregulatory theory gave new unity to previous strategies of containment: it also gave them a new coherence and transformed them into virtuous efforts to save the economy from irrational and harmful government intervention. As a result, both small firms and large corporations began to win on their traditional issues.

The desire of small firms for relief from enforcement had met with failure in the early 1970s, but between 1975 and 1981 all three branches of government gave relief to small business. In *Marshall v. Barlow's* (1978), the Supreme Court ruled that management could refuse entry to OSHA inspectors and demand that they obtain a search warrant. OSHA under both Morton Corn and Eula Bingham eased up on the smaller firms.[11] Finally, a succession of Department

---

9. Excellent examples of corporate executives' attitudes may be found in interviews with William Sneath, chairman of Union Carbide (*Business Today*, 1977) and Irving Shapiro, chairman of DuPont (*Business Today*, 1978).

10. The public relations departments of major corporations put out single glossy pamphlets, such as "Steel-making and the environment," (Public Affairs Department, Bethlehem Steel Corporation, 1976), or series of in-house magazines, such as DuPont's *Context*. The purpose of these publications was to show the companies' ecological consciousness and to oppose federal regulation. (See, for example, Roberts, 1978.) The effort in advocacy advertising is described by Noble (1979).

11. The proportion of inspection at firms with fewer than 50 workers dropped steadily under both Corn and Bingham, from 72 percent to 60 percent (Szasz, 1982:362).

of Labor appropriations bills in Congress increasingly limited OSHA's enforcement powers over small business. In fiscal year 1977, enforcement over small farmers was banned and first fines for non-serious violations were banned for firms with fewer than 11 workers. In fiscal 1980, OSHA inspections of small firms were prohibited if a state agency had inspected the firm in the previous six months, and fines were prohibited if a firm had used OSHA consultation services.

The corporate sector used deregulatory theory to link economic criteria to OSHA's standard-setting process. Here, too, gains were made in all branches of government. In 1974, Ford had required inflation impact statements to be written for each proposed standard. In 1977, the newly elected Carter was advised by his economic aides to intensify the White House's supervision of standards and to integrate "economic analysis into the early stages of the decision-making process." (*Reporter* 6[46]:1412). In 1978, Carter created the Regulatory Analysis and Review Group and empowered it to analyze the economic impact of proposed regulations. The application of economic criteria to standards was promoted in hearings by the House Banking Subcommittee on Economic Stabilization (*Reporter*, 8[27]:1127) and the Senate Government Affairs Committee (*Reporter*, 8[34]:1337). By 1980, both the Democratic and Republican parties had regulatory reform bills pending in Congress. These bills would, if passed, have formalized the policies already in effect in the executive branch. Finally, a landmark Supreme Court decision in the case of the benzene standard (*Industrial Union Department, AFL-CIO v. American Petroleum Institute*, 1980) declared that OSHA had to take economic factors into consideration when adopting standards and that there had to be a "reasonable relationship" between costs and benefits. Taken as a whole, the corporate campaign against standards was the fullest expression of deregulatory strategy, an attempt to get all branches of the federal government to accept the dominant importance of economic factors in any effort to protect workers from the effects of industrial production.

THE REAGAN DENOUEMENT

The November, 1980, election of Ronald Reagan as president signaled victory for industry in its decade-long battle against OSHA. Industrial lobbyists handed their policy shopping lists to the incoming Republican president and he moved quickly and dramatically after taking office in 1981 to meet their demands. Reagan appointed Thorne Auchter, a Republican activist and construction company official, to replace Eula Bingham, a trained occupational epidemiologist, as head of OSHA. Auchter declared that enforcement would no longer aim at "punishing" industry, but at seeking its cooperation instead. He declared that strict cost/benefit analyses would be applied to all new and existing standards, and that worker rights promoted by past OSHA heads would be re-examined. By 1984, all of industry's traditional demands had been satisfied. Calavita (1983), Grozuczak (1982), and Simon (1983) show the sweep of the policy initiative: work on new standards had come to a halt as OSHA devoted its energies to reviewing existing standards. Such reviews led to attempts to weaken the standards already in effect. Enforcement had been systematically weakened, as well. One third of the field offices had been closed and there were 20 percent fewer OSHA inspectors. On every significant measure – total number of inspections, number of workers covered by inspections, average time spent per inspection, fines levied, inspections due to worker complaints, reinspections following findings of violations – OSHA enforcement had suffered. Finally, there had been an unrelenting attack on the worker rights that OSHA had attempted to promulgate in the late 1970s. Worker education funds were severely cut and films, slide shows, and pamphlets designed by Bingham's OSHA for worker education were withdrawn. The right to be paid to accompany OSHA inspectors was withdrawn. The labeling standard, giving workers the right to know what chemicals they work with, was withdrawn. Thus, the Reagan administration completed the strategic offensive initiated by industrial actors and undid much of the environmental concessions that had been forced on industry during the previous decade.

DISCUSSION

Analysts of economic regulation have used the military metaphor of "capture" to conceptualize the relationship between regulatory agencies and industry (Bernstein, 1955:95; Mitnick, 1980; Stigler, 1975:114). My investigation of industry's role in the evolution of OSHA suggests that the military metaphor may also be appropriate for understanding the relationship between agencies and industry in cases of social regulation as well. When OSHA's supporters were strong and united, industry used defensive tactics; when conditions changed and the balance of power shifted in industry's favor after 1975, it went on the offensive. Industry finally "captured" OSHA in 1980 through the election of President Ronald Reagan.[12]

However, the "capture" of OSHA differs from the notion of agency capture described in the literature; in its uniqueness lies the key to understanding the fundamental difference between economic and social regulations. While most observers agree that economic regulations invariably serve the interests of industry, Freitag (1983) has shown that economic agencies have not been directly, physically captured by industry. Mitnick (1980:209) and Owen and Braeutigam (1978:1) describe several ways that industrial influence is exerted without actual capture: control of information, litigation, and manipulation of regulators through rewards such as friendship and promises of future employment. Through such actions industry can make an economic agency do for them what they find difficult or illegal to do for themselves, namely fix prices, block the entry of new firms into the sector, and reduce competition. In contrast, social agencies such as OSHA and the Environmental Protection Agency (EPA) have been directly captured by anti-regulatory businessmen and their allies under the Reagan Administration; yet, despite such direct capture, industries have been unable to make these agencies serve their interests in any *positive* sense. The most that industries have been able to achieve is to muzzle the agency; Reagan's OSHA only serves them in the negative sense of relieving them from the burden of complying with its mandate.

Why the difference in outcomes? I believe the answer lies in the relative compatibility of regulatory goals with the logic of the capitalist firm. The goals of economic regulation do not fundamentally conflict with the goals of firms who, in spite of the rhetoric of the free market, desire a predictable and controlled business environment. Economic agencies are acceptable and ultimately desirable because they regulate market relations. In contrast, social regulation means that "the government . . . becomes involved in . . . the most minute details of production" (Lilley and Miller, 1977:53). Because it regulates at the level of production decisions, social regulation is fundamentally and ontologically antagonistic to the logic of firms within a capitalist economy. Thus, even when captured, social agencies are useless as tools of business; moreover, the agencies continue to be at least potentially antagonistic to industry's interests. Ultimately, then, "captured" economic agencies and their regulations can be transformed into political puppets; social agencies and their regulations, once captured, remain, at best, political prisoners.

REFERENCES

Ashford, Nicolas A.
   1976   Crisis in the Workplace. Cambridge, MA: Massachusetts Institute of Technology Press.
Berman, Daniel M.
   1978   Death on the Job. New York: Monthly Review Press.
Bernstein, Marver H.
   1955   Regulating Business by Independent Commission. Princeton, NJ: Princeton University Press.

---

12. It should be noted that the attack was not limited to OSHA. Anti-regulatory administrators were also appointed to head the Consumer Products Safety Commission, the Environmental Protection Agency, and the Department of Interior. Deregulatory work was coordinated through the president's Task Force on Regulatory Relief, headed by Vice-President George Bush.

Boyer, Richard O., and Herbert M. Morais
  1955   Labor's Untold Story. New York: United Electrical, Radio and Machine Workers of America.
Brodeur, Paul
  1973   Expendable Americans. New York: Viking.
Bureau of National Affairs, Inc.
  1971– Occupational Safety and Health Reporter. Weekly journal published by Bureau of National
    81   Affairs, Inc., Washington, DC. Volume 1, number 1, to Volume 10, number 47.
  1973   "OSHA and the unions." Bureau of National Affairs, Inc., Washington DC.
Business Today
  1977   "BT interview: William Sneath, chairman, Union Carbide." Business Today 14(1):9–13.
  1978   "BT interview: Irving S. Shapiro, Du Pont." Business Today 15(1):45–48.
Calavita, Kitty
  1983   "The demise of the Occupational Safety and Health Administration: A case study in symbolic
         action." Social Problems 30(4):437–448.
Davidson, Ray
  1970   Peril on the Job: A Study of Hazards in the Chemical Industry. Washington, DC: Public Affairs
         Press.
Denton, John A.
  1978   Medical Sociology. Boston: Houghton Mifflin Company.
Donnelly, Patrick G.
  1982   "The origins of the Occupational Safety and Health Act of 1970." Social Problems 30(1):13–25.
Freitag, Peter
  1983   "The myth of corporate capture: Regulatory commissions in the United States." Social Problems
         30(4):480–491.
Gallup, George H.
  1972   The Gallup Poll: Public Opinion 1935–1971. New York: Random House.
  1978   The Gallup Poll: Public Opinion 1972–1977. Wilmington, DE: Scholarly Resources, Inc.
  1979   The Gallup Poll: Public Opinion 1978. Wilmington, DE: Scholarly Resources, Inc.
  1980   The Gallup Poll: Public Opinion 1979. Wilmington, DE: Scholarly Resources, Inc.
  1981   The Gallup Poll: Public Opinion 1980. Wilmington, DE: Scholarly Resources, Inc.
Grozuczak, Joanne
  1982   "Poisons on the job: The Reagan administration and American workers." Sierra Club Natural Heri-
         tage Report No. 4. San Francisco: Sierra Club.
Lilley, William, III, and James C. Miller III
  1977   "The new 'social regulation'." The Public Interest 47 (Spring):49–61.
MacAvoy, Paul W.
  1979   The Regulated Industries and the Economy. New York: Norton.
Marx, Karl
  1967   Capital, Volume 1. New York: International Publishers.
Mendeloff, John
  1978   Regualting Safety. Cambridge, MA: Massachusetts Institute of Technology Press.
Mitnick, Barry M.
  1980   The Political Economy of Regulation. New York: Columbia University Press.
Nation
  1981   "Labor disarray." The Nation 233(7):195–196.
Noble, David F.
  1979   "The chemistry of risk," Seven Days 3(7):23–34.
Owen, Bruce M., and Ronald Braeutigam
  1978   The Regulation Game: Strategic Use of Administrative Process. Cambridge, MA: Ballinger
         Publishing Co.
Page, Joseph A., and Mary-Win O'Brien
  1973   Bitter Wages. New York: Grossman.
Progressive
  1979   "Asbestos and its lessons." The Progressive 43(1):9–10.
Public Affairs Department, Bethlehem Steel Corporation
  1976   Steelmaking and the environment: A picture story." Booklet 3088. Bethlehem, PA: Public Affairs
         Dept., Bethlehem Steel Corporation.
Rickson, Roy E.
  1977   "Dimensions of environmental management: Legitimation of government regulation by industrial
         managers," Environment and Behavior 9(1):15–40.
Roberts, John A.
  1978   "Business takes a new approach on public issues." DuPont Context 7(1):10–14. DuPont Context is
         an in-house publication of the Public Affairs Department, E.I. duPont de Nemours & Co.,
         Wilmington, DE.

Rothstein, Mark A.
   1978   Occupational Safety and Health Law. St. Paul, MN: West.
Shabecoff, Philip
   1981   "Labor worries over decline in its influence." The New York Times, Jan. 4: sec. E, p. 3.
Simon, Philip J.
   1983   "Reagan in the workplace: Unraveling the health and safety net." The Center for Study of Respon-
          sive Law, Washington, DC.
Smith, Robert S.
   1976   The Occupational Safety and Health Act, Its Goals and Its Achievements. Washington, DC: Amer-
          ican Enterprise Institute.
Stigler, George
   1975   The Citizen and the State. Chicago: University of Chicago Press.
Stone, Peter H.
   1981   "Conservative Brain Trust," The New York Times Magazine. May 5:18.
Szasz, Andrew
   1982   "The dynamics of social regulation: A study of the formation and evolution of the occupational
          safety and health administration." Unpublished Ph.D. dissertation, University of Wisconsin,
          Madison.
   1984   "Accident proneness: A study of the career of an ideological concept." Psychology and Social
          Theory. In press.
U.S. Bureau of the Census
   1980   Statistical Abstracts of the United States, 1980. Washington, DC: U.S. Government Printing Office.
   1982   Statistical Abstracts of the United States, 1982-83. Washington, DC: U.S. Government Printing
          Office.
Weidenbaum, Murray C.
   1979   The Future of Business Regulation. New York: Amacon.
Weir, Stanley
   1970   "U.S.A.: The labor revolt." Pp. 466-501 in Maurice Zeitlin, (ed.), American Society, Inc. Chicago:
          Markham.
Wilson, James Q.
   1974   "The politics of regulation," Pp. 135-168 in James W. McKie, (ed.), Social Responsibility and the
          Business Predicament. Washington, DC: The Brookings Institute.

Cases cited:

Atlas Roofing v. Occupational Safety and Health Review Commission, 430 U.S. 442, 1977.
Chamber of Commerce v. Occupational Safety and Health Administration, 465 FSupp 10, 1978; 636
   F2d 464, 1980.
E.I. duPont de Nemours v. Finklea, 442 FSupp 821, 1977.
Frank Irey v. Occupational Safety and Health Review Commission, 430 U.S. 442, 1977.
Industrial Union Department, AFL-CIO v. American Petroleum Institute, 448 U.S. 607, 1980.
Leone v. Mobil Oil, 523 F2d 1153, 1975.
Louisiana Chemical Association v. Eula Bingham, 657 F2d 777, 1981.
Marshall v. Barlow's, 436 U.S. 307, 1978.
Marshall v. Daniel Construction, 563 F2d 707, 1977.
Usery v. Babcock and Wilcox, 424 FSupp 753, 1976.
Whirlpool v. Marshall, 445 U.S. 1, 1980.

State Implementation Effort and Federal Regulatory Policy: The Case of Occupational Safety and Health

Frank J. Thompson
University of Georgia

Michael J. Scicchitano
West Virginia University

The states play pivotal roles in implementing the protective regulatory policies of the federal government. In this capacity they often profoundly shape who gets what from these programs. A well-rounded theory of the policy process requires precise specification of why some states try harder than others to implement Washington's regulatory policies. This article tests four important theories (wealth, partisan, group, and organizational search) in an attempt to explain state implementation effort under one major regulatory program—the Occupational Safety and Health Act of 1970. State participation and enforcement vigor comprise the two major dimensions of implementation effort examined. The theories prove the most useful in explaining enforcement vigor. In this regard, a path analysis discloses that while wealth and interest group theories contribute to understanding, organizational-search theory is the best predictor of enforcement vigor. Partisan theory predicts the least. The study sheds light on a neglected aspect of regulatory policy and helps lay the cornerstone for a general theory of state implementation effort.

During the 1960s and 1970s, the federal government launched many new regulatory policies designed to protect the environment and public health. Unlike many distributive policies in which affected interests often promote implementation because they have something to gain, "protective" regulatory policies typically face an adversarial milieu where the targeted group resists implementation (Ripley and Franklin, 1982, pp. 132-33). Because of this opposition, implementing agents must usually exert considerable

* Our thanks to Charles Bullock, James Campbell, David McCaffrey, and our anonymous reviewers for helpful comments on a previous draft.

effort if these protective policies are to have much, if any, impact. Such effort cannot be assumed (Sabatier and Mazmanian, 1979). Agencies may fail to commit resources and engage in other actions that carry out the letter and spirit of the law. Problems of engendering implementation effort often become especially acute when Washington relies on other levels of government to execute the programs (e.g., Bardach, 1977; Ingram, 1977).

Many of the protective regulatory policies, such as the Water Quality Act, the Clean Air Act amendments, and the Surface Mining Control and Reclamation Act, assign pivotal implementation roles to the states (U.S. Advisory Commission on Intergovernmental Relations, 1984). In spite of the federal government's dependence on the states to realize its regulatory objectives, systematic examination of variations in *state implementation effort* under these programs remains scarce. This article takes a step toward remedying this neglect by examining state implementation effort under the Occupational Safety and Health Act of 1970. In its emphasis on the promulgation and enforcement of protective standards to reduce injury and illness in the work place, this law typifies many of the new regulatory initiatives in terms of both its goals and its enforcement technology. An examination of the sources of state implementation effort under this program can generate a more highly calibrated set of explanatory propositions that can be further tested in other regulatory contexts.

The essay begins by reviewing the related scholarly literature and then presents the measures of implementation effort. Subsequent sections test alternative explanations of two dimensions of implementation effort— state participation and enforcement vigor.

RELATED STUDIES

The role of the states in implementing and thereby shaping federal regulatory programs receives little attention in the literature on regulatory policy (e.g., Ripley and Franklin, 1982; Wilson, 1980). This neglect may in part reflect the fact that federal regulatory policies initiated before 1960 tended not to assign major implementation roles to the states. The gap may also spring from a propensity to pay more attention to the promulgation of protective standards rather than to their enforcement. Existing federal statutes give the states much greater discretion with respect to the latter function (Scholz, 1981).

Whatever the reason for neglect, the literature on state implementation of federal regulatory policy consists primarily of a few qualitative assessments of a specific program (e.g., Aron, 1979; Menzel, 1981) and of analyses of the legal issues embedded in "regulatory federalism" (e.g., Kanouse, 1980; Stensvaag, 1982). A handful of quantitative studies on the subject also exists.[1] These studies, however, require refinement and elaboration. Much of this quantitative literature tends to rely on expenditure data (Game, 1979) or formal policy mandates (Lester et al., 1983) to gauge state efforts. While these analyses yield valuable insights, it is critical that studies of state implementation also incorporate measures of enforcement at the street level. In this regard, Marvel's analysis (1982) of state performance under the Occupational Safety and Health Act is a noteworthy precursor to this study. Marvel, however, focused on only one dependent variable, inspections of work places. Other measures, such as the volume of citations and penalties, also deserve attention. Furthermore, Marvel's study focuses only in part on explaining differences in state performance, and it experiences modest success in accounting for this variation. Perhaps most important, her study focuses primarily on the early years after passage of the law before many state programs had a chance to surmount start-up problems. In sum, while the existing literature lays a useful foundation, further study is essential if a more satisfactory theory of regulatory policy is to emerge.

THE MEASUREMENT OF STATE
IMPLEMENTATION EFFORT

The Occupational Safety and Health Act affords an opportunity to study variations in two major dimensions of state implementation effort, participation and enforcement vigor. Participation is a dichotomous variable that indicates whether a state chooses to join the implementation process. Under the federal law, states are encouraged "to assume the fullest responsibility" for worker well-being. In support of this aim, the Occupational Safety and Health Administration (OSHA) generally pays about half of the cost of a state program. States that choose to participate must adopt safety and health rules "at least as effective" as those promulgated by OSHA and must meet certain vague stipulations about employing "qualified personnel" and appropriating "adequate funds." If a state will not agree to participate under these terms, OSHA claims jurisdiction and takes over implementation with its own federal personnel. Given these conditions, many states decided not to participate. By 1977, twenty-three states con-

[1] While suggestive, quantitative analyses that focus on the political and economic determinants of state policy outputs have several limitations in explaining state implementation effort. Many of these analyses focus on distributive policies such as welfare and education; factors shaping these programs probably differ from those producing variations in regulatory programs. Furthermore, the state policy literature infrequently analyzes state performance as a response to federal policy. The forces shaping regulation where the states possess considerable autonomy probably differ from those where a state administers a program on behalf of the federal government.

tinued to operate their own programs, and by the early 1980s this number had shrunk to twenty-one. (See note *d*, table 2 for a list.)

The second dimension of implementation effort, enforcement vigor, denotes the degree to which *participating* states monitor the enterprises targeted for regulation and apply sanctions for noncompliance. To measure this concept, this study draws on data assembled by OSHA on four aspects of state performance over a five-year period from fiscal 1977 through 1981. These are the mean amount of occupational safety and health inspectors, inspections, citations, and assessed penalties in a state per 100,000 members of the civilian work force.

Table 1 indicates that participating states vary substantially in enforcement vigor. This is hardly surprising since one would expect diverse motives to underlie a state's decision to participate. Some states may well get involved because their top officials believe that enforcement will be more vigorous if state employees, and not federal inspectors, carry out the program. In other states, participation may become an avenue to create a hospitable climate for business by undercutting "excessively zealous" enforcement. It deserves note in this regard that state programs differ considerably in the degree to which their enforcement scores reach the level that OSHA sustains in the nonparticipating states where it directly enforces the law. Ninety-six percent of the participating states had inspection and citation rates equal to or greater than OSHA's. But on the other enforcement indicators, many states lagged behind the federal agency. Fifty-two percent of the participating states had fewer compliance officers per 100,000 civilian employees than OSHA; 83 percent imposed monetary penalties at a lower rate than OSHA. In sum, participation for some states

TABLE 1

ENFORCEMENT VIGOR, PARTICIPATING STATES AND OSHA, 1977-81

| | COMPLIANCE OFFICERS | INSPECTIONS | CITATIONS | ASSESSED PENALTIES |
	(PER 100,000 CIVILIAN EMPLOYEES IN AREA SERVED)			
Mean of State Annual Rates	2.9	331	819	$15,667
State Range	1.3-9.3	80-859	206-2221	$3,859-$41,627
State Standard Deviation	2.6	206	547	$10,057
OSHA in Nonparticipating States	2.3	96	224	$21,794[a]

Source: Office of State Programs, OSHA.
[a]Estimate based on proposed penalties and partial data on assessed penalties.

411

appears to be an effective strategy for reducing certain aspects of enforcement.

HYPOTHESES

This essay explores the degree to which four theories—wealth, partisan, group, and organizational search—explain variations in state participation and enforcement vigor under the Occupational Safety and Health Act. *Wealth* might seem a likely source of state implementation effort (e.g., Dye, 1966; Thompson, 1981). On balance, however, one would not predict a linear relationship between wealth and a state's decision to participate. Some wealthy states might be more inclined to participate because they could better afford to pay their share of the financing. But poor states also have some incentive to participate in order to deflect regulatory pressures and to create an economic climate favorable to business. Among those states that do get involved, however, wealthier ones can better afford to hire inspectors and to engage in more stringent enforcement of federal policy. Hence, hypothesis 1 asserts:

Other things being equal, the wealth of a state will not be associated with a decision by that state to participate in implementing a federal regulatory policy; greater wealth will, however, be associated with greater enforcement vigor among participating states.

Per capita income and the percentage of the population below the poverty level comprise the indicators of state wealth.

The *partisan* hypothesis suggests that the particular party dominant in a state has an impact. The ideology generally espoused by Republican and Democratic leaders differs with respect to federalism and the regulation of business. Republican officials more readily oppose the concentration of power in Washington and excessive business regulation by government. This leads to hypothesis 2:

Other things being equal, the greater the dominance of the Republican party in a state, the more likely is the state to participate in the federal regulatory program but the less its enforcement vigor relative to other participating states.

To test this hypothesis, three indicators of Republican dominance during key time frames in the 1970s and 1980s receive attention: (1) Republican control of the governor's office; (2) the GOP's hegemony over the three major institutions of government—the governorship, the upper house, the lower house; and (3) a version of the Ranney Index.[2]

---

[2] The first index, Republican control of the governorship, measures the number of years that Republicans occupied that office. The second index treats control of each of the three institutions as a dichotomous variable and then adds the scores to achieve an overall measure of Republican dominance. The version of the Ranney Index derives from the proportion of

The strength of centralist and proregulatory *group pressures* seems likely to be important in explaining state implementation effort (Sabatier, 1975; Wilson, 1980). Centralist pressures increase to the extent that major groups in a state believe that their interests will best be served if the federal government takes over a program and lobby to this end. Proregulatory pressures increase to the degree that groups press for stringent regulatory standards and the vigorous enforcement of them.

In the case of occupational safety and health, the leadership of the union movement, especially the AFL-CIO, believed that states would be less committed to protecting workers than the federal government. Consequently, union officials in many areas lobbied against the involvement of their states so that OSHA would assume direct jurisdiction. Unions have also comprised the major group fighting for strict protective standards and energetic efforts to enforce them. These characteristics prompt hypothesis 3:

Other things being equal, the greater the strength of centralist interest groups in a state (the unions), the less likely is a state to participate in the program; the greater the strength of proregulatory groups (the unions), the greater the enforcement vigor of the program in participating states.

The following serve as measures of union strength: the proportion of the nonagricultural work force in a state that belongs to a union, the absence of a right-to-work law (legislation strongly opposed by unions), and a perceptual indicator of union strength based on the views of key state legislators (Thompson, 1981).[3]

The *organizational-search explanation* views implementation effort as a function of problem severity (Cyert and March, 1963). Occupational injury and illness rates comprise one stimulus that might lead state officials to perceive the presence of a problem and to activate search for a solution. A stream of complaints from employees about the hazards to health found in their work places might perform a similar function. The ability of either stimulus to produce awareness of a problem among state officials need not generate a predictable result in terms of state participation. Among participating states, however, it seems likely that identification of an occupational safety and health problem would trigger an increase in enforcement vigor. This leads to hypothesis 4:

---

seats in the upper legislative chamber controlled by the Republicans, the proportion of lower chamber seats similarly controlled, and the percentage of votes going to the Republican candidate for governor (see Tucker, 1982).

[3] The authors thank Joel Thompson (1981) for sharing his data on elite perceptions of union power in each state.

Other things being equal, the more that social indicators and members of the group targeted for protection point to the presence of a problem, the greater the enforcement vigor among participating states.

A state's mean annual rate of occupational injuries and illnesses from 1972 through 1976 comprised one measure of problem severity (U.S. Bureau of Labor Statistics, 1980). The number of complaints about occupational hazards filed per 100,000 civilian employees in a state from fiscal 1977 through fiscal 1981 became the second measure.

While wealth, partisan, group, and organizational-search hypotheses drove this investigation, certain literature suggests that regionalism (e.g., Grupp and Richards, 1975; Sharkansky, 1970; Walker, 1969) and political culture (e.g., Sigelman and Smith, 1980) may influence state implementation effort. These variables were, therefore, incorporated into the analysis. The concept of political culture employed here draws on the familiar typology articulated by Elazar (1975). Indicators developed by Johnson (1976) were used that rank each state in terms of the degree to which it features traditionalistic, individualistic, and moralistic cultures.[4]

State Participation

The hypotheses stress the relevance of two factors in predicting state participation under the Occupational Safety and Health Act, Republicanism and union weakness. As the first column of correlations in table 2 indicates, the data provide limited support for these predictions. Only Republican control of the governorship achieves much predictive power; it correlates at a modest .37 with participation. If one eliminates the South from the analysis, support for the partisan hypothesis does not increase.

While the data yield limited support for the hypothesized relationships, a regional phenomenon does appear to be operating. The states in the West are by far the most involved, with eight of eleven participating. By contrast, only one of ten northeastern states remained in the program by the early 1980s. Furthermore, the apparent regional effect cannot be dismissed by controlling for wealth, partisanship, union strength, or political culture. If one combines the two regional variables (East, West) and one partisan factor (Index of Republican Governors, 1970-75) into a regression equation, the three account for 32 percent of the variation in state participation.[5]

---

[4] To measure political culture, Johnson uses data concerning the dominance of certain religious groups.

[5] The values, which were derived using the ordinary least squares (OLS) technique, are .18 for Republican control of the governorship, -.37 for East, and .31 for West. Because OLS assumes that the dependent variable has an unrestricted range, some recommend alternative

TABLE 2

CORRELATES OF STATE PARTICIPATION AND ENFORCEMENT VIGOR UNDER THE OCCUPATIONAL SAFETY AND HEALTH ACT (Pearson r)

INDEPENDENT VARIABLES	PARTICIPATION AS OF 1981	INDICATORS OF ENFORCEMENT VIGOR, FY 1977-81			
		INSPECTORS	INSPECTIONS	CITED VIOLATIONS	ASSESSED PENALTIES
Wealth					
	$(N = 50)$		$(N = 23)$		
Per Capita Income	.12[a]	.53**	.40*	.35	.32
% Below Poverty Level, 1975	-.08	-.41*	-.46*	-.38	-.43*
Partisanship					
	$(N = 50)$		$(N = 23)$		
Index of Republican Governors, 1970-75	.37**	—[b]	—[b]	—[b]	—[b]
Index of Republican Governors, 1976-81	—[b]	.23	.17	.35	.33
Republican Institutional Dominance, 1970-75	.07	—[b]	—[b]	—[b]	—[b]
Republican Institutional Dominance, 1976-81	—[b]	.08	-.06	-.03	.30
Ranney Index of Republicanism, 1970-75	.06	—[b]	—[b]	—[b]	—[b]
Ranney Index of Republicanism, 1976-81	—[b]	.08	.07	.11	.23
Interest Groups					
	$(N = 50)$		$(N = 23)$		
% Union	.06	.40*	.64**	.61**	.44**
Right-to-Work	.07	-.28	-.34	-.41*	-.43*
Perception of Union Strength	-.08	.36	.43*	.48*	.27

415

TABLE 2 (CONTINUED)

CORRELATES OF STATE PARTICIPATION AND ENFORCEMENT VIGOR UNDER THE
OCCUPATIONAL SAFETY AND HEALTH ACT (Pearson r)

INDEPENDENT VARIABLES	PARTICIPATION AS OF 1981	INDICATORS OF ENFORCEMENT VIGOR, FY 1977-81			
		INSPECTORS	INSPECTIONS	CITED VIOLATIONS	ASSESSED PENALTIES
Organizational					
	(N = 43)			(N = 22)	
Injury and Illness Ratio, 1972-76	.16	.63••	.72••	.59••	.48••
			(N = 23)		
Complaints per Civilian Employees, 1977-81	—^{c}	.75••	.64••	.58••	.63••
Political Culture					
	(N = 47)			(N = 21)	
Moralistic	.11	.36	.36	.32	.18
Individualistic	-.05	.14	.16	.10	.24
Traditionalistic	-.02	-.35	-.36	-.29	-.31
Region^d					
	(N = 48)			(N = 21)	
Northeast	-.31•	.11	-.05	.19	-.05
South	.01	-.26	-.34	-.33	-.31
North Central	-.07	-.17	-.03	.00	.27
West	.37••	.31	.36	.19	.10

^{a}Since state decisions to participate were primarily made in the early 1970s, the per capita income figure for this column is from 1970. Otherwise, the 1980 figure was used.

^{b}Data excluded due to lack of theoretical justification for examining the relationship. (The missing correlations are low and do not achieve statistical significance.)

^{c}The data set does not include complaints in states where OSHA held direct jurisdiction.

^{d}The northeastern states are *Connecticut*, Delaware, Maine, Massachusetts, New Hampshire, New Jersey, New York, Pennsylvania, Rhode Island, and *Vermont*. The southern states consist of Alabama, Arkansas, Florida, Georgia, *Kentucky*, Louisiana, *Maryland*, Mississippi, *North Carolina*, Oklahoma, *South Carolina*, *Tennessee*, Texas, *Virginia*, and West Virginia. The north central states are Illinois, *Indiana*, *Iowa*, Kansas, Missouri, Nebraska, North Dakota, *Minnesota*, *Michigan*, Ohio, South Dakota, and Wisconsin. The West consists of *Arizona*, *California*, *Colorado*, Idaho, Montana, *Nevada*, *New Mexico*, *Oregon*, *Utah*, *Washington*, and *Wyoming*. The external states, *Alaska* and *Hawaii*, were not included because they lacked contiguous boundaries with other states in the region (Sharkansky, 1970). States participating in regulating the private sector as of 1977 are italicized. Connecticut and Colorado subsequently dropped out of the program.

416

Efforts to increase this percentage through the use of multiplicative models proved abortive. The variance explained represents a respectable start in accounting for participation but clearly demonstrates a need for additional research.

ENFORCEMENT VIGOR: CORRELATES AND CAUSATION

Table 2 provides more support for the hypothesized relationships concerning enforcement vigor. The variables associated with wealth, group, and organizational-search theories all correlate in the expected direction with the four measures of enforcement. The coefficients range in absolute values from .32 to .75. The data in table 2 do not support the hypothesis concerning partisanship. Republican dominance does not march hand in hand with weaker enforcement, a finding that holds when one eliminates southern states from the analysis.

The many variables correlated with enforcement vigor suggest the utility of constructing a recursive causal model. Such analysis can provide better understanding of both the direct and the indirect effects of a given independent variable, shed light on the relative importance of a variable, and yield clues about causal paths.

Preliminary analysis suggested that four independent variables in particular would be the more powerful predictors of enforcement vigor: percentage of the nonagricultural work force unionized, injury and illness rates, complaints about safety and health conditions, and per capita income. Wealth was assumed to be the basic antecedent, or exogenous, condition with the potential to affect enforcement vigor directly or by working through the other independent variables. The authors also reasoned that union strength would influence enforcement vigor directly and indirectly. The former effect presumably would stem from overt union pressure on elected officials and the bureaucracy to do more. The latter effect would

statistical techniques when the dependent variable is dichotomous (Fiorina, 1981, appendix A). Knoke (1975) and Goodman (1976), however, demonstrate that log-linear regression, a technique suitable for dichotomous dependent variables, and OLS yield substantially the same results when the split between the two categories of the dependent variable is between 25 percent and 75 percent. Gillespie (1977, p. 104) further argues that "when the split on the dependent variable is not extreme—dummy dependent variable regression can provide a more adequate description of the underlying causal structure." Other studies that use probit analysis to reexamine the findings produced by OLS analyses of a dichotomous dependent variable do not produce substantially different results (Fiorina, 1983, p. 162; Kinder and Kiewiet, 1979, p. 504). Because the split in the state participation variable did not fall outside of the 25 percent-75 percent range, OLS techniques were employed in this study. Additional analysis using alternative techniques failed to alter the findings.

*Significant at the .05 level.
**Significant at the .01 level.

JOURNAL OF POLITICS, VOL. 47, 1985

FIGURE 1

CAUSAL MODEL OF ENFORCEMENT VIGOR

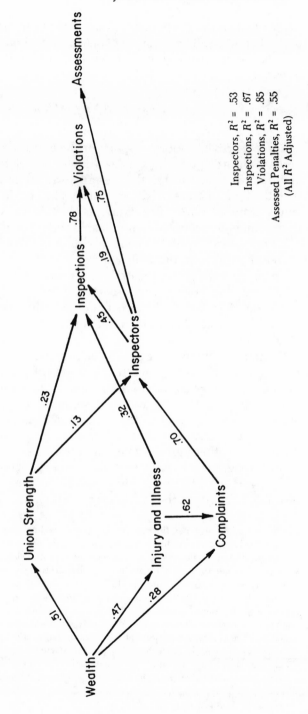

Inspectors, R^2 = .53
Inspections, R^2 = .67
Violations, R^2 = .85
Assessed Penalties, R^2 = .55
(All R^2 Adjusted)

spring from union activities at the plant level which both reduce employee inhibitions about filing complaints and encourage firms to collect and report data on industrial mishaps. The path analysis hypothesized that complaints as well as injury and illness would directly affect enforcement vigor. The analysis also tested for the possibility that injury and illness rates would indirectly influence enforcement vigor by stimulating complaints. Within the cluster of dependent variables, it seemed plausible that greater numbers of inspectors would result in more inspections which in turn would lead firms to be cited for more violations and to pay higher penalties. Ideally, it would be useful to incorporate a state's decision to participate as an endogenous variable in the path model. Given the patterns produced by empirical analysis and data limitations, however, this was not feasible.[6]

No firm consensus exists as to which causal paths should be retained or eliminated once coefficients have been computed for each path. It is reasonable, however, to eliminate all paths with coefficients of .1 or less (Asher, 1976). Figure 1 presents the results of this analysis.[7]

The model suggests that wealth works indirectly to promote enforcement vigor in three ways. First, it appears to foster greater union activity which in turn leads to more enforcement. Second, state wealth directly associates with higher injury and illness rates that then affect state inspec-

---

[6] The explanations of participation and enforcement vigor do not share common independent variables. Including participation in the model thereby heightens the risk of overlaying one analysis (enforcement vigor) with another (participation) in a confusing way. Furthermore, the addition of participation may well distort the estimates of enforcement. Data on enforcement in each state where OSHA holds jurisdiction were unobtainable. This leaves two major alternatives: (a) assign each of these nonparticipating OSHA states a missing value, in which case they would not provide any additional information; or (b) assign each OSHA state the mean value for all OSHA jurisdictions, in which case the absence of variation could create other statistical problems and distort the estimates.

The fact that some states did not participate means that the multiple regression analysis is based on a relatively small number of observations. Thus, the risk is present that the small "sample" contains too little information about variations among the variables to estimate effects accurately. Achen (1982, p. 82) notes that, theoretically, multicollinearity and having few observations are essentially the same problem. In such instances, parameter estimates may be sensitive to slight alterations of the model specification on the sample used (Hanushek and Jackson, 1977, p. 92). Concern with this potential problem prompted the authors to test different model specifications and to delete several of the more extreme observations in some analyses. None of these additional analyses provided any indication of instability. Nor did the small N result in a failure to find statistically significant relationships. To guard against the possibility that a small number of cases would yield an overestimated R^2, an adjusted R^2 was employed (Agresti and Agresti, 1979, p. 360).

[7] The path coefficients for the error terms of the endogenous variables in the model are as follows: union strength, .88; injury and illness rate, .91; complaints, .65; inspectors, .69; inspections, .57; violations, .39; penalties, .67.

tion rates. Richer states may house businesses that pose a greater challenge to health or that may simply do better at sustaining reporting systems that keep track of occupational safety and health problems (Viscusi, 1983). Third, wealth indirectly works through injury and illness rates to increase complaints; wealth also directly affects the propensity of employees to voice formal grievances about occupational hazards. Complaints in turn appear to increase prospects that a state will employ more inspectors per civilian worker. The direct effect of wealth on complaints could stem from the presence of better-educated workers in these states and greater worker expectations with respect to wages, hours, and working conditions. Their "high standards" could bolster their propensity to complain when they perceive a health threat.

Although the path coefficients are relatively low, the model suggests that union strength directly impinges on the number of inspectors and inspections. Apparently, union influence operates not only by encouraging states to hire more inspectors but by unleashing dynamics that result in more inspections per compliance officer.

The organizational-search variables also relate both directly and indirectly to enforcement vigor. Higher injury and illness rates appear to generate more complaints which in turn fuel a state's propensity to hire more inspectors. Like union strength, injury and illness data also act directly to spur a greater inspection rate. As with all the independent variables, the effects on cited violations and assessed penalties are indirect.

Conceivably, the explanatory power attributed to the organizational-search variables misses the mark. One could argue that enforcement vigor encourages workers to complain and prompts employers to report injuries and illnesses more accurately. On balance, however, the case for treating the organizational-search factors as causal rather than dependent variables seems stronger (although some reciprocal effects may well exist). The probability that a given firm will be inspected and seriously penalized for infractions is very low even in states that score high on enforcement vigor. Given this circumstance and other barriers to precise information about enforcement, one cannot readily assume that workers and employers will accurately perceive the enforcement vigor of a state agency. To the extent that one acknowledges the possibility of misperception, the case for viewing such vigor as the source of more complaints and better data on injuries and illnesses tends to weaken. Even if employers and workers accurately gauge a state agency's enforcement vigor, one cannot assume that it will automatically become a primary factor motivating their behavior. By comparison, it seems highly likely that the professionals who staff safety and health agencies will be knowledgeable about injury and illness data and will accurately perceive the volume of complaints that they receive. It is also probable that their professional ethos will strongly motivate them to

420

TABLE 3

EFFECTS COEFFICIENTS OF THE
FOUR MAJOR INDEPENDENT VARIABLES

MEASURES OF ENFORCEMENT VIGOR	PER CAPITA INCOME	UNION STRENGTH	INJURY AND DISEASE RATE	COMPLAINTS
Inspectors	.47	.13	.43	.70
Inspections	.48	.29	.52	.32
Citations	.46	.25	.48	.38
Assessed Penalties	.35	.10	.33	.53

respond to evidence of more acute problems with greater enforcement (Bardach and Kagan, 1982).

To summarize the causal implications of the model, an effects coefficient was computed for each of the independent variables. Lewis-Beck (1977) notes that in any causal system all effects of an independent variable are either direct or indirect. The effects coefficient is simply the sum of the variable's direct (e.g., the impact of union strength on inspection rates) and indirect effects (e.g., the path that flows from union strength to inspectors and inspections) on a dependent variable. An indirect effect for a given path is the product of the path coefficients that mediate the relationships between the explanatory and dependent variables. Table 3 presents the effects coefficients for each of the four independent variables for the measures of enforcement vigor.

These calculations tend to reaffirm the importance of the organizational-search theory in explaining enforcement. With respect to each of the measures of enforcement vigor, one of the two variables associated with the theory of search (injury and disease rates, complaints) features the largest effects coefficient. While working indirectly, state wealth also reveals a persistent effect on the various indicators of enforcement vigor, falling below .45 only in the case of assessed penalties. Union strength has the least effect.

CONCLUSION

The state role in implementing Washington's protective regulatory programs has received scant scholarly attention. When students of implementation consider the states, they often view them as potential veto points that can impede enforcement (e.g., Marvel, 1982). This pessimistic view is reinforced by the traditional justification for a new federal regulatory program, namely, that the states have failed to deal with some problem. This study presents a more mixed picture concerning state performance. The data indicate that states vary substantially in implementation effort. Some state programs evince less enforcement vigor than OSHA achieves in the areas where it holds direct jurisdiction; many other state agencies surpass OSHA. A state's decision to participate in a federal regulatory program may, therefore, be a strategy that enervates or energizes regulatory policy within its boundaries. Prospects that federal statutes will become so precise and constraining as to eliminate the enforcement discretion of participating states remain slim.

In explaining variations in state implementation effort, the findings point to the utility of wealth, group, and organizational-search theories in accounting for enforcement vigor. To a lesser degree they suggest the relevance of partisan control and regionalism for state participation. The limited explanatory power of partisan control could spring from several sources. State Republican and Democratic officials may not systematically differ in their attitudes toward occupational safety and health objectives and the means of attaining them. Or, the differences that do exist may get submerged beneath a commitment to administering programs in a "nonpartisan" way. Alternatively, Republican officials may prefer to reduce enforcement vigor but conclude that the investment in time and political capital needed to control the bureaucracy is too great. It deserves note that barriers to control may well be less evident in the case of a state's decision to participate. Hence, partisan control may persistently prove more important in explaining this dimension of implementation effort. The regional factor in state participation may derive from a propensity for some states to emulate a regional leader. Or, in light of the heavier participation in the West, it may be that officials more geographically removed from Washington come to experience this distance psychologically. Perceiving that the federal regulatory agency has limited sensitivity to their particular problems, these states may be more inclined to participate.

In considering these findings, one cannot assume that they will apply outside the regulatory arena (Kemp, 1981). Due in part to the resistance they provoke, protective regulatory programs confront many distinctive implementation problems. For instance, state participation is far less automatic under these regulatory policies than under federal programs that ask the states to deliver services or income. Factors that predict state participation in regulatory initiatives may explain little about state involvement in distributive or redistributive programs.

Consider also the findings concerning the importance of organizational-search variables. To some degree these results reinforce the idea that implementing agents will try harder if they have a vocal clientele at the street level and face a more serious outbreak of the problem they are supposed to correct (e.g., occupational injury and disease). Alternatively, states that feature more enforcement vigor may not have worse problems but simply record them more exhaustively. These indicators may then take on a life of their own and become independent variables in their own right. Whatever the dynamic, it may apply primarily to protective regulatory policies where broad agreement often exists both on how to interpret an index (occupational injury and disease are bad; something must be done) and on the appropriate response to the index (tougher rules and more enforcement). Many redistributive programs, such as those that strive to ameliorate poverty, cannot count on such broad agreement. Higher poverty levels in a state need not spawn a consensus on the appropriate course of action (e.g., more economic development, higher welfare payments, more education).

While the findings of this study seem most applicable to protective regulatory policies, this does not dismiss their broader relevance. Greater understanding of the state role under federal regulatory policy can help fuel the development of a more comprehensive theory of state implementation effort. Within this theory, policy type seems likely to be a critical intervening variable.

REFERENCES

Achen, C. H. (1982). *Interpreting and Using Regression.* Beverly Hills, CA: Sage.
Agresti, A., and B. F. Agresti (1979). *Statistical Methods for the Social Sciences.* San Francisco: Dellen Publishing.
Aron, J. B. (1979). "Intergovernmental Politics of Energy." *Policy Analysis* 5: 451-71.
Asher, H. B. (1976). *Causal Modeling.* Beverly Hills, CA: Sage.
Bardach, E. (1977). *The Implementation Game.* Cambridge: MIT Press.
Bardach, E., and R. A. Kagan (1982). *Going by the Book.* Philadelphia: Temple University Press.
Cyert, R. M., and J. G. March (1963). *A Behavioral Theory of the Firm.* Englewood Cliffs, NJ: Prentice-Hall.
Dye, T. R. (1966). *Politics, Economics and Public Policy Outcomes in the American States.* Chicago: Rand McNally.
Elazar, D. J. (1975). "The American Cultural Matrix." In D. J. Elazar and J. Zikmund II (eds.), *The Ecology of American Political Culture: Readings.* New York: Thomas Y. Crowell.
Fiorina, M. (1981). *Retrospective Voting in American National Elections.* New Haven: Yale University Press.
———— (1983). "Who Is Held Responsible? Further Evidence on the Hibbing-Alford Thesis." *American Journal of Political Science* 27: 150-64.
Game, K. W. (1979). "Controlling Air Pollution: Why Some States Try Harder." *Public Policy Studies* 7: 728-38.
Gillespie, M. W. (1977). "Log-Linear Techniques and the Regression Analysis of Dummy Dependent Variables." *Sociological Methods and Research* 6: 103-22.

Goodman, L. A. (1976). "The Relationship between the Modified and the More Usual Multiple Regression Approach to the Analysis of Dichotomous Variables." In D. R. Heise (ed.), *Sociological Methodology 1976*. San Francisco: Jossey-Bass.

Grupp, F. W., Jr., and A. R. Richards (1975). "Variations in Elite Perceptions of American States and Referents for Public Policy Making." *American Political Science Review* 69: 850-58.

Hanushek, E. A., and J. E. Jackson (1977). *Statistical Models for Social Scientists*. New York: Academic Press.

Ingram, H. (1977). "Policy Implementation through Bargaining: The Case of Federal Grants-in-Aid." *Public Policy* 25: 499-526.

Johnson, C. A. (1976). "Political Culture in American States: Elazar's Formulation Examined." *American Journal of Political Science* 20: 491-509.

Kanouse, R. (1980). "Achieving Federalism in the Regulation of Coastal Energy Facility Siting." *Ecology Law Quarterly* 8: 533-81.

Kemp, K. (1981). "Symbolic and Strict Regulation in the American States." *Social Science Quarterly* 62: 516-26.

Kinder, D. R., and R. D. Kiewiet (1979). "Economic Discontent and Political Behavior: The Role of Personal Grievances and Collective Economic Judgment in Congressional Voting." *American Journal of Political Science* 23: 495-527.

Knoke, D. (1975). "A Comparison of Log-Linear and Regression Models for Systems of Dichotomous Variables." *Sociological Methods and Research* 3: 416-34.

Lester, J. P., J. L. Franke, A. O'M. Bowman, and K. W. Kramer (1983). "Hazardous Wastes, Politics, and Public Policy: A Comparative State Analysis." *Western Political Quarterly* 36: 257-85.

Lewis-Beck, M. S. (1977). "The Relative Importance of Socioeconomic and Political Variables for Public Policy." *American Political Science Review* 71: 559-66.

Marvel, M. K. (1982). "Implementation and Safety Regulation: Variations in Federal and State Administration under OSHA." *Administration and Society* 14: 15-33.

Menzel, D. C. (1981). "Implementation of the Federal Surface Mining Control and Reclamation Act of 1977." *Public Administration Review* 41: 212-18.

Ripley, R. B., and G. A. Franklin (1982). *Bureaucracy and Policy Implementation*. Homewood, IL: Dorsey.

Sabatier, P. (1975). "Social Movements and Regulatory Agencies: Toward a More Adequate—and Less Pessimistic—Theory of 'Clientele Capture.' " *Policy Science* 6: 301-42.

Sabatier, P., and D. Mazmanian (1979). "The Conditions of Effective Implementation: A Guide to Accomplishing Policy Objectives." *Policy Analysis* 5: 481-504.

Scholz, J. T. (1981). "State Regulatory Reform and Federal Regulation." *Policy Studies Review* 1: 347-59.

Sharkansky, I. (1970). *Regionalism in American Politics*. Indianapolis, IN: Bobbs-Merrill.

Sigelman, L., and R. E. Smith (1980). "Consumer Legislation in the American States: An Attempt at Explanation." *Social Science Quarterly* 61: 58-70.

Stensvaag, J. M. (1982). "State Regulation of Nuclear Generating Plants under the Clean Air Act Amendments of 1977." *Southern California Law Review* 55: 511-96.

Thompson, J. A. (1981). "Outputs and Outcomes of State Workmen's Compensation Laws." *Journal of Politics* 43: 1129-52.

Tucker, H. J. (1982). "Interparty Competition in the American States: One More Time." *American Politics Quarterly* 10: 93-116.

U.S. Advisory Commission on Intergovernmental Regulations (1984). *Regulatory Federalism: Policy, Process, Impact and Reform*. Washington, D.C.: U.S. Government Printing Office.

424

U.S. Bureau of Labor Statistics (1980). *State Data on Occupational Injuries and Illnesses in 1976*. Washington, D.C.: U.S. Government Printing Office.

Viscusi, W. K. (1983). *Risk by Choice*. Cambridge: Harvard University Press.

Walker, J. L. (1969): "The Diffusion of Innovations among the American States." *American Political Science Review* 63: 880-99.

Wilson, J. Q. (1980). *The Politics of Regulation*. New York: Basic Books.

ACKNOWLEDGMENTS

Brown, William S. "Industrial Policy and Corporate Power." *Journal of Economic Issues* 19 (1985): 487–96. Reprinted with the permission of the Association of Evolutionary Economics. Courtesy of the Association of Evolutionary Economics.

Canto, Victor A. "U.S. Trade Policy: History and Evidence." *Cato Journal* 3 (1983/84): 679–96. Reprinted with the permission of the Cato Institute. Courtesy of the Cato Institute.

Chakrabarti, Alok K. "Reindustrialization of the United States: Three Perspectives on Organizational Adaptation." *Quarterly Review of Economics and Finance* 24 (1984): 51–56. Reprinted with the permission of the University of Illinois at Urbana-Champaign, Bureau of Economic and Business Research. Courtesy of Yale University Sterling Memorial Library.

DiLorenzo, Thomas J. "The Political Economy of National Industrial Policy." *Cato Journal* 4 (1984): 587–607. Reprinted with the permission of the Cato Institute. Courtesy of the Cato Institute.

Donnelly, Patrick G. "The Origins of the Occupational Safety and Health Act of 1970." *Social Problems* 30 (1982): 13–25. Reprinted with the permission of the University of California Press. Copyright 1982 by the Society for the Study of Social Problems. Courtesy of Yale University Sterling Memorial Library.

Eizenstat, Stuart E. "Reindustrialization through Coordination or Chaos?" *Yale Journal on Regulation* 2 (1984): 39–51. Copyright 1984 by the *Yale Journal on Regulation*, Box 401A Yale Station, New Haven, CT 06520. Reprinted from Vol. 2 by permission. All rights reserved. Courtesy of Yale University Law Library.

Fong, Glenn R. "The Potential for Industrial Policy: Lessons from the Very High Speed Integrated Circuit Program." *Journal of Policy Analysis and Management* 5 (1986): 264–91. Reprinted with the permission of John Wiley & Sons, Inc. Courtesy of Yale University Law Library.

Goff, David H. and Linda Dysart Goff. "Regulation of Television Advertising to Children: The Policy Dispute in Its Second Decade." *Southern Speech Communication Journal* 48 (1982): 38–50. Reprinted with the permission of the Southern States Communicaton Association. Courtesy of the *Southern Speech Communication Journal*.

Grady, Robert C. "Reindustrialization, Liberal Democracy, and Corporatist Representation." *Political Science Quarterly* 101 (1986): 415–32. Reprinted with the permission of the author and The Academy of Political Science. Courtesy of Yale University Law Library.

Hays, Samuel P. "From Conservation to Environment: Environmental Politics in the United States Since World War Two." *Environmental Review* 6 (1982): 14–41. Reprinted with the permission of the American Society for Environmental History. Courtesy of Yale University Foresty Library.

Kaufman, Allen, L.S. Zacharias, and Alfred Marcus. "Managers United for Corporate Rivalry: A History of Managerial Collective Action." *Journal of Policy History* 2 (1990): 56–97. Copyright 1990 by the Pennsylvania State University. Reproduced by permission of the Pennsylvania State University Press. Courtesy of Yale University Sterling Memorial Library.

Keiser, K. Robert. "The New Regulation of Health and Safety." *Political Science Quarterly* 95 (1980): 479–91. Reprinted with the permission of the author and The Academy of Political Science. Courtesy of Yale University Law Library.

Marcus, Irwin M. "The Deindustrialization of America: Homestead, A Case Study, 1959–1984." *Pennsylvania History* 52 (1985): 162–82. Reprinted with the permission of the Pennsylvania Historical Association. Courtesy of Yale University Sterling Memorial Library.

McIntyre, Richard and Michael Hillard. "Brave New Corporate World: An Assessment of Industrial Policy." *Monthly Review* 36 (1984): 14–23. Copyright 1984 by Monthly Review Inc. Reprinted by permission of Monthly Review Foundation. Courtesy of Yale University Sterling Memorial Library.

Miller, III, James C., Thomas F. Walton, William E. Kovacic, and Jeremy A. Rabkin. "Industrial Policy: Reindustrialization through Competition or Coordinated Action?" *Yale Journal on Regula-*

tion 2 (1984): 1–37. Copyright 1984 by the *Yale Journal on Regulation*, Box 401A Yale Station, New Haven, CT 06520. Reprinted from Vol. 2 by permission. All rights reserved. Courtesy of Yale University Law Library.

Norton, R.D. "Industrial Policy and American Renewal." *Journal of Economic Literature* 24 (1986): 1–40. Reprinted with the permission of the American Economic Association. Courtesy of Yale University Sterling Memorial Library.

Rockoff, Hugh. "Price and Wage Controls in Four Wartime Periods." *Journal of Economic History* 41 (1981): 381–401. Reprinted with the permission of Cambridge University Press. Courtesy of Yale University Sterling Memorial Library.

Scott, Bruce R. "Can Industry Survive the Welfare State?" *Harvard Business Review* 60 (1982): 70–84. Copyright 1982 by the President and Fellows of Harvard College. All rights reserved. Reprinted by permission of *Harvard Business Review*. Courtesy of Yale University Law Library.

Solo, Robert. "Industrial Policy." *Journal of Economic Issues* 18 (1984): 697–714. Reprinted with the permission of the Association of Evolutionary Economics. Courtesy of the Association of Evolutionary Economics.

Szasz, Andrew. "Industrial Resistance to Occupational Safety and Health Legislation: 1971–1981." *Social Problems* 32 (1984): 103–16. Reprinted with the permission of the University of California Press. Copyright 1984 by the Society for the Study of Social Problems. Courtesy of Yale University Sterling Memorial Library.

Thompson, Frank J. and Michael J. Scicchitano. "State Implementation Effort and Federal Regulatory Policy: The Case of Occupational Safety and Health." *Journal of Politics* 47 (1985): 686–703. Reprinted from the *Journal of Politics*, by permission of the author and the University of Texas Press. Courtesy of the *Journal of Politics*.

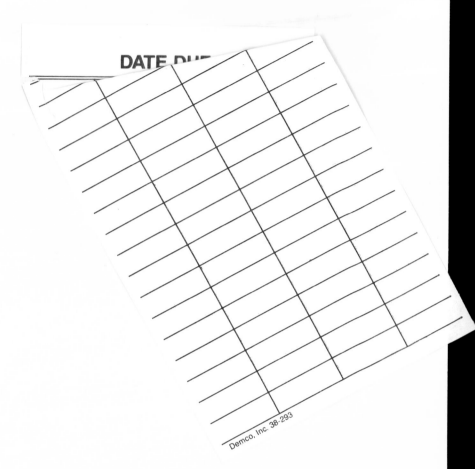

DATE DUE

Demco, Inc. 38-293